Korea's Political Economy

I0867161

Korea's Political Economy

An Institutional Perspective

edited by

Lee-Jay Cho and Yoon Hyung Kim

Routledge
Taylor & Francis Group
LONDON AND NEW YORK

First published 1994 by Westview Press, Inc.

Published 2018 by Routledge
52 Vanderbilt Avenue, New York, NY 10017
2 Park Square, Milton Park, Abingdon, Oxon OX14 4RN

Routledge is an imprint of the Taylor & Francis Group, an informa business

Copyright © 1994 Taylor & Francis

All rights reserved. No part of this book may be reprinted or reproduced or utilised in any form or by any electronic, mechanical, or other means, now known or hereafter invented, including photocopying and recording, or in any information storage or retrieval system, without permission in writing from the publishers.

Notice:
Product or corporate names may be trademarks or registered trademarks, and are used only for identification and explanation without intent to infringe.

Library of Congress Cataloging-in-Publication Data
Korea's political economy : an institutional perspective / edited by
Lee-Jay Cho and Yoon Hyung Kim.
p. cm.
Includes bibliographical references and index.
ISBN 0-8133-8859-7
1. Korea (South)—Economic conditions—1960– 2. Korea (South)—Economic policy—1960– 3. Industry and state—Korea (South) 4. Korea (South)—Politics and government—1960– 5. Korea (South)—Cultural policy. I. Cho, Lee-Jay. II. Kim, Yoon Hyung.
HC467.K627 1994
338.95195—dc20 94-16061
CIP

ISBN 13: 978-0-367-01683-8 (hbk)
ISBN 13: 978-0-367-16670-0 (pbk)

Contents

Preface

The countries of East Asia have emerged as viable, independent nations with excellent records of successful, dynamic economic growth and development, and East Asia has become a new center of world industry. Sustained high growth over three decades in the region has even led some to speculate about an East Asian–dominated twenty-first century. In particular, by any economic criterion, the Republic of Korea has registered outstanding material performance since the early 1960s and is now a semi-industrial, modern state.* Accordingly, it has attracted worldwide attention, because of the lessons it may teach other developing economies. One objective of this volume is to illuminate those lessons.

Korea still has problems to solve, to be sure, and hence new lessons to learn and to pass on to others. Within the short period of its modernization process, Korea instituted two development policy models: the Park Chung Hee regime's state-led economic development (1961–79) and the Chun Doo Hwan and Roh Tae Woo regimes' emphasis on private-sector market-oriented growth (1980–92). Under these three regimes, Korea achieved high-speed growth and rapid industrialization, but in the 1990s it faces a new critical challenge: how should its institutions dissolve the unfortunate by-products of rapid industrialization and uneven growth? Income and wealth distribution, which were quite equitable by world standards in the 1970s, deteriorated in the 1980s along with the public's perception of its own state of affairs; economic power has become highly concentrated in several major conglomerates; the relationship between management and labor has eroded and become belligerent. With a GNP growth rate as impressive as in the past, analysts and policymakers agonize about whether rising inflation and escalating real wages foretell a premature end to the Korean miracle.

In the search for economic and social institutions that will serve Korea well into the 1990s and beyond, the experiences of Japan, the European states, and the United States will provide valuable guides. By explaining these dominant models of the world market economy and relating them to each facet of Korea's economic

*Throughout this volume, "Korea" refers to the undivided peninsula up to 1945 and to South Korea—the Republic of Korea—after World War II. Likewise, "Koreans" refers to the entire Korean populace up to 1945 and thereafter specifically to South Koreans. References to modern North Korea should be clear from the context of the discussion. This terminology has been adopted for simplicity of style and does not imply any cultural or political judgment.

system—national management, taxation, banking, land ownership and use, trade and industrial strategy, and relations among business ownership, management, and labor—the scholars contributing to this volume provide valuable insights and proposals toward a new model for viable future social as well as economic modernization. Drawing this new model is this volume's second objective.

Such a model cannot, however, be structured without reference to Korea's cultural and historical heritage. Much current academic debate on the proper role of government in economic development, for example, is cast in a short time perspective. Economists who seek to draw lessons from or explain Korea's economic modernization have been dominated by a single hypothesis: that outward-oriented economic strategies, combined with deregulation of prices and relaxation of foreign exchange controls, have been the principal causes of Korea's rapid growth. This approach has tended to ignore or treat as incidental the non-economic factors that have also contributed to modernization. In contrast, *Korea's Political Economy* is designed to provide a more integrated understanding—a broadened view of the evolution and interaction of Korean economic, political, and sociocultural institutions. Such institutions mediate the movement between cultural values and economic progress; without understanding them, we cannot hope to understand, advance, or learn from the development of the modern Korean economy. Broadening our understanding of them is the third objective of this volume.

To understand the influence of culture on economic development, we must investigate how the interactions between culture and economy are mediated by institutions, both social and economic, and why certain institutions emerge in a given society. To this end, Chapter 1 links research on culture and on economic development, elaborating the mediating roles of religious, governmental, educational, corporate, and family institutions and values in order to expand our historical and cultural perspectives.

In many ways, Korea's challenges today are consequences of earlier institutional changes without regard for the traditional value system. Now the country must transform itself in conformity with its traditions while continuing along the path of political democratization and becoming a more respected member of the international community. The issue in the 1990s is how Korean society can adapt its political economy to the enormous changes in the political and economic domestic and international environments. In this volume, we address this issue through the specific systems that make up the political economy: the system of national economic management is covered in Chapters 2–5; the tax system in Chapters 6–8; the financial system in Chapters 9–11; the system of land ownership and use in Chapters 12–14; business ownership-management relations in Chapters 15 and 16; trade and industrial strategy in Chapters 17–19; labor-management relations in Chapters 20 and 21.

Within each category, Korean scholars present detailed descriptions and analyses of the historical development and current features of the Korean political economy as well as reform proposals. In companion chapters, Western scholars bring an outsider's perspective to the range of alternatives open to Korea. The final chapter argues for a new model of Korea's political economy—a set of institutions derived from the experiences of many developed nations and adapted to Korea's unique cultural and historical environment.

* * *

The editors gratefully acknowledge the Korea Development Institute and its president, Dr. Bon Ho Koo, for the generous financial contribution and intellectual assistance that supplies this book's foundation. Also deserving of our thanks is the Economic Planning Board of the Republic of Korea, for sustained encouragement, information, and support.

Mr. Chung Yum Kim, who served as Chief of Staff, Minister of Finance, and Minister of Commerce in the Park administration, was our most valuable source of guidance and inspiration. His appreciation of an institutional approach to economic policymaking has served the Republic of Korea and this volume well.

Finally, we acknowledge the work of a large supporting East-West Center staff to bring these many international manuscripts to their final, published form. The editorial and production skills of members of the Center's Office of Program Development, Program on Population, and Program on International Economics and Politics were important and appreciated elements of this project.

Lee-Jay Cho
Yoon Hyung Kim

Contributors

Robert Z. Aliber is Professor of International Economics and Finance, Graduate School of Business, University of Chicago.

Alice H. Amsden is Ellen Swallow Richards Professor of Political Economy, Massachusetts Institute of Technology, Cambridge.

Lee-Jay Cho is Vice President, Office of Program Development, East-West Center, Honolulu.

Michael L. Hoffman is Senior Research Associate, The Urban Institute, Washington, D.C.

Chalmers Johnson is Rohr Professor of Pacific International Relations Emeritus, University of California, San Diego.

Leroy P. Jones is Professor of Economics, Boston University.

Kwang Suk Kim is Professor of Economics, Kyung Hee University, Seoul.

Pyung Joo Kim is Dean of the Graduate School of Economics and Policies, Sogang University, Seoul.

Sookon Kim is Dean of the Graduate School of Business Administration and Professor of Management and Industrial Relations, Kyung Hee University, Seoul.

Yoon Hyung Kim is Professor of Economics, Hankuk University of Foreign Studies, Seoul, and Senior Fellow, Office of Program Development, East-West Center, Honolulu.

Thomas A. Kochan is George M. Bunker Professor of Management, Sloan School of Management, Massachusetts Institute of Technology, Cambridge.

Jin Soon Lee is Professor of Economics, Soongsil University, Seoul.

Kyu Uck Lee is Senior Fellow, Korea Development Institute, Seoul.

D. M. Leipziger is Lead Economist, Southern Cone, Latin America, and Caribbean Region, The World Bank, Washington, D.C.

Sang-Woo Nam is Senior Fellow, Korea Development Institute, Seoul.

Chong Kee Park is Professor of Economics, Inha University, Inchon, and President, Korea Tax Institute, Seoul.

Peter A. Petri is Carl Shapiro Professor of International Finance, and Director of the Lemberg Program in International Economics and Finance, Brandeis University, Waltham, Massachusetts.

Keesung Roh is Senior Fellow, Korea Development Institute, Seoul.

Jae-Young Son is Senior Fellow, Korea Development Institute, Seoul.

Raymond J. Struyk is Director of the International Activities Center, The Urban Institute, Washington, D.C.

John Whalley is Professor, and Director of the Centre for the Study of International Economic Relations, Department of Economics, University of Western Ontario, London, Ontario.

Seong Min Yoo is Senior Fellow, Korea Development Institute, Seoul.

John Zysman is Professor, University of California at Berkeley, and Co-director, Berkeley Roundtable on the International Economy.

PART I

Culture, Institutions, and Development

Chapter 1

Culture, Institutions, and Economic Development in East Asia

Lee-Jay Cho
East-West Center

Economic Development in East Asia

In this chapter I provide a framework for understanding the rapid progress of economic development in East Asia in broad terms that encompass culture and institutions. From a deep historical perspective one can hope to suggest institutional reform that is both necessary for sustained economic growth and at the same time compatible with the values and culture of Korea and the rest of East Asia.

Economic development in East Asia has been hailed in recent decades as a model of success. Japan, Korea, and Taiwan have maintained high growth levels in manufacturing and trade, even though they do not have essential natural resources within their national boundaries. When compared to economic growth elsewhere in the world, the growth rates of these three economies have obviously been substantially higher. Japan was a latecomer to industrialization, relative to Western Europe and America, but in the relatively short time between the Meiji period and World War II it became a major economic power. Then the rapid economic growth following its postwar recovery turned Japan into an economic superpower. Now, by utilizing industrial and technological innovation, Japan has the potential to launch a new chapter as a leader in global economic competition. Korea and Taiwan have shown consistent rapid growth since the 1960s. Although the growth rate of Japan's GDP began to slow during 1970–90, an average of above 5 percent per year was still achieved over these two decades, and the averages for Korea and Taiwan during the same period were almost 10 percent. All three countries achieved dramatic increases in exports. Between 1970 and 1990, the value of exports rose from $800 million to $65 billion for Korea, from $1.5 billion to $67 billion for Taiwan, and from $19 billion to $288 billion for Japan.

During the past fifteen years, China has adopted an open-door policy and a model for a mixed planned-and-market economy. The result has been a sustained high growth rate averaging 10–11 percent during the past few years—with a 15–16 percent growth rate in the manufacturing sector and an annual improvement of 4 percent on average even in the agricultural sector. As China relaxes the institutional rigidities imposed by the communist regime, adopts freer trade with other countries in the East Asian region, and makes more efficient use of its immense natural resources and well-functioning educational institutions, it has the potential to become a major economic power.

Other economic indicators from the East Asian countries suggest a similar picture of development. During the decade 1980–90, output per worker in the manufacturing sector increased by 75 percent in Taiwan and 62 percent in Japan. In Korea it nearly tripled. Although estimates of labor productivity are subject to a margin of error, it is clear that the increase in the three East Asian economies far exceeded that of the United States, which is estimated at 41 percent during the same period.

Household savings studies show that the ratio of savings to household income is 20–30 percent higher in Japan, Korea, and Taiwan than in other regions of the world. Government domestic savings rates have likewise been high, at a level of about 30 percent in all three countries.

Income distribution, as measured by the Gini index, is relatively equitable in Japan, Korea, and Taiwan, when these three countries are compared with other regions of the world. The Gini index for Japan in 1970 was 0.25, and by 1988 at 0.27 it measured only a slightly less equitable distribution. The Gini index for Taiwan changed very little between 1970 (0.29) and 1989 (0.30). The index for Korea was 0.39 in 1980, deteriorated somewhat thereafter, but had improved to 0.34 by 1990.

The quantitative evidence of development is clear. But how does one sustain such development? or regulate it? or adapt it to new cultural situations? Only by *understanding* it. And to do that, I suggest in this chapter, one must understand elements of an economy and a society not normally accounted for in traditional economic theory.

A Broader View of Economic Development

Most economists would agree that three basic requirements of economic development are maintenance of a market order, macro-management, and entrepreneurship. I propose to broaden this view of economic development by adding the institutional factors, the cultural milieu, and finally the current and rhythm of history.

By "market order" we mean maintenance of the institutional or legal framework within which economic interactions are facilitated and market forces operate. Macro-management is the societal management (including, for example, government policy, regulation, and intervention) in the economy. Entrepreneurship is characterized by individual or corporate motivation for achievement, creativity, and leadership in individual enterprises and corporations of a market economy.

Important components of this framework include the parameters of culture, institutions, and institutional change as they relate to economic development. Cultural and institutional parameters influence social behavior, which is economically significant particularly as this influence relates to conditions affecting changes in output of goods and services. Some of these cultural and institutional parameters are religion and traditional value systems (Confucianism, Taoism, Buddhism, and shamanism in East Asia), the educational system and curriculum, legal systems, labor institutions, political institutions, the concentration or diffusion of political and economic power (both geographic and in terms of socioeconomic strata), material aspirations, attitudes toward work, industrial organization, systems of landownership, administrative organization, and the family. All such cultural and institutional factors contribute to the milieu in which economic actors play their roles and in which economic development is either expedited or retarded.

Failure to recognize the significance of such factors can be illustrated by post–World War II "development" recommendations. The prevailing assumption among economists challenged to help the less-developed countries plan for their development was that modernization and adoption of Western technology and Western forms of economic activity require the simultaneous transformation of a society so that it will exhibit a Western social structure and assume most of the social values of the West. In a typical United Nations report on economic development in a specific country, the recommended procedure was to enumerate the economic structures and organizations of a developed (i.e., industrial Western) country, subtract what was already available in the object country, and propose the residual between the two as a "development program."

In his most recent analysis of economic development in the Republic of Korea, Duck Woo Nam (1992) identifies six principal factors to account for the rapid economic development that began in the 1960s. Among these six factors, four are dependent on cultural values, social solidarity, institutions, and the attitudes of the populace.[1] Although writing as an economist, Dr. Nam includes factors that suit neither quantitative analysis nor the terms most neoclassical economists prefer.

The view taken here is that economic development is broader than just an increase in per capita GDP. Rather, it is a complex process of social transformation. The implication is that a more appropriate analysis of economic development requires the study of the developmental process, incorporating relevant cultural and institutional changes. Economists, especially those with a neoclassical orientation in recent decades, have shied away from sociological, cultural, and institutional factors because such factors cannot easily be operationalized; that is, they cannot be readily quantified to meet fashionable rigorous analytical criteria. Not much progress has been made in the study of sociological and cultural dimensions of economic development. Some significant work has been carried out by Bert Hoselitz (founder of the journal *Development and Cultural Change* at the University of Chicago) in his *Sociological Aspects of Economic Growth* (1960).[2] Alexander

Gerschenkron's valuable works (e.g., 1962, 1970) on industrialization in Europe, especially with reference to Russia, have brought out the importance of the historical perspective and contributed to our understanding of the role of the state in the process of industrialization in countries of economic backwardness.

A broader view of economic development as social transformation requires a delineation of some of the basic sociological, cultural, and institutional variables either directly or indirectly linked to economic development. Culture in most cases is mediated by institutions, which either retard or expedite economic development. And therefore institutions, as defined broadly, are closely related to the economic development process.

In the eighteenth century, German economists first employed the term "institutional approach" in their study of the development process. The contribution of the German historical school was to point out noneconomic and metaeconomic factors—particularly political and social institutions—which profoundly affect economic development. Such theorists as Friedrich List and Brunoff Hildebrand rejected the purely economic theory of development and basically outlined various economic developmental stages which they considered to represent a generalized but empirically documentable form of economic life. By the mid-nineteenth century, however, economists had begun to concentrate on the relationships between purely economic variables, with the assumption that human motivations and the social and cultural environment of economic activity are relatively rigid and unchanging. Consequently, the modern theory of economic development has tended to be confined to the task of relating purely economic variables to one another. It tends to disregard the political and social changes that accompany the process of economic development, maintaining that cultural and institutional factors cannot be translated into operational terms. There are, however, some notable exceptions, such as the work of Joseph Schumpeter, who stated that "economic growth . . . is not a phenomenon that can be satisfactorily analyzed in purely economic terms alone" (Clemence 1990).

Since economic development is more than quantitative increase in production, a theory of economic development must explore a complex process of social transformation in more than purely economic terms. It must also be recognized that cultural and institutional factors may affect development directly or indirectly through the economic determinants of growth. The ultimate goal of the cultural and institutional framework of economic development is to expand our insights into the functional relationships between the economic and noneconomic factors that determine the tempo and direction of economic development.

Although great progress has been made in economics as a science, it is still far from performing the function of prediction. Even for simply understanding and explaining a development process, a more comprehensive perspective is desired. In the remaining sections of this chapter, I illustrate some of these relationships—in terms of culture itself and then as they appear in the realms of religion, government, symbols of authority, family, corporate and educational institutions, and land ownership.

Culture

To understand the role of culture in economic development, and the impact of cultural changes on economic development, one must consider how interactions between culture and economic development are mediated by institutions, both social and economic.

Let us look at culture. A distinction between material and adaptive cultures was proposed by William Ogburn (1966). I suggest adding another important type of culture, referred to in East Asia as *seishin bunka,* which I propose to call "spiritual culture." Material culture includes, among many man-made goods and artifacts, technological advancement and industrial products. It has occupied most of the timespan of human history evolving slowly over numerous millennia until the Age of Enlightenment and the technical and industrial revolution that followed the Renaissance. Adaptive culture represents social organizations and institutions required to cope with changes in material culture. But, because changes in material culture have come very slowly through most of human history, adaptive culture has solidified with ritualistic characteristics—seen in institutional as well as social and family organizations. Such rituals and practices have survived for centuries, together with their accompanying cultural and social values. Only during the past two centuries, with the rapid progress in scientific and technological innovation, have the modification and formation of institutions as adaptive culture become prominent. Spiritual culture is shaped by religious values, ethos, the *gemeinschaft* or community spirit. It includes religious and ethical values that pull individuals together into a social unit: a family, village, religious, ethnic, or racial community. Spiritual culture is a product of a historical process that has guided and supported the survival and prosperity of family, clan, race, and nation over a long span of time.

A lag exists between material culture and adaptive culture, and the distance between the two is quantifiable. Material culture is cumulative and progresses over a long time period. Adaptive culture adjusts to the changes in material culture, is itself subject to change, but is not cumulative. Once adaptive culture has evolved to a certain level, there is a great resistance to change, and this resistance is sometimes translated into cultural conservatism. Religious rituals and conventional folklore practices are examples of the stability and continuity of adaptive culture in the face of rapid change in material culture. The institutional arrangements or practices of some adaptive cultures are maintained and preserved both intentionally and consciously, to meet the psychological needs of the leaders and the public at large. As technology progresses and economic development is expedited, maladjustments due to the lags in the development of adaptive culture increase in scope and intensity.

The leaders and political ideologies of a nation may change, but institutions evolve as adaptive culture lags behind. In Russia today, for example, the leaders have abandoned the socially planned economic system and now espouse the free enterprise system. But over a period of seventy years, the socialist economic system and its institutional foundations have inculcated values and developed attitudes of their own. Although the former Soviet Union has now been divided into numerous independent states, the majority of the institutions that operated in the Soviet Union are still operating today, except that the element of corruption has been strengthened.

A simple change of symbols and national leadership cannot, in so short a period of time, bring about the kind of attitudes, values, and ways of thinking that would reform institutions and the way they govern the economic activities of the society. At immigration and customs posts today, one sees Russian soldiers stamping the same visa documents and customs forms that they used four years ago, when they were Soviet soldiers, and they still confiscate goods that were not purchased in a state-run store. The fascinating change is that, although the free market is supposedly in operation, the goods are still confiscated if they do not come from state-run stores—but now they are sold to other passengers on international departures from the airport in order to get foreign exchange.

Spiritual Culture and Development in East Asia

Max Weber maintained that, in the course of transition from traditional and developing society to modern and capitalist society, a nation must overcome hurdles to attain the basic characteristics of the capitalist system: rationality, continuity in production and markets, and labor mobility. It must overcome the hurdle of political and social structure, replacing patrimonialism and kinship with rational administrative organization, legal institutions, a separation of place of residence from place of work, and a distinction between corporate and private property.

On the individual psychological level, the hurdle is the development of the spiritual ethos according to one's "calling" (Weber 1958), the rejection of magic, and the cultivation of an existential tension between the real world and the ethical demand of a transcendent deity. In Western Europe these conditions were fulfilled by the Protestant ethic, in particular the Puritan concern for the salvation of the individual.

The followers of Weber have subsequently searched for analogues or counterparts of the Protestant ethic in Japan, Singapore, and elsewhere in East Asia. Robert Bellah, for example, in his *Tokugawa Religion* (1957) examined the nonpecuniary aspects of the samurai's handling of weapons and argued that a "central value system" in Japan provided a basis for competition for the sake of competition. According to his argument, this helped Japan enter the stage of modern capitalism during the Meiji period.

Michio Morishima argued that the Confucian traits of loyalty, nationalism, social solidarity, and collectivism contributed to successful economic development in Japan. The Confucianism practiced in China, Korea, and Japan (as outlined by Morishima 1982:4–9) emphasized in varying degrees the qualities of loyalty, filial piety, benevolence, faith, and bravery. The significant differences are that the Koreans shared their emphasis on the latter three qualities with China, whereas Japan (which gave no special place to benevolence) shared only the qualities of faith and bravery with its neighbors. These differences in emphasis highlight a distinct difference in philosophy. From very early in their history, the Japanese placed the strongest emphasis on loyalty, subordinating even filial piety to loyalty to the state and, moreover, giving no special consideration to benevolence (*ren*, which was a central concept in Chinese Confucianism) or moral obligations and concern for family, relatives, and friends. Hence Morishima concludes that, whereas the Confucianism of the Chinese and Koreans "is one in which benevolence is of central importance, Japanese Confucianism is loyalty-centered Confucianism" (Morishima 1982:8-9). Loyalty is given a preeminent place by the Japanese because social hierarchy is far more intensive in Japanese society. In Japan, loyalty to the ultimate ruler took precedence even over filial piety.

According to Ki-Jun Rhee, who translated Morishima's book *Why Has Japan "Succeeded"?* into Korean, the Chinese interpreted the term *chung* as a form of loyalty in which the subject serves his ruler with the greatest sincerity based on his conscience, whereas the Japanese interpreted it as absolute loyalty, to the extent that the subject may even have to sacrifice his own life for the ruler. For this reason, whenever a conflict arose in Japan between *chung* (loyalty to the ruler) and *hsiao* (filial piety), the Japanese had to opt for *chung*. Morishima recognizes the fact that, even though Japan imported science and industrial technology from the West, it failed to absorb Western liberalism, internationalism, and individualism because of this Confucian heritage.

Winston Davis's (1989) critique of "Japan theory," representing recent writings including Morishima's *Why Has Japan "Succeeded"?* which tend to exaggerate the uniqueness of Japanese culture in an attempt to explain Japan's successful development, is worth noting here. Especially relevant is his argument that each modern society has to be studied anew with respect to the decline of its religion. Pointing to some of the fallacies in the attempts by Weber's followers to explain the modernization of society in the context of the relationship between religion and development, he argues that there is an erroneous a priori assumption that religion is the source of some universal "spiritual ethos" or "central value system" which in turn influences all segments of society in the same way, and that this influence has a life of its own. Instead, "several different spirits" may emerge in the rise of capitalism. Buyers and vendors, for example, cultivate the spirit of credit worthiness. Entrepreneurs need a spirit that will inspire delayed gratification. Management needs a disciplinary spirit to impose on workers, as in the case of Japan.

The Weberian argument of secularization or disenchantment as part of the inevitable fate of modern civilization should not be taken for granted. Not all spirits may be secularized in the same way. Some may remain pure. Others may even undergo "resanctification." Weber's followers failed to deal with other social relations, such as the role of individual self-interest, competition, disloyalty, and conflict, which are more pertinent in explaining successful economic development in Japan. The emphasis on ethos must be balanced with the contributions of government, the banking system, tariffs, industrial planning, wages bonuses, and so on. Loyalty cannot exist in a vacuum; it is always situated in a network of incentives, rewards, patronage, coercion, and constraints which must be considered in examining the full dynamics at work in Japan, or anywhere.

In Davis's "barricades" theory of religion and development, instead of the hurdles proposed by Weber in the path of social transformation, barricades are set up to protect traditional values from the "economy." What traditional societies fear is not progress but the social turbulence and moral turpitude caused by unrestrained commerce. Both negative and positive religious "enablements" are proposed to explain Japan's economic development. One negative enablement is the passive outlook of Japanese Buddhism, which basically imposes no restrictions on choice of occupation by its adherents, allowing "economy" to extend beyond the encircled boundary. Japanese Buddhist institutions basically limit their services to rituals such as weddings, funerals, and other routine services, including the rites of ancestor worship. In addition, the coexistence of Confucianism, Buddhism, and Taoism and the interactions among them have resulted in a high degree of religious tolerance in East Asia. The Japanese, for example, have developed a value of multiple religious affiliations. Urbanization has expedited the secularization of Buddhist and Confucian practices. The prewar reemergence of and boom in religion has emphasized traditional values, ancestor worship, and ethnocentrism. The result has been to make magic and miracles compatible with the "rationality" of the industrial society. That many Japanese maintain "magic gardens" during weekends poses no serious threat to modern institutions, since they are seen to be situational and functional. In this connection, it is fascinating to recall the case of the Russian "Old Belief" (*starovery*), where mysticism rather than rationalism was the dominant feature of the faith. The "old believers" were "fanatical enemies of ecclesiastic reform and irrational adherents to letters and gestures of a religious movement, destitute of independent doctrinal contact and utterly conservative in outlook," but members of this group displayed impressive entrepreneurial talents and successfully engaged, for example, in the initial stage of the textile industry in late nineteenth-century Russia (Gerschenkron 1970:20–21).

One positive enablement is that religion is often called upon to enhance economic production. People go to a temple to pray for the fertility of their wives or their animals, for the elimination of a plague, or for the self-restraint, frugality, and diligence that are the basis of the common people's work ethic. Folk religion developed a work ethic for the common people. To be Japanese, it was believed, a person must work hard, be loyal, and be sincere. Both government and industry have supported and sponsored this concept to inculcate in the Japanese people the idea of work as a part of intrinsic Japanese values, alongside harmony, unity, consensus, loyalty, sincerity, and altruism toward the family, community, and nation. Japanese industry endeavored to inculcate the religious work ethic to workers from the top down through various initiation rites, training sessions, and "spiritual education."

A mixture of civil religion and work ethic has led to an amalgamation of civil religion and business ideology. This dynamic interaction during the early stage of economic development in the later Meiji period led to corruption in the business sector, which gave rise to the traditional Confucian barricades in the 1920s. This, in turn, led to the rise of militarism and fascism in Japan. By the 1980s little remained of the barricade that defended these traditions. Currently new values have risen to protect the economy from the intrusion of this society. The trend is now for the Buddhist religion, for example, to function to protect the economy, thereby transforming itself to accommodate a new role for religion in the development process. It is interesting to note that in the nineteenth century, during the late Tokugawa period, there was a period of persecution of Buddhism, which was perceived to be withdrawn, pessimistic, and aloof from reality. Then, between 1870 and 1876 the number of Buddhist temples in Japan decreased from 465,000 to a mere 71,000, and the number of Buddhist priests fell from 76,000 to 19,000. In spite of this decline, Buddhism was somehow transformed in the Meiji period, became a supporter of Japan's military policies, and collaborated with the government in the development of Japanese capitalism. Buddhist leaders moved from a pessimistic outlook to a more active and progressive one that dealt with real issues of the world. In the Meiji period, Buddhism even came to espouse the policy of "rich country, strong army" and placed great emphasis on the utility of religion. It contributed to value generation as part of the emergence of modern society: value generation toward a fundamental betterment of society.

In Western European countries the concept of individual rights was clearly defined and practiced in the early stages of capitalism. In East Asia, in contrast, where Buddhist, Confucian, and Taoist influences prevailed, the values of family, paternalism, cooperation, and loyalty were emphasized. Without concepts fundamental to free Western democracies (individualism, autonomy, individual rights, and a "loyal opposition"), no purely Western type of capitalism has evolved in Japan, and none is likely to evolve in the near future in any of the other East Asian countries.

Confucian Heritage in East Asia

Japan, Korea, and China share the heritage of Confucianism and its strong cultural influences. This is reflected concretely in the case of Japan in the imperial edict (or rescript) on education, and in Korea in the educational charter adopted in the 1970s. A strong Confucian family ideology is also reflected in today's corporate institutions.

Confucianism encompasses a large number of topics, ranging from philosophy to ethics, political theory, economic relations, and education. Confucian values include benevolence, righteousness, propriety, knowledge, and trust, but the core of Confucian thought in its role as a philosophy is the concept of benevolence (*ren*). Confucianism's ethical system includes the values of family, filial piety, loyalty, veneration, wisdom, and courage, but the core of these values is likewise benevolence. Confucianism places extremely high value on human ideals, morality, personal cultivation, and education.

Confucianism was adopted as official orthodoxy in China by the Han dynasty, during the reign of Emperor Wudi. Unlike Buddhism and Taoism, Confucianism did not bind its followers to a strict doctrine, established no religious organization, and did not resort to violent force to proselytize but instead influenced its followers mainly through education and moral training.

The core of the Confucian "Way" is benevolence. According to Confucius, "The genuine scholar and the man of virtue will not wish to live if it means injuring his virtue. He would rather give up his life so as to preserve his virtue" (Analects XV:8). To realize the ideal, one must possess both the Way and benevolence. If business managers are imbued with ideals and a spirit of voluntary service based on this Confucian philosophical perspective, they will become deeply concerned to plan for the future and avoid seeking purely short-term gains (Wen 1993).

During the last half-century, the economies of East Asia—particularly Japan, Korea, and Taiwan—have achieved new prominence in terms of rapid growth and demographic change. The paradigm developed by Western economists and social scientists has not been successful, however, in explaining the underlying causes and process of this rapid development, especially in terms of institutional factors and cultural values. These countries share East Asian cultural influences, such as the use of Chinese characters. In China, Japan, and Korea, the importance of achievement in education, motivation, frugality, and competitiveness is reflected in the values of the populace. In addition to sharing a common historical interactive background and geographic proximity, these countries all have similar cultural, social, and institutional frameworks. The past few years have witnessed dramatic regional political changes that have eliminated, for most practical purposes, the former political and military conflicts. Ideological barriers have eroded, leading to the reemergence and reassertion of cultural similarities in the region.

The Role of Government

The roles played by East Asian governments in their economies can be traced back to ancient history. During the Han dynasty in the second century B.C., just after the "Golden Expansion" period of Emperor Wudi, a great economic debate arose in the court of Emperor Zhaodi. The subject was the advantages and disadvantages of public as opposed to private management of the salt and iron markets. The debate was meticulously recorded, with the ministers in charge of agriculture and economic affairs and their key staff on one side, facing the opposing views of about sixty Confucian scholars. Although the discussion originated with the question of salt and iron production, it expanded into a full-blown debate on the political economy of China, ranging across topics of war, peace, trade, taxation, the monetary system, price controls, and resource allocation.

Some of that debate, translated into today's terminology and economic circumstances, still seems to be going on in China and Korea. It is fascinating to note that the Han dynasty government was accused of intervening too much, by controlling the production and sales of salt and iron. Prior to the Han dynasty, such decision making was in local hands. The local provincial leaders and the people who mined iron ore and produced iron products were the ones who planned and managed the production and sales operations. Salt production likewise was left in the hands of the people who lived either at the seaside salt flats or near inland salt deposits. The government's case for intervention was that the previous conditions inevitably enabled powerful individuals to conspire with local leaders to monopolize the trade, engage in hoarding, create artificial shortages, and then sell at a great profit when prices were forced up. The government therefore had to intervene to prevent periodic chaos in the markets. An additional reason for government intervention was the need to increase the intake of revenues to pay for military operations against the northern barbarians.

In the Han dynasty, taxes on farmers were lowered. But to obtain the revenues needed by the state, the government relied on taxing industries instead. According to the critiques of the scholars at that time, Chinese society was stratified into farmers and merchants. Merchants always reaped undeserved profits through unfair trade practices, with minimal labor on their part. And the merchants represented the social stratum that upheld Confucian values the least. According to this argument, private operations do not work for the national well-being in a Confucian society. Merchants inevitably become corrupt, and it is the responsibility of the state to educate them in Confucian values.

The moral of this debate is that government has always intervened in economic affairs. The lesson learned during the course of history is that the alternative model, which left economic affairs to the private sector, did not result in success. Even in Japan during World War II, the labor tax resembled exactly the labor tax levied during the Han dynasty, and the labor tax imposed by the Korean government during the Korean War was the same.

It is fascinating to find that, as far back in history as the Han dynasty, a public and scholarly debate was taking place about the advantages of government control over the production and sales of iron farm implements. It is also interesting that the argument in favor of private enterprise was that individual families have greater motivation to produce high-quality farm implements, because the quality of the product reflects the reputation of the family. When the government became the producer, on the other hand, the employees under the monopoly system were producing on a large scale, and the quality of products tended to be inferior for several reasons. The workers who supplied the labor (in lieu of a money tax) tended to be slack in their work and were less motivated than family-based workers. Less care was taken under the government monopoly, moreover, to time the production and sales of farm tools to coincide with the seasons when these products were in greatest demand. The debate can thus be translated in essence into a modern setting, in terms of the debate between nationalized enterprises run by the state and private enterprises.

The intriguing question in this debate is, Why did this early intellectual debate in China fail to flourish and evolve into a scientific analysis of economic relations? And why did China fail to experience a burgeoning of science and technology similar to the one that began in the West in the sixteenth century? Conditions were certainly right during the Tang dynasty and subsequent dynasties for China to become the world's leader in science and technology. The answer lies partly in the lack of continuity and the failure to build stepwise upon a succession of discoveries and ideas developed by the people with technical knowledge. Skilled craftsmen were ranked as an inferior stratum of society below agricultural laborers. They did not receive much respect, and often they were even killed to prevent the transfer of their skills to others.

Chinese history suggests that the answer also lies in the increasing emphasis on the development of spiritual and ethical culture, on human values based principally on Confucianism, Buddhism, and Taoism, and on social order and integration. For example, the selection of civil servants (the Chinese literati) by state examinations began in the Han dynasty. The system gradually placed more emphasis on what today's academic community would call the humanities and particularly on classical literature. From the Ming dynasty in the fourteenth century onward, much importance was attached to the ability to compose poems and essays. Even greater weight was placed in the Ching dynasty on the writing of stylized poems and essays, notably verse writing in *par-gu-wen* style, in which verses in couplets have to be rhymed and contain contrasts.

Over the centuries, especially beginning with the Sung dynasty, little emphasis was placed on the recruitment of military officers and warriors. In the civil service examinations, the least emphasis was placed on science, technology, economics, and craftsmanship. By the Ching dynasty, no emphasis at all was attributed to these subjects. Consequently, despite its early lead in scientific innovations (such as paper production, printing, and gunpowder), China fell behind the European countries, and Chinese culture did not produce the intellectual activity that might have ignited an explosion of scientific and technological ideas.

Ascriptive society holds that kings will be kings, scholars will be scholars, and peasants will be peasants. The basic bifurcation of society into the people who are trained to govern and those who are governed is implicit in the writings of Mencius, who observed that "those who work their minds rule the people, and those who perform physical labor are governed by the former" (Legge 1959:627).

The idea of virtuous government as prescribed by Confucianism is so widely accepted by the majority of the populace in China, Japan, and Korea that the positive role of government has been taken for granted. An important characteristic of the policymaking process common to these countries is the acceptance by the masses, both historically and today, of the role of intellectuals in policymaking. For a long time to come, the general public in all three countries will continue to accept leadership by intellectuals, and indeed the public expects intellectuals to play such a role. In contrast to Western-style public opinion, the public perspective with Confucian influence is based on the traditional respect shown to persons with superior intellectual training.

Gerschenkron found in Russia during the few decades before 1914 that the state played a dominant role in the inital stage of industrialization, for instance, generating the necessary financial resources through the state budget and transferring them to the emerging private sector. He argued that the intensity of economic backwardness is correlated with the extent of state intervention as well as with the strength of the spurt of industrial growth, and that nationalism and the nationalist ideology are important factors in the early stage of industrial development. By citing the examples of Hungary, Italy, and Germany, in addition to Russia, he pointed out that in the historical process of industrialization in Europe some of the prerequisities for development were missing in the late-comers, but these countries were able to work out substitutions for the necessary conditions for initial industrial development.

In this regard, Chinese, Japanese, and Koreans also expect the government to play an important role in industry. The public freely accepts the Japanese government's use of "administrative guidance" (*gyosei shido*) and the Korean government's "government instructions" (*chungboo chishi*) when intervening directly in industrial affairs. The Japanese and Korean public accept this terminology itself in a way Westerners find difficult to comprehend. Government-business relations in Korea have been characterized by strong leadership from a government that did not hesitate to intervene directly with markets by means of commands and discretionary measures. The government assumed the role of senior partner to business. The acceptance of the role of junior partner by large private enterprises was in part by necessity and in part cultural.

The rapid economic development experienced by Korea from the 1960s to the 1980s has been portrayed by some economists as the outcome of the free enterprise and market system and of economic management by American-trained economists employing the British-American system of free enterprise. In Cho and Kim (1991), which provided an economic development policy perspective, we proposed a more historical and institutional approach to explain rapid economic development in Korea, by examining eighteen policy measures that contributed to Korea's development from the perspective of the economic, institutional, social, and political environment in which the policies were introduced and implemented.

It is interesting to compare, for example, the roles of government in Japan and in the United Kingdom. In Britain the relationship between government and business has always been adversarial. The British bourgeoisie harbored a deep suspicion of the unelected officials in their bureaucracy. By contrast, the Japanese, like the Koreans and Chinese, always held their bureaucratic elites in high regard. Consequently, in Britain the role of bureaucrats was negative and regulatory, whereas in Japan the bureaucrats played a more positive and developmental role.

In the British-American case, there has always been an adversarial relationship between government and the business community, and government historically has not intervened in economic affairs except in its regulatory role. In Germany and France, on the other hand, government intervention in matters of economic development was more pronounced. In the nineteenth century, France and the German principalities formed government corporations, and Meiji Japan subsequently followed suit. In the Franco-German case, government evolved to provide guidelines and subsidies to business, and it continued to take measures to protect industries. The Germans also established a national bank to support and monitor private enterprise. Japan's experience during the early stages of economic development seems to fit the Franco-German model of institutional evolution more closely than the British-American one.

The Franco-German model may provide a closer fit for, and perhaps provide more useful and positive lessons for, the newly industrializing countries of East Asia, each of which has its own social, cultural, and political environment. In the case of Korea and Taiwan, the Japanese model of social transformation and economic change may provide a more appropriate basis for future institutional reform, as distinct from the predominant stress on neoclassical economics operating in Britain and the United States.

The induced economic development that has taken place in Japan and the newly industrializing economies of East Asia was accompanied by guided social transformation. To accomplish this, social forces had to be mobilized. In Japan, this included the induction and emergence of civil religion for purposes of social solidarity and cohesion to cope with external economic and military threats and to propel Japan out of its economic backwardness.

During the early stage of Japan's economic development, for example, the demise of the *daimyo* (feudal fiefs) led to unemployment among the lower ranks of samurai in the Meiji period. The samurai switched to economic activities, such as managing small-scale factories or government enterprises. This change did not really affect Japan's social structure and hierarchy, which was based more on ascription than on achievement. Later in Japan's economic development, the social structure loosened, but it remains fairly hierarchical and rigid although sometimes maintained only in symbolic form. Therefore, one can say that the initial economic development in Japan was brought about by a redefinition of the objectives of society on the part of Meiji elites, who were more competent and far-sighted than those who held political power during the Tokugawa period.

Leadership and Symbols of Authority in East Asia

The trend just noted suggests a proposition that might be formulated concerning institutionalized leadership for national development: in East and Southeast Asia, for historical, cultural, and sociopolitical reasons, institutionalized leadership based on the exercise of authority has been a necessary condition for rapid economic development. We must, however, note that this leadership must be combined with a free enterprise system.

A rough empirical basis for this proposition is provided by the countries with this type of institutionalized leadership, by virtue of the fact that they have succeeded in bringing about rapid economic development. In Japan the institution of the emperor, although symbolic, provides a sense of authority in the minds of the populace which overarches Japanese society. Korea had a presidential system with the authoritarian leadership centered on President Park Chung Hee. Taiwan remained under the authoritarian rule of the Kuomintang during the period of Chiang Kai-shek and Chiang Ching-kuo. Martial law in Taiwan was not relaxed until 1988, by which time the economy had already experienced rapid growth. In Thailand the monarchy is symbolic, yet it is perceived by the people as the center and ultimate source of authority for Thai society.

Singapore provides another example of rapid economic development in a society where the principles of liberal democracy appear to operate. In reality, Singapore established institutionalized leadership under President Lee Kuan Yew, who is Cambridge educated and understands Western society. He was able to merge his culture and Confucian values to provide the necessary elitist leadership in mobilizing the Singapore populace to achieve national economic development. In many ways, Singapore society is highly regimented, as seen in its management of the press, educational system, universities, city planning, housing, law and order, and the ethical standards of the populace.

In Indonesia, after the downfall of Sukarno in 1965 the political leadership provided by General Suharto established long-term political stability, under which Western-trained technocrats were able to formulate economic plans and translate the leader's vision of national development into specific policies. The result was the remarkable pace of economic progress achieved by Indonesia during the past twenty years. President Suharto is viewed by the majority of Indonesians as a symbol of authority and is looked up to as a leader who strives for the good of the nation.

The state sultans of Malaysia provide institutionalized leadership authority, which includes a monarchy that rotates among the sultans once every five years. Both symbolically and directly, this system serves as the basis for leadership authority. The parliamentary system practiced during the past few decades is tempered by culture and the ethnic idiosyncracies of Malaysia. A bare numerical majority of Malays and other indigenous groups wield political power, whereas business and the economy are dominated by the substantial minority (more than 30 percent of the total population) who are Chinese. For this reason, Malaysia may not have been able to achieve national solidarity for economic development to the same extent that was possible in Singapore and Thailand.

Given the factor endowments for economic development in Vietnam and some of the other Southeast Asian countries, the pattern of economic development will likely follow similar patterns in which institutional leadership is established to induce national economic development.

The Philippines is an interesting exception to the predominant pattern. For several decades early in the twentieth century, the United States attempted to induce the growth of an American-style liberal democracy in the Philippines. With American assistance after World War II, the free enterprise system appeared to have taken root. By 1960 per capita income in the Philippines was far ahead of practically all of East Asia, with the exception of Japan. Yet the Filipinos never evolved institutionalized leadership consonant with national goals of development.

Another exception is North Korea. Although the country has very strong authoritarian leadership under President Kim Il Sung, who depicts himself as the personification of national goals, the economy is aggravated by a distorted communist system. This provides a fascinating contrast to the kind of leadership needed for national development.

The People's Republic of China is currently undergoing an ideological and industrial transition, by opening its economy to the world and incorporating an increasingly pragmatic economic system. Deng Xiaoping, providing a new twist to the concept of the planned market that prevailed in the communist state prior to the 1980s, has remarked that there is a "market" in the planned system and a "plan" in the free market system. Given the recent political stability and the institutionalized leadership of Deng Xiaoping, the Chinese economy is currently growing at a rapid pace, almost equivalent to that of South Korea in the 1960s and 1970s. China is an exceptionally interesting case of institutionalized authoritarian leadership. Although Deng is completely outside formal institutional arrangements, he provides the ultimate political leadership, and the formal leaders still have to receive his sanction. In the minds of the great majority of Chinese, he represents the center of authority and leadership. In the absence of an institutional framework, he might be called an emperor without a crown.

The leadership characteristic in common among all these examples is the use of authority for the good of the nation and the moral discipline of the population. In most cases, leadership is also characterized by the absence of extreme ostentation and by an overt display of concern for the ordinary citizen. In some successfully developing countries, these leaders manifest an aura of personal austerity and emphasize their political integrity and aloofness from material greed.

All these cases include authoritarianism, although it ranges from strong to soft. East Asian history portrays its emperors, kings, and other leaders as authoritarian but also as benevolent and morally upright. The populace has always supported and followed such leaders. Considering the thousands of years of experience, traditions, and values inculcated in the populace, soft or strong authoritarian leadership in these economically successful countries is no anomaly.

Family Institutions

The rapid demographic change all East Asian countries have experienced during the past few decades provides an example of direct cultural and institutional influence on the economic development process. The populations in the East Asian sphere of Chinese cultural influence have consistently shown patterns of universal marriage. Among the females of childbearing age, nearly 100 percent are married. By contrast, the proportion who are married in other regions (about 75 percent in the United States, for example) is substantially lower and could hardly be termed universal. Moreover, East Asian women, once married, tend to have their first child without delay. Also, the proportion of childless couples is significantly lower among East Asian populations than among people elsewhere.

These phenomena are related to cultural values and norms that govern the formation of the family through the institution of marriage and childbearing. Deviation from this norm has traditionally been dealt with by punitive moral, social, and economic measures, contributing greatly to family cohesion. Yet, in spite of these phenomena, induced demographic change has been successful in the East Asian countries, leading to a reduction in the level of fertility and family size, and thus to a reduction of the dependency ratio and to higher-quality labor forces, through increased educational opportunities and investment, and consequently to higher rates of economic growth. This transition began earliest in Japan during the mid-1950s. By the late 1970s its level of fertility had been reduced by half, principally through induced abortions and the use of contraceptives. The transition in Korea and Taiwan began in the early 1960s. In both countries, the determined family planning programs implemented by the governments brought the total fertility rate down from a level of about 6 to below 3 by the second half of the 1970s. Mainland China was a late starter in family planning. Once the government's program was launched, it had to be carried out on a massive scale, because the population was already approaching the one billion mark. China was able to induce a reduction in total fertility from about 5 in 1970 to less than 2.5 by the mid-1980s.

In spite of the strong value attached to family continuity and the pro-natalist tendencies inherent in Confucian values, the national family planning campaigns in all four countries succeeded. People accepted the necessity of fertility reduction because it was perceived as directly relevant not only to national economic development but also to the economic well-being of the family. This perception reflects the pragmatic aspects of Confucian values in promoting the welfare of the family and thereby the national economic well-being. Given the strong Confucian values of the family function, continuity, and cohesion, however, the big challenge is whether the East Asian governments, having solved the population problem for the sake of present economic growth, can sustain family planning into the future.

Economic development in Japan, the rise of Japanese-style capitalism, and the outstanding performance of Japanese business enterprises since the Meiji revolution have strong linkages in the cohesive family system common throughout East Asia. At the end of the Tokugawa shogunate in Japan, scores of feudal lords were competing among themselves within a loose network, under the overall leadership of the Tokugawa family. This was a relatively peaceful period, and therefore most of the samurai (who served as warriors in times of trouble) in each fief were working as technocrats and engaging in rice production and other industries that helped generate revenues for the fief. With the external threat from Western powers, the lower echelon of samurai in the southwest of Japan (Kyushu and Shikoku) became involved in technology transfer from Europe, under slogans such as "increased national wealth and a stronger military" and "promote industry and economic prosperity." They increased their military capabilities and industrial production, thereby strengthening their respective fiefs' positions vis-à-vis rival fiefs.

The success achieved by the lower-echelon samurai through their efforts in southwestern Japan was subsequently applied throughout the nation. One barrier to the spread of this model, however, was the Tokugawa shogunate. To overcome this obstacle, the hitherto ignored imperial family was restored as the nation's supreme family, superseding the Tokugawa family. This change was perfectly in accord with the hierarchical structure of family and clan. There was no cultural or ideological basis upon which the Tokugawa family could resist the restoration of the supreme imperial family as the symbol of ultimate authority in the Japanese empire.

The most important point to recognize, with respect to the preservation of Japanese culture and the Japanese family system, is that the nation was restructured, under a strongly Confucian family ideology, to generate all the energy required to promote economic development and military capabilities. The Japanese family became defined not only in terms of perpetuating the family name and family functions but also on the basis of Confucian values, as a social unit of production and consumption—the former emphasizing management and the latter equated with family expenditure.

The Japanese knew that the process of industrialization, as it occurred in Western countries, was accompanied by a dissolution of the extended family system—that it created conflicts between family values, on the one hand, and industrialization and capitalist development, on the other hand. To preserve the Confucian family system, the Meiji government promulgated a strong civil law governing the family and household, giving authoritarian rights to heads of households and reaffirming patrilineal authority, "family virtues," and filial piety. Since the emphasis was on a hierarchical system of families, the imperial family became the ultimate object of loyalty at the summit of the new structure. In the same vein, the terminology was reinterpreted, so that filial piety, traditionally observed within the family, became an element of a hierarchical structure of loyalty with the imperial family at the pinnacle.

As Japanese workers migrated to new urban industrial sites in need of an expanding labor force, a fundamental contradiction—between capitalist development through industrialization and the traditional agricultural family—became apparent to the leaders of the Meiji government. Meiji legislation on this subject was therefore designed to encourage greater participation in the labor force by workers in younger age categories, but with provisions for return migration to the migrants' home areas. To sustain and uphold the family law, which was designed to keep intact the Japanese family system and values, the Meiji leadership issued an imperial edict establishing a new creed for public education, drawing primarily on Confucian values. Emphasis was placed on the emperor's ancestry, loyalty to the nation, filial piety toward one's parents, trust among friends, and harmony among community members, together with diligence in one's studies and development of skills and abilities. These measures were taken to mobilize the spiritual or psychological support of the populace for maintaining the family.

Tokugawa feudal society maintained a distinct social stratification. The highest respect was given to the warrior class, followed in descending order by farmers, craftsmen, and merchants. This class structure was common to China and Korea as well. In Japan, much greater weight and importance were given to the warrior class, because the Japanese fief was centered on the local warlord. The national administrative structure in Japan lagged behind that of China and Korea in terms of central control of local governments. In the feudal structure of Tokugawa Japan, the warrior family and the farm household provided a model for society at large. The function and structure of the warrior family were taken as models for Japanese social institutions, too, eventually including large corporations. Common characteristics cut across all households, whether warrior, farmer, or merchant. The warrior household placed the utmost importance on maintenance and continuity of the family, followed by the prosperity and good name of the family. These values were translated into the construction of a strong family-type nation and empire, which was called the "great Japan empire." The same values, in turn, were translated into the corporate organizations that began to emerge in the late nineteenth century.

Family succession in the Japanese system (which is almost the same as the systems in China and Korea) is patrilineal, and the main line of succession (from father to eldest son) is called *hongka*, or "main," family. There is a generational division into *bekka* representing the branch lines established by younger sons and the daughters, who establish separate, but still related, households. At the level of grandchildren, the main line continues and yet more branch lines are established. In addition, cousins working in the family also become part of the "associated" family. This model results in the creation of a kind of clan community.

The Japanese family and clan place the utmost emphasis on cohesion, loyalty, and filial piety. As the state modernized during the Meiji period, and as modern corporations began to form, the emerging administrative and business philosophy became imbued with these values. The evolution of the Japanese corporate structure was thus very distinct from the corporate structure built on the basis of capital in the Western world.

The Korean traditional family is patrilineal, the family as an entity is given preference over its individual members, and the family group is inseparably identified with the clan. The most important function of the family is to preserve the household within the traditional Confucian system. Accordingly, the central familial relationship is not that between husband and wife but rather that between parent and child, especially between father and son.

These Confucian principles of family relationships were projected into the community and national life and became important social values. The Korean family during the premodern period remained essentially Confucian in both ideal and practice. Moreover, even after national liberation in 1945, Korean family law emphasized the importance of blood relations and the authority of the male household head.

Because women had no right to inherit the position of head of household, they often lost out in the inheritance of property. The share of inheritance due an unmarried daughter was always given to the eldest son, who would pay for the daughter's wedding when she married. In practice, then, women received a share of the family property not as an inheritance but at the time of their marriage, and their shares were much smaller than the sons' shares. Korean inheritance practice was essentially the same as that in China, and it continued during the Japanese occupation of Korea up to 1945.

A law enacted in 1991 provides that when a man dies, his wife is to receive one-half his property, and the other half is to be distributed equally among the children, regardless of sex or marital status. However, division of property in other proportions, based on a properly executed will, takes precedence over this legal provision.

The deeply rooted preference accorded to patrilineal succession remains dominant. Regardless of whether separate households are maintained by the parents and by the eldest son, the relationship between parents and children is based on mutual reliance, and most children plan to rejoin their parents when the parents become too old to care for themselves. This trend indicates that, although industrialization has caused urban families to evolve into the nuclear type, parents and their grown children still depend upon one another to a great extent, in contrast to European and American nuclear families. There are, however, signs that in urban areas family ties and the importance attached to kinship are gradually weakening. Nevertheless, the Confucian influence on the Korean family is still strong, as evidenced by the preference for sons, the strong kinship bonds, and the persistent deference by wives to their husbands' status and role.

Corporate Institutions

Japan adopted the capitalist model of production and thereby accepted a corporate structure based on capital. By the nineteenth century, however, it was already evident that Western capitalism entailed a dissolution of the family and village community. To prevent this process from occurring in Japan, corporate leaders made a nationwide effort to meld the family ideology and functions into Japanese corporate structure. The "Japanese style" corporate structure and management that emerged is thus an amalgamation of the capitalist mode of production and traditional Confucian family ideology, within the larger framework of a family-type state capitalism.

The Japanese corporate world uses a family relationship term (literally "father" company) when referring to a business group's stockholding company or parent company. Similarly, the affiliated companies that are members of the corporate family are literally called the "son" and "grandson" companies. The parent company either controls or is a principal investor in these members of the corporate family, even though the affiliates are legally separate entities. In addition, there are branch companies that parallel the branches and associated members of the Japanese family structure, thus forming a corporate clan-type relationship. In the corporate structure, the branch company is related to the parent company and other members of the corporate family through capital investment in the branch by the corporate group, through management personnel who are sent from the parent company, and through coordination of some production, sales, and other operations between the branch company and other members of the corporate family.

Relationships between Japanese firms can be compared in some ways to the pyramidal structure of a typical family tree, which shows descent from a group of related forebears. The big corporations fill the primary leadership category at the top, below which are ranged the medium and small-scale enterprises that manufacture and supply many of the components the big corporations assemble into finished products. An interesting contrast is provided by General Motors, which had 120,000 employees in 1988 producing most of the parts for the corporation's car assembly, and Toyota, which had only one-twelfth as many employees. The difference is that the Japanese corporation has greater linkages with small-scale enterprises that provide such parts, manifesting a cultural difference based on family ideology.

One of the distinct characteristics of the Japanese family system is the tendency, whenever necessary, to adopt someone who has no blood relationship into the family. The amalgamation process brought this attitude toward adoption into the Japanese corporate structure, so that large corporations, particularly those in the heavy industry sector, introduced a system that included temporary employees, external employees, and subcontractors. Within the corporate family of firms, the main corporate family line remained 100 percent under the corporation's control, whereas other smaller firms were adopted into the corporate family as branch company lines (firms in which the corporate holding company held a relatively high percentage of ownership) and associated company lines (firms in which the percentage was relatively low).

Japanese corporate management has two important dimensions. The first comprises characteristics acquired as a consequence of being an integral part of the "family nation" within the Japanese empire. As in the case of the warrior family, which shares the same heritage, the main concerns of corporate management are focused on the maintenance and continuity of business activities. Emphasis is therefore placed on long-term planning and reliability in the company's operations, to ensure its future prosperity and reputation.

The second dimension is leadership. The style and philosophy of leadership in corporate entities are naturally predicated on the Confucian values of family cohesion, filial piety, and the wider national well-being. Within the corporate family, moreover, a natural emergence of leaders takes place, because the members of the family implicitly know who their best performers are. Those workers who demonstrate the most merit and superior performance thus emerge through a general consensus and rise through the firm's leadership hierarchy. Since this process is respected by the company unions, much greater harmony is achieved between management and unions than is the case in Western economies. It is accepted, moreover, that the head of a Japanese corporation, as the most respected person within the body of company employees, should be paid more than other employees. But, unlike corporate practices in the United States, the Japanese business leader is not paid vastly more than others within the same corporation. In this regard, Japan achieved a modernization of Confucian ideas.

One Confucian value obliges all members of a family to make their best effort when performing a duty for the family. In the company-family context, this characteristic is translated into mutual help. This value of mutual help is reflected in the willingness of employees to work overtime without extra pay, for the sake of the company-family, in order to accomplish a specific task. It naturally follows that entrance into the company is the most important step taken by the individual as a new family member. Entrants are initially treated on an equal basis, regardless of their abilities and qualifications. The process of socialization within the company prepares them through in-house training to become competent members of the company and possibly to emerge eventually as leaders. Hence, on-the-job training is greatly stressed.

The value placed on maintaining the good name of the family is recast by corporations in terms of the strong preference for expanding their respective market shares rather than pursuing short-term profits. An example is provided by the response to the increasing strength of the yen during the past two decades. As a result of U.S. pressure on Japan to allow the exchange rate to rise, the U.S. dollar declined over a long period beginning in the 1970s, from a rate of more than 360 yen to the dollar to a level close to one-third that rate in the early 1990s. As the exchange rate of the yen increased, however, Japanese exporters did not raise the dollar-denominated prices of their products to match the new exchange rates. Instead, they tried to keep selling prices abroad in line with existing dollar prices, not only to maintain their market shares but also to give them the necessary flexibility to expand exports even further. An interesting example is provided by Swallows, a manufacturer of silverware products in Niigata. Swallows assembles its final products, but it has more than twenty subsidiaries and subcontractors who either make various components or process the products at various stages of manufacture. In response to the upward valuation of the yen, these companies, working as a family corporative group, agreed to absorb the increases in costs, relative to the dollar, for their respective components or processes. By sharing the burden of these increases, they managed to maintain the dollar-denominated export prices of their products and thereby retained their market share. Today, this group has perhaps the biggest market share in silverware products. A similar approach was taken by Toyota and its component manufacturers, who likewise shared the burden of absorbing the increased dollar-denominated costs. This strategy illustrates an important institutional dimension of Japanese corporate behavior which businesses and governments outside Japan did not fully understand.

Relations between Japanese management and the workforce are characterized by lifetime employment, a system of automatic annual promotions (as distinct from Western-type promotions that depend on performance), and corporate labor unions. It seems natural that lifetime employment has been institutionalized in Japan, since it is based on the Confucian family characteristic of looking after the clan community and on the presumption that the prosperity of the family (in the corporate case, the achievement of the firm) is at stake.

A great third-century B.C. merchant, Bai Kuei, who is regarded as the founding ancestor of Chinese business philosophy, formulated a set of principles for success in business. He declared that businesses should be run according to the example set by Yi Yuen, a famous minister of the Cho dynasty. Business leaders should eat the same simple food and wear the same type of clothing as their employees. They should not expend their wealth extravagantly, since Confucius was opposed to extravagance and instead placed emphasis on the accumulation of savings. Bai further advocated that businesses use the famous Sun Wu military strategy, with emphasis on a strong will above all. Even after the passage of more than two millennia, these principles still exerted a strong influence over the modern Japanese style management that began to emerge in the Meiji period.

The lower-class samurai of the early Meiji period took charge of operating the enterprises established by the state. These enterprises were eventually sold or transferred to the private sector to avoid the hampering effects of bureaucracy on corporate operations. The samurai and government technocrats who entered private industry provided business with a philosophy and model for corporate leadership. Two men who typify the idea of business "for the sake of the society" rather than for the profit of the individual were Godai and Eiichi Shibusawa (1840–1931). Both were samurai early in life and later contributed to the development of Japan's private sector as great entrepreneurs and industrialists.

Shibusawa established the motto "Confucian Analects plus the abacus" as the motto of his company. He drew his inspiration in particular from a saying of Confucius: "Riches and honors are what men desire. If they cannot be obtained in the proper way, they should not be held." In this context, the "proper way" was interpreted to mean "for the social good." By combining this Japanese spirit with Western commercial techniques, Shibusawa was able to achieve an amalgamation of morality and economic development as the guiding philosophy of his company.

It is important to note that, during the Sino-Japanese and Russo-Japanese wars, all social organizations in Japan were mobilized, as though the nation were a single big family. In the process of these mobilizations, filial piety and loyalty to the state acquired quasi-religious connotations, almost like elements of a civil religion. In 1937, a few years before the start of World War II, the national government proclaimed a total "national spiritual" mobilization. In response, all Japanese united in an associated framework to "repay" the nation in the form of production and services. This response parallels the perception of position and obligation within the family, in the sense that all the people within the nation-family owed their existence and well-being to the nation and, at a critical juncture, were called upon for repayment.

The defeat of Japan led to a change in the legal foundation of the family system, which became much more democratic than before. The emperor was detached from the exercise of power and became a symbol of authority instead. Other social legislation and new labor laws opened up avenues for a stronger labor movement. Despite these changes, private corporations continued to adhere to the concept of the national good as a corporate priority. In the slogans still used by many corporations, the orientation toward the good of society and the nation is still a guiding principle. This spirit is illustrated in the Matsushida slogan "Industry for repaying one's debt to the nation" and the Toyota slogan "Never forget Japan!" Corporate patriotism based on Confucian family ideology thus lives on and sustains the traditional Japanese characteristics that underly its modern management behavior.

Typical of turn-of-the-century Japan is the creed of the Katakawa family, which was adopted as the creed of the textile firm established by the family during the

Meiji period. The creed can be paraphrased in ten basic points: (1) Pay homage to the Buddha, or worship some deity, and honor your ancestors. (2) Never forget the path of loyalty and filial piety. (3) Work hard and avoid extravagance. (4) Within your family maintain a simple and tranquil household, but at your workplace perform actively and vigorously. (5) Duties at work should always be carried out in the context of national goals and objectives and must coincide with the public good. (6) Perform your duties as best you can, as though nature has given them to you to perform, and receive whatever compensation naturally comes to you. (7) Never be lazy. (8) Always treat others better than you treat yourself. (9) Always try to help others who are in need. (10) Treat your employees as you treat members of your family. This creed is deeply imbued with Confucian thinking and establishes a whole Confucian-type philosophical system for the firm's management and employees alike.

The development of the relationship between management and workers required special attention in order to consolidate family ideology in the capitalist mode of production. Meiji period Japan experienced various types of exploitation common in the West, such as the use of children as industrial workers. Thus, in early industrial Japan, not only women but also children were sometimes temporarily separated from their village communities. In the longer term, however, the trend in Japan was a paternalistic approach to strengthen the national income, thereby raising the average income level of village households and in turn strengthening the village community.

As noted above, the creed of the Katakawa textile firm exhorted workers to accept the wages that naturally came to them. According to this philosophy, for purposes of getting higher wages, workers should not resort to industrial action but should increase their incomes through better peformance and higher productivity. Although Japanese workers suffered abuses and exploitation during the early stages of industrialization, with consequent pressure to form labor unions, organized labor as it is conceived today remained illegal until after World War II. In its place, each big prewar corporation established its own employees association, which provided mutual help to improve working conditions and to reduce human rights violations within the company. The original purpose of these associations was to obviate the need for unions by meeting the needs of workers within the respective corporations. To a great extent, these associations shielded the big Japanese corporations from the power organized labor unions would otherwise have exerted.

When this mechanism failed to work, and disruptions by workers took place on a large scale, the government responded not with legislation to legalize and regulate union activity but with greater police powers to preserve social order and maintain economic production. At the same time, a factory law was enacted—although never fully implemented—in an effort to establish a minimum age for employment and some regulations for other working conditions. It is interesting to note that, at the time these laws were promulgated, about 60 percent of factory workers were under the age of 20, and 30 percent were younger than 15.

Japanese workers endured a long and difficult period without effective enforcement of labor laws or support for basic workers' rights. But some positive aspects emerged in the course of postwar recovery and subsequent technological advance. This pattern of painful experiences eventually being transformed into relatively fortunate circumstances is reflected in an old Chinese saying: "It is not necessarily a blessing to get a beautiful horse. It is not necessarily a bane if your son breaks his leg when riding the horse, because in a subsequent outbreak of war the boy would be spared from conscription." Japanese-style management in the postwar era benefited from the earlier painful experiences when labor unions were still illegal. Although the factory law was never fully implemented, its provisions helped to persuade the big corporations to improve working conditions and maintain reasonable standards. It had much less influence among the small and medium-size enterprises, which were increasing in number and were responsible for most of the violations. For this reason, before World War II Japanese labor relations evolved along two separate planes: the big corporations gradually developed modern management-labor relations, whereas the smaller firms were not greatly influenced by labor legislation. The dual planes along which labor-management relations developed separately contributed to the evolution of the Japanese style of management. Labor-management relations were also influenced by the "national spiritual mobilization" that prevailed in Japan's modern wars and was perpetuated in essence among workers in the big postwar corporations. This spirit is exemplified by the importance attached to quality control of products (linked also to the corporate-family reputation) and the fact that the award most coveted by Japanese corporations is the Demming Prize—named after Edward Demming, who introduced the concept of quality control.

An instructive example of the development of management-labor relations in the postwar years is provided by Kanebo Textile Factory, under the leadership of Muto Sanji. He received his education at Keio University and was a student of Fukuzawa Yuichi. Subsequently he traveled to the United States, where he observed American labor-management patterns in the course of his employment as a tobacco factory worker and a restaurant waiter. After his return to Japan, he was employed by Kanebo. Although he supported the concept and goals of labor unions, he was unable to get his proposals for forming a union adopted. He remained personally committed to the improvement of working conditions and at Kanebo applied some of the ideas he had gained from his experience and observations in the United States and from the example of Germany's Krupp steel works. He raised the wages paid his employees substantially and provided them with incentives and benefits such as health services, hospital treatment, and housing. He made every effort to teach employees that their total dedication to the firm was a commitment that would be rewarded in the longer term. As a result of his efforts,

Kanebo quickly rose to the top stratum of Japanese firms in terms of production and sales. The model he established greatly strengthened the family-type management system in Japan and contributed to the Japanese system of lifetime employment and employee welfare.

Big corporations in Korea developed much later than in Japan and are essentially a postwar phenomenon. The Korean conglomerates grew out of government subsidies and government-guaranteed loans from abroad, which were integral to the rapid economic growth policies promoted during the tenure of President Park Chung Hee (1961–79). When President Park amended the Korean constitution and launched the Fourth Republic in 1972, he called the new system *yushin,* which was modeled after the *iishin* system of Meiji period Japan. In fact, these two terms differ only in pronunciation, since both are represented by the same Chinese character. During the Fourth Republic, the utmost emphasis was placed on loyalty and filial piety to promote economic and corporate development under the concept of state-guided capitalism. During this period, Korea retained the essence of the Meiji slogan for promoting a strong economy and a strong military, encouraging the rapid development of big corporations to generate, according to President Park's thinking, neither personal nor private interests but the greater public interests that were vital to the nation in the longer term.

President Park designed a system to deal with the conglomerates, which he expected to grow in size and economic power. During his tenure, the big corporations accepted and appreciated his leadership, and under his guidance their behavior remained docile. The long-term design for curtailing and balancing the economic power of the conglomerates was derailed in 1979 when the president was assassinated. Under the subsequent administrations of presidents Chun and Roh, who became directly involved with political funding, the administration lost some of the authority and respect that the head of a Confucian family system would otherwise enjoy. As the conglomerates grew in size, in share of GDP, and in political influence, the healthy structural balance achieved in the corporate sector of the economy was eventually lost. Whereas the Meiji regime lasted forty-four years, the *yushin* regime launched by President Park lasted only eight years, and the revolutionary spirit he generated was not perpetuated by his successors. By the beginning of the Sixth Republic, when President Roh introduced his own scheme of democratization for Korea, most of the institutional framework for achieving the Park vision of a strong country had been weakened.

Authoritarian behavior prevails in Korean business enterprises, including the medium-and large-scale conglomerates. The owner-head of a thriving Korean company, by virtue of his successful past endeavors, establishes himself in an authoritarian position comparable to that of a head of household. At the same time, in the case of a large corporation, the other executives consciously build up their leader beyond life size, partly with the rationale that his contacts among equally high elites in government and business will ultimately help the corporation to prosper. The chief himself encourages the construction of this facade, not only for personal gratification but also to lead the corporation (a surrogate big family) toward further economic success.

The management system in the corporate world, in contrast to that in politics and government, is far more authoritarian when an owner-founder heads the company. Once the corporate hero has been created and is perceived as such, the forum for a discussion of independent ideas ceases to exist. In the process, it becomes increasingly rare for subordinates to make critical evaluations of projects and policy decisions. Subordinates do not offer objections or even raise questions that might displease the hero. The hero, in turn, does not want to hear anything that might call his wisdom and abilities into question or that might detract from the aura of his past accomplishments. Eventually, rational evaluation of the owner-head's performance becomes almost impossible.

By never disagreeing with the leader or proposing alternatives, supporting executives cannot then play their proper roles. In the Korean corporation, decisions thus become strictly personal ones. This can be dangerous, especially when a single, overconfident chief makes a decision solely on a whim, while his executives hesitate to confront him with rational analysis. Even in an efficient business organization, therefore, at some point the undesirable facets of the authoritarian family system come into play. Later efforts to perpetuate earlier successes draw the corporation into rivalry with competitors and into risky ventures that may be economically unsound (such as acquiring nuclear electric power reactors for reasons of prestige). If a competitor has launched a new enterprise, the chief may want to follow suit immediately, to maintain parity with the competitor. The executives acquiesce, because they want to preserve the image of their corporation, even though it has been inflated beyond life size and beyond their resources to uphold. The economic consequences are not discussed in advance and are probably covered up once they become manifest, again to maintain the image.

Another negative aspect of the family authoritarian system without separation of ownership and management, as in Japan, is that heads of corporations want to bequeath not only ownership but also leadership to their sons, brothers, cousins, and relatives by marriage, who may not be equally dynamic or even fully qualified. The consequences to society may not be serious in the case of small and medium-size businesses. But can such a procedure be justified in a conglomerate—especially if the corporation's debt to the government is a large percentage of the entire business? One positive advantage is that a succession of brilliant leaders can stimulate the greatest possible advances for the corporation, particularly because personal trust and loyalty are highly valued within the corporation, as they are within the family. But objective, rational management is difficult to introduce when there are less capable heirs expecting to assume not only the chief's powers but also his undisputed authoritarian role.

In Taiwan, the healthy and gradual growth of small and medium-scale industries contributed to the long-term and higher growth rates of the economy. As in

Japan, the small, medium-size, and large corporations of Taiwan eventually became organized in a stable pyramidal structure. (The Korean corporate sector, by contrast, evolved into an unwieldy mushroom-shaped structure that is too heavy at the top.) Such economic growth and the healthy structure of the small and medium-size enterprises can be attributed in part to the political stability enjoyed by businesses in Taiwan, where martial law was maintained until 1988.

A recent Nihon University survey analyses the corporate structures in Japan, Korea, and China and reveals other important differences in business philosophy between East Asia and the West. For example, Japanese and Taiwanese businesses give the highest ratings to reliability and quality control, and responsibilities toward employees also ranks high. Profit seeking, on the other hand, is ranked low among company priorities in East Asia, whereas the reverse is true in the United States.

A preliminary analysis of the data available suggests that the dependence on the business group is loosening somewhat in Japan. Most new medium-size businesses in Japan are founded almost exclusively by family investments. The larger companies included in the survey tend to belong to the venture-capital category, and these companies are relatively more independent than other companies. Even so, about one-third of the larger companies belong to a business group, and more than half of the small and medium-size firms belong to a business group or form a *keiretsu* or have some other association with bigger companies; the proportion is even higher for companies in the manufacturing sector, especially those that produce electric appliances and automobile parts subcontracted by the larger corporations. About half the small and medium-size companies have a parent company as their main shareholder, and they are dependent on the parent company for business contracts.

The survey reveals an important difference in shareholders' perceptions of who wields the greatest power and influence over decision making within a corporation. In the majority of medium-size corporations in Japan, the chief executive officer is either the founder of the corporation or a son of the founder. Among the large corporations, the great majority (80 percent) of shareholders perceive the president as wielding the most power and influence over decision making, whereas only 10 percent view the chairman of the board as playing the most powerful role. By contrast, in Taiwan and Korea the chairman of the board (rather than the company president) is regarded as the most influential top executive. One reason for this perception is that about half the shares in the big Taiwanese corporations are held by the corporation's founder and his family; in the smaller and medium-size corporations, the proportion is about two-thirds.

In the case of Japan, the survey indicates that company presidents who rose through the ranks of management are most influential in their respective companies' affairs. This trend is attributable in part to the separation of ownership and management that has taken place over a period of several generations in Japan. Most Taiwanese and Korean companies, on the other hand, were established or have expanded into large corporations only during the period of rapid economic development of the past three decades. Thus, the founder, owner, and main shareholder in the Taiwanese and Korean company still exercises more direct control and retains more power over the operations of the company than the Japanese company president who has risen through the ranks.

Educational Institutions

From the time of the Meiji revolution onward in Japan, modern educational institutions were regarded as essential to train leaders for government, industry, and other sectors of the economy and to build the nation's military capabilities while also promoting overall economic development. General education was also provided for the populace at large, beginning with compulsory primary education. Prior to the Meiji revolution, education in Japan was confined to the study of the Chinese classics and training in the use of weapons such as swords. There was no national education system. Instead, each of the feudal fiefs provided the education and training deemed necessary for its administrators and samurai. In addition, some instruction was provided by Buddhist temples, and in some villages instruction in Chinese and Japanese was available through the private tutorial system.

Just before the Meiji revolution, sporadic efforts were made by some individuals to acquire the scientific, technical, and other Western-style knowledge necessary to begin the modernization of Japan. Among these men, the most prominent was Fukuzawa Yukichi (1835–1901), who established a *juku* (traditional place of learning) two years before the Meiji Restoration and later founded Keio University. Fukuzawa is regarded in Japan as the most important leader outside government who worked to promote the modernization of education, business, and social affairs. As a child, he thought that the knowledge necessary to modernize Japan could best be acquired through the language of the Dutch, who were the only Europeans permitted to trade in Japan before the opening of the country to the West in 1854. Fukuzawa subsequently switched his attention to English and made a long journey to the United States as a young man. On his return, he devoted his entire career to nurturing private higher education institutions and to the training of the leaders necessary to mobilize Japan's human resources and implement the government's policy of "rich country, strong army." Among his innovations was the teaching of Western economics (Adam Smith's *Wealth of Nations* was a basic text in Keio University classes), and his students ran the first modern bank in Japan. Fukuzawa's vision extended at least a century ahead of his time, and he is honored today by inclusion of his picture on the 10,000 yen note, the most frequently used banknote at the present time.

Other private universities were subsequently founded, including Waseda, Meiji, and Nihon. Christian missionaries also contributed significantly to the development of education in Japan and operated private schools at every level, from primary school to the International Christian University. Graduates of the private universities emerged as the nation's business and financial leaders. Political and administrative leadership, on the other hand, was largely the product of the public institutions of higher education

During the Meiji period, the government created eight "higher schools" to provide advanced education at the post-secondary level. According to the numbering system used for these schools, the most prestigious was located in Tokyo (number one), followed by those located in Sendai (number two), Kyoto (number three), and Kanazawa (number four). Parallel to these schools, but at a higher level, the government established the imperial universities, beginning with Tokyo Imperial University. To qualify for admission to an imperial university, candidates had to graduate from one of the higher schools (some of which were not among the eight "numbered" ones) and also pass a very difficult entrance examination that was open to qualified candidates nationwide. Tokyo Imperial University students were drawn mostly from the top-level higher schools (numbers one to eight).

The educational institutions at these two levels became the most prestigious in Japan and produced much of the successive new generations of national leaders. Most Japanese prime ministers, for example, were graduates of Tokyo Imperial University. The modernization of Japan was, then, made possible by the development of the higher schools, imperial universities, and private universities, which produced Japan's modern leadership in every sector: politics, public service, law, industry, finance, education, medicine, science, and technology.

In addition to the elite levels of post-secondary education, the Japanese government developed professional and technical schools to make advanced education available to a larger segment of the population, at levels ranging from middle school through junior college. These institutions were responsible for education in areas such as agricultural technology, commercial studies, and engineering. They also provided the corps of trained teachers needed for primary schools throughout Japan. In terms of teacher training, the most prestigious institution was the Tokyo Teachers High School, and the best of the high school graduates within such institutions tended to become the middle school teachers of the next generation. Some continued their professional education at higher levels: President Park Chung Hee, for example, was a graduate of a teachers middle school before his training at a Japanese-run military school in Manchuria and a military academy in Japan. Before World War II, most of the students in this system were male. Women attended the few schools and colleges open to them or else pursued their education at the private universities.

The authoritarian Japanese education system was geared to the national ideology of the greater Japanese empire until 1945. Postwar reforms made the system more open and democratic. But, far from attaining the research-oriented, interdisciplinary atmosphere necessary to stimulate innovation and create new knowledge, the traditional imperial universities (although still recruiting the best students) did not necessarily provide the type of training most appropriate for the future of Japanese economic development. Private universities that used to be in the second ranks have eliminated much of the former gap, in both teaching and the quality of students admitted each year. In economics and the medical sciences, for example, Keio University is now considered by some educators as more advanced than the University of Tokyo. One problem is that most economics departments in the postwar state universities were dominated or influenced by Marxist economists. The graduates of their departments pursued careers in government but were not successful in the corporate world. The graduates of private universities such as Keio, Waseda, and Hitotsubashi, on the other hand, trained in the economics of Western Europe and the United States, provided much of the corporate leadership, and have contributed greatly to the development of corporate institutions in Japan.

Under the Japanese colonial regime up to 1945, imperial universities and the Japanese educational system were also established in Taiwan and Korea. Taipei Imperial University was the forerunner of Taiwan National University, and Keijo Imperial University was the forerunner of Seoul National University. In northeast China, Japan helped to establish Kengkoku University, which was the equivalent of a Japanese imperial university, although it was operated by the puppet state of Manchukuo. Japan also established a system of middle schools and high schools in Korea and Taiwan, to generate the human resources required in the lower echelons for increased agricultural production, commerce, and the operations of the financial sector and to meet the demand for engineers and skilled technical labor in factories.

The modern education system in Korea, although under Japanese control from 1910 to 1945, was built on solid Confucian foundations. State civil service examinations on the Confucian model were introduced to Korea during the Koryo dynasty (918–1392). The strengthening of this examination system, particularly under the Yi dynasty (1392–1910), nurtured the growth of Korean scholarship and educational institutions. A Confucian university, four official schools in the capital, and official schools in provincial capitals became the great centers of learning for Koreans. Private schools also played an important role in the development of scholarship, as did private tutoring provided by individual scholars across the land. The outstanding intellectual achievement of the early Yi period was the Korean script, a scientific phonetic system institutionalized in 1446 by the scholarly King Sejong.

Modern concepts of education based primarily on the use of the Korean language were first introduced into Korea during the 1880s by Protestant missionaries. Their schools, which used Korean-language texts written in the easy-to-learn *han'gŭl* script, initially attracted the interest of very few Koreans, and enrollment in substantial numbers did not take place until the 1920s. A series of reforms was initiated by the Korean government in 1894 to create a primary school system, some high schools, and a normal college, but early in the twentieth century, as Japanese influence became predominant in Korea, education was still available only to the well-to-do. In the meantime, Korea's traditional suzerain (China) was eliminated as a rival for influence in Korea after the Sino-Japanese war of 1894, and Russia likewise was eliminated as a potential rival after the 1904–5 Russo-Japanese War. In 1905, Korea became a protectorate of Japan, and during the next five years a dual system of education (Korean schools for Koreans, Japanese schools for Japanese residing in Korea) was instituted. This dual system was retained when Korea was annexed to Japan in 1910, and it remained in force until 1938.

The concept of universal primary education was introduced to Korea during the period of Japanese rule from 1910 to 1945. The colonial government provided an increasing proportion of school-age children with minimal primary schooling, supplemented by a program of vocational education. The education system was intended, however, to train a subservient workforce of subjects loyal to Japan and capable of filling the growing number of menial and low-paying jobs for the benefit of the imperial economy. Numerous schools were built, and the enrollment of Korean children increased dramatically. The major accomplishment of this period, as shown in Table 1.1, was at the level of primary education.

Although Japanese-style education was a cultural shock for the Koreans and

Table 1.1

Registered students in Korea by type of school: Selected years, 1910–1937 (thousands)

Type of school	1910	1919	1930	1937
Primary schools (years 1–6)				
for Japanese	15.5	42.8	67.4	89.8
for Koreans	20.1	89.3	450.5	901.2
Middle schools (years 7–12)				
for Japanese	0.2	2.0	5.8	7.8
for Koreans and Japanese	0.8	3.2	11.1	15.6
High schools for girls				
for Japanese	0.5	1.9	8.3	11.9
for Koreans	0.4	0.7	4.4	7.1
Teachers' seminaries	0.0	0.0	1.3	3.8
Industrial schools	1.1	4.5	15.3	26.6
Colleges	0.4	0.9	2.5	4.0
University preparatory schools	0.0	0.0	0.3	0.4
University	0.0	0.0	0.6	0.5
Nonstandardized schools[a]	71.8	39.2	47.5	142.6
Total[b]	110.8	184.5	614.4	1,211.4

Source: UNESCO (1954:23).

[a]Includes short-course elementary schools.

[b]Column totals are subject to rounding errors.

deemed undesirable in the short term, it did bring rapid, positive change. It provided even the ordinary people with some exposure to modern education. It was accompanied by much-needed modern foreign technology, which the isolationist Yi dynasty had adamantly denied itself. The people born during the first three decades of the twentieth century are the first generation of Koreans to have received a modern, albeit Japanese, education. Significantly, they became the technocrats who contributed to economic and social development from the beginning of the Republic of Korea in 1948.

During the first half of the twentieth century, the educational systems of Taiwan, Korea, Japan, and the three northeast provinces of China were modernized along lines that fit the Japanese imperial concept of education. In all these areas, Christian missionaries played a substantial supporting role in developing modern education. Considering the decades of relatively rapid educational development under Japanese tutelage, it is not surprising that the educational institutions of the region, even long after the collapse of the Japanese empire, have retained certain similarities and common features. Although the emphasis placed on Confucian ethics and values in the Japanese curriculum, for example, was framed to serve Japan's nationalistic purposes up to 1945, all the countries of the region still share these Confucian values in essence.

Educational institutions developed by the Japanese contributed to the rapid economic development of both Korea and Taiwan. The individuals who received their education and training in the Japanese system constituted the core of government, business, the financial sector, engineering, medicine, and the sciences after the war. In the postwar period, substantial changes were made in Korea and Taiwan to expand the educational system and provide opportunities that were not available to the majority of the populace during the period of Japanese rule. Subsequently, enrollments have risen dramatically at all levels: by 1985, nearly 100 percent of primary-age children were attending school in Japan, Taiwan, and Korea; by 1980, attendance rates for secondary students were 95 percent, 90 percent, and 82 percent, respectively, in these three countries. These increased educational opportunities have in turn generated the high-quality workforce and other human resources that have made rapid economic development possible since the 1960s.

The modern educational system in Korea equipped the nation's workforce from 1945 to the 1980s with essential basic skills, which industry utilized as one of the driving forces for economic expansion and industrialization. Future development, however, especially in high-technology industries and in trade and services based on medium and high technology, will rely on higher standards of teaching, increased technological sophistication in educational curricula, and a more disciplined labor force. The greatest task for Korean educators as the nation moves through the 1990s is to achieve rapid improvements in the quality of education, particularly at the secondary and tertiary levels. Such advances are vital if the generation of Korean youth entering the labor market at the turn of the century are to be adequately prepared to meet the intensified international competition from other advanced industrialized countries.

System of Land Ownership

Land has always been one of the major factors of economic production, along with capital and labor. In the long history of China, various systems of land ownership have been developed, practiced over a period of time, and subsequently abolished. A broad generalization could even be made that practically all land ownership systems active throughout the world today have been tried in China, including the entire range from private individual landholdings to ownership of all land by the emperor or state. It is also important to remember that land has cultural meaning in East Asia. Countries under Chinese cultural influence share similar views about the value and significance of ownership of certain types of land. Some of these values differ from those in Western capitalist societies, such as the importance associated with plots of land containing cemeteries or temples which have been inherited over many generations.

During recent centuries, a system of landlordism developed in China and Korea characterized by extremely unequal distribution of land ownership. One major objective of the communist revolution in China and North Korea after World War II was to liberate poor peasants and tenant farmers from exploitation by landlords. Thus, as a result of the communist takeover and the establishment of socialist systems, the state became the owner of all land. After almost a half-century of experiments, however, China is gradually moving back in the direction of an essentially private form of ownership, based on long-term leasing. The past half-century of socialism in China and North Korea has demonstrated that increased agricultural productivity could not be achieved efficiently through state ownership of farmland and collectivization of agricultural production.

By contrast, rapid economic growth has taken place in Japan, South Korea, and Taiwan, where the land ownership systems followed a different course. One major factor contributing to this development was the land reform that took place shortly after World War II. In the case of Japan, land reform was imposed during the immediate postwar Occupation period. Land reform was perhaps the most important factor in promoting Japan's economic growth and averting social unrest. The main pillars of this land reform were the reduction of rent, the conversion of rent-in-kind to cash rent, the creation of more owner-cultivated landholdings, and the democratization of agricultural land committees. Land reform in Japan, together with labor reform and the dissolution of the big conglomerates, paved the way for Japan's economic expansion during the second half of this century. By providing a better standard of living in the rural sector and an enlarged domestic market for growing industries, it helped to establish a sound foundation for the stability that has characterized the past four decades of Japanese politics.

In South Korea and Taiwan, land reform was carried out by government initiative. As in the case of Japan, one of the major achievements of land reform in South Korea was to ensure domestic political stability in the midst of the confusion and chaos that resulted from the political division of the peninsula. Land reform was also a response to the redistribution of land being carried out in the north by the communist regime. South Korea experienced no significant increase in agricultural productivity immediately after the land reform, but in the long term the implementation of the government's policy contributed to higher agricultural productivity, which in turn was an important basis for the subsequent rapid industrialization of the economy. Land reform also brought direct social benefits to South Koreans, because the compensation to the former big landowners (provided in the form of bonds, which limited the recipients' reinvestment options) was invested in education and cultural activities, notably the establishment of private schools and cultural foundations.

In all three capitalist economies of East Asia, a relatively small number of landlords formerly owned a large proportion of the arable land. The traditional land ownership system was the basis for social stratification, dividing rich from poor and educated from uneducated. Postwar land reform in all three countries was aimed at inducing economic development through industrialization and at increasing farm household incomes, thereby developing a middle class that would protect traditional culture and provide a base of popular support for conservation factions within the political leadership. Land reform can thus be interpreted as a kind of social contract. In Japan the farming sector received protection for its products and subsidies from the government, and in turn the farmers became the backbone of support for the conservative alliance that remained in power for more than four decades.

Land reform served the primary purposes for which it was originally designed: to induce economic development and broaden the conservative middle class. But the industrialization and urbanization that have accompanied rapid economic development during the past few decades have made the land reforms of the 1940s and 1950s an anachronism. The small plots of land that resulted from the reforms cannot take advantage of much of the agricultural technology now available, but legal restrictions dating from the land reform prevent the conversion of small plots of land into larger landholdings on which such technology could be efficiently applied. Thus, in the East Asian countries' search for further development, with increasing emphasis on environmental safeguards, there is mounting pressure for a second land reform to keep in step with changed circumstances.

Another purpose of the postwar land reforms was to restrain the power of landowners while strengthening the rights of the cultivators. The reforms must therefore be examined in terms of efficiency in the use of farmland. In contemporary capitalist societies, land is regarded as a commodity, and in the constitutions of most countries land ownership is protected and guaranteed. As a major commodity, if land is used efficiently for economic production, the expected rate of return should be equal to the prevailing interest rate. In all three developed East Asian economies, however, there is strong evidence of the inefficiency of agricultural land use after the land reforms.

Demographic and industrial transitions have taken place in all three countries. The growth of cities and the migration from rural to urban areas have taken place at levels unprecedented in history. Now that only a small proportion of the original farming population remains on the farm, the basic premises of the postwar land reforms may no longer be valid. In both Korea and Japan, the original principle of supporting the tiller on his land is now seriously questioned in terms of efficiency.

The means for diversifying agricultural land use and raising production efficiency are now being debated. In South Korea, for example, after the land reform the government did not follow the Japanese example and never enacted an agricultural land law to promote and foster agricultural productivity and efficient use of agricultural land. According to an estimate by Professor Kanagawa of the University of Tokyo, almost 60 percent of agricultural land in Korea falls within the classification of absentee ownership. One explanation for this phenomenon is that much farmland has remained in the possession of former farming families, who have moved permanently to urban areas. They still retain legal ownership, although they have found tenant farmers to work the land. One possible solution debated in Korea is to increase the ceiling on landholdings from 3 hectares per farming household to 20 hectares, which would make it possible to convert small plots into larger landholdings on which modern technology could be applied.

In Japan there was an apparent inefficiency in agricultural land use even after the government began to deregulate the ownership market and rental system of farmland. The land problem in Japan reflects some of the failures of market mechanisms, which contributed to demoralization and increased burdens among the working class. Land prices in Japan, like those in the other two countries, outpaced interest rates and inflation rates, and land became a major commodity for speculation. The collapse of the "bubble economy" in Japan during 1992 was a result of the market failure in land transactions, both rural and urban, which ignited serious recession. After decades of constant increases, land prices in Japan have recently declined, and various sectors of the Japanese economy that had been speculating in land are now facing serious difficulties.

One recent phenomenon that deserves consideration is the globalization of the economy. In the global economy, as commodities and services are traded across national boundaries, the ownership of land as a commodity may also become subject to international modifications. Japan has already come under pressure from the United States and the European Community to open its land market. China seems to be preparing for similar international pressure and is already reverting to a system that permits virtual "private" ownership through land leases.

Systems of land ownership and associated institutions are clearly important at all stages of economic development. In retrospect it is obvious that the nationalization and redistribution of land, both rural and urban, carried out by the communist regimes at the initial stage of their industrial transitions contributed little to agricultural productivity and consequently failed to promote industrial productivity. In the capitalist economies of East Asia, on the other hand, the successful implementation of land reform not only provided political stability but also improved the standards of living for the majority of the population then engaged in agriculture. Subsequent increases in agricultural productivity paved the way for rapid industrial growth in all three economies. Today, however, the three economies are faced with the consequences of land reforms that took place almost half a century ago. They are facing the challenge of devising a new land system that will be compatible with the present-day industrial and agricultural structure, will make optimum use of current technology, will be responsive to demands for protection of the environment, and will also anticipate future economic changes.

NOTES

1. In presenting this retrospective view, Dr. Nam draws on his long and distinguished career as Finance Minister, Deputy Prime Minister and Prime Minister, and his service as one of the major architects and managers of Korean economic development in the 1960s and 1970s. The six factors elaborated by Dr. Nam are as follows: (1) Ethnic and cultural homogeneity and a strong Confucian tradition that places high value on education and loyalty to the nation. (2) The national security threat from communist North Korea, which helped the government forge greater national cohesion and a consensus in favor of economic development, while simultaneously preserving authoritarian rule. (3) Strong and effective leadership by an authoritarian government. (4) An outward-looking, export-oriented development strategy. (5) The faith of the South Korean people in the free-enterprise system, as opposed to the communist system operating in North Korea. (6) The favorable international economic climate that prevailed during the 1960s and 1970s.

2. For evidence that Japan's postwar growth cannot be fully accounted for by the usual economic variables alone, see World Bank (1993). Even some supporters of the conventional hypothesis that Korea's export-oriented development policies explain the country's rapid economic growth have suggested that other variables may be important in explaining why these policies were adopted in the first place and why they were so successfully implemented there. Political, historical, and institutional variables such as bureaucratic-dominated decision making, early land reforms, high levels of literacy, and firm and organizational behavior have recently been given attention by scholars of East Asia; see Cho and Kim (1991) and Chung-hua Institution for Economic Research (1990).

REFERENCES

Bellah, Robert. 1957. *Tokugawa Religion: The Values of Pre-industrial Japan*. Glencoe, Ill.: Free Press.

Cho, Lee-Jay, and Yoon Hyung Kim, eds. 1991. *Economic Development in the Republic of Korea: A Policy Perspective*. Honolulu: East-West Center, distributed by the University of Hawaii Press.

Chung-hua Institution for Economic Research. 1990. "Confucianism and Economic Development in East Asia." Proceedings from the May 1989 conference. Conference series no. 13, Taipei, Taiwan.

Clemence, Richard V., ed. 1990. *Essays of Joseph A. Schumpeter*. New Brunswick, N.J.: Transaction Publishers.

Davis, Winston. 1989. "Buddhism and the Modernization of Japan." *History of Religions* 28(4).

Feeney, Griffith, Feng Wang, Mingkun Zhou, and Baoyu Xiao. 1989. *Recent Fertility Dynamics in China: Results from the 1987 One Percent Population Survey*. East-West Population Institute Reprint 244. Honolulu: East-West Population Institute.

Gerschenkron, Alexander. 1962. *Economic Backwardness in Historical Perspective*. Cambridge: Harvard University Press.

Gerschenkron, Alexander. 1970. *Europe in the Russian Mirror*. Cambridge: Cambridge University Press.

Hoselitz, Berthold F. 1960. *Sociological Aspects of Economic Growth*. Glencoe, Ill.: Free Press.

Legge, James, trans. 1959. *The Four Books: The Great Learning, The Doctrine of the Mean, Confucian Analects, and The Works of Mencius*. Chinese text with English translation and notes by James Legge. Taipei: Culture Book Company.

Morishima, Michio. 1982. *Why Has Japan "Succeeded"? Western Technology and the Japanese Ethos*. Cambridge: Cambridge University Press.

Nam, Duck Woo. 1992. "Korea's Economic Take-off in Retrospect." Paper presented at the Second Washington Conference of the Korea-America Economic Association, Washington, D.C., 28–29 September.

Ogburn, William F. 1966. *Social Change*. New York: Dell.

Statistical Yearbook of the Republic of China 1991. Taipei: Directorate-General of Budget, Accounting, and Statistics, Executive Yuan.

Swedberg, Richard, ed. 1991. *Joseph A. Schumpeter: The Economics and Sociology of Capitalism*. Princeton, N.J.: Princeton University Press.

Tsuya, Noriko O., and Minja Kim Choe. 1991. *Changes in Intrafamilial Relationships and the Role of Women in Japan and Korea*. NUPRI Research Paper 58. Tokyo: Nihon University, Population Research Institute.

United Nations Educational, Social, and Scientific Organization (UNESCO). 1954. *Rebuilding Education in the Republic of Korea: Report of the UNESCO-UNKRA Educational Planning Mission to Korea*. Paris: UNESCO.

Weber, Max. 1958. *The Protestant Ethic and the Spirit of Capitalism*. Trans. Talcott Parsons. New York: Scribner.

Wen Xia Ren. 1993. "Confucianism and Business Management." Paper presented at the International Symposium on Economic and Social Development in East Asia: Policies, Management and Population, Nihon University, Tokyo, Japan, January 26–29.

World Bank. 1993. *The East Asian Miracle: Economic Growth and Public Policy*. Washington, D.C.

PART II

The System of National Economic Management

CHAPTER 2

An Introduction to the Korean Model of Political Economy

Yoon Hyung Kim
Hankuk University of Foreign Studies

Confucian Ethos and Heteronomous Modernization

One of the major characteristics of Confucian societies, such as China, Japan, and Korea, is their communitarian social order, centered on the family, which contrasts with Western societies' individualism. The Confucian doctrine of human communal life, with its principles of "top and bottom" based on the morality of loyalty and filial piety, has become one of the cornerstones of the Korean process of modernization. As Max Weber distinguished it, "whereas Puritan rationalism has sought to exercise rational control over the world, Confucian rationalism is an attempt to accommodate oneself to the world in a rational manner" (Morishima 1982:2). Because of this fundamental difference between Puritan and Confucian rationalism, the state-guided capitalist economy, which was managed in an absolutely different spirit from Western capitalism (the free enterprise system—that is, the competitive market economy founded on rational individualism and civil society), became well established in Japan, Korea, and Taiwan.

Recognizing the existence of such an interplay between "ethos" and "economy" would then become a first step in rejecting the monoeconomics claim asserted by orthodox economics. This would reinforce Albert Hirschman's (1981:3) assertion "that under-developed countries as a group are set apart, through a number of economic characteristics common to them, from the advanced industrial countries and that traditional economic analysis, which has concentrated on the industrial countries, must therefore be recast in significant respects when dealing with underdeveloped countries." Furthermore, it can be shown that, contrary to Weber's argument, capitalist management can be congenial to Confucian ethos as well as to Western ethos.

A second characteristic of the Confucian society is that, because the society is supported by the "two wheels of the principle of virtuous government and the principle of constitutionalism," and also because of the Confucian teaching of "Heaven's decree," the legitimacy of the government is regarded as having great importance.

A third characteristic is that Confucianism places great emphasis on the benefits of education. This emphasis is illustrated by the high educational standards and low illiteracy rates of the Confucian hemisphere. The influence of the Confucian ethos on education provided fertile ground in Japan, Korea, and Taiwan for nurturing a knowledge-intensive society and creating a large number of disciplined and skilled workers capable of acquiring the Western technology indispensable for modern industrial management.

Finally, the secular humanism of Confucian ethics has contributed positively to the modernization of Japan, Korea, and Taiwan. This secular humanism is secular realism (actualism): according to Confucian teaching, if one cultivates the moral principles necessary for ordering one's life, managing one's household, governing one's country, and maintaining peace in the world, and if one puts these principles into practice, thereby achieving social stability and political peace, then Heaven's will is fulfilled.

The Confucian moral culture of East Asia can, then, be seen as a secular culture attached to the realities of life in the sense that the Confucianist's ultimate goal is to realize today the "absolute virtue" attained by the ancient saint. Unlike Western Protestant culture, however, East Asian culture is a "static culture" of classicalism because it lacks a transcendental future ideal. Consequently, Confucianism's static classicalism lacks the reform spirit of reality-negation. This sort of mental attitude was a major factor in preventing the emergence of bottom-up autogenous modernization in Confucian culture.

To neutralize static thought and make it less resistant to modernization may be unachievable without an external shock. The modernization model of the Confucian culture is emerging as an alternative to the Western Puritan model of modernization. It is "top-down," heteronomous "modernization by political will," in contrast to the "bottom-up," autonomous modernization of Western society. Once the elite of the Confucian society open their eyes to Western modernization and perceive the challenge of the times before them, once they establish a powerful political leadership system with legitimacy and embark on the building of a modern state, then a national consensus on the goal of building a modern state can be established. The modernization program can receive the public's full support by virtue of the secular realism of Confucian ethics, thereby mobilizing all the national energy. When a communitarian society commands modern technology and modernization is set in motion by an external shock, the society can release an enormous amount of productive motive power. This is shown by the successful rapid industrialization of Japan, Korea, and Taiwan. Like the relationship between Puritanism and autogenous modernization, the Confucian national ethos can be compatible with the process of state-guided top-down modernization.

The Korean Pattern of Economic Modernization

The modernization processes of Japan and Korea, with their common heritage of Confucian static thought, are similar in that both countries adopted an alien, top-down route to modernization. The existing order of Confucian society in both Japan and Korea collapsed under an external shock, and both countries absorbed the modernized social system and organization of the West by political will, without modernizing their traditional cultural value system. When the Japanese encountered the steam-powered "black ships" commanded by Commodore Perry in 1853 awakened to the huge scientific and technological gap that existed between them and the West, the low-ranking samurai (warriors and bureaucrats) and intellectuals launched the Meiji Revolution by replacing the Tokugawa *bakufu* system with a modern structure under direct imperial rule, laying the foundation for a modern state built on the Western model. The very motive power by which Japan could meet the challenge of the times quickly, autogenously, and successfully lies in the Japanese ethical system, which is not a single religion but a flexible combination of Confucianism, Shintoism, and Buddhism—an ideological driving force for solving the problems Japan has had to confront. Japanese society has emphasized the Shinto elements in times of national crisis and the Confucian after drastic changes in its political regime, to maintain the stability of the new regime (Morishima 1982).

In contrast to the Japanese heterogeneous ethical doctrines, the Korean ethical system in the Yi dynasty was a single, one-sided neo-Confucianism which rejected all teachings that did not conform to neo-Confucianism. This neo-Confucianism was not only a self-righteous doctrine but also a rigid doctrine of principles based on the Absolute Truth and "black or white" logic. Because it lacked a heterogeneous ethical background, Korea did not possess the same motive power as Japan for altering its social conditions autogenously to meet the challenge of the times. Moreover, the *sadaebu*, who were then the social elite and bureaucrats and were thoroughly schooled in Confucianism, worshipped China as the country of Confucius and adhered to the doctrine of "China as the center of the world"; they were content to leave relations with the West to the Chinese. As a consequence, they were totally isolated from the outside world and failed to understand the challenge of the times. Ultimately, the static Confucian society of the Yi dynasty was destroyed not by the Koreans themselves but by Japanese imperialist military aggression.

To Koreans, imperial Japanese colonial rule represented not only the loss of political and cultural identity but also national and racial humiliation. Meanwhile, the Yi dynasty's static neo-Confucianism, which had been an obstacle to the modernization of Korea's traditional cultural value system, was denounced as the prime cause for having been annexed to an alien nation, particularly Japan. Accordingly, Korea's traditional cultural system was neutralized while Korea was modernizing. In addition, the resentment over Japan's occupation of Korea reinforced Korean nationalism and hatred of the Japanese. This nationalism has become the prime motive propelling economic modernization after 1960.

After being ruled by imperialist Japan for 36 years, Korea was emancipated in 1945. Contrary to the Korean people's expectations, however, emancipation did not automatically lead to the building of an independent modern state. A casual decision taken by Franklin Roosevelt and Joseph Stalin at Yalta in February 1945 divided the Korean peninsula between the American and Soviet military commands at the 38th parallel. A U.S. military government was then imposed on the south. The division of Korea shaped its modernization profoundly and indelibly. In the midst of the political and social turmoil that characterized the period of U.S. military occupation, Syngman Rhee, the charismatic spokesman for Korean independence, pressed the United States by all possible diplomatic means to assist in the formation of an independent country, even if only in the south. Elected as the first president of the newly proclaimed Republic of Korea in August 1948, President Rhee laid the legal and institutional foundations for the modern state. He successfully defended South Korea, with the direct involvement of United Nations forces, against a full-scale invasion by North Korea launched in June 1950. Agreeing to the Korean Armistice in July 1953, the Rhee government concluded a Korean-U.S. mutual defense treaty and greatly expanded the Korean armed forces, thereby making them the strongest organization in Korean society and solidifying the national security base.

Political Authoritarianism and State-Guided Capitalism

On the foundation of an anticommunist, independent modern state with a clear sense of national identity, General Park Chung Hee determined to begin the national task of industrialization after he seized power through a military coup d'état in May 1961. President Park set the nation on a forced march of state-guided, top-down materialistic industrialization. Korea's modernization was propelled by political will, the Park regime being unwilling to wait for the modernization of Korea's traditional cultural values. I have argued that the logic required by such a state-guided, top-down modernization process corresponds to the Korean ethos.

The priority given to economic development by the military government appealed to the country in the early 1960s. The vision of national economic development for solving the people's economic plight in the midst of resignation, poverty, and disorder provided the people the faith that the nation's economic development was congruent with the slogan "My Prosperity." It implanted in the people self-confidence and hope that they would have better livelihoods by working hard and participating in the nation's reconstruction. Economic development thus became a nationally supported goal. Convinced that social discipline and political stability were indispensable to the promotion of economic growth, President Park adhered to political authoritarianism. He nonetheless made every effort in accordance with necessary formalities to secure the legitimacy of his authoritarian regime. In the early 1960s as Korea embarked on economic development, capital was desperately scarce, the domestic savings rate was extremely low, and foreign aid was in sharp decline. Furthermore, a well-functioning financial and capital market was absent, and the public distrusted modern industrial activities. Under these circumstances, the military government became the primary agent of capitalist industrialization.

In July 1961 the Park regime established the Economic Planning Board (EPB) to formulate, implement, and monitor the government's industrialization strategy. The EPB was headed by a senior minister for economic planning, who was given the title of deputy prime minister. The board subsequently developed into a powerful bureaucratic organization, responsible for development planning and policy-making. In this capacity, it coordinated the functions of the ministries of Finance, Commerce and Industry, Transportation, Agriculture, Health and Social Affairs, and Science and Technology.

To create long-term capital for the strategic sector selected for development, the government brought the banking institutions under its direct control and instituted a new system of government guarantees for foreign-loan repayments. In accordance with the government's ambitious industrialization program, the commercial banks adopted an active overloan policy. Through the device of "rolling over" loans, they played the role of industrial investment banks designed to finance the long-term investment needs of the economy. Korean enterprises willing to conform to the government's development priorities were entitled to borrow from commercial banks and abroad well beyond the individual companies' net worth. The commercial banks, in turn, overborrowed from the Bank of Korea. This so-called indirect financing eliminated the financial risks associated with high debt levels of Korean enterprises because the Bank of Korea was the implicit guarantor of the debts of major companies. Moreover, the government provided tax concessions to those Korean enterprises willing to conform to government's development priorities.

In this way, Park succeeded in creating a nucleus of industrial capitalists cooperative with its development policy. The regime developed a collaborative relationship between government and business in which the nation's industrialization strategy could be carried out and at the same time free enterprise and the free market system could be maintained. In the meantime, the government devised various industrial policies to reduce the risks associated with productive investment, such as a price collapse through overproduction, competition from cheap imports, and losses through exporting. The government also perfected its market-conforming methods of state intervention in the national economy. Accordingly, industry could concentrate on increasing its productive capacity and on export promotion. Thus, within a fairly short period the Park regime created the nucleus of a modern industrial sector that was internationally competitive and could push forward modernization throughout the country by enlarging the nucleus.

Under the regime's political authoritarianism and state-guided capitalism, the government and the private sector developed a mutually beneficial, cooperative relationship. This strategic cooperation sparked productive forces so remarkably that rapid industrialization and economic growth were achieved during 1961–79, transforming the Korean economy from a state of extreme poverty (called "Asian stagnation") into a newly industrializing country. Central to the Korean success was the regime's political leadership, with its outward-looking strategy for industrialization, complemented by a vigorous and expanding group of entrepreneurs and an increasingly industrial, better-educated labor force operating in a favorable international economic climate.

Although President Park's economic orientation was a state-guided, goal-oriented approach, his regime was committed to free enterprise, private ownership of property, and the market. The private enterprises were owned and managed by a rapidly expanding and vigorous group of entrepreneurs. The fundamental problem of the capitalist developmental system is that of the public-private relationship. Harry G. Johnson (1962) has stated that "economic development is a process of cooperation between the state and private enterprise, and that the problem is to devise the best possible mixture." During the Park regime a unique mixture developed between the state bureaucracy and private business, a collaborative relationship in which, although private enterprise provided the principal operating units, the government was clearly in the driver's seat. The close association of government and business in Korea's economic development has been called "Korea, Inc." But as Jones and SaKong (1980) have argued, unlike "Japan, Inc.," whose policy reflects a consensus between government and business as equals, in Korea it is government that has set policies and businessmen who have followed.

Although this government-business relationship contributed greatly to Korea's rapid industrialization, government intervention was at times excessive and entailed serious costs. The biggest costs were distortion of the competitive market structure, misallocation of resources, and severe inflationary pressure and unbalanced development of the industrial structure. The government's direct control over monetary operations through preferential credit allocations and its controlled interest rates fixed at artificially low levels caused an excessive expansion of the money supply to accommodate the rapid growth of the real sector. The excessive liquidity, however, was not effectively absorbed by the organized financial markets because of suppressed interest rates and the inefficient financial sector, thereby creating inflationary pressure on the economy. At the same time, a system of government-controlled, subsidized credit allocations contributed to excessive investment in the heavy and chemical industries, to the neglect of the small and medium-size industries that constituted the backbone of the technologyintensive industrial structure. The overinvestment in the heavy and chemical industries also caused an imbalance between industrialization and agricultural development. This unbalanced development of the industrial structure, with its resulting economic power concentration, emerged as an aggravating factor in income and wealth distribution.

The rapid industrialization and high-speed economic growth, which contributed greatly to the legitimacy of the Park government, also brought about the growth of large-scale, private enterprises and big family fortunes during the latter half of the 1970s. This emergence of the conglomerates altered the public's perception of the benefits of the growth-first strategy. It became clear that growth had reinforced inequalities in income and wealth. And the Park government was, at that time, unprepared to use taxes or the public sector to offset the rising inequalities. Thus, the Park government's development strategy, which was based on "growth first and distribution later" and required continued sacrifice on the part of some sectors of society, made it difficult to sustain the enthusiastic public support the government had enjoyed earlier, as this strategy turned out to be "unfair" to them. In the public view, economic bureaucrats and the leadership failed to understand that "fair treatment is essential for a well motivated, cooperative, high-quality economic team. Equity is the essence of efficiency. Equity is one of the secrets of the Japanese success" (Thurow 1985:126).

President Park's state-guided, high-growth system depended on the existence of a widely accepted goal for the society. However, as Chalmers Johnson (1982:22) has asserted, "When a consensus does not exist, when there is confusion or conflict over the overarching goal in a planned rational economy, it would appear to be quite adrift, incapable of coming to grips with basic problems and unable to place responsibility for failure." Korea experienced this kind of confusion and drift during the latter part of the 1970s. As it emerged as a newly industrializing country, eliminating absolute poverty, people became more concerned about inequalities in income and wealth distribution, labor-management relations, and social welfare. In this new situation, the role of the economic technocrats became extremely difficult. The ruling party was not able to achieve a consensus on continued, rapid economic growth because the president was taking a long-term perspective in which defense and heavy industry had higher priority than measures designed to achieve greater equality. As a result, the ruling Democratic Republican Party polled 1.1 percent fewer of the total votes cast at the general election in 1978 than the opposition party. (The election outcome was also affected by various other factors, including noneconomic issues not discussed here.) As W. T. Easterbrook (1957) commented in another context, an economy that succeeds in finding a formula for growth tends to repeat that pattern after it has become inappropriate.

Subsequently, as Mason et al. (1980:56) have observed, a "serious political disturbance [was] occasioned [in September 1979] principally by the dismissal from the Legislative Assembly of the head of the New Democratic Party [the major opposition party] and the resignation of his followers. This disturbance was severely repressed." On 26 October 1979, President Park Chung Hee was assassinated by the head of the Korean CIA, abruptly ending his 18-year term of state control and bringing about the fall of the Fourth Republic.

When both benefits and costs are considered, how does one balance the national economy's ledger of rapid industrialization and growth accomplished by the

Park regime against the restriction of public participation and civil liberties? Although the costs of economic development have been by no means negligible, should not economic development be imperative, on balance, when it is the sole means of eliminating absolute poverty? It is a moot question, however, whether political development should be postponed until an economy has reached a certain level of development or whether economic development alone is in fact worthwhile without political development (Cho and Kim 1991).

Political Authoritarianism and Private Sector–Guided Capitalism

After the death of President Park, the public expected a greater opportunity for the establishment of a fully democratic state. These expectations were dampened by General Chun Doo Hwan's coup d'état in December 1979 and were destroyed by the brutal suppression of the Kwangju civil uprising for democratization in May 1980. The new regime reestablished law and order at the cost of infringing human rights. The Chun regime's search for legitimacy depended even more heavily than its predecessor's on economic performance, because of the specter of Kwangju.

Using the slogan of building a "Just Society," the Chun regime retired several older politicians belonging to both the pro-government majority and the opposition parties because it considered them to be obstacles to the formation of a new society. The regime also attempted to stifle freedom of the press. Under government pressure, more than 700 journalists were dismissed, and many newspapers and broadcasting operations were merged and placed under state control by the Chun administration. As part of a "purification" drive, the Chun regime purged nearly 8,000 civil servants in July 1980, thereby losing much of the administrative capability accumulated during the 1960s and 1970s. Thus, the loss of numerous senior economic bureaucrats considerably weakened the economic bureaucracy.[1] Korea thus experienced a radical discontinuity in its civilian bureaucracy and especially in its economic cadres, with resulting discontinuities in economic policies. These developments, coupled with a new orientation in economic policy emphasizing a free market ideology, propelled business leaders into the vacuum thus created, and private enterprise emerged with enhanced powers.

By advocating the free market ideology, which provided a conceptual foundation for the "Just Society" platform, some economists and civilian bureaucrats advanced their own careers as reformers in the new regime. The mottos of the Chun regime's free market ideology were "self-control," "trade liberalization," and "free competition." Whereas the main actor in economic policymaking under the state-guided, plan-rational system of the Park regime had been the economic bureaucracy, the main actors were now the reform economists.[2]

As Park's plan-rational system became increasingly counterproductive, given the sheer size and complexity of the Korean economy in the latter part of the 1970s, the pendulum swung in the relationship between governmental institutions and economic activity: a "private sector-guided, market-rational system" was adopted by the new Chun regime, which shifted away from high-speed growth to stabilization and liberalization as its overriding economic objectives. The macroeconomic policies this political authoritarian regime followed were essentially a restrictive monetary policy, fiscal austerity, and wage control. Committed to the stabilization policy, President Chun's political leadership successfully eradicated the chronic high inflation from which the country had suffered since the start of modernization and which had seriously undermined the growth potential itself, particularly in the latter part of the 1970s.

In addition to the stabilization program, the Chun government in 1981–82 undertook major structural adjustment programs a democratic government would have found difficult to implement. These economic reforms were aimed at dismantling the regulations that were constraining the capacity of the Korean economy to adjust to the new external and internal environments. As a first step toward financial liberalization, the Chun administration started denationalizing commercial banks in 1981 by disinvesting the government's share. By 1983 the government had turned all nationwide city banks over to private ownership and reduced its control over day-to-day operations. In addition, in 1982 the government abolished the system of direct credit controls for the deposit money banks and the preferential lending rates of policy loans. To promote competition among banks, two new nationwide commercial banks—joint ventures with foreign banks—were authorized. Perhaps the most important part of the financial reform was the rearrangement of the interest rate structure. Although monetary authorities still maintain interest rate ceilings on bank deposits and loans, the real rate of interest has been kept positive since 1981.

To improve industrial efficiency, a fundamental policy reform was instituted which aimed at reducing the government's direction of and control over investment decision making and at increasing the industry's exposure to market forces and external competition. A Fair Trade Law was promulgated in 1981 to guard against anticompetitive mergers, unfair advertising, and restrictive trade practices. Furthermore, the Chun government committed itself to reform the import regime, so that by 1986 it would reach the level of liberalization achieved by industrialized countries, and to overhaul the import tariff schedule to reduce the spread of tariff rates. The Tariff Reform Act, promulgated in 1984, included phased general reductions in tariff levels and charges in order to create greater uniformity of tariff levels.

Whereas the Chun government attempted to carry out decisive liberalization reforms, it overlooked the need to restructure the existing legal system and institutions necessary for the market-rational system to function properly and smoothly. Under the existing government licensing and approval authority, which remained intact, the "private-sector industrial guidance model" without operational apparatus turned out to be little more than a verbal slogan. Because the Chun regime adhered to the idea of political authoritarianism of the Park period, the state maintained its strong influence over private sector economic activity. Ultimately, the Fifth Republic's capitalism boiled down to a pseudo-free-market system that was not properly equipped with fair rules for private economic activity.

On the other hand, both the economic bureaucracy and private businesses were confused about their role in a "liberalized" economy. Moreover, the administration denounced many of the Park regime's high-speed growth policies and institutions as against the doctrine of economic liberalism. The government did not perform its proper role of managing the national economy well. In particular, the Chun administration was preoccupied with fiscal restraint for price stabilization and as a result overlooked public investment in social overhead capital such as railroads, harbors, and roads, thereby causing toda's traffic congestion and transportation bottlenecks.

In the meantime, symptoms of another legacy of the Park regime's rapid industrialization began to emerge: financially insolvent firms in the early 1980s due to the world recession. Unfortunately, however, by focusing exclusively on price stability, the Chun government failed to recognize the critical problems of insolvent firms—specifically, the shipping companies, some overseas construction companies, and some general trading companies. By the time the government grasped the gravity of the situation, the nonperforming assets of the commercial banks had grown so huge that the government lacked the political leverage to allow some firms to go bankrupt. Accordingly, to avert the immediate financial collapse of insolvent firms, it provided ad hoc relief loans and spent money to bail out failing enterprises. Because most of the "new" loans created by the commercial banks were sunk into insolvent firms, other firms were deprived of funds necessary for capital investment, thereby weakening the international competitiveness of Korean industry. Instead of resolving the fundamental problems related to insolvent firms, the Chun government let other conglomerates take over most of these firms and amended the Law Governing Tax Reduction and Exemptions to allow exemption from property and transfer taxes when insolvent firms disposed of their real assets to repay bank loans. There was, however, considerable public resentment against such tax exemptions, which amounted to yet another major subsidy to big businesses while small firms were being allowed to go bankrupt.

Under circumstances in which the state did not take on regulatory functions in the interest of maintaining fair competition and consumer protection, the principle of free competition of the Fifth Republic's ideology merely exacerbated the already excessive concentration of industry and economic power in the hands of the conglomerates. For instance, the big corporations were able to expand to immense size because of loans they received through government channels. If they were required to repay these loans, some of them (those with debt/asset ratios of perhaps 70–80 percent) would have few assets left. In effect, the assets of the Korean people (through government funds) were used to place greater economic power in the hands of corporate leaders. The economic power they wielded was thus far greater than their genuine corporate assets.

Because of their enormous size, moreover, the conglomerates (*jaebul*) were able to exert considerable influence over the direction the national economy was taking.

Furthermore, they no longer listened to the government bureaucracy. Thus, in some ways the model of "private-sector industrial guidance" under the Chun regime boiled down to a "*jaebul*-guidance" model. The necessary elements in the Korean economy have not been nurtured sufficiently to institutionalize this type of economy to the extent existing in the United States. A transitional period is needed while the Korean economy gradually moves in the desired direction.

In the meantime, the self-control principle caused investment distortion in the national economy. Under the policy of investment autonomy, and because the government no longer assumed the major risks of development, small and medium-size firms in pursuit of easy profits were inclined to invest in the leisure services industry—and larger businesses, similarly motivated, became preoccupied with real estate investment such as in commercial buildings and redevelopment projects. Combined with the erosion of export competitiveness caused by underinvestment in equipment, the trade liberalization principle of the reform bureaucrats' economic policy aggravated the already serious problem of foreign debt in 1985. Fortunately, however, the Korean economy as it entered 1986 started to revitalize and grow rapidly, thanks to the sharp decline in international oil prices, the fall in international interest rates, and the appreciation of the Japanese yen. Ironically, the Chun regime's stabilization and structural reforms contributed greatly to the robustness of the Korean economy, largely as a result of sudden and unexpected favorable external events.

The model reform economists' experimentation with the market-rational system without first laying the groundwork is a typical example of the failure of the orthodox version of laissez-faire. Commenting on the free market ideology as an instrument of economic development, Lester Thurow (1985:107) has argued in *The Zero-Sum Solution* that "market principles and forces have to be used, but 'leaving it to the market' is a recipe for failure." Nonetheless, the painful experience with the free market ideology was not wholly negative.

A more fundamental problem is the incompatibility of economic liberalization with a politically authoritarian regime. The model reform bureaucrats' ideal—that the free market economy would eventually bring about political democracy—is laudable. Nevertheless, the Korean experience has demonstrated, contrary to Milton Friedman's (1962) argument in *Capitalism and Freedom*, that political democracy itself is indispensable to the workability of the free market economy. In the market-rational system, the state is required to assume regulatory functions in the interest of maintaining fair competition and consumer protection. Rules of economic competition are needed by the state, not as a player but as an umpire. In the United States, which is basically a market-rational state, these rules are legislated by Congress. Thus parliamentary democracy is indispensable for guaranteeing the "fairness" of market competition. The success of the market-rational system as an instrument of development relies on a system of checks and balances: the bureaucracy checks the excesses of the business enterprises, the legislature checks the excesses of the bureaucracy, and a free press serves as a check on the three players, including itself. In retrospect, it seemed clear to the public that the coincidence of repressive authoritarianism in politics and free market ideology in economics during the Chun regime amplified the economic power concentration and political influence of the conglomerates and worsened the income and wealth disparity among social strata, regions, and the urban-rural sectors. Despite the initial attempts at building a "Just Society," the last years of the Chun regime were marred by major corruption scandals, public suspicion of a conspiracy between government and big business, and social injustice. From the public viewpoint, the Chun regime's slogan turned out to be mere rhetoric. Building a just society remains a critical social issue that today's Korea must tackle.

Political Democratism and Private Sector–Guided Capitalism

During 1961–87, Korea adopted the modernized social system and organizations of Western societies by sheer political will, without accommodating its traditional cultural values. Although it achieved rapid industrialization and high-speed economic growth in the period, thereby eliminating absolute poverty and transforming itself into a semi-industrialized, modern state, Korea's traditional cultural values began to conflict with the doctrine of one-sided, growth-first authoritarianism the government imposed on Korean society.

With 1987 as a turning point, the conflict manifested itself in the form of severe social disorder. Student demonstrators, opposing President Chun's plan to handpick his own successor, became violent in June 1987. They were joined by an increasingly large segment of the urban population. The pluralistic forces demanded changes in the authoritarian political mode.

Consequently, on 29 June 1987, the ruling Democratic Justice Party's candidate for president, Roh Tae Woo, abruptly pledged his support for the direct election of the president as well as other reforms for political democratization. In December 1987 the first popular election of a president since 1971 was held. Roh won the election, although with only 36.6 percent of the total vote. The ruling party, however, lost the subsequent National Assembly elections in April 1988. Thus, not only was the new president elected by a minority of the vote, but his party had a minority of seats in the National Assembly, which could be controlled by the combined opposition parties.

Although the Sixth Republic was founded on the ideal of political democratization, quite unlike the authoritarian system of the two previous regimes, it attempted to adopt the private-sector industrial guidance model of the Fifth Republic. However, the newly established government should have taken on the responsibility of redressing economic imbalances, in particular, the concentration of economic power and inequalities of income and wealth which were consequences of the previous compressed modernization.

The Sixth Republic accomplished considerable political democratization through the elimination of authoritarianism by force. Unfortunately, the populace confused democratization with "laissez-faire," and as a result social disciplined slackened, public order was disturbed, and government power weakened. At the same time, the Roh government left the correction of economic imbalances merely to the free competitive market forces. But reform of economically unfair institutions and policies is not achieved through mere "rational" market choices—energetic political determination is required; after all, the Sixth Republic's market-rational system undermined Korea's economic growth potential.

Four decades of autocratic government gave way to the politics of pluralism. The government of the Sixth Republic has turned out to be far weaker than governments in the past. A potentially more serious problem is the regional pattern of voting in both elections. The strong local appeal of the candidates in the two elections heightened regional emotions and dramatized the regional polarization. The sectionalism did much damage to the cohesiveness and rapport of the country. Yet the summer of 1988 played a pivotal role in drawing the Korean people together in a united effort to host the Olympic Games. This new challenge ignited the rising nationalism of Koreans for international prestige.

After the Olympic Games, however, a series of internal conflicts began to emerge in the new pluralist society. The Roh government's excessive publicity about the success of the Olympics and the emergence of trade surpluses during three consecutive years inspired public overconfidence in the nation's economic state. This, coupled with the exorbitant windfall profits from speculation in real estate and stock market shares during 1986–88, created an atmosphere in the affluent urban society of extravagant luxury consumption. The conspicuous consumptive trend became widespread and deepened the social disharmony between the haves and the have-nots. While the Roh government was preoccupied with its "Northern Policy," the symptoms of further internal conflict unfolded as new challenges to the Sixth Republic: protracted labor disputes, the specter of real estate speculation, Reverend Moon's illegal visit to North Korea, the prevailing violence on university campuses, and rampant social crimes.

Business groups and financial institutions vied with one another in greedy speculation in land, stocks, and bonds, and the pleasure-seeking business establishment continued to flourish. The allocation of available savings in the economy was increasingly distorted—away from the most productive investments and toward unproductive investments. Worse still, as speculative investment in urban apartment houses overheated, the prices of apartments skyrocketed in April 1989, and real estate speculation swept across the whole country. In general, the gainers have been the owners of wealth, whereas the losers have been the farmers and working classes. Workers were encouraged by social activists and students to claim higher wages, which led to explosive labor disputes. Fear of inflation was growing, creating a risk to economic stability. Korean society was experiencing a new situation—brought out by labor-management disputes and real estate speculation—of real or potential confrontation rather than harmony of interests among social classes. Just as the old harmony benefited the haves, the new confrontation was intended to be used to change the rules of the game in favor of the have-nots.

While the Korean economy, losing its vitality and international competitiveness, slipped into a deep slump, the whole country was swept into a heated debate in December 1989 as the National Assembly held special hearings on the suppression of the Kwangju civil uprising of 1980 and the irregularities of the Fifth Republic. The Korean political economy became mired in confusion and uncertainties, thus losing its focus and the ability to perform. Korea seemed ready to evolve from the dynamic entrepreneurial state of the Park and Chun regimes into a state preoccupied with zero-sum, renting-seeking processes.

In 1990, Korea entered a new era. To put an end to partisan politics characterized by rifts and confrontations and to place national development on a higher level, the ruling Democratic Justice Party and two opposition parties—the Reunification Democratic Party and the New Democratic Republican Party—were merged into a new conservative coalition: the Democratic Liberal Party (DLP). The DLP diagnosed the current condition of the Korean political economy as the "overall national difficulties."

In retrospect, the Sixth Republic was given a historical mission: to carry out drastic institutional reform so as to achieve harmony between social justice and economic growth. Korean capitalism was indeed at a turning point where economic development had to be balanced with distributive justice. The Roh government failed to grasp fully the nature of the new economic challenges, to give the nation a harmonious economic vision, or to restructure all economically unfair institutions and policies.

The New Challenges for Today's Korea

Within the short period of its modernization process, Korea has experienced three political economic models. Each model has its own merits and intrinsic flaws, but a common flaw has been unbalanced economic development. The past three decades may be regarded as an important stage in the learning process as the search continues for an appropriate model for the coming national economic management. When Kim Young Sam, the DLP's candidate, won the fourteenth presidential election in December 1992, the government inaugurated the slogan of building a "New" Korea. Kim's "New" Korea should be warranted to mend internal conflicts and reinvigorate its international manufacturing competitiveness.

To meet the new challenges, Korea will require some fundamental rebuilding of its political economy. Korea's is still a small developing economy in the catching-up process, and it has a long way to go on the forced march toward industrialization. Taking into account that Korean modernization has reached the stage in which economic development should advance side by side with political democratization, the question is, What is the best system of national economic management for Korea? In this regard, Johnson (1985:64) argues that the coincidence of soft authoritarianism in politics and capitalism in economics had much to do with the phenomenal economic performance of Japan. Very few any longer doubt that the guided market economy of Japan has outperformed the Anglo-American pluralist market economies. The state-guided capitalism has done as well in Korea, Taiwan, Singapore, and Hong Kong as it ever did in Japan. The political economic model of East Asia is a challenge both to the paradigm of a pluralist market economy without explicit political direction and to the command economies of explicit absolutism without capitalism.

Given such situational imperatives as its high population density, limited resources, utter dependence on international trade, and acute security threats, Korea should remain a capitalist developmental state and refine this form as best it can. The issue is to devise the best possible blend between political direction of the economy on the one hand and freedom of enterprise on the other, with adequate safeguards against the former crowding out the latter. Unlike the autarchic authoritarianism during the two previous regimes in Korea, democratic but strong political leadership could be achieved based on the least amount of political authoritarianism, that is, "soft authoritarianism." The Japanese soft authoritarianism, which perfected the compatibility of democratization and authority, could provide a source of new ideas for refining Korea's political-economic model.

The creation of the DLP could provide political stability as long as it dominates the National Assembly. On the other hand, the bureaucracy has to share power with the rising political elite, and the political elite becomes a captive of major business interests. Korea should find a creative solution to insulate national economic management from the ravages of zero-sum rent-seeking politics. A workable degree of technocratic insulation and autonomy in policy execution may be achieved by establishing state structures (of the type prevailing in Japan until 1972) in which the politicians reign and the bureaucracy rules. The politicians set broad national goals, protect the bureaucracy from political pressure, and perform "safety net" functions, while the bureaucracy formulates and implements economic policies and institutional reforms. The insulation process can be enhanced by extensive cross-penetration of political and administrative elites. Because the process of policy execution often generates various kinds of rental income accruing to the bureaucracy, a degree of integrity is required of all government officials, and strong political leadership is exercised to reinforce the social discipline of public servants.

Korea must find a creative solution to reduce the power of major business interests. Because the reigning politicians raise enormous sums of money for political campaigns, they are vulnerable to major business interests. One way to lessen the dominating influence of business groups over politicians would be for business to assume political responsibility. What is needed is for major businesses to build into their own values concern and responsibility for national goals. Major businesses could then provide contributions to political parties for the purpose of maintaining the system, not pursuing business interests. Alternatively, Peter Drucker (1989:105) suggests that "another way to reduce the power of business would be a change in financing campaigns for political office. Campaign contributions of any kind or from any source could be strictly prohibited. So would campaign expenses above a low level. Both winning and losing candidates (or parties) would then be reimbursed after the election on the basis of the votes they actually received."

Korea should also refine and perfect the cooperative public-private relationships involved in economic decision making. Because the private sector is now highly developed and competent, the government should encourage maximum popular participation in formulating development strategies through extensive use of expert panels. Where, then, should the Korean economy go? Because Korea is expected to undergo an extensive industrial restructuring in the coming years, it should invent a new form of cooperative relationship between government, the banking sector, and business to establish an industrial vision, to handle the risks facing industry, and to facilitate "industrial exit" for sunset industries. Government should play an active role in mitigating the inequalities of income and wealth.

Reducing inequality is not only an ethical good for its own sake but also a new source of soft productivity growth. Political democratization and economic liberalization, together with the expectations that accompany a more comfortable standard of living, have caused drastic changes in the people's value system. In the early 1960s when the nation embarked on industrialization, everyone started from nearly the same social and economic status. Today, however, income and wealth inequalities have greatly widened among social strata, regions, and the urban-rural sectors. The sense of relative deprivation among the alienated strata was the main cause of the acrimonious labor-management disputes in the spring of 1989. Thus, the disequilibrium of distribution has emerged as a new social issue in Korea.

In accord with such changes in social conditions and to cope with the challenges of the times, Korean modernization has to move from the stage of productive capacity expansion to a new stage in which productive capacity expansion advances side by side with distributive justice. The logic required by the developmental stage of productive capacity expansion is "efficiency" in the economic mechanical relations between people and things. During the capacity expansion stage, Korea successfully applied Anglo-American economics without major modification to national economic management and development planning. But in the stage of distributive justice, ethical judgments become influential in economic life. Accordingly, distributive justice cannot be solved only by "efficiency" but also requires "equity" in the social organic relations among people. The logic of "equity" as a criterion of social choice cannot be borrowed from Anglo-American modern economics, and Korean society should establish its own wisdom based on the national ethical system.

Korea's political economy is expected to be transformed in conformity with political democratization and the country's traditional cultural values. Rapid changes in social conditions will require some institutional reforms to keep economic management effective. Whereas the overriding goal of national economic management during the previous regimes was economic efficiency, this single-minded value system should be transformed into a pluralist value system that includes not only efficiency but also egalitarianism, humanitarianism, and coprosperity, reflecting Korea's traditional cultural values. Thus, the new challenge that the political economy of Korea faces as it approaches the year 2000 is to reform present economic and social institutions to achieve its new guiding principles: financial reform, tax reform, trade liberalization, a cooperative labor-management relationship, separation of management and ownership in businesses, and the system of land ownership and use.

There is a sense of urgency in academic circles to reform the Korean economy and position it favorably for this final stage in the development process. This is, however, a problem of political will rather than one of economics. What Korea needs is strong but democratic political leadership that possesses—instead of charisma—vision, moral seriousness, a deep sense of duty, and a willingness to get the best advice and to work very hard. By presenting a new "grand vision" for Korea in the twenty-first century, the political leadership can create hope, greater moral cohesion of society, more powerful centrifugal forces, and a new bond of national unity.

NOTES

1. In December 1988, after the establishment of the Sixth Republic under the constitution that came into force that February, the Roh Tae Woo government offered a formal apology and a pledge for monetary compensation to thousands of former civil servants who had been forced out of their jobs in the massive purge and to the victims of the Samchong reeducation camps. President Rho also called for early implementation of measures to restore honor and provide compensation for nearly two hundred victims killed during the suppression of the Kwangju civil uprising.

2. As Johnson (1982:26) has argued, "One further difference between the market-rational state and the plan-rational state is thus that economists dominate economic policy-making in the former while nationalistic political officials dominate it in the latter."

REFERENCES

Cho, Lee-Jay, and Yoon Hyung Kim, eds. 1991. *Economic Development in the Republic of Korea: A Policy Perspective.* Honolulu: East-West Center.

Drucker, Peter F. 1989. *The New Realities.* New York: Harper and Row.

Easterbrook, W. T. 1957. "Long Period Comparative Study: Some Historical Cases." *Journal of Economic History* 17(4):571–595.

Friedman, Milton. 1962. *Capitalism and Freedom.* Chicago: University of Chicago Press.

Hirschman, Albert O. 1981. "The Rise and Decline of Development Economics." In *Essays in Trespassing: From Economics to Politics and Beyond.* Cambridge: Cambridge University Press.

Johnson, Chalmers. 1982. *MITI and the Japanese Miracle: The Growth of Industrial Policy, 1925–1975.* Stanford: Stanford University Press.

Johnson, Chalmers. 1985. "Political Institutions and Economic Performance: The Government-Business Relationship in Japan, South Korea, and Taiwan." In Robert A. Scalapino, S. Sato, and J. Wanandi (eds.), *Asian Economic Development: Present and Future.* Berkeley, Calif.: Institute of East Asian Studies.

Johnson, Harry G. 1962. *Money, Trade and Economic Growth.* London: Allen and Unwin.

Jones, Leroy P., and Il SaKong. 1980. *Government, Business and Entrepreneurship in Economic Development: The Korean Case.* Cambridge: Harvard University Press.

Mason, Edward S., et al. 1980. *The Economic and Social Modernization of the Republic of Korea.* Cambridge: Harvard University Press.

Morishima, Michio. 1982. *Why Has Japan "Succeeded?" Western Technology and the Japanese Ethos.* Cambridge: Cambridge University Press.

Thurow, Lester C. 1985. *The Zero-Sum Solution: Building a World-Class Economy.* New York: Simon and Schuster.

Chapter 3

What Is the Best System of National Economic Management for Korea?

Chalmers Johnson
University of California, San Diego

Introduction

The basic question that this paper tries to answer—What is the best system of national economic management for Korea?—is raised by Yoon-Hyung Kim in Chapter 2 of this volume.

I am in broad agreement with Professor Kim on his periodization of development since 1961. He sees, first, a state-guided plan-rational system. This was followed, after 1979, by a never fully implemented private-sector-guided market-rational system based on the theories of "reform economists," but it actually boiled down to a *jaebul*-guided system. I also agree with his description of the Korean economy in the years since the Olympic Games: "Business groups and financial institutions vied with one another in greedy speculation in land, stocks, and bonds, and the pleasure-seeking business establishment continued to flourish. The allocation of available savings in the economy was increasingly distorted—away from the most productive investments and toward unproductive investments. Worse still, as speculative investment in urban apartment houses overheated, the prices of apartments skyrocketed in April 1989, and real estate speculation swept across the whole country. In general, the gainers have been the owners of wealth, whereas the losers have been the farmers and working classes."

Professor Kim is right in saying that Korea needs "a creative solution to insulate national economic management from the ravages of zero-sum rent-seeking policies" and to ask "What is the best system of national economic management for Korea?" I also concur with his conclusion, drawn from Lester Thurow, that "market principles and forces have to be used, but 'leaving it to the market' is a recipe for failure." Kim's proposed solution to these difficulties, "soft authoritarianism," is a concept derived from my own work but not fully developed in his chapter. Without a clear understanding of what is meant by soft authoritarianism and of the problems it is intended to address, this solution may be as much a prescription for disaster as leaving economic development to the market.

I am neither a specialist in the Korean political economy nor a Korean linguist. My conception of what is "best" for Korea does not presume to say what is morally or politically best for any or all Koreans. It is instead an exercise in applied social science—an attempt to say what policies and institutions are most likely to overcome the problems created by Korea's successful industrialization and allow it to continue to grow economically. My answer is rather succinct—soft authoritarian societal corporatism—but getting to it is a more long-winded process.

Social Values and Economic Activity

Between 1962 and 1986, South Korea advanced from being the ninety-ninth to becoming the forty-fourth richest country on earth in terms of per capita income. If this record of growth can be sustained, by the early twenty-first century South Korea will be as rich as Britain and Italy are today. Needless to say, this extraordinary economic development has generated many different explanations, all of them controversial and all of them reflecting to some extent the intellectual and ideological interests of their authors. These explanations range from those that stress Korea's reliance on market forces to an emphasis on Confucian values, the possibilities for growth offered by the Cold War and Korea's place in it, new management techniques, and new institutions of capitalism. In Chapter 2, Professor Kim stresses the influence of Confucianism and relates it to economic growth much in the way that Max Weber tried to associate Protestantism with early capitalism.

The heart of the matter is an accurate understanding of the sociopolitical forces that have fostered Korea's high-speed economic growth. Since these forces are not obvious but are highly controversial, the analytical task is one of determining which theories apply to the Korean experience and which ones offer misleading comparisons. Professor Kim, following a well-established school of English-language social thought, believes that the key to Korea's economic growth lies in the society's "traditional cultural values." In accordance with Western sociological theories that posit a connection between capitalism and religious values, he wants to find a link between Korean religion and Korean capitalism; and he consequently envisages needed reforms of the Korean economic system in terms of changes in basic social values. Here I believe Professor Kim goes off the tracks. In my opinion he is trying to interpret the Korean case using an inappropriate (and perhaps discredited) Western theory; and because of this theoretical inadequacy, he fails to identify the major drawbacks of "soft authoritarianism" as a solution to Korea's current economic problems.

Y. H. Kim is, of course, in good company. His colleagues Ki Jun Rhee ("Western Capitalism versus Oriental Capitalism," 1989), Young Hoon Kwun ("Cultural Values and the Economic System: Past and Present," 1989), and Lee-Jay Cho and Chung H. Lee ("Government-Business Interplay in Korea: Cultural Dimensions," 1989) all follow him to one degree or another down the path first pioneered by Weber. They accept as fact Weber's theory that a link existed between

Protestant religious values and the emergence of capitalism in the West, and hence they seek to find a similar link between the spirit of Korean capitalism and Korean religious values. I believe that such an approach is intellectually misguided and will generate wrong answers to the question, What is the best system of national economic management for Korea? Before introducing the theory that I believe actually applies to the Korean case—and that offers some comparative answers to the question, What is to be done?—let me explain why I think the Weberian approach is a dead end.

There are problems with Weber's theory of the Protestant ethic and the spirit of capitalism both on its own terms and in light of high-speed economic growth in Asia under capitalist auspices but without Protestantism—a development that Weber did not foresee and explicitly predicted could not occur. The most logical response to Weber's theory and the contraindicated developments in Asia would therefore be to reject the theory—to question whether there ever was any genuine connection between Protestantism and capitalism in the West since there assuredly was none in Asia. But the power of Weber's method and the influence he has had on English-language social science is such that this course is usually not followed. Instead it is argued that Asian capitalism differs because it rests on different religious values, or that Confucianism is the functional equivalent of Protestantism in providing the worldly but ascetic values that are alleged to be indispensable to capitalism. Y. H. Kim adopts the first stratagem. "Because of this fundamental difference," he writes, "between Puritan and Confucian rationalism, the state-guided capitalist economy, which was managed in an absolutely different spirit from Western capitalism (the free enterprise systems—that is, the competitive market economy founded on rational individualism and civil society), became well established in Japan, Korea, and Taiwan." While I agree that the state-guided capitalist economies of Japan, Korea, and Taiwan differ in fundamental ways from the Anglo-American model, I see no reason at all to suppose that such differences are caused by religion.[1]

The likelihood that religion has nothing to do with economic development—in either the West or Asia—is reinforced by attempts to explain Asian economic dynamism in terms of "Confucian capitalism." Weber himself thought of Confucianism as an impassable obstacle to economic development and blamed China's economic backwardness on the influence of Confucianism (Weber 1951: chap. 8). Similarly, the Western quest to find an equivalent of Protestantism in Japan in order to accommodate the Meiji achievements to Western theory produced some interesting speculation on Tokugawa religion. But no one has even come close to finding in the nineteenth-century Japanese the "mighty enthusiasm" that Weber posited (Bellah 1957). One of the biggest problems of conceiving Confucius as the god of wealth is timing. In the West the Protestant Reformation occurred about a century before the appearance of capitalism, thereby suggesting at least the possibility of a superficial correlation. In East Asia, Confucianism developed in the fifth century B.C.; thus it took two and a half millennia before it supposedly fostered any local capitalism. Even then one wonders what the role of Confucianism was, since it is opposed to and explicitly condemns all forms of mercantile activity.

I believe that Weber's contribution to social science theory has been seriously misunderstood. His theory is actually a philosophically idealist reaction to Marxist materialism. He and Marx were arguing about whether values are independent or dependent variables in the explanation of social phenomena. To divorce Weber's position from this intellectual context tends to trivialize it and make it overly mechanical. Today very few serious historians hold the view that Protestantism had much to do with the emergence of Western capitalism. They are more interested in developments such as the forces that promoted investment in things other than land by the upper classes and vigorous investment by the other classes; the appearance of social mobility, national transportation networks, information flows, and the ending of social barriers to entrepreneurship; and checks on the arbitrary power of rulers and institutions, thus providing predictability and accountability in government (Brewer 1989; Goodell 1985; Plumb 1973). Religion may promote or inhibit these developments, but many other things are just as important, including scientific breakthroughs, discoveries of new territories, and innovations in military organization. Weber was concerned above all to show that values and similar forms of belief influence these kinds of developments as powerfully as material forces and that, contrary to Marx, intellectual constructs could not be reduced to materialistic dynamics. Capitalism is not possible without the appropriate values, but there are many other sources of these values than religion. Kim actually knows this when he writes that Korean "nationalism has become the prime motive propelling economic modernization since the 1960s."

Most of the theorists who allege a link between Asian economic dynamism and "creative Confucianism" are actually not interested in Weber but have nationalistic, ideological, or journalistic motives. They want to explain Asia's competitiveness as due to primordial characteristics in order to get their own governments to protect them from it, or to cause the working people in Asian capitalist countries not to compare themselves with workers in other capitalist countries, or to find some new rallying cry for nationalism, or just to popularize very complex socioeconomic developments for readers of their newspapers. Influential examples of this type of writing include Herman Kahn, *World Economic Development* (1979); Kim Il gon, *Order and Economy in the Confucian Culture Area* (1986); Roy Hofheinz and Kent Calder, *The Eastasia Edge* (1982); Michio Morishima, *Why Has Japan "Succeeded"?* (1982); and Ronald Dore, *Taking Japan Seriously: A Confucian Perspective on Leading Economic Issues* (1987).

In addition to these writers, there are others who have tried seriously to address the relationship between social values and economic activity. Winston Davis, for example, argues that virtually all applications of Weberian thought to Asian capitalism cannot get around the fallacy of post hoc ergo propter hoc: because industry in modern Asia developed after particular systems of religious values were in place, it developed because of them. "Unless the connection between values and development," Davis writes, "can be made explicit there seems to be no way to turn Weberian speculation into defensible, testable, or falsifiable hypotheses. I would suggest that more attention be paid to the religious attitudes which appear while development is taking place." Davis is, in fact, the leading writer in English on the growth of new religions in Japan that help people manage the tensions of high-speed economic growth, and on the Japanese ideological use of religion to justify some of the inequities that economic development fosters (Davis 1987:221–280).

Albert Hirschman has also written a famous essay exploring the relationship between capitalism and social values and how theories of this relationship have changed over the course of capitalism's three centuries. He begins with the eighteenth-century thesis that capitalist relations of production civilized human society because they taught mutual benefit, the need to be prudent and reserved in order to obtain credit, and the virtues of frugality, punctuality, and probity. By the nineteenth century this view was replaced with a vision of capitalism as destructive of truly human values, leading not to civilization but to overindulgence, the cash nexus in all relationships, and alienation. The nineteenth century also inaugurated a new debate over whether capitalism had sufficiently penetrated society in order genuinely to supplant feudal values with bourgeois values. Many English-speaking observers concluded that what was wrong with Germany and Japan was that capitalism had not fully developed there and that these "late-developing" societies suffered from feudal survivals. At the same time in America, many social critics concluded that American bourgeois society was puerile and crass because it had no legacy of feudalism—as in Germany and Japan.

Perhaps Hirschman's most valuable insight in this essay is that neoclassical economic theory taken seriously leads to sociological nonsense:

> Economists who wish the market well have been unable, or rather have tied their own hands and denied themselves the opportunity, to exploit the argument about the integrative effects of markets [for society as a whole]. This is so because the argument cannot be made for the ideal market with perfect competition. The economists' claims of allocative efficiency and all-round welfare maximization are strictly valid only for this market. Involving large numbers of price-taking anonymous buyers and sellers supplied with perfect information, such markets function without any prolonged human or social contact among the parties. Under perfect competition there is no room for bargaining, negotiation, remonstration, or mutual adjustment, and the various operators that contract together need not enter into recurrent or continuing relationships as a result of which they would get to know each other well. . . . In this manner, [economists] have endeavored to endow the market with

> economic legitimacy. But, by the same token, they have sacrificed the sociological legitimacy that could rightfully have been claimed for the way, so unlike the perfect-competition model, most markets function in the real world. (Hirschman 1986:123)

A sociologically valid theory of the market must therefore incorporate not just Thurow's "market principles and forces" but also institutions, rules, histories, legal judgments, and cultural norms concerned with such things as gender, age, inheritance, and family obligations. This is the realm not of economic theory but of political economy.

In one sense the Japanese have built their economic system on a sociological rather than an economic theory of the market—one that recognizes the links and connections between manufacturers and consumers and tries to make the most of them. Thus, the Japanese system is filled with such institutions as *keiretsu* (developmental conglomerates), cross-shareholding, cartels of all kinds, insider trading, bid rigging (*dango*), linkages between banks and borrowers, and officially created trade associations. In short, the Japanese theory of the market rests on an assumption of the naturalness of oligopoly. By contrast, the American theory of the market is to regard all contacts among buyers and sellers as forms of collusion and to promote a huge, often parasitic apparatus of antitrust law and litigation.

Robert Bellah is another thoughtful writer on social values and economic activity. He is concerned with what happens to society when people actually attempt to create an approximation of the "ideal market with perfect competition." Following Tocqueville more than Weber, Bellah wants to identify as precisely as possible a "noneconomic normative order capable of supporting the extensive development of economic rationality" (Bellah 1982:112). Genuine economic rationality, Bellah holds, is relatively rare in human history because it is so destructive of all other forms of human relationships. It means subjecting all relationships to the test of efficiency; for example, if the shortest distance between two points happens to pass through a cemetery, economic rationality would dictate that society build its road through the cemetery. For people actually to tolerate periods of genuine economic rationality, they need some inner gyroscope that gives them a sense of orientation amidst continuous upheaval. Something like this developed in mid-nineteenth century America, and *Democracy in America* was Tocqueville's analysis of the gyroscope that made it tolerable to Americans.

The Liberal Democratic Party in Japan has arguably been more of an economically rational party than a conservative one—the true conservatives were the progressive coalitions that ruled postwar Kyoto—but the nature of the Japanese gyroscope is not fully understood. It may be religion, but it may also be based on group loyalties, nationalism, the bonding effects of international competition for market share, such Japanese values as *gaman* (uncomplaining perseverance, as long as all do their share), and ideologies of physical and ethnic distinctiveness. Such popular

Japanese fetishes as Nihonjinron (the theory of Japanese uniqueness) and racism may contribute to economic growth by persuading Japanese citizens to accept the personal, environmental, and political costs of their mercantilist industrial and trade policies. In other words, traditional social values can provide the raw materials for ideologists, whose intent is to keep the society docile and hardworking.

Late Industrialization Model

I hope that the discussion thus far has suggested that the problems of managing the Korean economy cannot be reduced to Korean religious values but that, at the same time, an effective managerial strategy is likely to be more political and social than economic.[2] The theory that I contend more accurately addresses Korea's economic problems than Weberian sociology can best be introduced by a quotation of Albert Hirschman, also quoted by Y. H. Kim: the "underdeveloped countries as a group are set apart, through a number of economic characteristics common to them, from the advanced industrial countries and . . . traditional economic analysis, which has concentrated on the industrial countries, must therefore be recast in significant respects when dealing with underdeveloped countries" (Hirschman 1981:3). What Hirschman has in mind is the theory of late economic development pioneered by writers such as Thorstein Veblen, Joseph Schumpeter, and Alexander Gerschenkron, a theory that is perhaps best represented today in the new books of Alice Amsden on Korea and Robert Wade on Taiwan (Veblen 1966; Schumpeter 1991; Gerschenkron 1962, 1989; Amsden 1989; Wade 1990).

By late development, all of these writers mean economic development following and in response to the original beneficiaries of the industrial revolution—or, in the cases of Korea and Taiwan, late-late development in response to the industrialization of Japan. Late developers—and the late-late developers even more so—differ from the original developers in that socioeconomic factors such as the rise of a bourgeoisie, private investment, entrepreneurship, and even perhaps Protestantism were not as important as the conscious political decision to industrialize. Gerschenkron generalizes that the later the timing of development, other things being equal, the greater the importance of the state in economic affairs. While this point is obvious with regard to the Leninist cases, classical economists have tended not to recognize its applicability to the other successful late developers because they have overgeneralized the Anglo-American experience and because they know too little about Germany and Japan. The theory of late development referred to by Hirschman is addressed above all to the two great non-Leninist late developers—Germany after 1870 and Japan after 1868.

In second-round late development, such as occurred in Germany and Japan, a mobilization regime forces its economic priorities on a society that may not necessarily be recalcitrant but that, in any case, has not evolved the bourgeois mores that press for industrialization from below. The two fundamental types of such mobilization regimes are the Leninist-Stalinist totalitarian model and the Bismarckian-Meiji authoritarian one. Both involve social goal setting, forced saving, mercantilism, and bureaucratism. They differ in that the Leninist-Stalinist strategy relies on a socialist displacement of the market to establish its goals whereas the Bismarckian-Meiji pattern is based on market-conforming methods of social goal setting and utilizes the market to implement its goals. The communist-type command economy characteristically retains all ownership and control in the hands of the state, whereas the capitalist developmental state (CDS) rests on genuine private ownership of property but indirect state control of economic decisions. The CDS is infinitely more efficient than its communist rival but not as efficient as the ideal market economy with perfect competition. At the same time it is much more effective in achieving its societal goals than its purely market competitor.

The major sociopolitical problem of all high-speed economic growth is that it generates acute social and political instability. This is doubly so for the late developers because industrialization is occurring in advance of and not in response to social evolution. But even for the original beneficiaries of the industrial revolution, where it occurred at a slower pace and was welcomed by some important elements of society, industrialization led to serious instability, as described and analyzed by Marx and Engels. In these early cases the state became the institution not for leading industrialization itself but for intervening to alleviate the tensions and inequities that industrialization caused. Where it intervened successfully, the state thus headed off the revolutions that Marx and Engels predicted. And in the process these governments became "capitalist regulatory states."

Leninist and CDS regimes deal with the forced sacrifices and political instability caused by industrialization in characteristically different ways. The Leninist approach is cruder and simpler—and, as the events of 1989 throughout the communist world showed, less effective. The Leninists rely on a penetrative, totalitarian organizational weapon, the Communist Party, to preempt, channel, or suppress unwanted developments in the society. The elites of the CDS have a quite different problem. They must reconcile their state goals with the mass politics inherent in modernized, mobilized nontraditional societies with highly developed markets, private ownership of property, and large cities—that is, sectors and locales in which a large measure of self-government and autonomy is the only feasible form of social organization. These regimes set the goals of the society in their elite state bureaucracies. But to implement these goals they must enter the market and manipulate and structure it so that private citizens responding to incentives and disincentives make the market work for the state. The term "soft authoritarianism" as used by Y. H. Kim and by me refers to the political arrangements through which the elites of the CDS attempt to implement their goals.

The political solutions that late nineteenth-century German and Japanese elites came up with can be approximated in the following four-part model. First, at the center is a covert establishment that perpetuates itself through a conservative alliance among the minimally necessary interest groups. Second, the elite takes preemptive measures to forestall formation of mass movements that could interfere with its goals, above all the emergence of a unified labor movement. Third, the elite develops and propagates ideologies to convince the public that the social conditions in their country are the result of anything—culture, history, feudalism, national character, climate, and so forth—other than political decisions. Fourth, the elite undertakes diversionary activities that promote national pride but that also deflect attention from constitutional development. The most common such diversion, learned from Bismarck and the Meiji oligarchs, has been imperialism, but in the atomic age Olympic Games, imperial weddings, anti-Americanism, and revanchist movements (Japan's northern islands, North Korea, the Chinese mainland) may serve as substitutes. By far the most important substitute for imperialism in the postwar era has been export promotion and competition for market share.

At the heart of this model is the covert conservative alliance that keeps the elite establishment in power. In Bismarckian and Wilhelmine Germany this included the two strongest economic interests in the country, the grain producers and heavy industry. The German alliance, like the creation of Japan's Liberal Democratic Party in 1955, was intended to wage an all-out attack on organized socialism and was underwritten by state subventions, tariffs, and protectionism. The chief unintended consequence of this arrangement was to stunt democratic development, which in turn provided fertile soil for the later development of fascism and militarism. Economic development in Germany and Japan produced economically capable but politically castrated bourgeoisies, which left the societies vulnerable to reactionary political movements. In the German case, Gordon Craig refers to "the whole miserable history of the German bourgeoisie, which had acquiesced in the powerlessness to which it had been reduced by its defeats in 1848 and 1866 and had compensated for its loss by combining an uncritical nationalism . . . with an idealization of private and cultural values (*Innerlichkeit*) which it used as an excuse for its lack of any sense of political responsibility" (Craig 1977:xi). The important pre-Nazi German historian Eckart Kehr labeled the resultant system "bourgeois-aristocratic neofeudalism," a term which could apply equally well to prewar Japan (Kehr 1977:118–119).[3]

In late Meiji Japan, after the promulgation of the Meiji Constitution, the conservative allies were the imperial household, the Meiji oligarchs, landowners, and the original *zaibatsu*. In the militarist era, after the seizure of Manchuria, the conservative allies were the imperial household, military leaders, the economic bureaucracy, and the new *zaibatsu*. In the era of high-speed growth, the conservative allies were the economic bureaucracy, the Liberal Democratic Party, and the leaders of big business. Since elections were now unavoidable, this last elite made the narrow interests of farmers and small retailers sacrosanct so long as they voted for the Liberal Democratic Party. Just as in Bismarck's famous alliance of "iron and rye," contemporary Japan rests on an alliance of rice and automobiles—or, in institutional terms, Nokyo (the agricultural cooperatives), who vote for the ruling party, and Keidanren (big business), who pays for it.

The key point here is the distinction between formal sovereignty—what the Japanese call *tatemae*—and concrete hegemony—what the Japanese call *honne*. The heart of soft authoritarianism is the concrete hegemony of a covert elite working within a formal system of legality and popular sovereignty. Such an elite can be extremely effective—as the modern histories of Germany, Japan, Korea, and Taiwan attest—but the attendant political underdevelopment can also be very costly in time of crisis.

It is obviously not my place, as it might be for Professor Kim, to recommend continued soft authoritarianism or further progress toward democracy for contemporary Korea (Johnson 1989). But I can perhaps outline the dangers inherent in either course. The danger of full democracy at this point is that it will not lead to political stability but merely reveal the great instability already created by Korea's industrialization thus far. Full democracy at this point in Korea's development might lead the country simply to spin out of control. On the other hand, further democratization could improve the society's endemic corruption, its inability to change basic policies because of the resistance of entrenched interests, and its vulnerability to violent groups.

The liabilities of soft authoritarianism have already been made clear. Its strengths are that long-term developmental goals for the economy can be set; serious investment in education and research can be depoliticized; and people can come to see their government as legitimate for what it has accomplished rather than because of the formal political philosophy it expresses. If Korea should choose this route, then it may want to take the postwar Japanese political system as a model but also as a guide to what to avoid. Following the Japanese course would involve expanding and consolidating the Korean elite beyond the narrow confines of ex-military officers and *jaebul* directors, certainly to include the incipient bourgeoisie of the cities. It would also mean reinforcing the integrity of the elite through the circulation of its members much as Japan does with bureaucratic *amakudari* ("descent from heaven," i.e., early retirement and posting to the private sector). Overt repression of the Kwangju variety must obviously be avoided.

The most important issue for the Korean elites is to depoliticize the Korean labor movement. One of Japan's major postwar achievements was, after 1960, meeting labor's demand for job security in return for labor's giving up any role in politics. Japan enjoys an unequalled comparative advantage in a labor force that is well educated, not exploited, and organized into company unions. Korean developmental elites must decide what they want from labor—and then be willing to pay for it.

Korea's elites are well positioned to employ the politics of diversion. The instability in the north and the possible collapse of communist legitimacy following the death of Kim Il Sung means that Korea's Nordpolitik is likely to be as diverting and as profitable as (former West) Germany's Ostpolitik. Further justification for elite guidance of Korea's development can be found in the need for very large financial reserves to pay for unification whenever it comes.

A compromise between democracy and soft authoritarianism might be found in a slow process of democratization using the Scandinavian countries as models. This would emphasize the further legal institutionalization of civil and property rights, a court system oriented toward administrative supervision of the bureaucracy and the enforcement of contracts, an up-to-date commercial code specifying the rights and obligations of buyers and sellers, and an accounting system that properly records and taxes values, gains, and losses. Such a course would be compatible with further economic development but would sacrifice a certain amount of direction over it and risk, as noted above, serious political instability.

However, in the long run, greater political instability may result from trying to maintain the current political status quo. The early industrializing states evolved—albeit painfully—in order to avoid the fate predicted for them by Marx and Engels (and many others). The capitalist development states may soon face similar internal challenges to their political and social norms. The maintenance of agricultural protection in Japan, for example, is increasingly opposed by many groups in the country as well as by its trading partners. How well the capitalist developmental states adapt to these and other international pressures will depend on the wisdom of their leaders and the degree to which ideological and other distractions lose their effectiveness with the people. Successful economic development from above does impart a degree of political legitimacy, but ultimately such legitimacy can come only from the consent of the governed. Delaying democratization is feasible for a while but not indefinitely.

Alternative Model of Korea's Political Economy

Looking at different forms of political economy in a very abstract sense, we may classify Korea's political economy as a type I have called the capitalist developmental state (Johnson 1982). It should be distinguished from a pure command economy, from a reformed command economy, and from a laissez-faire economy. If we take as variables public or private ownership of the means of production and public or private control of the means of production, as formulated by Yu-shan Wu (1990) of National Taiwan University, we come up with a fourfold matrix in which we can compare Korea's political economy with the other major forms.

	State ownership	Private ownership
State control	1	3
Private control	2	4

In the first combination, ownership and control are both in the hands of the state. This is the classic command economy, of which Stalin's USSR offers the best example. Such economies are capable of great feats of capital formation but they are very inefficient, a feature that is exacerbated by their isolation from international competition. The second combination is the reformed command economy, such as in Hungary and China before 1989. Here the state retains ownership of the means of production but devolves control over it to the level of the household or the enterprise. This change makes the economy more efficient but it still blocks the emergence of long-term entrepreneurship.

The third combination is the capitalist developmental state, of which Japan is the prototype. Here there is genuine private ownership of property, including its legal defense and the right to pass it on as an inheritance, which promotes entrepreneurship. But the state retains economic control, promoting productive investments and discriminating against socially unproductive investments even though they may be privately profitable (e.g., investment in land). In the fourth combination both ownership and control are in private hands; the economically weak state is restricted to regulatory roles. The primary example of this type of political economy is that in the United States, where with the exception of its military-industrial complex the state does not play a developmental role in economic affairs.

Although this seems to be an efficient way to classify economies, it is also intensely controversial. In the first three cases the main variable is the state; only in the last does the state have a diminished role. The explanation for the first three types is therefore primarily political. But the last case, the laissez-faire economy, has generated an elaborate set of theorems and measures that form so-called neoclassical economics. Because of the Cold War, which in part pitted the first type of political economy against the fourth, and because the fourth prevailed vis-à-vis the first, American economic theory has taken on a hegemonic quality. English-speaking economists claim that the fourth type is superior to the other three, but they are also very defensive about the achievements of the third, or CDS, type, which they did not anticipate and still cannot fully explain using their purely economic concepts.

This is not just a matter of ideology intruding into social science analysis. Because since 1945 the United States has played a global leadership role, American-style laissez-faire economics has had a disproportionate influence intellectually and in terms of the basic philosophy guiding the policies of many international economic organs such as the World Bank. Nonetheless, using neoclassical economic theories or taking the United States as a model in attempting to understand the third category of economies is highly misleading. If nothing more, the fundamental criteria for judging the success or failure of the first three and the fourth cases differ. In the first three the criterion is the effectiveness of state action whereas in the fourth it is the efficient allocation of resources.

It was because of these considerations that Jung-En Woo expressed alarm at the domination, during the 1980s, of the Korean Development Institute by some thirty-five economists, "every last one of them a Ph.D. from American universities" (Woo 1991:191). Similarly, Robert Wade, in advocating the creation of a "pilot agency" or "economic general staff" within the developmental state (such as Japan's MITI or Korea's Economic Planning Board), observes, "The activities of such an agency are likely to be uncongenial to economists trained to believe that targeting by officials will generally fail. This is one good reason for curbing the number and influence of economists in the industrial policymaking process, as was done in Japan, Korea, and Taiwan." He adds, "The United States is a model of what developing countries should avoid" (Wade 1990:372, 381).

Yu-shan Wu's fourfold schema is only one way that social scientists have tried to identify the strengths and weaknesses of various kinds of political economy. Another approach is via the theory of late development. This theory stresses that processes of industrialization differ fundamentally from each other over time. Among the causes of this variation are the availability of capital and the role of the state in mobilizing it and guiding its investment. The original industrial revolution was built on and proclaimed laissez-faire because the capital for it was already in private hands and the state was asked only to get out of the way. The second industrial revolution (Germany, Japan) required mobilization of capital by the state, which therefore played a more important role than the capitalistic bourgeoisie. The typical strategy of the second industrial revolution was the protection of infant industries.

The third industrial revolution (Korea, Taiwan) required both the mobilization of capital by the state and also the state's subsidization of private enterprises. As Alice Amsden writes with regard to Korea, "In late industrialization, the foundation is the subsidy—which includes both protection and financial incentives. The allocation of subsidies has rendered the government not merely a banker, as Gerschenkron (1962) [an important theorist of the second industrial revolution] conceived it, but an entrepreneur, using the subsidy to decide what, when, and how much to produce. The subsidy has also changed the process whereby relative prices are determined" (Amsden 1989:143–144).[4] In this conception the state does not just mobilize capital and then leave it to the market to put it to work. In a microeconomic sense the state actually augments the market by becoming the major source of discipline over firms' behavior. The third industrial revolution was a far more political process than the first, which was not political at all, or the second, which was political only in comparison to the first.

Let me summarize the discussion to this point. According to the contemporary theory of political economy, the high-growth economies of East Asia cannot be explained because of their values, or because of their innovations in managerial practices and industrial organization, or because of their alliances during the Cold War, or because they modeled themselves on the United States, although several of these factors may explain why the Asian experiences apparently cannot be duplicated today by other countries, for example in Latin America. Instead, the theory holds that Korea, for example, grew as fast as it did because of the policies implemented by the Korean state. These policies included guidance of investment through land reform and a publicly owned banking system; creation of a stable environment for long-term investment through control of foreign exchange rates, interest rates, and aggregate demand; protection of the domestic market from the full force of international competition; restriction of foreign companies in Korea to keep control of the economy in Korean hands; aggressive pushing of exports; and implementation of a sectoral industrial policy that favored progressively higher value-added manufacturing (Wade 1990:307; Gerefi and Wyman 1990; Dietrich 1991).

I have stated the theory baldly here for the sake of clarity; many other aspects of the developmental state need explication. But let me now relate it to Y. H. Kim's question. If one accepts the validity of this theory, then why need one ask what the best system of national economic management is for Korea? The answer should be obvious: more of the same. But Kim was not wrong in posing his question. The very success of the policies implemented in Korea between 1961 and 1987—that is, during the Third, Fourth, and Fifth Republics—has made their perpetuation impossible both domestically and internationally. An accurate understanding of why the old prescriptions no longer work is therefore prerequisite to prescribing the best ones for the future.

There are two fundamental aspects to any strategy of state guidance of the economy. The first is what the state must do to keep itself in power. The second is what the state must do to keep the economy healthy and growing. Each of these aspects is further subdivided into a structural dimension and a strategic choice dimension. As David Held notes, the concept of "state power expresses at once the intentions and purposes of government and state personnel (they could have acted differently) and the parameters set by the institutionalized context of state-society relations" (Held 1989:74). In other words, structures of state power may be similar in different countries but the results of policies differ because political leaders have quite different strategic intentions, as for example in Korea and Mexico. On the other hand, leaders' intentions may be the same, but different structures of state power will produce different outcomes, as for example in Korea and China.

During the late 1980s most of the structural and environmental conditions on which Korea had based its high-speed growth began to change. The authority of the military regime, for example, evaporated, leading to the revolutionary events of June 1987 (Johnson 1989). The Korean public had become too rich merely to continue to follow their authoritarian leaders unquestioningly. However, the generalization among political economists that a per capita income of around US$4,000 separates the era in which state repression of the population is effective from the era in which state repression generates more disaffection than it can control slightly overstated the amount in Korea's case (Wade 1990:375). The ROK's per capita income in 1987 was only $3,121 whereas, by contrast, Taiwan's was almost $5,000 when it brought the world's longest-running martial law (1949–87) to an end. Equally important, the main beneficiaries and instruments of Korea's economic development, the giant *jaebul* concerns, had become restive under the old structure. Fearing attacks on themselves, according to Woo, the *jaebul* "came to desire greater stability and the rule of law, even if that meant liberal democracy (especially if that meant 'liberal democracy' along Japanese lines)" (Woo 1991:201). By 1987 the *jaebul* had also acquired the financial strength to shift some of their operations abroad, thereby potentially slipping the leash of the Korean government.

The international environment in which Korea had flourished was also rapidly changing. The threat to South Korea's security from North Korea and from the international communist movement lessened both because the ROK itself had become very powerful and because during 1989 the European communist nations imploded. Korea was also able to implement a successful policy of isolating North Korea from Russia and China until Japan unilaterally opened relations with Pyongyang in September 1990.

The security threat was important to South Korean development because it kept the military focused on economic growth rather than on self-enrichment, as in so many other military regimes. It also legitimated the government during the Third and Fourth Republics, caused the South Koreans to accept the sacrifices involved in economic development, and persuaded the United States to tolerate Korea's trade surpluses. From approximately 1982 on, however, the United States began strenuously to demand that Korea open its markets and begin to liberalize its economy, meaning reform its economic institutions using models approved by the IMF and World Bank. All of these forces combined to present Korea with a demand for new structures and new strategic choices.

From a comparative perspective, what was happening in Korea during the late 1980s was both natural and familiar. One of the leading scholars of comparative political development is the Japanese political scientist Masumi Junnosuke.[5] His analysis is useful. In a comparison of the political development of Britain, France, Germany, and Japan, Masumi finds a correlation between political reform movements and the shifts of the population from agriculture to capital-intensive industry and again to services and knowledge-intensive industry. The first political reform movement, correlating with the decline of the agricultural population, was in Europe from monarchy to representative government and in Japan from government by feudal domains (*hanbatsu*) to government by political parties. A second political reform movement, correlating with heavy industry's absorption of the labor force, saw the emergence of powerful trade unions and the entrance of socialist parties into parliament. The third political reform movement, correlating with the preponderance of services and high-tech industries in the economy, ushered in a decline of the socialists, a rise of citizens' movements aimed at protecting the environment and consumers, the growth of interest groups, and the homogenization of the population into a mass of floating voters who can be mobilized only through the mass media.

Fueling Masumi's theory is, of course, an irony: whenever an aristocratic, oligarchic, or authoritarian regime succeeds in or permits the industrialization of its economy, it unleashes social changes that will ultimately overwhelm the original sponsors of development. Masumi believes that all three of his stages can be found in Britain, France, Germany, and Japan but not necessarily in other countries. He argues that the United States is exceptional in that it partly skipped the second stage, and that the late industrializers of East Asia, particularly Taiwan and Korea, may also, but for different reasons, skip stage two or merge it with stage three. Masumi explains the different history of the United States by the fact that, although it was born in an anticolonial revolt, the victors in the revolt were actually the colonialists. Because the United States lacked both a monarchy and a bureaucracy in its past and expanded through immigration into a virtually limitless territory, there were ready alternatives for it to avoid a socialist movement. Taiwan and Korea may also evade or mitigate demands for socialism because their states are less willing to allow the exploitation of labor than their European predecessors and because knowledge-intensive industries and services are growing as fast as capital-intensive industries.

Masumi believes that the first process of political reform is currently taking place in Taiwan and Korea. In Taiwan, the agricultural labor force fell from 55.6 percent in 1953 to 18.6 percent in 1983, a decrease over thirty years that took fifty years in Japan (1920 to 1970). In Korea, the agricultural labor force fell from 78.3 percent in 1956 to 23.6 percent in 1986, a bigger decrease over thirty years than Taiwan's and a change that took eighty years in Japan (1885 to 1965). In both Taiwan and Korea these changes have led to the emergence of labor movements and, in the case of Korea, to the rejuvenation of a long-standing movement of student protest. Masumi thinks the student protests in Seoul are more like the student movement in China than in Taiwan. In Taiwan the student movement is not so important because the Nationalist Party has gained considerable legitimacy and it has also preemptively organized the universities. Moreover, Taiwanese universities do not give their faculties tenure, thereby damping revolutionary fervor among professors.

Masumi believes that in both Taiwan and Korea the reform movements of stage two are rather attenuated when compared to his four older cases. He explains this by arguing that the high-tech superindustrialization of stage three is occurring simultaneously with stage two and driving both countries toward a media-coordinated mass society. In the case of Korea, Masumi suggests that Kim Dae-Jung's party is the equivalent of Japan's Socialist Party and that both have been weakened by the merging of stages two and three and by the emergence of large coalition parties that use the wealth generated by high-speed growth to co-opt dissident groups. The Japanese call this *kinken-seiji* (power-of-money politics); in Korea, Woo Jung-En sees its equivalent in such incidents as the creation of the Ilhae Foundation, which she describes as the "greasing of Korea, Inc." and as "state racketeering," terms that could apply equally well to Japan (Woo 1991:199–200). However, Masumi questions whether the merger in January 1990 of the parties led by Roh Tae-Woo, Kim Yong-Sam, and Kim Jong-Pil actually produced a Korean version of the LDP. In Japan the LDP's long rule (1955–93) was based on the backing and remote control of big business and the state bureaucracy. Have the *jaebul* and Korean bureaucracy forged the same kind of relationship with the Korean ruling party? Japanese-style *kinken-seiji* may weaken socialist forces, but without the backing of business and bureaucracy it is extremely corrosive of a regime's legitimacy.

Masumi's categories and analysis should not be applied mechanically to Korea and Taiwan. They are important primarily because they relate the need for new structures and policies in Korea to the success of its early industrialization and because they indicate that the direction of reform is away from authoritarianism and toward, but not necessarily requiring, socialism and democracy. There is actually a range of choices available to a country such as Korea and critically important sequences that should be followed in introducing any particular set of new structures and policies. The quicker a society moves through the labor reform period and into a high-tech, knowledge-intensive middle-class society, the less the chances that class antagonism and class warfare will develop and the greater the opportunities for low-intensity media-based politics to emerge.

These considerations, in fact, offer criteria for both new structures and new state policies. The structures should be those that will contain and defuse the potentialities for class warfare inherent in Masumi's second stage, and the policies should aim at the rapid expansion of the technical capabilities of the labor force and at keeping internationally mobile capital at home. These measures are required for a society to enter the stage of hyperindustrialization. It should be understood that I am not endorsing these changes in some philosophic sense as the "best" for Korea. I am only trying to indicate what is logical in the context of economic development and its effects on the polity and society—much as an architect must indicate what is a logical building for a given purpose and terrain.

In talking about the range of choices available for state structures, modern political science attempts to reduce the complexity by ranging them along two different dimensions: from authoritarian to democratic and from corporatist to pluralist. The first concerns the amount of political participation in the choice of leaders. Authoritarian regimes are indifferent to popular preferences in choosing leaders, whereas democratic regimes adopt methods that give as wide a scope as possible to popular sentiments. The second analytical dimension concerns relations between interest groups and the state. In a corporatist structure the state charters a limited number of major economic interest groups, granting them a near monopoly of representation, whereas pluralist regimes practice "free trade" in giving interest groups access to the state. According to some versions of pluralist theory, the contest among interest groups should result in a political equilibrium which, in Held's terms, "defines the policy options of a weak state" (Held 1989:64). Democracy is said to exist when the state acts in accordance with this political equilibrium. By contrast, part of the moral claim of corporatism is that it presupposes a shared interest in the state's existence by forging unity among societal factions.

Within authoritarianism and corporatism one can also make distinctions. Authoritarianism may range from hard to soft, and corporatism may vary from state corporatism to societal corporatism (or corporatism from above and corporatism from below) (Held 1989). By hard authoritarianism we mean single-party rule, rigged elections (if they are held at all), and de facto dictatorship or oligarchy regardless of what attempts may be made at legitimization. Taiwan and Korea before 1987 both belonged in this category.

Soft authoritarianism is less clear. I first coined the term to refer to the four-decades-long rule of Japan's Liberal Democratic Party since postwar Japan regained its sovereignty, but it should be noted that also from 1892 to 1937 no Japanese political party in power was ever replaced by election (Johnson 1987:143).[6] The essence of soft authoritarianism is the facade of democracy but the actual rule by a covert conservative alliance that has mastered the techniques of preventing the development of opposing political coalitions. In the Japanese distinction between *tatemae* (principle) and *honne* (actual reality), soft authoritarianism is part of the *honne*. Suffice it to say that, in Robert Wade's description, "For the past thirty years Japanese voters have gone to the polls with slimmer expectations that the result could be a change of government than in any other industrialized democracy; and the representatives whom they elect have had less influence on the major decisions affecting the national welfare than in any other industrialized democracy" (Wade 1990:374). That is soft authoritarianism.

Although the term "state corporatism" is often used by European writers to refer to fascist regimes such as those of Salazar in Portugal or Perón in Argentina, it is not restricted to those cases. It refers above all to states that are able not only to resist private demands but also actively to shape the economy and society, such as capitalist developmental states. By contrast, in societal corporatism, regimes share policy innovations with the private groups that they have created or authorized to participate in policy formation for the country as a whole. Japan's Keidanren (Federation of Economic Organizations) is a typical societal corporatist organization, one that accepts into its daily activities officials seconded or retired from the central state bureaucracy. Normally, labor is included as a recognized participant in societal corporatist governments, but it may be excluded, as in Japan, if the economy is growing fast enough to guarantee high labor demand.

Excluding from the analysis the totalitarian forms of social organization, we may range various regimes along a continuum from hard authoritarian state corporatism (Taiwan and Korea before 1987) to democratic pluralism (the United States). The European corporatist regimes—Austria, Norway, Sweden, and Switzerland—combine democracy with societal corporatism. Japan exists somewhere between them and Korea and Taiwan. Japan is formally democratic but soft authoritarian in practice. Although its propagandists like to describe it as a kind of modified pluralism (*tagen-shugi*), it in fact combines socially corporatist organizations, except for labor, with an interventionist bureaucracy that is sensitive to, not instructed by, a range of interest groups that both dominate the economy and, until 1993, kept the LDP in power.

Some analysts hold that corporatism is only an illusion, one that "temporarily obscure[s] the asymmetries in the distribution of power" or that engages in "mass co-optation" (Held 1989:67; Wade 1990:243). This may be partly true, but if it helps hold a society together during the transition from Masumi's stage one to stage three, it is a good strategy. All effective politics are complex combinations of camouflage, expectations, and actual substance. The great advantage of corporatism is that the interest groups that the state creates or authorizes gather large sections of the population into their activities and thereby constrain them from advocating narrow benefits that might damage national productivity or unity. Corporatist bodies are normally well staffed and have long institutional memories; their function is to process priorities for an industry and, ultimately, for all of a nation's industries before approaching the government. One does not see in corporatist regimes the common occurrence in America of competing industrial lobbying organizations, for example, the Semiconductor Industry Association and the American Electronics Association. Corporatism eliminates the free trade in lobbying that is the hallmark of pluralism. On the basis of the East Asian developmental experience, there is no longer any question that authoritarian corporatist or democratic corporatist regimes will outperform democratic pluralist regimes, other things being equal. This is not to deny, of course, that both democracy and pluralism might be desired on grounds other than their contributions to economic development.

Let me recapitulate. The Korean developmental state has succeeded in producing "capitalism without the capitalist class," a phenomenon that is at the heart of the changes in international power as the twentieth century comes to an end.[7] The fact that English-speaking economic analysis still dogmatically denies that such a development is possible strongly indicates that those nations and leaders who subscribe to such analyses are more than likely misled about the ways in which the world is changing. They continue to contend that bureaucrats cannot pick winners, failing to understand that in places like Korea they are not choosing winners but making them (Wade 1990:334).

To continue making progress, the Korean state must both keep itself in power and keep giving the economy the correct guidance. Each is requisite to the other. Korea can learn from the experiences and theories of others, but it is most likely to succeed if it concentrates inductively and empirically on its own history, culture, and experience. As one who first visited Korea in 1953, at the end of the Korean War, I can assure you that no foreigner then could have imagined the Korea of today; it seems to me that what was true almost 40 years ago still applies. The first lesson therefore is to be careful of foreign advice, including that offered here.

From a political point of view, Korea has a problem in that its big *jaebul* combines, which the Korean state itself created in its campaign of heavy and chemical industrialization during the 1970s, are now so big that they can act on their own-behalf but in ways that are not necessarily on Korea's behalf. This includes investing abroad, much as the American multinationals did in the 1960s and 1970s, which left the American labor force to fend for itself and, lacking serious state investment in human capital, created a problem that is all too apparent in the United States of the 1990s. The Korean state therefore should develop policies that promote industrial investment within Korea's national boundaries, thereby ensuring continuing demand for domestic labor. Such policies will also bolster the state's legitimacy as the indispensable agent of all Koreans. The essence of the developmental state as a political entity is to make the needs of state legitimacy cohere with the needs of national economic development. Talk from Japanese and American consultants about "borderless economies" has to be tempered with an understanding that they do not speak for the citizens whom the state represents. For the immediate future this means that state power should be used to make Korean labor more competitive and to keep the *jaebul* patriotic.

What is the "best" institutional structure to accomplish these tasks? As indicated earlier, Korea would be wise to preserve authoritarianism and corporatism as long as possible, shifting gradually to their soft and societal forms—not just as Japan has done but also as several rich nations on the European continent and in Scandinavia have done. Equally important, this institutional structure is probably the best for coping with Korea's changing external environment. The state is a human creation that performs certain functions for societies on which their existence depends but that they cannot perform themselves. Among these tasks external security is one of the most important. For Korea, the probable further decline of the security threat from the North has several, all too probable replacements.

First is the virtually certain attempt by the Japanese to recreate the Greater East Asia Co-prosperity Sphere, this time based on a great deal more prosperity than in the 1940s but with the Japanese again displaying their historical inability to ground their leadership in some universally appealing doctrine. The post–Cold War trends toward economic regionalism in Europe and North America make a

Japanese-based equivalent probable, and Korea will need all the national strength it can muster to negotiate a place in it that does not leave Korea subservient to Tokyo. Second is, of course, the challenge of unification of the Korean peninsula, a project that if carried out imaginatively and effectively offers the promise of balancing to some extent future Japanese power in the region. Third is the role the ROK or a unified Korea has to play in the economic development of China and Asiatic Russia. Korea can offer them models of governmental organization and economic policy that are effective, as well as technologies that are appropriate to their level of development, but this will require state leadership, including training cadres of Koreans who are fluent in Russian and Chinese.

The emphasis in Korea's institutional structure for the immediate future should be on developing corporatism in preparation for eventual democracy, gradualism in all reforms, an external orientation in order to provide early warning of global changes, and investment in human capital. The best evidence that the logic behind such an orientation is sound is that it is the same kind of logic underlying the success of the developmental state between 1961 and 1987.

NOTES

1. I distinguish the state-guided capitalist economies, which I call "capitalist developmental states," from the Anglo-American examples, which I call "capitalist regulatory states," in Johnson (1982).

2. The bulk of this section is reprinted from Chalmers Johnson, "The State and Japanese Grand Strategy," in Richard Rosecrance and Arthur A. Stein (eds.), *The Domestic Bases of Grand Strategy*. Copyright © 1993 by Cornell University. Used by permission of the publisher, Cornell University Press.

3. Kehr also writes, "The characteristic and distinctive feature of the Bismarckian Reich lies in the peculiar way in which the relationship between the state and nation was arranged, the method of regulating relations between the federal states, and the attribution of legal sovereignty to the *Bundesrat*, while real hegemony was reserved to the Emperor and Prussia" (1977:chap. 1). The exact nature of the conservative alliances in prewar Japan was the focus of one of the most important Marxist debates in this century; see Hoston (1986).

4. The work Amsden refers to is Alexander Gerschenkron, *Economic Backwardness in Historical Perspective* (1962).

5. Masumi Junnosuke is Emeritus Professor of Political Science, Tokyo Metropolitan University; see, in particular, Masumi (1990, 1991).

6. On prewar elections, see Scalapino (1968).

7. The phrase "capitalism without the capitalist class" is from Woo (1991:14).

REFERENCES

Amsden, Alice H. 1989. *Asia's Next Giant: South Korea and Late Industrialization.* New York: Oxford University Press.

Bellah, Robert. 1957. *Tokugawa Religion.* Boston: Beacon Press.

Bellah, Robert. 1982. "Concluding Remarks." In *The Japanese Challenge and the American Response: A Symposium.* Berkeley: Institute of East Asian Studies, University of California.

Brewer, John. 1989. *The Sinews of Power: War, Money, and the English State, 1688–1783.* New York: Knopf.

Cho, Lee-Jay, and Chung H. Lee. 1989. "Government-Business Interplay in Korea: Cultural Dimensions." Korea's Political Economy: Past, Present, and Future (a prepublication series). Honolulu: Population Institute, East-West Center. December.

Craig, Gordon A. 1977. "Introduction." In Eckart Kehr, *Economic Interest, Militarism, and Foreign Policy: Essays on German History,* trans. Grete Heinz. Berkeley: University of California Press.

Davis, Winston. 1987. "Religion and Development: Weber and the East Asian Experience." In Myron Weiner and Samuel P. Huntington (eds.), *Understanding Political Development.* Boston: Little, Brown.

Dietrich, William S. 1991. *In the Shadow of the Rising Sun.* University Park: Pennsylvania State University Press.

Dore, Ronald. 1987. *Taking Japan Seriously: A Confucian Perspective on Leading Economic Issues.* Stanford: Stanford University Press.

Gerefi, Gary, and Donald L. Wyman, eds. 1990. *Manufacturing Miracles: Paths of Industrialization in Latin America and East Asia.* Princeton: Princeton University Press.

Gerschenkron, Alexander. 1962. *Economic Backwardness in Historical Perspective.* Cambridge: Harvard University Press.

Gerschenkron, Alexander. 1989 [1943]. *Bread and Democracy in Germany.* Ithaca: Cornell University Press.

Goodell, Grace. 1985. "The Importance of Political Participation for Sustained Capitalist Development." *Archives of European Sociology* 26:93–127.

Held, David. 1989. *Political Theory and the Modern State.* Stanford: Stanford University Press.

Hirschman, Albert O. 1981. *Essays in Trespassing: From Economics to Politics and Beyond.* Cambridge: Cambridge University Press.

Hirschman, Albert O. 1986. *Rival Views of Market Society and Other Recent Essays.* New York: Viking.

Hofheinz, Roy, and Kent Calder. 1982. *The Eastasia Edge.* New York: Basic Books.

Hoston, Germaine A. 1986. *Marxism and the Crisis of Development in Prewar Japan.* Princeton: Princeton University Press.

Johnson, Chalmers. 1982. *MITI and the Japanese Miracle: The Growth of Industrial Policy, 1925–1975.* Stanford: Stanford University Press.

Johnson, Chalmers. 1987. "Political Institutions and Economic Performance: The Government-Business Relationship in Japan, South Korea, and Taiwan." In Frederic C. Deyo (ed.), *The Political Economy of the New Asian Industrialism.* Ithaca: Cornell University Press.

Johnson, Chalmers. 1989. "South Korean Democratization: The Role of Economic Development." *Pacific Review* 2(1):1–10.

Kahn, Herman. 1979. *World Economic Development.* Boulder, Colo.: Westview Press.

Kehr, Eckart. 1977. *Economic Interest, Militarism, and Foreign Policy: Essays on German History*. Trans. Grete Heinz. Berkeley: University of California Press.

Kim, Il gon. 1986. *Jukyo bunka-ken no chitsujo to keizai* (Order and economy in the Confucian culture area). Nagoya, Japan: Nagoya University.

Kwun, Young Hoon. 1989. "Cultural Values and the Economic System: Past and Present." Korea's Political Economy: Past, Present, and Future (a prepublication series). Honolulu: Population Institute, East-West Center. December.

Masumi, Junnosuke. 1990. *Hikaku seiji: Seio to Nihon* (Comparative politics: Western Europe and Japan). Tokyo Daigaku Shuppankai.

Masumi, Junnosuke. 1991. "Patterns of Modern History: East Asia and Japan." Unpublished paper. Wilson Center, Washington, D.C.

Morishima, Michio. 1982. *Why Has Japan "Succeeded"? Western Technology and the Japanese Ethos.* Cambridge: Cambridge University Press.

Plumb, J. H. 1973. *The Growth of Political Stability in England, 1675–1725*. Harmondsworth: Penguin.

Rhee, Ki Jun. 1989. "Western Capitalism versus Oriental Capitalism." Korea's Political Economy: Past, Present, and Future (a prepublication series). Honolulu: Population Institute, East-West Center. December.

Scalapino, Robert A. 1968. "Elections and Modernization in Prewar Japan." In Robert E. Ward (ed.), *Political Development in Modern Japan*. Princeton: Princeton University Press.

Schumpeter, Joseph. 1991 [1951]. *Imperialism and Social Classes.* Philadelphia: Porcupine Press.

Veblen, Thorstein. 1966 [1915]. *Imperial Germany and the Industrial Revolution.* Ann Arbor: University of Michigan Press.

Wade, Robert. 1990. *Governing the Market: Economic Theory and the Role of Government in East Asian Industrialization.* Princeton: Princeton University Press.

Weber, Max. 1951. *The Religion of China.* Trans. Hans H. Gerth. Glencoe, Ill: Free Press.

Woo, Jung-En. 1991. *Race to the Swift: State and Finance in Korean Industrialization.* New York: Columbia University Press.

Wu, Yu-shan. 1990. "Leninist State and Property Rights: The Industrial Reform in the People's Republic of China, 1984–1988." Ph.D. diss., University of California, Berkeley.

[illegible]

[illegible] Press.

[illegible]

[illegible]

[illegible] Press.

[illegible] Press.

[illegible]

[illegible] Press.

[illegible]

[illegible] Press.

[illegible]

Chapter 4

The Specter of Anglo-Saxonization Is Haunting South Korea

Alice H. Amsden
Massachusetts Institute of Technology

Issues

Drifting toward an Inappropriate Model of Political Economy

Ambiguity always characterizes economic development (or decline), since no one can ever be sure whether short-term or even seasonal fluctuations represent a temporary or permanent deviation from a long-run trend. Ambiguity is pervasive because of uncertainty over whether the fundamental structure that underpinned a country's Golden Age of growth has changed, or should change, in response to new developments in the global environment and success itself, which requires an ongoing process of industrial restructuring.

South Korea provides a case in point. As it entered the 1990s, with a GNP growth rate almost as impressive as in the past, there was agonizing over whether rising inflation, ballooning balance-of-payments deficits, and escalating real wages spelled a premature end to the South Korean miracle. This stimulated debate over whether or not a new model of political economy was warranted to mend these seams, and to match Korea's more advanced industrial structure.

The only possible advantage a foreigner has in analyzing another country is ignorance. A lesser familiarity with all the facts and frills of any particular political economy makes it easier to rise above the details and consider the general picture. Granted this limitation, I would suggest that in South Korea's case the essential structure of its business-government relations—which underscored its spectacular industrial ascent, and which has become a prime target of political unrest in the 1990s—remains more or less intact. Certain particulars have understandably adapted to changing circumstance, and more substantial adjustment is warranted in the future, as argued below. But the essential relationship between business and government continues to be one of the government intervening far more in the economy and exercising far more discipline over business than typifies what may be termed the "Anglo-Saxon model." This is the model of industrialization described in dominant mainstream economics textbooks, even if it is not the model that exactly depicts British or American economic history. Simply put, at the heart of the Anglo-Saxon model is the belief that, whatever the country, the free market is the best allocative mechanism.

By contrast, in South Korea the relationship between government and business has strongly resembled a mixture of the Japanese and German models of economic development. Certain added twists make South Korea a pioneer in what I have called the late-industrialization model (Amsden 1989, 1992). In all these models, the state plays a more interventionist role than stipulated in the free market paradigm—more from practical necessity than from theoretical conviction. Industrial policy and not just macroeconomic policy guide economic growth. The institution of big business is also more omnipresent than orthodox theory entertains. Additionally, there is a greater emphasis inside the firm on shop floor management, engineering capabilities, and labor skills than is the norm in the actual Anglo-Saxon experience since World War II.

I would suggest that what has exacerbated the problems South Korea has had to confront in the 1990s, and what has made it so hard for it to respond effectively to them, is the pressure being exerted on it by the U.S. government and American-trained Korean economists (A-TKEs for short) to abandon the Japanese-German late-industrialization model and adopt the Anglo-Saxon one. The A-TKE's conviction that adoption of the Anglo-Saxon model is necessary to sustain rapid economic growth has delayed South Korea's catching up process and has detracted from its need to reform big business directly. Although business-government relations in South Korea urgently require restructuring and uncompetitive elements in the economy need to be weeded out, the Anglo-Saxon model is a fundamentally inappropriate blueprint for South Korea to adopt, given structural differences in the paths to industrial development that the Anglo-Saxon countries and late industrializers like South Korea have had to follow.

In the case of England and the United States, the champions of the first and second industrial revolutions, respectively, their competitiveness was rooted in their *pioneering technology*. Although the institutions underlying industrialization in these revolutions were distinct, in both cases new products and processes were the driving force behind productivity increases and the capture of overseas markets. A stream of innovations at the world technological frontier was the foundation of U.K. and then U.S. international competitiveness. The competitive asset of pioneering technology allowed both countries' firms relative independence from government support, the ability to specialize in a single technology family, and a strategic focus on the staff functions, including R&D, necessary to develop and market new products.

By contrast, in countries like South Korea, Japan, and to a lesser extent Germany, industrialization has been a process of borrowing technology that has already been commercialized by firms from more advanced countries. South Korea, Japan, Taiwan, and other late industrializers have had to grow through a process of *learning*. Denied the competitive asset of new products and production techniques, even in leading enterprises, government intervention in these countries has had to be greater than in the Anglo-Saxon case, firms have had to be more diversified into technologically unrelated industries, and the strategic focus within these firms has initially had to be on the shop floor rather than the R&D laboratory or other administrative functions. The shop floor became a key focus because it was here that borrowed technology was first made to work, then adapted to suit local conditions, and eventually improved to the point where incremental improvements in productivity and quality supplemented low wages and enabled late industrializers to compete against firms from more advanced countries in "mature," expanding industries.

As a quintessential learner, Japan has carefully studied the economic, political, and social system of the United States. Nevertheless, even though it has borrowed selectively from the United States and has progressed to the point of becoming an innovator of major new technology, Japan has found it advantageous to retain two of the defining characteristics of a learner: by Anglo-Saxon standards, the Japanese government intervenes considerably to advance high technology and to regulate consumption, and Japanese companies invest considerably to deepen their laborers' skills and to advance their engineering know-how. However much progress South Korea has made in its industrial development, and however much South Korea has learned—and can continue to learn—from the United States, South Korea has still come nowhere near the point where its competitiveness rests on its capabilities to generate major technological changes. Therefore, the Anglo-Saxon model remains fundamentally inappropriate for South Korea to adopt. The restructuring of business-government relations required as a consequence of the emergence of political democracy and a higher level of industrial development must occur within the boundaries of the late-industrialization model if South Korea is to follow in the footsteps of Germany and Japan and catch up with the world technological frontier.

Late industrializers have included not just the fast-growth economies of Japan, South Korea, and Taiwan, but also the slower-growth economies of, say, India, Mexico, and Brazil. What has made the East Asian late industrializers distinct from the rest is not less government intervention in their economies but a different principle governing their allocation of subsidies. In the slower-growing late industrializers, subsidies have tended to be allocated according to the principle of *give-away*. Government support is not made contingent on the attainment of performance standards. Subsidies are thrown like a blanket over business, so that there is a greater tendency for, say, rampant nonrepayment of loans, persistent use of credit for purposes for which it is not intended, and failure to attain productivity levels near international norms.

While certain abuses associated with the allocation of subsidies are well-known in Japan, South Korea, and Taiwan, they are much less in evidence in these slower-growth countries. Instead, the principle governing subsidy allocation has tended to be one of *reciprocity*: subsidies are tied to concrete performance standards and are then monitored. In all late-industrializing countries the government has sternly disciplined labor. What is unique about East Asia is that its governments have also disciplined capital (Amsden 1989, 1991b, 1992).

The reciprocity principle was and is evident in Japan, although historically government intervention was less in Japan than in more underdeveloped East Asian countries. Japan had more competitive assets than merely low wages with which to industrialize, so government intervention could be lower. Furthermore, the rest of East Asia had to shoulder the additional burden of having to compete against Japan. Even in Japan, however, the government has intervened more than in the Anglo-Saxon case and has disciplined business more. In the postwar machine tool industry, for example, where government intervention in every country has tended to be below the norm for other industries, the Japanese government subsidized machine toolmakers with preferential credit and selective rather than across-the-board tariff protection. In exchange, the government set a target of 50 percent output in the form of numerically controlled machine tools (the target was reached in 1983, only three years after the specified date; Amsden and Hikino 1993). The American machine tool industry was unusual for the support it received from the government; it was considered vital for national security and could be said to have been coddled by the Department of Defense. Despite this, American machine tool builders successfully resisted the demands of the Defense Department for fulfilling certain performance standards, say, the standardization of machine tool components and parts (Wagoner 1966). When the government began protecting an ailing American machine tool industry in the 1980s, protection was not made contingent on the attainment of performance standards and failed to reverse the American machine tool industry's decline.

In Taiwan, the provision of subsidized working capital to industry in the 1960s was tied to the attainment of export targets; the system was similar to the one operating in South Korea, except that in Taiwan targets were monitored not by government officials but by an industry association of textile manufacturers, which acted as a cartel (Haggard 1990). By the 1990s, preferential credit to "star" industries (as opposed to "strategic" industries in the 1970s and 1980s) was contingent in Taiwan on performance standards, such as investing a minimum fraction of sales revenues in training and R&D or meeting certain environmental standards.

In both South Korea and Taiwan, the subsidy allocation process was corrupt to the extent that no firm could expect to receive substantial aid if it was openly critical of the government. No firm could expect to "make it big" unless it was a staunch government supporter. Nevertheless, in both countries by the 1960s even the government's political cronies had to execute and manage their investment projects relatively efficiently, or they would not be tapped again for any other major investment project. Additional forms of government control over business took various forms. For example, in South Korea firms in major industries were subjected to price controls and wage surveillance. There was a constraint on using subsidized credit for unintended purposes in the form of extraordinarily heavy penalties for illegal capital flight. In short, big business was handsomely subsidized, but it was also fairly tightly disciplined.

It is precisely this reciprocal relationship that had fallen into disrepute in South Korea by the 1990s. Popular resentment against big business has grown, so the government is wary of giving it further support. Big business has also increased its power vis-à-vis the government, in terms of both finance and knowledge of investment opportunities, so it has been more resistant to government discipline and more threatening to politicians fearful of losing businesses' financial backing. I would argue, however, that the solution to this standoff is reform *within* the existing Japanese-German late-industrializing paradigm. It is not a closer embrace of free market textbook economics, as many of South Korea's American-trained economists have vigorously advised.

American-Trained Korean Economists

To suggest that A-TKEs recommend free market economics as a solution to the standoff between big business and government is not to say that all of them do; rather, on average A-TKEs tend to regard the Anglo-Saxon model as the best solution to their country's woes. This is their philosophy despite the fact that their justifications for introducing radically freer markets have turned out to be fallacious. Free market economics in South Korea began to be championed by A-TKEs in direct response to (1) the inflation-cum-recession of the second energy crisis of 1980–82; (2) the drive to promote investment in heavy industry launched under Park Chung Hee after the first energy crisis of 1973; and (3) a rise in the number of Koreans receiving Ph.D.'s in economics from the United States. As Table 4.1 indicates, whereas the number of A-TKEs between 1970 and 1990 totaled 801, the decade of the 1980s accounted for 597 of the total. Although Japan's population is roughly three times greater than South Korea's, the number of A-TJEs (American-trained Japanese economists) was only about one-third of the number of A-TKEs (305) between 1970 and 1990. In retrospect, the negative impact of both stagflation and the push into heavy industry on the Korean economy was highly overdrawn, and the need for Southern Cone–style liberalization greatly exaggerated. On the other hand, the trend in the number of Koreans receiving American Ph.D.'s in economics continued sharply upward. The demand for such Ph.D.'s increased as the "old boy" network of A-TKEs widened, and promotions in government and research grants in academe came increasingly to depend on an Anglo-Saxon point of view.

In the case of the 1980–82 stagflation, the price surge the A-TKEs blamed on reckless expansionary public spending was cured almost overnight for reasons that had nothing to do with budget deficits. Prices began to fall in 1982 for exogenous reasons: a fall in imported oil prices (from an average annual growth rate of 38 percent in 1980–81 to 1.3 percent in 1982), better harvests (which witnessed a precipitous

TABLE 4.1
American-trained Korean and Japanese economists

Year	A-TKEs	A-TJEs	Year	A-TKEs	A-TJEs
1970	10	6	1981	26	14
1971	18	16	1982	30	15
1972	25	9	1983	31	14
1973	22	10	1984	22	9
1974	22	15	1985	33	12
1975	20	17	1986	66	21
1976	13	11	1987	70	13
1977	29	19	1988	70	12
1978	19	17	1989	88	11
1999	26	'21	1990	131	30
1980	30	13	Total	801	305

Source: Calculated from *Dissertation Abstracts International*, Ann Arbor, Mich., University Microfilms International.

Note: Number of persons who have received Ph.D.'s in economics from the United States. Numbers are estimates. The year listed indicates the date of publication, and not necessarily the year the Ph.D. degree was granted. The Japanese population in 1990 was approximately three times as great as the South Korean population. Some A-TKEs and A-TJEs stay in the United States after receiving their Ph.D.s, a phenomenon that is probably proportionately greater for the A-TJEs because the demand for their services in Japan appears to be relatively small.

decline in prices of foodstuffs), a steep decrease in real wage growth, and the return of political stability after the assassination of President Park. These probably made redundant the sharp contractions in monetary and fiscal policies the government introduced in response to A-TKE advice (Amsden 1987).

As for the big push into heavy industry, instead of being the catastrophe the A-TKEs portrayed, it turned out to be South Korea's economic salvation. Exports of heavy industry products were the major factor responsible for the resuscitation of growth after contractionary macroeconomic policies prolonged recession in the early 1980s. They continued to buoy employment and economic activity generally in the late 1980s, accounting for over half of all manufactured exports (EPB 1990). Nor was the big push into heavy industry responsible for what the A-TKEs feared would lead to massive financial collapse—namely, the banking system's burgeoning nonperforming loans (NPLs). Time series data on NPLs are hard to collect, but the evidence for one time point, in 1988, suggests that the banking system's burden of NPLs had little to do with underwriting the government's supposed

TABLE 4.2 Nonperforming loans (NPLs) by industry and type, as of July 1988 (Unit: 100 million won)

Industry	Type of loan				Total Share of NPLs[a]	Share of loans[b]
	Writeoff	Interest-exempt	Interest-deferred	Interest-adjusted		
Wood and wood products		1,111 (4.6%)	585 (5.3%)	200 (3.6%)	1,896 (3.7%)	(1.5%)
Textiles and wearing apparel		815 (3.4%)		876 (15.6%)	1,691 (3.3%)	(10.2%)
Chemicals and rubber	110.5 (1.1%)		910 (8.3%)	85 (1.5%)	1,105.5 (2.2%)	(7.6%)
Fabricated metal products	230.6 (2.3%)	320.5 (1.3%)		1,938 (34.5%)	2,489.1 (4.9%)	(16.9%)
General construction	3,495 (35.4%)	14,814 (61.1%)	9,526 (86.4%)	2,213 (39.4%)	30,048 (59.2%)	(19.0%)
Wholesale and retail trade	1,820 (18.5%)	2,338 (9.7%)		300 (5.3%)	4,458 (8.8%)	(8.3%)
Transport and storage	4,207 (42.7%)	3,731 (15.4%)			7,938 (15.6%)	(3.6%)
Recreational, cultural, service		1,097 (4.5%)			1,097 (2.2%)	(1.0%)
Total	9,863.1	24,226.5	11,021	5,612	50,722.6	—

Source: Amsden and Euh (1990).
[a]May add to less than 100 due to rounding.
[b]Share of outstanding loans and discounts of banks by industry as of December 1988.

overinvestments in heavy industry. As Table 4.2 indicates, heavy industry accounted for a smaller share of NPLs than its share of total loans outstanding. For example, fabricated metal products accounted for 16.9 percent of outstanding loans but only 4.9 percent of nonperforming loans. The two industries associated with the greatest absolute amount of NPLs, construction and inland shipping, were largely the responsibility of entrepreneurial "animal spirits" rather than the government.

Moreover, the disaster scenario about heavy industry drummed up by the A-TKEs and the World Bank (1987) was largely ideologically motivated.[1] There was evidence at the time, and not just retrospectively, that the government's investments in heavy industry, while hardly free from errors of judgment or excesses in several subsectors, were foresightful and productive overall (Auty 1991). Yet both the A-TKEs and the World Bank were blind to the positive side of the picture. For instance, despite the fact that the drive into heavy industry raised South Korea's foreign debt burden, the ratio of foreign debt to GNP was the same in 1973, when the heavy industry drive began, as it was in 1979, when for all practical purposes it ended (Amsden 1989). Evidently the performance standards the government had imposed on the big investors in heavy industry helped to push out production and exports.

Additional evidence from the 1980s argued further against the A-TKEs' advice that the problems associated with business-government relations be resolved by adopting the Anglo-Saxon model. The A-TKEs became fond of saying that the power of big business could be reduced by increasing imports (discussed shortly) and by allowing only market forces, with no government targeting, to decide which industries were to receive major investment loans. The A-TKEs believed that, with the end of government regulations forcing financial institutions to lend to targeted firms and industries, independent, efficient enterprises would flourish. Thereby, the power of the privileged big business groups would decline.

In fact, much of the liberalization that actually did occur in the 1980s worsened rather than improved South Korea's concentration of capital. Instead of weakening South Korea's big business groups, liberalization strengthened them. The allocation of resources to small and medium-size enterprises may have become more equal in the 1980s (see Cho and Cole 1986), but this was not due to the freer play of market forces. It was due to new government directives to make deregulated capital markets work better, markets which in the free market paradigm supposedly work best when left alone.

It is well known that in the 1970s the Korean government had discriminated against small and medium-size enterprises—in the grand tradition of virtually every major country that began to industrialize after 1880 (Chandler 1990). The rise of big business in South Korea was not out of the ordinary (whereas in Taiwan its retardation reflected government attempts to block individual businesses' expansion; Amsden 1991a). To reverse discrimination against the smaller firms in the

1980s, the Korean government did not and *could not* rely on market forces, because the newly created nonbank financial institutions and the privatized commercial banks, once given more discretion to choose their own clients, did not choose to lend extensively to them. In parallel fashion, foreign banks operating in South Korea, which were always free to lend to whomever they wished, did not lend extensively to them either. Like the government-controlled commercial banks, they preferred to lend to big businesses (Amsden and Euh 1993). Therefore, the government set a quota for all financial institutions which required them to set aside 30 percent of their loans for small and medium-size enterprises.

It was, of course, the A-TKEs who championed the liberalization of South Korea's domestic financial markets, only to wake up to the U.S. government's insistence on faster liberalization than the A-TKEs ever imagined. Ironically, the big business groups were probably the major beneficiary of whatever liberalization occurred, insofar as they became the predominant shareholders of both the privatized commercial banks and the new nonbank financial institutions. As a World Bank study acknowledged in a brief footnote (1987:82), "There are, perhaps surprisingly, some similarities between Korea's and Chile's reforms. In both cases, big conglomerates bought major interests in the national banks."

Not only did South Korea's big business groups increase their control over financial markets as a result of financial liberalization, they also appear to have extended their grip over markets for manufactured goods. With private ownership of financial institutions, the *jaebul* could buy up smaller companies, thereby making the distribution of capital *less* rather than more equal. Whereas the *jaebul* in the 1970s had grown organically, largely by rearing their own affiliates, in the 1980s they grew by acquisition, primarily by buying up other companies (Seok-Ki Kim 1987).

Obviously, in the presence of large agglomerations of economic power such as the *jaebul* (or *los grupos* in the Latin American Southern Cone), freer markets do not act as an equalizer. Given the rising trend toward inequality in income and wealth Simon Kuznets observed to be characteristic of almost every industrializing country, freer markets in South Korea after two decades of industrial growth made aggregate economic concentration worse.

That the A-TKEs could not anticipate this result possibly stemmed from flaws in the "technology" transferred to them in the average American economics Ph.D. program. Ph.D.'s in every field are one of the United States' most distinguished exports. Nevertheless, in the case of economics, Ph.D. programs even at the best universities tend to focus on mathematical manipulation of free market theory. As eminent economic historian A. W. Coats has observed, "American economics is in the grip of a narrow, technocratic species of professionalism" (Coats 1992). Often theory is not subjected to rich empirical analysis. Most American economics Ph.D. programs do not even include a core course in economic history. Moreover, as James Fallows observes, "Very few examples from Japanese (or Korean) industrialization can be found in American textbooks, since they don't fit the theories that the books contain" (1991:7). In the 1980s in particular, which is when the bulge in the number of A-TKEs occurred, the American economics profession became dominated by the conservative, antigovernment Chicago school, with an abiding faith in, rather than scientific demonstration of, the superiority of market outcomes over all types of government controls. Little wonder, then, that the A-TKEs were unable to anticipate how *institutions*, not even their own, could twist and turn the expected outcome of their textbook-inspired policies.

A Temporary Loss of the Art of Learning

I have tried to suggest that South Korea has demonstrated an inappropriate drift toward the Anglo-Saxon model of political economy. But I have also tried to suggest that South Korea has hardly definitively left the German-Japanese late-industrializing fold. A case in point is the financial liberalization of the 1980s mentioned above. Although South Korea officially liberalized its financial institutions, as masterminded by the A-TKEs and increasingly the American government, it never really said "good-bye to financial repression" (in the words of the late economist Carlos Diaz-Alejandro, 1985). The commercial banks in South Korea have been privatized, and the *jaebul* have gained access to independent sources of finance, but the Ministry of Finance's power over all financial institutions remains formidable. Moreover, Korean companies—even the largest ones—remain highly dependent on bank loans for their working capital and investment funding (Amsden and Euh 1990). Consequently, the government can put any manufacturing firm out of business in a matter of weeks by shutting off the faucet of working capital, or in a matter of months by impeding the rollover of short-term loans, which is a major source of long-term finance. There is no longer a three-tier interest rate structure, but preferential loans are still given to targeted firms in special industries. The new institutions the government has created to reduce the costs of capital—the Korean stock market, for example—were cultivated by extensive government intervention. The government even imposed a ceiling on the internal debt-equity ratio of businesses, which it then tried to monitor by preventing cross-investments within business groups. This halfway quality of liberalization partly reflects the ambivalence of the big business groups: they want more control over finance but also a continuation of government support (Amsden and Euh 1993).

Nevertheless, I would argue that the drift toward the Anglo-Saxon model has already taken some toll on the South Korean economy. It has raised false hopes that big business can be reformed by the market mechanism. It has prevented the government from proactively implementing an industrial policy, where an industrial policy may be taken simply to comprise two critical elements: a long-run competitive strategy, and a mechanism to increase the competitiveness of industry in the short run, which may or may not involve increasing the degree of competition firms face (see Chang 1991). The weak, half-hearted implementation of industrial policy has tipped the balance too far toward short-run profit maximization rather than long-run learning on the part of the private sector. The costs of passivity have increased due to the reliance on freer markets to achieve short-run ends.

A substantiation of the last point brings us back briefly to our discussion of the A-TKEs' conviction that big business can be made both less powerful and more efficient if it is subjected to greater competition from overseas. Nevertheless, import liberalization in the 1980s and early 1990s has generally not had the intended effect. As Kwang Suk Kim, a specialist on trade policy, has observed (see Chapter 17), there is no clear indication that import liberalization had any significant effect on industrial productivity. There are many potential reasons for this finding, which is ironic given the emphasis the A-TKEs have placed on import liberalization. Korea has always imported a lot of producer goods, as measured by its import/GDP coefficient and composition of imports (Amsden 1993). A large share of Korean imports have also been under the control of the *jaebul,* which tend to import only those products that do not compete with their own. Perhaps most probable, inefficiencies in the manufacturing sector were not nearly as pernicious as the A-TKEs portrayed.[2]

As for the drawbacks associated with not implementing a vigorous, unabashed industrial policy with a long-term competitive strategy, a possible cost so far has been *lost time,* in terms of catching up with the world technological frontier. The prosperity of the 1980s buoyed by earlier investments in heavy industry reflected the long time horizon of South Korea's economic planners. Whatever the military's motives for favoring the heavy industry drive, most other government bureaucrats recognized the need to move beyond light industry in anticipation of rising real wages in the future. This view was formulated as early as 1971, at a time when it was hard to imagine South Korea even approaching full employment (except under highly inflationary conditions). The foresight of planners was evident from a plan formulated in 1976, for example, to move the electronics sector beyond the stage of assembly operations. At the time, South Korea's per capita income was only about equal to that of Guatemala.

Unlike the 1970s, however, the drift toward the Anglo-Saxon model in the 1980s witnessed a much less active role by the government. It refrained from prodding the economy beyond borrowing basic technology to the next stage of learning: generating major product improvements in fast-growing "mature" industries (e.g., automobiles, consumer electronics, fine chemicals). Moreover, for all the talk in South Korea in the 1980s about shifting from a government-led to a business-led growth strategy, it is questionable whether the private sector provided a sufficiently energetic alternative source of leadership.

An examination of many Japanese and German firms suggests what it takes to move beyond the stage of mere manufacturing excellence. Even as many Japanese and German companies evolved to a higher stage of adding value to their products and began to invest heavily in major product and process innovations, they never ceased to regard the competitive process as one of learning. I mention Germany's emphasis on education later. As for Japan, one management guru, Peter Drucker (1991:10), makes this point very well with respect to Japanese R&D: "Every major Japanese industrial group now has its own research institute, whose main function is to bring to the group an awareness of any important new knowledge—in technology, in management and organization, in marketing, in finance, in training—developed worldwide." Thus, R&D in Japan means not just in-house technology development but also learning what others are doing with respect to both the software and hardware of new technology. Concerning what learning means in the case of product development, which became of immediate interest to South Korea by 1990, Drucker goes on to observe three tracks operating in Japanese firms, only one of which involves "pioneering": "One track (*kaizen*) is organized work on improvement of the product with specific goals and deadlines. . . . The second track is "leaping"—developing a new product out of the old. . . . And finally there is genuine innovation" (1991:10).

Industrial leaders in the private sector in South Korea certainly gave the *appearance*, even in the 1980s, of long-term profit maximization (ignoring their forays into real estate speculation). They invested heavily in R&D. Expenditures on R&D as a percentage of sales rose in South Korea from 0.58 in 1980 to 1.78 in 1987. By 1990 they were estimated to have reached 2.2 percent of GNP. The share of the private sector in R&D funding shifted from a minority to an overwhelming majority position, from 48.4 percent in 1980 to as much as 79.6 percent in 1987 (MOST, various years). Nevertheless, it is unclear what R&D activity in South Korea entails. To learn more about it, it is useful to examine one of the country's premier firms, the Samsung Electronics Company.

The Case of Samsung Electronics Company

Samsung Electronics Company (SEC) demonstrated leadership qualities in the startup of South Korea's semiconductor industry. Certainly it was in the vanguard of expenditures on R&D. Along with most other major Korean business groups, the Samsung *jaebul* established an R&D center in 1980, in clockwork response to a sharp increase in government incentives. By 1990, while the average share of R&D expenditures in sales for all of South Korean industry was about 2.2 percent, in SEC it was about 7 percent. SEC was also a leader in the training of its workforce. For instance, over the course of the 1980s it had established an internal engineering graduate school.

Nevertheless, SEC managers observed that their company really got into R&D only in 1988 and started focusing attention on consumer electronics a year after that. This was notwithstanding the fact that consumer electronics was the mainstay of SEC's business; if it started to fail, it would have jeopardized the jobs of a large number of employees (SEC's total employment in 1990 was 45,170). In 1990 consumer electronics still accounted for $3.44 billion of a total of $6.09 billion in SEC's sales, versus only $1.3 billion for semiconductors.

The delay in undertaking serious R&D, despite a heavy burden of royalty payments to foreign firms, was related to the steep investments necessary to generate major product improvements in consumer electronics. SEC, moreover, was not accustomed to competing on the basis of its product offerings. Like virtually every other Korean company, it was production-oriented. This orientation arose because SEC had grown by borrowing technology to manufacture mature products (see Amsden 1989, for the cases of steel, shipbuilding, and automobiles). The emphasis on process rather than product improvement was reinforced by a history in SEC of being able to sell just about any consumer electronics product it could make, either at home or abroad. SEC's attention, therefore, was focused on relieving production bottlenecks rather than on improving existing product lines or developing marketing skills.

Throughout most of the 1980s, then, SEC's R&D was primarily production-related. R&D was oriented toward making borrowed process technology work better, just as it had been in Japan at a comparable stage of industrial development (Ozawa 1974). Investments in SEC's R&D center throughout most of the 1980s probably helped raise sales and productivity, but SEC's owners can be faulted for having dragged their heels with respect to thinking in the long term and investing heavily in the development and marketing of new products.

It was only in the late 1980s that Samsung began to take major product improvement seriously. This was evident from its investments to learn what firms from technologically advanced countries were doing, the type of learning Japan had demonstrated as essential to reach and remain at the world technological frontier. In September 1989, SEC opened the Advanced Media Laboratory in New Jersey, close to the old Bell Laboratories and the RCA Corporation, with the purpose of undertaking research in VCRs, color televisions, and high-density televisions (its R&D branch in Tokyo, opened in May 1987, was largely responsible for the commercial end of R&D activity). A year later it opened an R&D branch in Osaka (the home of Matsushita) to undertake R&D in other consumer electronics (see Table 4.3).

A huge trade surplus, which South Korea began to accumulate in 1987–89, helped finance such overseas ventures, and the government's macroeconomic policy of raising domestic demand to encourage sales at home rather than in foreign markets gave Korean companies a breathing spell to invest long term. With greater dependence on the domestic market, moreover, the government's threats to liberalize South Korea's imports of consumer electronics (following pressure from Washington) became somewhat more credible.[3] Perhaps most important, the sluggish growth by 1990 in SEC's "cash cow" consumer electronics exports (e.g., televisions and microwave ovens) and the threat of competition from Japanese companies exporting from low-wage Southeast Asian countries added urgency to the whole transformation process.

South Korean industry's feet-dragging, whether in consumer electronics or automobiles, cannot explain the sharp contraction in export growth in 1989–90; that

Table 4.3
Chronology of R&D activities in Samsung Electronics Company

April 1980	Founded R&D Center
December 1984	Established CAD/CAM Center
May 1987	Opened Tokyo R&D branch in Japan (primarily to handle the commercial end of R&D activity)
October 1987	Established Samsung Advanced Institute of Technology (located near semiconductor production; for basic research in semiconductors)
September 1989	Opened Advanced Media Laboratory in New Jersey (for research in color TVs, high-density TVs, and VCRs)
September 1990	Opened Osaka R&D branch in Japan (located near Matsushita Corporation; for research in other consumer electronics)

Source: Samsung Electronics Company.

was due primarily to recession in the American market, appreciation of the won, and the fact that Korean exports were probably above trend in 1987–89 owing to an appreciated Japanese yen. Nevertheless, such a delay is significant to the extent that it threatened to retard the recovery of South Korea's export growth and ability to defend the home market. Therefore, it raises the issue of whether it is too costly socially to leave major investment decisions—such as those concerning a new stage of learning and catching up—exclusively to the private sector. Is this what people in Korea mean by "business-led growth"?

The Risks Inherent in Business-Led Growth

That the delays caused by big businesses' short-term profit-maximizing behavior in the 1980s did not, and probably will not, entail high social costs (in terms of unemployment and lost market shares) is partly due to the presence of an industrial policy. However apologetic the Korean government has been about having an industrial policy, and however much its rhetoric has hidden its existence, an industrial policy has operated nonetheless. Hence, one can only talk about a *drift* toward the Anglo-Saxon model, rather than a *shift* toward it.

For example, to develop high-tech industry in South Korea the government and business are cooperating in numerous R&D projects. In a representative case, three major enterprises and the central government are cooperating in a program to develop a 16 M DRAM memory, involving an outlay of $260 million, almost half of which will be financed by the government with concessional credit. In its Five-Year Plan (1987–91), the Ministry of Trade and Industry (MTI) also earmarked additional funding for R&D in priority sectors. Further support to high tech also comes indirectly, through infrastructure projects such as those involving telecommunications and transportation, most recently the transfer of foreign technology related to South Korea's investment in a high-speed railway system. South Korea's aerospace industry is booming in conjunction with military expenditures. To aid declining industries, the MTI and the Federation of the Textiles Industry have developed a long-term plan to expand domestic sales, improve product quality, and increase automation and personnel training. To prevent overproduction in the ("deregulated") petrochemicals sector, the government has imposed an export quota of 50 percent on two new market entrants. All these interventions operate alongside those related to financial markets and protection from foreign trade—for example, an outright ban on imports of Japanese goods made in low-wage Southeast Asian countries, and an "import diversification" scheme to please the American government and simultaneously protect South Korean industry from stiff competitors operating in Japan (for a perceptive summary of government intervention in electronics, see Clifford 1991).

It is noteworthy, however, that government encouragement of high tech appears lower-keyed in South Korea than in, say, Taiwan (e.g., the brief survey in OECD 1990). In part, this is due to the fact that by 1990 Taiwan had fallen behind South Korea in R&D, at least in terms of reported expenditure as a share of GNP. In 1987, South Korea was allegedly spending 1.78 percent of GNP on R&D, compared with only 1.16 percent in Taiwan. In part, however, the government has simply chosen to take a more openly interventionist approach to build high-tech capabilities in Taiwan (and Singapore) than that taken in South Korea. For example, all local enterprises in Taiwan are required by law to set aside between 0.25 and 1 percent of their sales (depending on their size) for R&D or to supply equivalent resources to government research centers.

Such measures would probably strike those South Koreans who have absorbed the *political* ideals of the Anglo-Saxon model as flagrant violations of liberty. One hears arguments to the effect that any indirect government measure not related to income taxes which forces business to do something against its will violates the sacred canons of liberal democracy. Yet this is a very Anglo-Saxon view of democracy, not a universal one. It could just as well be argued that to leave investment decisions that have the potential to make a major impact on the welfare of society in private hands is itself inherently undemocratic. Business-led industrial development is desirable when business is motivated to invest long term and acts in the interests of society, but not when it is short-term oriented.

To appreciate the downside of leaving an economy's fate to its business sector, take a hypothetical case concerning Samsung, which by the early 1990s was earning a very low profit rate, far below what it could have earned by investing in, say, U.S. Treasury bills. Moreover, SEC was sitting on land with high resale value. According to short-term profit-maximizing principles, SEC should have sold its land and laid off its 45,170 employees. It could then have taken its profits and invested them in still more profitable ventures, possibly employing even more workers at higher wages. On the other hand, there is a large risk of a much less desirable denouement: SEC's assets could have been bought by a foreign multinational, with a conflicting interest in global profit maximization and

Korean industrialization. Or SEC's land could have been used to build luxury housing, unemployment could have risen, and SEC's workforce could have ultimately found reemployment in agriculture or less skill-intensive jobs at lower average wages.

The point is that, if the market mechanism is allowed to work freely, its positive effects may possibly be great, but only after a costly and lengthy process of adjustment. This clearly is not what most Koreans have in mind when they talk of business-led industrial growth or a closer embrace of freer markets. But this clearly *is* a distinct possibility in the Anglo-Saxon model. How, then, should South Korea proceed, as its industrial structure and political economy grow more complex?

The Issues Summed Up

As I see the issues of the 1990s, reform is urgently required, but South Korea's problems cannot be solved by the adoption of the Anglo-Saxon model. Drifting toward that model has either failed to improve matters, such as the ineffectiveness of trade liberalization to stimulate greater efficiency, or has worsened them, such as lost time to reform big business and launch a new competitive strategy now that wages are almost as high as they are in regions of the Anglo-Saxon world—the north of England and the southern United States. That conditions in South Korea have not deteriorated further as a consequence of a drift toward the Ango-Saxon model I attribute to the fact that fundamentally South Korea's political economy remains within the Japanese-German late-industrializing tradition—and it should continue to remain within it.

The early 1990s, however, witnessed an impasse between business and government. Because of the unpopularity of the *jaebul*, it was hard for the government to support them, although support and general coaxing are still necessary to help South Korea reach the second stage of learning, associated with major product improvement, and move beyond to investments in basic research. On the other hand, because the market cannot be relied upon to discipline business in projects with long gestation periods, the government must continue to act as disciplinarian. Certainly the support and discipline of business by government were, and must remain, key components of South Korea's rapid growth. Yet, because business has grown so powerful, and because the politicians cradled by democracy are so eager to receive the financial patronage of the *jaebul*, the ability of government to discipline business has weakened (see, e.g., Kim 1988).

Because of these complexities, which are symptomatic of rising industrial sophistication, one hears again and again in South Korea an argument to the effect that the government can no longer intervene as it did in the past because the political economy has grown too complex. I turn, therefore, to an examination of the Anglo-Saxon, German, and Japanese models to see what they can teach about managing complexity.

The Anglo-Saxon, German, and Japanese Models

The Anglo-Saxon Model and Free Market Theory

To borrow intelligently from another country, it is necessary to appreciate the gap that exists between how its institutions supposedly work and how they actually work. The United States (and the United Kingdom) embrace a more extreme version of free market ideology than other industrialized countries. But there is still a sizable gap between actual British and American industrial history and the postulates of standard price theory. Any country wishing to emulate the Anglo-Saxon model should be aware of it.[4]

For example, although the United States became a staunch supporter of free trade after World War II, when it enjoyed global industrial hegemony, it was one of the most heavily protected economies during a long stretch of its industrialization (see the international comparisons of tariff levels in the early 1900s in Little, Scitovsky, and Scott 1970). Its import controls in the 1990s—say, on textiles, automobiles, and steel—were also significant.

Moreover, the United States heavily protected its home industry despite having enjoyed two competitive assets which Japan and South Korea have lacked and whose importance to industrial development generally are either assumed away or trivialized in standard market theory: economies of scale and pioneering technology. Standard price theory assumes constant returns to scale; increasing returns or economies of scale are not part of the orthodox doctrine. Yet no one would seriously dispute the advantage huge domestic markets bestowed to American industry (and, to a lesser extent, Japanese industry). New technology, moreover, is assumed in price theory to fall like manna from heaven: it is equally accessible to firms in all countries. In reality, pioneering technology is highly proprietary and has constituted a far more formidable competitive asset for the United States than low wages have for Japan and South Korea—low wages typically being the *only* competitive asset of many late-industrializing countries.

Finally, American industry enjoyed the price advantage of an abundance of raw materials: Wright (1990) argues that raw materials were the basis for American industrialization in the nineteenth century. The fact that rich raw materials were located in Western states, of which the U.S. government owned large tracts of land, enabled Washington to use its control over natural resources to help develop raw-material-processing industries throughout the country (Limerick 1987).

With all its advantages, it is little wonder American industry had less need for government intervention than Japanese or Korean industry. But not even American economic history provides strong empirical support for laissez-faire. The father of *institutional* theories of late industrialization, Alexander Gerschenkron, conceives of catching up as a process of "revolutionary," "eruptive" spurts, with the most backward countries promoting "those branches of industrial activities in which recent technological progress has been particularly rapid" (1962:9–10). Certainly in the nineteenth century, when British industry could not establish international entry barriers to protect its markets, leading American and German enterprises could and did follow a Gerschenkron-like competitive strategy: they leapfrogged ahead of England in the most dynamic sectors.

Nevertheless, the basic rules of international competition changed in the twentieth century, as global enterprises arose in the most dynamic sectors with "organizational capabilities" based on a core technology (Chandler 1990). The institutionalization of R&D in such enterprises allowed them to erect entry barriers around their proprietary technology family. Because of this historical condition, Gerschenkron's idea of leaping to the world technological frontier could no longer work. The only major country to attempt this strategy in the twentieth century was Russia, and despite partial and purely technical success it has failed to become a stable, industrialized economy (Amsden and Hikino 1992).

Thus, not only does early American economic history not conform with free market theory, the industrialization path it did follow cannot be replicated by late industrializers. (To the extent that Germany overcame its backwardness by leapfrogging to the world technological frontier, its model cannot be copied either.)

American industrialization went hand in hand with the rise of big business. The size and economic power of the American multidivisional firm were unprecedented in world history (Chandler 1990). How, then, did a young country like the United States handle the volatile social and economic problems unleashed by big business? Part of the answer lies in antitrust policy and regulation, as discussed shortly. Another part lies in the fact that the United States likely did *not* handle the problem in a way that would satisfy South Korea. The rise of big business in the United States was associated with great income inequality—inequality that remains far higher than has been observed in postwar South Korea, Japan, or Taiwan.

Big Business and Income Inequality Income distribution in the United States supposedly stayed more or less the same in the nineteenth century, then became more equal between the 1920s and 1950s, and then grew less equal again, although the accuracy of data on income distribution, and a fortiori on wealth, is problematic in all countries, the United States included. In 1929 the average income of the richest fifth, or quintile, of the American population was estimated to be 15.5 times that of the poorest fifth. By 1951 this ratio had dropped to 9.0. By 1980 it had risen to 10.7, and it reached 13.0 in 1989 in tandem with deregulation, liberalization, and their associated rise in poverty (see Table 4.4).

It is difficult enough to measure income distribution within a country, let alone to make meaningful intercountry comparisons. Such cross-sectional comparisons are tricky because of the tendency, observed by Simon Kuznets, for income distribution to change in the course of economic development. At any point in time, therefore, international differences in income distribution may reflect differences in

Table 4.4
Income distribution

Country	Year	Ratio[a]	Country	Year	Ratio[a]
South Korea[b]	1981	4.9	Denmark	1981	9.3
Japan	1979	4.3	France	1975	12.5
Taiwan[c]	—	4.3	Netherlands	1981	5.5
Singapore	1977–78	7.5	New Zealand	1981–82	8.8
Hong Kong	1981	12.1	Norway	1982	8.0
United States[d]	1929	15.5	Sweden	1981	7.3
	1951	9.0	Switzerland	1978	6.9
	1980	10.7	United Kingdom	1982	7.1
	1989	13.0	Brazil	1982	27.7
West Germany	1978	6.6	India	1975–76	10.1
Australia	1978–79	6.0	Philippines	1971	16.1
Canada	1981	9.0	Thailand	1975–76	11.2

Source: All countries except Taiwan and U.S., 1929, 1951, 1989: national survey data reported in United Nations Statistical Office (1985).

[a] Ratio by which the income of the top fifth of the population exceeds that of the bottom fifth.

[b] Urban only. Data for other countries are national, except those for Switzerland, which cover only three cantons.

[c] Statistic reported in Li (1988).

[d] 1929 and 1951: Williamson and Lindert (1984); 1989: *New York Times* (1992), based on data from the Bureau of the Census.

stages of development rather than intrinsic differences in distributional patterns. Moreover, income distribution is not necessarily a good indicator of wealth distribution. If income is properly measured, it should include returns to wealth. Often, however, returns to wealth are understated. The distribution ratio in South Korea may be more than suggested by Table 4.4 because in 1981 Koreans were still permitted to hold bank accounts under assumed names, one of the most contentious issues of the early 1990s.[5] Nevertheless, there are numerous tax loopholes in the United States as well which allow large accumulations of wealth to go undetected.

Whatever the mismeasurements, a special study by the United Nations in 1985 summarizes income distribution data that permit cross-sectional international comparisons (Table 4.4). The findings are intuitively plausible. They suggest that income distribution circa 1980 was considerably more equal in Japan, South Korea, and Taiwan than in the United States. This is plausible in light of the land reform that occurred after the war in all three Asian countries and the nationalization of the banking systems in two of them, Korea and Taiwan. Independent data for Japan, South Korea, and the United States related to the wage gap between managers and workers also suggest that the United States has a relatively unequal income distribution (Lee 1983). Even by comparison with Germany and some other European social democracies, income distribution circa 1980 was relatively unequal in the United States.

There is also evidence, although not of a quantitative sort, that postwar Japan, Korea, and Taiwan have had a relatively low tolerance for inequality. Although Anglo-Saxon ideology lauds equality, it also tolerates high doses of inequality that supposedly spring from differences in individual capabilities. On the other hand, while East Asian culture is considered authoritarian, with a huge appetite for hierarchy, one anthropologist has also observed a strong strain of egalitarianism, at least in South Korea (Brandt 1986). Therefore, in considering the merits of shifting toward the Anglo-Saxon model, a country with a strong egalitarian bent like South Korea should be aware that, in the past and at present, income distribution in the United States has been fairly unequal, American democracy and social mobility notwithstanding.

Big Business and Regulation The social unrest big business inspired in the United States at the turn of the century gave rise to progressive, muckraking social movements. These, in turn, were the catalyst for the gradual adoption of a wide range of laws to regulate the behavior of business. Generally, I would argue that regulation offers many positive elements for South Korea to adapt in order to restrict what may be called "private rent seeking," or speculative, antisocial behavior on the private sectors' part. The 1980s were, of course, a decade of "deregulation" in the United States, and many anachronistic restrictions on business activity were abolished. Nevertheless, deregulation did not go nearly as far as conservatives maintain, and the disastrous effects of too radical deregulation in some industries—for example, airlines and banking—merely reinforced the desirability of sensible regulation. The financial scandals that rocked Japan in 1990–91 attest to both the Japanese people's intolerance of special favors to big business and the need for regulation within the Japanese-German late-industrializing model.

Later in this chapter I discuss some of the specific types of regulation South Korea might consider adapting to reform big business. Suffice it to say here that regulation is probably a necessary but insufficient condition to create a dynamic, industrial sector. This is so because the Anglo-Saxon model of regulation is designed to restrict business malfeasance rather than to enhance global industrial competitiveness; it has not been developmental.

As observed by Harvard Business School professor Richard Vietor, "Government regulation in the United States has generally not been an affirmative public act" (1991:1). Rather, it emerged in spite of intense opposition to any form of government intervention in the economy. Vietor attributes the reluctance to regulate abusive business practices to the citizenry's suspicion of central government authority. I would argue that, in addition, regulation has not been an affirmative act in the United States because of the enormous power big business wields to oppose such controls, a power that the inequality of income distribution suggests.

Whatever the reason, regulation in the United States has had to operate defensively. Therefore, it has not been couched in an industrial policy. Whereas public utilities in Japan are managed by the government to increase technological capabilities, with few exceptions they are managed in the United States to serve the interests of consumers. Regulation has also had to function in the United States without any connection with measures to *support* business. Measures to support business operate largely in the context of the military-industrial complex and U.S. foreign policy, as discussed shortly. These support measures, however, have no regulatory element associated with them. Consequently, the support of business in the United States and the discipline of business are unconnected. As such, neither policy is capable of prodding the industrial sector to invest in the long term. Thus, regulation is a second best to industrial policy, which needs to include some regulatory elements but not exclusively.

Despite the rhetoric, the facts do not suggest that even during the period of deregulation in the 1980s the American government withdrew from the regulatory arena because the complexities thrown up by new technology and global competition were too great for it to handle—a line of argument conservative American economists, and the students they influence, often advance. The method of government intervention may have been designed better in the 1980s than in the 1930s, but it in no way reflected a closer approximation to laissez-faire. Vietor observes: "Besides cutting red tape and eliminating a few health and safety regulations that especially offended business, the Reagan administration had no overall plan for how to change regulation or what to replace it with. In fact, the Administration succeeded with only two deregulatory initiaties—the disastrous Garn St.-Germain Banking Act [which opened the door to a huge savings and loan crisis] and the Cable Television Act of 1984." Vietor goes on to observe that most important regulatory reforms were enacted between 1977 and 1981, during the Democratic Carter era, and continued to rely on government controls: "In telecommunications, for example, . . . [the new] system still entailed very complex regulatory determination. . . . In natural gas, [the new] system sought to emulate a competitive, nonintegrated market, but it was not exactly "deregulation." . . . regulation during the twentieth century has provided the United States with a politically acceptable means for preserving enterprise, *while still controlling it*" (Vietor 1991:53–56).

Nevertheless, antitrust legislation, which lies at the heart of the American regulatory system, has generally not done a good job handling the complexities of an advanced industrial structure. This is because antitrust legislation has accepted one of the analytical simplicities of standard price theory: that all industries (other than regulated public utilities) are intrinsically of equal importance to economic growth and therefore should all be treated alike. None allegedly deserves special treatment. This rule of thumb has lent an inflexibility to American government policy in the area of antitrust. Firms in the same industry have been prohibited from colluding even when their cost structures (e.g., with respect to R&D and sourcing of inputs) would make cooperation among them highly desirable to foster innovation. Such inflexibility has probably hurt the U.S. high-tech sectors. In parallel fashion, the relaxation of antitrust prosecutions beginning in the 1980s was equally undiscriminating. It allowed *all* mergers and acquisitions to occur, although the effects of many on long-term American competitiveness were probably negative (e.g., CBS's acquisition of Steinway, a high-quality piano manufacturer, or RCA's acquisition of Hertz Rent-A-Car; see Ravenscraft and Scherer 1987, for a general discussion of the American takeover phenomenon).

The German Model

I say the least about the German model because, in some major respects, I see it as a hybrid, or mixture, of the Anglo-Saxon and Japanese late-industrialization models. It has elements of the former because some German industries evolved on the basis of pioneering technology—for instance, heavy electrical equipment and chemicals. Government intervention to get the prices "wrong" therefore did not have to be as great as in Japan and other late industrializers, and firm structure has tended to be specialized around a single technology family (as in the case of, say, Siemens and Mercedes) rather than widely diversified into technologically unrelated industries (see Berghahn 1986, for a discussion of the Americanization of West German industry).

On the other hand, Germany experienced many of the same hardships of backwardness as Japan and other late-industrializing countries. Therefore, government intervention to stimulate industry has been greater than in the United States or Britain (see, e.g., Peacock 1980; Keck 1991). Firm structure has also been more cartelized, a process which, historically, the German government has encouraged (see, e.g., Braun 1990). There is also more cross-ownership of big companies in Germany than in the United States or Britain—or, for that matter, in Japan or South Korea (see Figure 4.1). Relations between financial capital and manufacturing capital have also been closer in Germany than in the Anglo-Saxon case (as John Zysman, an expert in this field, discusses in Chapter 5). The top supervisory boards of leading German companies include not only technical managers but also representatives from one of Germany's great banks. The management board, which is in charge of a company's actual operations, is entirely in the hands of technical people. This system allows industrialists to manage operations in the interests of efficiency, while a close integration of technical and financial expertise helps German companies to pursue long-term profit maximization.

Over the long run, the German and Anglo-Saxon financial systems converge: in both cases firms seek the lowest-cost finance. In the short term, however, companies in Germany tend not to shop around for the lowest-cost finance, as they tend to do in the Anglo-Saxon world. A long-term relationship is of more importance than a short-term bargain in interest rates. This tolerance for what is possibly short-run inefficiency, as well as a tighter integration between industry and finance generally in both Germany and Japan (and South Korea), violates the principles of

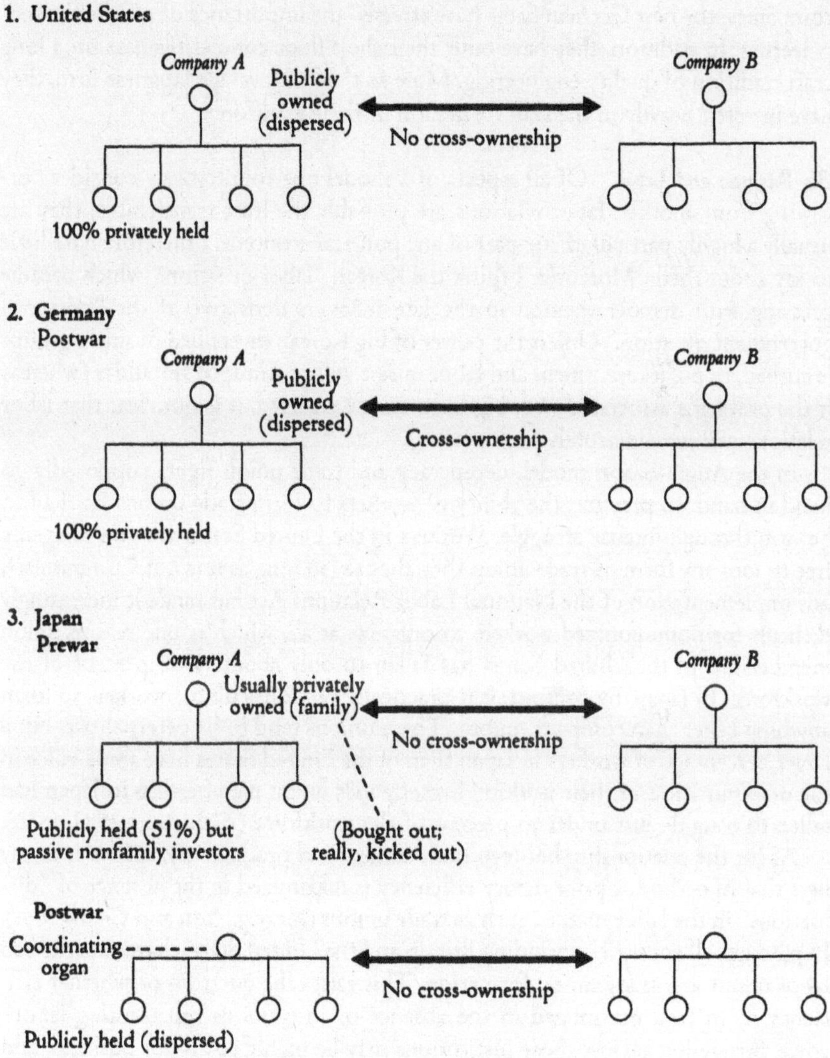

FIGURE 4.1 Organizational structure of large enterprises.

capital market theory in the Anglo-Saxon paradigm. But the German-Japanese financial system may be more favorable for long-run industrial development (for a historical perspective, see Sylla 1991).

In addition, due to the need to borrow technology in order to catch up, German companies have tended to pay more attention to the shop floor than the average American or British company. Like Japanese and other late-industrializing companies, the best German firms have stressed the importance of production engineering. In addition, they have built their shop floor competitiveness on a long craft tradition of quality engineering. More so than the average Japanese firm, they have invested heavily in the skill formation of their workforce.

Big Business and Labor Of all aspects of a model one country may consider borrowing from another, labor relations are probably the least transferable; they are usually a highly particularlistic part of any political economy. I therefore have little to say about them. Moreover, I think the Korean "labor question," which became pressing with democratization in the late 1980s, is derivative of the "business-government question." Unless the power of big Korean diversified business groups is curbed, popular resentment and labor unrest will continue to smoulder (whereas if the problems associated with big business are resolved, it is not clear that labor relations will remain acutely problematic).

In the Anglo-Saxon model, democracy and trade union rights supposedly go hand in hand. In practice, the ability of workers to form trade unions has had to be won through intense struggle. Workers in the United States are now allegedly free to join any form of trade union they choose (so long as it is not Communist), but implementation of the National Labor Relations Act has made it increasingly difficult for nonunionized workers to organize at all, which is one reason union membership in the United States has fallen to only about 17–18 percent of the workforce. In Japan, by contrast, it is practically very difficult for workers to form anything other than company unions. These unions tend to be paternalistic, but a larger percentage of workers in Japan than in the United States have some voice in the determination of their working lives; by 1985 union membership in Japan had fallen to roughly just under 30 percent of the workforce (Nakamura et al. 1988).

As for the relationship between trade unions and productivity, suffice it to say here that in orthodox price theory efficiency is maximized in the absence of "distortions" in the labor market, such as trade unions (see, e.g., You and Chang 1991). In practice, all countries, including Britain and the United States, have experienced labor unrest and trade union formation. This raises the question of whether efficiency is, in fact, maximized in the absence of institutions representing labor's voice. Struggling against those institutions may be highly costly for business, and the demoralizing effect on labor of not having a voice may reduce, not raise, productivity. Many unions in Japan are committed to more than improving the wages and working conditions of their members; in exchange for employment guarantees, and in the presence of highly segmented labor markets, they are also committed to increasing productivity. In this respect, certain labor market institutions may be a superior form of coaxing higher productivity from workers than a textbook, free labor market model (see Freeman and Medoff 1984, for a general argument to this effect).

The proportion of workers unionized in West Germany is high by Anglo-Saxon standards and has remained more or less constant (as it has in Scandinavia).

It jumped steeply after German unification. The proportion of workers unionized in United Germany in the early 1990s is roughly 40 percent. Unionization among industrial workers is as high as 90 percent. German workers (although not necessarily trade unions) also won the right after World War II to representation on the supervisory boards of their companies. What is most striking about German labor relations, however, is its interconnection with high levels of worker training. It is in the area of training where the German model especially excels.

Investments in technical capabilities have given Germany its competitive advantage in high-end engineering products. It is also arguable that these investments have provided German workers with a motive to continue being diligent and hardworking despite attaining high income levels. By the 1990s many Koreans seemed to have resigned themselves to the inevitability that, as income levels rose and Korean workers chose to consume more leisure, they would cease being diligent and hard-working. Nevertheless, while a preference for greater leisure is predictable under conditions of rising income, the German case suggests that workers need not necessarily work less diligently or hard on the job if they are properly challenged and provided with opportunities to improve their human capital.[6] The motivating factor of intellectual challenge, which is implicit in advancing toward the world technological frontier, may be the most important reason investments in learning raise productivity.

Authoritarian Politics Finally, the legacy of backwardness in German industrial history has manifested itself in authoritarian politics. Alas, an absence of democratic institutions is characteristic of most late-industrializing countries, South Korea included (see, e.g., Onis 1991). The peculiar frustrations associated with a mixture of backwardness and grandness in Germany and Japan, however, are probably partly responsible for the extreme militarism in both countries which erupted in fascism and war.

This fascist history should sober enthusiasm for borrowing from either the German or Japanese models. Certainly the rise of fascism should alert South Koreans and other late industrializers to the inherent danger of too close integration of the military, big business, and an authoritarian state (for a classic study on this integration in the industrialization process, see Moore 1966). Moreover, although South Korea managed to achieve political democratization in the late 1980s, its military-industrial complex may also be growing stronger. The postwar occupation period in Germany and Japan also offered an opportunity for the reform of big business, the likes of which South Korea has not experienced.

Germany's big businesses were discredited after World War II by their affiliation with the Nazis during the 1930s and 1940s. Japan's big businesses were not just discredited, they were "decapitated" during the postwar American military occupation (see Figure 4.1). The major *zaibatsu* family owners were forced out of power and their affiliated companies were made more independent (Hadley 1970). A similar decapitation and decentralization of management might be the ideal solution for South Korea's big business groups. Unfortunately, while American influence in South Korea may be as great in the 1990s as it was in postwar Japan, American policy is oriented toward opening Korea's markets rather than reforming its big business groups. Therefore, the reform of big business will probably prove harder to achieve in South Korea than in Germany or Japan.

Japan's Political Economy: A Subclassification of the Late-Industrializing Model

I do not think Japan's political economy represents a sui generis case, despite the insistence of many intellectuals on Japan's uniqueness. Because Japan had to industrialize by learning, or borrowing technology in "mature" industries from firms in highly industrialized countries (here, "mature" industries are those whose global demand may be growing but whose technology is for sale at competitive prices), Japan's political economy has much in common with that of other late industrializers. The absence of pioneering technology even on the part of leading Japanese enterprises necessitated more government intervention to support business than in the Anglo-Saxon case, a business structure involving wide diversification of groups into technologically unrelated industries (as exemplified by the *zaibatsu* and later *keiretsu*), and a business strategy of emphasizing incremental improvements in productivity and quality on the shop floor (Hikino and Amsden 1994).

To be sure, there are differences between Japan and other late industrializers, if for no other reason than that Japan's distance from the world technological frontier was less than that of other "backward" countries at the start of industrialization. The gap between developed and underdeveloped countries has widened over time such that Japan had more competitive assets with which to compete and, consequently, needed less government support of business than the typical late-industrializing case. Moreover, as noted earlier, countries attempting to industrialize after Japan have had the additional, nontrivial burden of having to compete against Japan itself, and of having to contend with competitors of Japan, like the United States, who have become frustrated with the late-industrializing model.

Even among the East Asian countries there are different variants of the late-industrializing model at work. A major method the Meiji government used to reduce the risks and costs facing private manufacturers was to build model factories. By contrast, South Korea and Taiwan have made little use of this method and instead have subsidized business more directly.

Despite these differences, there are enough similarities between Japan and these other countries to justify talking about a "late-industrializing," rather than a "Japanese," model of development. Nevertheless, Japan was the pioneer of the late-industrializing model, and it has also progressed the furthest by following it. Therefore, it is instructive to examine how Japan has managed the complexities of a more advanced industrial structure while remaining in the late-industrializing fold.

The major point to note is that these complexities have not been so great as to overwhelm the Japanese government's efforts to stimulate long-run growth.[7] The Japanese government has persisted in trying to create winners even as Japan has neared the world technological frontier. Sometimes it has succeeded (as in the case of high-density television), and sometimes it has failed (as in the case of fifth-generation computers), much as some private investments have failed (as in Sony's development of the Beta format VCR, against the advice of MITI). Judging by Japan's phenomenal growth rate, however, the government's successes have outnumbered its failures. Free market economists have argued that Japan could have grown faster with less government intervention (the same argument has been made by A-TKEs about Korea). But this counterfactual argument is merely doctrinal; there is no scientific evidence to back it up.

Theory behind the Late-Industrializing Model Whereas the Anglo-Saxon model purports to be anchored in a formal theory of markets, the theory behind the late-industrializing model has just begun to be formulated (for one attempt, see Amsden 1991a and 1992). The process of developing such a theory will not be easy because of the central role played by institutions in late industrialization. Suffice it to say here that neither the work of Alexander Gerschenkron (1962) nor that of Friedrich List (1956 [1841]) provides a promising starting point.

Although Gerschenkron appreciated the need for more government intervention the later the industrialization, he saw the government merely as an institutional substitute for the private banker rather than as an active player having to subsidize business to invest long term. List appreciated the need for government protection of infant industries, but Japan has demonstrated that government intervention in an industry is not a one-shot deal. Instead, for an industry to reach the world technological frontier, government intervention must be systematic, covering the life cycle of a single industry, and it must be flexible—on-again, off-again.

One may distinguish four on-again phases in the average mature industry of a late-industrializing country seeking to reach the world technological frontier: (1) the startup phase; (2) the major product-improvement phase, at which South Korea has found itself in the early 1990s, and which overlaps with (3) the basic research phase, to create an entirely new technology; and (4) the declining phase. Each of these switching points in an industry's catchup process (and decline) may necessitate government support, although for different reasons. Subsidies are required in phase 1 because low wages, if determined at free market prices, are usually an insufficient basis for a firm to enter competition against the higher productivity of more advanced countries.[8] Intervention is required in phase 2, the current phase of many of South Korea's industries, because the short-run profit maximization of private firms may delay investments in major product improvements at what are possibly high social and economic costs, as suggested in the example of the Samsung Electronics Company. The reasons behind the need for government intervention in phase 3 overlap with those in phase 2: the investments in R&D necessary for both major product improvement and basic research to create entirely new products involve many technology-related "market failures." As for the declining phase of an industry, government intervention may reduce the social and economic costs of dislocation and restructuring, as in Japan (Patrick 1991).

If one examines what the Japanese government has done to stimulate major product improvement, the second phase noted above, one finds similar policies in effect in South Korea; after all, as stated repeatedly, South Korea has not abandoned the German-Japanese late-industrializing paradigm. What is different is that the Japanese government appears to have been more aggressive in designing and implementing its industrial policy than has South Korea's. The Japanese government has tried to stimulate major product improvement with three types of approaches, as well as by increasing support for a wide spectrum of education. First, insofar as major product improvement is information-intensive—dependent on accumulating detailed knowledge of what many firms in advanced countries with different languages are doing, as noted above—the Japanese government has invested heavily in information collection. Some Koreans have begun to argue that the government's information about foreign firms is inferior to that of the private sector. This, however, is a self-fulfilling prophecy: if government bureaucrats are prevented from investing in information gathering, they will not be as informed as the private sector. The Japanese example suggests that both state and private investments to gather and disseminate foreign-language information are complementary and necessary. Typically such information has externalities, and there are benefits from information sharing among competitors within the same industry. Without the bird's-eye view that information collected by the government provides, firms within an industry may be unaware of the overall direction and pace of major product improvements abroad.

Second, the Japanese government was instrumental in setting industry-wide standards, the overall effect of which was to raise the level of product performance quality. A case in point is the Japanese machine tool industry, in which the government pressed machine tool companies to adopt the same set of numerical controls, developed with government support by the Fujitsu Fanuc Company. The adoption of a uniform control system by all machine tool makers helped the industry progress to a higher-quality market niche—the production of computer numerically controlled machine tools—and standardized controls made the adoption of such machine tools by small users easier as well.

Third, the Japanese government stimulated major product improvement by instituting progressively phased import controls (and subsidies more generally). To push firms into a higher-quality market niche, the government removed import controls on low-end products. This pressured firms to move into higher-end products, which the government then protected (while also leaving the highest-end products, as yet beyond the capabilities of local firms, duty-free).

Such progressive protection and flexible government intervention are precisely what go against the grain of the Anglo-Saxon model—as interpreted by such institutions as the World Bank and International Monetary Fund. Since the 1980s these institutions and the U.S. government have declared the best policy in the developing world to be no subsidies at all. The second-best policy has been declared to be low, uniform subsidy rates for all industries, a formula many A-TKEs have also advocated. The empirical evidence from Japan, however, suggests that discretionary policies may be preferable for catching up.

Exit: The "Off-Again" Aspect of Subsidies If a particular subsidy is to create efficient firms, it must eventually cease. Free market economists contend that subsidies are often prolonged by political pressure beyond their necessary time, and there is abundant evidence from many Latin American countries, India, and Turkey to support this case. On the other hand, the history of late industrialization suggests that, without subsidies, industrial development either does not start at all or does not progress beyond the processing of local raw materials.

Moreover, the Japanese evidence, and the evidence from South Korea and Taiwan as well, indicates that where subsidies are tied to performance standards, and where performance standards are continuously made progressively harder in order to drive firms to the world technological frontier, the "off-again," exit problem associated with subsidies is easily exaggerated. The East Asian experience teaches that the key to development is not to forego subsidization altogether but rather to follow a subsidy-allocation principle based on reciprocity: nothing is given to business without stipulating a concrete performance target in exchange. Under this condition the issue is not one of deciding whether to stop subsidizing a firm but *when* to do so. If too soon, the local industry may be destroyed, as in the case of Japan's commercial aircraft industry after World War II or major subparts of Taiwan's consumer electronics sector in the late 1980s. If too late, stagnation may occur with high economic costs.

One leaves the Japanese experience with the impression that there are no simple formulas to follow, either in theory or in practice. Since the mid-1970s, however, the real dangers of too lengthy protection have fallen sharply. This is thanks to the intense pressure waged by Washington for freer trade and easier access to the world's fastest growing product and financial markets—those of Japan, South Korea, and Taiwan.

Anglo-Saxonization by the Sword It is useful to return briefly to the Anglo-Saxon model, which, as noted earlier, supports its businesses partly through foreign policy. After the first energy crisis of 1973, this support for business took the form of the United States and the Bretton Woods institutions (the World Bank and

IMF) pressuring countries following the late-industrializing model to open their product and capital markets to foreign competition. Japan's response has been a series of delaying actions, reversals of promises, and general stonewalling. South Korea's response has been similar although less evasive, because of its lesser economic power and because the A-TKEs are proving to be a more vocal lobby than the A-TJEs.

Suffice it to say here that, in the absence of an industrial policy to restructure U.S. industry, American pressures on East Asia to liberalize have generally not had a significant, positive effect on American competitiveness. In parallel fashion, South Korean industry does not appear to have become more competitive simply through market liberalization, in the absence of explicit measures to restructure South Korean industry. In fact, in the period 1985–87, when the U.S. government's pressure on South Korea to liberalize its markets grew intense, the outcome was perverse for both the United States and South Korea. As Korea liberalized its markets, it began to import more, as theory would predict. But its increased imports came from Japan, not the United States. American exports did not grow substantially, nor did Korean industry become stronger—this in spite of South Korea's liberalization of one hundred products specifically requested by the U.S. government, a 65 percent devaluation of the dollar vis-à-vis the yen, and subsidized credit to Korean importers to "Buy American" (see Min 1989, and Min and Amsden 1991).

The Lessons Summarized

The simplest lesson from studying the Anglo-Saxon, German, and Japanese models—the models of the world's greatest economic powers, past and present—is that each was the product of both choice and the force of history, of opportunism and ideology. Certainly no one model is ideal, and each has its advantages, only some of which are transferable to other countries. Nor is any single model free of inconsistency and contradiction. Although the theory behind the Anglo-Saxon model is one of laissez-faire, the practice of American and British economic history represents a significant departure from theory. Moreover, although the great strength of the Anglo-Saxon model is democracy, that democracy is coupled in the United States with a much less equal distribution of income than in Germany, Japan, Taiwan, or South Korea.

One of the virtues of the American model that warrants partial adaptation in South Korea is the antitrust and regulation policies designed in response to popular protest and the Great Depression to curb abusive business practices. There is much to recommend the American approach to regulating health, safety, the environment, utilities, and banking. The good sense of this recommendation has been reaffirmed by the abuses unleashed by deregulation of mergers and banking in the 1980s in the United States, and by the scandals that erupted in the absence of sufficient regulation and monitoring of financial practices in the early 1990s in Japan.

Another virtue, if not of Anglo-Saxon practice then of free market theory, is simplicity. The great advantage of letting markets operate freely is zero implementation costs. The costs of the consequences of too-freely operating markets may, however, be substantial. Laissez-faire gives the appearance of being a simple solution to the policymaking problems posed by complex industrial structures, but not even the American government has shied away from intervention. Even the deregulation of the 1980s represented more a redesign of government interventionist policies than a reduction in intervention itself.

Moreover, liberalizing markets in the presence of big business groups does not necessarily bring the benefits promised in textbook theories. Given existing resource endowments and institutions—including the high concentration of capital that has characterized not just South Korean industrialization but nearly every major industrialization since the late *1890s*—the outcome of freer markets may be more, not less, economic inequality, with little if any increase in economic efficiency unless liberalization is combined with other policies. This general lesson, from any market reform that ignores institutions, has repeated itself not just throughout Anglo-Saxon history but also throughout the 1980s in the Latin American Southern Cone and South Korea.

The late-industrializing model, as pioneered by Japan, has also demonstrated that it is not necessarily true that the ability of government to intervene diminishes as a country's industrial structure grows more complex. The nature of government intervention has to change, as it has changed in Japan in tandem with Japanese industry moving closer to the world frontier and with U.S. pressures. But a proactive role for the government, to hasten the process of catching up and to minimize social costs, appears as necessary and as possible in the early stages of industrialization as in the later stages.

The theory behind the model of government intervention in late industrialization has only begun to be formulated, but the inspiration for that theory is unlikely to be Friedrich List. Although List pioneered the idea of protecting infant industries, the Japanese experience suggests that government intervention in any one industry attempting to catch up with the world technological frontier cannot be a one-shot affair, during the period of an industry's infancy only. Government intervention must, of practical necessity, be a flexible, on-again, off-again matter over an industry's life cycle, where the government systematically supports and disciplines business at strategic switching points, so that business invests long term and ultimately operates with state-of-the art technology, as well as with a set of human capabilities necessary to generate new technology.

The major point, as I stressed earlier, is that the role the government has to play to stimulate industrial growth is not a universal one. It depends on whether a country is an innovator or a learner; it depends, that is, on whether its leading enterprises already possess the capabilities to compete on the basis of generating pioneering technology, in which case government intervention can be less, or whether leading enterprises must rely on a transitory low-wage advantage and borrow technology from other firms in order to catch up, in which case government intervention must be more. If the government is to intervene more, then the discipline of business must also be more.

I have defined countries that have had to industrialize exclusively by borrowing technology as "late industrializers." By this definition, Japan, South Korea, and to some extent Germany are all late industrializers, and consequently the German-Japanese model is, on average, a far more appropriate model for South Korea to follow than the Anglo-Saxon one. This is all the more so since countries following this model appear to be outperforming the Anglo-Saxon countries.[9]

The Sequencing of Reforms

A foreigner has enough trouble understanding another country's political economy, let alone making recommendations to reform it. The latter is especially difficult because of the subtlety of political barriers to change. I proceed only with hubris and a strong caveat of this limitation in mind.

It seems to me that the most immediate problem South Korea faces is untangling the jumble of business-government-labor relations that emerged in the 1980s. In the past, these relations were rather simple: the government was autonomous from capital, and labor was kept in check by both capital and the state. As is to be expected, however, autonomous relations have eroded as labor has gained more power with democratization and as business has gained more power with capital accumulation.

This does not mean that the old relationships can be, or should be, resurrected; it would be highly undesirable if the repression of labor were to continue. What it does mean, however, is that, at minimum, labor must be convinced that business and government are not colluding to further their own interests against those of labor and society at large. Toward this end, and bearing in mind the necessity for South Korea's economy to continue to achieve high productivity growth, a possible sequence of reforms is the following.

1. Regulate Political Contributions One of the most effective American regulations concerns contributions to political parties. These are strictly controlled and monitored in the United States. Although abuses still persist, generally such controls have made politicians less the handmaiden of big business than previously. Similar controls in South Korea would help delink the influence of the business community on the political elite. The power of politicians in the National Assembly might also be curbed by limiting their tenure in office to, say, a total of two terms. The American public began to debate a similar law in the 1991 elections.

2. Enhance the Capabilities of the Government Bureaucracy Promotions within the government bureaucracy should also be delinked from political influence as much as possible. The capabilities of the bureaucracy to further economic development should also be enhanced. More investments are warranted to increase the information-gathering capability of the bureaucracy, with respect to gathering intelligence on what competitors abroad are doing or did in the past; what government policies in Japan, Germany, and other latecomers are or were in the past in strategic industries; and what major investment projects of the *jaebul* are in the pipeline to advance the capabilities of South Korean industry to generate major product improvements. The aim of strengthening the bureaucracy's capability to gather intelligence is not to have it supplant the intelligence-gathering capabilities of the private sector. Rather, it is to enable the government to both cooperate with and *compete against* the private sector in assuming leadership for driving industry closer to the world technological frontier.

To enhance the government bureaucracy's capability to pursue an active industrial policy, it may be warranted to merge the Economic Planning Board and the Ministry of Trade and Industry. This merger may be expected to create more diversity in the outlook of the economists who work in both bureaucracies and to provide the engineers in the MTI with more support services. Now the MTI economists seem to be predominantly concerned with free trade, while the economists in the Planning Board seem too distant from the engineering-oriented industry division of the MTI. As Korean industry becomes increasingly global, investing overseas as well as entertaining more inward direct foreign investment, an industrial policy unit with greater resources is necessary to keep ahead of developments and avoid possible bottlenecks.

3. Modernize the Jaebul Structure of Business: Debt-for-Equity Swaps and the Creation of Semipublic Institutional Investors With a political system and bureaucracy more independent from business influence, it should be easier for the government to impose increasingly rigorous performance standards in exchange for preferential credit, trade restrictions, and other incentives to move upmarket. The resumption of discipline of business should make support to business more politically palatable.

The fact of the matter is that, despite all the talk of financial liberalization in South Korea, loans to big business—short-term and long-term—remain under government influence and of critical importance to even the largest corporations (Amsden and Euh 1990). Henceforth, *jaebul* access to credit and other supports should be made contingent on their abiding by the following proposal. The more a *jaebul* agrees to the debt-equity swaps proposed here, the easier its access to credit, government contracts, and other government assistance should be.

Despite legal limitations in the past on family ownership of a corporation, the *jaebul* remain family-controlled and majority-owned through the use of fictitious names and other roundabout ownership methods. Large owners, moreover, use their power to pass on wealth from one generation to another. The ideal way to curb these practices is to legislate and monitor an end to fictitious name ownership and to tighten inheritance laws, as the government of Kim Young Sam has done. Moreover, the government may wish to introduce measures precisely targeted at the biggest business groups—which tend to have the highest debt-equity ratios, given their preferential access to capital in the past—and which allow monitoring by other than the government itself.

In countries with deeper financial markets, institutional investors (insurance companies, pension fund managers) often play the role of watchdog of corporations. They impede majority owners from reducing returns to assets by using such assets for family gains, such as the Hyundai group was charged with doing in 1991. They thereby protect the interests of the small investor. To make the *jaebul* more accountable to the interests of small shareholders (and small shareholding, including employee shareholding, is widespread in South Korea), the government may wish to create professionally managed semipublic institutional investors (SPIIs). With equity in each major *jaebul*, the SPIIs would act as watchdogs over the family owners' activities and ultimately serve to dilute family ownership itself. Specifics of such an institution might be as follows:

1. The government converts outstanding *jaebul* bank debt (or a part of such debt) into equity and makes a substantial part of further long-term loans to the *jaebul* in the form of voting equity shares (exact details decided later).

2. This equity is divided among several SPIIs—maybe five or six. (There should *not* be an SPII for each *jaebul*, since this would increase their vulnerability to capture.) Like mutual funds, these SPIIs should compete among themselves and ultimately be privatized, with their shares sold to the public on the Korean stock exchange.

3. These SPIIs have the capability to monitor the family management of the *jaebul* in which they are investors. They have access to the same information about management that is available to any owner. But unlike small, dispersed shareholders, they are able to monitor the performance of management and interfere with that management to make it more effective and accountable. To the extent that they increase rates of return, even the *jaebul* families might welcome their presence.

4. Competition among the SPIIs for the best performance makes them relatively independent of government control. Such competition can be expected to increase the efficiency of South Korean industry generally. Moreover, by reducing the debt-equity ratio of the big companies, the financial structure of Korean industry can be expected to be strengthened. The dispersion in the ownership of the *jaebul* will also be much faster than otherwise. Historically,

the transition from family-controlled to publicly controlled corporations takes around sixty years, or three generations, as exemplified by the Dupont, Ford, and Rockefeller families.

4. Give Labor a Greater Voice It is too soon to know what the fate of trade unions will be in late industrialization. All that is known is that in many advanced countries, including the United States and Japan, trade union membership has fallen with an increase in per capita income and a shift toward the service sector. Such a shift has not yet happened in South Korea, so trade unions may be an important part of the industrial landscape in the near future.

Whatever the trade union role, workers require a voice as their jobs involve a greater and greater degree of intellectual capabilities. Toward this end, large companies should be required to allow the formation of employee relations committees, or works councils, as well as the right to "codetermination" on the German model whereby workers are given a say in management decision making. Furthermore, given the abysmal record of job conditions in many large Korean corporations, health and safety committees should also be encouraged to organize.

5. Mobilize the A-TKEs The A-TKEs are an important resource, and steps should be taken to enable them to make a more positive contribution to the Korean economy in the future. Toward that end, they should be made less dependent on foreign financial support to undertake independent academic research. The government should make research grants available, through competitive screening, to Korean economists for the general purpose of discovering more about the actual process of late industrialization and about how systematic deviations of that process from the free market model influence policy objectives, particularly those of industrial policy.

NOTES

This chapter benefited from helpful discussions with the following people, many of whom are American-trained Korean economists: Ha-Joon Chang, Yoon-Dae Euh, Duck-Soo Han, Seung-Soo Han, Takashi Hikino, Eun-Mee Kim, Linsu Kim, Yoon Hyung Kim, Lisa Klein, Sunshik Min, Chung-In Moon, Won-Am Park, and Sang-Dal Shim. The research assistance of Cheol-Soo Park is much appreciated.

1. This became evident from a four-volume study, which the World Bank commissioned from its internal Operations Evaluation Department, on the newly industrializing economies. The report on Korea stated that the Bank used Korea's big push into heavy industry as an argument against a strategy of selective government intervention, whereas the evidence from Korea did not support this conclusion (World Bank 1992). The Bank agreed to release the overall volume of the study only after a strong protest from the Japanese delegation (see Awanohara 1992). The separate volume on Korea will not be released. Further Japanese pressure induced the Bank to undertake a more

comprehensive study of the "East Asian miracle" (see World Bank 1993, and *World Development* 1994).

2. It is noteworthy that, in the case of agriculture, prices have tended not to fall with a rise in the supply of imported foodstuffs. Housing prices have also not fallen with an increase in the housing stock—owing to shortages of land, labor, and possibly building materials.

3. That they were not entirely credible stemmed from a sobering fact about which both the Korean government and the business community were keenly aware: Taiwan had liberalized its domestic market for consumer electronics prematurely, and Japanese competition had wiped out local consumer electronics producers.

4. Only the American version of the Anglo-Saxon model is discussed here. The British version seems altogether inappropriate, since it evolved in accordance with Britain's being the first country in world history to industrialize. Britain also has the dubious distinction of being among the first major economies to decline, so it is probably not an attractive model to follow.

5. The Ministry of Finance reported that South Korea's financial firms were holding $2.6 billion, or 1.4 percent of their total deposit and trust accounts, under pseudonyms as of the end of July 1991. Accounts using assumed names had to pay a 60 percent tax on capital gains, whereas accounts using tax identification numbers paid a rate of only 20 percent. It was estimated that the figure of $2.6 billion might be even higher if accounts borrowing others' names were included, although there was no reliable method to identify such accounts (*Asian Wall Street Journal*, 3 October 1991, p. 4).

6. The average German worker puts in fewer hours per week than the average American worker; Keck 1991.

7. Chalmers Johnson's path-breaking work (1982) shows how MITI grappled with complexity throughout its history; see also Chapter 3 of this volume.

8. See Amsden (1989), for a discussion of the inability of the Korean and Taiwanese cotton textile industries to compete in the 1960s against the Japanese textile industry when the prices were "right," that is, in the absence of government subsidies.

9. According to recent estimates, there has been convergence in productivity levels among industrialized countries, with Japan and Europe finally catching up with the United States (see Abramovitz 1986, and Baumol, Nelson, and Wolff 1994, for a discussion of "convergence").

REFERENCES

Abramovitz, M. 1986. "Catching Up, Forging Ahead, and Falling Behind." *Journal of Economic History* 46 (June).

Amsden, Alice H. 1987. "Republic of Korea, Stabilization and Adjustment Policies and Programmes." Country Study no. 14. Finland: World Institute for Development Economics Research of the United Nations University.

Amsden, Alice H. 1989. *Asia's Next Giant: South Korea and Late Industrialization*. Oxford: Oxford University Press.

Amsden, Alice H. 1991a. "Big Business and Urban Congestion in Taiwan: The Origins of Small Enterprises and Regionally Decentralized Industry." *World Development* 19(9).

Amsden, Alice H. 1991b. "The Diffusion of Development: The Late-Industrializing Model and Greater East Asia." *American Economic Review* 81(2).

Amsden, Alice H. 1992. "A Theory of Government Intervention in Late Industrialization." In L. Putterman and D. Rueschemeyer (eds.), *The State and the Market in Development*. Boulder, Colo.: Lynne Rienner.

Amsden, Alice H. 1993. "Trade Policy and Economic Performance in South Korea." In Manuel R. Agosin and Diana Tussie (eds.), *Trade and Growth: New Dilemmas in Trade Policy*. New York: St. Martin's Press.

Amsden, Alice H., and Yoon-Dae Euh. 1990. "Republic of Korea's Financial Reform: What Are the Lessons?" Discussion Paper No. 30, United Nations Conference on Trade and Development, Geneva, Switzerland.

Amsden, Alice H., and Yoon-Dae Euh. 1993. "South Korea's 1980s Financial Reforms: Good-bye Financial Repression (Maybe), Hello New Institutional Restraints." *World Development* 21(3).

Amsden, Alice H., and Takashi Hikino. 1993. "Borrowing Technology and Innovating: Explorations of Two Paths of Industrial Development." In Ross Thomson (ed.), *Learning and Technological Change*. New York: Macmillan.

Auty, Richard M. 1991. "Creating Competitive Advantage: South Korean Steel and Petrochemicals." *Tijdschriftvoor Econ. en Soc. Geografie* 82(1).

Awanohara, Susumu. 1992. "Question of Faith: Japan Challenges World Bank Orthodoxy." *Far Eastern Economic Review*, 12 March.

Baumol, William J., Richard R. Nelson, and Edward N. Wolff, eds. 1994. *International Convergence in Productivity: Cross-Country Studies and Historical Evidence*. New York: Oxford University Press.

Berghahn, Volker R. 1986. *The Americanisation of West German Industry, 1945–1973*. Cambridge: Cambridge University Press.

Brandt, Vincent. 1986. "Korea." In G. C. Lodge and E. F. Vogel (eds.), *Ideology and Competitiveness: An Analysis of Nine Countries*. Boston: Harvard Business School Press.

Braun, Hans-Joachim. 1990. *The German Economy in the Twentieth Century*. London: Routledge.

Chandler, Alfred D., Jr. 1990. *Scale and Scope: The Dynamics of Industrial Capitalism*. Cambridge: Harvard University Press.

Chang, Ha-Joon. 1991. "The Political Economy of Industrial Policy: Reflections on the Role of State Intervention." D. Phil. diss., University of Cambridge.

Cho, Y. J., and D. C. Cole. 1986. "The Role of the Financial Sector in Korea's Structural Adjustment." Mimeo. Washington, D.C.: Korea Development Institute and the World Bank.

Clifford, Mark. 1991. "Taking on the Titans: South Korea's Electronics Makers Are Slowly Catching Up." *Far Eastern Economic Review* 154(44).

Coats, A. W. 1992. "Changing Perceptions of American Graduate Education in Economics, 1953–1991." *Journal of Economic Education* 23(4).

Diaz-Alejandro, Carlos. 1985. "Good-bye Financial Repression, Hello Financial Crash." *Journal of Development Economics* 19.

Drucker, Peter. 1991. "Japan: New Strategies for a New Reality." *Asian Wall Street Journal*, 4–5 October, p. 10.

EPB (Economic Planning Board), Republic of Korea. 1990. *Major Statistics of the Korean Economy.* Seoul.

Fallows, James. 1991. "The Crucial Difference: Japan's Inconvenient Refusal To Slow Down." *Times Literary Supplement*, 27 September.

Freeman, Richard B., and James L. Medoff. 1984. *What Do Unions Do?* New York: Basic Books.

Gerschenkron, Alexander. 1962. *Economic Backwardness in Historical Perspective.* Cambridge: Harvard University Press.

Hadley, Eleanor. 1970. *Anti-Trust in Japan.* Princeton: Princeton University Press.

Haggard, Stephan. 1990. *Pathways from the Periphery: The Politics of Growth in Newly Industrializing Countries.* Ithaca: Cornell University Press.

Hikino, Takashi, and Alice H. Amsden. 1994. "Staying Behind, Stumbling Back, Sneaking Up, Soaring Ahead: Late Industrialization in Historical Perspective." In William J. Baumol, Richard R. Nelson, and Edward N. Wolff (eds.), *International Convergence in Productivity: Cross-Country Studies and Historical Evidence.* New York: Oxford University Press.

Johnson, Chalmers. 1982. *MITI and the Japanese Miracle: The Growth of Industrial Policy, 1925–1975.* Stanford: Stanford University Press.

Keck, Otto. 1991. "The National System for Technical Innovation in Germany." In R. R. Nelson (ed.), *National Systems Supporting Technical Advance in Industry.* New York: Oxford University Press.

Kim, Eun Mee. 1988. "From Dominance to Symbiosis: State and Chaebol in Korea." *Pacific Focus Inha Journal of International Studies* 3(2).

Kim, Seok-Ki. 1987. "Business Concentration and Government Policy: A Study of the Phenomenon of Business Groups in Korea, 1945–1985." D.B.A. diss., Harvard Business School, Boston.

Lee, Joung-Woo. 1983. "Economic Development and Wage Inequality in South Korea." Ph.D. diss., Harvard University.

Li, Kuo-Ting. 1988. *The Evolution of Policy behind Taiwan's Development Success.* New Haven: Yale University Press.

Limerick, Patricia N. 1987. *The Legacy of Conquest: The Unbroken Past of the American West.* New York: Norton.

List, Friedrich. 1956 [1841]. *National System of Political Economy.* Philadelphia: Lippincott.

Little, Ian, Tibor Scitovsky, and Maurice Scott. 1970. *Industry and Trade in Some Developing Countries: A Comparative Study.* Paris: Oxford University Press for the Development Centre of the Organisation for Economic Co-operation and Development.

Min, Sunshik. 1989. "The Appreciation of the Yen and Japan's Exports to Korea." D.B.A. diss., Harvard Business School, Boston.

Min, Sunshik, and A. H. Amsden. 1991. "The Poor Performance of American Manufacturers in the Korean Market." *Seoul Journal of Economics* 4(4).

Moore, Barrington, Jr. 1966. *Social Origins of Dictatorship and Democracy.* Boston: Beacon Press.

MOST (Ministry of Science and Technology). Various years. *Annals.* Seoul.

Nakamura, Keisuke, et al. 1988. *Rodo Kumiai wa Hontoni Yakudatte Irunoka* (Are labor unions really useful?). Tokyo: Sogo Rodo Kenkyusho.

New York Times. 1992. "Even among the Well-off, the Richest Get Richer." 5 March, p. 1.

OECD (Organisation for Economic Co-operation and Development). 1990. *Industrial Policy in OECD Countries: Annual Review, 1990*. Paris.

Onis, Ziya. 1991. "The Logic of the Developmental State." *Comparative Politics* 24(1).

Ozawa, Terutomo. 1974. *Japan's Technological Challenge to the West, 1950–1974: Motivation and Accomplishment*. Cambridge: MIT Press.

Patrick, Hugh. 1991. "Concepts, Issues, and Selected Findings." In Hugh Patrick (ed.), *Pacific Basin Industries in Distress: Structural Adjustment and Trade Policy in the Nine Industrialized Economies*. New York: Columbia University Press.

Peacock, Alan. 1980. *Structural Economic Policies in West Germany and the United Kingdom*. London: Anglo-German Foundation for the Study of Industrial Society, St. Stephen's House, Victorial Embankment.

Ravenscraft, David J., and F. M. Scherer. 1987. *Mergers, Sell-Offs, and Economic Efficiency*. Washington, D.C.: Brookings Institution.

Sylla, Richard. 1991. "The Role of Banks." In R. Sylla and G. Toniolo (eds.), *Patterns of European Industrializaton*. New York: Routledge.

United Nations Statistical Office. 1985. *Special Study*. New York: United Nations.

Vietor, Richard H. K. 1991. "Government Regulation of Business in Twentieth Century America: An Overview and Synthesis." Business History Seminar, Harvard Business School, Boston (to be published in Cambridge Economic History, *History of U.S. Regulation*, forthcoming).

Wagoner, Harless. 1966. *A History of the American Machine Tool Industry, 1900–1950*. Cambridge: MIT Press.

Williamson, Jeffrey G., and Peter H. Lindert. 1984. *American Inequality: A Macroeconomic History*. New York: Academic Press.

World Bank. 1987. *Korea: Managing the Industrial Transition*, Vols. 1 and 2. Washington, D.C.

World Bank. 1992. *World Bank Support for Industrialization in Korea, India, and Indonesia*. Washington, D.C.

World Bank. 1993. *The East Asian Miracle: Economic Growth and Public Policy*. Washington, D.C.

World Development. 1994. "Symposium on the World Bank's *East Asian Miracle* Report." *World Development* 22(4).

Wright, Gavin. 1990. "The Origins of American Industrial Success." *American Economic Review* 80(4).

You, Jung-Il, and Ha-Joon Chang. 1991. "The Myth of a Free Labor Market in Korea." Mimeo. Faculty of Economics and Politics, University of Cambridge.

Chapter 5

Korean Choices and Patterns of Advanced Country Development

John Zysman
University of California

Introduction

What can Korea learn from the political economies and development experiences of the most successful advanced countries? The lessons, as we shall see, cannot be reduced to a bullet list of policies and practices to copy or avoid. As we look to the advanced industrial nations for lessons, we must keep in mind that each of them has found a distinct means to resolve the political as well as the technical problem of growth. The technical tasks are often evident: convert savings into investment, channel investment into the most productive uses, organize production competitively, and assure technological innovation and entrepreneurial activity. The political challenges are less precise, but economic development always implies social dislocations and the radical transformation of lives and communities. The losers from economic development will try to use whatever existing political position they have to resist changes that disadvantage them and to capture economic "rents," drawing subsidies that preserve their way of life but slow growth. Unless those who dislocated and disadvantaged are bought off and co-opted through compensation, or simply beaten politically, an endless series of conflicts and disputes will disrupt the market. When prices become unstable, market rules unclear, and profit calculations unpredictable, even ordinary transactions become difficult. Runaway inflation, for example, is a sure sign of unresolved political conflicts and can be a real threat to the normal functioning of an economy.[1] During an intense period of inflation in Argentina in the winter of 1989, a sign in a store window read: "Closed for lack of prices."[2] In the 1960s and 1970s, struggles between unions and management in the British automobile industry impeded and distorted both product development and production innovation. Case after case teaches us that political stability is essential to economic development. The primary political goal, then, is reasonably straightforward even if difficult to make precise: establish a stable means of allocating the gains and pains of growth among the winners who profit from the process and the losers who are disadvantaged. Unless a country is able to effectively allocate the gains and pains of growth, it will sink into a morass of conflicts, powerless to adopt cohesive development strategies or even focus on immediate technical tasks. This central political challenge must not, however, disguise the equally important need to match the policy and marketplace capacities to the everchanging economic tasks that must be resolved. These are precisely the challenges the advanced industrialized countries have met, and why we look at them today for lessons.

Unfortunately, the advanced country models are varied and can teach different—seemingly contradictory—lessons. To begin with, there are diverse forms of capitalism and a range of successful market systems. There is no such thing as a single, idealized, natural form of the market economy whose proper functioning is only distorted by political intervention. There is no single best way to structure an economy, to reconcile resources and demand, to organize and promote markets; each particular economic circumstance must be matched with an appropriate political strategy for growth. We must be clear that political rules and institutions create markets; markets do not exist apart from political rules and institutions that structure how buying, selling, and the very organization of production take place.[3] But, despite the great diversity of the political resolutions we observe in the advanced countries, similar technical tasks (how to channel resources and organize production) and political problems (how to assure a stable political foundation for markets) must be solved.

There is no single best way for a country to become rich and powerful. Firm strategies and government policies required for British success in the early nineteenth century, for example, were very different from those required by Germany toward the century's end (see Gerschenkron 1962). The organization of the shop floor that supported British industry was in turn radically different from the American system of mass manufactures in our century. Success does not come from copying a dominant form, but from adaptation and local innovation. The pattern of flexible specialization created and unveiled in Northern Italy resulted (unexpectedly) from efforts to implement traditional models of mass production, just as the Japanese production system emerged from efforts to imitate America. Industrial success is only assured by continuous adjustment and adaptation. Solutions that worked in one era become obsolete when new tasks emerge which cannot be addressed by old approaches. What worked fifty, even twenty years ago will almost certainly not work today.

Yet, at any moment, the most successful political economies become models for the others. The secrets of growth are sought in the particulars of corporate strategy, mechanisms of policy, and means of organizing political life. When in the 1960s America was at its peak of power, the airport bookstores carried titles like *The American Challenge* (Servan-Schreiber 1968) and *The Secrets of the American Giants* (Hetman 1969). Now, twenty years later, nearly identical titles substitute Japan for

America—books like *Trading Places* (Prestowitz 1988) and *Kaisha* (Stalk and Abegglan 1985). Unfortunately for those who yearn for simple political and economic equations, when the institutional arrangements of one country are copied by another, the economic results are rarely the same. The special difficulty for the analyst, then, is not only to describe different national arrangements but also to locate their critical and indispensable features. But even descriptions are problematic since there is no real agreement about how economies such as Germany or Japan actually operate. Different scholars often provide profoundly different pictures of the same place, almost as if they have visited different countries and accidentally put the same country name on their writings. Cartoon caricatures compete for attention. And the most visible features are not always the most significant. How, then, do we reason about the experiences of the advanced countries and draw implications for Korea or other industrializing nations?

Let us review the line of reasoning I undertake in this essay. The advanced countries often face quite similar problems in the effort to sustain growth, but they resolve them in different ways. The particular historical course of each nation's development creates a political economy with a distinctive institutional structure for governing the markets of labor, land, capital, and goods. That institutional structure shapes the dynamics of the political economy and sets boundaries within which government policies and corporate strategies are chosen. Predictable patterns of policy and strategy emerge. The institutional structure induces particular kinds of corporate and government behavior by constraining and by laying out a logic to the market and policymaking process that is particular to that political economy. These typical strategies, routine approaches to problems, and shared-decision rules create predictable patterns in the way governments and companies go about their business in a particular political economy. Those institutions, routines, and logics represent a distinct capacity to address particular sets of tasks.

As long as capacities match the tasks at hand, all is well. Unfortunately, growth demands that tasks evolve and capacities shift—creating a need for continuous political and technical adaptation. The tasks required to sustain economic development evolve as a function of internal growth. Rising incomes change consumer demand, for example, and wealth changes the process of investment. The locus of industrial growth may shift from one industry or technology to another as, for example, when textiles gave way to chemicals as the engine of growth in Europe in the nineteenth century—or, as in our own era, when electronics suddenly began to create new products, transform old ones, and alter the organization of production. Tasks also evolve as the country's place in the international system changes (the United States, for example, losing its capacity to organize international financial markets single-handedly). Similarly, policy and corporate capacities are not fixed for all times but grow and degrade. The institutional structure of the political economy evolves in response to shifting political balances, the emergence of new interests and groups, and changing markets. Thus, for example, the financial systems of each of the advanced countries have been reregulated and deregulated over the past decade, creating a global wholesale financial market and changing the national mechanisms for assuring industrial investment.[4] Solutions to new problems must always involve a new match between tasks and capacities.

This chapter develops the implications for Korea of the experiences of the advanced countries in four steps. The following section draws a baseline in the post–World War II political economies of the advanced industrial countries, with brief reviews of Japan, France, Germany, Sweden, Britain, and the United States. I then consider three models of industrial adjustment and change, models that represent three distinct ways of resolving the basic technical and political problems of industrial adjustment. The foundations of these models lie in the institutional structure of the economy. That institutional structure reflects the social arrangements and organizations in the market built by political settlements. In the next section I consider how the institutional structure, the foundation of each of these models, induces patterns of and sets boundaries to government policy and corporate strategy. Policy, corporate strategy, and arguably production organization in each country have distinctive features that reflect those structures. The result is that countries and companies tend to do what they are good at, that is, they have distinctive capacities and tend to apply those capacities to problems, usually without regard to what works. Crisis occurs when there is a mismatch between task and capacity. Several countries are considered. In this section I also argue that the Japanese production revolution and consequent success in international markets is best understood in this way. In the final major section I consider the evolution of the advanced countries' political economies in recent years. This is particularly difficult because there are multiple and sometimes contradictory trends, because many of the lines of development are not yet resolved, and because there is little agreement about what is in fact happening. As a last step, I speculate on the implications of both the experiences and recent developments of the advanced countries for the choices Korea faces.

Political Settlements and Industrial Development: Advanced Country Patterns in the Postwar Years

For the advanced industrial countries, the period immediately following World War II offered more than the burden of physically rebuilding; it represented an opportunity for political and institutional reconstruction. No one development strategy dominated all these countries. These different roads to development demonstrated that several patterns of industrial change were possible, and that there was more than one way of arranging governments and markets to achieve growth. Indeed, three distinct models of industrial development and adjustment emerged. Each model embodied technical capacities for state action in industry, a political settlement allocating the costs of industrial change, and a political process by which that settlement was reached. The three models of change were (1) state-led adjustment with developmental objectives in which a distribution of costs and gains is imposed by political manipulation of the market; (2) negotiated adjustment with a corporatist tone in which there were explicit bargains among elites representing segments of society; and (3) company-led growth with the government principally a regulator and umpire, with the political settlement simply left to the market, and with government providing some small compensation to those who complain the loudest.

The advanced countries shared the same central problem: how to reallocate resources among different economic sectors. In the quarter-century from reconstruction to the great oil crisis, growth rates were very fast in one set of countries (see Table 5.1). These were the countries that faced radical reconstruction and development—Germany, Japan, and France the are examples here—and transferred, in relatively short order, much of their resources out of agriculture and into industry. In the more mature economies—for example the United States and Britain—growth rates were slower; the challenge to reorganize production in already established industries proved surprisingly difficult. Industry and labor, whose political interests were deeply entrenched, had to be displaced. Political protection (in the form of trade restrictions and subsidies) was an alternative to the flexibility and adaptation that growth required. By the end of this long period of growth and development, all the countries eventually faced this problem of sustaining growth by reorganizing industry and adjusting it to competition in international markets (we return to this problem in the section "Adapting to the Permacrisis").

The Foundation of the Adjustment Models

These three models of industrial adjustment are distinguished from each other by the way their politics and markets are organized (Zysman 1983). Institutional arrangements of market and administration define the settings in which political fights about the economy occur. They structure the political conflicts over industrial change and economic policy. The institutions, both economic and political, in

TABLE 5.1

Rates of growth of total output (annual average, percentage)

	United Kingdom	United States	France	Germany	Japan
1950–60	2.66	3.26	4.56	7.97	8.92
1960–73	2.28	4.17	5.56	4.43	10.43
1973–83	2.22	2.04	2.23	1.64	3.7
1950–83	2.37	3.25	4.24	4.63	7.87

Source: Economic Statistics 1900–1983 (1985).

which those fights occur articulate how groups must organize to achieve their objectives, often who their allies will be, usually what their tactics must be, and certainly what can be obtained by them from government.[5] Of course, these arrangements are evolutionary: institutional arrangements have their origins in the processes of industrialization and political development; they are, in a sense, the products of past conflict, and they continue to respond to a country's economic and political shifts. But institutions, once created, are not infinitely malleable. Indeed, it is a fundamental feature of the advanced countries that their political and economic institutions do not radically change with each shift in the balance of political power. Rather, existing institutions are used for new purposes by new groups.

The institutional capacities that concern us as we examine the stories of the several efforts to maintain growth are the government's institutional capacity to shape adjustment by setting rules and allocating resources selectively toward purposes it defines; the possibility of negotiations among the major producer groups; and the flexibility of the shop floor. These capacities, in turn, hinge on the character of the state, the financial system, and the labor market. We return to the foundations of these capacities after reviewing several of the national stories.

State-Led Growth in Japan and France

State-led development in France and Japan was ultimately a conservative modernization in which agricultural and traditional businesses were cushioned against (but not protected from) the consequences of development. The central process in both was a shift of resources out of agriculture into industry and a modernization and then internationalization of industry. The political problem in both was that the very groups that had to be displaced—agriculture and like groups in traditional society—were the political base of the conservative governing parties. Although the patterns of development were in many ways similar, Japan surged to a position of real industrial power while French growth often stuttered and stammered, leaving Germany today as the industrial leader in Europe. The differences between the two countries lay in the depth of the political commitment to rapid industrial development, the intensity of internal industrial competition, and the creation of distinctive industrial advantage—in each case greater in Japan than in France. If we focus only on Japan, however, we may be deceived into believing that the developmental model or state-led model is in itself an automatic formula for development. It is not; there are substantial political and technical risks for those who attempt such a strategy. A strident political challenge by the outsiders and losers is automatically invited by this strategy. The principal technical risk of state-led growth is a government's temptation to try to compel markets to conform to its preferences and purposes, which often produces huge waste and market failures. The more successful government policy alternative is to use the instruments of support to accelerate market processes. For our purposes, the French story of state-led growth is as important as the more popular Japanese saga.

In the state-led model of development, the government bureaucracy attempts to orient the adjustment of the economy by explicitly influencing the position of particular sectors, even of individual companies, and by imposing its choices on the politically weakest groups in the polity. The state seeks to select the terms on which sectors and companies confront the market, either by explicitly providing resources to favored groups or by creating conditions that will force the recalcitrant to adjust. The state is an economic player, that is, an actor in the market system working toward purposes it defines, pursuing a specific agenda of economic development. It is not simply a regulator or administrator. When the state is an economic actor, finance can act as an instrument of the bureaucrats, permitting them to intervene in the affairs of particular firms and to allocate capital between competing uses. A state-led adjustment process politicizes and centralizes the process of industrial change. Those firms and groups excluded from the circle of the court favorites are evident, and they can plausibly blame whatever plights befall them on their political weakness rather than on their economic incapacity. Consequently, a government-imposed balance of the costs and gains of change rests on the continuing ability of the executive and the groups who are political winners to exclude the losing groups from policymaking. The system is inherently taut.

The institutional structures of our two state-led economies, Japan and France, are very similar. With an institutional map of the American economy as guide, an analyst or visitor would be lost in either Tokyo or Paris; but a visitor from Paris can find common institutional and political referents in Tokyo, and as a result such visitors often misunderstand how differently the economies of Japan and France work. What, then, are the common features between the two countries? First, there is a state executive with considerable autonomy from the legislature and some power to shape the interest groups that lobby it. Second, a credit-based financial system provides the executive of both governments instruments to shape—on a selective basis, without direct legislative intervention—the overall flow of funds in the economy. This financial system also allows the executive to intervene in a detailed way in industry. Indeed, this credit-based system was an important base of autonomy since the routine management of finance provided the executive with discretionary control over a truly significant piece of the nation's finance—discretion that could be used for purposes formulated by the executive alone. Third, there was no centralized coherent labor movement that linked power at the shop floor to power in politics. (The fragmentation of labor and the government's means for limiting autonomous influence in the factory were, however, very different in each country—with the result that Japan had fundamentally different capacities for production reorganization and technical innovation.) In each case a conservative coalition, facing the similar political problem of managing the transition to an industrial economy with a political base rooted in small towns and agriculture, used this structure to create a state-led strategy of development.

Japan The story told here is of Japan in its postwar development phase, a system of state-led growth (Johnson 1982; Zysman 1983:233–251). The character of growth and the logic of the political economy have evolved, but we need at least a clear baseline to understand those changes. The Japanese government, dominated in the years after World War II by a conservative coalition, used the institutions of a centralized state to create a developmental policy. Crucial elements of market arrangements that facilitated rapid adjustment and growth were the product of conscious choice in the postwar years. The Japanese government has pursued a conscious strategy of industrial development that has influenced the nation's patterns of domestic growth and international trade. The government influenced and shaped the dynamics of a highly competitive market economy, generating a system of controlled competition. Competitive markets induced the investment that underlay rapid growth and manufacturing innovation. The particular character of the interplay between policy, markets, and corporate strategy created and continues to sustain the logic that patterns Japanese development and foreign trade (Johnson, Tyson, and Zysman 1989; Okimoto 1989).

"Bureaucrats rule and politicians reign," a phrase popularized in the United States by Chalmers Johnson, captures the flavor of the system. The conservative-dominated legislature controlled by the Liberal Democratic Party (LDP) ensured support for the broad objectives of growth and development. The multiseat district helped mute substantive policy and personality conflict and certainly facilitated the emergence of the party that diffused and mastered opposition. The then secondary bureaucracies—such as post and telecommunication, education, construction, and transportation—provided means for patronage that could support a particularized electoral system. But the ministries with broader economic objectives, such as the Ministry of International Trade and Industry (MITI) and the Ministry of Finance, had substantial autonomy. The general concern of the government, both prewar and postwar, was development, leading it to be labeled a developmental system.

Policy had two crucial elements: controlling the links between Japan and the external economy, and promoting industrial development within. The government, to use T. J. Pempel's (1978) phrase, was gatekeeper and promoter. As gatekeeper it controlled the terms on which foreign investment could enter the country and on which technology could be licensed. This consequently broke apart the package of the multinational corporation, permitting Japanese-controlled firms to develop product and technology in Japanese markets. By preventing Japanese firms from bidding against each other for licenses, the government kept the price of imported technology low. As a promoter its efforts were diverse. The government supported corporate efforts to import foreign technology at low prices. It assured financing to favored sectors and helped sustain a flow of investment by guaranteeing bank lenders that the risk of industrial failure would be minimal. Its role in supporting domestic research to develop imported technology has been depicted in projects such as VLSI. Equally important, the government supported technology diffusion through joint research efforts and through networks of technology agents that spread advances to small and mid-size firms.

A crucial instrument in the promotional policy was the credit-based financial system. The financial system, as Kenneth Courtis of Deutsche Bank has often argued, was an instrument of policy, not an object of regulation. Without entering into the details of the system, administratively set interest rates and a shortage of capital investment encouraged industry's demand for bank funds, demands that exceeded the available supply. Firms therefore found themselves dependent on bank finance, and banks in turn found themselves dependent on the goodwill of the Bank of Japan and the Ministry of Finance, which created money to fill the excess demand for funds. The government thus assured funds to the most important growth sectors in the economy, setting up channels that collected funds from agriculture and funneled them into industry. Yet agriculture and small business were not denied funds either. Through subsidy and dedicated lending facilities their needs were also met.

As important as the policies for industry were, the character of the labor relations system created the basis for flexible adaptation and adjustment in industry. There were political arrangements that limited the direct national confrontation between labor and industry and effectively excluded labor from political power. At the same time, labor was effectively integrated into shop floor operations and given real responsibility. An odd mix, but it worked.

Industrialization is by no means a straightforward outcome of policy intent. Policy, as we have noted, only structures the logic of markets by creating a pattern of incentives and constraints, and in that sense it induces corporate response. An interpretation of industrial outcomes must therefore characterize the organization of industry. Japan is characterized at once by very intense domestic competition and by a range of mechanisms for cooperation or collusion. Whether it is joint planning of expansion in capital-intensive industries to avoid excess capacity and to ensure the introduction of plants of sufficient size to capture scale economies, or joint research on generic technologies, or reallocation of domestic market share in the aluminum industry to firms that move production offshore, or efforts to allocate domestic market to foreign firms—the evidence is overwhelming that competition is bound or orchestrated. The deals may or may not be stable; that is, the market divisions may or may not be fixed. But market outcomes are certainly different because mechanisms for collaboration, collusion, and bargains exist. Elaborating how this Japanese system works requires specifying the rules of controlled competition—in other words, the terms and circumstances of competition and the terms and circumstances of collaboration—a task not undertaken here.

A second major feature of the economy is that Japanese industry combines the strengths of large firms that are able to mobilize substantial resources in the pursuit of long-term objectives and the flexibility and innovative nature of small firms. And indeed Japanese government policy supports both.

Inflation reconciled the political and technical problems of growth in these years, as I argue in detail for the French case. Money was provided to meet the nominal demands, but those producers who could expand and increase productivity most rapidly were the winners. The expanding sectors could outbid (i.e., pay more than) the traditional sectors for productive resources. Thus, over time the market shifted the position of the different groups in the economy, but shifted them with inflationary consequences. Inflation was a means of avoiding direct confrontations. Excess money supply, itself inflationary, was tolerated. The cost of a resource shift out of industry generated demand-shift inflation. Winners were those sectors with the greatest potential for expansion and productivity growth which could pay the most in the competition for resources, drawing people and funds to them. Losers were those sectors that could not keep up with inflation or whose relative position deteriorated. The result was that the apparent direct contradiction between the technical requirement of satisfying industrial needs and the political requirement of satisfying an agricultural and small business constituency was sidestepped.

France In France very similar institutional arrangements were employed to shift the political balance in favor of policies that supported rapid growth and development. On balance, government policies before World War II supported the suppression of markets, or better, their control to limit social dislocation from growth and development. The broad consensus that existed in Japan to support development did not exist in France. After World War II, a coalition of modernizers had to be built and sustained. Indeed, only World War II and the later Algerian crisis permitted a small modernizing elite with limited popular support to reorient the economy. That elite broke the established group's hold on economic policies.[6] The Planning Commission was established and helped reformulate government purposes. The state treasury, the Tresor, transformed and expanded its function, giving the government the capacity to implement some of its ideas. But the electoral foundations of a developmental strategy did not yet exist.[7] This first phase of reform—the de Gaulle interregnum between the war and the creation of the new Fourth Republic—amounted to a reorientation of the state and creation of new instruments of policy.

The Algerian war generated a second break in French political life. When de Gaulle returned to politics, he established a presidential political regime that became the instrument of a growth strategy. In the name of French national glory, he rallied many social elements that would have opposed a project of development and economic transformation. Many traditionalist electoral elements, whose economic interests would lead them to oppose developmental strategies, found themselves trapped in a national coalition. The groups were held in place by nationalism and then transformed by the market. This established a new political base for a developmental strategy. It pitted the traditional elites of France's rural and small town past against the forces that favored industrial development. In response to this conflict, the state pursued competing and seemingly contradictory purposes—fostering growth while simultaneously containing its political consequences. The arrangements of the financial system enabled it to target financial flows to specific uses, and the government was able to subsidize groups that resisted change while strengthening the market forces that favored growth. In short, it can be said that the government devised a policy mix that force-fed the economy's high-growth engine high-octane fuel while at the same time stepping on the brakes.

One limit to the French strategy lies in the character of French industry. French industry after World War II was composed primarily of small to medium-size companies that had been insulated from foreign competition for decades. Long protected and often cartelized, most of the industry had experienced little internal competition. Following a growth strategy, government acted to force French firms to adjust to competition and international markets. Part of that strategy involved creating a more competitive domestic market by inviting foreign competition. The creation of the European Community exposed French industry to intense German competition and drove the weaker firms to turn to state assistance. The state assisted the transformation of the insular French firms into modern corporations. The specific industry policies, many of which were badly mistaken, must be measured against the political challenge of keeping French industry alive while it changed and adjusted. France, though, could never really implement a full-blown development strategy. It did not have the powerful mix of large and small firms such as existed in Japan. Nor could the French insulate their market, since French policymakers needed the EEC to force competition and corporate modernization. As a result, the French ended up with a state-led policy of limited development; indeed, political commitment to growth was partial and forced.

One real difficulty the French experienced in implementing a strategy of state-led growth arose from the government's inability to follow the market, that is, to use the instruments of intervention to amplify market signals. Instead, it had to create the market and generate market pressures. State policy tended to push firms to adopt strategies that were not viable in the international market, a problem we return to in a moment.

The deeper problem was political. A state-led strategy in which the government was thought to be capable of creating industrial and distributional outcomes made it difficult for government to avoid responsibility for virtually any economic or social outcome. As a result, the conservative political strategy inevitably became, at least in part, confrontational. It was a politics of social division. Part of the strategy turned on the need to isolate the Communist Party. Or, more precisely, because of the presence of the Communist Party, the conservatives could organize a nationalist strategy of confrontation against a class and country enemy. It was as well a strategy of labor exclusion, a strategy aided by the divisions inside the labor movement itself. For the conservatives, organizing against the Communist Party was an opportunity.[8] Remove from the political calculus the Communist Party's 20 percent share of the vote, and the electoral arithmetic meant that the non-communist left simply could not capture power.[9] The non-communist left could win (and in fact did win in 1981) only in alliance with the Communists. Consequently, the conservative parties consistently campaigned against the Communist threat to both private property and national integrity, suggesting that any left coalition was profoundly dangerous to French traditions. Without reviewing French political history between the world wars, we must simply note that the virtual civil war over both national and international political issues gave, in the end, even greater power to the conservative appeals. The strategy contributed to a sharply divided society and a sharply divided factory floor. The divisions inside the conservative party (the party conflicts between Gaullists and non-Gaullists, to simplify a quite complex political map) were, in turn, eventually exploited by the left. Led by Francois Mitterand, the Socialists in alliance with the Communists took power in 1981. Surprising to many, a decade of leftist power saw a steady relaxation of social and political tension.

In sum, the French commitments to development were weaker than those in Japan. They were commitments created only by marginal political victory and external pressure. The absence of the kind of broad political consensus Japan enjoyed prevented any possibility of a strongly focused national growth strategy. So, although France and Japan had similar institutions, they were used differently in each country.

Negotiated Growth in Germany and Sweden

Negotiated growth involves explicit and continued bargaining over the terms of industrial change by the predominant social partners. The notion of partner, in fact, is central. Although the several groups—labor, management, agriculture, for example—have distinct interests, those interests are thought by all to be pursued best within common frameworks. Bargaining among partners implies that some outcomes are recognized as legitimately being settled by discussion rather than in the market or by political dictate—that is, settled by compromise rather than imposition. Democratic corporatist bargaining implies that the stronger do not use their advantages to take away the negotiating rights of the weaker—do not deprive them of effective representation or attack vital interests (Katzenstein 1985).

The bargaining base of these social partners rests on both the organization of politics and policymaking and the institutional arrangements in the market. In the Netherlands, for example, the character of parties and interest groups creates the basis of negotiation. In Sweden, by contrast, labor market organization and the powerful labor party establish the foundation of the negotiated system. Although politics and policymaking were dominated for many years by labor, corporate decision making remained the norm of the economic system. In Germany, the powerful universal banks play an almost parapublic role in the financial system and in resolving the particulars of corporate crises. At the same time, a strong Social Democratic Party, strong unions, and effective mechanisms of labor representation within companies (they are not the same in Germany) create a second institutional foundation for bargaining. The Swedish and German cases suggest that a powerful position in one market—labor or capital—can provide the basis for entering into political bargains about the operations of other markets.

Note that this conception of the foundations of bargaining is much more extensive than the widely discussed notion of neocorporatism. The conception here includes the bargaining ties between finance and industry as a basis for social bargaining, as well as arrangements in the party/political system as a solution to divisions rooted in ethnic, religious, and language divisions. Neocorporatism focuses on the social democratic cases and the important place of labor as a foundation for negotiated settlements. Fritz Scharpf provides us with a clear definition of neocorporatist bargaining founded in social democratic parties:

> Neo-corporatism implies specific organizational structures of unions and employer associations, specific types of industrial relations, and specific relations between the "social partners" and government policy makers. As an ideal type, which was approximated in Scandinavia and Austria during the 1960s and 1970s, the neo-corporatist model is defined by the coexistence of the following characteristics: a monopolistic union movement without ideological cleavages or competing craft unions and concentration on the employer side; centralized collective bargaining; and participation by the peak organizations of labor and capital in the formulation of government economic and social policy. (1991:9)

The set of social democratic countries is particularly important because during the 1970s, and arguably during the early 1980s, these countries were quite successful in their fight against unemployment and inflation, even as they expanded the welfare system (Scharpf 1991:9). The response from a critic of these countries might well be that, though they were successful at managing the price and employment dislocations of the 1970s, they were much less successful in the 1980s arranging the structural and production reorganizations required by fundamentally changing patterns of international competition. The reason seems simple. In the first period, overall wage growth arrangements had to be reconciled with productivity growth to avoid inflation and to maintain competitiveness. In the second period, the problem became one of adjusting the relative wages of different sectors and rearranging shop floor labor rules.

Why are such bargaining arrangements useful? Again, Scharpf is helpful. He notes that, if government is to influence economic actors, those actors must be able to recognize unequivocally the direction of policy. In a chaotic world the overall direction of government policy as well as the action of other critical actors is difficult to determine. Therefore, when "union and management elites are continuously and jointly involved in economic policy making, they are likely to be fully aware of each other's interests and interpretations; and if opportunities for improving overall economic performance through joint action exist, they are more likely to make use of them" (Scharpf 1991:13). In the language of this essay, the search for a technical solution becomes entangled with the search for a political solution.[10]

For Korea, there are two particularly significant issues in the stories of the countries with negotiated patterns of industrial adjustment. First, in each of these cases a negotiated aspect to market processes did not occur automatically; it was not derived from historically rooted features of the society. Rather, each system of negotiation was created to resolve specific political conflicts that could at the time threaten to tear the society or paralyze industrial adjustment. The character of the political settlement is evident in the Scandinavian cases. Throughout the 1920s and 1930s, labor conflicts led to intense industrial conflict and the threat of authoritarian solutions. Then, quite abruptly, political deals were struck which moved many issues from the corporate to the policy arena, and strike rates dropped dramatically (Hibbs 1987). Second, in each case a legitimate position for labor within political and industrial life produced flexibility— policy flexibility and shop floor flexibility.

I consider two cases here, Sweden and Germany. Sweden is important because in the past it has demonstrated a full-blown form of social democratic corporatism. Germany is significant because of its evident central economic importance within Europe, which makes it crucial to the last part of this essay, but also because it suggests the importance of financial market arrangements in this model.

Sweden Sweden, along with its Scandinavian neighbors, is a small, wealthy country in a rich part of the world. It, like its peers, has become wealthy both by adding value to products often innovated elsewhere and by finding market niches it can defend. It also has a few powerful firms that are European and often world leaders, such as ABB in power generation, Erikson in telecommunications, and Electrolux. With enormous traded goods sectors, these small countries must adjust both their production structure and macro policy to international shifts. How they do this is the question.

The original corporatist pattern of governance emerged as a response to economic crisis during the 1920s. Sweden developed a strong centralized labor union movement, the LO, and a Social Democratic Party that has now governed—alone or in coalition—for almost all the period from the late 1920s to 1991 (with the exception of the years 1976–79). The September election brought the conservatives back into power. It is unclear whether this conservative government will simply be an interlude that closes with a recreation of a labor-agriculture alliance or, as the conservatives intend, an end to the welfare era.

After World War II, Sweden evolved a distinctive model of macroeconomic management, a model perhaps possible only in Sweden's institutional environment (Martin 1984; Scharpf 1991). The model operated from the late 1950s through the 1970s, though it really ended in the early 1970s—before the first conservative victory—when the farmers' party withdrew from the coalition.

The Swedish strategy at once settled macroeconomic issues and set the terms for the structural adjustment of industry. An industrial policy was pursued through wage policy. The elements were worked out self-consciously and executed purposively. First, there was a solidaristic wage policy aimed at raising low wages or, more precisely, at reducing wage differentials. This policy required centralized wage bargaining to harmonize wage rates among sectors and social groups. It also required mechanisms for limiting wage drift so that the broad national bargains would not be undermined by sector- and company-specific deals. Wage rates were set which could be accommodated, not just by the top few, but by most above-average firms. Since wage rates set for above-average firms would arguably limit profits for below-average firms, those weaker firms would be forced to adjust or exit. The policy notion was to run a budget surplus that would be rechanneled into industrial investment. Government savings would supplement company savings.

Those relatively high wage rates and the continuous pressure to reduce wage differentials did put real pressure on all but the best firms. It encouraged both structural shifts (the movement of resources from sector to sector) and production reorganization (changes within the firm). That was the intent. A retraining strategy to relocate labor to expanding sectors and firms, and away from less productive operations, proved a crucial element of the strategy.

Finally, the government distinguished firms engaged in international trade and facing sharp international competition from those in protected sectors that produced only for the domestic market. Government and corporate structures operated under the assumption that the competitive position of Swedish industry could be maintained only if the sectors exposed to international competition took leadership in wage negotiations. Protected sectors, therefore, had to follow the wage settlements of internationally competitive sectors. The Swedish model began to break down first with the end of the labor-farmer alliance and then in the late 1970s with the defeat of the Social Democrats. The central issue in the 1976 election was nuclear power, yet the radical shift in the broad competitive position of Swedish industry certainly created the basis for the defeat.

The competitive position of Swedish industry changed abruptly with the emergence of such countries as Japan and later Korea in global markets for autos and ships. The adjustment problem was profoundly altered. Previously, the task had been to shift labor from one metal-bending activity to another, or for firms to find the niches in which they could capture substantial value added. Suddenly, as a set of Swedish firms found themselves in trouble, the task changed. At the same time, changes in the international financial system added competitive pressure. The collapse of the dollar-centered international system saw a mark-based European financial system and limited devaluation strategies of adjustment. Production had to be reorganized internally to meet dramatically new competition. Workers required reeducation, not just retraining.

In power, the conservatives during 1976–79 found no policy alternatives to the Social Democratic adjustment formula. Without fully mastering the situation, conservative governance saw a sharp expansion of the public sector and the deficit. The Social Democrats retook power in the election of 1979, but the negotiated arrangements of adjustment were never recreated. Both the management of the public sector and the adjustment within firms became an enduring problem. In the last few years, the Social Democrats have sought a new adjustment strategy as their electoral position weakened. Sweden applied for membership in the European Community and radically reorganized the tax system. Once out of whack, an adjustment strategy is hard to recreate. It will be some time before we can assess whether the conservatives can invent a new formula.

Germany West Germany projects the image of a liberal market economy in which the most important decisions about the uses of the nation's economic resources are made by company management driven by profit motivation and responding to price signals, not by bureaucrats following their plans or by politicians simply following their voters. Indeed, during the 1970s the German case was used to demonstrate that, if government would only ignore business leaders and workers in their demands to be protected from foreign competition and to be insulated from domestic change, inflation-free growth would result—benefiting even those who bore the direct costs of adjustment. The inflation-free nature of Germany's industrial resurgence was facilitated by an industrial structure well suited to the needs of postwar competition. The German economic success also suggests that it is much easier to avoid protection and restriction when rapid growth does not involve major structural change within industry. Nonetheless, the image of a liberal German economy—with individual and self-contained firms competing in markets umpired but not managed by government—is overdrawn. There are important elements of negotiated capitalism in the German story.

The German version of negotiated market capitalism has more diverse foundations than the labor-based social democratic model in Sweden (*Economist* 1991). The foundations consist of a centralized society and economy (a bank-dominated financial system; a corporatist structure of interest group representation with centralized semiofficial trade associations; a strong union movement with labor rights in corporate management) and a decentralized state with considerable political autonomy in the *Lander*, or state governments (Katzenstein 1987).

Let us begin with the centralized economy and society. German capitalism developed a quality of organization, concentration, and centralization which

Andrew Shonfield labeled "organized private enterprise" (1965). German industrial development, as Alexander Gerschenkron (1962) has taught us, required the rapid mobilization of resources for deployment in capital-intensive sectors. Consequently, it followed a distinct course, different from that of, say, Britain. The commercial threat of its industrial predecessors and the military threat of its political rivals both urged quick growth and protection from competitors. The development of heavy industry required substantial concentrations of capital. A development strategy was constructed on trade protection with large firms, cartels, semiofficial trade associations, and large banks. From the beginning, giant export-oriented firms were instruments of industrial growth in many sectors of the German economy. But concentration alone does not distinguish the German case. Giant firms and industrial concentration are typical of all advanced countries, though some countries such as France came to large firms late and others such as Japan and Italy maintained pools of small firms throughout industrial development. Organized arrangements between businesses were never viewed with automatic hostility but were thought to provide elements of order in the unsteady world of market relations. Policy debate has asked whether particular cartels serve a useful public purpose, not whether they should exist at all. In Germany even small and middle-size firms have been highly organized. An indispensable element of industrial development and export success, these largely independent firms (organized in many cases in industrial districts) have been a crucial part of the capital-goods and production-equipment expertise that distinguished Germany throughout the years. Yet they too are organized into important trade associations and industrial districts.

Banks are an important cornerstone of organized German capitalism—"prefects" monitoring order and leaders in the process of industrial adjustment. What is unclear is whether securitization and liberalization in the financial markets or the financial integration of the 1992 process will truly alter that system. The power of the German banks in industrial affairs rests on a foundation of legal allowances and unique financial structure. The legal right to own substantial stock in corporations and to exercise proxy votes for other shareholders permits a special latitude for the German universal banks. There are no prudential limits on banks' holdings, giving them the possibility of direct control. As recently as a decade ago the banks held enough proxy accounts to vote 85 percent of all privately held shares and fully half of all shares outstanding. That voting power was concentrated in the three largest banks, which in the 1970s voted 35 percent of the shares at annual meetings of the seventy-five largest companies. The unique structure of the German financial system forms the second foundation of bank influence (Readman 1973; Vittas 1978). The banks as a group have a distinct place in the German system of financial markets. The securities market has traditionally been small, forcing firms to obtain capital through bank loans, which meant that access even to equity was mediated by banks. Moreover, access to the securities markets was controlled by the banks. The major banks with industrial voting rights and influence over access to equity and debt sit at the center of the system of corporate finance.

German society, not just the economy, is centralized, which also contributes to a style of elite negotiations by creating political parties. The institutions of interest representation are quite centralized and, equally important, often define semiautonomous policy arenas. The result of this interest group centralization is to create for specific social groups the basis for negotiation from coherent islands of influence. Traditionally, when German interest groups are small with sharply defined boundaries, they often do not face institutionalized opposition (Katzenstein 1987). The rules and regulations for that particular subgroup are then structured by the subgroup for itself, keeping the community at large at arm's length. This is the case of doctors and farmers, for example. Recently, in policy arenas such as finance and international competition, European Community proposals have forced adaptation on these previously autonomous groups (Webber 1990).

The dominant economic interest groups, employer associations, and unions are centralized and class-based. Since the mid- to late-nineteenth century, employer associations have been centralized—in part to help promote the economic integration of the German community. Different business associations represent broad policy interests (Bundesverband der Deutschen Industries, BDI) and collective bargaining problems (Bundesvereinigung der Deutschen Arbeitgeber-vebande, BDA). Also, a separate association for small business exists (Deutscher Industrie-une Handelstag, DIHT). The workers are much less organized (40 percent or less are in unions) than the business community (80–90 percent). While unions are organized principally along sectoral lines and a few principally white collar unions and civil service groups keep independence, there is a centralized union association (Deutscher Gewerkschaftsbund, DGB) representing the bulk of the organized working class with some 7.5 million members. Importantly, on collective bargaining matters the unions act independently, with their own strategies and strike funds. But one union, the metalworkers with 2.5 million members, has set broad patterns of wage and technology bargaining (Thelen 1991; Turner 1991; Katzenstein 1989).

Three elements of the labor movement must be highlighted to explain the framework of negotiated bargaining in industry within Germany. First, the unions and the dominant left party, the SDP, both stepped away from socialist commitments three decades ago (1963 for the unions and 1959 for the party). Consequently, both are committed to pragmatic resolutions of concrete problems. Second, the SPD is a viable alternative to the conservatives, having held power alone or in coalition often since the war. Labor concerns are therefore expressed both through the political system and through the labor relations system, and labor positions are entrenched in both. Third, the system of codetermination, of worker participation in corporate management structures, is entrenched in Germany throughout the bulk of industry. The representatives are elected from a company's workers, not appointed by the unions. This both extends labor's voice and provides an independent institutional counterpoint to the unions. Equally important for challenges of industrial adjustment, the mechanisms of codetermination have linked the shop floor to general management. Although these mechanisms were seen as a threat to capitalism and community when they were created, they now provide within firms an important means for adjusting to the new requirements of production.

In contrast to the highly centralized society and economic community, the state structure is very decentralized—a characteristic that permits multiple points of discussion and initiative. German federalism, reminiscent of the United States, is remarkably strong when compared with that of Japan, Britain, France, or Sweden. Germany, recall, was created as a forced bargain among independent principalities to provide a single market and common defense. West Germany was recreated after World War II with the intent of restraining central authority. The states have real and primary authority in many areas, from education and cultural affairs through the organization of the bureaucracy and the regulation of local government. Moreover, the administrative system itself is highly decentralized. The result is that the "federal (i.e., central) government has no choice but to negotiate and cooperate with centers of state power over which it has no control" (Katzenstein 1989:16). Consequently, issues that cannot be negotiated at a national level will often be resolved at a regional level.

This decentralization of the state has significant industrial consequences. For example, small and mid-size businesses have always been crucial in Germany, despite the evident importance of the big business sectors. It is not simply that these firms are dependents of the larger companies; they also provide an autonomous source of product development, innovation, and exports. There are several different sets of small and medium-size firms (with quite distinct historical roots) that now depend heavily on local community institutions. Without this political autonomy, it is doubtful such sets of firms could have emerged or adapted to survive in international competition (Herrigel 1989).

The national system of centralized society and decentralized state is stitched together by the overlap of administrative responsibilities between states and the federal government, by political parties, and by a group of parapublic institutions (Katzenstein 1987). For example, Germany's central bank, the Bundesbank, has considerable independence—greater than any other European central bank—and is a fixed point for policy. The Bundesbank's clear commitment has been to control inflation and the money supply. The strong union movement and labor-based political party apply pressure to maintain employment, but over the long haul the Bundesbank's control of critical monetary variables has proved dominant, and its weight generally falls on the side of inflation control at the expense of growth and employment. This was particularly evident in the consistent decisions to maintain high interest rates even at the risk of pushing up the value of the mark and risking export markets. As the mark strengthened over the years, creating the basis of a German mark–dominated European Monetary System, German industry faced a perpetual adjustment and adaptation. Helping industry adapt to these measures formed a second kind of parapublic institution: the German (really West German) system of vocational training that links public education to private industry. "Public vocational schools teach for a day or two each week general subject and some theoretical aspects of occupational training. The rest of the workweek apprentices acquire practical skills at the workplace" (Katzenstein 1987:12). There are more than four hundred programs set up jointly by business and unions which are officially sanctioned and jointly funded but supervised by the chambers of commerce. The result has been, for the most part, slow and iterative change rather than radical policy redirections: continuity with experimentation (Katzenstein 1989).

As political party coalitions shift, the direction of this system of centralized society and decentralized state has also shifted. In the first phase, from the late 1940s to the mid-1960s, the conservative party (under the primary leadership of Adenauer) oversaw the creation of a welfare state, the inclusion of labor into the institutions of politics and corporate management, and the entrenchment of a commitment to market principles. The second phase lasted from the late 1960s to the end of the 1970s and was dominated by a center-left coalition of the SPD/FDP in the first years and by a broad national coalition of conservatives and social democrats in the later phase. This period saw collaboration among "the major producer groups, senior civil servants, and political leaders . . . [to] bolster West Germany's competitive position in international markets" (Katzenstein 1989:8). The third period, one of a conservative government, has seen a troubled struggle to establish new lines of growth and development, culminating in the collapse of the Berlin Wall and the recreation of a unified German nation.[11]

The West German political economy's style of negotiated adjustment has been very successful. Economic and industrial growth from the reconstruction after World War II to the unification has been remarkable. Both growth and productivity rates have been, compared to the other OECD countries, quite high, although the rates have not been as rapid as those of Japan or the East Asian NICS (see Table 5.1). The Germans have consistently chosen price stability over accelerated growth when choices had to be made. The German pattern of trade shows broad strength across a range of sectors: advanced technology, scale intensive, and production equipment (see Figure 5.1). German producers have even maintained strength in so-called traditional sectors by reorganizing production and product mix. The adaptation of industry must be broken into several groups (Guerrieri 1991). In the capital equipment sector, German industry has been very powerful, often competing with innovation in sectors that are not price sensitive.[12] In science-based sectors, German industry has been powerful in chemicals and pharmaceuticals. Its position in advanced electronics, by contrast, has been weak, as indeed has been true of European industry as a whole. In scale-intensive sectors, German

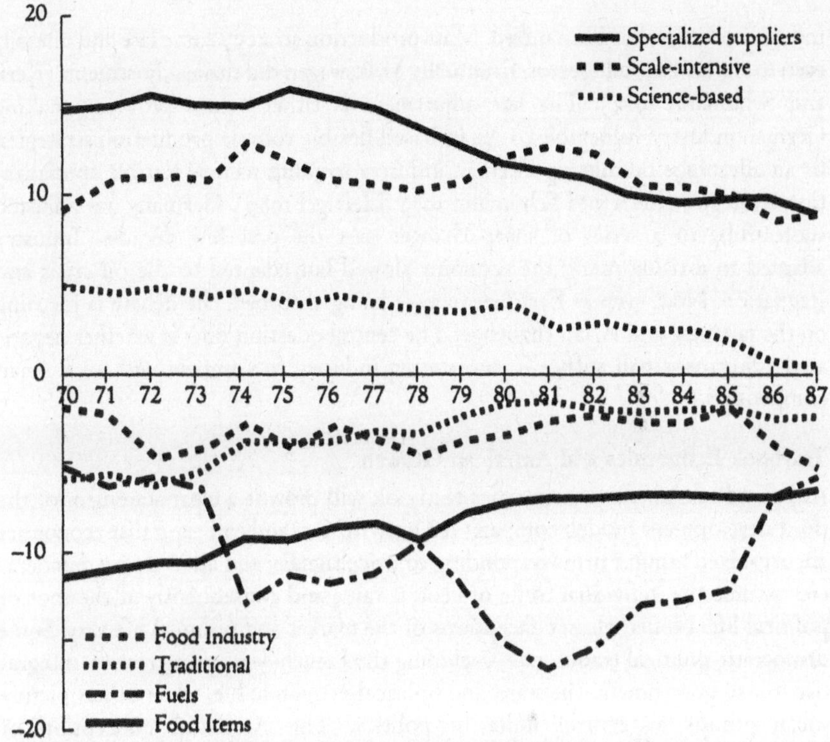

FIGURE 5.1 Patterns of West German trade specialization.
The indicator of the contribution to trade balance (ICTB) of a country with respect to a given group of products i is the following:

$$\mathrm{ICTB}_i = \frac{100(X_i - M_i)}{(X+M)/2} - \frac{100(X-M)}{(X+M)/2} \times \frac{(X_i + M_i)}{(X+M)}$$

X_i = total exports of country in the product group i.
M_i = total imports of country in the product groups i.
X = total exports of country.
M = total imports of country.

Positive ICTB values indicate those product groups whose positive contribution to the trade balance is greater than their weight in total trade (import plus export). Therefore, they represent comparative advantage sectors in the trade specialization of a given country. Opposite considerations are associated with negative ICTB values. The sum of the indicators with respect to the various product groups (i) is equal to zero (see CEPII 1983; figure adapted from Guerrieri 1991 and 1993).

industry position has been mixed. Mass production strategy came late and uneasily even to the automobile sector. Eventually Volkswagen did make adjustments (Kern and Schumann 1989). The late adjustment is either a new problem, making German industry vulnerable to Asian-based flexible volume production strategies, or an advantage permitting German industry to jump to new flexible specialization strategies (Kern and Schumann 1989; Herrigel 1989). Germany has adjusted successfully to a series of sharp changes over the past few decades. Industry adapted to a rising mark; the economy slowed but adapted to the oil crisis and stagflation. Now, even as East Germany is being absorbed, the debate is focusing on the Japanese and Asian challenge. The central question now is whether negotiated adjustment will suffice in supporting industry to compete with new Asian competitors.

Textbook Economics and American Growth

Any standard American economics textbook will provide a clear statement of the third development model: company-led growth. Certainly all capitalist economies are organized around firms responding to price signals, and all Western democracies assume the individual to be of central value and consequently at the root of political life. Nonetheless, conceptions of the market and political life vary. Some democratic political traditions—including the French—assign a creative, integrative role to government, the state, and political-economic life, while others picture social groups as central units in politics. The American conception of company-led growth is, then, a stark version of market capitalism and pluralist politics rooted in extreme notions of individualism (Hartz 1955).

In the American model of company-led growth, the government's only appropriate role is as an umpire assuring that rules are followed, and indeed even regulation itself is often viewed as an improper interference with market processes, benefiting a few at the expense of the many. Instead of social partners seeking common technical solutions within a politically agreed frame, there are interest groups that have to be beaten back to maintain the market. Instead of an *etatiste* or corporatist style of politics, we have classical pluralism. In this arrangement, the government cannot, and indeed should not, have a strategic view. Only the market can signal the economic future, and only pluralist interest groups competing in an open system can determine political values. Consequently, government action in the market can only mean distortion and inefficiency on behalf of arbitrarily selected objectives.

Thus, in this system of company-led growth with a regulatory state, the basic choices are made by individual firms without negotiation with government or other social groups. The result leaves workers or communities who are displaced or damaged to fend for themselves or to seek compensation as special interests making special pleas. The costs and gains of change are fundamentally allocated through the market. And because market outcomes are assumed to be legitimate, they are politically difficult to challenge. To be clear, there are analytic mechanisms for judging "market failure" and determining when private decisions based on prices do not express the best economic outcomes. Notions of "externalities"—gains not expressed in price signals to individual parties, or spillovers and linkages between activities that affect future prospects—are expressed in theory. Those notions, though, are not the core of the theory and are awkward to use in practice or debate. Above all, the government does not take a view of the long-run development of the economy, nor does it assume a developmental strategy other than to follow the market. All economic activities are judged by their current return, and future prospects are revealed, not created, so that a dollar's worth of semiconductors has the same inherent value as a dollar's worth of potato chips. The financial system, then, becomes a vehicle that allocates resources among competing uses, not an instrument for social negotiation or state intervention.

The American model of textbook liberal markets is a twentieth-century creation. This model was in fact very different in the nineteenth century, when there was an implicit, often even an explicit, strategy of development. America's de facto policy for industry now has three components. First, there is autonomy for corporate management, guaranteeing freedom from outside interference and particularly from government intervention. The extensive interchange and conversation between senior executives and the bureaucracy typical in much of the rest of the world is not present. Second, there is a basic consensus on the process of union management conflict and collaboration, a consensus which, though open to negotiation, has in practice reserved to management the right to select production and technologies and lay off workers. (America is sometimes said to have a comparative advantage in closing plants.) Third, although there has been principled opposition to national and international trade restrictions, in practice policy has accommodated demands for protection by specific troubled sectors. So, although a strategy is eschewed, there is an extensive web of ad hoc government policies that promote and control industry. The myriad efforts of state and local governments to promote their own firms or attract plants are not seen as an industrial policy. In a sense, then, America has a multitude of industry policies that compete with each other while it denies having any policy at all. And if industry policy is understood as a conscious federal strategy linked to tactics at the macro policy, regulatory policy, and sectoral level, then indeed there is no policy.

This "policy of no policy" rests on a set of structural features that constrain a government's executive discretion and autonomy and limit the instruments of intervention available. First, and critically, the apparatus of government divides powers and makes the system responsive to particular interest group demands. At the federal level the legislature has a remarkable control of detailed policy, and the weakness of the political parties fragments authority even further. The extensive authority of state and local government in central policy domains further decomposes the government as a unitary actor. The extent of the effective sovereignty of subnational politics is usually difficult for those outside the United States to fully grasp. Second, the decentralized and independent judiciary constrains executive authority, as it was designed to do. In essence, the judiciary is a third party introduced into the dealings between business and the state which cannot be controlled by the executive and may serve as a means for those outside limited alliances of government and business to enter into their dealings. Third, the financial system rooted in equity markets with power diffused into markets deprives the executive of an instrument that is important to state action in France and Japan. American policy sought to fragment markets and limit national banking precisely to avoid a concentration of financial power. The result, of course, is that government not only is disallowed instruments of direct intervention but also has no financial partners to develop or implement a policy for industry. The American system did, however, work effectively in the period after World War II. As the industrial and financial leader with the most developed economy, the United States did not require structural change to achieve its domestic purposes. The market was producing satisfactory results.

The entrenched patterns of American political economy have come under pressure from foreign competition in the past decade. That pressure was first felt in textiles, then steel, consumer electronics, and later automobiles. Now it is felt in advanced technology sectors—from semiconductors and computers through aircraft—as well as in finance, where the once internationally powerful American banks have been displaced as the dominant global players. The American response has been murky, in part because policy reaction has been to either deny that there is a problem or blame others for our troubles. This is expressed in part by the core policy strategy of the past decade—an aggressive strategy of unthinking deregulation which has provoked extremely expensive problems, particularly in finance. But we return to these issues later.

Common Problems, Diverse Solutions: The Institutional Structure of the Political Economy

The institutional structure of the political economy represents a set of capacities. When those capacities are appropriate to the tasks that must be resolved, growth and political stability unite. Real political difficulty often results when new tasks require new capacities. Consider the case of Britain. The first, and long the dominant, industrial power, it grew to preeminence in the nineteenth century with financial and political institutions suited for company-led growth. After World War II, however, it could not find a stable model of development. No longer a leader and on the slope of decline, the United Kingdom required a new solution—a new technical approach and a new political bargain. The efforts to create new capacities for either a state strategy of development or a more negotiated approach to growth shattered on institutional limits and the political problem of lifting those limits. Britain, which had been governed from the political center after the war, found the swirl around this issue radicalizing its political life as the extreme left and right captured control of the labor and conservative parties, respectively. Indeed, Margaret Thatcher represented a political resolution, her basic strategy being to recreate the conditions of company-led growth.

Let us recall the political-economic capacities that concern us: the government's institutional capacity to shape adjustment by setting rules and allocating resources selectively toward purposes it defines; the possibility of negotiations among the major producer groups; and the flexibility of the shop floor. As previously noted, these capacities rest on the character of the state, the nature of the financial system, and the arrangements of the labor relations system.

The Character of the State Differences in the character of the state—or, more specifically, the structure of the political executive—produce differences in the process of adjustment because such arrangements affect a government's capacity to construct a long-term economic strategy and mobilize economic resources to serve it. State-led strategies of adjustment require state structures that permit bureaucrats partial autonomy from parliament and from the interest groups attempting to influence them. Bureaucrats have both the legal discretion to discriminate between firms when implementing policy and the administrative and financial instruments to exert their will. Negotiated adjustment also demands a state with the capacity to formulate and implement a view of where the industrial economy should go. Without this capacity the state cannot be a negotiator, because it would have no notion of what to negotiate for. In market-led growth the state does not need a view or conception of industrial development.

A state structure's capacity for influencing strategic policy can be defined by four characteristics: (1) the method by which it recruits the national civil service; (2) the extent to which its power is centralized; (3) the legal extent of administrative discretion; and (4) its degree of autonomy from the legislature and interest groups. This last element, the degree of executive and bureaucratic autonomy, requires several comments. The place of the legislature and the character of interest groups are essential. The ability of the legislature to control the executive in a detailed way (as is the case in the United States but was not in France or Japan during the high-growth years) is certainly one element. But the nature of interest groups is also powerfully important.[13] In the pluralist model that prevails in the United States, interest groups can be formed spontaneously, passing demands from the populace up through the legislature. Consequently, intense policy pressures from these groups can constrain the state. At the other extreme, the state forms and authorizes interest groups, or promotes them by rewards or special policy access. This has been the case in France, Japan, and Germany at various times. In this case, the corporatist interest arrangements can serve the purposes of the government. The state executive's autonomy and influence is increased in circumstances where the legislature does not have detailed or effective control over the bureaucracy or where interest groups do not easily or autonomously form. The greater the degree of administrative discretion in making and applying rules, the greater the state's capacity for autonomous action.

The Nature of the Financial System The state cannot act in the economy without tools to implement its objectives. In some countries, the financial system acts as a hand to implement the will of the state; in others, it represents a clear barrier to state intervention. In the postwar years, certainly up through the early 1980s, there were three distinct types of financial system, each with different consequences for the political ties between banks, industry, and finance as well as different implications for the process by which industrial change occurs. The most crucial feature differentiating the three financial systems is how savings are transformed into investment and how those funds are allocated among competing users (Scharpf 1991). A complete picture of the systems would also need to elaborate how investments and loans are monitored and how bankruptcy is managed. The political implications of marketplace arrangements in the financial system are set by three elements: (1) Does one or several financial institutions exert discretionary power over financial flows, that is, influence who uses funds on what terms? (2) Is market power used selectively and intentionally to affect the decisions of firms or the organization of an industry (the alternative being that any market power is used simply to achieve financial gain rather than to influence industrial behavior)? (3) Can government employ the financial system or institutions as an instrument in its dealings with the industrial economy, either by discriminating between firms or sectors in granting access to funds or by creating financial packages that can be used to bargain with companies?

I consider changes in the financial system later. For now I note the three types. One is a capital market-based system with resources allocated by prices established in competitive markets in which security issues—stocks and bonds—are the predominant source for the long term. This model places banks, firms, and governments in distinct spheres from which they venture forth to meet as autonomous bargaining partners. A second model is a credit-based system with critical prices administered by government. Market relations are dominated by the government: administered prices, generating inherent disequilibriums in the market, provide the government a menu of discretionary actions it can use for varied purposes. The stock and bond market is not easily accessible to private borrowers, though it is often used by the government as a means of raising money for its projects. This state becomes a linchpin in the system of industrial finance; government is drawn in to bolster the system and to make the administrative choices about allocation. The borderline between public and private blurs, not simply because of political arrangements, but because of the very structure of the financial markets. A third model is also a credit-based system, but one in which a limited number of financial institutions dominate the system without themselves being dependent on state assistance. Markets, not administrative actions, determine prices, but the movement of prices in the markets reflects this concentration of financial power. In this model, the state pursues aggregate instead of allocative objectives, and it does so through market operations instead of administrative techniques. As a result, the financial institutions influence the affairs of companies through their lending power and their domination of access to securities markets. Government does not have the apparatus to dictate allocative choices to the financial institutions and consequently has no independent instruments in the financial system with which to influence companies. Banks, however, can serve as policy allies for government, on terms negotiated between the government and finance. To situate these models, the second and third are solutions to late development, whereas the first is tied to earlier industrial transformation. The market differences themselves become important elements in shaping the responses of each country to its present economic problems.

The Labor Relations System The institutional arrangement of the labor market, the character of worker representation and participation, sometimes labeled the labor relations system, is the other feature of the political economy important to our story. The role of labor both at the national political level and at the industrial level is an essential part of industrial restructuring, production reorganization, and technological change. In the past decade production reorganization and innovation have become viewed as critical elements in national industrial competition. Flexible production, which involves flexible work organization, seems to turn on labor's integration into managerial decision making, that is, substantial participation by unions or works councils in discussions with management regarding work reorganization before actual decisions on the new organization are made. This can happen as in Japan, through company-controlled unions and a labor movement that is weak in national politics; it can happen as in Germany, with a strong independent cohesive labor movement that has powerful legal rights to participate in management decisions at the company and plant while unions negotiate sectoral bargains; it can happen as in Sweden, where the powerful national political position is offset by substantial management rights within the company. As Lowell Turner argues, where unions are integrated into processes of managerial decision making, industrial relations practices have been relatively stable in the 1980s (1991:421). Strong effectively centralized labor movements are an essential feature of the negotiated patterns of industrial change, but labor integration into company decision making has apparently become essential in all countries. Price stability was the concern in the earlier period from the mid-1950s through the mid-1970s, and consequently the focus was on wage and benefits demands. The assumption was essentially that the key issue was keeping wage demands in line with productivity increases; the problem of production organization, though present, was of secondary consequence. The crucial question was how each of the several national political economies resolved this problem of setting wages and work conditions. In the 1980s and 1990s, of course, the issues become quite different.

Institutions, Governments, and Markets

Institutions do not adjust rapidly; political strategies do not evolve easily. To interpret the experience described in the previous section, we must understand clearly how institutions and market arrangements constrain national choices. I have already argued that the institutional structure—the foundation of each of these models of national adjustment—induces patterns of and sets national boundaries for government policy and corporate strategy. In each country, policy, corporate strategy, and arguably production organization have distinctive features that reflect those structures. The result is that countries and companies tend to do what they are good at. They tend to apply their distinctive capacities to problems, usually without regard to what will work effectively. Crisis occurs when there is a mismatch between task and capacity. These policy and corporate patterns are not immutable, but they are deeply entrenched. The institutions evolve slowly, radically altered only by political conflicts and the settlements that follow.

In this section I look more closely at the link between the structure and patterns of policy and corporate strategy. For convenience I focus on policies for industry in France and the policy and corporate strategies that led to the Japanese production revolution. Then, in the next section I turn to the mismatches that emerged in the 1980s between the tasks of a new era and the institutional capacities that had been built to respond to the problems of an earlier epoch.

Patterns of Policy in France

French political-economic institutions produced constant responses to a diverse set of industrial problems in the period from the end of World War II until the mid-1980s. A core strategy was implemented in four waves after World War II: initial reconstruction, modernization in the late 1950s and 1960s; management of outside structural adjustments in the 1970s; and the effort to reinforce the structure of state intervention and influence after the socialist victory in 1981. By that time, the governing socialists, led by President Francois Mitterand, had discovered the limits of a purely national development approach in Europe and therefore adopted a strategy of economic liberalization, producing a new political settlement and a reform of the institutional structure (Zysman 1977).[14] This in itself was an odd and unexpected outcome of years of socialist-communist alliance, but that is a separate story.

The core French strategy for industry has been evident. The French executive has the capacity to formulate and pursue an interventionist strategy: the executive has considerable autonomy from selective legislative interference; the administrative system is centralized with considerable discretion in its implementation of the law; and the financial system is under the influence of the state. Viewed from the vantage of a senior political executive, the French system could be understood as a series of circles of power and influence emanating out from a core defined by the prestigious Tresor in the Ministry of Finance. Beyond the core would be the parapublic banking institutions; beyond them, the commercial financial institutions. Since market relations among these groups were defined by the credit-based system of administered prices, each circle contained a series of instruments of intervention and influence in industry. The limits on that influence were defined by the political buffers of trade associations, which acted as insulation from state authority, and by the industrial structure, which consisted of noncompetitive, tradition-bound small firms that had been historically protected from foreign threats while competition was organized at home. Consequently, the state preferred large projects with goals that could be centrally defined and large institutions with which it could deal directly.

The French solution worked when the tasks at hand required the mobilization of resources, when it was possible to define a limited number of technological results, and when the competitive market could be suppressed, controlled, or oriented by the state. Success is evidenced by Ariane, Airbus, the TGV, and the Minitel system. The French strategies in competitive industries therefore concentrated on the means to control market signals and the creation of large domestic players to act in oligopolistic markets. But when France could neither dominate nor negotiate the markets, it simply suppressed market signals and insulated its firms, hindering their adjustment. To limit dislocation, the government encouraged growth by merger rather than by victory of the stronger, often leading to awkwardly structured and clumsy giants. Not surprisingly, the strategy did not work when a company had to rapidly adapt its products and processes to changing international market conditions. As a result, the French position in consumer electronics and now high-volume digital electronics has been weak, and its position in electronic components untenable. Overall, French trade reflects this pattern: it is strong in capital goods sectors and armaments, where government support is effective in developing products and selling goods; but consumer durable sectors are weak, since there these strategies are often harmful.

The pattern of French policy is evolving in the 1980s. Each of the elements of concern are changing: the character of the state is transforming in light of EEC integration; financial markets are liberalized and are evolving as France becomes more wealthy; the labor relations system has been altered by a decade of expanded socialist power and the decline of the Communist Party. Perhaps a new pattern will become clear only when the institutional structure of the new Europe is settled.

Policy and Corporate Innovation: Production Revolution in Japan

The institutional structure of an economy shapes not only policy but corporate strategy and, as a result, even production organization. Japanese interventionism produced a distinct pattern of policy and market response. The government acted, as suggested earlier, as a gatekeeper to develop the technology in an insulated market under Japanese control. Japanese policy produced intense internal competition, but the competition it created was managed and controlled. In this system of intense but managed competition, pursuit of market share was the best way to pursue profits (Tyson and Zysman 1989). This had two important consequences: production innovation in the firm combined with a search for technology around the world, and waves of excess capacity translated into dumping abroad.

Let us examine this situation more carefully. The logic rests on three aspects of the Japanese political economy. First, the Japanese market was relatively closed to the implantation of foreign firms. Consequently, competition was restricted to Japanese firms. Second, there was a rapidly expanding domestic demand. Financial resources channeled to expanding sectors by government policy permitted firms to satisfy demand by building production capacity. Third, foreign technology was easily and readily borrowed. Under these conditions, market logic encouraged Japanese firms to pursue market share aggressively as a means of maximizing profits—goals traditionally assumed to be contradictory. Formally, firms faced long-term declining cost curves. They could jump quickly from one product or process generation to the next by borrowing technology abroad during the catchup years of an expanding domestic market. That meant that as firms increased volumes—ideally capturing more market share in the expanding market—costs would fall, allowing prices to drop to increase sales, thus starting the cycle over. A firm borrowing product or process technology abroad could drive down its costs by steadily expanding production, and it could also capture both scale and learning economies by building pricing and building capacity in anticipation of demand. Borrowing again, it could start the process over. Faced with long-term declining cost curves, firms developed the ability to move new technology to market quickly, price and build capacity in anticipation of market, and implement rapidly what they learned as production expanded. These became basic characteristics of Japanese companies.

Because all firms sought to maximize market share by heavy capacity investment, excess capacity and excessive competition resulted. This in turn led to efforts to regulate competition which included creating cartels or production controls negotiated among firms. Equally important, constant efforts to import and develop foreign technologies created a basis for government-organized technology consortia, which likewise structured and bounded competition. None of these arrangements are stable, however, because, as Kozo Yamamura (1982) notes, the imperatives of pushing down the cost curve farther and faster will induce firms to break industry agreements or seek special advantage in consortia. Nonetheless, these arrangements have often served to bound or regulate the consequences of excess capacity.

The interplay of public policy and corporate strategy also affected trade and trade politics. Very simply, the pursuit of market share spilled over into international markets, as Yamamura (1982) and others have argued. Companies in Japan competed for market share, which required them to build production capacity in anticipation of demand. Excess capacity was almost inevitably the result (this excess capacity would necessarily be even greater with any market downturn). What would happen to that excess capacity? It would be sold abroad. Since much of the production capacity was then a fixed cost, the temptation was to sell at marginal production cost in foreign markets. As long as the domestic market was insulated and foreign markets open for sale of excess capacity, Japanese firms had a constant incentive to build in anticipation of demand and offload the consequences of overambitious judgments onto foreign markets. In fact, when the domestic market became saturated, a group of firms would begin to export at the same time. The result, in the phrase translated from the Japanese debate, was a "downpouring of exports." The sudden flood of exports into the major export market—the United States—caused intense political conflict with America in a series of sectors beginning with textiles and continuing through televisions, automobiles, and, later, semiconductors (see Johnson, Tyson, and Zysman 1989).

Market share competition pushed, then, in two directions. The effort by all firms to capture market share by building capacity in anticipation of demand inevitably resulted in bouts of excess capacity in the domestic market. That excess in turn encouraged firms, Yamamura and others argue, to sell abroad at marginal costs. The periodic battles over Japanese dumping are thus a function of the domestic pattern of competition in which market share is key.

With large protected domestic markets and access to borrowed technology, Japanese firms were encouraged to grow rapidly, to pursue market share, and to exploit increasing returns. The corporate practices fashioned in the era of rapid growth significantly affected the tactics of production organization in the factory. The key to organization became flexibility. Those Japanese firms that could organize themselves flexibly to capture the gains of introducing successive waves of borrowed technology had an advantage domestically. Competition among Japanese firms turned, in no small part, on manufacturing innovation and the introduction of new product. Consequently, firms were organized to sustain constant evolution in their production processes to improve productivity and sustain the flow of product. In fact, the particular strategies for production that emerged in Japan created distinct and enduring advantages in global markets.

Summary

This section suggests that, although the growth puzzle can be resolved in a variety of ways, the particular political and institutional solutions set down enduring patterns of policy and create a market logic that induces patterns of corporate strategy. Those patterns and strategies represent capacities for addressing categories of tasks. We have here looked at industrial intervention policies for two countries with state-led growth, but the same arguments about the particular influence of institutional arrangements can be made by looking at macroeconomic stabilization policies in social democratic political economies. These capacities are not immutable; they evolve slowly as institutions are restructured and as markets are recast. Developments occur with incremental reforms to institutions and market rules as well as with the more basic restructuring that results from the settlement of deeper political fights.

The obvious question, then, is what happens when there is a mismatch between structural capacities and the tasks at hand? If the tasks are not important, then the policy failures will be inconvenient, inefficient, and expensive but not central to the fate of economic growth or political stability. If, on the other hand, the new tasks are essential, affecting the capacity of the economy to adjust and compete, or the ability of politics to allocate the costs and gains of change, then the disjuncture may prove critical. Thus we next consider what happened to the models of adjustment built in the advanced countries after World War II when the tasks they confronted shifted dramatically.

Adapting to the Permacrisis

For two decades after World War II the advanced countries found solutions that supported enduring growth with political stability. Some were more successful than others. There were real battles and losers, let there be no mistake. That era ended sometime around 1970. Beginning perhaps with the French upheaval in 1968 and the Italian "hot summer" in 1969, but certainly by the oil crisis of the early 1970s, the old bargains began to unravel. The national postwar settlements and institutional structures were suddenly found wanting or inappropriate; the economic problems the advanced countries faced had changed. In search of new economic solutions and in response to changing domestic politics, the national systems began to transform. To capture the essence of the changing strategies of development, I proceed in two steps. First, I characterize some of the problems and pressures that have affected all the advanced countries. Then I review specific responses by the United States, Japan, and Europe. Note that suddenly we must consider Europe rather than the singular responses of France, Germany, and Sweden. That in itself is a dramatic shift. But most of all we find that clear, stable solutions—new definable models of adjustment—have not yet emerged.

The Permacrisis of the Advanced Countries[15]

Beginning in the early 1970s, a seemingly independent series of problems, crises, and disasters plagued the advanced countries, forcing them to alter the way they did business. The basic tasks of development and industrial adjustment were changing, and the adaptation was difficult. Highlighted here are several of these developments.

We start with the oil crisis of the early 1970s, since several processes were either first evident or amplified then. Politically, stagflation in the 1970s exploded the distributional settlements made in the preceding decades. The oil price increase of the early 1970s is itself best characterized as a tax by oil producers on the oil-consuming countries.[16] The question was who would pay the tax. Each social group's effort to avoid the tax, and force another group to pay it, generated inflationary pressures. Each country's political capacity to impose a distributional solution produced the basis for a return to macroeconomic stability (Lindberg and Maier 1985).

Stagflation and the distributional fights that followed the oil shock were common to all the advanced countries, but the politics in each was defined by preexisting political arrangements and divisions. In Britain, which had once been among the richest countries and was rapidly losing its position, inflation and rising taxes provoked radical labor responses as real take-home incomes stopped growing (Bacon and Eltis 1978). It became clear that those most organized would become the relative winners; consequently, Britain's white collar middle-class workers began to unionize (Gaster 1986). Strike waves suddenly swept not only industry but public services. Both conservative and labor governments would fall in the face of these conflicts until Margaret Thatcher finally imposed radical solutions that weakened the position of labor. For France and Japan, where the conservatives had managed industrial development, there was a common problem. In each case the conservatives' electoral support derived primarily from traditional sectors of peasants and small business. It was precisely these traditional groups who were displaced and whose worlds were transformed by industrial development. This political balancing act—the need to create political support in a newly industrial society—was made more difficult by the economic downturn in the 1970s which imposed additional stress on all. The Japanese LDP was able to manage this, but the French conservatives were not. In Germany, Sweden, and Austria, where a negotiated process of adjustment prevailed, the challenge of the 1970s was to maintain the bargaining processes while new macroeconomic solutions were sought.

At first glance, the inflation and slowed growth of the early 1970s formulated a new task: reestablishing macroeconomic stability by sticking to a more disciplined economic strategy (McCracken et al. 1977). Or, by extension, it was a matter of reestablishing, or modifying, the political bargains on which macroeconomic policy rested. But there was more: the macroeconomic crisis that began the 1970s had by the end of the decade become a matter of structural adjustment. Sustained growth increasingly required a fluid movement of resources from one sector to another. Then global competition amplified this pressure for structural adjustment. Those nations that could not make structural adjustments would be less competitive and face more difficult economic futures. Success in export markets, or lack of it, became for all countries important to maintaining employment and restraining inflation. Again, at the beginning of the 1960s and the beginning of the 1970s it appeared that national winners, the more successful economies, would be those countries that controlled wages and prices without disruptive political combat. Negotiated corporatism was in vogue in political debate. By the end of the decade, the key to success was competitiveness and adjustment.

The first part of the adjustment problem was tied to the oil crisis. The advanced countries had to focus on reorienting production both to sustain output in the face of the downturn and to export to pay the new oil bill. The painful oil readjustment was really only a one-time reorientation. But then new dynamics of international trade and competition, more permanent and structural in nature, were also revealed. It soon became clear that crucial assumptions about trade among the advanced countries were incorrect, and that a substantial reassessment was needed to understand the new, emerging patterns. In the 1960s and 1970s it was hoped that an expansion of *intraindustry* trade would permit countries to become interdependent and grow rich together. Everyone could have a car industry; Germans would buy Renaults and Americans would buy Volkswagons. Intraindustry trade was a congenial game that all could win. It would replace the earlier, nastier game of *interindustry* trade in which the British, for example, would specialize in textiles and industrialize while the Portuguese specialized in port and remained poor. Intraindustry trade promised to expand trade since technology was widely available and production costs would converge. Production costs among the advanced countries, it was believed at the time, would steadily converge as factor costs of labor and finance converged. Trade between nations would then be based on differences in national taste as producers specialized in particular niches. Fundamental structural adjustment—closing an auto industry or shipbuilding industry—would not be necessary. Trade would then be, if not frictionless, at least not politically disruptive. All countries would grow together, and consequently the goals and interests of all advanced countries could be accommodated if each bore the temporary pains of industrial adjustment. The original conceptions of interdependence, we should note, rested on these ideas; but these notions were, if not wrong, quite limited (Cooper 1968).

Production costs did diverge, for two reasons. First, labor costs diverged. As we all know, standard production technologies spread to a group of countries, of which Korea is one, which became known as the newly industrializing countries (NICs). These countries could initially enter a range of industries—from textiles through steel—on the basis of lower wages and lower production costs. Producers could then often combine their low-cost labor with subsidized finance and often protection. The advanced countries limited access to their markets, often using restrictions such as voluntary restraint agreements (VRAs) which encouraged new products in new locations and prodded existing producers to move to higher value-added market segments. NIC producers eventually moved to an ever wider range of products and to industries that included automobiles, automotive parts, and electronics. Firms in the advanced countries were constantly pressured to move into more defensible high-value niches by a range of means that included differentiating product, speeding product entry, and raising quality. And of course their competitors followed. The second reason for production-cost divergence was that innovation in production processes allowed some advanced countries' producers to gain an enduring advantage over competition.

So production costs did not converge, and technological advantage on which product and production rents were built could be created by government policy and corporate strategy. Instead of Japanese consumers buying Fords and Renaults, Japanese producers simply displaced production in America and then in Europe. The results were significant. The countries that most successfully adjusted and innovated became the most able to sustain growth over the next years. Those countries that did not adjust well found their positions more troubled. A related result was that this domestic adjustment often expressed itself in a very strong export position (Boyer 1990). In fact, a production revolution had begun that would soon affect the development and position of all the advanced countries.

By the mid-1980s it was clear that a profound revolution in the organization of production was under way. That revolution expressed itself in a series of operational codewords such as "flexibility" and "just-in-time production" and metaphysical historical codewords such as "post-Fordism." An evolution in production control clearly intersected the need to create new, more defensible high-value niches in world markets. Substantively new ways of approaching production which at once lowered cost, raised quality, and speeded up product introduction emerged. These innovations came from both Japan and Europe, Japan introducing forms of volume-flexible production and Europe introducing forms of flexible specialization in regional communities. While both forms represented new and important innovations, Japanese models proved the most powerful for international trade as a whole. Industrial adjustment and trade success, then, suddenly required recognizing, understanding, and implementing new forms of production. That required, as it turned out, a broad range of specific innovations from accounting changes to labor relations. In passing we must note, first, that these innovations were mostly generated in Europe and Japan, and second, that the United States was slow in adjusting and adapting to these developments (Cohen and Zysman 1987, 1988; Piore and Sabel 1984; MIT Commission 1990). The results are evident in global trade patterns (Guerrieri 1991). Importantly, these innovations seem most effectively introduced where labor is integrated into decision making, at least at the plant level, and where job tasks are broadly defined, which requires forms of labor-management reconciliation—again, at least at the plant level.

In the 1970s, also, it seemed that the world economy was going global, a conclusion that remains premature. But the economies, and their policymaking processes, did become more interconnected. For example, the oil crisis accelerated, if it did not actually cause, the development of global wholesale financial markets as the banks of the industrialized countries recycled the oil tax, that is, the deposited funds of the OPEC countries (Strange 1986).[17] Many analysts now hold that globalization, or at least the globalization of wholesale markets, then drove domestic financial liberalization, that is, the deregulation of the domestic financial markets (Meerschwam 1991). It is argued that price competition in international wholesale financial markets created disequilibria in domestic national financial markets, compelling national deregulation to create greater freedom of price movement. An alternate view contends that the national processes of deregulation demonstrated a very different logic, rooted in each case in national politics but justified by the economic ideology of deregulation pouring out of the United States.[18] In this view, markets were not deregulated but reregulated; the purpose of the regulator was often not to accommodate international financial markets but to influence the national place within those international markets. The outcome of the individual national deregulations and reregulations was an adaptation of national financial systems.

Even in Europe, where in principle a single financial market is being created, national retail financial channels remain firmly in place. Consider France. Following the decision in 1983 not to withdraw from the European Monetary System, the French socialist government took on a liberal market orientation. In the name of eliminating privilege (but practically to reduce the expensive state subsidies by removing the costly and contradictory layers of financial incentives) the French minister of finance radically reoriented and indeed liberalized its financial system. Or consider Japan, whose national system remains firmly in place. At its core, Japanese firms' high profits reduced their dependence on bank finance, deconstructing the development-based financial system. Rising government debt affected the terms on which banks and the Ministry of Finance dealt with each other (Yamamura 1982). Foreign pressures to open Japanese financial markets meant altering the terms of regulation. Some new form of regulatory structure, quite apart from any global financial pressure, was needed. The eventual resolution created the basis for a capital investment boom in the mid 1980s as well as an investment free-for-all. Finally, consider the United States, where an unconsidered belief in markets created the intellectual basis for a policy strategy of deregulation. Deregulation would itself increase financial market efficiency, the story went, though as it turned out—financial theory aside—deregulation did not increase the effectiveness of finance in supporting the real economy. Ideology and political purposes—as much as market pressures—changed national financial structure, readjusting markets to fit government notions of crucial problems and central interests. In sum, converging global wholesale financial markets and securitization of the process of transforming savings into investments have altered the national financial markets, but national markets remain, and national institutions and regulatory systems continue to be crucial to financial intermediation. Interconnected international financial markets were not a first step in economic globalization which would force national economies to converge, creating a more homogeneous, not simply interdependent, world. That convergence has not happened, but the broader debate surrounding liberalization and deregulation has been important.

Deregulation emerged as one political strategy for dealing with the problems of stagnant growth. But deregulation is a catchall phrase that expresses not only diverse national policies for varied sectors but also two quite different intents. Viewed one way, deregulation can mean the withdrawal of government intervention and regulation from market processes, leaving pure market processes to determine outcomes. Those outcomes, being market outcomes, are then assumed to be the best possible results. In reality, though, market rules are never eliminated, and market outcomes always reflect politically constructed institutional and regulatory arrangements. Viewed a second way, however, rules can be changed to produce specific outcomes, a process that should really be labeled reregulation, not deregulation. When those objectives are the intentional development of industry or the creation of an infrastructure that will support a more competitive industry, then we should refer to it as "developmental reregulation."[19] Thus in Japan the process of administrative reform in telecommunications is one of developmental reregulation to establish the infrastructure for the economy and help position firms in global competition.[20] In the United States, by contrast, a simplistic conception of deregulation has prevailed. The deregulation of American telecommunications is largely the application of antitrust laws intended to ensure a more competitive market place. Unfortunately, the results are an unthinking opening of the domestic market without negotiated reciprocity; an enormous experimentation with new telecommunication services; the risk that the most advanced new services will not be widely available; and the danger of an incoherent telecommunications infrastructure.

Regions and Nations in a Global Economy

National politics and national regulatory policies remain important even in a supposedly global and interdependent economy. A more global international economy is certainly visible in trade, direct investment, and finance. Yet the responses to the new competition are generated within particular places, not by world corporations that stand outside a home base, and the foundations of economies remain national, or at least regional. Multinational corporations and global financial institutions do not sweep away the national foundations of trade, finance, and technology. Perhaps someday that will happen, but not yet (Coriat 1991). To continue our discussion of the politics of advanced country economic adjustment, we must sketch the regional economic context.

The increasingly regional character of the global economy is now evident. It has emerged over the past two decades. We know that there are three increasingly coequal and distinct, though interconnected, regional economies. The United States/Canada and Western Europe each represents about 25 percent of the global GDP. In 1987, Japan plus the four Asia tigers represented 15.8 percent and were growing more rapidly than the others. Each of those regions trades predominantly and increasingly with itself. Numbers suggesting a general growth of international trade now disguise the even more rapid growth of intraregional trade. Europe has been coalescing as a trade and political region over the past three decades, a process that has accelerated in recent years. Japan has increasingly become the center of an Asian region constructed around Japanese trade and financial flows.

We must focus on the critical problems this regionalization poses for the dominant countries in each area. Consider the Japan-centered and increasingly yen-based Asian trade and investment region. By almost any measure, Japan rather than the United States is now the dominant player. The regional production network appears to be very hierarchically structured and dominated by Japan. Japanese technology lies at the heart of an increasingly complementary relationship between Japan and its major Asian trading partners. In 1987, MITI noted a growing tendency for Japanese industry, especially the electrical machinery industry, to view the Pacific region as a single market from which to pursue a global corporate strategy (Zysman and Borrus 1992). The crucial question here is whether the region will remain a staging ground for Japanese global corporate strategy or whether the other Asian countries can establish an independent position. Much will turn on Japanese trade and investment policies.

The European story must be understood in relation to the competitive advance of Japan and the difficulties of the United States. The European community was created after World War II when Europe found itself no longer at the center of the international system but rather a frontier and cushion between two new superpowers. There were two objectives of the original bargain in the 1950s: to contain Germany by binding it to the rest of Europe, and to restart European growth (Hanrieder 1989). In the 1980s, the real shift in the distribution of economic power was one of the sparks to reignite the European integration process. Plainly put, relative American decline and Japanese ascent forced European elites to rethink their roles and interests in the world economy. The United States was no longer the first source of leading technologies; in crucial electronics sectors, for example, Japanese firms now led the world. Moreover, Japanese innovations in organizing production and in manufacturing technologies meant that the United States was no longer necessarily the most attractive model of industrial development. In monetary affairs, some Europeans argued that Frankfurt and Tokyo—not Washington—were now in control. In short, shifts in relative technological industrial and economic capabilities were forcing European to rethink their goals and the means of achieving them (Zysman and Sandholtz 1992). In light of the weakening of the socialist/communist left, European elites searching for a new growth formula turned to market-oriented strategies. The details of the process leading to Europe 1992 are not important here. It is crucial only to understand what kind of issues will shape the options for the dominant European economies.

The third region is North America. Organized around the United States, the North American free trade region seems to be emerging from two quite different deals. The American-Canadian agreement brings together two complementary advanced countries that already have extensive ties. Though the American economy and population are each roughly ten times the size of Canada's, the institutional and economic matches are such that arrangements seem fairly straightforward. The second bargain, however, that with Mexico, raises several issues. After stymied growth in a debt trap created in the 1970s, Mexico is attempting a dramatic change in economic direction, shifting from an aggressive, state-sponsored import-substitution strategy to one focused on adaptation to global markets and a search for competitive advantage. This bargain proposes two advantages for the United States. First, Mexican migration to the United States, which creates serious social problems and direct budgetary costs, would potentially slow. Sustained growth in Mexico and an increase in Mexican incomes would relieve the migration into the United States (Hinojosa-Ojeda and Robinson 1991). Second, there are direct economic advantages. Some suggest that, since the Mexican economy is only 5 percent the size of the U.S. economy (its population is about one-third), it will have only limited consequences in any case. The Mexican-American bargain hinges on the expansion of the Mexican economy, which should in principle lead Mexico to import capital goods while exporting labor-intensive products. Integrating Mexico into a North American region should provide North American firms a more differentiated production network so that they can source more labor-intensive components within North America rather than Asia, thus creating their own regional base for global competition. But will things work out this way? Not necessarily. American capital goods have lost competitive position in global markets, and Mexico may subsequently purchase equipment from Europe and Japan while continuing to export standard industrial products to the United States. Labor displaced from labor-intensive sectors in the United States will not smoothly move to sectors requiring capital and education. In fact, recent studies suggest that because of the lack of skilled workers American firms have deskilled production—perhaps introducing a slide of declining wages and slowing productivity. The crucial question, then, is whether the United States will adjust upward toward a higher-skilled high technology economy—or slip, at least relatively, in international competition.

In each region, but most centrally in both Asia and North America, the regional "architecture of supply"—the structure of markets through which components, materials, and equipment technologies reach producers—is a central issue (Zysman and Borrus 1992). There are two questions: how does the structure of the supply base influence the competitive position of each region? what is the degree of autonomy (or, conversely, the extent of interdependence) of the three regional networks, and as part of that what economic/industrial influence (or dependence) exists?

For Korea, the implication of a regionalization makes its technology and market position in relation to Japan all the more critical. Will Japan, in effect, regulate Korean development by its allocation of markets and technology? Or can Korea develop an autonomous strategy?

Continuity and Change: The Response of the Advanced Countries

The American Strategy of Unregulated Markets The Reagan revolution was at its core a response to the era of stagflation. As an aggressive recommitment to a company-led strategy, it reasserted the image of untrammeled market competition. The movie image of the American nineteenth-century settlement is of the lone pioneer: Daniel Boone, moving west, the single gunfighter standing off the bad guys at the OK corral. The reality of the nineteenth century was the cooperation of wagon trains and the support of the government in agricultural and transportation development. There was a conscious development strategy of state support for settlement and industrial development. The movie image of the American twentieth century is perhaps of Horatio Alger or Henry Ford, the single entrepreneur creating a new world. But the reality of the twentieth century also included state support for the diffusion of agricultural technology (in the form of the Agricultural Extension Service) as well as the massive government support for the construction of national highway, air travel, and communications infrastructure. The movie image of the Reagan revolution was the freeing of industry from the heavy hand of regulation and taxation. In practice, the Reagan strategy has shattered the coalition for growth that for years subordinated distributional fights to a joint consensus for consumer-led growth. Whether measured by international competitiveness, domestic debt, international debt, family or manufacturing income growth, or income distribution, the past decade has not been the remarkable success hoped for. The central problems of American industrial adjustment have simply been postponed for a decade.

The Reagan argument presumed that the stagflation had been created by an extension of the state into the market. Substantial intellectual support was mustered for the notion that market processes were slowed, and the gears of the economy clogged, by selfish interest groups using government to capture private benefits (Olson 1982). Business had been unfairly burdened by unnecessary regulated costs that were disadvantaging them in international competition. In transportation, telecommunications, and finance, many felt that regulatory distortion was depriving the economy of real gains. Markets were conceived as a form of self-regulating natural phenomena that would produce the best of all economic worlds. This conception of the public interest fitted the self-interest of particular business groups, so a strategy of deregulation was adopted across a whole range of sectors. Rather than rethinking the purposes of regulations and creating a regulatory regime that would use competition as an instrument, deregulation expressed ideological zeal. The results have been, at best, mixed. Consider the case of telecommunications. Firms have become competition-driven, aggressively experimenting with new technologies and business strategies based on their development. The competition is not simply in long-distance voice and data networks or in equipment but also in local loops. Cable television companies will, if allowed by regulators, attempt to become alternate local phone companies. But the risk for the United States is substantial. Chaotic fragmentation of networks may keep the nation from capturing the full possibilities of twenty-first-century telecommunications technology despite the head start provided by the initial deregulation. Consider the case of finance. Deregulation has initially produced disaster—whatever the final balance sheet. By any measure, the several hundred billion dollar direct cost of the collapse of the American savings and loan system will have to be set against any gains of efficiency. Deregulation, as demonstrated by both of these cases—telecommunications and finance—did not increase gains, or it increased gains at the expense of structural health. Although these sectors found new competition, the lack of direction—the lack of cohesive, long-range strategy—produced outcomes arguably worse than those of the preceding regulatory era.

The second measure taken to spark an economic resurgence through private sector initiative was to reduce government expenditures and cut taxes so as to release investment. In principle, this would reduce the government deficit and raise private savings and investment. The tax cut was seen to be self-financing. Its proponents argued that the loss of revenue from tax cuts would be made up in part by expenditure cuts. More important, tax revenues would grow again with the economy and make up the losses. The reality, however, was a spectacular domestic deficit. The deficit then became a constant pressure to restrain domestic social spending. It also induced an influx of foreign capital to finance the deficit, which drove up the dollar's value, amplified the trade deficit, and weakened American firms. In the short run, the strategy financed a boom based on a government deficit, a new financing twist on a classic Keynsian strategy. Instead of an investment boom based on increased domestic savings, the United States was left with a consumption boom based on increased national deficits. In the longer run, the average growth over the past decade has not been higher than that of the decade before.

The United States is now in a critical political trap that makes it difficult to solve its policy problems. The country faces dramatic domestic/internal adjustments to new competition. This challenge will undoubtedly require investment in several areas: skills and health of the workforce, new products and production techniques, and infrastructures for the next century such as telecommunications. Yet there is no longer a political coalition for public, or private, investment. The tax cuts that financed a sustained expansion in the 1980s helped solidify a presidential electoral coalition that also elected Bush. Tax increases to support public investment would be difficult, moreover, because real incomes in the United States have declined; family incomes, which rose for a time as women entered the workforce, have now again flattened out. The slowed relative growth of the United States then becomes a barrier to the investments needed to rebuild the basis of continued development. The enormous deficit means that further unfunded expenditures cannot pay for the public investments. Only a new political coalition, organized within either the Republican or Democratic parties, can break the lock on America's trap. In sum, the United States responded to the 1970s by seeking to perfect an idealized image of company-led growth.

The Response in Japan The crucial question about Japan is whether the core of the Japanese developmental system of state-led growth is still in place, and whether, if in place, its use to create position and advantage for Japan disadvantages its trade partners. Has the old mold been broken or has adaptation simply updated the original strategy? The power of the Japanese economy created in the decades of fast growth (and the continuing level of investment at home and abroad which is entrenching advantage created in a diverse set of sectors) makes the domestic political choices of global interest. The concern outside Japan is that the basic developmental policy objectives remain, but that the instruments have become more subtle. The tasks of development may have changed, the argument goes, but the central purposes of the state and the society may not have.

Certainly there have been important changes. The balance of relations among government, industry, and finance in Japan has clearly shifted from the mid-1970s. The growing competitive strength and profitability of the firms unquestionably give them a new independence from both banks and government. Governments always have the most influence when firms are weak and need support; conversely, profitable firms that are competitive in global markets have the greatest independence from state influence. In the thirty years following World War II, Japanese firms were—loosely speaking—short of capital and technology followers, often depending on government and trading companies for a knowledge of foreign markets. Now these firms are among the strongest in the world, technology leaders in many fields, and marketing innovators in many countries. There are fewer things government can give or deny them. Yet government mechanisms for regulating competition, such as recession cartels in declining sectors, are still in place. In advanced sectors, the government tools of promotion remain pervasive and crucial to global market outcomes.

The politics of industrial policy have also changed, but a loosening of the developmental system does not mean government withdrawal from policies aimed at creating the market outcomes it prefers. Reform does not mean that the developmental system has simply been dismantled and that the government has simply assumed the role of umpire. It can simply reorient policy objectives and recalibrate policy instruments. Consider the reregulation and sometimes privatization (what the Japanese call "administrative reform") of a range of services including railroads, telecommunications, and finance (Vogel 1993). The railroads were privatized in part to shift labor conflict from the public to the private sector. Telecommunications were reregulated and Nippon Telephone and Telegraph (NTT) privatized—the reregulation serving a complex set of agendas and reconciling a set of competing political purposes (Johnson 1989; Yamada and Borrus 1992). The list of winners in the reform is long. The process led by

NTT to establish an integrated broad-band telecommunications network as the infrastructure for twenty-first-century growth was launched. Several industrial groups will gain a share of the network markets as competitors, albeit controlled competitors. Privatizing NTT removes telecommunications issues from government control, relieving direct trade and political pressures. On balance, promotional objectives in telecommunications are not eliminated, but the winners in industry and government are reshuffled. Similarly, the financial system was reregulated, not deregulated to approximate a liberal order. It was restructured to manage finance in the 1990s better. Part of those adjustments were successful. In the past five years, for example, Japan has invested $2.3 trillion in capital equipment for a new industrial era, adding to its industrial muscle. Moreover, Japan has not only reinvested its trade surplus abroad but also reorganized its domestic market and production position. It takes a special and focused analysis of Japanese finance to decipher the story, but several elements stand out amid the positioning for political and market advantage. Whether by calculated intent or accident, land has dominated the story. The financial foundations of Japanese banks were reinforced to meet Bank of International Settlements (BIS) standards, and the mechanism of doing so was revaluation of land. The land boom in turn permitted Japanese firms to raise borrowing. Increasing land prices then fueled a stock market boom, which raised values all around again. Recognized industrial players were insulated from speculation by their brokers. As of the fall of 1991, there were very few casualties and no real regulatory restructuring. On balance, though, financial reregulation looks very much like an effort to structure the financial system to carry the Japanese economy, under the continuing tutelage of the Ministry of Finance, into the twenty-first century. Even severe political and market abuses have not weakened the Ministry of Finance's control or created a truly liberal system.

At the core of the Japanese developmental system were the twin tools of promotion and an insulation. Mechanisms for promotion, formed in government-industry compacts, have not been abandoned, though their importance is diminished in many industries. Nor has the market been truly opened. Certainly the insulation has loosened and formal tariff walls are very low. Although manufactured imports have risen in recent years, the absolute levels of imports remain very low. In sectors where Japan has created defensible advantage in world markets (in other words, where entry for foreign firms is now most difficult), the Japanese markets are the least restricted. However, in sectors where Japan has lost advantage or sectors where it is attempting to create advantage, markets are much less open. Recession cartels and other restrictions limit sectors losing position; certainly in all countries, sectors in trouble receive protection from imports. But where Japanese firms are seeking advantage, the mechanisms of outright restriction—nontariff barriers—remain substantial (see Johnson, Tyson, and Zysman 1989). The character of business arrangements replacing outright government restriction is suggested by the corporate cross-holdings that emerged in the 1970s prior to market liberalization. Those cross-holdings protect firms against outside takeovers. Moreover, the list of firms compensated for market losses by investment banks in 1991 includes no foreign firms, suggesting both the continued, closely held character of Japanese business and the apparent exclusion of foreign firms from its critical inner circles.

On balance, the argument that the government still actively seeks to assist firms to create enduring competitive advantage in global markets and that domestic markets are still reserved for Japanese firms is supported by substantial evidence. Many of the elements of a state-led system of industrial development are still in place, even though the precise mix of policy and corporate strategy has changed.

Recasting the European Bargain Europe is in flux; policy processes are being profoundly altered. The European bargain has been recast by national governments seeking to adapt to the problems of a changed global economy and a suddenly altered security situation. Europe 1992 must be understood as an effort by European governments and business elites to meet the permacrisis of slowed growth and higher levels of unemployment; respond to the changing American and Japanese capabilities; and promote their collective position in the international order. The political economies of the European countries must now be understood as part of an increasingly important European structure. The national arrangements continue, and continue to matter, but they are being altered by the expanding reach of Europe. Before even thinking about the national cases, we must consider how the political-economic game has changed in Europe. There will be a European Monetary Union, but the form and governance will be settled over the next years. There will be some version of a European Political Union, but whether Europe will begin to act as a single protagonist in foreign and security policy will be decided only by the crises that are collectively addressed—or not—in the next decade. But it is not simply that the big questions are unsettled; rather, the dynamics of European and national politics are being reset.

European choices, both decisions made by the Brussels institutions and those made jointly by the governments outside those institutions, increasingly bind national choices. But the pattern of Brussels influence is varied and uneven. Brussels has more power in competition policy than in trade policy, more in monetary policy than in tax policy (Goodman 1991). Within the category of competition policy, Brussels has more influence over mergers than state aid. In trade policy, European positions are created in negotiation among commission and national governments. The 1979 creation of the European Monetary System of linked national currencies has forced a coordination of national monetary policy (though a single European central bank and common currency have not yet been adopted). But in tax policy the governments have retained a strong hold (Goodman 1991).

At the same time, the logic of national politics in each European country has been increasingly altered in important though diverse ways by the growing influence of Brussels. Policymaking in Brussels mixes together elements of intergovernmental bargaining represented institutionally (e.g., by the Council of Ministers) and of supranational governance represented institutionally by the Commission and the Court, which are only distantly controlled by Parliament and very distantly connected to any electorate. Who should national constituencies hold responsible? Critically, governments can use the ambiguity of responsibility at the European level and the lack of an electoral check to implement policies they favor but cannot implement within the constraints of national politics. A second consequence may be the unwinding of national corporatist bargains. In most European countries there are tight bargains between interest groups and the state, which in many countries involve labor; that is, government certifies particular groups as privileged interlocutors, which is an exchange of special status for influence. These national corporatist arrangements are dissolved, or at least weakened, by moving decisions to Brussels. No particular group will retain special status and all will have to compete as lobbyists. The result may be that diverse national interest groups will compete to influence policy in a competitive environment in Brussels rather than manage policy in corporatist bargains in their national capitals. A final example would be the possibility—not likely but a possibility nonetheless—that Europe will become a community of subnational regions as much as of nations.[21]

It is not simply the European evolution that is uncertain. The political development of several countries is also ambiguous. Consider Germany. With unification Germany becomes, at first glance, the dominant player in Europe. It has the largest population and the strongest industry, and it occupies historically pivotal geography between Western and Central Europe. But the first glance assumes a smooth transition of eastern Germany into the unified state. That, so far, has not happened. Indeed, a separate eastern identity may endure. The scale of the transformation has generated a budget deficit, trade deficits, stunning unemployment, and new concerns. The political bargain that allowed quick unification involved merging currency and labor rules, which suddenly made the east an unproductive and high-wage region. The costs of construction and reconstruction have been and continue to be astronomical. It remains unclear how rapidly the transformation can be managed, and more signs show Germany heading down the worst-case path: eastern German requirements sap investment and raise interest rates; higher interest rates drive up the mark, which raises export prices for German industry. Industry in western Germany, which has withstood similar increases, might not be overly troubled. But producers in eastern Germany (where productivity is in any case too low to support viable integration) are being devastated.

A closer look also suggests that the bargains and the bargaining process in German adjustment may be altered. The political basis of German negotiated adjustment has rested on a strong Social Democratic Party capable of governing on its own or in alliance with the centrist Free Democrats and a strong labor movement. That balance could be transformed by an entrenchment of a conservative hegemony based on the unification, a radicalization of eastern unemployed who have no clear attachment to the major parties, or (though less likely) an extension of union power that channels the discontent. At the time of this writing, speculation on the outcome is rife, but there are no clear lines of development. European competition and financial services rules may loosen the institutional foundation for bargained adjustment in Germany.

Likewise in France, the pillars of the traditional national model (in this case, state-led growth) are, if not eroding, at least taking different form. In fact, the past decade is a confusing saga. The 1970s saw slowed growth and high unemployment, which culminated in Conservative defeat at the hands of the Socialists in 1981. Socialist economic strategy first rested on an expansionary macroeconomic policy that would restart growth, thereby lowering unemployment and a commitment to nationalization which would hold the coalition with the Communists together while providing instruments for state-sponsored efforts to create globally competitive firms. The implementation of the policy of nationalization may have damaged the job possibilities of a certain segment of senior Conservative bureaucrats on leaving office, but it did not harm the middle-class stockholders and rarely changed the core of the management structure. Ironically, in many ways the real authority of the state was reduced. The strategy of expanded demand, implemented in a period of global downturn and American recession, had the consequence of sparking a trade deficit and currency crisis, which brought about a policy reversal that had the Socialists implementing the Conservative policy mix. So, by the mid-1980s the Socialists were cooking an odd policy brew of nationalization, demand restraint, and market liberalization. They came to power at the beginning of the decade advocating a nationally based strategy of state-led industrial adjustment and were leading the call for a European-centered policy of market shocks and demand restraint.

It simply is not clear how much of the French postwar *etatiste* apparatus and strategies will endure. Consider three diverse elements. First, postwar modernization strategies rested on a refinement of the state bureaucracy. It was not simply that its power was extended or its instruments refined. Rather, the state bureaucracy became the institutional bastion of the modernizing coalition through changes in recruitment and training. The fundamental task of supporting the market-driven shift of resources from agriculture to industry is completed. In developing an industrial policy, the state bureaucrats had considerable administrative discretion in applying law, increased their autonomy from the legislature, and preserved a tradition of status and influence. That discretion is now limited by Brussels, particularly in the arena of state aid and market access. Increased competition in the domestic market, moreover, limits the utility of state action. Yet the traditional role of the state as promoter and market maker continues in large-scale technology projects such as Airbus, the high-speed train, Minitel, and HDTV. And many of the French government's development strategies are now being implemented through Brussels. Second, the financial system has been reformed, making its prices more a function of market processes and reducing the pervasiveness of the influence of the state in the selective allocation of credit. The emergence of a commercial paper market, for example, limits the dependence of large firms on the banks. The state's role may be diminished, but it is not eliminated. Yet that role may be further diminished if new Continental reforms create even more integrated European financial markets.[22]

In sum, the European national growth models of the postwar years are all being recreated. For each there is the same, new fact—Europe. The expansion of policy and policy initiative in Brussels is dramatic and significant. The balance between national capitals and Brussels is yet to be set, and indeed the balance between nation and region may itself be altered. Equally, the economic dislocations of the past years have shaken the national models themselves, which is part of the reason the governments have supported the relaunching of the European idea. No new model—either at the national or European level—is yet in place.

Do the Models Still Matter?

Certainly the tasks of sustained growth and development have changed. The new, common problems to be resolved by the advanced countries include the reorganization of production the new industrial revolution demands, the reregulation of service and industrial markets, and the adjustment of domestic macroeconomic policy to a more integrated, but regional, world of trade and finance.

The particular countries are now experimenting to create new solutions. New models do not yet exist. But for the moment the original adjustment models still distinguish the national responses because they set the frameworks of national experimentation. The American policy pattern has been reinforced, but arguably without addressing—and indeed postponing—needed industrial and economic adjustments. The result may be a period of sharper and more sudden policy shifts based on possibly radical—and not clearly imagined—political bases. Japanese policies have evolved, as Japan has become richer, with the result that the interplay of government and industry has changed. But the developmental objectives remain the same. Europe is watching both the recasting of the bargain among nations and a reconfiguration of policy processes within them. The past decade simply emphasizes the intense difficulty of creating new "models" of political economy, the difficulty of both identifying the problems and creating new institutions and tools to address them.

Korean Choices: Inventing New Solutions for Growth

Let us return to where we began. What can Korea draw from the experiences of the advanced countries? Since my knowledge of Korean politics and economics is at best superficial, let me base my remarks on the core idea developed in this chapter. While there are a several alternative political strategies for growth, a successful solution must resolve the technical problem of how to move and reorganize productive resources, both within and between sectors, and maintain political stability while allocating the costs and gains of development. As the economic tasks evolve and political possibilities are redefined, mismatches between tasks and capabilities emerge. National development strategies must be adapted to refit policy capabilities to economic requirements. But those adaptations are difficult political moments.

Korea seems, from even my superficial understanding, to face several delicate junctures. Authoritarian development solutions that worked in an era of fast industrial growth may not provide either viable technical economic policies or effective political strategies today. The political problem seems evident. Economic development is the transformation of poor, rural agricultural societies into richer, urban industrial ones (failed development may, of course, leave a country urban but neither rich nor industrial). Korea's successful development has already transformed the society by creating urban working and middle classes, consequently transforming the political problem.

Political stability almost certainly requires that mechanisms be found to involve and incorporate the emerging middle class and labor communities into politics. The question is, on what terms, or rather whose terms, will that incorporation come? State-orchestrated development has generally involved conservative leadership structuring the terms in which labor, and often the mass political community in general, participates in politics. In the late nineteenth century, the Prussian leader Bismarck created the first self-conscious welfare system, shocking his conservative allies, precisely to tempt the emerging working class to forsake its political ambitions for material advantage. In the mid-twentieth century, Japanese leadership managed to orchestrate party politics and labor organization to limit the direct voice of the labor movement in forming governments and making policy. But labor in Japan has gained real influence in wage formation, real participation in work reorganization, and very substantial material gains. There has been real incorporation at the firm level if not at the political level. In France, by contrast, we have seen that long-standing social rifts, ideological confrontations, and sharp divisions within labor prevented the Conservatives from implementing a similar strategy of co-optation and integration of labor into a Conservative-dominated society. The tense confrontational atmosphere in large-scale industry complicated French development and finally contributed to political realignment. Stability and growth in Conservative-led development has required substantial material gains and even an entrenched place in the processes of wage and work formation. By contrast, the societies with a negotiated style of adjustment—in this chapter, Sweden and postwar Germany—have empowered highly organized labor and business groups. True corporatism involves real political positions for labor. The problem for Korea is not just one of political stability and order.

The evolving economic tasks sharpen the political choices. Let us consider three issues.

1. As I argued in the previous section, a profound transformation in industrial production is altering the dynamics of international competition. The codewords of the transformation have become flexibility and speed. The new production model allows producers to gain static flexibility (the capacity to produce a range of products from a single process) and dynamic flexibility (the capacity to advance the process and introduce new product more quickly). At the same time, quality, measured in such forms as defects, is raised and costs often reduced. The production transformation at its core is not technological but rather emerges from new understandings of the production problem, new conceptions of how to organize work, and new notions of how to link steps in the production process. We are watching, as one IBM engineer remarked, a shift in paradigms about what is to be done and how to do it. Now highly automated versions of flexible volume production are emerging, but the technology serves to amplify the power of the new paradigms. It is the new paradigms, not the technologies that implement them, that are core. Product variety and speed to market are capabilities firms use to carve up standard markets into groups of niche markets. The capital-intensive volume production strategies used to force entry into standard goods markets are becoming obsolete; producers who do not adapt will be perpetually forced into low value-added segments of important sectors.

On the surface, responding to this shift in production paradigms is a technical task, but more fundamentally it is proving to be a social and political matter of the place of labor and small firms in production and politics. This revolution in production demands the effective integration of labor into production. The classic image of a shop steward's control of recalcitrant workers to extract surplus value simply evaporates (Lazonick 1990). The images that guide us must become ones of labor collaboration, responsibility, and, of necessity, trust. Endemic confrontation becomes an impediment to the continuous adjustment and adaptation that flexible production requires. Shop floor peace is necessary but not sufficient; broad job definitions, worker initiatives, and toleration for reorganization are needed. Skilled workforces become key to decisions about how to organize production and arrange the process of product development. Labor must be committed to the effective functioning of the production system to maintain and improve rapidly adjusting production processes and implement constantly shifting product mixes. Effective links from shop floor to strategic management are ultimately required. Japanese firms have managed to incorporate labor into production and planning while excluding them from political power or formal corporate position. In Germany, a strong industrial union movement and formal labor rights in corporate governance complement a strong Social Democratic Party capable of governing. A political settlement must achieve more than simply labor acquiescence and political stability; it must assure the labor foundations for flexible volume production.

2. Networks of small to mid-size firms provide an important element of the networks of suppliers that create the basis of production flexibility so essential in global markets. In Germany, Japan, and Italy these small firms were dismissed twenty years ago as anachronisms of an earlier capitalism, anachronisms that survived with subsidy and would eventually vanish (Berger and Priore 1980). Now they are admired as elements of just-in-time supply networks or flexible specialization. These smaller firms adapted to the needs of the new production organization and provided flexibility in the economy as a whole. This adaptation was facilitated by policies and programs as diverse as robot leasing firms, regional banks, and trade associations acting as technology brokers. Will Korea manage to find a policy balance to support large firms that provide muscle in international competition and smaller firms that create crucial flexibility? This, of course, comes to central policy choices: what will be the political and market role of the large firms and what purposes will financial reregulation pursue?

3. The global economy has become increasingly regional, and the Asian region has become increasingly centered around Japanese finance and technology. If the three major trade groups begin to cordon themselves off in competition, creating some version of a twenty-first-century neomercantilism in which the prize is an advantage in development, then Korea's position within Asia and its ties to Europe and Japan may become all the more critical. The problem, simply put, is this: how can Korea avoid dependence on the strongest regional power, Japan? This is partly a matter of product development, partly one of markets for exports, and partly one of technology access and development. One approach might be development alliances for advanced products with European and American firms, with individual product arrangements embedded in joint market strategies that permit partners to understand the longer-term mutual gain. Korea may represent a volume production platform for European companies having difficulty in the American market. Possibilities for such alliances might exist in sectors such as electronics and cars.

We return at the end to what seems to this observer to be the central issue. The Korean domestic political problem is altered by the social transformations industrialization has brought. Political strategies that permitted the state to influence both the course of economic growth and the distribution of the gains of development must be adapted to accommodate the emerging middle and working classes. The alternative is confrontational politics that undermines or derails growth. At the same time, economic strategies that emphasized capital-intensive volume production of standard product must be reconsidered. As the twenty-first century unfolds and high-technology products are rapidly introduced to the market by skilled workforces, the integration of labor into corporate operations will prove even more crucial than in the past. For once, the political imperative and the economic necessity are the same.

NOTES

1. That is, as a government fails to reconcile the claims on its resources, it simply prints more money. See Lindberg and Maier (1985).

2. Reported to me by Fernando Saboya de Castro.

3. Political scientists now debate how to characterize these relationships, using notions such as the strong or weak state, "policy compacts," state-led growth, developmental system, and corporatism. Rarely, however, do they try to establish that these institutional relationships, by whatever characterization, shape market behavior. Economists, by contrast, generally ignore or caricature the role of institutions and proceed with their analysis either as if institutions did not exist and history did not matter or by reducing the role of institutions to an arrangement of transactions and the roots and processes of historical development to the jargon of historisis.

4. There is a progression in each national case from the emergence of the industrial economy through a series of major economic and political crises. The functions and logic of the institutions of a political economy are a product of how they were created and evolved. The institutional structure, the institutions of the market, forms the artifacts for an archeology of these economies so that we can understand their dynamics and the shifting matches of tasks and capacities.

5. Seen in this way, variation in the power of social groups accounts for policy and economic outcomes within each national economy or adjustment model rather than distinguishing between them. Changes in social power within a society are reflected by changes in the groups that benefit from policy, but those changes do not easily alter the basic political processes associated within industrial change in the advanced countries.

6. During World War II, significant elements of the elite collaborated with the Nazi occupiers or worked with the puppet Petain government. After the war, in a political vacuum and before groups rooted in the traditional economy could reorganize themselves, Charles de Gaulle, the one national symbol of French resistance, established new state institutions committed to growth.

7. When the Fourth Republic was constituted, and de Gaulle withdraw from politics for a decade, the traditional economic groups reestablished their political position.

8. As important, deep divisions ran through society. Fights about the very character of French society dating from the French Revolution in 1789, fights that divided both the left and the right, rose to the surface of French political life.

9. There are many analyses of this issue. My favorite is Johnson (1981).

10. To that I would add that the failure to find a technical solution in the first round of effort need not lead to antagonistic and disruptive actions by the individual actors.

11. The final complexity is that German domestic politics and the politics of the economy have been profoundly shaped and constrained by the effort to reconstruct postwar Europe. One of the purposes of the creation of the European Economic Community was to contain Germany, and part of the German objective in forming the Community was to bind itself to the West. Adenauer's commitment to national unification was a check that he never expected to cash, but one that was honored with great political gain by Kohl nearly forty years later.

12. The capital equipment and heavy industry orientation, though, may have created a line of technology oriented away from the flexible volume production that has formed the core of Japanese production strategy.

13. The clearest estimate of this is made in the introduction of Berger (1981).

14. The same position was adopted by the Review of French Innovation Policies (1986).

15. My thanks to my colleague Steve Cohen for this adaptation of his title.

16. For non-oil-producing developing countries with limited capacity to expand exports to pay the tax, the burden was certainly the greatest. But it did create serious problems in each advanced country.

17. The emerging Eurocurrency markets expanded as the funds of the OPEC countries were moved about, ultimately connecting wholesale money markets around the world. When Citibank's view that sovereign nations would not default on loans proved painfully wrong, the American banks retreated. The statistics of trade and finance became understood more widely: despite global wholesale profits, banks remained rooted in their national economies. The global position of these banks rested on the investment of the national trade surplus, on the support of the nation's industrial firms, and—in general—on their domestic deposit base. The retreat left European and Japanese banks the global giants (see Wellons 1987).

18. For a different version of this, see Vogel (1989).

19. Michael Borrus was among the first to use this phrase.

20. Steven Vogel's doctoral dissertation "Changing the Rules: The Politics of Regulatory Reform in Comparative Perspective" (1992), is a remarkable piece of work on this subject; see also Johnson (1989) and Yamada and Borrus (1991).

21. Because of the funds Brussels offers, some regional groups seek to bypass their national capitals. Regional autonomy is, in fact, routinely increased when the local authorities, as in Germany, already have the capacity and responsibility for policymaking. The national government continues to intermediate when authority is more centralized. For example, the Basques in Spain actively seek autonomy from national authorities. In some cases national governments resist EC intervention as part of a broader political drama.

Reinforcing a tendency toward regional responsibility is the fact that many of the most innovative dynamic segments of European industry are concentrated in regional agglomerations such as Prato in Italy or Bad Wurstenberg in Germany. These industrial districts consist of horizontal connections among firms that cooperate to provide an infrastructure even as they compete in international markets. These regional interests are potentially creating new political attachments.

22. Several comments cannot be incorporated in the text but should be made. First, the Conservative defeat was triggered by a strategy of economic management that emphasized the necessity of policy discipline to return to the orderly normal growth of the 1960s, a strategy that over time developed a political tone of conflict and confrontation. The left exploited that tone to give credence and meaning to its ideology of class conflict. Second, Mitterand was faced with two choices when his initial policy failed: the Socialist-left's aggressive national strategy that demanded abandoning the EMS and many other European commitments, or an imitation of the Conservative policy. Mitterand chose the latter. That policy decision also meant a political break with the Communists. Third, the modernizing coalition began to erode after deGaulle's defeat in 1969, and by the time of the victory of the Socialists in 1981 the political base of the Gonservatives had narrowed dramatically. Now the base and reach of the Socialist Party dwindles, and its rival but ally to the left collapsed as a political force long before the fall of the Berlin Wall. In fact the collapse of the Communist Party has directly fed the emergence of the racist National Front and the demagogue Le Pen. The nature of the next political settlement, the basis of the next enduring governing coalition, and the policy strategies that coalition may follow are not at all clear.

REFERENCES

Bacon, Robert, and Walter Eltis. 1978. *Britain's Economic Problem: Too Few Producers*. London: Macmillan.

Berger, Suzanne, ed. 1981. *Organizing Interests in Western Europe*. New York: Cambridge University Press.

Berger, Suzanne, and Michael Piore. 1980. *Dualism and Discontinuity in Industrial Societies*. Cambridge: Cambridge University Press.

Boyer, Robert. 1990. *The Regulation School*. New York: Columbia University Press.

CEPII. 1983. *Economie mondiale: La montéé des tensions*. Paris: Economica.

Cohen, Stephen, and John Zysman. 1987. *Manufacturing Matters*. New York: Basic Books.

Cohen, Stephen, and John Zysman. 1988. "Manufacturing Innovation and American Industrial Competitiveness." *Science* 239 (4 March): 1110–1115.

Cooper, Richard N. 1968. *The Economics of Interdependence: Economic Policy in the Atlantic Community*. New York: McGraw Hill.

Coriat, Benjamin. 1991. "Globalization and Production." Berkeley Roundtable on the International Economy (BRIE) Working Paper no. 45. Berkeley, Calif.: BRIE.

Economic Statistics 1900–1983. 1985. Pindar Group.

Economist. 1991. "The Wallenbergs: The Empire Strikes Back." *Economist* 318 (March 2): 62–63.

Gaster, Robin. 1986. "The Politics of White Collar Unionism in Great Britain." Ph.D diss., University of California, Berkeley.

Gerschenkron, Alexander. 1962. *Economic Backwardness in Historical Perspective.* Cambridge: Belknap Press.

Goodman, John. 1991. "Political and Social Changes in the 1990s." In Norman Ornstein and Mark Perlman (eds.), *The United States Faces a United Europe.* Washington, D.C.: American Enterprise Institute.

Guerrieri, Paolo. 1991. "Technology and International Trade Performance of the Most Advanced Counties." Berkeley Roundtable on the International Economy (BRIE) Working Paper no. 49. Berkeley, Calif.: BRIE.

Guerrieri, Paolo. 1993. "Patterns of Technological Capability and International Trade Performance: An Empirical Analysis" In M. Kreinin (ed.), *The Political Economy of International Commercial Policy: Issues for the 1990s.* London: Taylor and Francis.

Hanrieder, Wolfram. 1989. *Germany, America, Europe: Forty Years of German Foreign Policy.* New Haven: Yale University Press.

Hartz, Louis. 1955. *The Liberal Tradition in America.* New York: Harcourt Brace.

Herrigel, Gary. 1989. "Industrial Order and the Politics of Industrial Change." In Peter Katzenstein (ed.), *Industry and Politics in West Germany.* Ithaca: Cornell University Press.

Hetman, Francois. 1969. *Les secrets des geant Americans.* Paris: Seuil.

Hibbs, Douglass. 1987. "On Political Economy of Long Run Trends and Strike Behavior." *British Journal of Political Science* 8:153–175.

Hinojosa-Ojeda, Raul, and Sherman Robinson. 1991. "Alternative Scenarios of U.S.–Mexico Integration: A Computable General Equilibrium." U.S. Department of Agricultural and Resource Economics Working Paper no. 609 (April).

Johnson, Chalmers. 1982. *MITI and the Japanese Miracle.* Stanford: Stanford University Press.

Johnson, Chalmers. 1989. "MITI, MPT and the Telecom Wars: How Japan Makes Policy for High Technology." In Chalmers Johnson, Laura D'Andrea Tyson, and John Zysman, *Politics and Productivity: The Real Story of Why Japan Works.* New York: Ballinger.

Johnson, Chalmers, Laura D'Andrea Tyson, and John Zysman. 1989. *Politics and Productivity: The Real Story of Why Japan Works.* New York: Ballinger.

Johnson, R. W. 1981. *The Long March of the French Left.* London: Macmillan.

Katzenstein, Peter. 1985. *Small States in World Markets.* Ithaca: Cornell University Press.

Katzenstein, Peter. 1987. *Policy and Politics in West Germany.* Philadelphia: Temple University Press.

Katzenstein, Peter, ed. 1989. *Industry and Politics in West Germany.* Ithaca: Cornell University Press.

Kern, Horst, and Michael Schumann. 1989. "New Concepts of Production in West Germany." In Peter Katzenstein (ed.), *Industry and Politics in West Germany.* Ithaca: Cornell University Press.

Lazonick, William. 1990. *Competitive Advantage on the Shop Floor.* Cambridge: Harvard University Press.

Lindberg, Leon, and Charles S. Maier, eds. 1985. *The Politics of Inflation and Economic Stagnation: Theoretical Approaches and International Case Studies.* Washington, D.C.: Brookings Institution.

McCracken, Paul, et al. 1977. *Towards Full Employment and Price Stability.* Paris: OECD.

Martin, Andrew. 1984. "Trade Unions in Sweden." In Peter Gourevitch (ed.), *Union and Economic Crisis: Britain, West Germany, and Sweden.* London: Allen and Unwin.

Meerschwam, David M. 1991. *Breaking Financial Boundaries: Global Capital, National Deregulation, and Financial Services Firms.* Boston: Harvard Business School Press.

MIT Commission. 1990. *Working Papers of the MIT Commission on Industrial Productivity.* Cambridge: MIT Press.

Okimoto, Daniel. 1989. *Between MITI and the Market.* Stanford: Stanford University Press.

Olson, Mancur. 1982. *The Rise and Decline of Nations.* New Haven: Yale University Press.

Organisation for Economic Co-operation and Development (OECD). 1991. *Historical Statistics 1960–1989.* Paris: OECD.

Pempel, T. J. 1978. "Japanese Foreign Economic Policy, the Domestic Bases for International Behavior." In Peter Katzenstein (ed.), *Between Power and Plenty.* Madison: University of Wisconsin Press.

Piore, Michael, and Charles Sabel. 1984. *The Second Industrial Divide.* New York: Basic Books.

Prestowitz, Clyde. 1988. *Trading Places: How We Allowed Japan to Take the Lead.* New York: Basic Books.

Readman, Peter. 1973. *The European Money Puzzle.* London: Joseph.

Review of French Innovation Policies. 1986. *French Examiners Report.* Paris: OECD.

Scharpf, Fritz. 1991. *Crisis and Choices in European Social Democracy.* Ithaca: Cornell University Press.

Servan-Schreiber, Jean Jacques. 1968. *The American Challenge.* New York: Atheneum.

Shonfield, Andrew. 1965. *Modern Capitalism: The Changing Balance of Public and Private Power.* London: Oxford University Press.

Stalk, George, and James Abegglan. 1985. *Kaisha: The Japanese Corporation.* New York: Basic Books.

Strange, Susan. 1986. *Casino Capitalism.* Oxford: Basil Blackwell.

Thelen, Kathleen. 1991. *Union of Parts.* Ithaca: Cornell University Press.

Turner, Lowell. 1991. *Democracy at Work: Changing World Markets and the Future of Labor Unions.* Ithaca: Cornell University Press.

Tyson, Laura D'Andrea, and John Zysman. 1989. "Developmental Strategy and Production Innovation in Japan." In Chalmers Johnson, Laura D'Andrea Tyson, and John Zysman, *Politics and Productivity: The Real Story of Why Japan Works.* New York: Ballinger.

Vittas, Dimitri, ed. 1978. *Banking Systems Abroad.* London: Inter-Bank Research Organization.

Vogel, Steven. 1989. "Japanese High Technology, Politics and Power." Berkeley Roundtable on the International Economy (BRIE) Research Paper no. 2. (March). Berkeley, Calif.: BRIE.

Vogel, Steven. 1993. "The Politics of Regulatory Reform in the Advanced Industrial Countries." Ph.D. diss., University of California, Berkeley.

Webber, Douglass. 1990. "Institutions, Structures, and the Intermediation of Interests under the Christian-Liberal Coalition in West Germany." Paper presented to the Institutions, Structures, and Intermediation of Interests ECPR Joint Sessions, Bochum, West Germany, April 2–7.

Wellons, Philip. 1987. *Passing the Buck: Banks, Government, and Third World Debt.* Boston: Harvard Business School Press.

Yamada, Takahiro, and Michael Borrus. 1992. "Change and Continuity in Japan's Telecommunications Policy." Berkeley Roundtable on the International Economy (BRIE) Working Paper no. 57. Berkeley, Calif.: BRIE.

Yamamura, Kozo, ed. 1982. *Policy and Trade Issues of the Japanese Economy*. Seattle: University of Washington Press.

Zysman, John. 1977. *Political Strategies for Industrial Order*. Berkeley: University of California Press.

Zysman, John. 1983. *Government, Markets and Growth*. Ithaca: Cornell University Press.

Zysman, John, and Michael Borrus. 1992. "Industrial and American National Security." In Wayne Sandholtz, John Zysman, and Michael Borrus (eds.), *The Highest Stakes: The Economic Foundation of the New Security System*. London: Oxford University Press.

Zysman, John, and Wayne Sandholtz. 1992. "Europe's Emergence as a Global Protagonist." In Wayne Sandholtz, John Zysman, and Michael Borrus (eds.), *The Highest Stakes: The Economic Foundation of the New Security System*. London: Oxford University Press.

PART III

THE TAX SYSTEM

Chapter 6

Tax Policies and Institutional Reform

Chong Kee Park
Inha University

Introduction

This chapter concerns one aspect of institutional change—the development of the tax system in Korea. I have two objectives: to examine tax reforms and their consequences in Korea during the modernization period, and to evaluate Korean tax policy options for the future. Tax reform in Korea is an ongoing process of trying to keep up with the rapidly changing economic structure and social policies. I also attempt to differentiate and compare international variations in tax policy changes in Korea and other industrial countries, particularly Japan, with a broad objective of offering some generalizations about the sources of international differences in the development of tax systems that will be instructive for Korea as well as other developing countries.

Evolution of the Tax System in Korea

There have been three important and distinct periods in the evolution of the Korean tax system since the beginning of rapid industrialization in the early 1960s: (1) the decade of the 1960s, which included the 1961–64 period of disruption and two epoch-making tax reforms; (2) the economic adjustment period of the 1970s, highlighted by the oil crises and two economic emergency measures; and (3) the economic restructuring and stabilization of the 1980s with limited tax reforms. The objectives and successes of tax reform have differed between these periods. Therefore, I analyze the general characteristics of tax changes and the types of institutional reforms undertaken since the early 1960s with reference to the specific problems pertaining to each period.

Tax Reform during the 1960s

The period 1961–64 was one of sociopolitical upheaval and drastic change in economic policy. The military government that came to power in 1961 adopted an expansionary policy and launched the ambitious First Five-Year Economic Development Plan in 1962, which resulted in rapid increases in government expenditures.

The 1961–64 disruption period is often referred to as a time when the foundations were laid for a more permanent contribution of tax policy to the development process. During this disruption period the tax/GNP ratio declined from 12 percent in 1960 to 7.2 percent in 1964. Data presented in Table 6.1 clearly indicate that after 1962 the growth of tax revenues failed to keep pace with rising levels of price and GNP in this period.

The weakening position of taxation in the fiscal system was a cause of major concern for government tax officials and planners. The government was also faced with a sharp decline in receipts from foreign aid during this period. Implications for tax and fiscal policies were clear. Beginning from such a low level of tax revenue and having given itself the mandate to substantially increase the tax share of GNP over the planning period, the government would have ample opportunity to reshape the tax structure in a short period of time. This it did through a series of tax reforms and institutional changes. First, the government overhauled the organizational structure of tax administration and considerably improved tax enforcement. Second, there was a comprehensive and productive reform in the structure of the tax system.

The Tax Reforms of the 1960s and Their Impact on Revenue As in many other developing countries, lack of compliance, corruption, and inept administration have been persistent problems in the tax system of Korea. Recognizing that improved administration is an important element of tax reform, the military government that came into power on 16 May 1961 began to work on structural tax reforms and measures to improve tax administration. To encourage voluntary taxpayer compliance, the Tax Collection Temporary Measures Law and the Tax Delinquent Special Measures Law were enacted, whereby the government relinquished all existing claims to penalties for past tax delinquencies but pledged to deal more stringently with future delinquencies. In addition, a tax reduction was allowed for voluntary filing of tax returns. To assist taxpayers in filing voluntary tax returns, a tax accountant system was instituted through enactment of the Tax Accountant Law. Additional measures included the strengthening of the tax withholding system, the reorganization of regional tax offices, and the screening and retraining of tax officials.

In December 1961 the military regime undertook tax reform through extensive revisions in the tax laws. The basic objectives of this reform as set forth by the government were (1) to simplify the tax structure in order to promote voluntary compliance; (2) to improve the tax yield and elasticity of the tax system; (3) to redesign the tax system to promote savings and investment; (4) to bring about a more equitable distribution of the tax burden; and (5) to increase local government tax revenues (ONTA 1967:9).

Although the 1961 tax reform was extensive in nature and coverage, additional revisions and minor changes in tax laws have been enacted almost every year since

Table 6.1
Tax revenues, growth rates, and inflation, 1960–65

	Tax revenue as % of GNP			Nominal GNP growth rate (%)	GNP price deflator (1965 = 100)	Inflation rate (% per year)
	National taxes	Local taxes	Total tax revenue			
1960	11.1	0.9	12.0	11.6	41.9	9.1
1961	8.7	0.9	9.6	20.3	48.4	15.5
1962	9.3	1.5	10.8	17.4	54.9	13.4
1963	7.4	1.5	8.9	40.0	70.4	28.2
1964	6.0	1.2	7.2	42.8	92.9	32.0
1965	7.2	1.4	8.6	15.7	100.0	7.6

Source: ONTA (1962–67); Bank of Korea (1962, 1967).

1961. Subsequent to the large tax law reform of December 1961, there were relatively minor revisions of tax laws between 1962 and 1966 in conjunction with the implementation of the First Five-Year Economic Development Plan (1962–66).

In the 1962 tax law change, the number of personal income tax brackets was increased from three to four, and corporate income tax rates were increased to meet the rising revenue requirements of the government. In 1963–64 the tax laws pertaining to the corporation income tax, the commodity tax, and the petroleum tax were revised. The corporate income tax was made progressive with two income brackets and rates. The commodity tax base was expanded by adding 24 new taxable commodity items, including jewels and precious metal products, and the tax rates on certain luxury consumer goods were raised. The Petroleum Products Tax Law was also revised to reduce the gasoline tax rate from 300 to 100 percent while doubling rates on diesel oil and heavy oil.

In 1965 administrative reforms in the personal income tax, registration tax, and liquor tax systems substantially increased revenues from these sources. For the personal income tax, a heavy penalty was imposed for failure to file a proper return or make prompt payment. To provide incentives to invest in certain key industries and to foster foreign exchange earning by export, the Tax Exemption and Reduction Control Law was promulgated in 1965. This law in effect consolidated into a single piece of legislation all provisions pertaining to tax concessions to businesses, which had previously been included in separate tax laws.

These tax incentive measures were provided to achieve growth objectives. The incentives included tax exemptions, special allowances, accelerated depreciation, investment tax credits, and tax-free reserves. These concessions served specific economic purposes but were granted at the cost of the principle of tax equity. During the latter half of the 1960s and the 1970s, these tax incentives proliferated in Korea.

Tax exemptions for a specified number of years for certain designated industries were an early form of incentive. Major business enterprises engaged in such key industrial activities as shipbuilding, electronics, iron and steel manufacturing, chemical fertilizer manufacturing, and power generation were given a full tax exemption for the first three years and a 50 percent tax exemption for the following two years.

Recognizing the importance of stimulating the self-financing of industrial expansion, the law also provided tax incentives for the reinvestment of profits. Under this provision, a 50 percent tax reduction was allowed on profits retained for reinvestment in plant and equipment. This provision of favorable tax treatment, criticized as inefficient, costly, and a major source of tax evasion, was replaced in 1968 by an investment tax credit (Musgrave 1965:40). Another major tax concession, which provided a tax exemption of 50 percent of income accruing from foreign exchange earnings, was repealed in 1974 in favor of a special depreciation allowance of 30 percent for fixed assets used by foreign exchange-earning enterprises.

The rationalization of exemption and allowance provisions tends to offset any serious effects that corporation income taxation might have on the incentive and ability to invest in the private corporate sector. The benefits from these and other exemptions do not come without costs. It is estimated that the revenue loss from various exemptions and allowances under the corporation income tax amounted to approximately 25 percent of corporate income taxes actually collected in the mid-1960s. For the 1963–73 period, tax exemptions and allowances averaged more than 20 percent of corporation income tax revenue (Bahl, Kim, and Park 1986:85).

In 1967 a comprehensive tax revision was enacted. As the government embarked on the Second Five-Year Economic Development Plan (1967–71), another major tax reform was needed to provide fiscal support. The tax reform of 29 November 1967 was the most comprehensive reform since that of 1961. In all, thirteen existing tax laws were revised and two new tax laws were enacted as an integral part of the government's effort to promote rapid economic growth and industrialization. The stated objectives of this reform, however, did not differ substantially from those of earlier reforms.

The 1967 tax reform brought about major changes in the personal income tax, including the partial introduction of a globalization of the existing schedular system, under which tax rates varied among five different schedules of income; an increase in the number of income tax brackets from five to seven for wage and salary income and from five to six for business and real estate income; and an increase in the exemption level for wage and salary earners from 5,975 won to 8,000 won per month.

An important change in the corporate income tax was the introduction of discriminatory rates between closely held family corporations and open corporations, by which the former were subject to rates from 5 to 10 percentage points higher than the latter. The objective was to provide an inducement to transform family-type enterprises into widely held corporations. In another area of direct taxation, the 1967 tax reform introduced a new land speculation control tax to discourage speculative investment in real estate. This was a capital gains tax levied at 50 percent on profits from transfers of urban real estate.

In the area of indirect taxation, the list of items subject to the commodity tax increased from 46 to 80. Tax rates on luxury commodities and imported goods were also increased. To make liquor taxes more responsive to price changes, they were shifted from a unit basis to an ad valorem rate schedule. Another new tax introduced in the 1967 tax reform was a 10 percent tax imposed on telephone services.

The 1967 tax structure reform, together with the 1966 tax administration reform, brought about dramatic improvements in Korea's tax efforts and sharp increases in tax revenues. These two back-to-back reforms resulted in a doubling of the tax/GNP ratio between 1965 and 1969, a shift in revenue emphasis toward modern income taxation, and a very large increase in the savings rate. National internal tax revenue as a percentage of GNP increased from 5.2 to 10.5 percent in the 1965–69 period. The share of personal income tax in total tax revenue also increased, from 27.8 percent in 1965 to 32 percent by 1969. These spectacular increases in tax revenue were accompanied by increased savings in the government sector, boosting the government saving share in total domestic savings from 23 to 31.4 percent (Table 6.2).

The Organizational Reform of Tax Administration In 1966 the Office of National Tax Administration (ONTA) was created as an independent agency to improve the efficiency of tax administration. The president gave strong personal support to the administrative reform by appointing one of his most trusted assistants to the position of commissioner of taxation. This event thrust the tax administration authority into a position of prominence unparalleled in Korea's history. The establishment of ONTA was part of a reorganization that split the former Bureau of Taxation in the Ministry of Finance into the Office of National Tax Administration and the Tax Systems Bureau. The former was charged with responsibility for the administration

Table 6.2
Revenue impact of the 1966/67 tax reforms

	1965	1966	1967	1968	1969
Tax revenue as % of GNP	5.2	6.8	8.2	9.8	10.5
Annual growth rate of tax revenue	44.1	66.5	48.3	50.6	39.4
Personal income tax as % of total tax revenue	27.8	28.9	29.8	30.5	32.0
Government saving rate	1.7	2.8	4.1	6.1	5.9
Domestic saving rate	7.4	11.8	11.4	15.1	18.8
Government saving as % of domestic saving	23.0	23.7	36.0	40.4	31.4

Source: ONTA (1970); Bank of Korea (1970).
Note: Tax revenue refers to national internal tax revenue.

of national tax laws; and the latter, which remained in the ministry as one of several bureaus, became responsible for tax policy, legislation, and tax treaties. In addition to the separation of these functions, the reorganization provided an upgrading of the status of the tax administration agency and an expansion of investigation and inspection activities.

The primary concentration of the initial effort of ONTA was on fraud investigation and internal audit, and it is in these areas that the most significant breakthrough in organizational and operational concepts occurred, that is, the creation of the new position of inspector-general reporting directly to the commissioner. For the first time, permanent audit and inspection staff were internally organized to investigate misconduct of all tax officials. The primary responsibility of the inspector-general is to audit the service performance and accounting practices of the ONTA national office as well as the field offices and to take disciplinary action against corrupt tax officials.

As a means of encouraging voluntary compliance, ONTA introduced a new "green-return" system (so named for the color of the form used), which encouraged individuals and firms to file tax returns on a self-assessment basis rather than under government supervision. The green-return system was the first step away from the traditional method of having tax officials prepare returns for taxpayers. The pilot operation initially selected taxpayers who kept satisfactory accounting records and brought them under a voluntary system. Taxpayers under this system then became entitled to self-assessment. Various other advantages were offered such taxpayers, including the privilege of offsetting profits with reserves used for the exploration of export markets.

One important consequence of the strengthened tax enforcement and compliance was that "the government also has had a more powerful instrument for monitoring business performance and applying pressure to businessmen who were not operating in ways consistent with national policy objectives" (Mason et al. 1980:322). Another important aspect of the improvement of the tax administration was the insulation of the tax officials from frequent political interference.

Tax Reforms during the Economic Adjustment Period

Third Five-Year Plan, 1972–76 Increasing sectoral and regional imbalances during the 1960s led to a shift in policy emphasis from the rapid economic growth of the previous two development plans to less rapid growth combined with economic balance in the third plan. In support of this strategy of the Third Five-Year Development Plan, another major tax reform took place at the end of 1971 and new tax laws became effective on 1 January 1972. The 1971 tax law reform was designed to accomplish the following specific objectives: (1) to reduce the tax burden on low income earners; (2) to provide tax inducements to encourage savings by individuals and businesses; (3) to reduce excessively high marginal rates; and (4) to improve horizontal equity in taxation (Ministry of Finance, Korea, 1972:11).

In line with these objectives, personal income tax rates on wages and salaries and on business income were lowered, and the minimum income subject to the global tax was reduced from 5 million to 3 million won. Interest income from bank deposits, previously exempted, became subject to a 5 percent tax. Corporate income tax rates were also adjusted downward, and the investment tax credit was expanded to cover a wide range of businesses and industries. Ten major tax laws were affected by the 1971 reform. In 1973 the inhabitants tax to be administered by local governments was introduced. This is levied as a surtax on the national personal income tax.

The 1972 Emergency Decree for Economic Stability and Growth In the early 1970s there was a noticeable decline in investment demand, partly caused by the tight credit policy, and prices were increasing at a rapid rate. With a fall in real investment, the Korean economy slowed considerably during 1970–72. Against this unfavorable economic development, on 3 August 1972 the government took a series of emergency measures designed to strengthen the financial position and the structure of business enterprises and to dampen inflation. These measures provided generous, although temporary, depreciation allowances and 10 percent investment tax credits for investments using domestic resources. In addition, the Emergency Decree abolished the existing revenue-sharing scheme with provincial governments, which was pegged to central government tax revenue, and made equalization grants dependent on the budgetary conditions of the central government at any given time.[1] The intention of this decree was to support anticyclical flexibility in budgetary procedures of the government.

The Presidential Emergency Decree of 1974 The favorable economic developments of 1973 were abruptly interrupted in 1974 by external developments: the oil crisis, recession in the advanced industrial countries, and the high level of foodgrain and raw materials prices. The impact on the Korean economy of higher prices for energy, foodgrains, raw materials, and other intermediate product imports was particularly severe. To assist hard-pressed low-income groups, on 14 January 1974 the government adopted the Presidential Emergency Decree for National Economic Security, providing substantial income tax relief for low wage earners.

The magnitude of tax reduction for wage and salary earners was 50 percent for annual incomes between 600,000 and 840,000 won and 30 percent for incomes ranging between 840,000 and 1,200,000 won. Incomes below 600,000 won were completely exempted from personal income tax for one year (see Park 1978:74). In addition, transportation taxes on train, city bus, and passenger ship fares were suspended to sustain the standard of living for low-income persons. To restrain consumption and recoup the revenue losses caused by reductions in the tax burden for the low-income groups, the government raised tax rates for certain commodities including gasoline and liquor products.

Table 6.3 shows the revenue impact of two emergency measures taken in 1972 and 1974 as well as that of the 1971 structural reform. Data presented in the table clearly indicate that these tax measures had an adverse effect on revenue yields. The sharp decline in the tax/GNP ratio from 15 percent in 1971 to 12.5 percent in 1973 is largely attributable to discretionary rate reductions in personal and corporate income taxes which resulted in actual decline in the absolute amount of revenues from these two sources in 1972. In addition, the President's Emergency Decree of 1972 led to a sharp decline in the absolute amount of corporation income tax yields in 1973.

This chain of events also brought about a gradual shift in the pattern of Korea's tax structure. As the lower half of Table 6.3 shows, the share of personal and corporate income taxes in the overall tax structure sharply declined, whereas the reliance on indirect taxes, including customs duties, increased markedly over the 1971–75 period.

The 1974 Tax Reform Until 1974, Korea's personal income tax system consisted of both schedular taxes and a global tax. Under the schedular system, exemptions, deductions, and rate structures varied considerably, depending on the type of income. As a result, the system was complex, inequitable, and difficult to administer.

The major objective of the 1974 reform was to correct these defects in the personal income tax by replacing the schedular system with one in which virtually all personal income previously included in the five different schedules would be taxed under a global system (Ministry of Finance, Korea, 1975b:9–78). The new system also provided an additional exemption for bonus income, increased the number of allowable deductions to reduce the tax burden on families, increased the maximum level of deductions, and reduced tax rates over most ranges of taxable income.

Other taxes were affected by the reform of 1974. The land speculation control tax, which had been in effect since 1968, was replaced by a capital gains tax. In addition, the Basic Law of National Taxes was enacted to clarify the legal basis of taxation, promote fair tax administration, and protect the taxpayers' rights and interests. Under this law, the National Tax Tribunal was created as an independent agency under the Ministry of Finance to deal with tax appeals.

Enactment of the Defense Surtax Law The declaration of the Nixon Doctrine for self-defense in the early 1970s brought about gradual increases in national defense expenditures for Korea. In July 1975 the Defense Tax Law was enacted to finance the modernization of a self-reliant national defense force. Under this law, a surtax at rates ranging from 0.1 to 30 percent was applied to both national and local taxes (Ministry of Finance, Korea, 1975a:14–18). The defense surtax, adopted as a tem-

Table 6.3
Revenue impact of tax changes in the early 1970s (percentage)

	1971	1972	1973	1974	1975
Tax revenue as % of GNP					
Total tax revenue	15.0	13.0	12.5	13.9	15.8
Personal income tax	3.4	2.7	2.5	2.4	2.2
Corporate income tax	1.8	1.4	1.0	1.6	1.4
As share of total tax revenue					
Personal income tax	23.8	22.0	21.4	18.0	15.2
Corporate income tax	12.5	11.5	8.6	12.1	10.0
Commodity tax	7.7	7.7	8.7	8.7	9.0
Customs duties	11.5	12.4	14.2	13.9	13.9

Source: Derived from ONTA (1972–78).

porary measure in 1975, was originally scheduled to expire in 1980, but the expiration date was postponed to 1990.

In terms of revenue contribution, the defense surtax producing 2,911 billion won in 1988 represented 14.9 percent of total national tax revenue and 2.3 percent of GNP. And, of the total defense tax revenue, about 47 percent came from surtax levy on direct taxes and roughly 43 percent from those on indirect taxes including custom duties. Local taxes accounted for almost 10 percent of total defenses surtax revenue in 1988 (Ministry of Finance, Korea, 1990:21).

Adoption of the Value-Added Tax System In a drastic change in the existing indirect tax structure, the 1976 tax law reform adopted a new value-added tax (VAT) system. The objective of this tax reform was to simplify the then complicated system of indirect taxation and its administration, to promote exports and capital formation, and to preserve the neutrality of indirect taxes (Ministry of Finance, Korea, 1977). In return for the transfer of local entertainment and restaurant tax to the national government to be consolidated with the newly introduced VAT, the national registration tax was transferred to the local governments.

On top of VAT, special consumption taxes were also levied on luxury consumer goods and services at rates ranging from 5 to 100 percent for selected commodities and from 500 to 15,000 won for certain services. The value-added tax law provided for a single basic rate of 13 percent, adjustable within a range of 3 percentage points without legislative approval. To minimize the inflationary effects of a 13 percent value-added tax, however, a temporary rate of 10 percent was initially applied and is still effective. Exempted from the VAT were unprocessed foodstuffs and basic daily necessities such as tap water, coal briquettes for home heating, and medical services. A zero rate was applied to exports.

At the time the VAT was introduced, there were fears that the tax would have undesirable economic effects, particularly on the general price level and the distribution of the tax burden. The introduction of VAT, however, did not appear to have had a major impact on the rate of price increases in Korea. Most of the increase in prices was attributable to the general inflationary situation in the economy at the time (for a detailed analysis, see Choi 1984:34–40). However, the regressivity issue of the VAT continued to be a topic for hot debate in Korea. Studies carried out to estimate the distribution of VAT burdens in Korea generally conclude that the value-added tax is regressive with respect to income. A study by Kye-sik Lee (1986), for instance, shows that Korea's VAT burden declines from 4.696 percent of disposable personal income at the lowest decile to 1.958 percent at the highest decile.

The introduction of the VAT system had significant impacts on the government's tax receipts and on the structure of the tax system, as reflected in the share of indirect tax revenue in the overall tax system. Korea's tax structure changed significantly between 1976 and 1977—the year the VAT was introduced. The share of indirect taxes jumped from 56.2 percent in 1975–76, to 61.4 percent in 1977–78, and to 65.4 percent in 1980. On a five-year average basis, the indirect tax share in the total internal tax revenue rose from 53.6 percent in 1972–76 to 62.7 percent in the 1977–81 period (Table 6.4).

The Economic Restructuring and Stabilization Period of the 1980s

The Comprehensive Stabilization Program announced in April 1979 represented a turning point in Korea's economic policy. It was the first serious and comprehensive stabilization effort ever launched by the government. The major objective was to restructure the economy so as to enable the nation to make full use of its potential for continued stable growth.

To deal with overinvestment in heavy and chemical industries, the government temporarily suspended all new projects in these industries and realigned credit priorities in favor of light industries. To eliminate price distortions and promote competition, the government decontrolled prices of many items and stepped up import liberalization efforts. To achieve these objectives, several reform measures were adopted, such as reduction of tariff rates and removal of nontariff barriers. Other policy reforms included financial liberalization, reduction of the government budget deficit, and restructuring of the industrial incentive systems.

Soon after the stabilization program was launched, however, the nation was hit by a series of oil price increases. In 1980 the economic situation began to deteriorate in the midst of political and social unrest. Korea had a negative economic growth rate for the first time, and the wholesale price index increased by almost 40 percent.

Tax Policy Measures in the Early 1980s A major focus of fiscal policy during this period was the reduction of the government deficit, which was contributing to in-

Table 6.4
Direct and indirect tax shares of total tax revenue, 1972–1981 (percentage)

	Direct tax	Indirect tax		Direct tax	Indirect tax
1972	50.1	49.9	1978	38.6	61.4
1973	47.7	52.3	1979	38.4	61.6
1974	46.6	53.4	1980	34.6	65.4
1975	43.8	56.2	1981	36.5	63.5
1976	43.8	56.2	1972–76 avg.	46.4	53.6
1977	38.6	61.4	1977–81 avg.	37.3	62.7

Source: Derived from ONTA (1973–83).

flation. The government decided to reduce the deficit by cutting back on the rate of increase in expenditure rather than by revising tax laws to further raise tax revenue. The tax/GNP ratio remained fairly stable during the 1982–86 period at about 19 percent. But the ratio of the total budget deficit to GNP was reduced from the 4–5 percent level during the 1980–82 period to 1.6 percent by 1983 and to 1 percent by 1985. With such an effort and determination on the part of government, accompanied by reduction of the special consumption tax for selected consumer durables, inflation was finally brought under control by 1984 (Moon 1987).

With regard to specific changes in tax policy, in 1981 the government began to work on restructuring the tax incentive system for industries to facilitate greater efficiency in investment allocation and to distribute the tax benefits more equally among industries. Accordingly, the list of special tax measures and the range of tax preferences were reduced.

In 1982 the government adopted a substantial reduction in the highest marginal rate for both personal and corporate income taxes in an attempt to minimize distortions in resource allocation caused by an extremely progressive tax rate structure. The range of personal income tax rates was gradually reduced from 8–70 percent in 1979 to 6–55 percent in 1982, and that of corporate income tax from 25–40 percent in 1980 to 20–30 percent in 1983.

The Education Tax of 1982 A notable change in the structure of the tax system during the 1980s was the introduction of an education surtax in 1982 to relieve hard-pressed educational financing. This tax, adopted as a five-year temporary measure, was to expire at the end of 1986 but in fact did not expire until the end of 1991. The major objective of this earmarked tax was to finance the improvement of teachers' salaries and allowances and the expansion of school construction programs to ensure the minimum standards of education.

Revenue from the four sources of the education surtax amounted to about 512 billion won in 1988, accounting for 2.6 percent of total central government tax revenue. Tobacco and interest and dividend income provided over 73 percent of the education tax revenue, and the rest came from the liquor tax and finance companies (Ministry of Finance, Korea, 1990).

The 1988 Tax Reform During the three-year period from 1986 to 1988, the Korean economy achieved a remarkable growth performance along with a substantial current account surplus. It recorded an average annual growth rate of over 12 percent for three consecutive years from 1986. In the balance of payments, the current account surplus exceeded US$14 billion in 1988, much larger than anticipated. Despite the good performance of these macroeconomic indicators, the Korean economy was faced with structural adjustment difficulties. Consumer prices, which had been stabilized since 1982, rose 7.2 percent in 1988. Rising food prices, in particular, placed a disproportionate burden on the lower income groups.

In addition, the rapid transition toward political liberalization created social desires for more balance and equity among various sectors of the economy. Farmers, factory workers, small merchants, and other low-income urban dwellers alike felt that the recent rapid economic growth had passed them by. The government, with minority seats in the National Assembly, was subject to heavy sociopolitical pressures to implement policies to maximize the economy's potential by ensuring fair distribution of the fruits of economic growth among social strata.

The tax reform of 1988 thus represented a first step toward a more equitable distribution of income in response to a mounting social and political demand for greater economic democracy. The major highlight of the reform package was a lowering of the tax burdens of low- and middle-income classes through reductions of personal income tax and excise taxes.

The reform effected changes in seven tax laws altogether and resulted in a net revenue loss of 1.6 trillion won in 1989. The total breaks down to losses of 580 million won from personal income tax, 300 million won in special excise tax, 290 million won in telephone tax, 190 million won in liquor tax, and 500 million won from import tariff cuts. These revenue losses were partially offset by an increase in revenue resulting from repeal of various tax incentives (Ministry of Finance, Korea, 1989a:20). The major contents of the 1988 tax reform are summarized below.

1. The reform reduced the personal income tax burden on low-income people by raising the tax exemption levels and expanding various tax deductions, as well as adjusting the tax rate structure. The annual tax exemption for a five-person family with wage and salary income was lifted from 2,740,000 to 4,600,000 won. This adjustment, occurring for the first time since 1982, takes account of the increase in basic deductions, deductions for spouse and dependents, and special deductions for wage and salary workers. In addition, the reform reduced the number of tax rate brackets from sixteen to eight and also cut the marginal tax rate for the top income bracket from 55 to 50 percent (Table 6.5).

Table 6.5
Personal income tax rates, before and after the reform of 1988

Pre-reform		Post-reform	
Taxable income (1,000 won)	Rate (%)	Taxable income (1,000 won)	Rate (%)
1,800	6	2,500	5
1,801–2,500	8	2,501–5,000	10
2,501–3,500	10	5,001–8,000	15
3,501–4,800	12	8,001–12,000	20
4,801–6,300	15	12,001–17,000	25
6,301–8,000	18	17,001–23,000	30
8,001–10,000	21	23,001–50,000	40
10,001–12,500	24	>50,000	50
12,501–15,500	27		
15,501–19,000	31		
19,001–23,000	35		
23,001–29,000	39		
29,001–37,000	43		
37,001–47,000	47		
47,001–60,000	51		
>60,001	55		

Source: Ministry of Finance, Korea (1989a).
Note: In addition, surtaxes of 7.5 percent for local inhabitants tax and 10–20 percent for defense tax are levied.

2. The number of tax brackets for inheritance and gift taxes was reduced from fifteen to eight. Progressive tax rates, ranging from 7 to 60 percent for inheritance tax and from 7 to 67 percent for gift tax, were adjusted downward to 5–55 and 5–60 percent, respectively. Exemption levels for inheritance tax were also substantially increased.
3. The amount of dividend tax credit allowed for shareholders was raised from 8 percent of dividend income (4 percent for incomes exceeding 10 million won) to 12 percent (6 percent for incomes exceeding 10 million won) so as to minimize the impact of double taxation on corporate profits and to encourage internal financing of corporations through the stock market. In addition, the period for deduction of carried-over losses was extended from three to five years. To improve tax equity among different types of corporations, tax treatment of nonprofit corporations and public corporations was changed. Interest and dividend income of nonprofit corporations, formerly tax-exempt, became subject to tax, and the tax rate for public corporations was increased from 5 to 10–15 percent.

4. With regard to indirect taxes, the rate structure of the special excise tax was simplified and certain commodities such as black-and-white TV sets were removed from the excise tax list. Furthermore, the telephone tax rate was reduced from 15 to 10 percent and the tobacco consumption tax previously levied by the central government was transferred to local governments.

Tax Reform under the "New Economy" In 1990 there was a major tax reform, reducing tax burdens of wage and salary earners and enhancing tax equity among income sources by strengthening taxation of financial assets, inheritances and gifts, and capital gains from real estate transfers. The defense surtax was repealed as of 1 January 1991, and the education tax became part of the permanent taxes.

With the inauguration of Kim Young Sam as president in 1993, Korea's new administration unveiled its Five-Year Plan for a New Economy, which includes tax reform measures. The highlights of the long-term tax reforms are (1) strengthening the role of income tax, (2) increasing the effectiveness of property taxation, (3) effective management of tax incentives, (4) structural adjustment of consumption-related taxes, (5) structural reform of the tariff system, and (6) improving tax enforcement and administration.

One of the new government's most drastic acts was the August 1993 proclamation of a presidential emergency decree of immediate implementation of the real-name financial transaction (RNFT) system. The two previous presidents felt the need for the RNFT system but were unable to enforce it. This new system will eventually ensure equity in tax burdens and prevent tax evasion. It will force underground money into the legitimate money market.

Tax Reforms and the Modernization Process: A Summing Up

Major tax reforms were undertaken in eleven of the twenty-seven years between 1961 and 1988. In six instances—1961, 1967, 1971, 1974, 1976, and 1988—the changes were substantial enough to be labeled "comprehensive" (Table 6.6).

The objectives of these comprehensive tax reforms during the 1960s and the early 1970s were to make the tax system more supportive of economic development programs. Thus the tax reforms of 1961, 1967, and 1971 were undertaken in conjunction with the Five-Year Economic Development Plan and constituted an integral part of the government's efforts to promote rapid economic growth. One of the most important reforms in the evolution of Korea's tax system may have been the creation of the Office of National Tax Administration in 1966. This reform signaled the governnment's long-term commitment to increasing the tax effort, and a sustained period of growth in revenue mobilization followed.

The economic adjustment period of the 1970s was marked by severe economic difficulties, which had largely originated from the worldwide oil crises and two

Table 6.6
Tax reform and major tax law changes, 1961–1988

Date	Major tax measures
5/61	New military government initiated improvement of tax administration • Strengthened the tax withholding system • Reorganized regional tax offices • Screened and retrained tax officials • Enacted: Tax Collection Temporary Measures Law Tax Delinquent Special Measures Law Tax Accountant Law
12/61	Comprehensive tax reform (First Five-Year Economic Development Plan)
1962-64	Minor tax law changes
12/65	Tax Exemption and Reduction Control Law
3/66	Office of National Tax Administration (ONTA)
11/67	Comprehensive tax reform (Second Five-Year Economic Development Plan) • 13 tax laws revised • Two new tax laws enacted (Land Speculation Control Tax Law)
12/71	Comprehensive tax reform (Third Five-Year Economic Development Plan) • 10 tax laws affected • Interest income subject to 5 percent tax • Corporate tax rates reduced • Investment tax credit expanded
8/72	Emergency Decree for Economic Stability and Growth • Provided generous investment tax credits • Abolished the existing revenue-sharing scheme for local governments
12/73	Inhabitants tax (local tax)
1/74	Presidential Emergency Decree for National Economic Security • Provided substantial tax relief for low-wage earners • Public transportation service taxes suspended
12/74	Comprehensive tax reform • Introduced the global personal income tax system • Land speculation control tax replaced by a capital gains tax (real estate) • Enacted the Basic Law for National Taxes • Established the National Tax Tribunal
7/75	Introduced the defense surtax
12/76	Comprehensive tax reform • Adopted the value-added tax • Replaced 8 of 11 indirect taxes
12/81	Introduced the education surtax Personal income tax rates and corporate tax rates reduced
12/86	Introduced the excessive land holding tax (local tax)
12/88	Comprehensive tax reform • Revised 7 tax laws • Reduced personal income tax, special excise tax, telephone tax, liquor tax, and customs duties
8/93	Emergency Decree for the Implementation of the Real Name Financial Transaction System

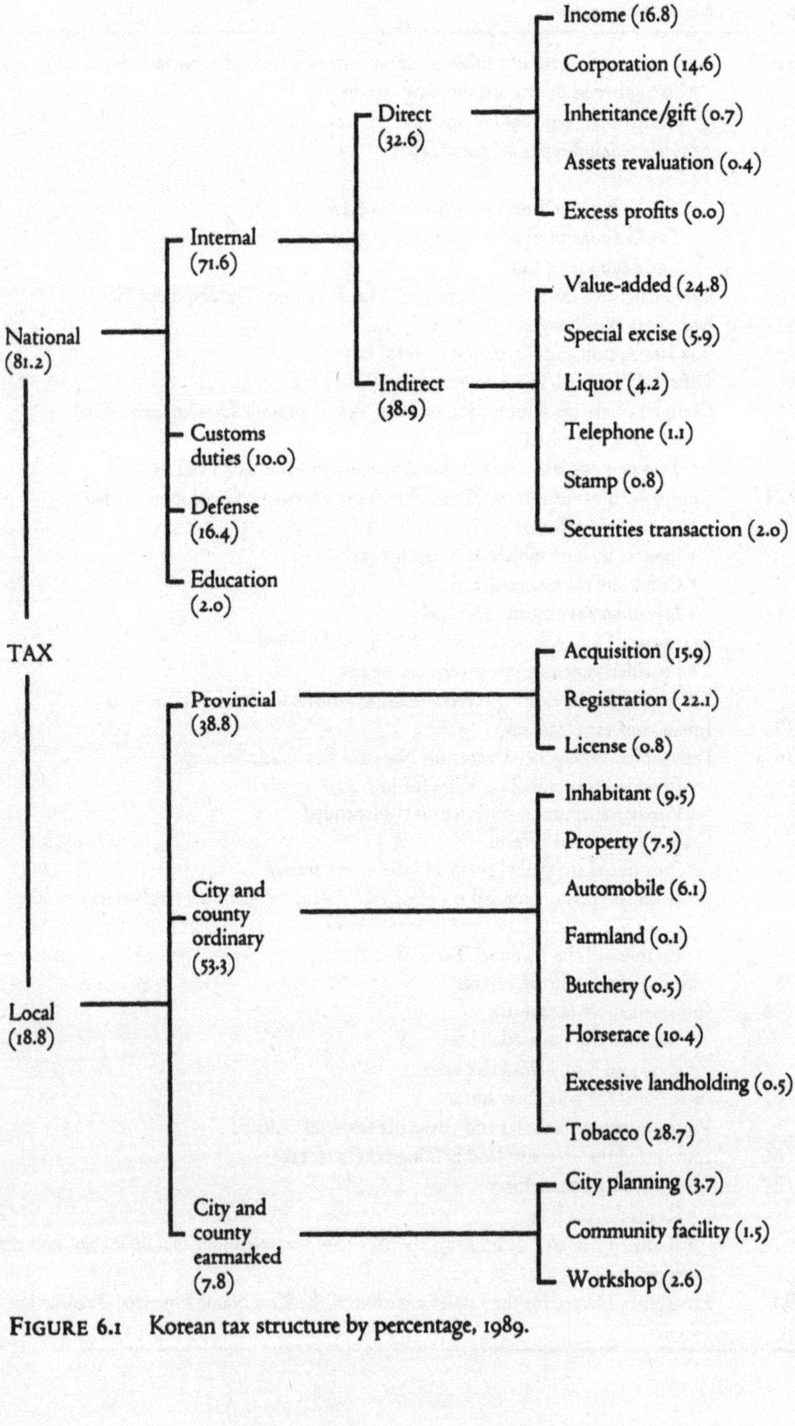

FIGURE 6.1 Korean tax structure by percentage, 1989.

emergency tax measures adopted in 1972 and 1974. The major highlight of this period is, of course, the introduction in 1976 of a broad-based value-added tax system in place of eight of eleven existing indirect taxes. The 1970s also saw the introduction of two other taxes—the local inhabitants tax in 1973 and the defense surtax in 1975.

The decade of the 1980s is one of economic restructuring and stabilization with much less tax reform activities. In keeping with a policy of structural adjustment and liberalization, the range of tax incentives was reduced in the early 1980s. The education surtax was adopted in 1981 as a temporary tax measure to boost public financing of elementary and secondary schools. The issue behind the 1988 comprehensive tax reform was the fair distribution of the fruits of economic growth and of the tax burden among different social groups. One of the most drastic measures on the early 1990s was the 1993 implementation of the RNFT system.

The current tax system has gradually evolved from the history of discretionary change in tax laws. The Korean tax system is composed of a large number of national and local taxes (Figure 6.1). As of 1989, eleven different kinds of internal taxes were levied by the central government. Of these, five were direct taxes, accounting for 45 percent of total internal tax revenues. The remaining six indirect taxes accounted for 55 percent of total internal tax revenues, and the valued-added tax alone contributed nearly 35 percent of the total.

The local government units—provincial, municipal, and county—also levy fourteen different kinds of taxes, three of which are provincial taxes. Municipal and county taxes include eight ordinary taxes and three special earmarked taxes. Local government sources provided less than 20 percent of all taxes collected in the nation in 1989. There is little overlap in the tax bases for the national and local taxes. The major tax revenue source of local units of government is property-related taxes, whereas that for the central government is consumption and income taxes.

Comparison of Tax Policies in Korea and Other Countries

In this section I briefly analyze and compare the experiences of Korea and Japan in the formulation and implementation of tax policy. These two neighboring countries share a common sociocultural background, and though there are many similarities, there are some striking differences as well.

Tax System and Revenue Structure

Compared with other advanced industrial countries, the aggregate tax level in Japan is relatively low. In 1987 tax revenue/GNP in Japan was 21.4 percent, compared with 30.2 percent in Great Britain and 21.6 percent in the United States. France's tax ratio in 1987 was 25.4 percent (Ministry of Finance, Japan, 1989).[2] The aggregate tax/GNP ratio for Japan was quite stable throughout the 1950s and 1960s: until the first oil crisis of 1973 it held steady at around 14–15 percent. The

TABLE 6.7
Composition of national tax revenue: Korea and Japan, 1988 and 1989 (percentage)

	Korea[a]		Japan	
	1988	1989	1988	1989[b]
Direct taxes	36.4	43.0	73.4	72.1
Personal income tax	18.9	21.1	34.2	34.1
Corporate income tax	16.2	20.6	35.8	34.5
Inheritance tax	0.7	0.8	3.3	3.6
Other	0.6	0.5	—	—
Indirect taxes	62.0	55.1	26.6	27.9
Value-added tax or consumption tax	21.6	24.8	—	8.5
Special excise tax	8.1	7.0	—	—
Commodity tax	—	—	3.8	—
Gasoline tax	—	—	3.6	3.5
Liquor tax	5.3	5.6	4.2	3.4
Tobacco tax	—	—	2.0	1.7
Securities transaction tax	1.3	2.0	3.6	2.1
Stamp tax	0.6	0.8	4.0	3.5
Customs tax	16.3	13.1	1.4	1.4
Telephone tax	2.4	1.5	—	—
Other	6.4[c]	0.3	4.0	3.8

Source: Ministry of Finance, Korea (1989b); Ministry of Finance, Japan (1989).

[a] The defense surtax and the education surtax were allocated to individual tax categories.

[b] Budget estimates.

[c] Monopoly profits and receipts from previous years.

ratio fell somewhat in 1975 due to the recession caused by the oil crisis. It quickly recovered, however, and is now much higher than its previous level.

The relatively low level of taxation in Japan can be explained partly by the low level of defense spending in the budget. But this low tax burden also reflects the reluctance of the government to permit the public sector to expand in relation to the private sector of the economy. Korea, even with its heavy defense burden, has also kept the tax share of GNP at a moderate level during the modernization process. Korea's tax/GNP ratio in 1987 was 17.5 percent (Ministry of Finance, Korea, 1989b:8).

The tax structure in Japan is very similar to that of the United States. Tax revenues at the national level are largely derived from personal and corporation

Table 6.8
International tax revenues by direct and indirect tax share (percentage)

	1975		1987	
	Direct	Indirect	Direct	Indirect
Korea	38.5	61.5	34.0	66.0
Japan	69.3	30.7	73.3	26.7
United States	88.4	11.6	91.5	8.5
England	63.7	36.3	53.9	46.1
West Germany	52.8	47.2	52.8	47.2
France	36.4	63.6	40.2	59.8
Italy	39.3	60.7	58.5	41.5

Source: Ministry of Finance, Japan (1989); Ministry of Finance, Korea (1989b).

income taxes (nearly 70 percent of total national tax revenue), and there was no general sales or value-added tax until 1 April 1989, when Japan introduced the consumption tax. Korea's tax system, however, resembles those of the European countries more than that of the United States. Like most European countries, Korea relies more heavily on indirect taxes, including value-added tax, than on direct taxes (Table 6.7). No European country except France still relies so heavily on indirect taxation as does Korea (Table 6.8). Achievement of a well-balanced tax system through an appropriate mix of taxation on income, consumption, and assets remains a major objective of tax reform for both Japan and Korea.

Despite these sharp differences between the Japanese and Korean tax systems, there are striking similarities. Both countries have a unitary fiscal system, with limited fiscal responsibilities and powers at the local units of government. Local taxation is largely controlled by the central government in both countries. Japanese and Korean tax laws contain many special provisions designed to encourage or discourage specific types of consumer and business behavior.

Tax Policy

Tax policy has been oriented heavily toward rapid economic growth in both Japan and Korea. Tax incentive schemes and other measures of tax preferences illustrate the strong orientation of both countries toward economic growth in their economic planning. Tax incentives, of course, are not unusual in many other countries; what is unusual is the heavy emphasis both Japan and Korea placed on special tax measures to promote national objectives. Both countries seem to have relied extensively on tax incentives as a means of stimulating desirable economic activity.

The two countries have adopted a wide variety of tax incentive measures, such as tax-free reserves, accelerated depreciation, and tax credits. In Korea various types of generous tax incentives were provided under the Tax Exemption and Reduction Control Law enacted in 1965. There appears to be general agreement among Japanese government and business circles that the tax system has been actively employed to promote economic growth and that special tax measures were major factors contributing to rapid economic growth in the 1950s and 1960s (see Ishi 1989; Pechman and Kaizuka 1976).

The proliferation of these tax preferences are, however, believed to have contributed to the low effective tax burden in these two countries. The erosion of the tax base and revenue losses through such tax preferences were enormous in both countries. The revenue loss resulting from the direct tax incentive schemes in Korea amounted to 15.8 percent of total income tax (both personal and corporate income tax) revenues in 1988 (Ministry of Finance, Korea, 1990). It ranged between 12 and 13 percent in Japan during the 1958–66 period but gradually declined to about 5 percent in the mid-1980s (Ishi 1989).

It is generally believed that the investment tax incentives enacted in most advanced industrial countries in the past encouraged business enterprises to invest for tax advantages rather than to improve their economic performance. Thus, a major trend of the tax reform plans of most European countries as well as those of the United States and Canada has been to eliminate tax preferences for investment. This policy was largely motivated by the conviction that free market operations allocate resources more efficiently than those driven by tax incentives (Pechman 1988). Korea needs to reexamine its tax structure critically in light of efficiency criterion to determine whether it can achieve additional revenues by eliminating unnecessary deductions, allowances, or tax credits. It should also be kept in mind that tax preferences complicate the tax laws and often raise difficult administrative and compliance problems.

Another important goal of the worldwide tax reform movement is the improvement of horizontal equity. In most industrial countries, horizontal equity receives more emphasis does vertical equity. In Japan, in particular, the "9-6-4" phenomenon is widely regarded as the most serious problem of the tax system.[3] Korea is faced with exactly the same problem. The personal income tax burden of wage and salary workers is considered much heavier than that of business proprietors, the self-employed, and recipients of income from real estate and financial assets. Therefore, correcting the unfair distribution of the tax burden among different income sources remains the ultimate objective of the tax reform plan of Korea.

Japanese policymakers relied heavily on annual tax cuts and reforms to offset the mounting pressures for tax concessions and to make the general direction of the government's tax policy acceptable to the public. Japan's tax policy throughout most of the postwar period was guided by the principle that tax provisions should be adjusted frequently to keep total tax revenues at about 20 percent of national income.

Because income taxes are highly responsive to economic growth, and because growth was rapid, Japan was able to reduce income taxes every year. The elasticity of the Japanese personal income tax was around 2.0 during the 1960s. In contrast, the income elasticity of Korea's personal income tax was only slightly over 1.0. With this low elasticity of the personal income tax, combined with the smaller income tax share in the total tax system and with its large defense commitment, Korea could hardly afford the luxury of annual tax reductions. The income elasticity of the overall tax structure, particularly that of the personal income tax, needs to be kept well above unity to improve the built-in flexibility of Korea's tax system so that it can be used to promote more stable growth.

Social Attitudes and the Tax Process

Although there are many similarities in the tax practices of Korea and Japan due to their similar cultural and historical backgrounds, there are also marked differences in their social attitudes in the formulation and development of national policies. In Japan we find a strong inclination toward consensus and gradualism in the development of national tax policies. It is interesting to note that it took exactly ten years for Japan to get the value-added tax reform bill through the legislature. Politico-institutional characteristics of Japan as well as its perceptions, attitudes, and value systems may have played an important role.

This inclination toward a slow, gradual approach to resolving differences does not necessarily hinder needed changes in tax rates and other tax provisions, but it prevents abrupt changes in the tax structure and in the general direction of tax policy. This bias partly reflects the attitude of the traditionally conservative and business-oriented government that was in power for so long. A danger of this type of social attitude is, however, that it might perpetuate or even aggravate certain tax practices that are considered undesirable.

In contrast, Korea's experiences in the development of tax policies reveal a strong tendency toward drastic and sometimes sudden changes in the tax structure and taxation policy. Contrary to the Japanese experience, the value-added tax legislative process took only one and a half years before it became effective on 1 July 1977 (Choi 1984). The major differences between Korea's and Japan's tax policies, then, lies neither in their objectives nor in their achievements but in the much more forceful and aggressive spirit with which Korea's policymakers and officials pursued their objectives.

If there is anything Korea can learn from the Japanese experiences at this stage of development, it would be the decision-making process based on consensus and the gradual approach to resolving differences of opinion. The basis for tax policy changes and decision making in institutional reforms in Korea should be enlarged to incorporate the views and opinions of various segments of the society. To accommodate all these elements, the tax process needs to be modified and improved as necessary.

In Japan, the Tax Advisory Commission plays a significant role in the tax process. This commission, established in 1955, advises the prime minister on the formulation of long-range policy in institutional reforms of the tax system. It also reviews and recommends tax changes in the annual budget. The members of the Tax Advisory Commission, appointed by the prime minister, come from various segments of society. But none of the members is a government official. The intent of this diversity of membership is to allow the commission to act as arbiter among the various interest groups that influence tax policy. The commission's recommendations are transmitted directly to the prime minister, and they are generally adopted intact, although some changes occasionally are made by the government (Pechman and Kaizuka 1976).

Korea established a similar commission, known as the Tax System Deliberation Committee, in 1970. But the committee members are appointed by the minister of finance, and the committee also includes government officials among its members. The major task of the committee is to assist the Tax Bureau in the Ministry of Finance in the formulation of long-term policies for institutional changes of the tax system.

To have more efficient and consensus-based decision making in the tax process in Korea, the status of the Tax System Deliberation Committee needs to be upgraded so that it will have more influence on policy recommendations. The functions of the committee should also be broadened, so that it can review and recommend short-run tax changes on an annual basis as well as recommend long-range tax policy on the structure of the tax system.

The Future Tax System of Korea: Major Issues and Institutional Reforms

Tax reform is currently an important policy issue in many countries. The major industrial countries are undertaking or have already implemented tax reforms, partly stimulated by the successful U.S. tax reform of 1986. Through that tax reform, the United States was able to broaden the tax base and reduce high income tax rates.

Over the past few years the tax burden in most industrial countries has become heavier and criticism of the inequity and complexity of the tax system has become widespread. Major tax issues common to all these countries are (1) inequities and distortions created by very high nominal tax rates, (2) misallocation among industries and firms, (3) the proliferation of ineffective tax preferences, and (4) noncompliance with tax laws (Pechman 1988).

Although the specific tax reform measures adopted or being discussed in each country differ somewhat, certain trends are discernible. Most countries have lowered personal and corporate tax rates, particularly in the top brackets, to achieve "flattening" in combination with the reduction of brackets. The United States, for instance, lowered the top individual income tax rate by 22 percentage points and reduced the number of brackets from fourteen to two. Including local taxes, the top bracket rate in Japan was cut by 23 percentage points—from 88 percent to 65 percent—over three stages. Japan also reduced the number of brackets from twelve to five.

Another noticeable trend of the worldwide tax reform movement is the broadening of the tax base. Most countries undertook a critical examination of their tax structure to determine if eliminating unnecessary deductions or tax credits would generate additional revenues. The United States, the United Kingdom, and Canada, for example, eliminated or reduced investment allowances or investment tax credits. In Australia and Denmark, deductibility of entertainment expenses was largely curtailed. In some countries, capital gains became taxable as ordinary income.

To some extent, Korea's tax reform is in the purview of this universal trend of the tax reform movement, with some of the reform measures proposed here for Korea reflecting experiences and lessons from the countries that have already undertaken extensive reforms.

Taxation Policy: Its Changing Role and Emphasis

Since the early 1960s, the government of Korea has made a strong commitment to accelerating national development, leading to export-led rapid economic growth. The government introduced many institutional reforms and other policy initiatives, expanded its planning functions, and implemented successive five-year economic development plans. During the past quarter-century, Korea's priority in the allocation of public resources has been investment in plant and equipment to expand the productive capacity of the economy. Public finance policy during this modernization process played a supporting role by contributing to overall savings and productive investment, and thus to rapid economic growth. A greater emphasis was placed on incentives for increased saving and investment and, to a large extent, equity was ignored.

Recent developments in Korea, however, have made it necessary for the nation to redefine its development strategies for achieving further advances and to redirect future economic policy. In particular, the political reform movement toward democratization in 1987 and the subsequent surge of outspoken demands by various social groups for socioeconomic justice, increased wages, additional welfare, better housing, and other amenities made it inevitable that macroeconomic management and the priorities for economic and social policy be adjusted. There is a growing awareness today that, while growth-oriented development policies are of fundamental importance, they cannot be relied upon to reduce social imbalances and distributional inequities, except possibly over a longer time period than may be politically acceptable. The government has already made it clear through the revised Sixth Five-Year Economic and Social Development Plan that it will "strengthen support for the underprivileged and for lagging sectors of the economy so as to narrow the imbalances among different social strata and different industrial sectors and to promote a more equitable distribution of income" (Economic Planning Board 1988). This change has important implications for the kind of tax system Korea needs to develop in the future.

Thus, the coming decade will witness the turning point in Korea's public finance policy, for the major focus will gradually shift from one-sided support of "quantitative growth" by simply providing physical expansion to meeting rising social needs and demands for improvement in the quality of life—that is, "qualitative growth." The emphasis of taxation policy should be shifted to issues so often dominant in the latter stages of modernization, such as promoting social stability, improving income distribution and equity in taxation, and enhancing international competitiveness. As Yoon Hyung Kim puts it in Chapter 2, "Korean modernization has to move from the stage of productive capacity expansion to a new stage in which such expansion advances side by side with distributive justice."

To meet the challenge of becoming an advanced industrial society, it is essential that Korea readjust its national goals and priorities in the management of the national economy and resources. As Korea's per capita income exceeds $5,000 and the size of the national economy expands, it becomes necessary to implement more accommodating taxation policies to avoid difficulties in maintaining social stability and distributive justice.

In the past the Korean government failed to meet the rising need for social services and, as a result, there are now serious imbalances between social and economic development. The share of social development in total government expenditure remains relatively low at 17.2 percent in Korea (Table 6.9). In comparison, social development expenditures accounted for nearly 34 percent of total government expenditure in Japan, 36.8 percent in the United States, and 59.5 percent in France in the mid-1980s. It is evident that the budgetary commitment of the Korean government to health, social security, housing, and regional development is far from satisfactory. Korea's national goals and priorities for social development and welfare thus imply that additional tax revenue will have to be generated to finance increasing social development expenditure in the 1990s. The Sixth Plan envisages the nation's tax burden to rise from 18.3 percent of GNP in 1988 to 20.0 percent by 1992 (Economic Planning Board 1988). It has been suggested that the tax burden ratio needs to be increased to 25 percent by the year 2000 (Keesung Roh, Chapter 7 of this volume).

To meet the rising social development costs and social overhead investment of the 1990s and thereafter, tax revenue must increase substantially. The future role of taxation policy should be to facilitate the most effective and equitable mobilization of the required volume of tax revenue to support increasing government expenditure needs, particularly social services and welfare. Within Korea's prevailing social and political context, anticipated increases in government expenditures

Table 6.9
International government expenditures (percentage)

	Korea (1988)	Japan (1986)	United States (1986)	United Kingdom (1986)	West Germany (1984)	France (1985)	Sweden (1987)
General adminstration	14.5	4.7	8.6	6.3	7.1	6.0	3.9
National defense	21.2	5.7	17.1	11.3	5.7	7.4	9.3
Education	15.9	8.8	13.7	11.7	8.5	7.8	8.9
Social development	17.2	33.9	36.8	45.2	61.9	59.5	62.2
Economic development	24.4	7.3	9.3	9.9	11.1	7.9	9.2
Miscellaneous[a]	6.7	39.6	14.6	15.6	12.9	11.4	6.5
Total expenditures/GNP	23.1	17.0	37.4	44.8	49.2	44.7	43.8

Source: International Monetary Fund (1988) and K. Lee (1990).

Note: Data for France, Sweden, and Japan refer to central government expenditures; all others are for general government expenditures.

[a] Repayment of debt, subsidies, etc.

should first come from incremental tax yields accruing from steady economic growth. Introducing new taxes or sharply raising nominal tax rates within the existing tax system is probably not the best way for the government to increase revenues. Instead, greater emphasis needs to be placed on changes in tax structure to make it more responsive to economic growth and distributional needs. Taxation policy and institutional reform efforts should also be directed toward broadening the tax base within the existing revenue structure, by eliminating unnecessary tax preferences and tax loopholes.

Objectives of the Tax Reform

The primary function of a tax system is to raise enough revenue to cover government expenditures. The growing conviction among taxpayers that tax reform is urgently needed, however, seems to be based on criteria other than revenue requirements. These criteria include equity, efficiency, and simplicity. These broad guiding principles are also supplemented by more specific issues such as tax evasion and the influence of taxation on savings and investment, economic growth, distribution of income and wealth, and socially desirable or undesirable forms of behavior.

The Korean tax system is widely regarded as unfair, inefficient, and extremely complicated. A large number of taxpayers believe that the tax system favors wealthy individuals and large business firms at the expense of the average taxpayers. Another general perception is that people pay widely different taxes even though they have the same amount of income. This taxpayer discontent has been increasing steadily in recent years, with the tax structure becoming more complicated and new preferences introduced to achieve various objectives. Consequently, the public is demanding tax reform to improve the distribution of tax burdens, simplify the tax structure, and eliminate tax distortions in the economy.

Another criticism of the tax system is that it is unproductive and does not raise sufficient revenue from potential tax sources. It is quite difficult, however, to raise taxes when the tax system is widely considered unfair, with further taxpayer discontent effected by the belief that outright evasion is widespread. Therefore, the objectives of tax reform and the need for more revenue are closely related.

The main purpose of tax reform is to design a tax system that promotes the broad objectives of economic and social policy: a fair distribution of income and wealth, a satisfactory rate of growth, and economic stability. Within this framework of reform, tax administration must be improved and major parts of the tax structure modified, keeping in mind that tax policy should not be treated in isolation but instead viewed as an inherent part of overall economic and social policy.

Equitable Distribution of Income and Tax Burden

The mere existence of a market system and free competition does not always guarantee the fair distribution of income and wealth. Consequently, government policies, including fiscal policy, should be directed toward promoting equity. Through its tax and expenditure policies, the government can exert substantial influence on the distribution of income and the incidence of poverty. Only when the principles of equity and fair competition are upheld can goals of economic efficiency and social justice be attained.

One of the most important emerging issues and tasks facing Korea today is institutional reform of the tax system to promote equitable distribution of income and the tax burden (Roh 1990). Despite rising levels of income and living standards, many Koreans feel more relative poverty than ever before. This trend may reflect an increasing sensitivity to the concentration of income and wealth and a widespread feeling of relative deprivation and exclusion (see, e.g., S. U. Kim 1989). There is now a growing awareness of the failings of Korean tax and fiscal policy in redistributing real income.

The degree of income inequality in Korea, as measured by the Gini coefficient, increased from 0.33 to 0.39 between 1970 and 1976. It remained at about 0.39 until 1980, when it declined slightly. The 1988 figure was 0.34 (Economic Planning Board 1989). Although Korea's income distribution has improved somewhat over the past ten years, it still compares unfavorably with its two neighboring countries, Japan and Taiwan. The Gini coefficient for Japan and Taiwan were 0.28 and 0.30, respectively, as compared with Korea's 0.34 (Kim and Koh 1989).

Another important factor underlying the feeling of relative deprivation in Korea is the skewed distribution of financial wealth. For financial assets such as securities and savings, which are largely held by wealthy persons in Korea, the distributional inequality is much greater than for income distribution. The Gini coefficient for these assets is 0.56, considerably higher than 0.34 for overall income.

TABLE 6.10
Distributional regressivity measure by type of tax, 1984

	Weights of tax revenue	K-P index[a]
Total tax[b]	100.0	1.086
Individual direct taxes	28.3	1.745
Corporation income tax	9.0	1.196
Indirect taxes	46.7	0.918
Customs taxes	16.0	0.918

Source: Shim (1988).
[a] Khetan-Poddar index: KP > 1 means progressivity; KP = 1, proportionality; and KP < 1, regressivity.
[b] Includes both national and local taxes.

While the top 20 percent of the asset holders owned 58.6 percent of total financial assets, the lowest 40 percent owned only 7.9 percent.

It would be interesting to see if Korea's tax system plays a significant role in equalizing incomes. It is generally agreed that in Korea's tax policies the issue of income redistribution has remained secondary to that of economic growth during the modernization process. The redistribution of income has not been a major concern of government economic policy. Neither has it been a major concern of tax institutional reforms in the past (Bahl, Kim, and Park 1986).

A recent study that attempted to assess the redistributional impact of taxes provides some evidence that Korea's overall tax system is only mildly progressive and that it does not appear to have any significant effect on the distribution of income (Shim 1988). Table 6.10 presents the measure of distributional regressivity of the total tax system by different categories of tax using the K-P (Khetan-Poddar) index. According to data presented in this table, Korea's overall tax system with the K-P index of 1.086 is close to proportional with respect to income. Whereas the distribution of the individual direct tax burden is highly progressive (K-P index, 1.745), indirect and customs taxes, which account for nearly 63 percent of total tax revenues, are regressive (0.918).

This lack of progressivity in Korea's overall tax system partly reflects a tax structure that relies heavily on indirect taxes. In 1987, Korea relied on indirect taxes such as the value-added tax and special consumption tax for two-thirds of tax revenues. Direct taxes, including individual and corporate income taxes, provided only about 34 percent of total tax revenues for that year.[4] In comparison, direct taxes accounted for 40 percent of national taxes in France, over 58 percent in Italy, 73 percent in Japan, and over 90 percent in the United States (Table 6.8).

The fact that the direct tax share is much too small partly reflects an element of weakness in the Korean tax structure. Thus, the tax reform should accord a high priority to correcting this structural deficiency in direct taxes. A capital gains tax scheme needs to be rationalized and income from financial assets such as interest and dividends should be brought into the global income tax system. The reform of inheritance and gift taxes must also be undertaken and, above all, financial transactions in anonymous accounts should no longer be allowed.

Korea's tax system violates the principle of equity in other aspects. In the past too many special tax provisions have been introduced into tax laws, benefiting selected groups of taxpayers. Special application of reduced tax rates to certain capital incomes favors high-income classes over low-wage and -salary earners. Likewise, special exclusions, deductions, and tax credits erode the tax base and create large differences in the tax burden among people with equal incomes. It is noteworthy that the revenue loss from various tax exemptions and allowances provided under the Tax Exemption and Reduction Control Law amounted to 1,478 billion won in 1989, representing nearly 10 percent of total internal taxes collected in that year (Ministry of Finance, Korea, 1990).

Thus, for reasons of equity and social stability, tax reform is badly needed in Korea. Tax institutional reforms should aim at eliminating lopsided tax favors and improving the distribution of the tax burden. Maintaining equity and balance in the tax structure is essential to promoting the well-being of taxpayers and enhancing efficiency. Therefore, equity-oriented adjustments should be made with respect to all possible tax policy instruments. Tax policies should, however, emphasize equity in taxation and income without adversely affecting economic efficiency and productivity.

Strengthening the Role of Personal Income Tax

Of all taxes, the personal income tax is widely recognized as having the greatest potential for distributing tax burdens most in accordance with the ability to pay. It thus constitutes an essential component of any tax system that would otherwise rely heavily upon indirect taxes, none of which are closely related to the taxpayer's personal circumstances. Despite these advantages, a general discontent with the personal income tax prevails in Korea.

Personal income tax does not play as significant a role in Korea as in other industrial countries. In comparison with most Western industrial countries and even some of the more developed Asian countries, the ratio of personal income tax revenue to GNP is relatively low in Korea. Korea's personal income tax represents about 2.4 percent of GNP, compared with 4.6 percent in Japan and 8.2 percent in the United States (Table 6.11). It accounts for only about 24 percent of total central government tax revenue in Korea, compared with nearly 35 percent in neighboring Japan and 46 percent in the United States.

For the Organisation of Economic Co-operation and Development (OECD)

TABLE 6.11

Personal income tax revenue in Korea, 1965–1988 (percentage)

Revenue	1965	1970	1975	1980	1985	1988	Japan (1988)	U.S. (1986)
As % of GNP	1.3	3.0	1.1	1.8	1.9	2.4	4.6	8.2
As % of total tax revenue[a]	16.8	21.2	12.8	10.1	10.9	13.1	21.4	23.2
As % of total central tax revenue[b]	27.9	29.8	19.6	18.0	19.8	23.6	34.7	46.2

Source: Ministry of Finance, Korea (1989b); Ministry of Finance, Japan (1989); U.S. Bureau of the Census (1989).

[a] Includes local tax revenue.

[b] Internal tax revenue.

countries as a whole, personal income tax accounted for 11.7 percent of GDP. Among individual countries, it ranged from a high of 24 percent in Denmark to a low of 6 percent in Greece. Even in France, where, as in Korea, the tax system relies heavily on indirect taxes including the value-added tax, personal income tax revenue accounted for 6 percent of GDP (OECD 1987).

This low level of personal income tax in Korea may reflect the high level of personal exemptions, the low initial tax rates, and the inadequate taxation of capital income in the Korean income tax law. The amount of personal exemptions provided in Korea in 1987 was equivalent to 116.9 percent of average monthly earnings of manufacturing workers, as compared with 73.9 percent in Japan, 68.3 percent in Singapore, and 43.1 percent in the United States. Moreover, Korea's initial tax rate of 5 percent for the lowest income bracket is much too low in comparison with Japan's 10 percent and the United States' 15 percent (Ministry of Finance, Korea, 1989b).

The inadequate taxation of interest and dividend income is one of the most serious problems pertaining to Korea's personal income tax system. Interest and dividends are largely subject to a separate withholding tax rate of only 10 percent in contrast to a maximum rate of 50 percent for wage and salary income, and they are not included in the global income tax base which is subject to progressive taxation. According to unpublished data of the Korean Ministry of Finance, in 1987, 99 percent of interest income and 63.6 percent of dividend income were subject to a withholding tax rate of 10 percent under the schedular tax system. Less than 1 percent of interest income and 36.4 percent of dividends were taxed at the progressive rates under global taxation.

In addition to such favorable tax treatment, a significant amount of interest and dividend income is said to be unreported and thus tax-free. It has been a general practice to collect more taxes from sources readily identifiable and taxable, that is,

Table 6.12
Personal income subject to taxation by income source, 1983 (100 million won)

	National income	Taxable income	Income subject to taxation (%)
Wage and salary	255,875	191,855	75.0
Capital income	77,316	24,811	32.1
Rental income	23,722	2,799	11.8
Interest	49,247	19,794	40.2
Dividends	4,347	2,218	51.0

Source: Tax System Advisory Committee (1985).

employees with fixed wages and salaries. In 1988, for instance, roughly 50 percent of personal income tax revenue was derived from taxes on wages and salaries withheld at the source, while only 17 percent was contributed by interest and dividends. It was estimated that about 75 percent of wages and salaries is captured by the tax authorities through the withholding system, as compared with only 12 percent of property income and roughly 40 percent of interest income (Table 6.12). Since business and property rental incomes are largely taxed according to the taxpayers' self-assessments, it is difficult for the tax administrators to trace the entire income. This deficiency, which is inherent in the existing personal income tax system, is partly responsible for the growing feeling of tax inequity in Korea.

The ultimate objective of structural reform in Korea's discriminatory personal income tax is thus to move from the current mix of "global" and "schedular" income taxes to a genuine, fully integrated (globalized) personal income tax system. Full globalization is vital if personal income tax is to achieve equity in taxation and efficiency. All interest and dividend income should be fully included in global income in addition to wages and salaries. If this tax reform measure is to be implemented successfully, the use of false names in financial transactions should be made illegal as soon as possible.

Deposits with the nation's banking institutions under false names were recently estimated at about 769 billion won, with the percentage of deposit accounts under false names at 3.4 percent, or 1,426,000 accounts. Securities companies topped the list of false-name accounts with 7.5 percent, followed by trust companies with 6.2 percent, banking institutions with 3.4 percent, short-term financing companies with 2.5 percent, and mutual savings and finance companies with 0.3 percent (*Korea Herald*, 19 May 1988).

The first major task in achieving goals of distributional justice and fair economic order, and at the same time securing additional revenues, is to introduce a "real-name" financial transactions system, banning the use of anonymous names. It is widely known that a large number of people, particularly loan sharks and usurers, are using aliases on their financial transactions in an attempt to avoid personal income taxes. This practice of using fictitious names in financial transactions has long been criticized as being inequitable and providing tax shelters for various underground economic activities. The function of the real-name system is not, however, single-purposed; it serves several functions, including maintenance of equity in the tax burden, restoration of economic order, and generation of additional revenue.

It is essential that the government clearly identify the adverse effects a real-name system might have on the economy and carry out appropriate policy measures to rectify them. There is certainly a limit to what the government can do with the personal income tax reform unless a real-name system is implemented.

Once the real-name financial system is enforced, a personal income tax system based on a full globalization of all incomes accruing from financial assets could be gradually implemented. This will allow for the combined income of interest, dividends, and capital gains from taxation at progressive rates. At present, capital gains from the sales of securities are completely exempted from personal income taxation. This practice has long been criticized as a favor given to the wealthy class. The criticism has become stronger as stock prices recently skyrocketed. It is interesting to note that the composite stock price index increased at an annual rate of 45.1 percent during the 1987–88 period, in sharp contrast to 4.7 percent for the consumer price index during the same period.

In addition to remedying the problem of inequity in taxation, the transition to a real-name financial transaction system, coupled with the gradual implementation of a fully global personal income tax system, is expected to generate substantial increases in tax revenue. The revenue effect of taxing capital gains from stock sales would be particularly significant. It was estimated that under given assumptions the new tax scheme for capital gains from the sales of securities would generate tax revenues equivalent to 1,258 billion won in 1991 and 1,656 billion won in 1992 (Kang 1989). This additional revenue of 1,656 billion won is compared with the personal income tax of 2,694 billion won actually collected in 1988. Besides the equity goal of taxation, the government would thus be able to secure additional tax revenue so critically needed to finance increasing social programs.

Improving Taxation of Personal Wealth

Personal wealth is an ideal measure of an individual's ability to pay tax under an equitable tax system. The taxation of wealth has often been suggested as a desirable supplement to the income tax and also as a means of improving the uneven distribution of wealth. In a country like Korea, where economic classes tend to be fairly stable, with very little mobility throughout succeeding generations, taxation of wealth should play a larger role in the overall tax system.

Korea's current tax system, however, fails to impose effective levies on personal wealth. There are many loopholes and defects in the existing system of taxing the wealth of individuals. At present, wealth-related taxes affect only a small number of taxpayers because wealth is unevenly distributed, and many people who should be paying taxes are able to avoid them.

Korea's tax efforts for personal wealth and real property are relatively low, compared with other advanced industrial countries. Government revenues from all wealth and property taxes accounted for less than 10 percent of total national and local government tax revenues. In 1986 most of these revenues (93.7 percent) were derived from real property taxes or taxes on real estate transactions that took place at the local government level, whereas national government taxes on personal wealth provided only 6.3 percent of the total (Table 6.13).

The amount of inheritance and gift tax collected by the national government increased steadily through the 1980s, but their revenue yield was disappointing. Inheritance and gift tax revenues accounted for only 0.4 percent of total tax revenues in 1987 compared with 1.5 percent in Japan in 1986, 0.8 percent in the United States in 1986, and 1.0 percent in Taiwan in 1987. The number of persons who paid inheritance and gift taxes in 1987 represented only 1.5 percent of the total persons deceased in that year. This may be compared with 6.4 percent in 1985 for Japan and 7.3 percent in 1980 for the United States (M. S. Kim 1989).

As in most developing countries, personal wealth is unequally distributed in Korea and is likely to become more so unless appropriate policy measures are taken. The only available data on the distribution of personal tangible wealth such as residential structures and consumer durables indicate that the relative wealth share of the bottom 40 percent of all households was 10.6 percent, compared with over 58 percent for the top 10 percent (Choo 1982). The distribution of financial assets shows a similar pattern. For savings assets, for example, the relative share of the lowest 40 percent of households was only 13.1 percent, in comparison with 41 percent for the top 10 percent (Bank of Korea 1989). The excessive concentration of personal wealth in the top income groups is seen to be socially undesirable, and a tax on transfers of wealth is perhaps the best instrument for moderating the skewed distribution of wealth. The present system of inheritance and gift tax, however, is not expected to halt the trend toward greater inequality in the distribution of wealth, because special provisions for deductions and exemptions reduce the effectiveness of the tax system and add to the many ways of escaping taxes.

The objective of the inheritance and gift tax reform is to check the excessive accumulation of undue concentrations of personal wealth and to raise appropriate taxes from transfers of personal wealth. Reform proposals include broadening the tax base by partially abolishing deduction and exemption provisions. The present inheritance tax law provides for five different kinds of personal deductions, which creates structural problems and complicates the tax system. The number of these deductions should be reduced to, say, three, as suggested by one economist (M. S. Kim 1989). Deductions are also allowed for specific types of estates such as farm-

TABLE 6.13
Composition of wealth and property taxes in Korea (percentage)

	1975	1980	1984	1986
National taxes	13.8	6.2	7.3	6.3
Inheritance and gift	9.4	1.7	3.9	3.9
Asset revaluation	4.4	4.0	2.9	1.9
Securities transaction	—	0.5	0.5	0.5
Local taxes	86.2	93.8	92.7	93.7
Property	24.8	21.3	17.4	18.4
Acquisition	36.4	29.1	28.0	26.0
Registration	—	21.8	27.5	27.8
City planning	11.7	9.1	8.3	8.8
Fire-fighting facilities	2.4	2.3	2.9	3.0
Automobile	10.7	10.2	8.6	9.5
Wealth and property taxes as % of total taxes	9.1	10.6	11.1	9.8

Source: J. K. Lee (1987:6).

land, grasslands, and forest. Serious consideration should be given to revising this provision, for the rationale for providing discriminatory tax treatment simply based on the type of property is unsound and inequitable. Another area of reform involves the improved coordination between the inheritance tax and gift tax. Since the inheritance tax is closely associated with the gift tax, the rate schedule and exemption levels of the two taxes should be unified. For the sake of simplicity, top marginal tax rates (currently 55 percent for the inheritance tax and 60 percent for the gift tax) will have to be lowered in combination with the reduction of brackets.

One of the critical structural problems of the inheritance and gift taxes has to do with the contribution of estates to religious, charitable, and educational foundations, which are tax-exempt. One of the major avenues for tax avoidance has been the use of tax-free private foundations to maintain control without paying taxes on the bulk of estates. Although the majority of these foundations operate in the public interest, some have been suspected of abusing the tax exemption privilege. There is a prevailing feeling that their activities should be subject to stricter public controls and careful scrutiny by the tax authorities. In this regard, we may learn lessons from the experiences of the United States, where a series of legislative measures adopted in the tax reforms of 1950 and 1969 considerably curtailed many abuses of the private foundations' tax exemption privilege (Pechman 1987).

Property tax constitutes another important element of the taxation of personal wealth. The local property tax in Korea is presently grossly underutilized, and the current effective tax rates are considered much too low. One of the major reasons for the underutilization of property tax in Korea is the extremely low and uneven assessment of real property for tax purposes. In 1988, for instance, the average assessment for property tax was estimated to be only 23 percent of actual value in Seoul and 46.2 percent in Gyeong Bug Province. There is a wide variation in the assessment ratio among different regions and among different uses or types of land (Kwack and Lee 1990). Although lands acquired for speculative purposes as well as residential land are subject to progressive rates ranging from 0.2 to 5.0 percent under the newly introduced comprehensive land tax scheme, their effective tax rates are still considered very low due to underassessment of property value.

In 1985, total tax revenue from local taxes on property was 237 billion won, representing only 1.8 percent of total tax revenues in Korea for that year. By comparison, the equivalent ratios for Taiwan and Japan were 8.4 and 4.8 percent, respectively. In terms of national income, local property tax revenue in Korea was 0.3 percent of GDP, compared with Taiwan's 1.2 and Japan's 1.4 percent. Property tax revenue represented 4.0 percent of GDP in the United Kingdom (M. S. Kim 1988). The central problem of property taxation in Korea thus lies in its current state of underutilization. Inadequate property taxation is costly, not only from the revenue point of view, but also for its negative effect on the development process.

Like most developing countries, holding wealth in the form of real estate and other physical assets still predominates in Korea. In 1987, for instance, over 85 percent of the personal wealth assessed for the inheritance tax was made up of physical assets such as land and residential structures. Corporate securities and bonds, on the other hand, accounted for only about 8 percent (ONTA 1988). The strong preference for real estate investment may be explained by several factors, including landholding as a hedge against inflation and the desire to secure long-range stability and social prestige. The continuing demand for land has the effect of inflating real estate values and results in the large accrual of capital gains for the landowners. The distribution of land ownership is also heavily concentrated, with 76.9 percent of the nation's land being held by the top 10 percent of individual landowners (Korea Research Institute for Human Settlements 1989).

A notable feature of land prices is that they increase much faster than the general price index. In 1988, for example, the average land price increased by nearly 30 percent, whereas the wholesale price registered an increase of only 2.7 percent in the same year. The demand for land in Seoul and other urban centers has resulted in land prices increasing by as much as 8.4 times between 1975 and 1988, as compared with an increase by a factor of 2.9 for wholesale prices during the same period (Table 6.14).

Tax reform should play some role in halting land speculation by imposing heavy taxes on capital gains accruing from skyrocketing land values. Rising land

Table 6.14
Land prices and other economic indicators, 1975–1988

Indicators	1975	1980	1983	1985	1987	1988	Factor increase (1975–88)
Land price	100.0	328.1	440.5	533.5	656.5	839.0	8.4
Housing price	100.0	355.3	328.7	397.0	400.8	466.5	4.7
National income	100.0	142.1	178.6	204.2	256.9	287.9	2.9
Wholesale price	100.0	225.4	284.4	289.0	286.1	293.9	2.9

Source: Ministry of Construction, Korea (1988); Bank of Korea (1988).

prices have spurred calls for a comprehensive land tax system, a scheme to levy taxes with progressive rates on the combined value of all lands owned by an individual or a company. Property must be correctly identified, valued at reasonable approximations to market prices, and globalized to ensure that all properties in a single person's ownership are aggregated.

The taxable base of property should be raised to the actual transaction level if the capital gains tax on real estate is to produce any result. To prevent real estate speculators and tax evaders from taking advantage of administrative loopholes, the government must work out a plan for more extensive reform (for more detailed proposals for land tax reform, see Jae-Young Son, Chapter 13 of this volume).

Taxation of wealth and real property should be an important element of the overall tax structure in Korea. As Korea grows richer and accumulates more wealth, taxation of personal wealth should assume increased importance. There is a strong case for a comprehensive tax on personal wealth on both equity and economic grounds. The major argument is that income, taken by itself, is an inadequate measure of taxable capacity, and a tax system based on income alone tends to discriminate against persons with no accumulated wealth (Tanabe 1967). Therefore, a well-designed tax scheme for personal wealth will certainly supplement the personal income tax and also improve the distribution of income and wealth in Korea. In this connection, it has often been suggested that Korea adopt a net wealth tax in place of property tax (see, e.g., M. S. Kim 1989).

Administrative Improvements

Improved administration is an important aspect of tax reform. With the initiation of a major tax reform designed to halt speculative transactions in the land market, along with the implementation of a real-name financial transaction system, problems of tax administration are of paramount importance.

The complexity of the tax law can erode public confidence in the law's fair treatment of everyone. Although improvement in administration involves simplification—making administration and compliance simple—it sometimes requires more complex procedures to secure consistent enforcement of the law. In both cases, the objectives are to eliminate unnecessary administrative burdens on the taxpayer and to secure a more equitable and effective application of the tax. Achievement of these objectives should improve the morale and cooperation of the taxpayer and establish a better revenue structure.

It is now generally believed that the loss of tax revenue resulting from evasion, underreporting, and tax avoidance is substantial. There may be a considerable loss of tax revenues caused by administrative failure to reach a greater portion of potentially taxable income. The so-called compliance gap is enormous by anyone's estimate and is growing larger. This situation creates serious equity problems: the honest taxpayers are bearing an ever-increasing burden because of the growing number of citizens who are not paying their full share of taxes. If the situation continues to worsen, it could lead to the disruption of the economy and eventually to a breakdown in society.

The part of the economy that consists of income concealed from the tax authorities is often referred to as the "underground economy," which seems to thrive in many countries. In Korea the underground economy has been roughly estimated at 20–40 percent of the regular economy or GNP (Choi 1987). Comparatively, figures of 30–35 percent for Italy, 25 percent for France, and 10–25 percent for the United States (AICPA 1983) would indicate that the underground economies abroad are similar to that in Korea.

A comprehensive survey and further research must be undertaken to investigate the nature and causes of underreporting and to develop innovative methods of bringing the widespread underground sources of income and wealth within the tax net. Equal and effective application of the tax law to all taxpayers must be assured to curtail the high degree of tax avoidance and evasion now prevalent among certain groups. To accomplish this objective, new techniques of tax administration are needed. Additional and more effective enforcement is needed to alleviate the inequities, contain the growth of the underground economy, and assure the recovery of tax revenues. Real progress in this area will require the coordinated efforts of the National Assembly, the Ministry of Finance, the Office of National Tax Administration, other relevant government agencies, the academic community, and perhaps major assistance from the private sector.

To alleviate the growing problem of underreporting, the Office of National Tax Administration should redirect some of its efforts toward the underground economy. ONTA can improve its effectiveness by reallocating some of its present enforcement personnel and efforts. Many tax experts feel that too much time and effort are being devoted to unproductive and trivial matters when they could be utilized to uncover underground income and wealth. ONTA may have to increase its personnel to have an impact on the underground economy. It should consider early retired CPAs and other business executives as a new source of qualified personnel. An increase in the resources devoted to the underground economy should also be contemplated. Additional manpower and resources could be applied to increased surveillance of those who are underreporting. An increase in ONTA's budget can be expected to produce a substantial increase in tax revenue.

In addition to the expansion of enforcement activities, current penalties for both civil and criminal fraud should be reexamined. Encouraging the use of checks and credit cards and discouraging the use of currency might deter transactions that are common to underground activities.

One of the possible causes of underreporting in Korea is said to be the change in social mores and general morality that have been evident in recent years. Many people seem to have less confidence in our society's rules and institutions and instead have a growing feeling that it is acceptable to ignore "unfair" laws. National educational programs should be addressed to this particular problem so that society's misguided view toward the tax system and its responsibilities to society and to government may be modified. Some of these efforts in educational programs would have greater credibility and acceptance if provided or sponsored by groups outside the government, such as professional organizations, trade associations, labor groups, and civic organizations.

A perception of widespread waste and inefficiencies in government is often used by some to justify their underreporting. In this connection, it is suggested that the government's extralegal reliance on "quasi-taxes," long in practice in Korea, be discontinued. These "taxes," being unbudgeted and likewise not accounted for, are frowned upon by business people and the general public as sources of financial abuses and inefficiencies in government. The accountability for the tax money spent should be publicly and clearly reported to secure the understanding and cooperation of taxpayers.

NOTES

1. A revenue-sharing system, which set aside 17.6 percent of total central government internal tax revenues as subsidies to local governments, was suspended by the Emergency Decree of 1972. But the system was restored in 1983, with the sharing rate of 13.27 percent instead of 17.6 percent.

2. Tax revenues do not include social security contributions.

3. The "9-6-4" phenomenon refers to the inequitable distribution of tax burdens among the three major groups of income sources. The government fully taxes about 90 percent of the actual earned income of salaried employees, 60 percent of that of small and medium-size businesses, and only 40 percent of that of farmers.

4. The direct tax share, however, has increased to nearly 40 percent since 1987.

REFERENCES

American Institute of Certified Public Accountants (AICPA). 1983. *Underreported Taxable Income: The Problem and Possible Solutions.* Washington, D.C.: AICPA.

Aoki, Torao. 1986. "The National Taxation System." In Tokue Shibata (ed.), *Public Finance in Japan.* Tokyo: University of Tokyo Press.

Bahl, Roy, Chuk Kyo Kim, and Chong Kee Park. 1986. *Public Finances during the Korean Modernization Process.* Cambridge: Harvard University Press.

Bank of Korea. 1962, 1967, 1970. *Economic Statistics Yearbook* (in Korean). Seoul.

Bank of Korea. 1988. *Monthly Research and Statistical Bulletin* (April). Seoul.

Bank of Korea. 1989. *Survey of Savings Market: 1988* (in Korean). Seoul.

Choi, Kwang. 1984. "Value-Added Taxation: Experiences and Lessons of Korea." Working Paper 84-06. Seoul: Korea Development Institute.

Choi, Kwang. 1987. *A Study of the Underground Economy in Korea* (in Korean). Seoul: Korea Economic Research Institute.

Choo, Hakchung. 1982. *Korea's Income Distribution and Its Determinants* (in Korean). Seoul: Korea Development Institute.

Economic Planning Board, Republic of Korea. 1988. *The Revised Sixth Five-Year Economic and Social Development Plan (1988–1991).* Seoul.

Economic Planning Board, Republic of Korea. 1989. *Social Indicators* (in Korean). Seoul.

Hinrichs, Harley H. 1966. *A General Theory of Tax Structure Change during Economic Development.* Cambridge: Harvard University Law School.

International Monetary Fund. 1986, 1988. *Government Finance Statistics Yearbook.* Washington, D.C.

Ishi, Hiromitsu. 1989. *The Japanese Tax System.* Cambridge: Clarendon Press.

Kang, Bong Kyun. 1989. *Economic Development Strategies and Income Distribution in Korea* (in Korean). Seoul: Korea Development Institute.

Kim, Kwan Young, and Il Dong Koh. 1989. "Distribution of Income and Wealth and Policy Issues." In *Policy Conference on the Equitable Distribution of Income and Wealth* (in Korean). Seoul: Korea Development Institute.

Kim, Myung Sook. 1988. *Analysis of Korea's Property Tax Burden* (in Korean). Policy Research Material 88-02. Seoul: Korea Development Institute.

Kim, Myung Sook. 1989. "Estate and Gift Taxation in Korea." *Korea Development Research* (Summer) (in Korean). Seoul: Korea Development Institute.

Kim, Sun Ung. 1989. "Social Perception and Attitude toward Equitable Distribution of Income and Wealth." In *Policy Conference on the Equitable Distribution of Income and Wealth* (in Korean). Seoul: Korea Development Institute.

Korea Research Institute for Human Settlements. 1989. *Research Report of the Research Committee on the Concept of Communal Land* (in Korean). Seoul.

Kwack, Tae-Won, and Kye-sik Lee. 1990. "Tax Reform in Korea." Paper presented at the NBER/KDI Conference on the Political Economy of Tax Reforms and Their Implications for Interdependence, Seoul, 14–16 June 1990.

Lee, Jai Ki. 1987. *Current Status and Problems of Korea's Property Tax* (in Korean). Seoul: Ilhae Institute.

Lee, Kye-sik. 1986. "Analysis of the Distribution of Indirect Tax Burden in Korea" (in Korean). Paper presented at the annual meeting of the Korea Society of Public Finance, Seoul, 15 March 1986.

Lee, Kye-sik. 1990. "A New Role for Fiscal Policy and Financing Social Development in Korea." KDI Working Paper no. 9002. Seoul: Korea Development Institute.

Mason, Edward S., et al. 1980. *The Economic and Social Modernization of the Republic of Korea.* Cambridge: Council on East Asian Studies, Harvard University.

Ministry of Construction, Republic of Korea. 1988. *Trends in Land Prices* (in Korean). Seoul.

Ministry of Finance, Japan. 1989. *Zaisei Kin-yu Tokei Geppo* (Monthly statistics of government finance and banking). (May). Tokyo.

Ministry of Finance, Republic of Korea. 1972. *An Outline of the 1971 Tax System Reform* (in Korean). Seoul.

Ministry of Finance, Republic of Korea. 1975a. *Defense Tax Law* (in Korean). Seoul.

Ministry of Finance, Republic of Korea. 1975b. *Summary of Revised Tax Laws* (in Korean). Seoul.

Ministry of Finance, Republic of Korea. 1977. *Value-Added Tax* (in Korean). Seoul.

Ministry of Finance, Republic of Korea. 1989a. *Korean Taxation.* Seoul.

Ministry of Finance, Republic of Korea. 1989b. *Cho Se Kai Yo* (Summary of tax statistics). Seoul.

Ministry of Finance, Tax Bureau, Republic of Korea. 1990. *Juyo Semu Tong-ge Jaryo* (Major tax statistical sources). Seoul.

Moon, Hi Gab. 1987. "The Impact of Fiscal Restraint on Stabilization: A Case Study of Korea." Paper presented at the East-West Center, Honolulu, 29 July 1987.

Musgrave, Richard A. 1965. *Revenue Policy for Korea's Economic Development.* Seoul: Ministry of Finance.

Noguchi, Yukio. 1988. "Tax Reform Debates in Japan." Paper presented at a conference on world tax reform in San Francisco, 7 October 1988.

Office of National Tax Administration (ONTA), Republic of Korea. 1962–67, 1970, 1972–83. *Statistical Yearbook of National Tax.* Seoul.

Office of National Tax Administration (ONTA), Republic of Korea. 1967. *An Outline of Korean Taxation.* Seoul.

Office of National Tax Administration (ONTA), Republic of Korea. 1988. *Statistical Yearbook of National Tax.* Seoul.

Organisation of Economic Co-operation and Development (OECD). 1987. *Taxation in Developed Countries.* Paris.

Park, Chong Kee. 1978. *Taxation and Economic Development in Korea.* Seoul: Korea Development Institute.

Pechman, Joseph A. 1987. *Federal Tax Policy.* 5th ed. Washington, D.C.: Brookings Institution.

Pechman, Joseph A., ed. 1988. *World Tax Reform: A Progress Report.* Washington, D.C.: Brookings Institution.

Pechman, Joseph A., and Keimei Kaizuki. 1976. "Taxation." In Hugh T. Patrick and Henry Rosovsky (eds.), *Asia's New Giants: How the Japanese Economy Works.* Washington, D.C.: Brookings Institution.

Shim, Sang Dal. 1988. "Analysis of Benefit Distribution of Government Expenditure," In *National Budget and Policy Objectives: 1988* (in Korean). Seoul: Korea Development Institute.

Tanabe, Noboru. 1967. *The Taxation of Net Wealth.* International Monetary Fund Staff Papers (March). Tokyo.

Tax System Advisory Committee, Ministry of Finance, Republic of Korea. 1985. " A Research Report on the Future Development of the Tax System: Summary" (in Korean). Seoul.

U.S. Bureau of the Census. 1989. *Statistical Abstract of the United States: 1989.* Washington, D.C.: GPO.

Chapter 7

A Proposal for Tax Reform in Korea

Keesung Roh
Korea Development Institute

Introduction

Korean society experienced dramatic changes in the latter part of the 1980s. The strong demand for democratization has led to the reformation of various sectors in Korean society, including taxation. The tax system influences each agent in the economy as well as the economy as a whole in several ways: through income redistribution, resource allocation, and the stabilization or destabilization of the economy. Therefore, the establishment of a desirable tax system is a matter of great importance with far-reaching implications. The purpose of this chapter is to suggest adding a tax reform option with a long-term perspective to the institutional reforms already under way in the Korean economy.

The Current Korean Tax System

Recent Tax History

I sketch the evolution of the Korean tax system only briefly here; it is well summarized by Professor Park in Chapter 6 of this volume.

Korea pursued economic stability and independent fiscal employment when it was emancipated from Japanese rule and the government was established in 1948. But the Korean economy failed to achieve these ends due to the outbreak of the Korean War. The tax system at that time existed mainly to finance war-related expenditures. In 1953 the Korean government shifted its tax system toward rehabilitation after the war. As the new government under President Park launched the first economic development plan in 1962, the tax system was changed once again, this time to support economic development. In particular, due to the expanded need for efficient tax management, the government established the Office of National Tax Administration (ONTA) in 1966 and gave the tax administration function to that office.

In 1968, for the purpose of equity improvement, a global income tax was introduced, such that income greater than a certain amount (5 million won/year) would be taxed at higher rates. To finance and meet increased fiscal demands for economic development, two earmarked taxes, those for defense and education, and a value-added tax (VAT), were introduced in 1975, 1982, and 1977, respectively.[1] In 1975 the income tax system was made more progressive and changed to a complete global income tax system, at least under the tax law itself. Thereafter, the progressive structures were gradually weakened by successive tax law amendments, including the recent one of 1990.

This amendment also weakened the corporate income tax and brought on the repeal of the defense tax, while estate and gift taxes have grown smaller due to lowered tax rates and increased deductions. Although the defense tax has been repealed, the education tax remains as an education concession tax. The government introduced two strong measures in 1990 to curb land speculation, the Concept of Public Ownership of Land (CPOL) and the global land tax. The property tax on housing remained unchanged, however.

The Personal Income Tax

The Korean personal income tax system has the dual characteristics of schedular and global income taxes. Global, retirement, capital gains, and forest incomes are taxed separately in accordance with different statutory tax rate schedules. Global income, which includes interest, dividends, wages and salaries, business income, and rental income, is taxed at the rate schedules shown in Table 7.1.[2] The tax schedule in 1991 had marginal rates of 5–50 percent and a tax-free income of 5.81 million won. Statutory rate schedules have been simplified since 1975, when it had sixteen brackets and the highest rate was 70 percent.

Business and rental incomes are supposed to be reported by taxpayers for global income tax determination by the tax agency. Also, those who have two sources of income should report global income to the tax agency. For example, a taxpayer who has rental income in addition to labor income on which the withholding tax is imposed should report rental income by May of the next year. Exemptions for business income are permitted just as in the calculation of taxable income for corporate entities.

It should be noted that there had been favorable treatment of interest and dividends until 1990; they were taxed at an exceptionally low rate of 10 percent. However, stockholders with shares amounting to more than 1 percent of the total capital of a corporation and who have more than 100 million won pay the global tax.

The capital gains tax has been a key instrument for the government's antispeculation policy for land and apartments (Table 7.2). Basically, speculation on real estate is an outcome of the government's regulation of land price and usage, as well as of its macroeconomic policy. Nevertheless, the government has resorted heavily to tax measures. Tax rates were leveled up or down according to the pace of the real estate market. Currently, progressive tax rates fall in the range of 40–60 percent, whereas

Table 7.1
Global income and labor income tax rate schedules (10,000 won, percentage)

	Brackets	Lowest rate	Highest rate	Upper limit of lowest bracket	Tax-free income[a]	Tax rate on dividend/interest[b]
1970	9	7	50	12	12	15/5
1975	16	8	70	24	78	25/5
1980	17	6	62 (79.05)	120	238	25/5
1981	17	6	62 (79.05)	120	238	10 (16.75)
1982	17	6	60 (76.5)	120	268	10 (16.75)
1983–88	16	6	55 (70.13)	180	274	10 (22.6–28.5)[c] (16.75)
1989	8	5	50 (63.75)	250	460	10 (52)[c] (16.75)
1991	5	5	50 (53.75)	400	581	20 (60)[c] (21.5)

Note: Figures in parentheses except those for 1991 are tax rates including defense, inhabitant, or education taxes. Figures in parentheses for 1991 include only the inhabitant tax.

[a]Family of five.

[b]In case of separate taxation.

[c]Tax rate on anonymous account.

uniform tax rates were applied to capital gains before 1984, when assessed value was far below actual value. However, capital gains from stocks are not taxed at all.

The Corporate Income Tax

The Korean corporate income tax system is somewhat complicated (Table 7.3). Corporate entities are classified into general corporations, unlisted corporations, nonprofit organizations, and so on, and different rate schedules are applied to each entity. In the amendment to the tax law in 1990, rate schedules were integrated and simplified to improve international competitiveness by cutting down tax burdens on industry sectors. Furthermore, the government tries to treat various corporate entities as equally as possible. In addition, the government permits larger tax credits or deductions on research and development investments by expanding the deductible limit and coverage.

The distinctive feature of the system is that the government adopted a partial

Table 7.2
Capital gains tax rate schedule (percentage)

	Before December 1978	1979[a]	1981[a]	April 1984[b]	1989[c]
Land	50	50 (70)	25 (35) 40 (50)	40 (50)	40–60
Buildings	30	50 (70)	25 (35) 40 (50)	40 (50)	40–60

[a]Tax rate applied when the holding period is less than two years. The 1981 figures on the upper rows are actually applied tax rates, i.e., flexible rates.

[b]Actually, the government applied a flexible tax rate of 25 and 35 percent rather than a statutory tax rate of 40 and 50 percent.

[c]Capital gains from small apartments are taxed at 30 percent and capital gains from land or buildings without filed titles are taxed at a far higher rate of 70 percent.

Table 7.3
Corporate income tax rates (percentage)

Taxable income	1990	1991
Less than 100 million won	20 (24)	20
More than 100 million won		
General	30 (36–37.5)	
Unlisted	33 (39.6–41.3)	34
Nonprofit	27 (32.4–33.5)	

Note: Figures in parentheses are tax rates including defense, inhabitant, or education taxes.

gross-up method to integrate dividend income and corporate taxes. Double taxation of returns to capital by personal and corporate income taxes is a well-known problem. The government permits a deduction of one-third of corporate income tax from the global income tax when dividend income is subject to global income taxation.

The Wealth and Property Tax

Various Korean wealth taxes are closely related to antispeculation policy. CPOL, one of the two pillars of antispeculation policy, contains three measures: (1) restric-

TABLE 7.4
Property, estate, and gift tax rates (percentage)

	1990	1991
Property tax (on assessed value of house)	0.3–7 (6 brackets)	same as in 1990
Estate tax	6–66 (8 brackets)	10–55 (5 brackets)
Gift tax	6–72 (8 brackets)	15–60 (5 brackets)

tion of residential lot holding, to directly control housing lot size in different classes of local government, such as in the six largest cities; (2) a tax on excessive gains from land, to tax accrued capital gains above a normal increase (due to land development, changes in zoning, etc.); and (3) a tax on land developers by which developers pay 50 percent of the evaluated profit from the project as a capital gains tax. The other pillar, the global land tax, is nothing but a significantly strengthened property tax in the sense that it is not based on the physical size of each parcel of land but on the total value of all lands held by a person. Its progressive tax structure has basically nine brackets and two different marginal rates, 0.3–2 percent for commercial land and 0.2–5 percent for speculatively held land and residential land.

The property taxation of land has given way to the global land tax. The property tax is now mainly imposed on the assessed value of houses, and its rate schedule is progressive, from 0.3 to 7 percent.[3] The estate and gift taxes are sometimes called "taxes paid by fools," meaning that these taxes can be easily evaded. In the amendment in 1990, their tax rates were lowered by 5–10 percent and the number of brackets was also reduced (Table 7.4). Also, taking into account the rapid increase in land and housing prices, the government increased the deduction limit by a considerable amount.

Emerging Issues in Korea's Tax Reform

Traditionally, public finance economists have placed primary emphasis on the tax policy objectives of equity and efficiency. There is no need to restate the tradeoff between equity and efficiency, nor the two concepts of equity—horizontal and vertical. Besides these two objectives, the simplicity, flexibility, stability, and neutrality of the tax system can be taken into account as well. However, the most important issues related to tax reform in Korea are the unequal distribution of income and wealth, the weakened distributive role of direct taxes, the necessity of a consistent buildup of growth potential and capacities, and the liberalization of the Korean economy.

Distribution of Income and Wealth

While the distribution of income has been a widely adopted research topic, the distribution of wealth has not been as popular, due possibly to data problems in the case of Korea. Wealth and income are too closely related to be considered separately; wealth, after all, is a stock from which income is produced. Statistics show a recent improvement in the income distribution of Korea. Estimates for the Gini coefficient were 0.3355 in 1988, while those for the worst case in 1977 were 0.437 (Table 7.5). It should be noted, however, that the incomes of self-employed households and unrealized capital gains from real and financial assets were not included in these statistics.

Recent reports on wealth and land distribution by Kwon (1990) and the CPOL Committee (1989) provide notions that there might be a discrepancy between statistics and the actual or perceived state of income distribution. According to Kwon (1990), the distribution of wealth was far worse than that of income. The Gini coefficient of wealth distribution is 0.58, which is 0.24 greater than the coefficient for income distribution. The top 30 percent of assets holders own 72.1 percent of financial and real assets in nominal terms (Table 7.6).

The report from the CPOL Committee (1989) shows that the Gini coefficient of land ownership distribution is 0.85, with the top 5 percent of holders owning 65.2 percent of privately held land. It is quite likely that the unequal distribution of financial and real assets (land in particular) severely deteriorates income distribution, partly because the assets are the main sources of income and partly be-

Table 7.5
Gini coefficient (urban households)

1970	1975	1977	1980	1985	1988
0.3455	0.4119	0.4370	0.3787	0.3657	0.3355

Source: Kang (1989).

Table 7.6
Distribution of land ownership (percentage)

	Share of real and financial assets (1989)	Share of private land ownership	
		Nationwide	Seoul
Top 5 percent	–	65.2	57.7
Top 10 percent	43.1	76.9	65.9
Top 25 percent	–	90.8	77.8
Top 30 percent	72.1	–	–
Gini coefficient (1985)	0.58	0.85	–

Source: CPOL (1989); Kwon (1990).

cause rapid price increases of real assets such as land and housing generate a lot of unearned capital gains. According to one rough approximation, capital gains from rapid land price increases amounted to more than 60 trillion won in 1988, which was 55 percent of Korea's GNP. This approximation reconfirms the notion that the unequal distribution of wealth is the key determinant of inequality in income distribution.

Another statistic also supports this view. Table 7.7 shows the inequality of income distribution perceived by different occupations. Industrial workers and farmers claimed that they were poorer than they had been five years earlier relative to the average Korean citizen, while employers, the self-employed, and professionals responded that they were at least as rich as before or richer than they were five years earlier.

Comparing the equality of income distribution in Korea with that of other countries, it appears that Korea has achieved a relatively equal distribution of income (Table 7.8). But the fact that 72 percent of total assets and 76.9 percent of private land were held by the top 30 percent and top 10 percent of holders in each category, respectively, indicates that the problem of inequitable wealth distribution in Korea might become a potential source of the unequal distribution of income when the price of real estate and the interest rates soar. Therefore, the principle of the right instrument for the right target suggests that taxes on property or wealth are as appropriate as income taxes in improving the distribution of income.

The Redistributive Role of Direct Taxes

It is somewhat surprising that Korea has faced a budget surplus in the general account for a decade while developed countries, including the United States, are suffering from burgeoning budget deficits. The Korean budget surplus amounted to 3.1 trillion won, or 14 percent of the total budget, in 1989 (Table 7.9). The surplus existed not only because the Korean economy enjoyed a boom in the favorable

Table 7.7
Perceived inequality in income, by profession (percentage)

	Richer than before	Similar	Poorer than before
Employers	28.6	34.7	36.7
Self-employed	17.7	40.1	42.2
Employee			
Professionals	15.6	42.3	42.1
Blue-collar	14.0	35.4	50.6
Farmers	13.6	26.0	60.5
Average	14.5	32.6	52.8

Source: Kwon (1990).

Table 7.8
International comparisons of income distribution (Gini coefficient)

Korea (1988)	Italy (1977)	U.K. (1978)	Philippines (1975)	U.S. (1978)	Canada (1977)
0.3355	0.36	0.372	0.45	0.364	0.402

Source: Ministry of Finance (1990).

Table 7.9
Surpluses in the general account, 1980–1989 (billion won, percentage)

	Budget	Surplus[a]		Budget	Surplus[a]
1980	5,804.1	23.5 (0.4)	1985	13,800.5	189.0 (1.4)
1981	9,578.1	81.5 (0.9)	1986	15,559.6	551.2 (3.5)
1982	10,416.7	142.3 (1.4)	1987	17,464.4	1,364.9 (7.8)
1983	10,966.7	315.2 (2.9)	1988	19,228.4	3,305.0 (17.2)
1984	12,275.1	496.5 (4.0)	1989	22,046.9	3,123.0 (14.2)

Source: Ministry of Finance (1990).
[a]Figures in parentheses are ratios of surplus to budget.

environment fostered by low international interest rates, low foreign exchange rates, and low oil prices but also because politically the government feared a recurrence of high inflation and wished to avoid an overexpansionary budget. Consecutive budget surpluses in the 1980s raised the issue of the overburden of taxpayers, especially of wage earners, and their claims for a tax cut. Therefore, the government cannot help but reform the tax system. The government's keen interest is placed on a personal income tax and, in particular, on a labor income tax.

Along with this, it can be argued that direct taxes are relatively small in comparison to indirect taxes and thus do not play a proper income redistributive role. The trend of direct and indirect tax structures in Korea shows an interesting U-shaped curve over time, as pointed out by Hinrichs (1966). In the early stages of economic development, the government was heavily dependent upon direct taxes for about 50 percent of total internal taxes. In the 1970s the share of direct taxes dropped to 30 percent but has recovered recently to almost 46 percent (Figure 7.1). The highest share of direct taxes during the period, 50 percent, can be considered an achievable target.[4]

Direct taxes in Korea consist of factor income taxes (personal and corporate income taxes) and taxes on wealth (property tax, estate tax, gift tax, capital reassessment tax, capital gains tax, etc.; Table 7.10). Although the capital gains tax is classified as a personal income tax, it is considered a kind of tax on wealth

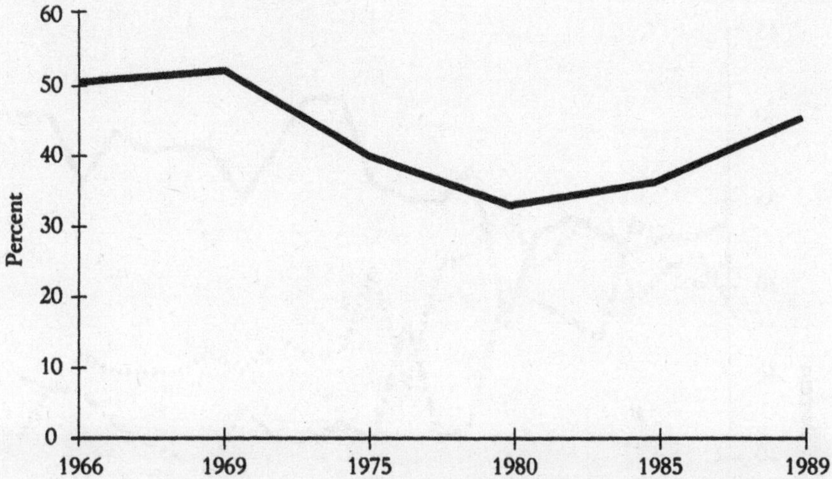

FIGURE 7.1 Share of direct tax in the internal tax (data from Ministry of Finance 1990).

TABLE 7.10
Direct taxes

Tax on factor income			
Personal income tax			
Labor income tax	Capital income tax	Corporate income tax	Tax on wealth
Labor income tax	Interest income tax	Corporate income tax	Property tax[a]
Retirement income tax	Dividend income tax		Capital gains tax
	Business income tax		Gift tax
	Global income tax		Estate tax
	Rental income tax		Capital reassessment tax

[a]Local tax.

in the sense that capital gains are neither value added nor counted in the national income account. Income taxes are levied separately on some different sources of income. The labor income tax undoubtedly includes the retirement income tax, while the capital income tax includes interests and dividends, rental, business, and global income taxes.[5] Business income and rental income taxes are also placed in the capital income tax category, since they mainly contain returns from capital.

Figure 7.2 shows the structure of direct tax revenues over time, with total yields increasing by 26 percent annually from 32 billion won in 1966 to 5.6 trillion won in 1988. The labor income tax's share of total direct tax revenues declined steadily until 1982 but has increased since then, while the share of taxes on wealth peaked

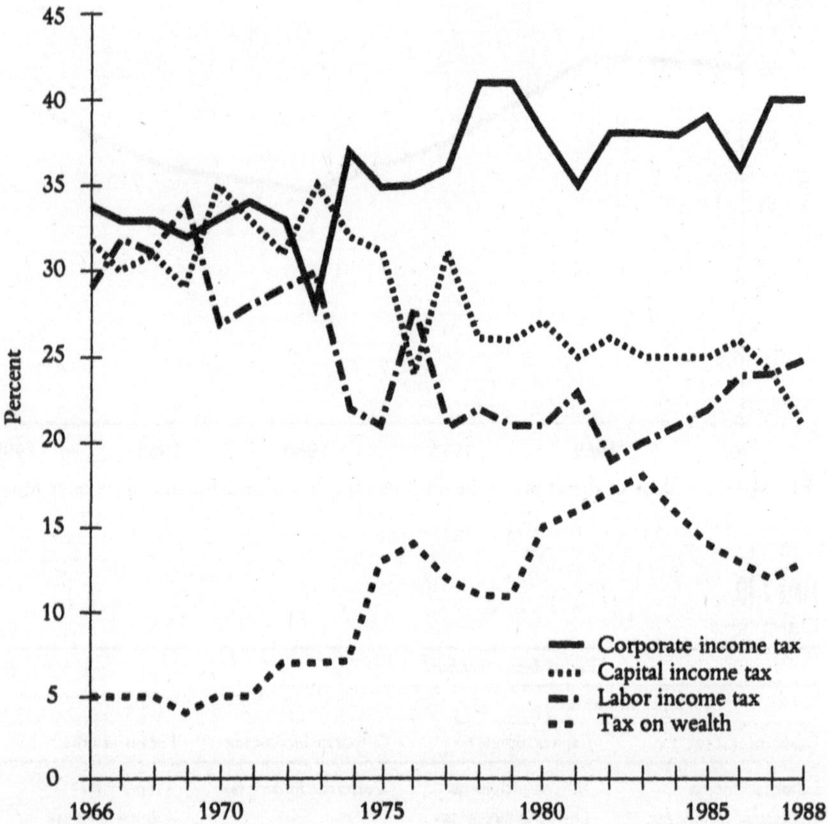

FIGURE 7.2 Changes in the composition of direct tax revenues (data from Ministry of Finance 1990).

at 10 percent in 1983 and has decreased since then. The corporate income tax's share was shifted upward in 1974 by 5 percentage points from 33 to 38 percent, while the capital income tax's share has steadily declined, reaching 21 percent in 1988.

One interesting observation is that labor income and corporate income taxes have recently increased and shifted upward, while the capital income tax and the tax on wealth have recently declined. In this respect, it is generally known and argued that wage earners are taxed more heavily relative to capital income earners. However, Table 7.11 shows that statistics vary substantially from prevailing perceptions. Wages and salaries constituted 52 percent of the national income in 1975, increasing to 60 percent in 1989, but the labor income tax was 40 and 54 percent of total factor income tax in 1975 and 1989, respectively. From these figures it appears that, contrary to popular belief, labor income and surplus taxes are keeping pace with the respective corresponding tax bases.

Table 7.11
National income and personal income taxes, 1975–1988 (percentage)

	National income			
	Wages and salaries	Surplus[a]	Labor income tax	Tax on surplus[b]
1975	52.2	47.8	40.1	59.9
1980	56.9	43.1	42.7	57.3
1985	58.5	41.5	45.9	54.1
1988	59.7	40.3	53.8	46.2

Source: Ministry of Finance (1990); Bank of Korea (1990).

[a]Surplus includes noncorporate income, interest, dividends, and rents. However, income from the agricultural sector is excluded.

[b]Surplus taxes include the global income tax, the business tax, the interest income tax, the dividend income tax, and the rental income tax. If the corporate income tax revenue is included in the tax on surplus, then the share of the labor income tax is far smaller than shown here.

Instead, prevailing perceptions arise mainly because a large part of wage earners below a threshold income did not pay at all, and those who did pay an income tax felt a somewhat heavier tax burden (Roh 1991b).[6] Therefore, the problem is not that an excessive burden is placed on wage earners as a whole, but that some of them, those wage earners in the middle class in particular, bear too much of the burden. Another problem is that an imbalance among direct taxes and leakage in tax bases of some income sources such as business and interest incomes exist, a large part of which are neither subject to taxation nor measured in the national account. In particular, business income and tax are significantly underreported due to a unique tax-reporting system: the tax agency sets a level above which proprietors report income ratio to total sales and are considered to have truly reported their income and tax. This system, unlike those of advanced countries, induces proprietors to underreport true income and tax. As shown in Table 7.12, the estimated ratio of reported income and tax paid to actual income and tax due was in the range of 8–25 percent and 13–39 percent in the latter 1980s.

Growth Potential and Capacity

The scheduled liberalization of Korea's trade and capital market will inevitably result in a restructuring of the country's industrial makeup. Furthermore, this

Table 7.12
Ratio of reported to actual business income and tax (percentage)

	Income		Tax	
	At average income	Upper limit	At average income	Upper limit
1986	12.1	24.8	18.2	39.0
1987	11.3	11.3	17.7	17.0
1988	7.9	14.8	12.8	21.4
1989	11.9	18.4	19.8	24.5

Source: Roh (1992).

inevitability will and should be fueled by the high quality of labor, sufficient social overhead capital, and new high technology in order to make this process as smooth as possible while minimizing social costs.

In fact, nobody can deny that the Korean economy has achieved rapid growth. The problem is that the top national priority has been placed on the growth of volume rather than of quality. It is therefore time to build up growth potential and production capacity for sustained social development. This requires a high rate of savings, which leads to a high rate of investment and rapid capital accumulation. Only heavy investment in research and development and human capital can allow the Korean economy to survive in the extremely competitive world economy.

In reforming the tax system, the effects of taxes on savings and investments should be taken into account. Although most adverse effects are manifested only after a long period of time, a high priority should be placed on the consistent nurturing of growth potential and production capacity.

Recognizing the International Context

The recent movement toward world political and economic openness and the new detente between East and West have come to the fore as the main global trends. The implication of this movement for the Korean economy is that, as the world becomes more liberalized and interdependent in finance and trade, Korea's economic policies may conflict with those of other countries. Taxation of factor inputs such as capital and labor in a country affects international factor flows and thus domestic as well as foreign factor prices, interest rates, and wage rates. This in turn alters the balance-of-payments positions of related countries. Consider, for example, a reduced corporate income tax in an open economy; this may cause foreign capital to flow in, so that the after-tax return to capital rises very little. There may also be a substitution of capital for labor, which will cause a decrease in wages. Ultimately, a change in factor prices will affect international trade patterns through final price changes.

TABLE 7.13
Tax rate changes in developed countries (highest bracket) (percentage)

	Personal			Corporate		
	1979	1989	% change	1979	1989	% change
Britain	83	40	43	52	35	17
Italy	72	50	22	36	36	0
United States	70	28	42	46	34	12
France	60	57	3	50	39	11
Australia	60	50	10	46	39	7
Japan	75	50	25	40	42	2
West Germany	56	53	3	56	56	0
Canada	43	29	14	46	28	18

Source: The Economist, January 5, 1991, 11.

Since the 1970s there have been interesting developments in the tax policies of developed countries. Many industrial countries reacted against the unprecedented flourishing tax levels and structures; the slower growth of real incomes, increased distortions resulting from inflation, and growing dissatisfaction with government's ability to provide goods and services effectively expedited tax reforms. The United States, the United Kingdom, Canada, and Australia produced possible tax policy options for the 1980s that deserve careful consideration.[7] There has been a clear tendency toward significant cuts in personal and corporate income taxes in developed countries. Table 7.13 shows the changes in the top tax rates for personal and corporate income taxes in major developed countries. It is important that Korea acknowledge the international trade consequences of these tax reforms and take appropriate measures to meet this challenge from abroad. Recent tax cuts in developed countries do not, however, provide Korea with the basic direction for tax reform. Nor do they necessarily justify any cut in Korea's personal and corporate taxes. But, at least, taxes on domestic factors might be reduced, with no preferential tax treatment for foreign factors at home.[8]

Theory and Practice of Tax Reform

Theories on optimal taxation explore the most desirable tax structures for an economy. The pioneering paper by Ramsey (1928) gives the optimal commodity tax mix. This rule, sometimes called the inverse elasticity rule, is connected and extended to the optimal taxation of income. When the utility function is weakly separable to leisure, Ramsey's rule is reduced to uniform commodity tax rates and is equivalent to the proportional income tax (only labor income exists). Even Mirrlees (1971) suggests a linear income tax system for Britain. When equity enters the domain of tax reform, Ramsey's rule is modified to contain the distributive characteristics of commodities (Stern 1987).

The progressive income tax system is supported by the classical equal-sacrifice theory. It parallels the "ability-to-pay" principle in which the utility taken as tax should be equal for everyone.[9] If marginal utility decreases with income, then a person who has higher initial utility should be taxed more heavily.[10] But the theory of optimal taxation does not suggest, in a practical sense, how direct (income) and indirect (commodity) taxes should be mixed, how progressive the direct tax rate schedule should be, and in what combination labor and capital income taxes are desirable.[11] A tax system is largely dependent on a country's unique socioeconomic and cultural environment, which includes the technology of tax administration available and the attitudes and expectations of the tax-paying citizens.

Tax is, in effect, the price of government services and expenditures. In the constituent's calculations of utility, tax and government activities are distinct factors related to the same issues. Each constituent measures the benefits and costs of fiscal activities and taxes and then decides to vote for or against that combination of activities and taxes. Wicksell and others stress this simultaneity in the tax and public expenditure decisions and further suggest that taxation enjoys unanimous approval just because someone would become worse off otherwise. This implies that tax reform, coupled with considerations of expenditure, should be supported by at least the majority of constituents for successful results. In other words, taxes are quasi-constitutional.[12]

Furthermore, a change in the tax system over time is not a matter of simple legislation; rather, it is a matter of establishing a socioadministrative infrastructure that will be ready when certain taxes are necessary and productive. Hinrichs (1976) suggests the following sequence of preconditions for tax reforms: (1) infrastructure (finding and training the right people); (2) formal tax reform (passing the right law); (3) substantive tax reform (enforcing these laws); and (4) tax process reform (developing an institutional framework that will continue to adapt to a changing reality).

Future Budget Requirements Necessary for Tax Reform

It is more or less a political issue whether and to what extent the government should meet increasing demand for social overhead capital and welfare-related expenditures such as transfer expenditures and expenditures on public housing, environmental improvement, interregional balanced development, and medical aid. Once the government decides to get involved in these kinds of spending, the question then becomes how to finance these expenditures.

On the one hand, this sort of strong demand for public expenditures, transfer expenditures in particular, has exploded in the process of recent democratization because the demand has been modestly tolerated. But this seems to be only a transitional phenomenon; such demand is not likely to grow as fast in the near future as it does at present. Sooner or later, people will recognize that an exces-

TABLE 7.14
Tax burden ratio to GNP (percentage)

	National tax	Internal tax	Total taxes
1988	15.8	10.1	18.3
1990	15.9	11.4	19.7
1995	17.7	12.7	22.0
2000	19.7	14.2	24.5

Source: Ministry of Finance (1990).
Note: Forecasts of the tax burden are based on nominal economic growth rate forecasts of 11 percent, GNP elasticity of national tax revenue of 1.2, and GNP elasticity of tax burden ratio of 0.2 (Roh 1990, 1991a; Roh et al. 1990).

sive increase in transfer expenditures does not always benefit them, since it raises efficiency costs. On the other hand, the rapid economic growth and national wealth accumulation of the past require greater expenditures for social overhead capital and a higher quality of life, which is income elastic. It has generally been proven that social welfare expenditures are a normal good; thus, as the economy moves up to higher stages of economic development, these expenditures are needed more.[13]

It is difficult to grasp the desirable size of government expenditures, since desirability depends upon the constituent's willingness to pay as well as his demand for each category of expenditure. But one analysis (KDI 1990), though not a direct study on expenditure but one on taxes, regressed the tax burden ratio on per capita GNP, import ratio to GDP, and social security expenditure ratio to total expenditure based on data across thirty-three countries and suggests that the desirable tax burden ratio will be 25 percent in the year 2000.

However, the tax burden ratio to GNP of total taxes is expected to reach 24.5 percent, if nominal GNP increases by 11 percent annually, as shown in Table 7.14. As a result, actual tax revenues will be a little short of desired revenues and will not meet fiscal requirements, if additional tax reductions are manifested in such measures as the repeal of the defense tax. In future tax reforms, this budget requirement should be considered a high priority.

Tax Reform Proposals

Personal Income Tax

It is needless to reemphasize the importance of the income distributive role of the personal income tax. Therefore, the progressivity of this tax should satisfy vertical equity. In fact, it is impossible to derive optimal progressivity of a personal income tax. There may be no optimal level. The current personal income tax system shows a simplified rate schedule (fewer brackets and lower rates). The problem may be that 20 percent of interest income is supposed to be paid as a withholding tax even though the income is of a real-name account. Savings from the financial market may be redirected to the real estate market, causing instability in the latter.

One might temporarily defend the position that, until the real-name-based financial transaction system (RNFT) is deeply rooted, the tax rate should be maintained at a high level. But RNFT does not necessarily mean taxation of interest income combined with all other income by the global income tax rate schedule. The RNFT system is also related to taxation of dividend income and capital gains from stocks. These two taxes are closely related to the corporate income tax. The current corporate income tax system has lowered rates. Accordingly, there is room for taxation of dividends and capital gains from stocks. Also, the gross-up system will lower the dividend tax burden. Therefore, gradual strengthening of the tax on capital gains from stocks based on RNFT is necessary and will be important for the financially liberalized Korean economy of the near future.[14]

Another recommendation is that a greater part of business income be subject to taxation. The purpose of tax administration should be to detect concealed sources of income. Also, the balance between labor and business income taxes should be restored to their state before the global taxation system was fully introduced in 1975. Business entities should be induced to follow regulations and to file their total sales honestly for the value-added tax.

It is sometimes asserted that all incomes, regardless of source, should be combined and then taxed by a progressive tax scheme (fully global income tax system). Also, some prefer the recommendation of a flat income tax such as a negative income tax (Tobin et al. 1967). Others cautiously recommend an expenditure tax system instead of a personal income tax. But these recommendations have flaws. The fully global income tax system itself violates horizontal equity—one of two equity rules—even though the system is designed to realize this rule (Feldstein 1975:17–19). The flat income tax system seems neither politically viable nor vertically equitable. Although this system is recommended for its simplicity and broadening of the tax base, it might neglect vertical equity since the complexity of the tax system arises from careful consideration, to the extent possible, of the differences in the situations faced by each taxpayer. In the real world, the flat income tax system might not be practical and therefore not recommended. The expenditure tax is equivalent to the personal labor income tax. It is efficient in that, with no capital income tax, there is no intertemporal distortion and no disincentive to save. In this sense, a recommendation of the expenditure tax system is not compatible with the strengthened capital income tax in a fully global income tax system. Moreover, this system might be impractical (Pechman 1990).

In sum, my recommendation is that the capital income tax, in particular the interest income tax, be imposed by a separate and mildly progressive tax schedule, with consideration given to consistent capital financing and accumulation for economic development.

Wealth and Property Taxes

The right instruments for the improvement of income distribution are taxes on wealth such as property taxes on land and housing, the capital gains tax, the estate tax, and the gift tax—those that can directly tackle the determinants of unequal income distribution. In particular, the land tax removes a large part of the unearned income of capital gains resulting from the high rate of increase in land price. The global land tax and CPOL have already been introduced and are in effect little more than reinforced taxation of wealth (i.e., a capital gains tax on unrealized gains and a tax on the total value of all land held). Therefore, it is strongly recommended that the complicated rate structures of the global land tax be simplified, and that CPOL be activated only when the land price soars abnormally, since CPOL brings the problems of taxing unrealized capital gains and inefficiently advancing construction on idle lands. And it is also necessary for all taxes on wealth to be harmonized at the same time, since estate and gift taxes, with low effective rates and many loopholes, weaken these taxes.

In other words, estate and gift taxes should be strengthened through strict tax administration. More specifically, I recommend that property taxes imposed on land and other real assets amount to 1 percent of the total actual value of properties. Between financial and real assets, they are inevitable substitutes. If the net return from real assets is higher than the return from financial assets, undesirable investments in real assets will take place and lead to an increase in land price. The government has promulgated the official price of land that should be used for the assessment of property or wealth-related taxes. Furthermore, it is expected that this official price will be adjusted gradually to match actual prices. Therefore, the shift from real to financial assets will be made, and this will partly curb land speculation through increasing landholding costs.[14]

Concluding Remarks

I conclude this chapter by drawing a picture of the tax structure in the near future. The desirable ratio of tax burden to GNP seems to be 25 percent for the year 2000. To meet this budget requirement, the government should maintain its current rate of tax revenue increase. If wealth and capital income taxes are strengthened as stated above, with other taxes being changed automatically, the target tax burden can be achieved with the direct tax share to total tax revenue raised to the proper level—that is, higher than 50 percent. But there still is room for the reform of personal income taxes as well.

Lowering the income tax rate will give rise to tax revenue losses, but some of these losses will be offset by the widening of the tax base, which becomes more transparent under the RNFT system. The net revenue effect as a whole, combining revenue gains from the strengthening of wealth and capital gains taxes, will be positive. Therefore, the Korean tax system will play a far greater redistributive and growth-supporting role by depending more on direct taxes than on indirect taxes and a moderate capital income tax.

NOTES

1. The defense tax is added to personal and corporate income taxes, estate and gift taxes, special consumption tax, and so on. The education tax is imposed on interest and dividend incomes.
2. Most (more than 90 percent) interest and about 50 percent of dividend incomes are taxed separately.
3. All taxes on land are imposed on values that are periodically and officially assessed.
4. Whalley (see Chapter 8 of this volume) and Browning (1978) argue that indirect taxes in general and sales taxes such as VAT are not really regressive. In fact, they may even be progressive for the bottom and top deciles. Still, it cannot be denied that direct taxes are progressive.
5. More than two sources of income, or rental and business incomes alone, are subject to global income taxation. But rental and business income taxes constitute almost all of the global income tax. Interest and dividend incomes are not subject to global income tax but are instead taxed separately at 10 percent.
6. In 1989, 50.8 percent of wage earners paid no taxes at all (MOF, Korea, 1990:70).
7. Blue Print of the United States, the Meade report of the United Kingdom, and the Carter report of Canada are among them (Head and Bird 1983).
8. The Foreign Capital Inducement Law, amended in 1983, provides foreigners with investment incentives including a five-year tax holiday for individual corporate incomes, royalties, accelerated tax depreciation, and special consumption taxes.
9. A study by Young (1990) confirms that American and Japanese income taxes are progressive in accordance with this theory.
10. The degree of progressivity of income tax is dependent on the marginal utility curve of income.
11. See Shoven (1976), Boskin (1978), Chamley (1981), Feldstein (1978), and Gandhi (1987) on capital income tax coupled with savings, economic growth, or its welfare cost. Various studies using the general equilibrium model report simulation results in which expenditures tax is superior to income tax. Since these results are derived under unrealistic, strong assumptions concerning the utility function, they can be used as supporting evidence for a tax design drawn from scratch, rather than for gradual tax reform. Tait (1989) even borrows the statement of Atkinson and Stiglitz, that "their aim is not so much to yield policy recommendations but rather to explore the grammar of the arguments." Also see Pechman (1990) for income tax. In a different perspective, Tobin et al. (1967) suggest the negative income tax system, which is considered impractical.

12. There can be no doubt that the best and indeed the only certain guarantee against such abuses of power lies in the principle of unanimity and voluntary consent in the approval of taxes (Wicksell [1856] 1967).

13. Expenditure for social development is only 10 percent of total central government expenditure in Korea, while the corresponding ratio is 15 percent in Japan. See Chapter 6 for details of the expenditure structure of Korea. According to Gould (1983) and Kohl (1983), social welfare expenditures are highly elastic to GDP (around 1.3 for its elasticity).

14. In August 1993, the new government legally launched an RNFT system by presidential order.

15. My belief is that the taxation of land by itself cannot solve the land speculation problem, even though it can be a subsidiary instrument. Land speculation arises largely from information asymmetry among agents and changes in macro variables such as rapid increases in the money supply and wealth.

REFERENCES

Bank of Korea. 1990. *National Account.* Seoul.

Boskin, Michael J. 1978. "Taxation, Saving, and the Rate of Interest." *Journal of Political Economy* 86(2):S3–S27.

Browning, E. K. 1978. "The Burden of Taxation." *Journal of Political Economy* 86(4).

Chamley, Christophe. 1981. "The Welfare Cost of Capital Income Taxation in a Growing Economy." *Journal of Political Economy* 89(3):468–496.

Concept of Public Ownership Committee (CPOL). 1989. *The Concept of Ownership Committee Research Report* (in Korean). Seoul.

Feldstein, Martin. 1975. "On the Theory of Tax Reform." Paper presented at the International Seminar on Public Economies, Paris.

Feldstein, Martin. 1978. "The Welfare Cost of Capital Income Taxation." *Journal of Political Economy* 86(2):S29–51.

Gandhi, Ved P. 1987. *Supply-Side Tax Policy: Its Relevance to Developing Countries.* Washington, D.C.: International Monetary Fund.

Gould, R. 1983. "The Growth of Public Expenditures." In Charles L. Taylor (ed.), *Why Governments Grow.* Beverly Hills, California: Sage.

Head, J. G., and R. M. Bird. 1983. "Tax Policy Options in the 1980s." In Sijbren Cnossen (ed.), *Comparative Tax Studies.* Amsterdam: North-Holland.

Hinrichs, H. H. 1966. *A General Theory of Tax Structure Change during Economic Development.* Cambridge: Harvard University Law School.

Kang, B. 1989. *Korean Economic Development Strategies and Income Distribution* (in Korean). Seoul: Korea Development Institute.

Kohl, Jurgen. 1983. "The Functional Structure of Public Expenditures: Long-Term Changes." In Charles L. Taylor (ed.), *Why Governments Grow.* Beverly Hills, California: Sage.

Korea Development Institute (KDI). 1990. "Directions of Fiscal Policy and the Optimal Size of the Budget" (in Korean). Mimeo. Seoul.

Kwon, S. 1990. Korea: *Income and Wealth Distribution and Government Initiatives to Reduce Disparities.* Korea Development Institute Working Paper 90-08. Seoul.

Ministry of Finance (MOF), Korea. 1990. "Main Tax Statistics." Seoul.
Mirrlees, J. A. 1971. "An Exploration in the Theory of Optimum Income Taxation." *Review of Economic Studies* 38:175–208.
Pechman, Joseph A. 1990. "The Future of the Income Tax." *American Economic Review* 80(1).
Ramsey, F. P. 1928. "A Mathematical Theory of Saving." *Economic Journal.*
Roh, Keesung. 1990. "Estimating the Tax Revenue Function of the Personal Incomes" (in Korean). *Korea Development Review* 12(4).
Roh, Keesung. 1991a. "Long-Term Forecasts of Public Expenditures in Korea" (in Korean). *National Budget and Policy Objectives.* Seoul: Korea Development Institute.
Roh, Keesung. 1991b. "The Rate Structure of Income Tax and Vertical Equity" (in Korean). *Korea Development Review* 13(4).
Roh, Keesung. 1992. "The Estimation of Under-reported Business Income Tax" (in Korean). *Korea Development Review* 14(4).
Roh, Keesung, I. Ryu, J. Lee, and K. Yun. 1990. *A Study of Tax Revenue Forecasting Models* (in Korean). Seoul: Korea Development Institute.
Shoven, John B. 1976. "The Incidence and Efficiency Effects of Taxes on Income from Capital." *Journal of Political Economy* 84:1261–1284.
Stern, N. 1987. "The Theory of Optimal Commodity and Income Taxation: An Introduction." In D. Newbury and Nicholas Stern (eds.), *The Theory of Taxation for Developing Countries.* New York: Oxford University Press.
Tait, A. 1989. "Not So General Equilibrium and Not So Optimal Taxation." *Public Finance* 44(2): 169–182.
Tobin, James, J. A. Pechman, and P. M. Mieszkowski. 1967. "Is a Negative Income Tax Practical?" *Yale Law Journal* 77(1).
Wicksell, K. [1856] 1967. "A New Principle of Just Taxation." In R. A. Musgrave and A. T. Peacock (eds.), *Classics in the Theory of Public Finance.* New York: Macmillan.
Young, H. Peyton. 1990. "Progressive Taxation and Equal Sacrifice." *American Economic Review* 80(1).

Chapter 8

Does Korea Need a Tax Reform in the 1990s?

John Whalley
University of Western Ontario

Introduction

With the background provided by Chong Kee Park and Keesung Roh in Chapters 6 and 7, I propose to address questions of how Korean tax policies can best be focused to foster growth, yield a more equitable income distribution, and avoid nonneutralities and resource misallocation—particularly against the context of recent tax reforms in Japan, Germany, the United Kingdom, the United States, and other OECD countries.

It is always tempting for a public finance economist, when asked to discuss possible tax reforms for specific countries, to think in terms of grand proposals for yet more change. But the theme of this chapter is that there does not really seem to be a need for major wholescale reform of the Korean tax system at this point. Over the years of strong Korean economic performance (since the late 1950s), the tax system has not really been a major impediment to growth, nor is there compelling evidence that the tax system is excessively regressive or the income distribution in Korea unequal compared to OECD economies. In short, major policy reform in Korea that seeks to dramatically further improve economic performance (if that is possible in Korea) should perhaps look elsewhere than the tax system.

From my own somewhat limited knowledge of Korean policy matters, it has always seemed to me that tax reform in Korea has never been part of the leading edge of an overall activist policy strategy. Instead, tax policy has been largely accommodative, adapting to developments elsewhere in the policy mix rather than defining new directions for policy. This approach to tax policy in Korea seems to have worked well in the past, and so perhaps it should remain the approach for some time to come.

In this chapter I stress that the history of tax policy in Korea over the postwar years has been one of accommodation to broader changes in policy orientation, which in turn have been driven by non-tax considerations. In the initial outward-oriented growth phases of the late 1950s and the 1960s, the policy focus on export promotion was accommodated through indirect tax rebate schemes and export promotion initiatives using the corporate and personal income tax as supportive of other mechanisms. The switch in the early 1970s to a focus on industrial incentives (the heavy and chemical industry growth phase) was accommodated through sectoral incentives in the corporate tax with tax-based export promotion deemphasized. And in the more recent structural adjustment phase, the general policy direction of moving toward policy neutrality has once again been accommodated by further changes in the tax system. As the Korean economy has grown, so has the tax system matured and changed, with replacement of commodity-specific indirect taxes by a value-added tax and base-broadening measures in personal and corporate taxes throughout the 1970s and 1980s.

Over the period of Korean growth, therefore, the tax system has slowly matured toward that of an OECD country, with only a few exceptions such as the remaining relatively high trade taxes, which reflect trade policies in Korea more than choice of tax policies per se. Given the substantial uncertainty that exists in public finance literature in OECD countries as to the effect of taxes on redistribution and efficiency, the indications that the income distribution in Korea is more equal than that in many OECD countries, and the lack of evidence of regressivity of the Korean tax system, there seems to be no clear requirement for yet more change in the Korean tax system at this time. The issue is more the level at which taxes should be collected to finance infrastructure improvements than the structure of the tax system.

Taxes and Economic Performance in Korea

Much of the literature attributes Korea's postwar economic success, in part, to a major change in policy direction in the 1960s from import substitution to export promotion (see Brown 1973; Hasan and Rao 1979; Krueger 1979; Kwack 1988; and Scitovsky 1985).[1] In this discussion, tax policy does not figure prominently as a contributor to growth, even though tax measures, such as indirect tax rebates, have been part of this strategy.

The mean growth rate in Korea from 1961 to 1986 has been high—around 8.3 percent—but there have been repeated and major policy changes. From 1961 to 1972 policy was strongly outward oriented and was characterized by duty remissions, tax rebates on exports, registration schemes for importers, and other measures tied to export performance. Between 1973 and 1979 the emphasis switched to development of heavy and chemical industries, including iron and steel, nonferrous metals, shipbuilding, general machinery, chemicals, and electronics. Many earlier export promotion policies, including tax holidays and other outward-oriented incentives, were withdrawn. Since 1980 policies have focused instead on structural adjustment and trade liberalization, with a pronounced move toward neutrality in policy and the removal of most existing incentives. In this 30-year process, tax policy has generally been adaptive, changing as each new policy regime has been entered into.

Growth in Korea has been remarkably resilient to these switches in both broad policy approach and accompanying tax regimes. Taxes played a role in the early outward-oriented phase through the rebating both of cascading sales and excise taxes and of a portion of corporate taxes on earnings of export industries. As protection has been reduced in the trade liberalization and structural adjustment phase, however, duty remissions have become progressively less important. Furthermore, some of the tax rebate schemes linked to exports in the early growth phase have been eliminated over the past 10 to 15 years. In the process, the Korean tax system has matured from a relatively narrowly based system, relying largely on traditional excisables, trade, and other taxes, to one with a broadly based value-added tax that accounts for a major portion of revenues and income and corporate taxes with much wider coverage and more sophisticated administration than is the case in most other developing countries (see Han 1986).

Early outward-oriented Korean policies included preferential credit for exports; indirect tax exemptions on inputs for export production and export sales; a reduction of corporate and income taxes on export earnings; wastage allowances on imported raw materials for export production; accelerated depreciation allowances for fixed capital directly used in export production; foreign loan guarantees; and import and export financing assistance.

As can be seen from Table 8.1, under these policies exports grew rapidly, initially reflecting major expansion in the production of labor-intensive manufactures (textiles, apparel, plywood, and footwear). The annual growth rate of exports (in value terms) was about 30 percent between 1961 and 1972, and real GNP grew at an annual rate of 8.2 percent. Manufactured exports were 18.2 percent of total exports in 1961 but reached 88 percent by 1972.

Disentangling the contribution of tax policy in Korea to this strong growth is a difficult task, however, not only because of changes in tax policies but also because many other factors have influenced Korean growth. The importance of taxes, as measured by tax revenues as a proportion of GNP, rose from 9.1 percent in 1962 to 15.5 percent in 1987 (see Table 8.2). This increase financed infrastructure development, which contributed to growth. But the growth in taxes was uneven, reflecting periods of lower growth, as in 1963–65, when revenue to GNP ratios fell, and in 1972–73, when substantial tax cuts were used for incentive purposes.

Also, since the introduction of the value-added tax (VAT) in 1977 (accounting for 25.3 percent of tax revenues in 1987), indirect taxes have become the most important source of revenue; the shares of direct and indirect taxes in revenues were 42.3 and 26.6 percent, respectively, in 1976, but then switched places, moving to 23.4 and 40.3 percent in 1987. This has raised concerns over regressivity[2] in the Korean tax system: sales (VAT) taxes are traditionally viewed as regressive, since richer households save more of their income.

TABLE 8.1
Major economic indicators of Korean growth, 1955–1986

	Per capita GNP (US current $)	% growth rate of GNP (1975 constant won)	% inflation rate (GNP deflator)	Gross fixed investment to GNP ratio	National saving to GNP ratio	% growth rate of exports	Exports to GNP ratio	Manufacturing exports to total exports ratio
1955	65	4.1	62.1	10.2	5.2	22.1	2.9	na
1956	66	–1.4	34.0	10.3	–1.9	–9.0	2.3	na
1957	74	7.6	22.2	10.6	5.5	33.9	2.2	na
1958	80	5.5	–1.3	10.2	4.9	24.6	2.8	na
1959	81	3.8	1.3	11.0	4.2	15.0	3.4	na
1960	79	1.1	11.7	10.8	0.8	20.8	4.1	na
1961	82	5.6	14.0	11.7	2.9	38.7	6.3	18.2
1962	87	2.2	18.4	13.7	3.2	13.0	6.0	27.0
1963	100	9.1	29.3	13.5	8.7	9.0	5.4	51.7
1964	103	9.6	30.0	11.3	8.7	23.5	6.7	51.6
1965	105	5.8	6.2	14.8	7.4	35.9	9.5	62.3
1966	125	12.7	14.5	20.2	11.8	42.4	11.9	62.4
1967	142	6.6	15.6	21.4	11.4	32.7	13.6	70.0
1968	169	11.3	16.1	25.0	15.1	39.5	14.7	77.3
1969	210	13.8	14.8	25.8	18.8	36.1	15.4	79.0
1970	252	7.6	15.6	24.7	16.2	19.6	15.0	83.6
1971	288	9.1	12.9	22.5	14.5	21.1	16.1	86.0
1972	318	5.3	16.3	20.4	15.7	36.0	20.6	87.7
1973	395	14.0	12.1	23.2	21.4	53.0	30.0	88.2
1974	540	8.5	30.4	25.6	19.3	–0.8	28.4	90.2
1975	590	6.8	24.6	25.3	16.8	19.0	28.2	88.3
1976	797	13.4	21.0	24.4	22.2	41.5	32.0	89.8
1977	1008	10.7	15.9	27.3	25.4	23.3	32.7	87.5
1978	1392	11.0	21.6	31.3	27.3	12.5	30.6	89.9
1979	1640	7.0	20.0	33.2	26.5	–1.1	27.7	90.1
1980	1589	–4.8	25.3	32.3	20.8	10.2	34.4	92.3
1981	1719	6.6	15.4	28.7	20.5	15.0	37.8	92.9
1982	1773	5.4	6.7	30.5	20.9	6.5	36.9	93.7
1983	1914	11.9	3.9	31.3	25.3	15.5	37.5	94.4
1984	2044	8.4	3.8	31.3	27.9	10.0	38.7	95.0
1985	2047	5.4	4.1	30.8	28.6	2.1	37.7	95.4
1986	2300	12.3	2.7	31.4	32.6	26.5	42.5	94.6

Source: Trela and Whalley (1990, 1991), who draw on Choi (1988:tab. II-I); Economic Planning Board (1976, 1988).
na = not available.

Table 8.2

Structure of national taxes in Korea, 1962–1987 (as percentage of total national taxes)

	Direct taxes				Indirect Taxes								
	Income tax	Corporation tax	Business tax	Others	VAT	Special Consumption tax	Liquor tax	Commodity tax	Others	Stamp revenue	Custom duties	Defense surtaxes	National taxes as % of GNP
1962	16.2	7.2	6.9	3.1			8.9	16.7	13.8	2.3	23.9		9.1
1963	19.1	9.6	8.2	2.7			8.9	12.1	14.5	2.3	23.9		7.1
1964	23.0	11.0	8.6	2.8			7.9	8.8	12.6	2.3	22.0		5.9
1965	21.4	10.4	8.0	2.8			6.9	12.9	12.3	1.4	23.0		7.2
1966	23.2	12.4	8.3	3.0			7.2	11.8	11.2	1.7	20.1		9.2
1967	23.9	12.3	8.9	3.3			6.3	11.9	11.1	1.8	19.7		10.9
1968	24.5	12.7	9.0	2.8			5.7	11.4	12.5	1.3	19.5		12.7
1969	26.5	212.6	8.8	2.7			6.1	11.7	12.6	1.2	17.0		13.3
1970	25.2	12.7	9.3	3.5			6.5	9.5	17.1	4.9	15.2		13.1
1971	26.4	13.9	9.3	3.5			6.8	8.6	17.7	0.6	12.8		13.3
1972	24.2	12.6	11.2	3.7			6.5	8.5	16.8	1.8	13.6		11.4
1973	23.7	9.5	11.5	4.8			6.5	9.6	16.4	1.6	15.8		10.8
1974	19.5	13.1	11.5	4.5			6.3	9.4	18.2	1.6	15.0		12.1
1975	15.8	10.4	15.8	4.1			6.54	9.4	13.7	1.0	14.4	5.0	13.8
1976	16.7	8.9	13.6	3.0		4.9	8.7	13.0	0.8	14.4		14.0	15.1
1977	14.7	9.8	8.7	0.8	10.11	4.2	5.1	5.0	9.3	0.8	16.1	14.2	14.8
1978	13.9	10.6		0.5	24.9	9.7	5.8	0.0	0.7	0.7	19.2	14.0	15.3
1979	14.0	11.2		0.4	24.7	11.0	6.0		0.8	0.8	16.6	14.4	15.5
1980	12.5	9.2		0.6	27.8	11.0	5.6		1.0	0.6	14.5	16.2	15.8
1981	13.5	9.0		1.0	27.4	10.7	5.7		1.1	0.8	13.5	16.6	16.1
1982	13.2	10.2		1.2	27.4	8.7	5.2		1.4	0.7	13.3	15.4	16.6
1983	12.3	9.4		1.0	27.8	8.6	4.8		1.4	0.7	15.9	14.2	17.0
1984	12.2	9.2		0.8	26.9	8.9	4.9		1.6	0.7	15.9	14.7	16.4
1985	13.4	10.2		0.6	26.3	8.9	4.5		1.6	0.7	14.2	15.1	16.3
1986	14.1	9.4		0.6	25.9	8.6	4.4		1.7	0.7	15.4	14.6	16.2
1987	13.6	9.3		0.5	25.3	8.8	4.5		1.7	0.6	17.0	14.4	15.5

Source: Trela and Whalley (1990, 1991), who draw on Economic Planning Board (1982, 1988).

1961–72

In the 1960s, the main objective of Korean policy was to achieve export growth, which the government of the day equated with nation building.[3] It saw tax incentives as forming part of this policy strategy and as one way of helping to promote the growth of foreign exchange earnings, particularly from labor-intensive exports in which Korea was believed to have a comparative advantage. The most prominent tax measures used were rebating indirect taxes on inputs used in export production (whether imported or domestically purchased), and indirect taxes on export sales.[4] These tax rebates operated alongside tariff exemptions on capital equipment and raw materials imported for export production.

Export incentives also included special depreciation arrangements in the corporate tax. These were introduced in 1962, with machinery and equipment used in export production or sales eligible for an additional allowance equivalent to 30 percent of the normal depreciation allowance. In 1966 the scheme changed slightly, making the allowance 30 percent if the export share of total revenues exceeded 50 percent, and 15 percent if the share was less than or equal to 50 percent. In 1971 the rule applicable to the latter case was changed to 30 percent times twice the share. Equipment used by small and medium-sized firms was also eligible for an additional 30 percent special depreciation allowance from 1968 onward.

Beyond these were direct tax exemptions on income from export business and a 20 percent exemption on income from tourism and sales of goods and services to U.N. military forces in Korea; however, from 1962 on, all incomes from activities earning foreign currency were given this same treatment, and the exemption rate was raised to 50 percent.

Other features of the tax regime in these years, although not directly tied to trade performance, affected growth performance. Tax holidays had been provided since 1949 for selected industries deemed important for national economic development, including shipbuilding, machinery, basic metals, petrochemicals, and chemical fertilizers. Typically such industries were classified into one of two groups, each with a different tax schedule. The first group (including oil refining, steel, shipbuilding, iron and steel, copper, cement, and chemicals) were eligible for a five-year tax holiday. For a second group, a three-year tax exemption applied. Over the years, minor changes were made to these schedules, but the notion of using incentives for selected industries became a central element in the tax system.

In 1968 a 6 percent investment tax credit was given to qualifying firms in selected industries, notably shipbuilding, iron and steel, chemical fertilizer, synthetic fiber, autos, machinery, straw pulp, food processing, petrochemicals, electronic equipment, electrical machinery and equipment, construction, and some mining industries. In 1970 a 6–10 percent investment tax credit was given for investment in machinery and equipment in iron and steel manufacturing, with larger firms receiving the higher rate. Tax incentives under the 1972 Emergency Decree included a 10 percent temporary credit for investment using domestic capital goods manufactured before 1975 and a 40–80 percent special depreciation allowance for fixed assets employed by firms in selected industries. From 1970 on, the five-year tax holiday was given only to selected petrochemical industries.

The initial outward-oriented phase of Korean growth therefore featured several tax measures to spur development, including tax rebates and exemptions for exports. Although it did not necessarily play a central role to the growth strategy, tax policy clearly contributed to outward orientation and growth during the period.

1973–79

In the early 1970s, Korea began to scale back its export promotion policies, giving higher priority to sectoral development and focusing primarily on heavy and chemical industries. There were accompanying changes in direct taxes and their incentive features.

In 1973 the 30 percent corporate tax exemption on export earnings was replaced by two tax-free reserve funds, one to develop new foreign markets and the other to defray export or foreign investment losses. Under the former, licensed exporters could deduct 1 percent of their foreign exchange earnings from taxable income and deposit this in a reserve fund. After a grace period of two years, the amount was to be added evenly to taxable income over the following three years. Under a new export and foreign investment program, any firm earning foreign exchange could deduct an amount not exceeding either total foreign exchange sales or 50 percent of total income, depending on which figure was the lowest, and, as in the foreign exchange market reserve system, add it back to taxable income after a two-year grace period.[5]

There were other changes. In 1974 the system of prior tariff exemptions for capital equipment imported for export production was changed to an installment payment system. In 1975 tariff exemptions on raw material inputs for export production were dropped in favor of a drawback system, which required exporters to pay tariffs and indirect taxes when importing their inputs, but these were rebated when exports were actually shipped out.

Indirect tax rebates on exports were changed in 1977. A destination-based VAT replaced eight existing indirect taxes, making rebating of indirect taxes both easier and more transparent. The VAT was regarded in Korea as a simpler and more effective way of rebating taxes on exports because exports are zero-rated under the VAT.[6] Indirect tax refunds for exports increased sharply after the introduction of the VAT, in part because the tax rate increased. For example, the indirect tax refund, as a percentage of export values, increased from 6 percent in 1976 to 9 percent in 1978 and to 10 percent in 1982 (Choi 1984:tab. 14).

Tax changes also occurred outside trade-based incentives. In 1974 a new "special tax treatment for key industries program" was instituted. Under this program, eligible firms in selected industries could get either (1) a tax holiday for five years, with 100 percent tax exemption for the first three years and 50 percent exemption for the following two years, (2) an 8 percent investment tax credit for machinery and equipment (10 percent for investment using domestically produced capital goods), or (3) an additional 100 percent special depreciation allowance. Industries selected for this treatment included shipbuilding, naphtha cracking plants, selected machine and electronics manufacturers, iron and steel, fertilizer, copper, lead and zinc smelting, selected mining and refining, and electric power generation. Firms in iron and steel, petrochemicals, shipbuilding, chemical fiber, chemical pulp, marine food processing, and other food processing industries not qualifying for these benefits were entitled to a 60 percent special depreciation allowance on machinery and equipment; the special depreciation rate for small and medium-sized firms was also raised from 30 to 50 percent.

Thus, in the heavy industry promotion phase of Korean growth, export tax incentives no longer played the central role, which instead was played by industry incentive schemes, whose effect was to concentrate Korean investment over this period on a relatively small number of industries.

Since 1980

In 1980, in the face of financial losses and structural distortions caused by the drive for heavy and chemical industries, Korea began pursuing a policy of structural adjustment and liberalization that stressed neutrality in policy instead of industrial targeting. Once again, tax policy was changed.

Substantial modifications were made to the tax system in 1981. Effective in 1982, petrochemicals, steel, nonferrous metal refining, chemical fertilizer, and power generation were excluded from the industry beneficiary list. The 60 percent special depreciation system and the tax holiday option were terminated, and eligibility for special tax credit was limited to the machinery and electronics industries. Also, the investment tax credit was reduced to 6 percent (10 percent for investments using domestic capital goods) and then halved to 3 percent in 1983 (5 percent for investments using domestic capital goods).

The tax incentives now in use are not designed to affect the structure of the economy but rather to promote neutrality by correcting market failures or compensating for them. Thus, the government has attempted to promote small and medium-sized firms to offset the power of conglomerates and to speed the adoption of new technologies. Up to 15 percent of the book value of fixed business assets at the end of the previous accounting period can now be reserved as a taxable income deduction. If after a four-year grace period actual investment expenditures exceed the reserved amount, they are added evenly to taxable income over the succeeding three years. If, on the other hand, the reserved amount exceeds actual investment expenditures, the difference is added to taxable income in the fourth year.

Further changes include a six-year personal income tax exemption for owners of newly established smaller firms in rural or sea districts in manufacturing, mining, construction, transportation, or fishery industries, and those organized in technology-intensive industries (100 percent for the first four years and 50 percent for the subsequent two years). Furthermore, such newly organized smaller firms are given a 50 percent deduction from property taxes for five years and a 50 percent reduction in acquisition and registration taxes for two years. Tax incentives for companies investing in these new firms include tax-free reserves for investment losses, 100 percent exemption from capital gains tax, and a special 10 percent tax rate on dividend income.

Establishing the exact effect of all these measures on Korean economic performance is difficult, but Kwang Suk Kim has estimated the export subsidy effect of a range of tax and non-tax policies in Korea over the period 1958–83 (see Chapter 17, Table 17.1). Kim focuses on policies for which consistent and quantitatively significant time series data were available. These include direct cash subsidies, exchange rate premiums, interest subsidies, indirect tax exemptions, tariff exemptions, and direct tax reductions (exclusive of accelerated depreciation provisions and reserve funds both for developing export markets and for covering exports losses).

The export subsidy effect of direct tax exemptions was derived as the difference between tax liabilities in the absence of any such exemptions and actual direct tax payments. The incentive effect of different interest rates was determined in any analogous fashion. The interest subsidy was the difference between the interest paid at the nonpreferential commercial bank lending rate and the interest actually paid. Similar calculations were made for the various other tax and non-tax export incentives.

Several interesting observations flow from Kim's data. Exchange rate policy, via the foreign exchange premiums, seemed to play an important role in stimulating exports during the late 1950s and early 1960s, before being changed in 1965. Furthermore, the largest export incentives occurred during the 1960s and early 1970s, which was also the period in which the effects of export promotion schemes increased markedly. Beginning in the early 1970s, however, the Korean government tried to reduce the scope of export incentives, as is clearly evident from the fluctuations in these subsidies, from 29.6 percent in 1972 to a low of 16.7 percent in 1975 and, with subsequent rises, to a high of 21.3 percent in 1980. Gross export subsidies declined from 136.2 percent of the official exchange rate in 1960 to 18.1 percent in 1961 mainly because of the substantial depreciation of the won and the resulting rapid increase in exports. Net exports subsidies per U.S. dollar declined from 23 percent of the official exchange rate in 1964 to about 4–7 percent during 1965–78, mainly because of the abolition of the export-import link system.

Table 17.1 also clearly indicates the role of tax policy to outward-oriented strategy in the 1970s. The direct tax reductions for exporters were consistently small and had disappeared by the early 1970s. But indirect tax exemptions for exporters grew from approximately one-third of gross export subsidies in 1965 to approximately one half by 1980. Adoption of the destination-based VAT system in 1977, under which exports are zero-rated, increased the border tax rebates on exports sharply.

These data seem to confirm the hypothesis that tax policy in Korea has involved a maturation of the tax system which has generally been accommodative of growth and resulted in the tax system broadly approaching an OECD style tax structure (a progressive income tax with a reasonably broad base, a corporate tax, a VAT) during the later-stage growth process. In all stages of this process, however, tax policy has been focused largely on the use of incentive schemes to promote the current growth strategy, with less use of tax policy to achieve other goals such as redistribution.

Comparing Korean and OECD Taxes

If the postwar history of tax policy in Korea has been one of adaptation and response to both internal policy developments and external factors, an evaluation of the next steps for tax policy in Korea might reasonably ask how different current Korean tax policies and objectives are from those in OECD countries. Perhaps the central distinguishing characteristic of Korean tax policy over the years of rapid development has been a seeming lack of emphasis on redistribution through the tax system. Although taxes on capital gains have been introduced in recent years, it seems fair to say that the main thrust of Korean tax policy has been to promote growth. In the various phases of growth promotion this has been through the chosen routes (export promotion, industrial targeting, etc.) rather than by using tax policy to achieve either growth or a more equitable income or wealth distribution per se.

At the same time, however, changes in tax policy in the most recent structural adjustment phase have yielded a tax system that today is structurally quite similar to those of the OECD countries. Also, the degree of equality in the income distribution seemingly generated during the rapid growth process has produced an income distribution which, if anything, is more equal than in OECD countries. Ironically, there is an argument that by promoting growth, which in turn has produced more equality in the income distribution, the Korean tax system may have been more egalitarian in impact than it would have been under a direct attack on redistribution through tax policy consciously designed with this objective in mind, as in some of the OECD countries.

In Tables 8.3, 8.4, and 8.5, a series of comparisons of tax structure and rates between Korea and various OECD countries are reported. Table 8.3 compares tax collections and revenue shares of taxes in Korea and OECD countries; Table 8.4 compares tax rates; and Table 8.5 compares tax structure across several countries. As Table 8.3 shows, the ratio of tax revenues to GDP in Korea still remains below that of major OECD countries. In part, this is because of the relatively low level of GDP per capita in Korea compared to the OECD countries. However, these levels seem approximately the orders of magnitude that held in Japan at comparable levels of development in the early 1960s. In terms of tax structure, the higher dependence on direct taxes in Japan and Europe is a noticeable difference relative to Korea, although the heavier dependence on indirect taxes in Korea also occurs in the United Kingdom and West Germany. The heavy dependence on trade taxes

TABLE 8.3
Revenue shares in Korean and OECD tax systems

	Korea (1987)	Japan (1989)	U.K. (1989)	West Germany (1989)	U.S. (1989)
Tax revenues as percentage of GDP	17.5	30.6	36.5	38.1	30.1
Revenue shares by tax (%)					
Direct					
Personal income	13.5	24.7	26.6	29.5	35.7
Corporate	9.3	24.4	12.3	5.5	8.5
Indirect					
VAT/Sales	25.2	3.3	16.8	15.4	7.4
Excise	13.3	6.6	10.8	6.7	4.7
Trade taxes	17.0	0.7	1.0	0.8	1.1
Other (incl. payroll and local)	20.0	40.3	32.5	42.1	42.6

Source: Economic Planning Board (1988:tab. 8-6); Park (this volume); OECD (1991:various tables).

in Korea reflects duties that still remain and are determined more by the orientation of current trade policies than by tax policies. Outside of this, the Korean tax system is structurally not that different from other OECD countries, and it is perhaps more similar to the European than the North American countries.

As Tables 8.4 and 8.5 suggest, Korea has corporate, personal, and sales tax rates not unlike those in OECD countries. The VAT rate is similar to rates in Western Europe; corporate tax rates are a little lower, with top personal marginal tax rates at a comparable level. Korea stands alone in not having, until recently, taxation of capital gains, although it has a similar tax treatment of imputed income of home ownership and a dividend tax credit comparable to those used in West Germany and the United Kingdom. Korea also still retains some degree of acceleration in depreciation allowances. Overall then, and at first sight, the Korean tax system seems to be not that dramatically different from those in use in the major OECD countries, with small differences in structure here or there.

Comparing the degree of progressivity implicit in the Korean tax system is, unfortunately, not a simple matter, since there seem to be no generally available studies of tax incidence in Korea (in English). There is also some ambiguity as to how Korea stands in terms of comparative income distribution relative to OECD countries. Chong Kee Park (see Chapter 6) argues that with Gini coefficients at 0.28 in Japan and 0.30 in Taiwan, the Korean economy is more unequal than its neighbors. Park also argues that the Gini coefficient in Korea was 0.33 in 1970, rising to 0.39 in 1976, and falling after 1980 to 0.34 in 1988. This suggests that the

TABLE 8.4
Tax rates in Korea and OECD countries

	Korea (1986)	Japan (1990)	United Kingdom (1989)	West Germany (1990)	United States (1990)
Standard VAT rate	13%	3%	15%	14%	none
No. of VAT rates	1	1	1	1	none
Basic corporate tax rate	20%	37.5	35%	50%	34%
Top marginal personal tax rate	37% plus 55% of an amount in excess of $60 million won	50%	40%	53%	28% with a 5% surcharge for some higher income individuals

Source: Ministry of Finance, ROK (1986); Ministry of Finance, Japan (1990); Dilnot and Kay (1990); Roh (this volume); Uelner and Merck (1988:tab. 1); Whalley (1990:tab. 9.1); International Tax Centre (1990).

TABLE 8.5
Tax structure in Korea and OECD countries

	Korea	Japan	United Kingdom	West Germany	United States
Taxation of captial gains	Yes	Yes	Yes	No	Yes
Tax treatment of housing	Imputed income tax free	Imputed income tax free	Imputed income tax free	Imputed income tax free	Imputed income tax free
Dividend tax credit	Yes	Yes	Yes	Yes	Yes
Accelerated depreciation	System of special depreciation	System of special depreciation	No	System of special depreciation	No
Investment tax credit	Yes	Yes	No	No	No

Source: Ministry of Finance, ROK (1986); Ministry of Finance, Japan (1990); Whalley (1990); OECD (1991).

Korean growth process has not been accompanied by a monotonic reduction in inequality, as some maintain. However, Keesung Roh (see Chapter 7) quotes comparative data on Gini coefficients for income distributions, with Korea (1988) at 0.336, Italy (1977) at 0.36, the United Kingdom (1978) at 0.372, Philippines (1975) at 0.45, United States (1978) at 0.364, and Canada (1977) at 0.402. These data seem to suggest clearly that Korea has a more equal distribution of income than many OECD countries.

It is more than inequality in the income distribution per se that has been used by pro–tax reform proponents in Korea to argue that a redistribution-driven tax reform is now in order; they see the heavy reliance on indirect taxes as the larger factor. C. K. Park, for instance, argues that, for reasons of equity and social stability, tax reform is badly needed in Korea. The low direct tax shares in Korea in Table 8.3 have already been emphasized above, and Park argues that one reason for contemplating reform is that Korea collects only around 34 percent of revenues from direct (corporate and personal) taxes, as against 40 percent in France, 58 percent in Italy, 73 percent in Japan, and 90 percent in the United States.

One issue is how important this difference in tax structure is for the impact of Korean taxes and hence the extent of regressivity generated in the Korean tax system by this heavy reliance on indirect taxes. As the next section makes clear, much recent OECD-based literature in public finance has challenged the long-standing and traditional view that indirect (sales or VAT) taxes are inherently regressive. Perceived regressivity is in part a reflection of the fact that higher-income households save a larger fraction of their income, and hence taxes on consumption are seen to favor them. But if savings today are dissaved, and if a lifetime (or even dynastic) view of tax incidence is taken, then it is no longer clear that savers should be treated as not bearing the burden of consumption taxes, and the argument that such taxes are regressive comes under challenge (see Browning 1978; and Davies, St-Hilaire, and Whalley 1985). Thus, despite these differences, whether there remains a need for tax reform in Korea on redistributive grounds depends on how one evaluates the impact of current policies, as well as how equal or otherwise the income distribution is.

Evaluating Korean Tax Policy Options

In light of the success of Korean tax policy in accommodating the Korean growth process, the relatively small differences remaining between the Korean and OECD country tax systems, and the seeming equal income distribution in Korea, it seems reasonable to ask what impact further modifications to the Korean tax system could have on future economic performance, particularly on distribution, growth, and efficiency. Is further change merited? Perhaps the most direct way of answering these questions is to draw on recent studies of tax policy in the OECD countries and assess their implications for Korea.

Here there is a large literature, which seems to indicate that in the OECD countries the tax system probably has had only mild effects on income distribution (and may have been somewhat progressive in impact) but more major effects on overall economic efficiency and aggregate performance. The implications for Korean tax policy seem to be that little current inequality in Korea should perhaps be attributed to taxes; that raising more revenues to use to redistribute incomes may have adverse incentive effects; and that tax policy that seeks to be more than accommodative to the Korean growth process through minimizing resource misallocation as part of a structural adjustment approach needs careful justification.

One of the more prominent themes in recent OECD public finance literature is that distortions caused by taxes have associated with them an excess burden. The term "excess burden" is used synonymously with "distortionary loss." It provides a measure of the cost to society of the misallocation of resources induced by distorting taxes.

There are different ways to calculate the excess burden of a tax. Perhaps the most famous is associated with Harberger (1959, 1962, 1964a, 1964b, 1966), who calculates the changes in consumer and producer surpluses involved with distorting taxes. These are not limited to distortions of consumer choice; taxes also cause distortions in the allocation of resources on the production side of the economy. The corporate tax, for example, has long been analyzed as a productively distorting tax, since it distorts the allocation of resources between the incorporated and unincorporated sectors of the economy (especially between the manufacturing industry and housing). Other tax distortions affect intertemporal allocation decisions of households by distorting the allocation of resources through time; this form of distortion has also been analyzed in terms of the associated deadweight loss.

Taxes also affect the distribution of income, and these effects have been analyzed in OECD literature. The personal income tax with progressive tax rates seeks to make the distribution of net of tax personal incomes more equal, while the taxation of capital income through the corporate tax changes the functional distribution between capital and labor and thus feeds back on personal distribution. The incidence literature, in calculating tax burdens, seeks to analyze the impact of taxes on the personal distribution of income, while model-oriented incidence analyses focus on the functional distribution.

In the following two subsections, I briefly summarize some recent evidence on the distributional and efficiency impacts of taxes in OECD countries and assess how this may relate to possible Korean tax policy. A reasonable benchmark evaluation may be to suggest that the overall efficiency effects of taxes for OECD countries are significant, especially so at the margin, whereas the combined distributional impacts of OECD tax systems are small but possibly somewhat progressive.

Efficiency Losses from Taxes

For the OECD economies, calculations of the welfare cost to the economy of tax distortions have been pioneered by Harberger (whose papers are collected in Harberger 1974), who has drawn on Hotelling's (1938) earlier work in providing calculations of the social cost of several tax distortions.[7] In more recent years, this work has been carried further through more complex numerical general equilibrium models constructed to evaluate the interacting effects of tax distortions in various economies.

Piggott and Whalley (1985) considered most of the major distorting elements of the U.K. tax-subsidy system in the 1970s. The conclusion from this work is that, aside from distortions associated with inflation, the distorting loss from the whole U.K. tax-subsidy system appears to be in the region of 7–9 percent of GNP per year. In terms of revenues, about one-quarter of total tax collections are "destroyed" through the misallocation of resources caused by the tax-subsidy system. For an assumed 10 percent inflation rate, their estimate of the distortionary loss of the tax-subsidy system increases by about 2 percent (of GNP). Under this modified calculation, roughly one-third of total taxes collected are "destroyed" through the misallocation of resources in the economy. Similar ranges of estimates for the welfare cost of the U.S. tax system are given in Ballard, Shoven, and Whalley (1985).

Examining individual tax distortions, calculations by Harberger (1964b) and by Piggott and Whalley (1985) evaluate labor supply distortions through the income tax alone. This distortion involves a commodity for which the supply elasticity is low (according to current evidence). The tax distortion involved is less significant than some of the other tax distortions of economic behavior (less than 0.5 percent of GNP), and welfare loss estimates are minor. The larger number produced by Browning (1976) for labor supply distortions from taxes (0.9 percent) reflects the combination of the income, sales, excise, and social security taxes.

Interestingly, the Browning calculation considers not only the total welfare costs to the economy from various tax distortions but also the marginal welfare costs per dollar of additional tax revenue raised. Because further taxes would need to be collected by increasingly distortionary taxes, the marginal welfare cost to the economy from increases in taxes in a distorting tax system is larger than the average welfare cost calculated for the whole of the system. For the income tax alone, Browning calculates that, for every additional dollar collected through the U.S. income tax, 14–16 cents is "lost" through further labor supply distortions.[8] This conclusion suggests that a calculation of the marginal welfare cost for the whole U.K. tax-subsidy (extrapolating from the Piggott and Whalley calculations) would have a marginal welfare cost substantially in excess of one-quarter to one-third of additional tax revenues. Estimates of this order of magnitude for the U.S. economy are reported in Stuart (1984) and in Ballard, Shoven, and Whalley (1985).

A further set of tax distortions affect the interindustry use of capital. Here the focus is on the distorting effects of the combination of corporate, property, and personal income taxes on the industrial allocation of capital. The corporate sector in the economy has to pay the corporate tax, while personal income taxes give preferences to housing which, in turn, are partially offset through the property tax. The combined effect of these taxes is to distort the interindustry allocation of capital in the economy. A first calculation by Harberger (1964b) suggested that a loss of 0.3 percent of the U.S. GNP is involved. In a later paper, Harberger (1966) analyzes the combined effects of the U.S. corporate, property, and personal income taxes and calculates a production loss of 0.4–0.6 percent of GNP. Shoven's (1976) recalculation of the Harberger estimate does not substantially change these earlier figures.

Ballentine (1978) produces a combined intersectoral and intertemporal welfare loss estimate of 1.6–2.3 percent of GNP for the United States, and Piggott and Whalley (1985) produce a larger 2.1 percent welfare loss from the U.K. corporate and property tax distortions. The tax rates involved for the United Kingdom are more sharply differentiated than in the U.S. case. In these two studies, the welfare losses from consumer distortions as well as producer distortions are included. The Ballentine calculation suggests that about half the revenues collected through the corporate tax are "lost" through the distortions produced.

Fullerton, King, Shoven, and Whalley (1981) analyze the removal of consumer and producer distortions associated with corporate and personal tax integration in the United States and also include some calculations of the effects of intertemporal distortions of the corporate tax. Based on U.S. data for 1973, their results suggest that the welfare loss from distortions in the corporate tax are in the region of 1 percent of GNP. Approximately 30 percent of corporate income tax collections are "lost." The last-mentioned three studies thus clearly suggest that on efficiency grounds tax distortions of interindustry use of capital are more important than distortions of labor supply.

Analysis of tax distortion of savings has also attracted considerable attention in OECD countries. Summers's (1981) well-known paper suggested that the distorting loss to the U.S. economy could be as much as 10 percent of GNP, although some features of this study have been questioned in subsequent work (see Auerbach, Kotlikoff, and Skinner 1983; and Davies, Hamilton, and Whalley 1989). The Fullerton, Shoven, and Whalley (1983) and the Piggott and Whalley (1985) estimates are not as large; welfare costs are more modest, but still more significant than distortions of labor supply.

For home ownership distortions—an area public finance economists have long been interested in for possible tax reform initiatives—the most widely quoted welfare loss estimate is by Laidler (1971): 0.1 percent of GNP for the United States, using 1960 data. Piggott and Whalley (1985) show that this estimate is heavily dependent on the inflation rate assumed, because of the absence of any taxation on nominal capital gains on housing. If the inflation rate of the economy is large enough, the welfare loss becomes much larger. For a 20 percent inflation rate in the United Kingdom, they estimate that homeowner preferences inflict an annual welfare loss on the economy of 1.7 percent of GNP.

Excise taxes typically involve high tax rates and therefore larger distortions. A problem with a simple interpretation of these distortions is the suggestion that their removal will result in sharp increases in consumption of drink and tobacco, and this would represent a beneficial change in the economy. Under the usual assumption of sovereignty of consumer choice, Piggott and Whalley (1985) show a distorting cost involved of 1.6 percent of GNP. Browning (1976) confirms the importance of excise tax distortions with his estimate that the marginal welfare cost in the United States per dollar of additional tax collection amounts to 26 cents.

Subsidies have not attracted much attention in terms of their distorting costs, but Piggott and Whalley (1985) report a welfare loss estimate of over 3 percent of GNP for the United Kingdom. The largest portion of this loss is accounted for by subsidies to public housing. Piggott and Whalley (1985) also estimate a significant welfare loss from inflation-induced tax distortions. These distortions affect the tax treatment of housing and also the treatment of stock appreciation in the corporate tax.

Two other general distortion studies are relevant here. Boskin (1975) looks at the differential tax treatment of the market and nonmarket economies, focusing heavily on homeowner and labor supply distortions. His loss estimate from these distortions (using 1972 U.S. data) is 1.7–3.4 percent of GNP (5–11 percent of total taxes collected). Browning (1979), in a study of tax preferences in the U.S. income tax (which includes home owner preferences), suggests that 0.6 percent of GNP is lost through a misallocation of resources. A marginal welfare cost of 13 cents on the dollar is involved.

Other distortions in OECD tax systems have received less quantitative analysis. A potentially important distortion arises with the tax treatment of human capital formation (see Davies and Whalley 1991). Distortions within the social security system, especially of retirement decisions and displacement of private sector capital accumulation of anticipated social security benefits, are also stressed by Feldstein (1974). Welfare cost estimates are not, however, included in the literature. One last "distortion" arises through the operation of the "underground" economy. There have been recent suggestions (e.g., Feige 1979) that the total value of "underground" activity in the United States may be as large as 30 percent of GNP. Since the underground economy is untaxed, a large "distortion" operates.

Another issue relevant to an evaluation of the efficiency impacts of tax systems in OECD countries is the possibility that a distorting tax may improve the domestic terms of trade of individual countries; in such a case, from the point of view of a national economy, the tax may involve, not a welfare loss, but a welfare gain (a welfare loss is, however, imposed internationally). Whalley (1980), for instance, produces some calculations for the United States which suggest that significant tax exporting occurs within the U.S. capital taxation system.

Distributional Effects of Taxes

Available studies of distributional impacts of tax policies in OECD countries largely reflect detailed data analyses and attempts to collect information on incomes, expenditures, and other characteristics of households, and on their payment of income taxes. The best known of these studies are by Pechman and Okner (1974) for the United States. The alternative approach of constructing an analytical model with more limited data, in an effort to provide a clearer indication as to the incidence of particular taxes, is associated with Harberger (1962) and his work on corporate and other capital income taxes in the United States.

In recent years, this latter approach has been taken further in larger-scale general equilibrium models (such as those mentioned earlier, by Piggott and Whalley 1985 for the United Kingdom, and by Ballard, Fullerton, Shoven, and Whalley 1985 for the United States). These models provide a capability of analyzing the impact of tax policies on the personal distribution of income within a consistent model framework; however, the data they employ are less detailed than those used in studies of the Pechman and Okner type. Devarajan, Fullerton, and Musgrave (1980) seek explicitly to compare the general equilibrium and the Pechman and Okner shifting approaches to incidence analysis.

Until relatively recently, a widely held view was that in the OECD countries total tax systems did not redistribute income to any significant degree. The assumptions underlying these studies have been increasingly questioned, however, with several researchers coming to a different conclusion, namely, that there is considerable redistribution inherent in tax systems. This conclusion is suggested by Browning (1978) for the United States and is implicit in some of the general equilibrium incidence calculations for the United Kingdom reported by Piggott and Whalley (1985). Evaluating the assumptions and procedures used in these studies is therefore a necessary part of any possible evaluation of the distributional impact of taxes in Korea.

Table 8.6 presents a summary table from the Pechman and Okner study. These analysts used several different shifting assumptions in determining the allocation among households of the burden of individual taxes. In spite of the common belief that they show the tax system not to be redistributive, there is a sharp contrast between their most and least redistributive variants. Table 8.6 reports their effective tax rates by income ranges for 1966 U.S. household incomes for these two variants. The least redistributive variant produces the result that the effective tax rates for the whole tax system are approximately uniform across income ranges. For the lowest income range, where family income is between zero and $3,000 per year, the total effective tax rate is 28 percent; for households with an annual income of a million dollars and over, the effective tax rate is 29 percent.

The reason for this result is that the income tax is somewhat redistributive, but not as redistributive as might appear from legal tax rates. The corporate tax is only mildly redistributive, with effective rates varying from 6.1 to 9.8 percent, and a range of other taxes are less redistributive: property tax rates change from 6.5 to 0.8 percent moving from poor to rich; sales and excise tax rates similarly range from 9.2 to 1.3 percent; a comparable regressive picture holds for the payroll tax. The combined effect is a mildly redistributive income tax whose redistribution is offset by the regressivity in three other taxes—property, sales, and payroll.

The critical importance of the shifting assumptions adopted by Pechman and

Table 8.6

Summary of Pechman and Okner's (1974) analysis of U.S. tax incidence

Effective rates of federal, state, and local taxes, by type of tax, by adjusted family income class, 1966

Adjusted family income ($1,000)	Individual income tax	Corporation income tax	Property tax	Sales and excise tax	Payroll taxes	Personal property and motor vehicle taxes	Total taxes
Most redistributive variant[a]							
0–3	1.4	2.1	2.5	9.4	2.9	0.4	18.7
3–5	3.1	2.2	2.7	7.4	4.6	0.4	20.7
5–10	5.8	1.8	2.0	6.5	6.1	0.4	22.6
10–15	7.6	1.6	1.7	5.8	5.8	0.3	22.8
15–20	8.7	2.0	2.0	5.2	5.0	0.3	23.2
20–25	9.2	3.0	2.6	4.6	4.3	0.2	24.0
25–30	9.3	4.6	3.7	4.0	3.3	0.2	25.1
30–50	10.4	5.8	4.5	3.4	2.2	0.1	26.4
50–100	13.4	8.8	6.2	2.4	0.7	0.1	31.5
100–500	15.3	16.5	8.2	1.5	0.3	0.1	41.8
500–1,000	14.1	23.0	9.6	1.1	0.1	0.2	48.0
1,000 and over	12.4	25.7	10.1	1.0	—[b]	0.1	49.3
All classes[c]	8.5	3.9	3.0	5.1	4.4	0.3	25.2
Least redistributive variant[a]							
0–3	1.2	6.1	6.5	9.2	4.6	0.4	28.1
3–5	2.8	5.3	4.8	7.1	4.9	0.4	25.3
5–10	5.5	4.3	3.6	6.4	5.7	0.3	25.9
10–15	7.2	3.8	3.2	5.6	5.3	0.3	25.5
15–20	8.2	3.8	3.2	5.1	4.7	0.3	25.3
20–25	9.1	4.0	3.1	4.6	4.1	0.2	25.1
25–30	9.1	4.3	3.1	4.0	3.6	0.2	24.3
30–50	10.4	5.8	4.5	3.4	2.2	0.1	26.4
50–100	10.5	4.7	3.0	3.5	2.6	0.2	24.4
100–500	14.1	5.6	2.8	2.4	1.3	0.1	30.3
500–1,000	17.7	9.0	1.7	1.4	0.4	0.2	30.3
1,000 and over	16.6	9.8	0.8	1.3	0.3	0.2	29.0
All classes[c]	8.4	4.4	3.4	5.0	4.4	0.3	25.9

Source: Pechman and Okner (1974:tabs. 4-6, 4-8).

[a]For an explanation of the incidence variants, see St-Hilaire and Whalley (1982:tab. 8).

[b]Less than 0.05 percent.

[c]Includes negative incomes not shown separately.

Okner comes out in the results of their most redistributive variant. In this case, total effective tax rates by income range move from 18.7 percent for the income range zero to $3,000 to 49.3 percent for the income range of a million dollars and over. These results thus present a sharply different picture from that for the least redistributive variant. There is some redistribution in the income tax, but redistribution through the corporate tax is more pronounced, with tax rates changing from 2.1 to 25.7 percent. The property tax is changed from a regressive tax to a sharply progressive tax, with tax rates changing from 2.5 to 10.1 percent; sales and payroll taxes have tax rates largely unchanged. The sharp changes in corporate and property tax rates between the most and least redistributive variants alter the perceived redistributive impact of the whole tax system.

The conclusion from the least redistributive variant in the Pechman and Okner study (the variant that is widely cited) is that there is only limited redistribution through the U.S. tax system, and certainly much less than many people suppose on the basis of an examination of the income tax. It is, however, incorrect to infer that government activity in total has no effect on personal income distribution. A further issue is the redistribution within income ranges, which has been highlighted by Atkinson (1980).

When pressed to choose between alternative variants, recent OECD literature points toward the most redistributive variants, if not beyond. This has been emphasized by Browning (1978), who suggests a key feature of the Pechman and Okner results which may misrepresent the redistributive impact of the tax system. Browning considers the most redistributive variant of Pechman and Okner and suggests that the "standard" incidence procedure of allocating sales and excise taxes on the basis of consumption of taxed commodities is inappropriate. He argues that it is reasonable to assume that, on the income side of household activity, the real value of transfers is unchanged in any experiment made to evaluate the incidence of sales and excise taxes. He suggests that, in order to allocate tax burdens using consumption data, prices must rise by the amount of an equivalent broadly based tax, and transfers should remain unchanged. Given that U.S. transfer policies exhibit extensive indexation, low-income groups who have a large fraction of incomes in the form of transfers cannot bear the burden of these taxes, as is widely supposed, since only factors can bear this burden. On the expenditure side of household activity, Browning shows that, unless there are pronounced differences in consumption patterns (which evidence seems to indicate is not the case when normal or permanent income is considered), ignoring tax effects on the uses side introduces only a small bias into the estimates. Examining the burden of the entire tax system in this fashion, Browning demonstrates a pattern of effective sales tax rates by household that is progressive, especially for the bottom two and top deciles.

The picture of a tax system significantly redistributive between the top and bottom deciles, which emerges from Browning's (1978) study, is also reported by Piggott and Whalley (1985) from their general equilibrium evaluation of the U. K. tax-subsidy system. Their differential incidence calculation replaces all existing taxes and subsidies in the United Kingdom by a yield-preserving broadly based single-rate sales tax. The authors show that the bottom 6 percent of households are made worse off and the top 10 percent of households are made better off, by about 25 percent in each case. The use of the general equilibrium framework does not involve one particular set of shifting assumptions, although a configuration of elasticity values has to be selected, which significantly affects results. The results from this model indicate that the U.K. tax-subsidy system is noticeably redistributive in the tails of the income distribution.

This work is clearly relevant for incidence discussions of the Korean tax system, as these may relate to any future Korean tax reform. Because of the heavy reliance on indirect taxes and steady growth in importance of the VAT, traditional incidence literature, which sees indirect taxes in general and sales taxes in particular (such as VAT) as inherently regressive, will tend to come to the conclusion that the Korean tax system either redistributes income to only a small extent or is regressive. If, however, these alternative and more recent analyses of the incidence effects of VAT are taken into account, the evaluation will change, and with it the strength of the argument for redistributive tax reform in Korea.

Implications for Korean Tax Reform

What does one make of the arguments advanced in previous sections, and where does it leave possible Korean tax reform? As I argue in the earlier sections, over the past 30 years Korea has passed through a series of developmental phases in which major changes have taken place in the overall policy orientation toward growth: outward orientation in the 1960s, industrial targeting in the 1970s, and, subsequently, structural adjustment and policy neutrality in the 1980s.

The striking feature of Korean tax policy over the years has been its ability to adapt to these wider changes in policy direction and, generally, to facilitate the strong growth performance of the Korean economy. In the process, the Korean tax system has matured and grown to the point that it is now similar in structure to those of the major OECD countries, perhaps with the exception of a relatively heavier reliance on trade taxes. Through this 30-year developmental phase, Korean tax policy can thus be seen as having contributed positively to Korean growth in not blocking growth performance. The remaining issue in this policy stance is redistribution. Korean society has traditionally shown major concern over income distribution, and in tax policy debate such concerns have frequently been voiced—more strongly, if anything, in recent years. Hence, if there is to be a major tax reform in Korea in the 1990s, it would likely be oriented toward redistributive objectives.

There are, however, strong arguments against such a major tax reform initiative. First and perhaps foremost, the Korean income distribution is seemingly already one of the most equal among countries around the world, even OECD countries.

Available data seem to indicate in comparative exercises with OECD countries that it is more equal than the United States, the United Kingdom, Germany, and others in terms of the Gini coefficients (and implicitly percentile shares). The argument is that, if the income distribution is that equal, why the need to mount a redistributive tax reform?

In addition, and as is emphasized in the preceding section, literature on OECD countries is now in a substantial state of flux as to the redistributive effects of tax policies, questioning how much redistribution takes place, in practice, through the tax system. In the 1960s it was commonly argued in the OECD countries that tax systems did little to redistribute income, and that reforms to make the system more redistributive were needed. This view has, however, recently come under serious challenge, with several analysts suggesting that OECD tax systems are substantially more redistributive than had been thought. Much of this debate has focused on incidence analysis of indirect (VAT) and sales taxes, which in previous literature were thought to be regressive. But these taxes are increasingly viewed as progressive when analyzed over a lifetime or on an intertemporal basis. Given that the Korean tax system has matured and grown, and that one of its more important taxes is now the VAT, the arguments in favor of mounting a major redistributive tax reform in Korea seem further weakened.

Finally, there seems no doubt that throughout the 1980s the Korean tax system has moved in the same direction as that taken by the United States, the United Kingdom, West Germany, Japan, Australia, and other OECD countries. In all these countries, the general drift of tax policy throughout the 1980s has been to lower tax rates and broaden tax bases, and to do this by eliminating investment incentives and accelerated depreciation in the corporate tax as well as by engaging in more minor base broadening at the personal level. Through the 1980s the Korean tax system seems to have passed through a similar process to the point that its rates and structure are now relatively similar to the overall stance toward tax policy taken by the OECD countries. Hence, any major further tax policy change in Korea might now be viewed as something of an aberration—and indeed could have negative implications for trade flows in terms of competitiveness effects, especially given the approximate trade neutrality of the VAT.

Thus, given that the Korean tax system has proved itself able to accommodate the wider policy changes the Korean economy has had to confront, and given that the tax system has not blocked the growth strategies pursued in the past, at this point there seems no compelling reason to introduce major tax reform in Korea. What has worked in the past is likely to prove more than adequate for strong Korean growth performance in the future, which has, if anything, tended to be a pro-equality factor. This would seem to suggest continuing a facilitative and adaptive tax policy rather than a more interventionist tax policy, potentially into uncharted territory.

NOTES

1. This section draws on a longer discussion of Korean tax policy and growth performance in Trela and Whalley (1990, 1991).

2. The share of local taxes (also often viewed as regressive) in total revenue has remained small in Korea. During the period 1962–87, the local tax share ranged from 8.1 to 17.3 percent; see Economic Planning Board (1982, 1988).

3. This and the discussions of subperiods of Korean growth to follow draw on Westphal and Kim (1977), Hong (1979), Scitovsky (1985), World Bank (1988), and Choi (1988).

4. There is a substantial literature that stresses the neutrality for trade of switches between origin-based (or production-based) indirect taxes with no border tax adjustments and destination-based (or consumption-based) indirect taxes under which such adjustments occur; see Johnson and Krauss (1970), and Whalley (1979). In Korea, however, the export tax rebate was seen as undoing existing biases in the policy structure as much as it was an explicit export incentive. Thus, one can argue that it had a favorable influence on exports.

5. A further tax-free reserve scheme was introduced later (1977) to deal with price fluctuations. Under this plan, any licensed exporter could deduct additions to a reserve fund from taxable income within a limit of 5 percent of inventory asset value, at the end of the accounting period. This amount was also added to taxable income after a one-year grace period.

6. One can also argue that no export subsidy is involved with VAT rebates on exports, since they compensate for taxes on imports and have no effect on trade flows. Results from Choi (1984), however, show that the government had underestimated the border tax adjustment under the previous tax system. In this sense, the adoption of the VAT had a positive effect on trade flows.

7. This and the following subsection draw on the discussion in St-Hilaire and Whalley (1982).

8. Empirical evidence on labor supply elasticities seems to indicate that, for selected groups in the labor force, labor supply elasticities are high, while for the main portion of the labor force elasticities are low. For primary workers (head of household), elasticities in the range of 0.1–0.2 are often quoted; but for secondary and tertiary workers (spouses, older people, potential labor market entrants with schooling options that would delay entry) elasticities are considerably higher (0.5–0.6 are values sometimes quoted).

REFERENCES

Atkinson, A. B. 1980. "Horizontal Equity and the Distribution of the Tax Burden." In Henry J. Aaron and Michael J. Boskin (eds.), *The Economics of Taxation.* Washington, D.C.: Brookings Institution.

Auerbach, A. J., L. J. Kotlikoff, and J. Skinner. 1983. "The Efficiency Gains from Dynamic Tax Reform." *International Economic Review* 24 (February): 81–100.

Ballard, C., D. Fullerton, J. Shoven, and J. Whalley. 1985. *General Equilibrium Analysis of U.S. Tax Policy*. Chicago: University of Chicago Press for the National Bureau of Economic Research.

Ballard, C., J. Shoven, and J. Whalley. 1985. "General Equilibrium Computations of the Marginal Welfare Costs of Taxes in the United States." *American Economic Review* 75 (March): 128–138.

Ballentine, J. G. 1978. "The Cost of the Inter-sectoral and Inter-temporal Price Distortions of a Corporate Income Tax." Mimeo. Wayne State University, Detroit.

Boskin, M. J. 1975. "Efficiency Aspects of the Differential Tax Treatment of Market and Household Economic Activity." *Journal of Public Economics* 4 (February): 1–25.

Brown, G. T. 1973. *Korean Pricing Policies and Economic Development in the 1960s*. Baltimore: Johns Hopkins University Press.

Browning, E. K. 1976. "The Marginal Cost of Public Funds." *Journal of Political Economy* 84 (April): 283–298.

Browning, E. K. 1978. "The Burden of Taxation." *Journal of Political Economy* 86 (August): 660–661.

Browning, J. M. 1979. "Estimating the Welfare Cost of Tax Preferences." *Finance Quarterly* 7 (April): 199–219.

Choi, Kwang. 1984. "Value Added Taxation: Experiences and Lessons of Korea." Korea Development Institute Working Paper no. 84-06. Seoul.

Choi, Kwang. 1988. "Tax Policy and Tax Reforms in Korea." Mimeo. Department of Economics, Hankuk University of Foreign Studies, Seoul.

Davies, J., B. Hamilton, and J. Whalley. 1989. "Capital Income Taxation in a Two Commodity Life Cycle Model: The Role of Factor Intensity and Asset Capitalization Effects." *Journal of Public Economics* 39 (June): 109–126.

Davies, J., F. St-Hilaire, and J. Whalley. 1985. "Some Calculations of Lifetime Tax Incidence." *American Economic Review* 75 (September): 633–649.

Davies, J., and J. Whalley. 1991. "Taxes and Capital Formation: How Important Is Human Capital?" In B. D. Bernheim and J. B. Shoven (eds.), *National Saving and Economic Performance*. Chicago: University of Chicago Press.

Devarajan, S., D. Fullerton, and R. A. Musgrave. 1980. "Estimating the Distribution of Tax Burdens: A Comparison of Different Approaches." *Journal of Public Economics* 13 (April): 155–182.

Dilnot, A. W., and J. A. Kay. 1990. "Tax Reform in the United Kingdom: The Recent Experience." In M. J. Boskin and C. E. McLure, Jr. (eds.), *World Tax Reform: Case Studies of Developed and Developing Countries*. San Francisco: ICS Press.

Economic Planning Board, ROK. Various years. *Major Statistics of Korean Economy*. Seoul.

Feldstein, M. 1974. "Social Security, Induced Retirement and Aggregate Capital Accumulation." *Journal of Political Economy* 82 (September–October): 905–926.

Feige, E. L. 1979. "How Big Is the Irregular Economy?" *Challenge: The Magazine of Economic Affairs* 22 (November–December).

Fullerton, D., T. A. King, J. B. Shoven, and J. Whalley. 1981. "Corporate Tax Integration in the United States: A General Equilibrium Approach." *American Economic Review* 71 (September): 677–691.

Fullerton, D., J. B. Shoven, and J. Whalley. 1983. "Replacing the U.S. Income Tax with a Progressive Consumption Tax: A Sequenced General Equilibrium Approach." *Journal of Public Economics* 20 (February): 3–33.

Han, Seung-Soo. 1986. "Korea's Recent Tax Reform Effort: Personal Observation of

Reform Effort in 1984–1985." Provisional Papers in Public Economics no. 85–32. World Bank.

Harberger, A. C. 1959. "The Corporation Income Tax: An Empirical Appraisal." In *Tax Revision Compendium*. House Committee on Ways and Means, 86th Cong., 1st sess., Vol. 1.

Harberger, A. C. 1962. "The Incidence of the Corporate Income Tax." *Journal of Political Economy* 70 (June): 215–240.

Harberger, A. C. 1964a. "Taxation, Resource Allocation and Welfare." In J. Due (ed.), *The Role of Direct and Indirect Taxes in the Federal Reserve System*. Princeton: Princeton University Press for National Bureau of Economic Research.

Harberger, A. C. 1964b. "The Measurement of Waste." *American Economic Review* 54 (May): 58–85.

Harberger, A. C. 1966. "Efficiency Effects of Taxes on Income From Capital." In M. Kryzaniak (ed.), *Effects of Corporation Income Tax*. Detroit: Wayne State University Press.

Harberger, A. C. 1974. *Taxation and Welfare*. Boston: Little Brown.

Hasan, Parvez, and D. C. Rao. 1979. *Korea: Policy Issues for Long-Term Development*. Baltimore: John Hopkins University Press for the World Bank.

Hong, Wontack. 1979. *Trade, Distortions and Employment Growth in Korea*. Seoul: Korea Development Institute.

Hotelling, H. 1938. "The General Welfare in Relation to Problems of Taxation and of Railway and Utility Rates." *Econometrica* 6 (January): 242–269.

International Tax Centre. 1990. *Taxation of International Transfers of Technology*. Amsterdam: Klynveld Peat Marwick Goerdeler.

Johnson, H. G., and M. Krauss. 1970. "Border Taxes, Border Tax Adjustments, Comparative Advantage and the Balance of Payments." *Canadian Journal of Economics* 3 (November): 595–602.

Krueger, A. 1979. *Studies in the Modernization of the Republic of Korea, 1945–1975: The Developmental Role of the Foreign Sector and Aid*. Cambridge: Harvard University Press.

Kwack, Taewon. 1988. "Public Finance, Trade, and Economic Development: The Role of Fiscal Incentives in Korea's Export Led Economic Growth." Paper presented at the 44th Congress of the International Institute of Public Finance, Istanbul, August.

Laidler, D. 1971. "Income Tax Incentives for Owner-Occupied Housing." In Arnold C. Harberger and Martin J. Bailey (eds.), *The Taxation of Income from Capital*. Washington, D.C.: Brookings Institution.

Ministry of Finance, Japan. 1990. *An Outline of Japanese Taxes*. Tokyo.

Ministry of Finance, ROK. 1986. *Korean Taxation 1986*. Seoul.

OECD. 1991. *Revenue Statistics of OECD Countries: 1965–1990*. Paris, France.

Pechman, J. A., and B. A. Okner. 1974. *Who Bears the Tax Burden?* Washington, D.C.: Brookings Institution.

Piggott, J., and J. Whalley. 1985. *U. K. Tax Policy and Applied General Equilibrium Analysis*. New York: Cambridge University Press.

Scitovsky, Tibor. 1985. "Economic Development in Taiwan and South Korea: 1965–1981." *Food Research Institute Studies* 14 (3): 215–264.

Shoven, J. B. 1976. "The Incidence of Efficiency Effects of Taxes on Income from Capital." *Journal of Political Economy* 84 (December): 1285–1292.

St-Hilaire, F., and J. Whalley. 1982. "Recent Studies of Efficiency and Distribution Impacts of Taxes: Implications for Canada." In W. R. Thirsk and J. Whalley (eds.), *Tax Policy Options in the 1980's*. Toronto: Canadian Tax Foundation.

Stuart, C. 1984. "Welfare Costs per Dollar of Additional Tax Revenue in the United States" *American Economic Review* 74 (June): 352–362.

Summers, L. H. 1981. "Capital Taxation and Accumulation in a Life-Cycle Growth Model." *American Economic Review* 71 (September): 533–544.

Trela, I., and J. Whalley. 1990. "Taxes, Outward Orientation, and Growth Performance in Korea." World Bank Staff Working Paper no. 519. Washington, D.C.

Trela, I., and J. Whalley. 1991. "Taxes, Outward Orientation, and Growth Performance in the Republic of Korea." In Javad Khalilzadeh-Shirazi and Anwar Shah (eds.), *Tax Policy in Developing Countries.* A World Bank Symposium. Washington, D.C.: World Bank.

Uelner, A., and T. Menck. 1988. "Germany." In J. A. Pechman (ed.), *World Tax Reform: A Progress Report.* Washington, D.C.: Brookings Institution.

Westphal, L. E., and K. S. Kim. 1977. "Industrial Policy and Development in Korea." World Bank Staff Working Paper no. 263. Washington, D.C.

Whalley, J. 1979. "Uniform Domestic Tax Rates, Trade Distortions, and Economic Integration." *Journal of Public Economics* 11 (May): 213–221.

Whalley, J. 1980. "Discriminatory Features of Domestic Factor Tax Systems in a Goods Mobile-Factors Immobile Trade Model: An Empirical General Equilibrium Approach." *Journal of Political Economy* 88 (December): 1177–1202.

Whalley, J. 1990. "Foreign Responses to U.S. Tax Reform." In J. Slemrod (ed.), *Do Taxes Matter?* Cambridge: MIT Press.

World Bank. 1988. *Korea: Managing the Industrial Transition,* Vol. 1: *The Conduct of Industrial Policy.* Washington, D.C.

PART IV

THE FINANCIAL SYSTEM

Chapter 9

Financial Institutions

Pyung Joo Kim
Sogang University

Introduction

The modern financial system in Korea began under the influence of foreign advisers to the treasury of the Yi dynasty at the turn of the twentieth century and was subsequently tailored to the needs of the Japanese colonialists after annexation. The role of indigenous entrepreneurs should not, however, be underestimated; they established and maintained their own modern banking institutions under the adverse circumstances of occupation.

By the time World War II had ended, the colonialists had left behind a financial system with a fair degree of specialization. At the apex of the system was the Bank of Chosun, which performed paracentral banking functions as well as engaging in the commercial banking business. Below were a host of "specialized banks": the Industrial Bank specialized in long- and medium-term credit, the Savings Bank in saving accounts, the Trust Company exclusively in the trust business, and the Mutual Aid Company in the lottery (called *mujin*) business. And the Korean Commercial Bank and the Choheung Bank engaged in general commercial banking. In rural areas there were financial associations, which were essentially agricultural cooperatives providing credit facilities and other services to their members (primarily farmers). The Federation of Financial Associations performed the role of central bank and coordinating agency for the financial associations. There were also life and nonlife insurance companies, largely branches of Japanese companies. The Post Office was part of the financial system in that it maintained postal savings accounts, a form of checking system, a postal annuity system, and a life insurance business. Finally, a stock exchange in Seoul was engaged in some underwriting activities. These various institutions were all closely linked to the developed financial system of Japan. Their operations were mainly designed to serve Japanese interests within and outside Korea.

In sum, banking institutions dominated the financial system of Korea, and banking itself was heavily tilted toward specialization and compartmentalization. As Hubert Schiffer put it, "The rise of Japan as a world power in the early part of the twentieth century was facilitated by the vigorous and politically oriented development of a system of government-sponsored 'special banks'" (1962:12). In other words, the financial structure in Korea was in effect a mechanism to expedite the mobilization of Korean savings and the diversion of resources into selected Japanese industrial projects and the Japanese war machine.

In the banking business, the stock of human capital is a crucial factor overriding physical and other elements. The fact that a cadre of well-trained and experienced indigenous bank employees had been created in the pre-1945 period had far-reaching implications for the evolution and direction of the Korean financial system. It was this human factor that prepared reform-minded people as well as ordinary bank operators to accept the financial structure evolved in Japan. In the early phase of Korea's nation building, an attempt was made to erase the imprints of the colonial heritage, but in the subsequent period the benefits of Japanese experience were overtly and eagerly sought.

Evolution of the Financial System in Korea

Setting up Institutional Arrangements, 1948–60

The Immediate Postwar Period Immediately after Korea's liberation in 1945, a strong wave of emotion and determination to eradicate the remnants of the colonial past swept through the nation. In the financial sphere, however, radical departure from past experiences was neither feasible nor desirable. Thus adjustments had to be made to serve the needs of a new nation in the throes of fundamental restructuring.

The special banks were forced to concentrate on straight commercial banking business, since their specialized functions related to the Japanese industrial-military complex had been largely suspended. The Federation of Financial Associations was established to carry out a wide range of nonbanking activities: the collection and distribution of rice and other grains, the purchase and distribution of imported fertilizers, and so on. The federation was treated as a government agency to the extent that it performed such functions on behalf of the government.

In August 1948 all Japanese-owned properties in Korea were transferred to the newly formed government. Through this process, the government acquired controlling shares in all Korean banking institutions except for the Choheung Bank (the shareholders of which were largely Korean) and the Federation of Financial Associations and its member associations. The virtual nationalization of banking institutions had long-term effects in that this led to government pressure and interference in various aspects of banking such as management, personnel, and budgeting.

The Beginning of Banking Reforms In 1950, on the eve of banking reforms under the influence of the United States, what was the state of financial development in Korea? There were two apparently contradictory views.

1. "Though the Korean economy shares the characteristics typical of an agricultural and underdeveloped economy, Korea has a relatively well-developed banking system, and in a sense, even an excess of commercial banking facilities relative to the stage of economic development of the nation" (Kim 1965:55–59).
2. "The [Korean] financial structure is . . . underdeveloped. There are no money or capital markets in the accepted sense of the terms and no really adequate facilities for mobilizing such savings as are currently made and for channeling them into productive investments. . . . The use of the check is highly undeveloped and the bulk of the country's monetary transactions [are] consummated in currency" (Bloomfield and Jensen 1965:45).

A clue to unraveling the puzzle of this disagreement lies in the different points of view taken by these observers. Arthur Bloomfield and John P. Jensen, coming from the United States, took a broad view, noticing obvious lacunae in a modern spectrum of financial institutions and activities. Byong Kuk Kim's view reflects a domestic bank insider's perspective, confined to the lending function of banks (especially commercial banks). According to this latter view, frequent irregularities are attributed to competition among bankers for creditworthy customers, a clear manifestation of which is the overcrowding of bank offices in some major cities. However, in light of the heavy demand for bank loans at the time—caused by rampant inflation and acute shortages of goods and services—it is fair to state that competition was on the borrowing instead of the lending side. Because there were relatively few creditworthy firms, the process of adverse selection set in, and the less scrupulous borrowers, often with the aid of outside influences, succeeded in securing the credit rationed by banks. Hence, irregularities related to bank loans and subsequent defaults were frequent.

Attempts were made to start afresh in the financial sphere in the early days of the administration of President Syngman Rhee, even though Rhee's regime was subjected to the criticism that it inherited unsavory aspects of the colonial legacy such as police personnel. The highlight of the attempts to begin anew was the invitation of Bloomfield and Jensen in 1949 to draft recommendations for the reform of the central bank and other financial institutions in Korea. These suggestions for reforms were submitted in the form of new statutes to the minister of finance in early 1950.

In drafting new statutes for the central bank and other financial institutions in Korea, Bloomfield and Jensen were guided by three major factors. Since a grave inflationary trend was prevailing at the time, the first consideration was to include provisions to check this trend. The second factor was the violent upheavals and uncertainties caused by the sudden disengagement from the Japanese economy and by the division of Korea into two parts. Hence the idea was to draft new statutes "in terms sufficiently broad to permit flexibility and ready adaptations to future developments as they may arise" (Bloomfield and Jensen 1965:42). The third consideration was the underdeveloped state of the Korean economy and financial system. As a consequence of these factors, the primary purposes of the statutes were (1) to convert the Bank of Chosun (Bank of Korea), previously a paracentral bank, into a genuine central bank and to enable it to start afresh, free of the structures of the past; (2) to protect the central bank as much as possible from political pressure and arbitrary interference by placing its management and operations under the control of the Monetary Board; and (3) to strengthen the Korean banking system as a whole and promote its more efficient functioning, thereby furthering the progress of Korea's economy. It would be a digression at this point to go into details of the central bank statute that resulted from the efforts of Bloomfield and Jensen (1963:83–98). Suffice it to note the following two goals, which appear to have guided their efforts: (1) as much flexibility as possible should be retained in the emerging financial system, and (2) the central bank and other banking institutions should be protected from undue pressure and interference. In the following decades, however, these two goals have been stymied or evaded. This growth with singular atrophy has been closely related to the Japanese colonial inheritance, which can be summarized into two characteristics: the segmentation or compartmentalization of financial markets, and the strong control and influence of the government.

Bloomfield and Jensen took a negative position on the alleged necessity and desirability of greater specialization of banks such as prevailed before liberation. They also recommended that a thorough structural reorganization, except that of the central bank, should be postponed, at least until the overall financial situation could be placed on a sound footing. They asserted that premature attempts to develop an advanced financial system should be avoided. Interestingly enough, the Korean Banking Act allows a further degree of flexibility in that the term "banking institutions" (*eun-hang kigwan*) in the English-language version of the act drafted by Bloomfield and Jensen became "financial institutions" (*gum-yung kigwan*) in the Korean-language version. Through the approval of the Monetary Board, a banking institution may be engaged directly in business other than that related to banking (Article 25). It appears that no one perceived serious potential problems in distinguishing banking institutions from financial institutions since the overriding majority of financial institutions in Korea at the time were banks, and the functions of a commercial bank could be expanded as the need arose for other financial services (conventionally considered nonbank businesses). A "universal banking" system could have been constructed out of the new banking statutes.

The first of Bloomfield and Jensen's two points to become entangled with the government and hence eventually thwarted was the idea of and measures for protecting financial institutions from government interference. The coign of vantage regarding this matter is the central bank (Kim 1976:26–28). The central bank system created on 12 June 1950, in accordance with the new statute, consists of the bank itself, the Monetary Board, and the Bank Superintendent's Office. The basic idea is that the Monetary Board deliberates, the bank executes, and the superintendent's office oversees. The Monetary Board is intended to be the supreme authority in the domain of monetary credit policies in both the letter and spirit of the statute. It is vested with wide-ranging authority over the policies, management, and administration of the Bank of Korea and over the management and operations of the banking system as a whole. As one example of its power, the board may advise the shareholders of any banking institution to dismiss its director if any legislation or regulation issued by the board is deliberately violated.

The Monetary Board was composed of seven members, which included two ex-officio members—the finance minister and the governor of the Bank of Korea—and five government-endorsed members. The fulcrum of the board was the finance minister, who was its chairman. Originally the finance minister's presence on the board was conceived as an arrangement for avoiding possible conflict and for facilitating close coordination and integration between the fiscal policy of the government and the monetary policy of the bank. In practice, however, the minister has dominated the board. Whenever rare cases of conflict between the minister and the governor of the Bank of Korea have developed, it has invariably been the latter who is forced out. In hindsight, however, the period from 1950 to 1960 witnessed a less rigid financial system compared with the later period: the attempts of the government to control and interfere were less frequent and less systematic. Generally speaking, the administration of Syngman Rhee had a better appreciation of market mechanisms than did Park Chung Hee's regime following the military coup in 1961.

The Major Developments Three major developments in the period before 1961 deserve special attention. The first was the privatization of commercial banks that had been previously nationalized in the process of divesting Japanese interests. The government shares of commercial banks were put on the block beginning in 1954 and on a massive scale in 1957. The auctions were conducted in such a fashion that the result was the high concentration of stock in a few hands. Later it was alleged that these new private major shareholders (owners of large enterprises) extended credit lines exclusively to their own firms and were also susceptible to solicitation for political contributions. This situation met a sudden end in 1961 when the military regime revoked the previous privatization, branding it a form of illicit wealth accumulation.

The second development worthy of mention was the establishment in 1959 of the Bank of Seoul as a bank exclusively funded with private capital. The Bank of Seoul was the first new entry into commercial banking since liberation.

The third new development was the initiation of the Financial Stabilization Program beginning in 1957 on the recommendation of the United States' AID and the International Monetary Fund. In the preceding period, the fiscal and monetary policies of the Korean government had been highly dependent on the magnitude and direction of U.S. aid and grants and therefore were not stable and systematic. The late 1950s saw a trend of dwindling economic aid and grants, and the Korean government was notified of their imminent termination. Thus the

Financial Stabilization Program signified the start of meaningful self-management of economic policies. This began under the influence of the United States and international organizations, which diminished over time. The target variable of monetary policy was M1, a narrowly defined monetary aggregate: currency in circulation plus demand deposits. The annual and quarterly targets of M1 were set by the monetary authorities—that is, the Ministry of Finance and the Bank of Korea—and in order to curb monetary increases within preset targets, direct and selective control instruments were used. Direct control on bank credit was necessitated by the fact that the traditional indirect control instruments, such as open market operations, rediscount policy, and reserve requirement manipulation, were by and large inappropriate to an economy with undeveloped financial markets.

Institutional Rearrangements and Experiments, 1961–71

The vision and determination of Park's military regime was different from that of either Syngman Rhee or John M. Chang. In a fundamental sense, Park's regime was philosophically more susceptible to Japanese historical lessons and influences. It was also technically better armed with administrative techniques learned from U.S. military training. Park's regime paid little respect to market mechanisms and was determined to steer the Korean economy through a comprehensive economic plan. The term "government-led growth policy" represents the main tenor of economic policies during this period. The much-touted "can-do" spirit had the negative effect of disregarding the cost of doing something. The growth during this period, which was remarkable, was sustained largely at the expense of repressing the financial institutions and their development.

The character of financial sector development during this early phase of Park's regime may be described as a flow of waters, the main currents of which were Japanese influences (i.e., government control and interference with financial institutions as well as preference toward market segmentation such as specialized banks). During this period a host of U.S. advisers (E. S. Shaw, John Gurley, Hugh Patrick, and others) visited Korea frequently under the auspices of USAID and international organizations. Their recommendations were put into practice with much fanfare and had an apparently dramatic effect for a while. These experiments, imbued with American ideas and implemented by officials more susceptible to U.S. influence, made ripples on the surface of Korea's financial structure. In most cases, these experiments were short-lived, distorted, ignored, and eventually overwhelmed by the main currents flowing steadily under the surface. There were, however, some major developments in the financial sector during this period.

Subjugation of the Central Bank The strengthened control of the government over the financial system is most evident in its relationship to the central bank and the Monetary Board. In May 1962 the Bank of Korea Act was amended. The official Korean appellation of the Monetary Board was changed from *gumyung tongwha* *wiwonhui* to *gumyung-tongwha unyong wiwonhoi.* This titular change—*unyong* means "management"—has since been interpreted as an expression of the government's intention to downgrade the function of the board from policy deliberation to policy management discussion.

The board's membership was expanded to nine, with two more appointed members. The power of the finance minister was strengthened; the minister could request that the board reconsider a resolution previously passed. If the request was overruled by the board with a two-thirds majority, the final decision would be made at a cabinet meeting, at which the minister's view would be ensured a hearing. But the process of appointing the governor of the Bank of Korea and the seven non-ex-officio members was such that the strengthening of the position of the minister in the board was unnecessary. The board was divested of the function of formulating foreign exchange policy; this task was transferred to the finance minister.

This singular division of monetary policies between those directly related to domestic currency and those related to foreign exchange might have been made with an intention of expediting the introduction of foreign savings through bypassing the possibly cumbersome deliberation process of the board. The absurdity of this artificial division has increased as the significance of the foreign sector has become more pronounced and the inseparability of factors affecting money supply has become more evident. As final proof of its subordination, the central bank was made subject to examination by the finance minister at least once a year, and its annual budget was to be approved by the cabinet.

Nationalization and Comprehensive Control of Commercial Banks Korean entrepreneurs, perennially short of funds, are heavily dependent on external financing for their operation and expansion. The "over-loaning" of commercial banks has been the mirror image of their client firms' "over-borrowing." In other words, the commercial banks of Korea have been confronted with a chronic excess demand for funds since 1945. To cover the shortage of funds they have had recourse to the discount window of the central bank. As a result, a door has been opened wide for the central bank's application of "window guidance" to restrict increases in bank lending.[1]

In addition, those commercial banks privatized in the late 1950s were once again nationalized as a result of confiscating "illicit" wealth accumulated under the previous regime immediately after the military coup. Furthermore, it was legislated that the voting power of major shareholders (except the government) owning 10 percent or more of the total stocks outstanding of a bank should be circumscribed. The annual budgets of commercial banks were made subject to the approval of the finance minister, although there was neither binding statute nor legislated rule to that effect. The case was the same with the top management of banks. The organizational structures of banks were made identical. In essence, the presence of the government was felt in commercial banks almost to the same extent as in special banks, which were fully government-owned and -controlled. In sum, the role of banks, whether commercial or special, was to be that of credit-rationing outlets (or "windows") at the behest of the government.

Specialization of Banks The colonial legacy of compartmentalization of financial institutions, namely, special banks, has been noted. Specialization in finance takes several forms (Wallich and Wallich 1976:278–290).[2] This specialization in finance meshes well with the aim of Korea's economic planners to encourage economic growth in selected projects and industries with policy-directed loans.

The specialized banks of Korea were established mostly during the 1960s for purposes specifically defined by their respective statutes. One feature of specialized banks is that they are owned, directed, and supervised by the government and, in principle, are outside the purview of the Monetary Board. Some areas of their business operations are, however, subject to the control of the Monetary Board. Minimum reserve requirements and maximum interest rates decided by the Monetary Board and the governor of the Bank of Korea are universally applied to specialized banks as well as to commercial banks. Specialized banks are also subject to the Bank Superintendent's Office, empowered by the finance minister. Another feature is that their major sources of financial resources are borrowing from the government, debentures issues, and deposits received from the public.

The Korea Development Bank was founded in 1954 to supply long-term credit for key industries. In the latter half of the 1950s the bank contributed to the rehabilitation of industrial facilities destroyed during the Korean War. The bank was reoriented to financing major development projects in line with the First Five-Year Economic Development Plan launched in 1962. The Small and Medium Industry Bank was established in 1961 to reinforce financial support for small- and medium-sized firms, since they had difficulty in competing with large firms for the limited funds of banks. Several mutual finance companies were consolidated into the Citizen's National Bank of Korea in 1962; a year later this was reorganized as the Citizen's National Bank. This bank was to specialize in small loans to small firms with poor credit standing as well as to households. The National Agricultural Cooperative Federation and its affiliated cooperatives were reorganized in 1961 via the merger of the former Agricultural Cooperatives and the Agriculture Bank. Similarly, the National Federation of Fisheries Cooperatives and its affiliated cooperatives were established in 1962 to meet the financial needs of fishermen and fisheries manufacturers.

The most hectic year for establishing specialized banks was 1967. First, the Korea Exchange Bank was established with the specific task of supporting foreign exchange transactions of firms, which had previously been handled mainly by the Bank of Korea. The need for a bank specializing in this field had increased with the rapid growth of foreign trade volume beginning in 1966. The Korea Housing Bank was also founded in 1967 to finance housing for low-income households. As rural-to-urban migration increased with the pace of industrialization, the housing shortage in urban areas became an acute issue, and the establishment of a specialized bank was deemed necessary to mitigate this problem. A third bank, established in 1969, was the Korea Long-Term Credit Bank (reorganized from the Korea Development Finance Corporation). It was empowered to extend medium- and long-term credit to firms in the form of loans, discounts, equity investments, and guarantees. This bank is unique in that it is a privately funded institution with specialized functions assigned to it.

Booming exports necessitated the inauguration of the Export-Import Bank of Korea in 1969, with its paid-in capital funded by the government, the Bank of Korea, and the Korea Exchange Bank. Its main tasks are financing medium- and long-term export-import transactions; investing overseas, including natural resource development projects abroad; underwriting export insurance for domestic corporations and foreign institutions; and extending credit to foreign buyers for importing capital goods and technical services from Korea.

The initiation of a local banking system also took place in 1967. As mentioned previously, the Bank of Seoul was founded in 1959 and regionally restricted to the Seoul area, but in 1962 it became a nationwide bank. During the period from 1967 to 1971, ten local banks were established, one for each province. This was most likely an echo of the "one bank in each prefecture" principle from Japan (Bank of Japan 1978:64). The branch network of these banks was allowed within each province, in which their head offices were located. These local banks have been privately owned from the outset, in contrast to the nationwide commercial banks.

The year 1967 was noteworthy in yet another respect: it witnessed the inauguration of foreign bank branch offices. The Seoul branch office of Chase Manhattan Bank was the first, and other foreign bank branches soon followed. The major purpose of allowing foreign banks into Korea was to facilitate foreign capital inflows and to give incentives for domestic banks to improve their banking practices and managerial skills by borrowing ideas from their international competitors.

Korea's banking system was to be developed with a fair degree of flexibility in the range of business allowed for commercial banks, as noted in connection with the new statutes regarding the central bank and commercial banks. But the Park regime became more inclined toward specialization of finance as its growth drive through selected projects and industries intensified.

Financial Experiments One of the major characteristics of economic policies during the Park regime was the unabashed adventurism manifested in frequent trials and errors or sudden starts and abrupt reversals. Most of the drastic experiments were attempted in the sphere of finance. To illustrate the period's experiment-happy spirit, the following examples may be cited:

The adventuristic posture of Park's regime was evident when a monetary reform was announced on 9 June 1962. Later it became known that the idea of monetary reform had been conceived by a group of indigenous advisers to General

Park soon after the coup. The avowed objective was to force domestic savings by freezing portions of large-scale old currency holdings and mobilizing them into investment in key industries. However, forced savings as a part of monetary reform was soon revoked because of the unexpectedly small amount of such frozen funds and the presumed pressure from the United States. This had a shock effect that made the public wary of the new regime.

The interest rate reform enacted on 30 September 1965 was the best-known and best-documented event during this period. Korea's exports began to increase rapidly around this time, with the export composition shifting from primary products to the manufactured goods of labor-intensive industries such as textiles. According to the development stage hypothesis, export substitution involves a major shift of policies from financial repression toward financial liberalization, through readjustment of exchange rates and interest rates among other measures (Ranis 1977). In May 1964 the exchange system was unified, and the won was depreciated from 130 per U.S. dollar to 255 per U.S. dollar. Through the interest rate reform of 1965, deposit rates were doubled, the maximum rate on one-year time deposits being raised from 15 to 30 percent per annum. The interest rate was set at 27 percent per annum (raised from 16 percent) on banks' commercial loans on bills with maturity up to one year. To make up for losses to the banks due to inverted rates (i.e., loan rates set below deposit rates), interest at the rate of 3.5 percent per annum was paid to banks on reserve deposits with the central bank.

During the three-year period from 1966 to 1969, deposits and loans grew rapidly, at annual rates of 72.5 and 26.5 percent, respectively. Real GNP increased at the average annual rate of 12 percent during the same period. Meanwhile, inflation was running at the average annual rate of 3.5 percent, providing a remarkable respite from the rate of 17.5 percent in the preceding five years.[3]

At this time, a package of readjustment or "realization" policies, including interest rate reform, which had originally been recommended by U.S. advisers (Gurley, Patrick, and Shaw 1965:58–59), was adopted by the Korean government. One goal was to encourage foreign capital inflows by creating a wider spread of domestic interest rates in excess of foreign money market rates. The dramatic increase in bank deposits and loans was brought about by the combination of the reform itself, inflows of foreign capital, and strengthened restrictions on real estate speculation.

In this heady environment, cases of insolvency and bankruptcy became more frequent and noticeable. Firms long accustomed to an inflationary milieu could not adjust to the stabilizing overall prices and the shifting demand pattern that had developed since 1965. Recipients of relatively cheap foreign loans in the form of plant and equipment were often selected irrespective of their net worth and debt-servicing capacities. They had to resort to borrowing from domestic sources, including the curb market, to make up for shortages in working capital. The ratio of current liabilities to net worth of manufacturing firms soared precipitously from 56 percent in 1965 to 113.3 percent in 1968. In addition, a brake was applied on bank credit expansion beginning in the last quarter of 1969 in connection with the

Financial Stabilization Program. The configuration of these forces eventually paved the way for the Emergency Decree Concerning Economic Stability and Growth, promulgated on 3 August 1972.

A point to be made clear at this juncture is, not that the reform of 1965 was an unmixed success (which is definitely not the case), but that a policy posture of financial liberalization was not maintained for a period long enough to alter the basic texture of accustomed practices of financial repression. Financial liberalization culminating in the interest rate reform of 1965 remained a short episode in the midst of financial repression rather than an epoch-making event ushering in a new phase of financial liberalization.

Relations between the Government and the Banks Much has been said concerning the relationship between the Korean government and the banks. The government's role may be summarized as one of direction and management. The weight of policy-directed loans was increasingly heavy; the magnitude and allocation of commercial loans was tightly controlled; and other aspects of bank management such as personnel management, budgeting, and organization were also subject to the approval of the government. Consequently, commercial banks were virtually credit-rationing outlets of the government to nearly the same extent as the specialized banks.

The conventional wisdom now appears to hold that the role of the government has been crucial in the rapid economic growth of Korea, as it was in Japan. The relationship between the government and business approximates the hierarchical relations found in a large corporation, and it is even more hierarchical in Korea than in Japan. The government has played the role of senior partner, selectively influencing the decisions of private firms. It has done this both directly and indirectly, altering market incentives by manipulating prices and sometimes even quantities of goods and services as well as affecting the availability of financial resources (Mason et al. 1980:263–272). Financial institutions are more tightly controlled in Korea than in Japan, due to the latecomer's zeal to achieve economic development. The less advanced a country is, the greater the role of the government and of government financing (Gerschenkron 1962:353–355).

A useful way to examine Korean finance may be to observe the tripartite relationship between the government, business, and financial institutions rather than a bilateral relationship of the government versus banks. During the drive to high growth, the primary objective of enterprises was growth (or sales) maximization rather than profit maximization. The goal was for enterprises to grow at top speed to achieve a critical minimum size, at which the government would be unable to allow insolvency or bankruptcy. After all, widespread unemployment ignited by the failure of large corporations would cause social unrest and loss of reputation overseas for the Korean economy. Fuel for the rapid expansion of firms was provided by high leverage or heavy dependence on debt financing. Firms raced to the brink of bankruptcy with one eye ever fixed on the government, which played the role of referee in this game of brinksmanship. It exercised discretionary power for determining which firm would get the benefit of financial credit and thus be saved from going over the edge. Thus, the maintenance of a good relationship with the government was the most crucial element for success in business. The stance of banks was a passive one; they simply responded to the commands of the government to extend or withdraw credit to designated firms. A natural and inevitable consequence of this tripartite relationship was the increase in insolvent firms or nonperforming assets on the balance sheets of the banks.

By the same token, bank credit was extended normally on the basis of client firms' real estate collateral instead of their credit standing, which tended to bring into motion a cumulative process of bank loans utilized for the acquisition of more real estate, which in turn led to further bank credit next round. Coupled with the inflationary milieu and the lack of alternative investment opportunities, this cumulative process constituted a fertile ground for whirlwinds of land speculation, which often swept across the landscape.

Financial Repression Reinforced, 1972–79

Several landmark events combined to initiate the later phase of Park's regime. First of all, the sociopolitical life of the nation began to be overshadowed by more authoritarian leadership as the *yushin* (revitalization) measure—an appellation highly reminiscent of Japan's Meiji revolution—was announced in October 1972. Korea's economic growth showed signs of slackening: after double-digit growth rates in two consecutive years (1968 and 1969) it plummeted sharply to a mere 5.3 percent in 1972. Symptoms of economic strain began to appear. The development strategy up to that time had been based on the availability of abundant labor, but surplus labor began to diminish and labor shortages became an issue due to the rapid pace of economic growth. Another major shift in economic policy occurred when the government announced its intention to accelerate the development of projects related to heavy and chemical industries. Since heavy and chemical projects involve a long gestation period and huge capital outlays, the need to mobilize large amounts of long-term funds and direct them into this sector became urgent. In addition, the government preference for large enterprises and conglomerates grew more pronounced. Soon the worldwide oil shock took a heavy toll on the Korean economy, which was totally dependent on imported oil. A scramble for foreign capital ensued.

This string of events had inevitable repercussions for Korea's finance system: reinforced financial repression, proliferation of policy-directed loans, and endeavors to devise mechanisms to facilitate foreign capital inflows. The general characteristics of the earlier phase became intensified.

Freeze on Curb Markets Korea's official or organized financial markets have always suffered from excess demand for funds. Aggravating this situation was negative interest charged to borrowers as a result of high inflation and interest rates of financial institutions artificially held below a market-clearing level. For many applicants, obtaining access to bank credit was very difficult—in the vernacular, "the doorsill of banks was too high." Even those who were successful in acquiring credit rationed at the banks could not fully satisfy their need for borrowed funds. Thus, frustration at official financial markets abounded, and borrowers sought other sources of funds. On the supply side, Koreans in every walk of life have had close contact with unofficial or unregulated money markets (notably *kyes*), and under protracted inflation and low official interest rates the preference for this type of market instead of official institutions was strong. Thus fertile ground was created for unofficial or unregulated money markets.

As mentioned previously, economic growth performance began to sour in 1970 and worsened in the first half of 1972. Businesses began to blame their troubles on mounting financial burdens and voiced their demand for lower interest rates (partly as a delayed reaction to the interest rate reform of 1965) through organizations representing their interests such as the Federation of Korean Industries.[4] The Park regime, never sympathetic to the finance community, was ready to accommodate the alleged needs of business. The Emergency Decree Concerning Economic Stability and Growth was promulgated on 3 August 1972.

The Emergency Decree was designed to reduce the financial costs of businesses, primarily by removing the burden of loans from unofficial or unregulated money markets. In addition, measures were taken to lower the interest rates of banking institutions; to convert portions of outstanding bank loans into long-term, low-interest loans; to establish a credit guarantee fund; and to improve the financial structure of firms. According to the decree, it was the obligation of both the creditors and the debtor firms to report to the tax offices or the banking institutions the total amount of curb loans plus unpaid interest as of 2 August 1972. Incentives and penalties were combined to enhance reporting. These included exemption from taxation on all interest income previously unpaid or evaded; no questions asked as to the source of funds; in cases of false reporting, no benefits of tax exemption; in cases of no reporting, suspension of the legal protection for the claims of loans and collateral involved. Reported curb loans were to be converted into long-term loans having a three-year grace period and thereafter a five-year repayment period with an equal amount (corresponding to 10 percent of the loan amount) to be repaid every six months. Interest rates were to be reduced to 1.35 percent per month (from the prevailing curb loan rate of about 3.5 percent per month) if the contracted rate exceeded that; otherwise, the contracted rates were allowed.

The total amount of curb loans reported within the seven-day reporting period was staggering: 357.1 billion won reported by the creditors and 345.6 billion won by the debtor firms. Even using the lower figure, this was tantamount to 88 percent of M1 and 32.4 percent of loans and discounts outstanding of the demand deposit banks as a whole (i.e., virtually all commercial banks and specialized banks, with the exception of the Korea Development Bank, the Export-Import Bank of Korea, and the Korea Long-Term Credit Bank). The often-heard official evaluation of the Emergency Decree and its consequences is that it was a tour de force as a package of policies. As a reflection of its success, in 1973 the growth rate of GNP soared to 14 percent, nearly tripling that of the previous year, and inflation was lessened to 6.9 percent in 1973 from 13.8 percent per annum in 1972. This sanguine evaluation based on short-term growth and stability should, however, be tempered by the consideration that world economic circumstances were favorable to the expansion of Korea's exports in 1973, which recorded about an 80 percent increase and thus propelled the economy.

In a longer-term perspective, the Emergency Decree had only a small effect on the operation and magnitude of the unorganized money markets. In the early 1980s, a decade after the Emergency Decree, the curb markets were still in operation, and they sometimes erupted into major financial scandals. But the steady growth of official financial institutions has made the curb markets relatively insignificant in contrast with ten years before.

The Proliferation of Nonbank Financial Institutions In connection with the Emergency Decree, a trio of nonbank financial institutions was created in 1972 to absorb curb market funds into the organized or official financial markets: (1) investment and finance companies, (2) mutual savings and finance companies, and (3) credit unions and mutual credits (the mutual credit facilities of agricultural and fisheries cooperatives).

Investment and finance companies. Investment and finance companies (*danja hoisa*) were officially created in 1972 with the promulgation of the Short-Term Financing Business Act. These companies were designed to attract funds from the curb market and to develop the money market.[5] The model for these kinds of finance companies was the investment banks of the United States, and the International Finance Corporation promoted this idea to the Korean government. The idea was to allow a fairly wide range of financial activities, including securities business. However, the types of businesses specifically listed in the act were narrowed, and in actual practice they were restricted further, especially after the creation of another financial institution comprising a comprehensive range of businesses. The principal function of these finance companies consists of meeting short-term financial needs of the business community with funds raised through selling papers drawn on themselves and trading in papers issued by other firms. Subject to the authorization of the finance minister, these finance companies may engage in securities transactions such as underwriting, buying and selling, and acting as brokers or agencies. For a long time, these securities transactions were not fully allowed; for instance, the finance companies were not authorized to participate in the management of underwriting securities. The companies also serve as dealers in treasury bills issued by the government. Until the door was opened to new entries again in

1982, twenty-four of these companies (of which seven were located in Seoul) were operating. They had only the head office; no branch offices were allowed.

Mutual savings and finance companies. Previously, a large number of *mujin* companies were catering to the financial needs of small-scale merchants and manufacturers as well as households. The traditional Korean savings and loan scheme (*kye*) was a ubiquitous phenomenon. Again, in order to absorb curb market funds into the organized financial markets, the existing mujin companies were reorganized and new mutual savings and finance companies were allowed in accordance with the Mutual Savings and Finance Company Act of 1972. The Korean name for these companies was *sang-ho sin-yong kum-go*, which strongly reveals the Japanese influence on the conception of these companies. *Sang-ho* ("mutual") was derived from the *sogo-ginko,* mutual savings banks of Japan; *sinyong-kumgo* was derived from the *shinyo-kinko,* the credit associations of Japan. Whereas *sogo-ginko* are incorporated, all *shinyo-kinko* are cooperatives. The Mutual Savings and Finance Company Act of Korea allows both types of legal structure for *sang-ho sin-yong kum-go*. As time has passed, the majority of these companies took on the incorporated framework, which jibes with the trend that in Korea every nonbank financial institution aspires to become a bank and every local bank wants to become a nationwide bank. Initially over 400 of these companies came into being, but after several waves of insolvencies, mergers, and government-guided consolidations, the number of companies was trimmed to 199 until the onrush of new entrants in 1982.

The main business of these companies consists of providing mutual credit (*kye*) and mutual installment savings with remuneration. Through a history of business bottlenecks and measures designed to alleviate them, borrowings from the public and loans on discounted bills have become the primary source and use of funds for these companies. The importance of *kye* has almost disappeared. Essentially, the borrowing of these companies is not much different from deposits to banks, and their loans are also similar to the commercial loans of banks.

Credit unions and mutual credits. The jurisdiction of a third piece of legislation, namely, the Credit Union Act of 1972, was over three different types of financial organizations: credit unions, agricultural and fisheries cooperatives, and Saemaul (New Community) finance associations.

The first credit union in Korea was related to a church organization in Pusan in 1960. As cooperative organizations designed to meet the financial needs and promote the economic welfare of their members on a mutual basis, credit unions burgeoned in churches, businesses, and even government offices. Credit unions were established and operated on a purely spontaneous and autonomous basis and were outside the influence of the government. With the enactment of the new legislation, their establishment became subject to the approval of the finance minister and their operation came under government guidance and supervision. It is difficult to say whether this new legal framework has been beneficial to the sound development of credit unions or detrimental to their spontaneous growth and flexible operations. In any case, official involvement clearly reflected the regimentation-prone and control-minded mode of the government during that time.

In Korea, the National Agricultural Cooperative Federation and the National Federation of Fisheries Cooperatives have always been under government control. In many aspects of their operation they have acted as government agencies. Theoretically their member cooperatives are autonomous organizations run by the members themselves, but practically they have been operated by a board selected by the government until recent years. The Credit Union Act also applies to the mutual credit facilities handled by these cooperatives.

After the *yushin* measure, the Saemaul movement was increasingly encouraged, particularly in rural communities, to promote a spirit of self-help and demonstrate visible benefits from cooperation, such as improved roofs and roads. As a credit arm of the Saemaul movement, *saemaul kumgo* (new community finance associations) were established and operated under the auspices of local governments throughout the country. The Credit Union Act also applies to this type of financial organization. The responsible government office is the Ministry of Internal Affairs rather than the Finance Ministry. Since its inception, *saemaul kumgo* has remained the most doubtful part of the organized financial structure of Korea.

After the initiation or reorganization of the three institutions just mentioned, another nonbank financial institution was introduced in 1976—the merchant banking corporations. The oil crisis exacted a heavy toll on Korea's foreign exchange reserves. The existing channels were inadequate to replenish the coffers, and new ones had to be found to facilitate foreign capital inflows. The Merchant Banking Corporation Act was promulgated to meet this task. The official title for these institutions was *jong-hap kumyung hoisa* (literally, comprehensive finance companies). The range of business allowed to these firms is indeed comprehensive and includes (1) brokerage of foreign capital inducement, overseas investment, and international financing for enterprises or inducement of foreign capital inflows on their own account and subleasing to enterprises; (2) loans for equipment and working capital; (3) discounts, purchases, sales, acceptance, and guarantee of papers issued by enterprises; (4) underwriting and brokerage of securities sales; and (5) consulting services including business management guidance. In addition, securities investment trusts and leasing are permitted by the finance minister. In short, these firms are "department stores" for financial commodities. The model for this type of financial institution was the merchant banking institutions of Great Britain.

As noted, the official primary purpose of the merchant banking system was to expedite foreign capital inflows. In line with this purpose, all of the six merchant banking corporations were to be incorporated as joint ventures between domestic and foreign interests. At that point, the domestic interest groups, which had missed the opportunity when the door for investment and finance companies was open, rushed to form joint ventures. Merchant banking represents a unique deviation from the accepted financial structure of Korea, which has the same compartmentalized structure as in Japan. The merchant bank in Great Britain is a counterpart to the investment bank in the United States, and Korea has two types of financial institutions that play virtually the same roles under different names. There appears to be a tendency for a newly appointed minister to try to leave his imprint on the institutions and conventions under his control. When merchant banking was introduced, the finance minister at that time had an outstandingly ambitious personality. Thus, merchant banking may have been introduced unnecessarily, since it seems to duplicate the functions of investment and finance companies. At any rate, Korea's financial structure became a confusing hodgepodge, a crazy quilt too bewildering to reveal a consistent pattern. Conflicts between merchant banking corporations and other types of financial institutions (especially investment and finance companies) were inevitable. A trend frequently noted in the Korean bureaucracy is that a new institution conceived by the current minister is often nurtured at the expense of other institutions initiated by former ministers.

Accordingly, short-term financing of businesses with funds raised through issuance of a financial company's own papers (one of the main businesses of investment and finance companies) was permitted to merchant banking corporations on a limited basis. Securities-related transactions of investment and finance companies were restricted, to the benefit of merchant banking corporations and securities companies. To any financial reformer, merchant banking corporations present either a challenge or an opportunity.

Development of the Capital Market The Korean Stock Exchange came into existence in 1956, and the Securities and Exchange Law was enacted in 1962. For more than a decade afterward, the major business of the securities market was transactions of government and public debentures; hence, the market was of only minor significance as far as corporate financing was concerned. The number of listed companies was limited, and returns on securities investment were much lower than those on alternative investment opportunities. Furthermore, in the early 1960s immediately after the coup, scandals involving manipulated speculation of securities had hurt many small investors to the extent that they chose to stay out of the market for a long time. In September 1968 the Law on Fostering the Capital Market was enacted, and under this law the Korea Investment Corporation was established to induce firms to go public and to encourage public participation in the securities market. In 1969 regular-way transactions were instituted in place of forward transactions, which were prone to encouraging excessive speculation.[6]

It was after the enactment of the Public Corporation Inducement Law in 1972, however, that the securities market really began to put on steam. The intent of the law was to invest the government with the power to designate firms eligible to go public and to issue ordinances to that effect. The Securities and Exchange Commission and its executive body, the Securities Supervisory Board, were established in 1977.

The institutional players in the securities market are the securities companies, the Korea Securities Finance Corporation, and the securities investment trust companies. Securities companies are engaged in the following businesses: (1) buying and selling securities for their own accounts or on consignment; (2) buying and selling securities as brokers, intermediaries, or agents; (3) underwriting securities as members of the underwriting syndicate; and (4) making arrangements for public offerings of securities. The Korea Securities Finance Corporation was established in 1955 as an institution specializing in securities financing, an intermediary between the banking institutions and the securities market. Its main sources of funds are subscriptions and borrowings from banks, and it extends loans to underwriters, securities companies, and individuals. It also lends securities, conducts bond trading on repurchase agreements, and acts as a custodian of securities. Securities investment trusts were introduced in 1970 as a specialized business to be handled by institutions established specifically for this purpose to prevent conflicts of interest. In addition to securities investment trust companies, merchant banking corporations were also authorized to engage in this business.

A glimpse at securities market activities during the 1970s shows that the number of listed companies in the stock market increased sluggishly from 48 at the beginning of 1970 to 66 at the end of 1972. This number began to grow sharply, reaching 355 at the end of 1979 after being stimulated by the new government policy. The total value of listed stocks increased 18.4 times (from 119.9 billion won to 2,202.3 billion won) during the 1970s. The increase in the total value of listed public and corporate bonds in this period was more spectacular, increasing by 88.1 times (from 17.5 billion won to 1,541.5 billion won). The stock market experienced a boomlet from 1976 to 1978: the composite stock price index rose from 104.04 at the end of 1976 to 144.86 by the end of 1978. Then a crash occurred, and the composite stock price index plummeted to 118.97 at the end of 1979. Meanwhile, the bond market picked up steadily, with the value of transactions soaring 14.3 times between 1976 and 1979.

Policy-Directed Loans Policy-directed loans have been an indispensable channel by which the government has directed the flow of funds into selected sectors such as export-related industries and heavy and chemical industries. These sectors were deemed strategic to economic development. The government was determined to steer the economy through the development of heavy and chemical industries after the *yushin* measure, and the need for mobilizing and directing funds increased greatly in magnitude. The conventional method of credit extension to selected industries via specialized banks was not sufficient for the new task. A set of measures had to be designed to bring other financial institutions (especially commercial banks) in addition to specialized banks into the process. The participation of commercial banks in policy-directed loans had previously been limited primarily to export-supporting finance with the aid of rediscount facilities at the central bank.

Thus, the National Investment Fund was instituted in January 1974 to meet the challenge of supporting investment in major industries including heavy and chemical industries. The formulation of an annual program of fund raising and lending for the National Investment Fund is prepared by the Ministry of Finance, and the actual operation of the fund is entrusted to the Bank of Korea. Its resources are raised (1) by compulsory deposits from banking institutions, national savings associations, insurance companies, and various public funds managed by central and local governments and other public entities, and (2) by transfers from various government budgetary accounts. Compulsory contributions of banking institutions make up the bulk of the fund's resources; they are required to deposit 13 percent of the increase in time and savings deposits to the fund. This required contribution rate varies over time. National savings associations, which are a scheme of mandatory savings by public and private employees, also contribute a minor portion by depositing 100 percent of their savings with the fund.

The line of demarcation between commercial banks and specialized banks has become increasingly blurred because of the increased role of commercial banks in policy-directed loan activities and the allowance of deposit taking to specialized banks and subsequently the increased weight of deposits as a source of their funds. With commercial banks and specialized banks steadily being homogenized, the profitability of commercial banks declined and the gap between the profitability of commercial banks and that of nonbank financial institutions widened.

Commercial Banks under Financial Repression Until privatization, the government was the unchallenged single major shareholder in all nationwide commercial banks. The top management of banks (whether commercial or specialized) was largely hand-picked by the government. Annual budgeting and other major activities of the banks were subject to approval by the Ministry of Finance. Under these circumstances, it is natural that the overriding concern of the top management of banks has been, not to maximize profits or operating efficiency, but rather to obtain a higher "grade" from the government. The rate of increase in deposits has been a key criterion in this grading for a long time. Thus, annual and quarterly targets of deposits are established for each bank, and these are disaggregated into targets for each branch office.[7] The top management of banks has paid little heed to profitability but has placed a great emphasis on achieving deposit goals and extending credit as directed by the government. Government-controlled finance is doubly harmful in that it represses the evolution of banks as autonomous business entities and also protects personnel unfit for the banking business. Top managers have not been held accountable for poor profits by the major shareholder (i.e., the government), private shareholders' views have been regarded as nothing more than a nuisance, and banks' profits have been illusory and frequently manipulated by the payment of interest on reserve deposits with the central bank.

Enterprises that chose to engage in government-selected industries (in other words, those that played the game of brinksmanship well) benefited by being designated recipients of policy-directed credit; hence, they were able to grow rapidly and eventually turn into conglomerates. In the early years, in addition to lacking the needed finance, they were short of high-quality personnel, who were attracted by banking institutions offering job security and better pay. Afterward (from the mid-1970s on), however, banking institutions faced shortages of qualified personnel. With top management hand-picked by the government and opportunities for promotion limited, enterprising and innovation-minded middle-echelon banking personnel were lured away through aggressive scouting by rapidly expanding conglomerates. Deliberately or not, the government contributed to this en masse migration from banking institutions to conglomerates and newly formed nonbanking financial institutions by keeping the remuneration level of bank employees lower than that of private enterprise employees. These factors explain why nonbanking businesses grew at the expense of banking institutions in the process of Korea's economic development in the late 1970s.

Attempts at Financial Liberalization, 1980–86

At the beginning of the 1980s, opinion within and outside the government began to shift toward changing economic helmsmanship, that is, switching from government-led to private-led management of the national economy. The preamble of the Fifth Five-Year Economic and Social Development Plan was noteworthy for frankly admitting mistakes that had arisen from the government-led mode of economic development involving comprehensive planning and for expressing the need to promote private initiative and steer the national economy along the lines of indicative planning. Thus far, though, there has been a disquieting gap between the stated intentions and the deeds of the government.

Price Stability At the start of the 1980s the Korean economy plunged into serious stagflation, registering a slow and negative growth of GNP (7.0 percent in 1979 and −4.8 percent in 1980 after double-digit growth performance in the previous three years) and soaring price levels (18.8 and 38.9 percent per year as measured by the WPI in 1979 and 1980, respectively, after an inflationary but relatively stable period). Three factors contributed to this situation: (1) the OPEC-engineered second worldwide oil crisis hiked the nation's oil import bill dramatically, and the import price index rose 25.7 and 27.5 percent in 1979 and 1980, respectively, as compared with 5.1 percent in 1978; (2) the value added of the primary sector (agriculture, forestry, and fisheries) actually decreased by 19.9 percent in 1980, primarily due to a poor rice harvest; and (3) in the aftermath of President Park's death in

1979, a turbulent atmosphere of instability and uncertainty affected the nation's political and social life amid a scramble for power. On the economic scene, a relaxation of the authoritarian government's grip began to be manifested in various ways. In particular, cases of labor unrest became more frequent.

An external concomitant of this poor economic performance was a deterioration of the international balance of payments. The current account deficit increased sharply from US$1.1 billion in 1978 to $4.1, $5.3, and $4.6 billion in 1979, 1980, and 1981, respectively. Consequently, the nation's foreign indebtedness began to increase rapidly, from $14.8 billion at the end of 1978 to $32.4 billion at the end of 1981 and then to $46.8 billion at the end of 1985.

The new regime that finally emerged under the strong hand of President Chun Doo Hwan affirmed its dedication to tame runaway inflation and maintain price stability. On the one hand, the resort to market mechanisms has allegedly been the basic posture of the government in bringing about an overall balance of supply and demand. On the other hand, the Price Stabilization and Fair Trade Act of 1975 was enforced primarily to control the prices of basic commodities and products of monopolistic and oligopolistic industries. Although the Anti-Monopoly and Fair Trade Act was enacted in 1980, a part of the 1975 act concerning direct control of the prices of basic commodities has been kept intact. Moreover, the government has maintained a system of listing commodities under price watch as well as a means of direct control over prices of goods produced by government-controlled enterprises. Therefore, the government's direct and indirect control of prices has been very much in effect in the 1980s. Some examples can be cited to demonstrate the government's emphasis on price stability.

In January 1980 interest rates on deposits and loans of banking institutions were increased. Interest rates on deposits over one year were raised from 18.6 to 24 percent a year. It was significant that this unpopular contractionary measure—almost anathema to the heavily indebted business community—was taken in the politically most difficult period. Another example was a freeze on the government's general fiscal budget in 1984. This measure was noteworthy because a general election for the National Assembly was scheduled to be held the following January. The government party sustained a major setback in that election, in part because of that budget freeze. Government stabilization measures and stabilizing forces overseas (a steady fall in oil prices and international money market rates) contributed to sustained price stability in the period after 1982—a remarkable achievement for a nation long accustomed to an inflationary milieu. In contrast to the double-digit inflation Korea had experienced for a decade, WPI rose 2.4 percent in 1982 and maintained that level in the subsequent three years, then fell by 2.6 percent in 1986. The movement of the CPI showed a similar trend but remained a few percentage points higher. In 1986 the CPI crept up by 1.4 percent. Price stability was essential for a great surge of exports and domestic savings, and thus the way had been paved to financial liberalization.

Privatization of Nationwide Banks A tentative first step toward the denationalization of nationwide commercial banks was taken in 1973 when government-owned shares in the Commercial Bank of Korea were transferred to the Korean Traders Association. But this transfer of shares did not constitute genuine privatization, however, since the Traders Association is under the authority of the Ministry of Commerce and Industry. Earnest privatization endeavors had to await a change of position on the part of the government. The process of privatization was accelerated in the early 1980s as a result of a shift in the government's views on economic leadership, with a greater role being assigned to the private sector. Government-owned shares in the remaining four nationwide commercial banks were put on the block: the Hanil Bank in June 1981, the Korea First Bank and the Bank of Seoul and Trust Company in September 1982, and finally the Choheung Bank in March 1983. A ceiling of 8 percent was placed on individual shareholding in nationwide commercial banks to prevent the concentration of economic power.

Event-Forced Financial Changes The evolution of the financial sector in Korea has rarely proceeded smoothly or in accordance with a program well prepared in advance with an overall grasp of the outcomes. More often than not, changes have been forced on financial institutions in tandem with the government's hasty response to unexpected turns of events. Financial institutions and money markets were rocked to their foundations by large-scale irregularities and scandals on several occasions in the early 1980s.

In the early spring of 1982, a fraud involving private bills on an unprecedentedly large scale nearly brought Seoul money markets to collapse. The protagonists in the scandal, C. H. Lee and Y. J. Chang, allegedly had a close relationship with a top-echelon power group. On the heels of this scandal, the Myung Sung Group, which had a highly leveraged capital base, grew rapidly in the atmosphere of real estate boom and invested heavily in condominiums and recreational facilities in various resort areas throughout the country. In the summer of 1983 the bubble finally burst, and the group went bankrupt, plunging banks into a deep morass of bad debt. Apparently C. H. Kim, mastermind of the group, had hinted to unwary investors about connections to high-level officials and their kin. It is widely believed that these two instances starkly revealed the vulnerability of bankers to clients who claim a relationship with the holders of power. A third instance was a growth of unofficial bond transactions *wan-mae-chae,* that is, transactions of borrowed bonds on repurchase agreements, which occurred for about a year in the wake of the Myung Sung Group incident. When the government finally decided to put an end to this wayward practice in November 1984, the disintegration of the Kukje Group (one of Korea's major conglomerates), which had overextended itself out of its core business (shoemaking), became unavoidable. The fact that *wan-mae-chae* met with a sudden death was unfortunate, since it was perhaps the first spontaneous, market-created product, different from other financial instruments, which had been initiated or endorsed by the Ministry of Finance.

The frequent occurrence of large-scale financial irregularities in such a short span of time (three major scandals in as many years) was rooted in the financial pressures caused by the government's stabilization posture during this period, which adversely affected those enterprises still tied to the accustomed way of doing business in an inflationary milieu.

Each time a financial scandal occurred, officials groped for workable stop-gap measures, which all too often turned out to be ill conceived and shortsighted. Of the three scandals previously described, the Lee-Chang fraud has probably caused more significant and far-reaching consequences than the others in terms of its impact on the nation's financial structure. To cope with the Lee-Chang fraud, two sets of measures were instituted by two succeeding finance ministers—the so-called June 28 and July 3 policy packages. The major intent of these packages was three-pronged.

One of the intents was to lower a whole spectrum of interest rates of banks drastically (e.g., rates on discounts on commercial bills were slashed from 14 percent to 10 percent a year) so that the new rate would be uniformly charged on loans irrespective of maturity, collateral, and use of funds. Reduction of loan rates was deemed necessary to alleviate the debt service burden of financially besieged firms.

The next intent of the new policies was to phase out financial transactions via anonymous accounts and to require that every financial transaction be carried out on a real-name basis. Curb market transactions are an ancient, ubiquitous, and tenacious phenomenon in Korea. Two fundamental factors accounting for the persistence of curb markets are the Koreans' preference for higher returns at the cost of some risk and their desire for anonymity in financial matters. The Lee-Chang fraud highlighted the delicate nexus between official and unofficial money markets. Government officials decided to try a carrot-and-stick approach. Real-name accounting, which was to remove the comforting cover of anonymity, constituted the stick aspect of the policy packages for financial transactors. Anonymous financial transactions were not confined to the curb markets, and a large number of accounts at official financial institutions (including commercial banks) were also held anonymously. However, the idea of making real-name financial transactions mandatory turned out to be premature. Profound concern arose about the possibility of piercing a hole in the fragile texture of the nation's socioeconomic life such a short time after the big ruptures of the previous two years had barely been patched over. Thus the law making real-name financial transactions mandatory was promulgated but came to be not enforced. Afterwards, however, differential tax rates on interest incomes applied to real-name and anonymous accounts.[8]

The third prong of the policy packages represented the carrot for curb market dealers. To attract and absorb curb market funds into official financial institutions, doors sprang open for curb market dealers to start new financial institutions. The government's resorting to market mechanisms and stimulation of competition—slogans often repeated and also abused by officials during this period—was congruent with this open-door policy. In this climate, the Shinhan Bank (funded exclusively by Korean residents in Japan) and the KorAm Bank (a joint venture between Korean interests and the Bank of America) were established in July 1982 and March 1983, respectively.[9] The new open-door policy was aimed primarily at nonbank institutions familiar to curb market dealers, namely, investment and finance companies and mutual savings and finance companies. After the barriers to entry were lowered, 12 new firms were added to 20 existing investment and finance companies, and 41 new mutual savings and finance companies were added to the existing 199 by the end of 1983. Branch offices of financial institutions were also allowed to expand in number. Finally, amid outcry over too much competition, the open-door policy was phased out.

With more competitors in the market, with financial services overlapping and contractionary monetary policies in full swing, financial institutions found it increasingly difficult to attract funds from the public. Funds shifted, sometimes with great volatility, from one type of financial institution to another and even between different institutions of the same type in search of a better deal. In particular, "disintermediation" (i.e., the shift of funds away from banking institutions and toward nonbank financial institutions) became an increasingly serious problem. Naturally this situation caused a clamor for new financial instruments with attractive terms. From time to time the Finance Ministry was inclined to calm the furor by issuing a new commodity to any institution that marshalled greater influence and presented a more pressing case at a given moment. Sooner or later it would become evident that, though the new commodity was a boon to one type of financial institution, it was a curse to another. This usually occasioned another cycle of outcry and assuagement. By and large, the clamor for new commodities and better terms for existing commodities came from three sources: commercial and special banks, investment and finance companies, and securities companies. Negotiable certificates of deposit (CDs), a new breed of commercial papers (CPs), sale of bonds on repurchase agreements (RPs), and cash management accounts (CMAs) were the major commodities newly created or reactivated in the early 1980s. CPs were authorized for investment and finance companies in June 1981 and extended to the five large securities companies in April 1984. At the same time, CMAs were issued to investment and finance companies, partly to compensate them for the "inequity" caused by the extension of CPs to other financial institutions. Securities companies were allowed to engage in RP business as of February 1980, and banks joined this business in September 1982. CDs, which had been created in 1974 and then lay dormant, were reactivated in June 1984 to help staunch the outflow of funds from commercial banks to nonbank financial institutions.

Financial Liberalization In the early 1980s a major shift of the government's posture on economic helmsmanship from the government-led to the private-led mode was loudly heralded, but cynics remained unconvinced. For government officials, however, the fast-growing magnitude and increasing structural complexity of the national economy left little option but to make changes by which the private sector would be cast in a more prominent role than in the past.

By inclination and through professional training and experience, officials on the Economic Planning Board tend to be relatively reform-minded (if and when their interests are not directly involved), whereas those in the Finance Ministry are relatively conservative and more mindful of protecting their turf. Perhaps deliberately, a reshuffle of top-level ministerial personnel was made on a couple of occasions. As a result, key posts in each ministry were filled by those from the other ministry. In retrospect, however, the overall effect of this interministerial shift has been mixed. While it helped facilitate the speedy introduction of often drastic measures (such as the June 28 and July 3 policy packages), the compromising side effects of these measures could have been avoided by officials properly trained and seasoned within the competent ministry.

The need for reforming financial institutions as a main method for streamlining the national economy began to gain credence as early as the late 1970s. At the beginning of the 1980s it became widely accepted both inside and outside the government. Eventually the idea was anointed by the Finance Ministry, and the culminating rite was the formation of the Financial Development Council as an advisory group to the finance minister in 1982. Financial Development Council meetings were frequent in its first two years, and its agenda covered a wide range of issues in financial liberalization and development.

Against the backdrop of this realignment in the government's mood and allocation of human resources, four developments paved the way for further liberalization:

1. A feeble but significant first step was taken toward the deregulation of interest rate determination. In January 1984 a measure of this was put into force, as a narrow band of rates ranging from 10 to 10.5 percent a year was introduced to permit banks to charge different rates on the basis of borrowers' creditworthiness. The band was widened and the upper limit raised to 11.5 percent a year in November 1984. In addition, the ceilings were lifted on interbank call rates and issuing rates of unsecured corporate bonds.

2. In the previous decades of financial repression, financial institutions were nearly suffocated with a multitude of regulations, ordinances, instructions, and directives issued by the Finance Ministry and the Bank Superintendent's Office. Commercial banks were particularly entangled in the web of regulations. In the early 1980s hundreds of regulations and directives were abolished or simplified. Moreover, efforts were made to pry the power to appoint top-level bank officials out of the government's hands. At first, bank executives were unconvinced and wondered whether their new option was a blessing or a trap. Reportedly they went to the Finance Ministry, and the minister made news by turning them away with unopened envelopes containing lists of candidates. However, suspicion of outside interference persisted.

3. Policy-directed loans made in previous decades had turned sour in many cases. Insolvent firms became nonperforming assets (i.e., more or less irredeemable loans to be written off in due course) of commercial banks. Unless this burden was somehow relieved, autonomous and profitable operation of banks would be difficult. Methodical but determined endeavors were made in the early 1980s to reduce policy-directed credit (e.g., by limiting further growth of the National Investment Fund to which commercial banks are obligated to contribute) and to adjust the backlog of insolvent firms with the aid of the central bank's facility as lender of last resort. Although this adjustment and drastic consolidation of insolvent cases inevitably bred charges of favoritism and inequity, it is fair to say that it went a long way toward clearing the way for further liberalization of commercial banks.

4. Also during this time, the allocation of credit for large-scale projects in the heavy and chemical industries was deemphasized. In contrast, the promotion of small- and medium-sized firms was highlighted. Commercial banks were required to extend at least 35 percent of their loans to small- and medium-sized firms. The required ratios for local banks and foreign bank branches were 55 and 25 percent, respectively. In addition, nonbank financial institutions (notably investment and finance companies) were also assigned specific target credit ratios for small- and medium-sized firms.

The Erosion of Compartmentalization The demarcation of boundaries defining what business practices can be carried out by specific financial institutions has gradually been adjusted. The range of commercial banking has been expanded since 1982 to include ancillary businesses such as sale of commercial bills, sale of government and other public bonds on RPs, factoring, trusts, credit cards, CDs, and mutual installment savings business. As already mentioned, a new breed of CPs and the business of CMAs (a Korean variation of the money market fund in the United States) were introduced through investment and finance companies and merchant banking corporations in 1981 and 1984, respectively. CP business was also extended to large securities companies in 1984.

Computerization and Financial Innovations In the early 1980s, there was a rush to computerization and mechanization among banks and nonbank financial institutions at the expense of lump-sum investments, often deteriorating their short-run profitability. Because of the installation of electronic data processing systems, however, they have been able to reduce the cost of financial intermediation significantly and thus offer new financial services. With interest rate competition virtually eliminated, for instance, commercial banks have actively pursued the diffusion of nonprice competitive practices such as the payment of salaries through bank remittances, the debiting of bank accounts for credit card usage, and the payment of taxes and public utility charges via automatic fund transfer between bank accounts. Other services of banks that have newly been made possible by technological advances include on-line accounts, cash dispensers, and night depositories.

Financial Internationalization To facilitate the ever-expanding export and import activities of the national economy and in the name of motivating domestic banks to improve their banking services and skills, financial internationalization has been one of the government's major directions in the 1980s. Another 24 foreign bank branches have been allowed to operate in Korea while three have folded since 1981, bringing the total to 53 by the end of 1986. Korean financial internationalization has proceeded partly in response to competition from overseas. The success of Korean commodity exports brought about the United States' demand for reciprocity in service industries. Financial businesses have become the primary target of U.S. demands for reciprocity, or "national treatment," and lowered entry barriers. In this atmosphere, discriminatory restrictions on foreign banks in the domestic financial market have been gradually phased out. In 1985 foreign banks were permitted to handle trust business and make use of rediscount facilities at the Bank of Korea for export financing. In 1986 the rediscount facilities of the central bank were made available for all operations of foreign bank branches. In the spirit of "national treatment," foreign bank branches have been asked to comply with requirements such as the obligatory ratio of loans to small- and medium-sized firms (that is, 35 percent or more) effective 1 August 1986, the same as the ratio required of domestic nationwide commercial banks. As of the end of 1986, the opening of foreign life insurance and securities businesses remained a hot issue on the agenda for trade talks between Korea and the United States.

Developments in the Securities Market Efforts to upgrade the securities market continued to gain momentum in the 1980s. In January 1980, bond transactions on RPs were institutionalized to enlarge the scope of the bond-issuing market. Furthermore, in July 1983 the securities authorities announced the Measures for Reinforcement of Capital Market Function, the main intent of which was to induce corporations in good credit standing to sell stock and help stimulate security issuance at the market price. As a measure for liberalizing securities markets further, two open-ended types of investment trusts exclusively for foreigners, namely, the Korea International Trust (KIT) and the Korea Trust (KT), were established and sold for US$15 million each in November 1981. The amount of KIT and KT funds was increased by $10 million each two years later. Buoyed by their popularity among foreign investors, three additional investment trusts of $30 million each were sold to foreigners in March and April 1985, namely, Korea Growth Trust (KGT), Seoul International Trust (SIT), and Seoul Trust (ST). A most significant event was the establishment in New York in May 1984 of the Korea Fund, a closed-end, company-type investment vehicle of $60 million. Later this company was listed in the New York Stock Exchange. The aim of the Korea Fund was to allow some leeway for foreigners to participate in capital appreciation through long-term investment in equity securities of fast-growing Korean enterprises, yet without prematurely opening the domestic capital market.

An overview of securities market activities during the period from 1980 to 1986 may be gained from surveying the following facts. The composite stock price index did not rebound to the level of 1978 until 1985. Because of this slackness of the stock market, which in turn reflected a sluggish national economy, the number of listed companies dwindled to 328 at the end of 1983 and then increased again to 355 (the same as in 1979) at the end of 1986. The total paid-in capital of listed companies increased only 2.6 times (from 2,202.3 billion won to 5,649.7 billion won), whereas that of listed public and corporate bonds jumped 11.1 times (from 1,541.5 billion won to 17,112.6 billion won) in the seven-year period up to the end of 1986. Meanwhile, the stock market has turned increasingly bullish from mid-1985 on, bringing the year-end composite stock price index up from 142.46 in 1984 to 163.37 in 1985 and 272.61 in 1986. The boom was sustained, with the composite stock price index reaching 525.1 at the end of 1987, apparently impervious to Black Monday repercussions. The total market value of listed stocks amounted to 11,994.2 billion won at the end of 1986, 1.8 times the level of one year earlier.

Current Status of the Financial System

Financial Institutions: An Overview As shown in Figure 9.1, financial institutions in Korea can be classified into the central bank (Bank of Korea) and two other broad categories—banking institutions and nonbank financial institutions. Notwithstanding the retardation of their development under governmental control, Korean financial institutions are highly diversified and specialized. The functions of most of the financial institutions listed in the figure have been described at least briefly in the previous chapters (for more information, see Bank of Korea 1985).

Nonbank financial institutions were rather insignificant in the early 1970s. Since then they have grown rapidly and have substantially eclipsed the dominance of banking institutions due to preferential interest rates and less government interference in the earlier phases of their existence. At the beginning of the 1980s, government control in the sphere of nonbank financial institutions was increased with a view to correcting the relatively disadvantaged position of banking institutions. Deregulation has been steadily progressing in banking institutions, but the market share of nonbank financial institutions in terms of deposits has climbed from 16 percent in 1971 to slightly over 50 percent in 1986.

The shortage of national savings relative to gross investment has been a chronic feature of the financial scene of Korea. In 1986, however, for the first time a surplus was recorded in the national savings-investment balance. The ratio of national savings to GNP increased to 32.6 percent (a big rise from 28.6 percent in 1985) while the gross investment ratio was 29.8 percent (a decline from 31.1 percent in 1985). A primary impetus came from the remarkable growth in savings of the business sector, reflecting a sizable surplus in the international trade balance. The household savings ratio also inched up a bit but still remained at a considerable distance

Category	Subcategory	Institution	Total Assets (in billion won)
Central Bank		The Bank of Korea	40.406
Banking Institutions (Deposit Money Banks)	Commercial Banks	Nationwide Commercial Banks (11)	64.301
		Local Banks (10)	14.331
		Foreign Bank Branches (66)	12.630
	Specialized Banks	Industrial Bank of Korea	8.841
		Citizens National Bnak	8.937
		Korea Housing Bank	7.778
		National Agricultural Cooperatives Federation	11.658
		National Federation of Fisheries Cooperatives	1.260
		National Livestock Cooperatives Federation	768
Nonbank Financial Institutions	Development Institutions	Korea Development Bank	17.687
		Export-Import Bank of Korea	2.214
		Korea Long-Term Credit Bank	3.961
	Savings Institutions	Trust Accounts of Banking Institutions (50)	44.698
		Mutual Savings and Finance Companies (334)	8.392
		Credit Unions (including Village Finance Associations) (4,606)	7.466
		Mutual Credits (1,696)	9.989
		Postal Savings	3.034
	Investment Companies	Investment and Finance Companies (32)	12.618
		Merchant Banking Corporations (6)	4.229
		Investment Trust Companies (8)	23.783
	Insurance Companies	Life Insurance Companies (22)	20.803
		Postal Life Insurance	1.000
Securities Market		Securities Supervisory Board	
		Korea Stock Exchange	
		Securities Companies (25)	45.733
		Korea Securities Finance Corporation	865
Quasi-Financial Institutions		Credit Guarantee Funds (2)	
		Leasing Companies (17)	
		Venture Capital Companies (31)	
		Credit Administration Fund	

FIGURE 9.1 Financial institutions in Korea. Figures in parentheses represent the number of institutions at the end of 1989.

from that of either Japan or Taiwan. National savings relative to gross investment were 109.4 percent in 1986, as compared with 92 percent in 1985 and a mere 73.1 percent in late 1982. Doubt lingered about the sustainability of this situation. In 1987 the national savings ratio rose to about 35.6 percent, again outstripping the gross investment ratio. As a result, the need for net inflow of foreign savings waned, and the size of foreign debts diminished rapidly from the peak of US$46.8 billion at the end of 1985 to $35.6 billion at the end of 1987. How long will this fair weather be sustained? What are the appropriate measures to maintain national savings at a level commensurate with gross investment, regardless of what happens in the international trade balance? These and other questions should be weighed carefully in formulating any grand design of reforms for making Korean financial institutions more efficient in coping with future challenges.

Profitability, Efficiency, and Soundness of Financial Institutions

Thus far this discussion on the evolution of financial institutions has been primarily descriptive. In what follows, an attempt is made to present a quantitative analysis of the performance of commercial banks, the backbone of any financial system, from the early 1960s up to 1989. The coverage of commercial banks for this analysis includes seven nationwide commercial banks (five banks established decades ago plus the Shinhan Bank and the KorAm Bank) and ten local banks. Therefore, foreign bank branch offices and the three nationwide commercial banks founded in 1989 are excluded. The performance of banks is evaluated in terms of a few easily available indicators of profitability, efficiency, and soundness.

The ratios of net profit to net worth (paid-in capital plus reserves) and to total assets are taken as profitability indicators of commercial banks. As shown in Table 9.1, the banks were better off in the early 1960s when the government's comprehensive drive for economic development had not yet shifted into high gear.

Nationwide commercial banks' profitability indicators kept sliding downhill to 8.52 and 0.30 percent in 1973, a drastic fall from the average annual ratios of 20.36 and 2.07 percent in the 1962–65 period. But profitability improved from 1974 to 1981, with average annual profitability ratios of 17.34 and 0.76 percent. It seems rather paradoxical to witness the synchronization of a more repressive financial regime and an improved profitability of banks in this period.

One of the clues to solving this conundrum may be found in the shift in the sources of bank revenue. Funds that cost less than deposits to mobilize were made available to the banks through foreign capital inflow and central bank credit. At the same time, income and fees from foreign exchange transactions and income other than operating income took a greater share in the banks' total income (as shown by columns D and G in Table 9.2). The profitability of banks in the financial liberalization in the 1980s looks pale beside that in the immediately preceding period, with the average annual figures of the two indicators being 4.96 and 0.27 percent in the 1982–89 period. Major culprits for this deterioration of profitability

TABLE 9.1
Ratios of net profit to net worth and total assets of nationwide commercial banks and local banks (percentage)

	Net profit/net worth		Net profit/total assets	
	National[a]	Local	National[a]	Local
1962	18.41	—	2.29	—
1963	17.90	—	2.15	—
1964	20.45	—	2.03	—
1965	24.67	—	1.80	—
1966	11.13	—	0.88	—
1967	10.01	3.05	0.56	0.91
1968	7.89	10.74	0.47	1.95
1969	9.81	13.30	0.42	1.67
1970	10.58	13.57	0.39	1.80
1971	5.07	16.57	0.28	1.98
1972	5.44	16.97	0.21	1.10
1973	8.52	14.25	0.30	1.04
1974	28.89	15.13	0.78	1.13
1975	16.73	16.92	0.62	1.06
1976	21.49	19.72	0.99	1.66
1977	13.49	21.81	0.69	0.60
1978	17.69	19.80	0.84	1.43
1979	12.02	16.69	0.70	1.29
1980	14.36	18.17	0.79	1.38
1981	14.06	13.43	0.68	0.90
1982	5.19	5.51	0.23	0.35
1983	2.74	4.90	0.12	0.25
1984	6.81	13.65	0.30	0.68
1985	3.90	9.53	0.15	0.47
1986	4.04	8.00	0.16	0.39
1987	4.38	4.71	0.19	0.27
1988	6.56	4.55	0.36	0.60
1989	6.06	3.53	0.66	0.60

Source: Research Department, Bank of Korea.

[a] Seven nationwide commercial banks including the Shinhan Bank and the KorAm Bank.

were a big drop in banks' lending interest rates in 1982 and the snowballing nonperforming loans in the wake of the government's industrial restructuring endeavors in the subsequent period (as shown in Table 9.3).

In the financial liberalization period of the 1980s, a remarkable shift can be discerned in the banks' income sources away from conventional routes and toward new ones. The shares of interest income (on won and foreign currency deposits) and income from foreign exchange transactions decreased from 65.5 and 17.7

Table 9.2

Composition of income sources of nationwide commercial banks (percentage)

	Sources of income						
	A	B	C	D	E	F	G
1962	76.5	6.6	2.3	2.3	12.3	100.0	0.0
1963	80.1	5.7	3.1	3.0	8.0	100.0	0.0
1964	69.1	11.6	3.9	5.3	10.2	100.0	0.0
1965	74.3	3.3	3.5	4.9	10.9	96.9	3.1
1966	76.0	2.1	2.2	3.7	14.2	98.2	1.8
1967	72.3	1.5	5.1	4.7	14.5	98.0	2.0
1968	76.7	1.3	6.1	4.3	10.3	98.8	1.2
1969	82.5	2.6	4.3	3.6	6.1	99.2	0.8
1970	82.7	1.2	4.2	4.6	6.4	99.0	1.0
1971	83.1	1.1	4.3	6.6	3.3	98.4	1.6
1972	76.2	1.0	5.6	7.8	8.4	98.8	1.2
1973	72.6	1.1	5.7	12.9	6.0	98.3	1.7
1974	77.0	0.9	4.5	11.6	1.8	95.7	4.3
1975	74.1	1.2	6.2	9.1	3.2	93.7	6.3
1976[a]	66.1	1.0	8.3	9.8	9.4	94.6	5.4
1977[a]	51.3	1.0	9.6	12.4	10.4	84.7	15.3[b]
1978	62.8	0.9	6.5	17.4	8.1	95.6	4.4
1979	63.8	0.6	7.1	15.6	8.0	95.1	4.9
1980	64.3	0.5	6.8	17.1	6.1	94.7	5.3
1981	65.5	0.4	6.8	17.7	9.3	99.6	0.4
1982	61.0	0.6	9.8	17.2	9.8	98.5	1.5
1983	58.7	0.8	11.4	11.1	16.2	99.3	0.7
1984	59.0	1.0	12.8	9.7	16.7	99.2	0.8
1985	59.4	1.1	12.4	7.2	19.3	99.4	0.6
1986	57.8	1.1	14.2	8.2	18.1	99.3	0.7
1987	56.8	1.3	13.6	8.3	19.3	99.3	0.7
1988	53.5	1.5	13.3	7.9	22.6	99.0	1.0
1989	56.8	1.9	12.3	5.9	22.3	99.2	0.8

Source: Research Department, Bank of Korea.

Note: For seven nationwide commercial banks, including the Shinhan Bank and the KorAm Bank.

Sources of income: A = interest income; B = fees received; C = income from securities holding; D = income and fees from foreign exchange transactions; E = others; F = total operating income (A + B + C + D + E); G = non-operating income (including real estate-related incomes).

[a] Based on the second half-year accounting.

[b] Irregular revenue increase due to actual savings in bad-loan allowance associated with guaranteeing business to overseas construction companies.

TABLE 9.3
Ratio of nonperforming loans of nationwide commercial banks and local banks (percentage)

	National[a]	Local		National[a]	Local
1962	0.5	—	1976	2.87	1.46
1963	0.4	—	1977	1.67	1.35
1964	0.2	—	1978	1.08	1.43
1965	0.1	—	1979	3.43	4.63
1966	0.1	—	1980	2.74	8.89
1967	n.a	n.a	1981	7.25	6.85
1968	n.a	n.a	1982	6.95	5.51
1969	0.3	0.0	1983	8.57	6.90
1970	1.51	0.37	1984	10.85	8.47
1971	2.46	0.14	1985	10.22	8.18
1972	2.24	0.47	1986	10.53	8.54
1973	0.92	0.02	1987	8.42	7.36
1974	0.63	0.03	1988	7.44	6.16
1975	0.40	0.04	1989	5.86	4.11

Source: Research Department, Bank of Korea.

Note: Ratio of nonperforming loans (the sum of three categories of loans: fixed, doubtful, and estimated loss) to total credit outstanding (the sum of total deposits, acceptances and guarantees, and other credits) for the period since 1976; for the period prior to 1976, the ratio represents that of nonperforming loans (excluding fixed loans) to total deposits only.

[a]Seven nationwide commercial banks, including the Shinhan Bank and the KorAm Bank.

percent, respectively, in 1981 to 56.8 and 5.9 percent in 1989, while fees received, income from securities holding, and miscellaneous operating incomes (including incomes from trust business, credit card business, interest on reserve deposits, and monetary stabilization account with the central bank) increased rather steadily from 0.4, 6.8, and 9.3 percent in 1981 to 1.9, 12.3, and 22.3 percent in 1989. One may add that the share of fees received is underreported in Table 9.2 because of the classification of fees on the foreign exchange transaction in another category (that is, in column D instead of column B).

The official profitability statistics of banks in Korea more often than not do not represent the real situation of the banks under the changing modes of the government's financial repression. In this connection it is recommended that the reader bear in mind the tripartite relationship between business, the banks, and the government. The government's repression of the financial sector has been double-edged to the banks: protection as well as control. It is commonplace to note solely the side of financial repression that taxes the management of banks: heavy-handed control of every aspect of bank operation, restricted scope of business, policy-directed loans, lending rates lower than market rates, and so on. Along with this negative side, however, the government's handouts to the banks should be mentioned: the government's safety net against banks' insolvency, which helps to dispense with a formal deposit insurance scheme; the central bank's low-interest rate credit to banks; deposit rates lower than market rates; payment of interest on reserve deposits with the central banks to window-dress banks' financial statements and keep a semblance of profitability at a minimum acceptable level, and so on.

To approximate implicit subsidy and taxation under financial repression, the following adjustments are made to the official profitability statistics of banks. On the implicit subsidy side, the following two items are taken into consideration:

- The subsidy to banks from the central bank's low-interest-rate credit, which is estimated by the Bank of Korea's (BOK) average nonpolicy-related loans outstanding to the banks multiplied by the interest rate differential between the BOK lending rate and the market rate.[10]
- The subsidy to banks on account of the deposit rate being lower than the market rate, which is estimated by average savings and time deposits of banks multiplied by (market interest rate minus one-year time deposit rate)/(1 minus required reserve ratio).

On the implicit taxation side, one item is taken into consideration:

- Taxation on banks caused by the required holdings of the low-paying Monetary Stabilization Account and Monetary Stabilization Bond (MSA and MSB, respectively, hereafter), which is estimated by average MSA holdings multiplied by the interest rate differential (= interest rate paid on MSA minus the market interest rate) and by average MSB and other public bonds holdings multiplied by the interest rate differential (= MSB rate paid by the BOK minus the market interest rate).

The result of adjustments to banks' official profitability statistics is shown in columns A and B of Table 9.4. Column A takes into account the subsidy from the central bank's low-interest-rate credit only, while column B includes the subsidy from the deposit rate being lower than the market rate as well. Readers are advised to take the absolute level of our calculated effect of implicit subsidy cum implicit taxation on the official statistics with a grain of salt because of incomplete and arbitrary coverage. Rather, attention should be paid to differentials between implicit and official profitability in the last two columns of Table 9.4. The trend of implicit profitability is interesting enough: (1) implicit profitability, even with the narrow concept of implicit subsidy (column A), almost always looks

TABLE 9.4
Estimated implicit profitability of commercial banks under financial regulation (percentage)

	Implicit profitability		Official profitability	Differential	
	A	B	C	(A–C)	(B–C)
1971	0.48	1.10	0.39	0.09	0.71
1972	0.40	4.24	0.29	0.11	3.95
1973	0.19	3.73	0.39	−0.20	3.34
1974	1.30	2.98	0.83	0.47	2.15
1975	1.06	2.10	0.68	0.38	1.42
1976	1.22	2.15	1.03	0.19	1.12
1977	0.78	1.41	0.77	0.01	0.64
1978	0.82	0.93	0.73	0.09	0.20
1979	1.29	3.50	0.79	0.50	2.71
1980	0.72	3.51	0.86	−0.14	2.65
1981	0.67	3.01	0.67	0.00	2.34
1982	0.63	4.58	0.24	0.39	4.34
1983	0.42	3.40	0.14	0.28	3.26
1984	0.86	3.27	0.35	0.51	2.92
1985	0.56	2.41	0.19	0.37	2.22
1986	0.43	1.62	0.19	0.24	1.43
1987	0.52	1.79	0.20	0.32	1.59
1988	0.69	2.66	0.39	0.30	2.27
1989	0.89	3.15	0.65	0.24	2.50

Note: Nationwide commercial banks, including the Shinhan Bank and the KorAm Bank, and local banks.

A = implicit subsidy (narrow concept) net of implicit taxation to the total assets of commercial banks; B = implicit subsidy (wide concept) net of implicit taxation to the total assets of commercial banks; C = weighted average profitability of nationwide commercial banks and local banks (as reported in Table 9.1).

better than the official profitability except for 1973 and 1980, which to an extent substantiates the existence of benefits along with well-recognized banes to banks under the regime of financial repression, and (2) the conundrum mentioned above of the higher profitability of banks under a more repressive financial regime in the 1974–81 period as compared with both the preceding and following periods virtually disappears.

So much for the profitability of banks. Now let us turn our attention briefly to the efficiency and soundness of banks. It appears to me rather difficult to find a handy guide to check on the efficiency of credit allocation via banks. A plausible argument for the allocative efficiency of bank credit based on the actual performance of Korea's overall economic growth is easily demolished by the sheer size of banks' large nonperforming loans outstanding in the late 1980s. The importance of allocative efficiency notwithstanding, the complication and extent of work involved to tackle this task properly would take me beyond the purview of this paper. Thus, suffice it here to look into the mobilization efficiency of banks with the help of Table 9.5. The ratio of expenses to deposits of nationwide commercial banks declined steadily from 6.15 percent in 1962 to a record low of 3.03 percent in 1973. Despite a jump of nearly one percentage point to 3.92 in 1974, the ratio managed to remain below a 4.0 percent level with mild ups and downs until 1980. Having surpassed a 4.0 percent level in the first half of the 1980s (possibly at the influence of banks' deposit hemorrhage to nonbank financial institutions to which the entry doors were open in 1982–83), the ratio fell again to a level less than 4.0 percent, presumably as a result of price stability and double-digit growth in GNP in the late 1980s. The case of local banks initiated in 1967 presents a similar trend but a consistently worse efficiency in deposits mobilization. Local banks' disadvantageous position vis-à-vis nationwide commercial banks is natural in that, under a repressive financial regime, the network of a bank's branch offices is essential to its deposit mobilization. The branching network of a local bank is limited in principle to the province where the head office is located. Thus, local banks are virtually off limits to the Seoul metropolitan area, where deposit funds were much easier to tap except for two branch offices as of the end of 1989. By the same token,

TABLE 9.5
Ratio of expenses to deposits of nationwide commercial banks and local banks (percentage)

	National[a]	Local		National[a]	Local		National[a]	Local
1961	—	—	1971	4.49	7.03	1981	4.12	5.28
1962	6.15	—	1972	3.49	5.40	1982	4.22	5.17
1963	6.71	—	1973	3.03	4.97	1983	4.29	5.16
1964	8.73	—	1974	3.92	5.95	1984	4.19	5.01
1965	8.16	—	1975	3.43	5.36	1985	4.14	5.10
1966	6.89	—	1976	3.28	4.59	1986	4.03	4.75
1967	9.21	8.73	1977	3.40	4.72	1987	3.49	4.14
1968	5.57	10.89	1978	3.68	4.92	1988	3.30	4.11
1969	4.37	7.92	1979	3.65	4.78	1989	3.67	4.08
1970	4.80	8.12	1980	3.90	5.11	1990	—	—

Source: Research Department, Bank of Korea.
[a]Seven nationwide commercial banks, including the Shinhan Bank and the KorAm Bank.

a large number (even two-thirds in some cases) of local banks' branch offices have run on a chronic deficit basis.

Finally, we come to the issue of banks' soundness. Although sporadic bouts of financial crisis in the 1970s and 1980s could have brought some banks to a collapse, the government's visible and invisible hands have guaranteed the absence of even a single case of actual bankruptcy in the banking history in Korea. Table 9.3 shows the ratio of nonperforming loans to the total credit outstanding of nationwide commercial banks and local banks. Caution is due for a discontinuity in the basic data. In the period prior to 1976 the ratio represents the share of nonperforming loans (the sum of doubtful loans and estimated loss) in the total loans outstanding, whereas in the subsequent period the coverage of both the numerator and denominator is wider: nonperforming loans include fixed loans in addition to the aforementioned two categories of loans and the denominator comprises acceptances and guarantees and other sundry credit items in addition to total loans outstanding. This discontinuity notwithstanding, an interesting trend over time is clearly discernible: in the 1960s the banks' burden was kept at a pretty low level; the ratio began to soar sharply at the turn of the 1970s and then fell plumb down in 1973, most likely in the wake of the Emergency Decree on 3 August 1972. In the period of a more repressive financial regime from 1974 to 1980, however, the ratio rose again gradually but was kept at a manageable level of about 3 percent largely on account of the banks' bookkeeping practice of sweeping bad loans under the carpet at the nod of the authorities. In a financial regime more open to liberalization in the 1980s, the long covered-up bad loans were brought into the daylight all at once. In addition, the government's industrial restructuring endeavors focused on shipping, overseas construction, and other heavy and chemical industries had a snowballing effect on the magnitude of bad loans held in the banking sector. Having reached a scary double-digit height in the mid-1980s, the ratio came down to a manageable level again thanks to the upturn of the business cycle of industries concerned and the banks' lump-sum recapitalization in the late 1980s. The case of local banks offers a similar story.

Table 9.6 shows the ratio of net worth or equity to total assets of nationwide commercial banks and local banks. Here again, the equity-to-assets ratio appears to indicate the effects of a distinctive demarcation in financial control. In the early 1960s the ratio was kept above the 10 percent level. From 1965 to 1972 it declined more or less steadily. An abrupt fall in the equity ratio was made in 1972, a record low (2.68 percent) was reached in 1974, and subsequently the situation began to improve. At the outset of the 1980s, the ratio fell sharply and then picked up again to 10.83 percent in 1989 with the aid of banks' large-scale recapitalization in the booming securities market of the late 1980s. In this connection, it is noteworthy that 1989 saw the entry of three new nationwide commercial banks, which are not included in Table 9.6.

Table 9.6
Ratio of net worth to total assets of nationwide commercial banks and local banks (percentage)

	National[a]	Local		National[a]	Local
1961	—	—	1976	4.59	6.49
1962	12.47	—	1977	5.10	5.47
1963	12.04	—	1978	4.76	7.22
1964	9.84	—	1979	5.85	7.76
1965	7.37	—	1980	5.47	7.62
1966	7.91	—	1981	4.53	6.67
1967	5.66	33.33	1982	4.35	6.46
1968	5.91	17.86	1983	4.63	5.30
1969	4.29	12.39	1984	4.51	5.46
1970	3.70	13.39	1985	3.77	5.25
1971	5.52	11.92	1986	3.95	5.05
1972	3.84	6.53	1987	4.42	5.70
1973	3.57	7.27	1988	5.72	11.27
1974	2.68	7.46	1989	10.83	17.09
1975	3.68	6.26	1990	—	—

Source: Research Department, Bank of Korea.

[a]Seven nationwide commercial banks, including the Shinhan Bank and the KorAm Bank.

The Future of Financial Institutions

Lessons from Abroad

Financial liberalization or deregulation has been in effect in so many countries for so many years that by now it seems to have had a bandwagon effect. In the United States, powerful innovative forces unleashed by rising inflation and advancing technology have substantially eroded the restrictive bank regulatory structure that emerged from the Great Depression. This has had strong and sustained effects on three fronts. First, due to gradual deregulation of interest rates, the structure, cost, and stability of bank funds have changed dramatically since the early 1980s. In the process, the character of banking operations has been greatly altered. Second, although the separation of commercial banking and other financial activities (mainly investment banking)—"the Chinese Wall" epitomized in the Glass-Steagall Act—remains in force, the boundaries have become increasingly blurred due to the ability of nonbank institutions to offer deposit-like products (normally bearing higher interest rates) and the expansion of banks and bank holding companies into nonbanking operations (sometimes taking advantage of various loopholes in the regulations). Finally, geographic restrictions on banking operations have lost much of their force in recent years, again through the exploitation of loopholes. In the rapid progress of the financial revolution, however, a host of insolvencies and near-bankruptcies as well as outright frauds on Wall Street have necessitated a reappraisal and strengthening of the supervisory oversight of financial institutions. The net effect of deregulation and reregulation, however, has still been in the direction of financial liberalization (Furstenberg 1985; Broaddus 1985).

The forces motivating financial innovation and liberalization in Japan were inflation and interest rate volatility; increasing interest rate preference and financial assets accumulation; large-scale issue of government bonds and the development of open markets; increasingly active international capital flows under the floating exchange rate system; and technological innovations in electronics and telecommunication. Additionally, pressure from the United States has played an important role in speeding up change in the rigid Japanese financial structure (Suzuki 1985).

As for the risk involved in the speedy implementation of financial liberalization, the experience of the Latin American Southern Cone (Chile in particular) provides some useful lessons. First, prudence is warranted when instituting financial liberalization in developing countries, particularly in determining the speed and extent to which interest rates should be freed. Second, cautious attention should be paid to the schedule of liberalization of the capital account and relaxation of exchange controls. The opening of the capital account should be delayed until foreign trade has been opened and the trade account has registered a surplus. Third, it is essential that the process of financial reform be accompanied by strict supervision of the banking and nonbanking sectors to prevent fraud and circumvention of sound banking practices. The enforcement of supervision should be particularly strict when conglomerates play a crucial role in the national economy (for a detailed discussion, see Corbo 1985; Corbo, de Melo, and Tybout 1986; Dornbusch 1983; Edwards 1985; and Harberger 1985).

So much has been borrowed from Japan for so long and built into the current financial system of Korea that there appears to be nothing left for further emulation. Yet, it has become habitual for would-be Korean reformers to look closely at things Japanese once again and grope for clues to mend and improve what is amiss in the Korean system. But lessons from Japan should be weighed and carefully selected in the broad context and long perspective of the Japanese experience. Historical as well as contemporary events deserve scrutiny. Immersion in things foreign as such is often fruitless, and the Korean perspective should always be borne in mind. In this manner only, international comparison and assessment can throw light on the Korean situation.

Lessons, both positive and negative, can be learned from the Japanese experience. A gradual approach to major shifts of fundamental policy is laudable from the viewpoint of Koreans accustomed to frequent trial and error on the part of the government. Japanese officials appear not to rush to change. They have no predilection for drastic measures but rather strive for cautious consensus building prior to major shifts in policy. Still, Japanese gradualism can be carried to an extreme and become nothing more than procrastination.

The Japanese financial system has so far worked well in terms of the mobilization and allocation of funds, in spite of its "outdated" framework (Suzuki 1985:136). Government interference in the operation of financial institutions, including the central bank, although well enshrined in various laws and regulations, has been less pronounced than in Korea. What has made the Japanese financial system function so efficiently? Two major factors have contributed to its smooth operation.

One factor is the high national savings rate. When ample funds are forthcoming, the mobilization function of financial intermediaries is automatically expedited. Their allocative role is made easy, and even some cases of gross misallocation are tolerable. In other words, the high rate of savings can propel the outmoded system, and high growth of the economy is sustainable even with old-fashioned financial institutions. In my view, this has been the case in Japan, West Germany, and Taiwan. The reverse can be found in the United States and Great Britain. Their financial institutions constitute a busy and prosperous sector in the economy, and most recent financial innovations have been created in their money markets. Yet their national savings rates remain at deplorable levels and their economies lack vitality.

The other factor that spares the Japanese financial system from the possibly detrimental effects of an outdated financial framework (and potentially excessive repression) lies in an accepted set of conventions or practices. The most conspicuous case is in the relationship between the Ministry of Finance and the Bank of Japan. In terms of verbatim interpretation of Japanese law, the position of the Bank of Japan is weaker than that of the Bank of Korea vis-à-vis the government. In actual practice, however, the reverse is true. Perhaps the clue lies in Japanese conventions, including such a gimmick as the virtual alternation of appointment to the governor of the Bank of Japan between the former vice minister of finance and Bank of Japan senior officials, which helps to remove friction between the two organizations. There are a host of unwritten Japanese practices and conventions that apparently serve to lubricate the rigid and seemingly archaic financial system of Japan.

Naturally, the latecomers' advantage follows from its capacity to learn from a predecessor's experiences, especially past mistakes and the corrective measures addressed to them. In this sense, events of the past are more illuminating than contemporary events. In the recent years of financial liberalization, the trend toward "universal banking" is often accepted as a forgone conclusion, and every erosion of compartmentalization is deemed commendable and desirable. However, if not checked properly, this course is fraught with conflicts between diverse interests and a high degree of market risk. A case in point is a Japanese experience of the early 1960s, when a securities trading and a securities investment trust were combined in one company, resulting in a debacle known as the Yama-Ichi Securities Company scandal. The Japanese government was prompted to reverse its policy and keep the two kinds of securities businesses in separate houses again. Korea can learn from this sort of experience and guard against the conflicts of interest and risks associated with breaking down protective regulatory walls.

The control- and regulation-mindedness of government bureaucrats permeates multifarious aspects of the Japanese financial system. Their laws and regulations strongly exude this attitude. This is particularly so in the relationship between the Ministry of Finance and the Bank of Japan, on the one hand, and between the Bank of Japan and banking institutions, on the other. In addition, excessive care for vested interest and strong territorial instincts are pronounced among the bureaus, departments, and sections within the Ministry of Finance. This hampers the intraministerial flow of information, causes tunnel vision, and tends to make ministry-wide endeavors difficult. In sum, the specialization or compartmentalization manifest in the existing financial system of Japan is excessive. Because of this, institutional barriers have been crumbling in recent years.

Toward Reform

Basic Directions of Reform What the diverse threads of future trends and their implications in the financial sector have in common may be epitomized in the following four basic directions:

- liberalization (or deregulation)
- scale and scope economization for aggrandizement (with room for financial boutiques)
- internationalization
- equity-mindedness

What do these four basic directions for reform signify for the functioning of financial institutions? Do they involve any conflict of objectives or divergence of signals to would-be reformers? Liberalization, aggrandizement, and internationalization are not necessarily conflicting and can be construed as complementary—they tend to converge in one of two major objectives of financial reform. In other words, they should be conceived and pursued so that they are conducive to maximization in fund mobilization and optimization in fund allocation as well as minimization in intermediation cost in the financial sector. In short, liberalization, aggrandizement, and internationalization are means to meet the objective of efficient financial reform. Equity-mindedness in financial reform is, of course, needed to meet the objective of equity. It goes without saying that there exists a conflict between efficiency and equity criteria. It is an art indeed for policymakers to achieve the delicate balance between efficiency and equity, maximizing complementarity while minimizing substitutability and conflict.

Two Basic Approaches Two basic approaches can be recommended for financial reform in Korea. One is what can be called a holistic approach. The other is a gradual or stage-by-stage approach.

The financial system of a developed economy is a network of intricately related institutions and an interwoven framework of legal structures and conventions. More often than not, this system is at the very vortex of conflicting interests and is even at the mercy of overt and covert interplays between politics and business. Piecemeal alterations of the existing financial system tend to lead to a loss of proper perspective on the part of policymakers and to a series of claims and counterclaims on the part of financial interest groups, which tend to invoke the explicit and implicit assistance of the political arena. Hence the development and implementation of balanced financial reform programs require a proper perspective in which the whole picture can be viewed constantly, as opposed to peeping at parts. Courage and probity are also required. For this purpose, the mental exercise of constructing what might be called a "financial matrix" may be effective. The rows and columns of a financial matrix represent financial institutions and financial commodities. By comparing this matrix with the actual existing financial needs of the corporate and household sectors, the deficiencies or superfluities of a given financial system are easily identified. By repeating this mental exercise for projected future financial needs of an economy, both as a whole and by sector, the direction and content of financial reform can be conceived in a rational way and at any desired level of sophistication.

It is true that there has been no historical precedent in any modern state of across-the-board comprehensive financial reform, as if writing on a clean slate. Most major financial reforms in modern states (except possibly in socialist regimes) were made for exigencies such as financing wars or coping with financial crises. In other words, they were executed in emergency operation rooms, so to speak, in a hurried fashion; they were not conceived leisurely in a planner's clean room prior to actual implementation. Nevertheless, the case can still be made for the holistic approach and for being prepared for the future. It can be argued that a dreamer with a vision of topography covering the entire financial system (however rudimentary it may be) can be expected to design a better system than a tinkerer occupied solely with patchwork. A would-be reformer equating his job to that of a fire fighter or an emergency-room operator is the worst kind.

The case for gradualism is based on the existence of hurdles to a sweeping reform at one step and on the future's innate uncertainty.[11] Financial reform can be effected in the following three stages. The first stage, the preparatory consolidation period, is required to clear the way for full-fledged reform efforts via the reduction and rearrangement of policy-directed loans among other things prior to amendments of banking and other financial laws. The second stage, an active realignment and incipient development period, is intended to modify the existing system and relieve its inadequacies through active legislative amendment efforts. The central task of reform is the restructuring of the scope of business of financial institutions. The third and final stage, a period of maturity and competition promotion, is projected to stimulate competition among financial institutions and to open domestic and capital markets to a greater extent.

The idea of such a three-stage financial reform was conceived and developed in a research project commissioned by the Korean government (for the outcome of this research, see Park, Kim, and Park 1986). The original idea was to divide the 15-year period from 1986 to the year 2000 into three five-year subperiods or stages, allowing periodic review of the financial system. One might wonder about the advisability of the rather lengthy period of preparatory consolidation in the plan. The rationale was predicated on (1) the perennial shortage of national savings vis-à-vis gross investment, (2) the deficit in the current account balance of payments, (3) the backlog of nonperforming assets of commercial banks, and (4) the authoritarian tenor of the nation's political and social life at that time.

In view of what has actually evolved since, it appears that the nation's events overtook the just-mentioned rationale for a lengthy preparatory consolidation period except for the issue of banks' nonperforming assets. The beginning of the 1990s appears to be an opportune time to initiate the second stage of active realignment and development in the financial system.

Minefield Ahead Warning seems to be in order at this juncture. The financial world in the future is likely to be strewn with booby traps of high risk. To put it another way, money markets will be occasionally rocked by speculation, crises, and crashes. The direction in which the future society and financial reform is about to evolve leads to a minefield of high risk. Financial liberalization or deregulation will run into a beehive of risk, namely, interest risk, liquidity risk, credit risk, exchange rate risk, and stock price change risk. Internationalization or globalization will accentuate, among other things, interest risk, exchange rate risk or currency risk, and country risk, whereas securitization is likely to bring about liquidity risk, stock price change risk, and off-balance-sheet risk. In summary, financial reform may be undone by its own doing if not properly guarded against the future's high risks.

More significant, politics and money tend to attract each other (for the case of the United States, see Adams 1990). It is open to question whether an authoritarian or a democratic regime is more conducive to overt and covert interplays between power and money. It may be argued, however, that in a democratic society the chances and room for collusion between politics and business tend to be wide open and widespread, whereas such collusion is mainly concentrated at the center in an authoritarian regime. In the electronic mass communication age, electioneering is extremely expensive. In the recent and future Korean context, the democratization process, which requires frequent elections at both the national and local levels, will tend to hike electioneering bills and to be afflicted by alliances between power and money. Efforts to prevent democracy's degeneracy deserve top priority in Korea's future agenda. In the meantime, however, the synchronization of democratization and financial deregulation as well as internationalization in the first half of the 1990s could lead to financial turbulence. It follows that measures should be taken for the protection of the financial system from a political-business alliance, on the one hand, and from a host of risks in the wake of financial reform, on the other.

In this connection, the systems for financial regulation and supervision, deposit insurance, and disclosure by banks need to be carefully reexamined.

Agenda for Reform

The agenda for financial reform in Korea may be summarized in the following three broad categories: mobilization of private sector savings, removal of impediments to reform, and institutional realignments,

The fundamental function of financial institutions in any economy is the efficient mobilization, channeling, and allocation of funds. Sufficient savings mobilized through financial institutions go a long way to help alleviate deficiencies of the financial system. Financial institutions as such in Japan, Taiwan, and Germany have not reached the level of sophistication of those in the United States and Great Britain. Nonetheless, sufficient savings over fund demand in the aggregate terms have more than compensated for apparent shortcomings in the financial system of the former countries. Even in the overall surplus economy of recent years, the saving propensity of the household sector has been relatively low as compared with Japan in the past and Taiwan in the current years. In this connection, bear in mind the demographic shifts in the decades to come and their expected negative effects on private savings.

Two major stumbling blocks stand in the way of expediting comprehensive programs of financial reform. One is the magnitude of the nonperforming assets burdening banks, which is closely related to heavy intervention by the government in resource allocation. The other is the infeasibility of reducing policy-directed loans in a short span of time. As observed in Table 9.3, the ratio of nonperforming loans to total credit outstanding of commercial banks has been sharply chalked down in the late 1980s. As long as the backlog of nonperforming loans remains on the banks' books, however, the competitive edge of commercial banks cannot be expected to be effective enough to meet the challenge of foreign banks in the coming years of deepening internationalization. One much-talked-about idea is to consolidate all commercial banks' nonperforming loans into one specialized bank (the KDB, or a part of the KDB if it were subdivided) and subsequently to digest them gradually with the aid of government budget surplus earmarked for this specific purpose. Even more important than the backlog caused by the past mistakes, the government should restrain itself from the excessive use of policy-directed loans that could pile up another layer of nonperforming loans on top of the existing hill. In this respect, downright abolition of policy-directed loans would be most desirable. Realistically speaking, however, policy-directed loans are likely to remain in force for the foreseeable future as long as the government's intention appears to have some credit leverage in correcting market failures.

As for institutional realignments, the following considerations should be borne in mind: (1) the need to redefine the government's role in the economy and in the financial sector, and to realign financial institutions to conform to the fundamental shift in the process of democratization, internationalization, and liberalization; (2) the need to redress the mismatch of financial institutions and their instruments vis-à-vis the anticipated needs of future society; and (3) the urgent need to promote domestic financial institutions so that they can compete with foreign players in money and capital markets both at home and abroad.

NOTES

1. The terms "over-loan," "over-borrowing," and "window guidance" were endemic to the Japanese prewar and postwar financial experience until the period of balance-of-payment surpluses in the early 1970s (see, e.g., Wallich and Wallich 1976:284; Bank of Japan 1978:64; Goldsmith 1983:162; and Horiuchi 1984:28). I use this terminology deliberately to indicate a strong similarity between the two countries' experiences for much of the postwar period.

2. One form of specialization is based on the types of financial operations, particularly lending, underwriting and trading in securities, and trust administration. A second form of specialization defines finance on the basis of maturity terms, that is, short- and long-term credit. Other forms of specialization involve concentration on selected areas of the economy (such as agriculture, housing, and exports); on the size of client firms (such as small and medium-sized versus large firms); and on the region of business (such as nationwide versus local banks). Most of these forms of specialization are well represented in the financial system of Japan.

3. This episode of interest rate reform and its consequences was regarded as "financial reform without tears" and as a good example of "financial deepening" (McKinnon 1973:105–11; Shaw 1973:chap. 5).

4. The three constant credos of Korea's business organizations are that interest rates should be lowered, tax exemptions extended, and the money supply expanded.

5. The Korea Investment and Finance Company, an offspring of the International Finance Corporation's joint venture, was actually chartered before the promulgation of the act.

6. In regular-way transactions, the settlement or delivery of stock is to be made on the second business day following the contract date, as against within two months in the case of forward transactions.

7. This practice in banking institutions reflects the growth-oriented, sales-maximizing behavior of private enterprises as previously described.

8. Since this period, the question of reopening this issue has been politically tense. Finally, a real-name financial transactions system came to light on 12 August 1993, in the form of a presidential emergency decree. A two-month period was provided for converting false and borrowed names into real names and for confirming real names for all accounts at every financial institution. As a final stage of enforcing the real-name system, a comprehensive income tax is scheduled to be levied sometime in 1996 on total earnings including various financial incomes except for capital gains on securities.

9. In fact, the establishment of these two nationwide commercial banks had been authorized before the Lee-Chang incident.

10. In this exercise, the yield on corporate bonds is taken as a proxy for market interest rate out of other candidates.

11. For the unsuccessful experience of South American countries, see Corbo (1985), Corbo, Melo, and Tybout (1986), Dornbusch (1983), and Edwards (1985).

REFERENCES

Adams, James Ring. 1990. *The Big Fix: Inside the S&L Scandal.* New York: Wiley.

Bank of Japan, Research Institute. 1978. *The Financial System in Japan* (in Japanese). Tokyo.

Bank of Korea. 1985. *The Financial System in Korea* (in Korean). Seoul.

Bloomfield, Arthur I., and John P. Jensen. 1963. *Banking Reform in South Korea.* Seoul: Bank of Korea.

Bloomfield, Arthur I., and John P. Jensen. 1965. *Reports and Recommendations on Monetary Policy and Banking in Korea.* Seoul: Bank of Korea.

Broaddus, J. Alfred, Jr. 1985. "Financial Innovations in the United States: Background, Current Status and Prospects." In *Korea Federation of Banks, Financial Innovation and Financial Reform.* Seoul.

Corbo, Vittorio. 1985. "Reform and Macroeconomic Adjustment in Chile during 1974–84." *World Development* 13(8).

Corbo, Vittorio, Jaime de Melo, and James Tybout. 1986. "What Went Wrong in the Southern Cone?" *Economic Development and Cultural Change* 34(3).

Dornbusch, Rudiger. 1983. "Remarks on the Southern Cone." IMF Staff Paper, March.

Economic Planning Board. 1988. *Recent Population Status and New Population Estimates.* Seoul: Statistics Bureau, Economic Planning Board.

Edwards, Sebastian. 1985. "Stabilization and Liberalization: An Evaluation of Ten Years of Chile's Experiment with Free Market Policies." *Economic Development and Cultural Change* 33(2).

Furstenberg, George M. von. 1985. "Financial Innovations in Developed Economies and Financial Reforms in the Process of Economic Development." In *Korea Federation of Banks, Financial Innovation and Financial Reform.* Seoul.

Gerschenkron, Alexander. 1962. *Economic Backwardness in Historical Perspective.* Cambridge: Harvard University Press.

Goldsmith, Raymond W. 1983. *The Financial Development of Japan, 1868–1977.* New Haven, Conn.: Yale University Press.

Gurley, John G., Hugh T. Patrick, and E. S. Shaw. 1965. *The Financial Structure of Korea.* Seoul: Bank of Korea.

Harberger, Arnold. 1985. "Reflections on the Chilean Economy." *Economic Development and Cultural Change* 33(2).

Horiuchi, Akiyoshi. 1984. "Economic Growth and Financial Allocation in Postwar Japan." Discussion paper. Tokyo: University of Tokyo.

Kim, Byong Kuk. 1965. *Central Banking Experience in a Developing Economy: Case Study of Korea.* Seoul: Korean Research Center.

Kim, Pyung Joo. 1976. "Does Monetary Policy Work and How: Toward a Model of Monetary Management in Korea." Ph.D. diss., Princeton University.

McKinnon, Ronald I. 1973. *Money and Capital in Economic Development.* Washington, D.C.: Brookings Institution.

Mason, Edward S., et al. 1980. *The Economic and Social Modernization of the Republic of Korea.* Cambridge: Council on East Asian Studies, Harvard University.

Park, Yung Chul, Pyung Joo Kim, and Jae Yoon Park. 1986. *Gum-yung San-op Bal-jon-e Gwan-han Yon-gu: 1985–2000* (Research report on financial development: 1985–2000). Seoul: Korea Development Institute.

Ranis, Gustav. 1977. "Economic Development and Financial Institutions." In Bela Balassa and Richard Nelson (eds.), *Economic Progress, Private Values and Public Policy: Essays in Honor of William Fellnor.* Amsterdam: North Holland.

Schiffer, Hubert F. 1962. *The Modern Japanese Banking System.* New York: University Publishers.

Shaw, Edward S. 1973. *Financial Deepening in Economic Development.* New York: Oxford University Press.

Suzuki, Yoshio. 1985. "Financial Innovations in Japan: Background, Current State and Prospects." In *Korea Federation of Banks, Financial Innovation and Financial Reform.* Seoul.

Teranishi, Juro. 1989. "Financial System and the Industrialization of Japan: 1900–1970." Mimeo. Tokyo: International Development Center of Japan.

Wallich, H. C., and Mable I. Wallich. 1976. "Banking and Finance." In Hugh Patrick and Henry Rosovsky (eds.), *Asia's New Giant.* Washington, D.C.: Brookings Institution.

CHAPTER 10

Institutional Reform of the Korean Financial System

Sang-Woo Nam
Korea Development Institute

Introduction

Korea has a specialized banking system in which restrictions are placed on the types of financial services offered by different financial institutions. The establishment of a specialized as opposed to a universal banking system in Korea was largely an outgrowth of the government's policy of using commercial banks as conduits for the direct allocation of credit to targeted sectors and industries.

Since the early 1980s, however, the specialized banking system has undergone some modifications, and the business boundaries of some intermediaries have been expanded in such a way that they now overlap. In connection with government efforts to develop the money market, bank and nonbank institutions are allowed to participate in wider areas of the money market business, including repurchase agreements, commercial papers, certificates of deposit, cash management accounts, and bond management funds. Banks in particular also added many peripheral services such as credit cards, factoring, and trust.

In the absence of an overall blueprint for a desired financial market structure, the broadening of business boundaries has mainly been motivated by a need for financial deepening and the desire for fair treatment of the different intermediaries; that is, the government has sought to prevent the growth of banks from falling too far behind that of nonbank intermediaries in the presence of government-imposed interest rate controls that have been more restrictive for banks. But long-term efficiency requires a fundamental reassessment of the structure of the financial system rather than an arbitrary and piecemeal approach. To that end, I address three principal questions involved in the sector's restructuring in the Korean context: Can commercial banks enter into investment banking? How should investment banking institutions be restructured? May business groups own financial intermediaries? In addition, I discuss complementary institutional safeguards which should be strengthened in tandem with the reform of the financial system to minimize financial instability during the transition.

Rationale for Reform of the Financial System

Restructuring the Korean financial market now seems timely for two reasons. First, past government policy has created both uncertainty and problems for some categories of intermediaries. Second, the Korean financial sector is facing significant changes in its environment, including interest rate deregulation and the external liberalization of the domestic financial market.

Uncertainty The opening up of new businesses to different categories of financial institutions has mainly been guided by the need to correct emerging imbalances in the competitiveness and relative growth among financial intermediaries. The changing imbalances themselves have resulted mostly from government regulations on the interest rate structure and from the government's policy of allowing particular categories of intermediaries to enter new areas of business. The absence of a blueprint for the future financial market, while every aspect of the market is still regulated by the government, has encouraged financial intermediaries to undertake unproductive rent-seeking activities rather than concentrating on financial innovation and other badly needed efforts to enhance the efficiency of intermediation. This is undesirable and calls for rather comprehensive reform.

Emerging Problems The evolving financial structure and business boundaries have brought about some obvious problems and concerns. For instance, some financial institutions designed to meet specific needs of the economy, such as specialized banks, have gradually been changed in ways that have obscured the rationale for their existence. Other intermediaries like investment and finance companies (IFCs) have found their business base eroded substantially, as much of their basic money market business has been opened up to banks as well as securities companies (SCs). The same is true of investment trust companies (ITCs), which must now compete with several services provided by banks and SCs.

Other less obvious problems may also become critical in due course. These include the banks' ownership of SCs and IFCs as subsidiaries and bank involvement in money market and other securities businesses. Both phenomena raise questions of the extent to which commercial and investment banking should be mixed, and of how restrictive the formation and activities of bank subsidiaries should be. In view of these and other questions, prudent guidelines should be established before the current situation is too deeply entrenched to be easily corrected.

Interest Rate Deregulation With a wider range of interest rates being deregulated, there will remain only one major policy tool, adjustment of business boundaries, to ensure balanced financial growth (although there is no convincing reason why balanced financial growth should remain as a major policy objective). Thus, the impact of adjusting business areas is now likely to be larger than before. However, just as an arbitrary change in the interest rate structure should not dictate the relative growth of financial intermediaries, neither should an ill-grounded regulation of business areas. Thus, it is advisable to review the current demarcation between financial market lines along with interest rate deregulation.

External Financial Liberalization Growing pressure from abroad, often on the basis of reciprocity, together with Korea's liberalization policy will work to increase the openness of the Korean market to foreign investors and financial intermediaries. At the same time, Korean financial institutions will also increasingly be engaged in overseas financial services and find their way to international financial markets to meet the needs of their customers.

Recent Trends in the Overseas Financial Markets

Concern over International Competitiveness With the trend toward internationalization and increasing interpenetration of national financial institutions, many countries are now more concerned about the global competitiveness of their financial sector. Major policy efforts aimed at improving the competitiveness of the financial system have been directed to increasing its efficiency through deregulation and external liberalization and developing a modern technological infrastructure which helps strengthen its linkages with other international financial centers. Ensuring safety of the financial market through adequate prudential regulation is also an important complementary element.

A good example is the comprehensive stock exchange reforms (Big Bang) of the United Kingdom in 1986, which included adopting negotiable commissions, abolishing the system of separate brokers and jobbers, opening the stock exchange membership, and introducing a more efficient trading system. These reforms were followed by the establishment of a new regulatory authority and new rules for investor protection.

Concern over international competitiveness in the financial services markets in the presence of substantial country differences in financial regulations often leads to bilateral negotiations for market access, or "leveling the playing field." For instance, countries with universal banking systems would like to apply the reciprocity principle, which means "better than national treatment" in the host country.

In this connection, the European Community financial market integration is certainly a big challenge and is having a grave impact on the shaping of financial markets worldwide. The single banking license enables EC financial institutions to expand their activities throughout the EC, either via branches or by offering cross-border services. Although banks are supervised by the authorities of the member country first granted the licenses, uniform standards have been set up for bank licensing and supervision. Financial services permitted under the single banking license include all forms of securities business but not insurance business.

Concerning the entry of non-EC banks, the EC may withhold issuing licenses to applicants from a country that does not provide effective market access and genuine competitive opportunities to EC banks. Although "effective market access" is somewhat vague, it appears to require reciprocity that involves more than host-country national treatment. Though the reciprocity principle may be a powerful tool for encouraging countries to decompartmentalize their financial markets, some tension may be unavoidable between countries with different regulatory framework.

Prudential regulation and investor protection are other areas where national financial systems feel need and pressure for convergence, as they have stronger linkages and more compatibility with the international markets. For any markets aspiring to be growing financial centers, they have to be well regulated and supervised as well as functionally efficient. The Basel agreement on minimum capital standards of banks is a result of such a need.

Trend toward Decompartmentalization of Financial Services Markets Since the beginning of the 1980s, there has been an obvious trend toward blurring the demarcation lines between different types of financial institutions. While financial institutions have attempted to diversify their services to cope with rapid changes in the financial environment, the authorities have tended to accommodate this trend with a view to strengthening the competitiveness of their financial systems through more vigorous competition.

Canada may have taken the boldest approach. The Canadian financial system, which had been divided into four territories—banking, trust and mortgage, securities, and insurance—was largely decompartmentalized under the New Directions for the Financial Sector of December 1986. Depending on the riskiness of particular types of financial services as determined by prudential considerations, financial institutions have been allowed to enter into new financial services areas either directly or via separately capitalized subsidiaries.

This trend has been evident even in countries such as the United States and Japan where commercial banking and securities-related activities are still legally separated. In the United States, commercial banks have been allowed to provide securities brokerage and investment advisory services through subsidiaries, engage in the placement of commercial paper, and underwrite (deal in) corporate bonds (private placements), mortgage bonds, and securities outside the United States under some restrictions. The U.S. securities firms have also expanded into real estate, insurance, "nonbank" banking, money market funds, cash management accounts, as well as commercial banking (subsidiaries) abroad.

In Japan, securities-related new banking services include selling newly issued government bonds "over the counter" and trading them in the secondary market, participating in bond futures markets, offering integrated bond-deposit accounts, and dealing in public sector foreign currency bonds. Securities firms have also been allowed to undertake such banking activities as offering medium-term government bond funds and loans against collateral of government bonds and trading CDs and yen-denominated BAs in the secondary market.

The majority of advisory bodies and expert studies in both the United States and Japan are clearly in favor of decompartmentalizing financial markets further. With an important competitive challenge posed by the EC single market for financial services, the United States and Japan may have more comprehensive reform in store, which will no doubt accelerate their financial restructuring.

Progress in external financial liberalization has implications for the restructuring of the Korean financial system. Domestic financial institutions are in a disadvantageous position in international (as well as domestic) financial markets since they compete with foreign intermediaries whose business dealings in their domestic markets have been more comprehensive. Reciprocity requirements by countries with universal banking systems will have a direct bearing on the shaping of the Korean financial system. Furthermore, for the Korean market to achieve respectable growth, its rules for prudential regulation and supervision need to be compatible with those of the major international markets. Given these considerations of competitiveness, the redemarcation of business areas should precede any major moves toward opening domestic financial markets.

Major Issues and Suggestions for Reform

The broadening of business areas for an intermediary must be evaluated on the basis of the trade-off between the potential gain in efficiency of financial intermediation and the associated risk of financial instability and conflict-of-interest abuses. Broader business boundaries are generally expected to reduce the cost of intermediation due to economies of scale or scope, make information more readily available, improve the resource allocation of the economy, and stimulate economic growth. These benefits, however, are normally difficult to measure and less visible, while financial instability is typically very visible, particularly in the case of bank runs and failures, and is likely to result in a tendency toward overregulation.

When restrictions on business areas are lifted, each financial institution is expected to choose a combination of services it can provide most efficiently. However, institutions may misjudge and overestimate the potential gains of economies of scope or scale, with the resulting failures imposing a heavy cost on the economy. This is why financial intermediaries are not allowed to provide some services whose mode of business and information requirements are dissimilar to others. On this basis, few seem to disagree on the separation of banking and insurance, for instance. Views on the desirability of separating investment banking from commercial banking are, however, sharply divided.

It is clear that institutional reform of the Korean financial system should be based on the realities of the Korean markets. More specifically, the following three questions should provide the central focus of the pursuit of a desirable financial system.

1. Are the current business areas broad enough to allow adequate portfolio diversification and to ensure stability under the anticipated new financial environment characterized by increasing competition?
2. What are the major constraints in the pursuit of a universal banking system? Are the market structure and other conditions as well as supervisory and regulatory institutions in Korea comparable to those of advanced countries where the mix of commercial and investment banking allegedly poses few problems?
3. To what extent can the existing institutional safeguards be relied on to protect the safety and soundness of the financial system, and what improvements are most needed?

The issue of readjusting business boundaries for financial intermediaries is further complicated in Korea by the extensive ownership of the intermediaries by large business groups possessing market-dominating positions in many areas. Thus, in connection with the restructuring of investment banking institutions, where concerns arise over conflicts of interest and economic concentration, the ownership of these intermediaries by large business groups must be reevaluated.

Can Commercial Banks Enter into Investment Banking?

The major arguments against allowing commercial banks to enter into investment banking in Korea include these: (1) some investment banking activities such as underwriting corporate securities are too risky for commercial banks to undertake; (2) financial difficulties of securities affiliates will undermine consumer confidence in the commercial banks; (3) commercial bank entry into investment banking gives banks unfair competitive advantage over nonbank competitors; and (4) conflicts of interest associated with combining commercial and investment banking businesses by affiliated firms can easily lead to abuse.

Underwriting Risks It has been argued that many of the risks involved in underwriting corporate securities can be hedged or diversified away. Underwriters' risk associated with changes in bond prices resulting from changes in the general level of interest rates can be diversified away by hedging in the futures market or reducing other bond holdings in their portfolios. Of course, losses can still be incurred as prices of underwritten corporate securities change during the holding period due to firm-specific changes in default risk or earnings prospects. In the current Korean market, however, the possibility of hedging is limited because various options and financial futures markets are not available. Shortening the holding period is also difficult for corporate bonds due to substantial interest rate disparities between the primary and secondary markets. The secondary market and other sales networks for corporate bonds are not sufficiently developed in Korea to allow quick sale of bonds without a capital loss. Corporate bond underwriters, facing a large capital loss due to interest rate control in the primary market, have limited capacity to dispose of the bonds in the secondary market and therefore let the issuing firms share the sales responsibility. The shallowness of institutional investor groups is also responsible for the unreliable and risky bond market. Furthermore, the lack of underwriter financing makes the risk of capital loss and the unintended lengthening of the holding period all the more damaging to underwriters. These factors indicate that the underwriting activity itself in the current Korean market could be rather risky for commercial banks to undertake.

Nevertheless, any loss in corporate bond underwriting tends to be compensated for by other profitable business given to the issuing firms in return for the underwriting. Furthermore, however risky the underwriting service may be, it is a far less important source of revenue than other securities businesses such as trading (own investment activity) and brokerage.

Question of Confidence Financial difficulties of a securities affiliate can damage the reputation of a bank and lead to a loss of confidence in the bank's safety and soundness. Korean banks have not yet suffered a serious lack of public confidence, despite their accumulation of huge nonperforming loans. This follows from the public's understanding that the government is responsible for the situation by mandating loans to support its development objectives and would not allow banks to fail, making their deposits de facto fully protected. With the privatization of commercial banks, commercial bank entry into the corporate securities business through a subsidiary of an affiliated firm may lead to declining confidence in bank stability and a need to establish some type of deposit insurance. Notwithstanding this possibility, experience in West Germany and the United States (before the Glass-Steagall Act) indicates that it is unlikely to threaten the safety and soundness of the whole banking system.

The shareholders of a holding company can maximize their interest by transferring risk to an affiliate where their relative capital investment is the smallest. In the Korean context, many business groups have predominant equity shares in their securities affiliates (SCs and IFCs), while their equity shares in commercial banks are typically much smaller. By transferring, wherever possible, questionable assets from a securities affiliate to a bank, they shift part of their portfolio risk onto other shareholders of the bank. The current predicament of Korea banks might be somewhat attributable to risk transfer from other financial institutions controlled by large business groups.

Fairness in Competition It has frequently been argued that commercial banks should not be allowed to enter into the securities business because this represents unfair competition in favor of the banks. This argument is based on the belief that commercial banks enjoy captive markets or can tie their services for their own interest, mobilize capital at lower cost, and have cost advantages in providing financial services.

According to the captive market argument, a commercial bank underwriter, as an investor and a trustee with many correspondent banks, has unfair advantage in being able to sell underwritten securities to these captive markets. Commercial banks are also said to be in a position to provide commercial loans on the explicit or implicit condition that the borrowing firms give their underwriting business to the banks' securities affiliates.

However, tying bank services is possible only when the bank has market power in the business in question. Even if a bank has market power in commercial loans, it can charge a higher loan rate rather than opting to tie other services, and even with regulations on lending rates the banks still have ways to exploit their market power, such as requiring borrowers to maintain compensating balances. If the Korean commercial loan market continues to be characterized by chronic excess demand, some banks may be in a position to tie their loans to other services, to the disadvantage of nonbank competitors. With deregulation of interest rates, however, such tying of services would be difficult to impose.

It is also argued that the deposit-taking function of commercial banks allows them easy access to low-cost funds, giving them unfair competitive advantage over other financial intermediaries. But as long as the financial market is reasonably efficient, marginal and opportunity costs of mobilizing funds for different financial institutions are expected to be roughly comparable. Commercial bank access to central bank rediscounting is also said to give a cost advantage to banks. In Korea, however, general-purpose borrowing from the central banks is often available only at high penalty rates. On the other hand, Korean securities companies pay very little interest on customers' deposits held for securities investment. If anything, the cost of these deposits seems to be lower than that of bank deposits.

The large size, diverse services, and extensive branch networks of commercial banks are often suggested as factors giving banks unfair competitive advantage over nonbanks. In dealing with customers, commercial banks obtain various information about creditworthiness as well as the diverse financial needs of the customers. The same information obtained in connection with one banking service can obviously be used in the bank's other services. Thus, banks (or any financial intermediaries) are in a better position to provide services at lower cost when they expand the scope of their business.

Should Korean commercial banks succeed in solving their current difficulties associated with nonperforming loans (many of which have accumulated while banks followed government credit allocation regulations), their entry into all aspects of the securities business, through a subsidiary or a securities affiliate, will pose a potential threat to nonbank competitors. To be fair, either commercial banks should not be allowed to enter into investment banking or investment banking institutions should also be permitted to undertake commercial banking.

The first option, however, would be grossly "unfair" to customers, since it limits the efficiency of financial intermediation. Thus, the desirable long-run solution would be a blurring of the demarcation between commercial and investment banking institutions.

Conflicts of Interest Making accurate corporate information readily available to all potential investors and allowing that information to be immediately reflected in securities prices, free of unfair practices or distortive institutional factors, are essential for the efficiency of the market and the protection of investors. Incentives for abuse tend to be stronger when information asymmetry is large and the search for accurate information costly.

A good corporate disclosure system that fully and accurately informs investors of the business and financial situation and management performance of firms is vital for the efficiency of the securities market. The Korean corporate disclosure system is not well established. Disclosed information is not sufficient, and information on future prospects is particularly lacking. Corporations tend to be reluctant to disclose corporate management directions and strategies, and they avoid or delay disclosing unfavorable information. Furthermore, the nationwide information delivery system is inadequate, and coordination and cooperation are poor among information-generating and -handling institutions such as the Securities Supervisory Board, the Korea Securities Dealers' Association, and the Korea Stock Exchange.

Auditing by independent and qualified outsiders, enhancing public confidence in regularly published financial statements of corporations, is essential for the protection of investors and other interest groups. Currently, all stockholding companies in Korea with equity capital or total assets over specified amounts are required to undergo external auditing. The competitive bidding system for audit contracts, however, tends to strengthen the position of the firms to be audited, calling into question the independence of the outside auditors and the quality of the audit.

Reliable credit rating by an independent institution would compensate for the limitations in the corporate disclosure system by reducing information asymmetry between corporate insiders and investors through the analysis of both undisclosed and disclosed information and industry prospects. In Korea, corporate credit rating institutions have been operating only since 1985 and have yet to play their full expected role, mainly because of government control of interest rates and repayment guarantees of financial institutions for corporate bonds, which largely obviate the need for credit ratings.

Regulation of insider trading is grossly inadequate in Korea. The fact that just a few cases of insider trading have ever been disclosed in Korea indicates the difficulty of proving the use of inside information. Relying entirely on the reports of insiders for the identification of their changing equity ownership is a critical limitation. The Korean stock market has also suffered from frequent price manipulation through self-dealing, bull cornering, and dumping. Due to the poor stock price monitoring system, most of these transactions have not been exposed. An amendment of rules shifting the burden of proof from plaintiffs to the suspects of insider trading will help enforce the law more effectively. The scope of insiders should also be extended to include not only those who obtain confidential information while fulfilling their duties or by their positions but also those who inform them.

Various other institutional factors have also resulted in inefficiencies in the Korean securities market. Restrictions on maximum daily price changes for equity stocks prevent the prompt reflection of all available information in stock prices. This pricing rule is intended to protect investors but tends to reduce incentives for information gathering. The absence of an efficient over-the-counter market for unlisted securities, which can serve as an experimental market for firms planning to go public, makes useful information on stock pricing unavailable.

Institutional investors in advanced countries play an important guiding role in the capital market as they invest huge amounts of capital on the basis of thorough market analyses. In Korea, even though the scope of institutional investors was broadened recently to include various funds, their participation in the stock market has not been active. As for investment consulting firms, these began operations only in early 1988 and still lack sufficient know-how in investment analysis to contribute significantly to enhancing the quality and availability of investment information in the market.

Conclusion on Commercial Bank Entry into Investment Banking Commercial banks' entry into securities business will certainly contribute to their efficiency in the long run by allowing them to benefit from economics of scope. Priority should, however, probably be given to restructuring investment banking to allow the intermediaries to provide various services of a broader scope, inducing them to realize economies of scope in a more fair and competitive environment. They are generally overly specialized, and the broadening of business boundaries in recent years for some intermediaries has left others relatively squeezed in their business scope. There are other reasons as well why commercial bank entry into investment banking might be premature in the short run, as explained below.

Given interest rate controls in the primary securities market and the lack of various hedging instruments, underwriting corporate securities is a risky business in Korea. Commercial bank asset portfolios may be exposed to serious risk if the banks engage in distress financing for their securities affiliates, or if business groups attempt risk shifting among their financial subsidiaries or affiliates. Furthermore, as long as bank loan rates remain controlled, banks may be able to tie loans to securities business, thus unduly undermining the business bases of nonbank competitors. Moreover, without solutions to the nonperforming loans resulting from the government's past abuse of banks, allowing investment banking institutions to enter into commercial banking would be unfair to the existing banks.

Finally, combining commercial and investment banking leaves open the possibility of conflicts of interest. While such conflicts are difficult to exploit profitably in a competitive market, in the Korean market institutions that encourage generation of complete and reliable information and prevent unfair transactions are yet to be firmly established. These constraints should not, however, be interpreted as implying that a transition to universal banking is a remote possibility within a decade or so. As a matter of fact, such a transition would help ease the constraints considerably.

How Should Investment Banking Institutions Be Restructured?

Investment banking institutions in Korea include securities companies (SCs), investment and finance companies (IFCs), merchant banking corporations (MBCs), and investment trust companies (ITCs). Among these four categories of intermediaries, IFCs and ITCs are most in need of adjustment, since their unique services or similar ones are now fairly open to both securities companies and commercial banks.

Investment and Finance Companies With the short-term securities business opening to other intermediaries, it is unfair to limit IFCs to their narrow business boundaries. It is also economically inefficient. A logical solution would be to allow IFCs to convert to, or merge with, other investment banking institutions. It would be preferable to limit IFC mergers or conversions to investment banking institutions, because entry into commercial banking would be unfair to the existing commercial banks, which have been burdened with carrying out the government's industrial policies. As discussed below, some IFCs may specialize as dealers or brokers in the money market.

The restructuring alternatives among investment banking activities should be as wide as possible, with minimum government discretion in determining the future of these institutions. IFCs should choose their future disposition in light of current and expected future business opportunities as well as their own comparative advantage. This will tend to equalize economic rents throughout investment banking and will maximize customer welfare. By holding the companies responsible for their decisions, the government will also be relieved from any pressure for another round of adjustments.

The restructuring of IFCs began in 1990 with the enactment of the Law on Mergers and Conversion of Financial Institutions, which allowed IFCs in Seoul to merge and convert to banks or securities companies. Of the sixteen IFCs located in Seoul, five converted to securities companies, one to a bank, and two others merged to become another bank. In addition, the government allowed provincial IFCs that satisfied its requirements to convert to merchant banking corporations. Most provincial IFCs that meet the requirements are planning to convert to MBCs in 1994. Some others in Seoul will also convert to MBCs eventually, and a few will remain specialized money market dealers or brokerage firms.

Investment Trust Companies ITCs specialize in securities investment trust, with portfolios in public and private bonds and equity stocks. Investment trust in bonds is also allowed to MBCs. In recent years, several financial services similar to the investment trust of ITCs were also introduced by other intermediaries. They include money in trust for households and corporate trust accounts offered by banks, cash management accounts of IFCs and MBCs, and the bond management funds of securities companies. Securities companies have also been seeking more general investment trust in bonds.

It is well known that conflicts of interest arise between investment trust and underwriting or trading (dealing). Currently, bond issues in Korea are mostly of standard types, and most corporate bonds are repayment-guaranteed by financial intermediaries to limit the possibility of conflict-of-interest abuses. With the issuing of more diverse and unguaranteed corporate bonds, incentives for abuses involving conflicts of interest are expected to increase. However, the market environment is likely to improve at the same time, making profitable abuses more difficult. Any remaining risk may also be controlled by rules concerning disclosure, bond rating, and other regulations. In sum, the potential conflicts of interest associated with permitting investment trust, specializing mainly in bonds, to merchant banks and securities companies do not seem to be serious enough to justify its prohibition.

Reorganization of the three existing nationwide ITCs should focus on the utilization of their accumulated expertise and manpower. Given their experience in long-term securities business, ITCs may be encouraged to establish SCs and investment consulting firms as their subsidiaries. Branch offices of an ITC can be converted to branches of its SC, also serving as sales windows for the certificates of the ITCs' trust beneficiaries. Since ITCs are owned mainly by financial institutions, the probability of conflict-of-interest abuses arising from ITC ownership of an SC does not seem high.

Money Market Dealers and Brokers The money market in Korea is not well developed, and corporate bills and liquidity control bonds account for most of the market. Despite the market's fairly rapid growth in size, such money market functions as integrating various financial markets and serving as a resilient market for monetary control do not operate adequately. In spite of the recent integration of the call market, it is still divided in its operation, with implicit collusion on interest rates among banks and often directly negotiated transactions between borrowers and lenders. With large gaps between regulated primary market interest rates and free secondary market yields, development of the secondary market is also restricted.

Several IFCs are serving as brokers for the call market. Specializing as money market dealers and brokers, IFCs may play a key role in promoting a repurchase agreement market for financial intermediaries. Central bank open-market operations would be directed to this market, with the money market dealers as counterparts. The current system of "allocating" issues of liquidity control bonds to financial institutions should be replaced by a system in which money market dealers function as a buffer and the impact of open-market operations, reflected in short-term market interest rates, is more smoothly transmitted to all financial markets.

Integration of Short- and Long-Term Securities Businesses The separation of short- and long-term securities businesses in Korea can be traced to the establishment of IFCs in 1972 for the purpose of absorbing curb market funds by the formal market. These two services, however, are complementary for investors and offer a means of achieving economies of scope when supplied together, with benefits such as greater convenience, lower transaction costs, higher investment yields, and reduced financing costs. Thus, the case for blurring the business boundaries between MBCs (IFCs) and SCs by permitting them to undertake both short- and long-term securities businesses seems to be very strong. This may may not be a threat to MBCs (IFCs) given that SCs are already in the commercial paper business and operate the bond management funds. On the other hand, as long as MBCs (IFCs) are prohibited from having branch networks, they are at a disadvantage in providing securities brokerage services and may have to concentrate on primary market businesses.

In view of the market instability that might result from keener competition or high short-run costs, it may be argued that the integration of these services should be postponed until the medium term. Since the short-term securities business is the major service of IFCs and entering into new businesses requires costly preparations, opening the business to SCs during the transition may indeed impose a serious financial strain on MBCs (IFCs). An abrupt change in regulatory environment and enhanced competition may at the same time encourage the affected institutions to restructure (e.g., merge among themselves) and improve efficiency as quickly as possible.

May Business Groups Own Financial Intermediaries?

Risks of Mixing Financial Services and Commerce It is widely agreed that the potential for economies of scope is typically very high for financial services. However, opponents of allowing the mix of financial and nonfinancial products within a firm or a business group argue that the mix would (1) lead to concentration of economic power and undue influence over the political process, (2) increase the probability of conflict-of-interest abuses, and (3) endanger the stability of financial intermediaries because nonfinancial businesses are likely to be riskier.

The first two assertions are valid only when entry into financial services is restricted. Even though free entry may produce financial supermarkets, some of which include nonfinancial products, they are not likely to have stronger political power. Rather, regulations restricting entry result in excess profits, part of which tend to be used for lobbying for the continued restriction of entry. Likewise, conflict-of-interest abuses are best prevented by free entry and more competition. A firm or business group providing many products including financial services may be more careful about, and refrain from, abusing interests because such action, by damaging its reputation, is likely to turn its customers to competitors in all its service areas.

Even when financial markets are competitive with free entry, the mix of financial and nonfinancial products increases the probability of abuses involving conflicts of interest as long as the firm has market power in the nonfinancial product. Tie-ins of two or more services and interlocking directorships among member firms of business groups are common means of exploiting interests. In an imperfect financial market, a firm providing both financial and nonfinancial products may try to discriminate against competing nonfinancial firms or their customers by limiting, or charging higher prices for, credit and other financial services.

Finally, the effect of mixing financial and nonfinancial products on the stability of financial intermediaries (including commercial banks) and the financial system will depend on many factors. These include (1) the riskiness of the nonfinancial business compared with the financial business; (2) the likelihood of exploiting conflicts of interest arising from the product mix, which in turn depends on the perfectness of markets for both financial and nonfinancial products; (3) the correlation of profits from financial and nonfinancial businesses; and (4) the existence (or nonexistence) of deposit insurance.

The Korean Situation and Policy Suggestions The ownership of commercial banks by large business groups in Korea has given rise to much concern. The largest five business groups, owning 97 manufacturing firms, accounted for 22 percent of total manufacturing shipments in 1987. The largest thirty business groups had a market share of over 40 percent in 335 of a gross total of 1,499 (873 excluding double counts) commodity markets in which they operated in 1987. The maximum equity share of a nationwide commercial bank that can be held by a shareholder is now limited to 8 percent of the total. At present, however, there are no ownership restrictions for nonbank financial institutions.

With constantly changing financial environments, the following observations should be considered regarding ownership control for financial intermediaries.

1. Banks no longer dominate the Korean financial market. To the extent that bank ownership restriction was due to concern about concentration of economic power, similar restriction may also be extended to their intermediaries like securities companies.

2. The uniqueness of commercial banks will be weakened in the future. Nonbank deposit-taking institutions may offer saving accounts on which checks

can be drawn. Investment banks may, in connection with their involvement in asset management accounts, be allowed to provide fund transfers, automatic bill paying, and loans to depositors. These developments will bring nonbank institutions under money and credit policies on more equal terms with banks. In that case, ownership restrictions on commercial banks based only on their uniqueness among financial intermediaries may not be justified.

3. With the deregulation of interest rates (elimination of the subsidy element in bank loans) expected in the future, banks will no longer be particularly susceptible to temptation to abuse interests. On the other hand, with heavier reliance of corporate financing on the securities markets, abuses involving conflicts of interest by investment banking affiliates of business groups will have relatively greater consequences. Conflicts of interest arise from all areas of their major activities of underwriting, dealing, and brokerage.

4. If concerns about the concentration of economic power and abuses involving conflicts of interest are the major reasons for bank ownership restrictions, there may be no strong rationale for applying the restriction in an indiscriminate way to those without interest in nonfinancial firms. Limiting the ownership restriction only to large business groups could be an alternative. It may be much easier to monitor and regulate any abuses where few firms are involved in a business group.

5. Most of the problems to which bank ownership restriction is directed result from entry barriers. Of course, even with free entry into financial markets, conflicts of interest would still be a problem as long as the firm or business group had market power in the nonfinancial product. Nevertheless, substantial reduction of entry barriers to financial markets will go a long way toward controlling conflicts of interest as well as enhancing efficiency in financial services.

The following broad suggestions may be made to improve policies on the ownership restrictions of financial intermediaries. First, restrictions on bank ownership may be eased for stockholders without affiliations with, or controlling shares in, large business groups. In such cases there is little concern about the concentration of economic power. To rule out the possibility of collusion that may result in control of banks by business groups, any controlling shareholders of business groups and those with special relations to them may be disqualified from top bank management. Second, a maximum permissible ownership share might be introduced for (controlling shareholders of) large business groups owning investment banking institutions such as SCs and MBCs. The maximum share may be high enough to allow them to keep management control but low enough to make it difficult for them to abuse interests because of the participation of other major shareholders in the management and board of directors. Third, ownership restrictions for large business groups owning investment banking institutions may be designed to be more selective, directed toward cases involving a high risk of abuse. For instance, restrictions can be made contingent on an intermediary's engaging in certain financial businesses like securities investment trust, or made variable depending on the degree of a group's presence in financial businesses. The risk of abusing conflicts of interest is supposed to be high when nonfinancial businesses are combined with both underwriting corporate securities and investment trust in equity stocks.

Complementary Institutional Safeguards

With financial intermediaries expanding their services and operating in an environment of more competition and less government protection, the financial market is likely to experience instability at least during the adjustment period. Institutional safeguards should therefore be introduced to reduce this instability and maintain an efficient financial system. De facto government protection of deposits will have to be replaced by a more rational deposit insurance scheme, prudential regulation should be strengthened, and an institutional framework for efficient restructuring of troubled financial intermediaries should be developed.

Deposit Insurance Deposit insurance is supposed to be essential to avoid bank runs and demonetization of the economy and, thereby, to protect the payment system. Bank runs or bank failures have not occurred in Korea thus far because depositors know that the government would not let banks fail. This practice of de facto deposit protection is undesirable for at least two reasons. First, it encourages banks to take risks by effectively providing a subsidy to risk taking, and as risky banks attract deposits by offering high interest rates resource allocations are distorted. Second, the implicit deposit guarantee is also inequitable because the cost is borne by taxpayers who do not benefit from the scheme. The de facto protection should therefore be replaced by another system in step with the growth of banks as healthy and truly commercially based intermediaries.

A flat rate premium for deposit insurance will not discourage risk taking and the distortion of resource allocation. However, a variable rate premium scaled to bank riskiness is not operationally very feasible. On the other hand, bank capital serves as a cushion protecting depositors as well as the deposit insurance agency. Thus, a risk-related capital requirement scheme may be another alternative, although it suffers from the same problem of measuring bank risk.

In Korea, where deposit-taking institutions are relatively few in number, variable rate premiums may be more feasible than in other countries. The large number of policy-directed nonperforming loans held by banks is, however, a constraint to the adoption of variable rate premiums, because it is unfair to charge a higher premium for a bank with a greater number of policy-directed nonperforming loans.

The risk-based premium may still be workable by taking these loans into special consideration (implicitly presuming that the government will assume their default risk). Deposit insurance may aim at protecting small depositors only in order to induce large, better informed depositors to impose discipline on banks. But if the maximum limit of deposit protection is set too low, the objective of deposit insurance to prevent bank runs may be undermined.

Prudential Regulation Like deposit insurance, the primary goal of prudential regulation is to prevent financial panic and protect the payment system. In the absence of deposit insurance, prudential regulation achieves this goal by protecting depositors. Under a flat rate insurance premium that subsidizes bank risk taking, the fear of excess risk taking calls for prudential regulation by the deposit insurance agency. By providing various rules of sound banking practices such as capital adequacy and limiting credit concentration, prudential regulation helps banks avoid insolvency.

A unique trait of financial intermediaries, unlike nonfinancial firms, is that insolvency usually precedes illiquidity, which enables troubled banks to hide their insolvency problem for some time with the cosmetic manipulation of their financial statements. While the banks buy time trying to solve the problem, they usually further damage their portfolio position by paying above-market rates for deposits, involving themselves in speculation, and charging high interest rates to borrowers in distress. Bank supervision helps in the early detection of insolvency by requiring banks to provide periodic reports containing detailed information, to disclose disaggregate bank accounts, to be audited by external auditors, and to comply with rules for classifying loans, interest accruals and, write-offs.

Prudential regulation is also essential for the development of a healthy capital market. Its major tasks are to enhance transparency in the market and adequately control price manipulation and other unfair transactions by the development of an efficient information system and the establishment of a strong government institution supervising capital market activities. In line with the expansion of business areas for financial intermediaries as well as the innovation and sophistication of financial technology, the supervisory system has to be strengthened and the divided supervisory function should be better combined in a more comprehensive supervisory body. Extensive ownership of financial institutions by large business groups makes financial supervision a particularly demanding task in Korea.

Coping with Financial Crisis The experiences of other countries indicate that the largest losses to deposit insurance agencies and uninsured depositors have been due to delays in resolving bank failures. If, in fact, every troubled depository institution were reorganized shortly before it became economically insolvent, there would be no bank runs and no need for deposit insurance or prudential regulations. Restructuring troubled depository institutions is thus an essential complementary action to be closely coordinated with prudential regulation and the management of deposit insurance.

Resolution of a financial crisis involves the allocation of past losses and restructuring of the related firms and financial intermediaries. Past losses are distributed through one or more of three mechanisms: (1) inflation combined with ceilings on interest rates and other measures to improve bank profits; (2) across-the-board assistance; and (3) case-by-case restructuring and assistance. The inflationary approach has proven to be very costly since it destabilizes the economy with the erosion of growth potential and the creation of a further financial crisis. Across-the-board assistance is also grossly wasteful because the assistance is given to firms that either do not need it or are not viable regardless of the assistance. A case-by-case restructuring program involves reorganization, recapitalization, or closure based on a judgment of the firm's or financial intermediary's viability.

As for the restructuring of involved nonfinancial firms, a decentralized approach encouraging negotiations between the debtor firms and banks is believed to be superior to government-guided solutions. After agreements are made on the rationalization of management, part of the debt is written off or converted into equity or quasi-equity. The latter method permits the banks to share the eventual profits of the restructured firms. To prevent the banks from controlling the firms and thus facing conflicts of interest in credit decisions, the firms should be sold as soon as possible or the debt converted into nonvoting or preferred stock. The owners or managers should not be protected except in cases where their survival is indispensable to the operation of viable firms.

Restructuring troubled banks involves purchasing debt-ridden portfolios, rationalizing management, and selling the shares of the reorganized banks. This task would be best handled by a deposit insurance agency whose major responsibility is preventing bank runs at minimum cost to the insurance system. The agency takes partial or total ownership of distressed banks in return for the cash purchase of bad assets and takes measures to rationalize management. After cleaning up the banks' portfolios, the agency sells the equity shares to the private sector. In the bail-out process, the existing bank shareholders and managers should not be protected. The managers should be replaced even in cases where the banks are not taken over by the insurance agency, since the management style responsible for the failure of banks is difficult to correct without removing the managers.

REFERENCES

Bank of Korea. 1985. *Financial System in Korea* (in Korean). Seoul.

Bank of Korea. 1988. *Restructuring the Financial Industry* (in Korean). Seoul.

Benston, George J. 1988. *The Separation of Commercial and Investment Banking: Evidence on the Glass-Steagall Act's Passage and Continuation.* Boston: Kluwer Academic.

Benton, George J., and George G. Kaufman. 1985. *Risk and Solvency Regulation of Depository Institutions: Past Policies and Current Options.* Monograph Series in Finance and Economics, Monograph 1985-4/5. Salomon Brothers Center, New York University Graduate School of Business Administration.

Benston, George J., Gerald A. Hanweck, and David B. Humphrey. 1982. "Scale Economies in Banking: A Restructuring and Reassessment." *Journal of Money, Credit, and Banking* 14 (November, Part I):435–56.

de Juan, Aristobulo. 1987. "From Good Bankers to Bad Bankers: Ineffective Supervision and Management Deterioration as Major Elements in Banking Crisis." Mimeograph, World Bank.

England, C., and T. Huertas, eds. 1988. *The Financial Services Revolution: Policy Directions for the Future*. Washington, D.C.: Cato Institute.

Foreign Bankers Group in Korea. 1987. *Proposal for a Korean Money Market System*. Seoul.

Hinds, Manuel. 1987. "The Economic Effects of Financial Crises." Mimeograph, World Bank.

Jensen, Michael C., and William H. Meckling. 1976. "Theory of the Firm: Managerial Behavior, Agency Costs, and Capital Structure." *Journal of Financial Economics* 3:305–360.

Kang, Moonsoo. 1990. "The Challenge of the European Single Market to Korea's Banking Sector." Mimeograph, Korea Development Institute, May.

Krummel, Hans-Jacob. 1980. "German Universal Banking Scrutinized." *Journal of Banking and Finance* 4:33–35.

Lee, Duck-Hoon. 1985. *Development of Nonbank Financial Institutions and Adjustments of Business Boundaries* (in Korean). Korea Development Institute, Seoul.

Nam, Sang-Woo. 1988. "Readjustment of the Business Boundaries of Financial Intermediaries in Korea." KDI Working Paper no. 8822, Korea Development Institute, Seoul.

OECD. 1990. "Main Issues for Policies towards Efficient Financial Systems," and "Recent Trends in the Structure and the Regulation of Securities Markets." Background Papers 1 and 3 for the Informal Workshop with Dynamic Asian Economies, Paris, 26–27 February.

Park, Y.C., P.J. Kim, and J.Y. Park. 1986. "A Study on the Development of the Financial Industry (1985–2000)" (in Korean). Korea Development Institute, Seoul.

Pozdena, Randall J. 1987. "Commerce and Banking: The German Case." *FRSF Weekly Letter* (Federal Reserve Bank of San Francisco), 18 December.

Saunders, Anthony. 1985. "Securities Activities of Commercial Banks: The Problem of Conflicts of Interest." *Business Review* (Federal Reserve Bank of Philadelphia), July/August:17–27.

Walter, Ingo, ed. 1985. *Deregulating Wall Street: Commercial Bank Penetration of the Corporate Securities Market*. New York: Wiley.

Chapter 11

Financial Reform in South Korea

Robert Z. Aliber
University of Chicago

Introduction

The economic success of Korea in the past twenty-five years has been phenomenal—almost without parallel in modern economic history. Korea has moved from among one of the most backward of the developing countries in the early 1960s to one of the most advanced of the newly industrializing countries in the early 1990s. Per capita income first doubled from 1960 to 1965, then doubled a second time, and then a third. This sustained rapid increase for more than twenty-five years has no effective parallel in other countries.

If Japan had "catching up with the West" as one of its objectives in the 1950s and 1960s, then Korea may have felt that "catching up with Japan" was its primary economic objective during the 1970s and 1980s. In the past several decades the growth rate in Korea has been nearly twice that in Japan. Though published data suggest that per capita income in Japan is three to four times higher than in Korea, impressions of diet, housing, clothing, transport, and education suggest that the living standards in metropolitan Seoul may be 65–75 percent of living standards in metropolitan Tokyo.[1]

Part of this discrepancy between reported data and impressions reflects Korea's larger rural sector, and part reflects incomes significantly lower in these rural areas than in the urban areas, and by a larger amount than in Japan; part may reflect that the Japanese yen is relatively overvalued.[2]

Korea has shared one characteristic of most high-growth countries:a high rate of personal saving. In recent years gross saving has surged to about 35 percent of gross domestic product; in the 1970s this ratio increased from 15 to 30 percent. Until the early 1980s, Korea was one of the largest international borrowers, with an external debt surpassed only by those of Mexico and Brazil. Still, foreign loans financed only a small part of total domestic investment in Korea, in part because access of foreign investors to the securities market in Korea was, and remains, tightly regulated.

The high rate of household saving has facilitated a high rate of business investment; rapid growth and high investment were bootstrapped on the back of a high rate of personal saving. Governmental fiscal deficits were modest.

The Korean financial system—the combination of the central bank, the eleven nationwide commercial banks, the ten local banks, the sixty-six foreign branch banks, the six specialized banks, the six thousand savings institutions, and hundreds of nonbank lenders—has been instrumental in both the creation of credit and the allocation of credit to various borrowers. Virtually all credit flows, from households to business and government borrowers, have been indirect and have flowed through the financial system and initially primarily through the commercial banks and specialized banks. With the exception of currency, direct credit flows in the form of household acquisition of the security issues of business borrowers and of government borrowers have been modest (again in sharp contrast with Japan, where public shareholding is extensive, although two-thirds of shares are held by other firms and banks in a form of mutual crossholding). The market value of Korean equities is low as a share of total Korean income and presumably as a share of total Korean wealth, because many large Korean firms are still privately owned; at the end of 1989 the ratio of the market value of equities to GNP was half that in Japan (Table 11.1).

In Korea as in most other economies, achievement in terms of growth of per capita income can be weighed in comparison with the inputs of labor and capital associated with the observed increase in output. A significant part of the increase in income reflects the redeployment of labor from agriculture, where its marginal product was low, to industry, where its marginal product was much higher, partly because the capital employed per worker was significantly higher in industry. With an average annual savings rate of 30 percent and an average annual increase in the national income of 8 percent, the marginal capital output ratio has been in the range of four to five—not especially low when compared with other developing countries.

The implication of the relatively high marginal capital output ratio suggests that the Korean growth performance can be characterized as one of "brute force": the remarkable achievement in the rate of growth of income is more nearly the result of the use of abundant inputs than of the efficient use of these inputs.[3] The implication is that the growth achievement could have been even more impressive if the resources of a disciplined labor force and a large increase in new plants and equipment had been combined more efficiently.

One factor contributing to inefficient use of resources has been that the macrofinancial environment for business decision making has bordered on the unstable, with substantial variations in the inflation rate, real interest rates, and real exchange rates (Table 11.2). At times real interest rates have been positive and at other times negative; at times the Korea won has been overvalued and at other times undervalued. The 1970s was a period of severe financial repression, and the Korean banks

Table 11.1
Household financial portfolios, 1991 data (US$ billion)

	No. claims on banks (1)	Market value, equities (2)	GNP (3)	1/3(%)	2/3(%)
Korea	87	116	238	36	48
Japan	3,480	2,095	2,961	118	98
Taiwan	180	131	162	111	81
Singapore	32	53	35	90	151
Malaysia (1990)	24	60	40	60	150
Thailand	53	30	80	66	38

Source: Fortune, Oct. 7, 1991, pages 128-129; *International Financial Statistics,* selected issues.

were being slowly decapitalized. In contrast, the 1980s was a period of financial liberalization; however, the move from negative to positive real interest rates meant that many insolvent borrowers could no longer be carried without an increase in their insolvency.

A second factor contributing to inefficient resource use was the combination of a severe system of credit rationing and the extensive concentration of business and industrial activity in a relatively small number of large business conglomerates—the *jaebul.* The combination of the prospect of continued rapid growth, and hence a high anticipated profit rate, and a low real interest rate meant that frequently there has been an excess demand for credit, much as in Japan. Household savers have been subject to a high and variable inflation tax; the proceeds of the tax were transferred to business borrowers in the form of negative or low real interest rates. In the 1970s this inflation tax was large, perhaps as much as 8 percent of national income, since the inflation tax affects the public's holdings of money, quasi-monies, and most other financial assets (the sum of these assets may approximate national income). Credit rationing was necessary because interest rate ceilings meant that interest rates on bank loans were substantially below market-clearing levels.[4]

A third factor contributing to inefficient use of resources was the extensive administrative and political, and even military, involvement in business decision making. A large amount of the available credit was allocated to a small number of large business conglomerates.[5] Government authorities adopted policies to stimulate investment in accordance with the economic plan, and firms involved in exports were given priority in receiving credits.

Changes in macropolicies led to an unstable financial environment, and so some

Table 11.2
Nominal and real interest rates and exchange rates (percentage)

		Interest, nominal		Interest, real		Change in exchange rate	
	Inflation	Discount	Deposit	Discount	Real	Nominal	Real
1970	16.1	19.0	22.8	2.90	6.70	4.0	–6.9
1971	13.4	16.0	20.4	2.60	7.00	17.8	15.2
1972	11.7	11.0	12.0	–0.70	0.30	6.9	–8.2
1973	3.2	11.0	12.0	7.80	8.80	–0.3	2.6
1974	24.3	11.0	15.0	–13.30	–9.30	21.8	3.6
1975	25.3	14.0	15.0	–11.30	–10.30	0	–17.8
1976	15.3	14.0	16.2	–1.30	0.90	0	5.05
1977	10.2	14.0	14.4	3.80	4.20	0	5.2
1978	14.5	15.0	18.6	0.50	4.10	0	–2.6
1979	10.3	15.0	18.6	4.70	8.30	0	0.2
1980	28.7	16.0	19.5	–12.70	–9.20	36.3	31.1
1981	21.3	11.0	16.2	–10.30	–5.10	6.2	–4.3
1982	7.2	5.0	8.0	–2.20	0.80	6.9	–9.8
1983	3.4	5.0	8.0	1.60	4.60	6.2	–6.4
1984	2.3	5.0	9.2	2.70	6.90	4.0	10.7
1985	2.5	5.0	10.0	2.50	7.50	7.6	–0.2
1986	2.8	7.0	10.0	4.2	7.20	–3.2	–17.6
1987	3.0	7.0	10.0	4.00	7.00	–8.1	2.4
1988	7.1	8.0	10.0	0.09	2.90	–13.7	–9.5
1989	5.7	7.0	10.0	1.30	4.30	–0.6	17.9
1990	8.6	7.0	10.0	–1.60	1.40	5.4	4.8

financially overextended firms were provided with loans at below-market interest rates. One result was that excess capacity developed and remained extensive in some industries. Banks became loaded, and overloaded, with loans whose implicit market value was much below book value.

In this chapter I discuss the political economy of the credit allocation process in Korea and the advantages of alternative institutional arrangements for the allocation of credit. My objective is to identify the types of financial arrangements that are likely to be efficient in the allocation of credit, robust in their stability in response to various shocks, consistent with both the competitive spirit and traditional cultural values of Korea, responsive to the changes in the technology of money payments and financial intermediation, and consistent with both Korean population demographics and the probable changes in Korea's international economic position. I also consider the ability of Korean financial institutions to adjust to changes in the global competitive environment in finance.

In the next section I discuss the theory of financial development and the criteria for a successful and efficient financial system. The financial system allocates credit among competing uses; this system provides a mechanism for the appraisal of the risks of various projects or activities and the risks of the portfolios that include loans undertaken to finance these activities.

The third section I examine some of the popular concerns about the operation of the financial system in Korea and then seek to determine how many of these concerns may be a result of the system of financial regulation, and especially of interest rate ceilings. This section is responsive to the view that the dominant characteristic of organized financial markets in Korea has been a persistent excess demand for funds (see P. J. Kim, Chapter 9 of this volume).

Borrowing from a brief discussion of financial liberalization in the United States, Germany, and Japan, the fourth section presents some proposals for the regulation and organization of the Korean financial system which are both responsive to Korean values and traditions and likely to lead to a more efficient allocation of credit and to a set of Korean financial institutions that are more competitive internationally.

Efficiency and Equity in Financial Systems

Financial systems are mechanisms for the allocation of scarce capital among competing uses and borrowers, including both business borrowers and government borrowers. Household savers may allocate capital directly on their own ("direct finance"), or they may acquire claims on banks and other types of financial intermediaries which then allocate capital to the business borrowers ("indirect finance").

The allocation of scarce capital among competing uses is responsive to both (1) the evaluation of the prospective returns on the several types of financial liabilities issued by business borrowers and the various financial intermediaries, and (2) the evaluation of the risks attached to these various uses of scarce funds. The financial systems provide a mechanism for distinguishing the risk of particular firms and their projects from the market risk.

Many universal statements can be made about the demands on a financial system and the features of an ideal financial system. Household savers could engage in direct finance and choose among the security issues of primary borrowers, including business firms and various government units. Or household savers could buy the financial liabilities issued by banks or some other financial intermediary. Household savers choose between direct finance and indirect finance in response to several financial needs, including both returns available on the securities they might acquire if they engage in direct finance and the returns available on the securities if they acquire the liabilities of financial intermediaries. Household savers want an efficient means of payment, and they want a positive real return on their financial assets; they want a safe and relatively riskless way to save for retirement, a low-cost source of finance for the purchase of housing and other durables, and an efficient way to reduce the losses associated with unanticipated health and casualty events.

Household savers want to acquire securities that will minimize their sensitivity or exposure to default risk and want to be compensated for carrying such risks.

Business borrowers want to maximize their access to credit and minimize net financing costs. Moreover, they want to avoid credit squeezes or pinches at the time of refinancing and minimize the intrusion of lenders in their investment decisions.

Household savers acquire the liabilities of financial institutions rather than of business borrowers because of the advantages of diversification, professional risk appraisal, liquidity, and lower transaction costs. Household savers accept a rate of return on the liabilities of the financial institutions lower than the rate of return on the liabilities of the primary borrowers because of the advantages of diversification, professional risk appraisal, and liquidity.

The financial system performs an important signaling function. Information about the time preferences and risk preferences of household savers and business borrowers is assembled in the financial markets. The financial system provides a means for investors to estimate the risk of various investments or activities and the risk to their portfolios of combining these investments or activities with other activities and investments. The capital market provides a mechanism for comparing the current costs of investment and the future return of these same investments, and it provides a mechanism for comparing returns on short-term and long-term investments.

The financial system reconciles the divergent preferences of household savers and business borrowers. Savers want high rates of return, while borrowers wish to pay low interest rates. Households want liquidity, while borrowers want long-term finance. Both household savers and the business borrowers want a financial system that minimizes transaction costs and their share of the transaction cost.

The liquidity preferences of household savers mean that the maturity of securities preferred by household savers is generally substantially shorter than the maturity of securities business borrowers prefer to issue. The challenge for banks and other financial firms is to accommodate this difference in preferred risk/maturity profiles.

Financial intermediaries borrow short and lend long, and they incur a transformation risk; they seek to be compensated for carrying this risk. The risk is that long-term interest rates can change relative to short-term interest rates; in the absence of such changes, transformation risk would be trivial. The fallacy of composition is relevant; the demand of household savers as a group for liquidity is significantly smaller than the demand of individual households for liquidity. Nevertheless, these financial intermediaries still must be concerned that short-term interest rates may increase significantly relative to long-term rates.

Both household savers and business borrowers want a system that is robust in response to shocks. And they want a system with internal buffers, so that a shock to the financial system will be dampened rather than amplified. The system needs a mechanism to provide an increase in liquidity in response to an increase in the demand for liquidity.

Both household savers and business borrowers want a transparent financial system, which means that the decisions of the financial institutions are open and responsive to risk and return considerations and that favoritism is not the basis for these credit allocation decisions. The test of a transparent financial system is that the officials making the credit allocation decisions not be embarrassed by having the basis for their decisions printed on the front page of the *Wall Street Journal*, the *Financial Times*, and their counterparts in other countries.

One question raised by this review of the functions of the financial system is whether household savers in Korea have secured a significant share of the gains from the growth of the economy. A second question is whether the financial market in Korea provides information on the pricing of various risks. A third question is whether the system is efficient and provides household savers with liquidity, risk diversification, and payment services at reasonably low costs; one aspect of this question is whether the Korean financial intermediaries are competitive on an international scale. A fourth question is whether the Korean financial system provides adequate credit for newly established firms. The fifth question is whether the decisions in the Korean system, and especially the credit decisions, are transparent.

Efficiency in the Korean Financial System

The contrast between the impressive growth of the Korean economy and the lack of stability in its financial policies is strong, where the lack of stability is shown by the year-to-year variations in the inflation rate, the real interest rate, and the real exchange rate. There has been a remarkable improvement in the stability of the Korean financial economy from the 1970s to the 1980s, at least in the sense of a reduction in the inflation tax on money balances and other fixed-price securities. Korea participated in the late 1980s bubble in equity markets and real estate markets which affected Japan and Taiwan.[6]

The criticisms of the operation of the financial system are extensive. One criticism is that of corruption: individual bank officers are said to have been bribed by various borrowers.[7] A second criticism is that the commercial banks have been inefficient, which might be judged by the average markup between deposit interest rates and loan interest rates. Moreover, the bank lending officers have developed little experience in credit analysis, in part because of the override the administrative guidance and in part because firms that have become bankrupt are nevertheless permitted to continue operations. The Korean banks still carry large amounts of nonperforming loans; the implication is that the capital of banks may be modest or even negative.

The contrast between the rate of economic growth in real income and the real interest rate paid to household savers is especially sharp. The inference from the golden rule approach to growth theory is that the real interest rate should approach or more or less equal the rate of growth of real income, since the rate of growth of real income is the return on capital. The more competitive the financial environment and the more nearly the system is in equilibrium, the more nearly the real rate of growth of income and the real interest rate approximate each other.

As long as real interest rates were negative or low, as in the 1970s, debt was the "name of the game"; the larger the leverage of the firms (the larger the ratio of debt to equity), the higher the income of the owners. When real interest rates became positive in the 1980s, the operating profits of many Korean firms proved low relative to interest payments, and many firms became insolvent. And though individual firms could fail, the failure of a large number of firms was not permissible, and so government measures were necessary to subsidize these insolvent firms.

Financial regulation and especially interest rate ceilings have meant that the real rate of return to household savers in Korea has been low or at times negative—and hence substantially below the rate of growth of real income. In effect, an amount equivalent to the product between these two interest rates and liquid household saving has been diverted from household savers to the owners of businesses.

These interest rate ceilings and regulations have had a significant impact on the behavior of household savers and investors, banks and other financial institutions, and borrowers. Moreover, there is a significant impact on the structure of industry; the ability of new and would-be startup firms to obtain credit at the prevailing low rates is severely handicapped. The ability of Korean banks and other financial firms to be competitive with their foreign counterparts is adversely affected by interest rate ceilings, since profits for financial firms are assured.

Japan also relied extensively on interest rate ceilings during the 1950s and 1960s and even until the early 1980s. Some of the problems of Japanese finance that surfaced in the early 1990s can be attributed to the fixed-price commissions and interest rate ceilings. The high prices of land and equities in Japan relative to the prices of land and equities in other countries are responses to the low and negative rates of return on financial securities; household savers were willing to pay very high prices to acquire those assets and securities, which offered a positive real return. The increase in the price of equities and real estate can be viewed as the mechanism necessary to ensure a more or less constant share of debt and equity in the portfolios of investors in a period of rapid growth and high saving rates. The large loan losses experienced by the affiliates of major city banks in Japan probably reflect their limited experience in credit appraisal; in a rapid-growth environment, with substantial cross-subsidization from household savers to business borrowers, relatively few firms are likely to fail. the payment of compensation for losses on equities of a small group of relatively large investors can be considered a price-discounting concession in a fixed-commission environment. The bubble in Japanese equity prices can be traced in part to this money-back guarantee—virtually every investor would be willing to buy securities and to pay exceptionally high prices for them if guaranteed against losses should the equity prices decline.

One basic feature of interest rate ceilings in Korea is that both the interest rates paid household savers and the interest rates charged business borrowers are not responsive to increases in the demand for and supply of credit, or to the changes in the anticipated inflation rate in Korea. Credit rationing becomes more or less extensive, depending on changes in the demand for credit relative to the supply. However, the information available to both the authorities and private parties from changes in the scope of credit rationing is less precise and meaningful than the information available from changes in interest rates.

A second feature of interest rate ceilings, or more precisely of the excess of the anticipated profit rate on new investments over the nominal interest rate on the loans incurred to finance these investments, is that there has been an excess demand for credit. Those borrowers fortunate enough to receive loans at the interest rate ceiling receive an economic rent; the amount of this rent varies with the amount of credit and the difference between the nominal interest rate and the interest rate that would clear the credit market. (This economic rent is the mirror image of the inflation tax.) Those firms that can borrow at the ceiling interest rate can secure a substantial income by arbitraging these funds into the curb financial market.

As in many rent-seeking activities, the borrowers have an incentive to share some of the economic rent with the lenders—or with the representatives of the bank lenders—so as to increase the amounts of credit they receive and the economic rent. The corruption of bank lenders is a consequence of the interest rate ceilings; if interest rates were allowed to increase to clear the credit market, the borrowers would not have an incentive to make side payments to bank lending officers to increase their access to credit.

A third consequence of interest rate ceilings is that they reduce the incentive for banks to limit costs or to be concerned with economic efficiency and technical innovation; ceilings mean banks operate as if they were a cartel. The market share of an individual bank is not dependent on the skill of its offices in pricing deposits. While the thrust of the competition among banks might be directed at cost reductions in the absence of price competition, this alternative appears to have been dulled by the interest rate floors and ceilings, which appear to suffuse banks with a lethargy with respect to competition. The incentives to economize on the use of labor and to adopt labor-saving devices in the banks are limited by the assured profits. Because Korean banks have not developed experience in operating in an environment characterized by variations in interest rates, they are poorly prepared to compete with American, Japanese, and other foreign banks.

A fourth consequence of interest rate ceilings is that the attention of the bank lenders to credit analysis and risk appraisal of particular loans is limited, since losses any borrower might incur can be made good by the interest rate subsidies the lenders can provide the borrowers under new loans. The banks have less restraint in throwing "good money after bad" and less incentive to curtail the unprofitable activities of particular borrowers.

A fifth consequence of interest rate ceilings is that individual firms can obtain much of the capital they need for expansion from the economic rent they receive from subsidized loans, and so they have less need to sell securities to the public to finance their expansion. In effect, part of all economic rents attached to subsidized loans is transferred to the owners of firms that are able to borrow at the regulated interest rates. The interest rate ceiling partly explains the change to a less equal distribution of income and wealth and the growth of large family fortunes.

A sixth consequence of interest rate ceilings is that new and somewhat riskier firms may find it more and more costly or difficult to obtain credit. If the lenders cannot set the interest rate at a level that matches the riskiness of the borrower, they have an incentive to provide credit to borrowers who are deemed less risky. New entrepreneurs are stalled or shunted into the curb market, where they pay significantly higher interest rates than the established firms. And the less risky borrowers will be the established firms or groups of firms.

As long as interest rate ceilings remain and banks are compelled to engage in nonprice credit rationing, some scope for administrative guidance remains. If these ceilings were removed and interest rates changed to clear the market, the scope for administrative guidance would decline.

Although the Korean banks were privatized in the 1980s, they still operate much as if they were government-owned. Interest rate ceilings and administrative guidance are an extension of government. There is implicit 100 percent deposit insurance, much as if banks remained government-owned. As long as the sentiment prevails that banks cannot be allowed to fail, there remains little incentive for senior officials and managers of these banks to accept responsibility for credit decisions and for various managerial decisions.

Despite the remarkable economic progress in Korea, household savers have been inadequately compensated for their contribution to this achievement. Because of the extensive reliance on interest rate ceilings, the economy has not provided information on the risk of various projects. Investment resources have been wasted by too large a volume of investment in big-ticket projects. Because credit is cheap, large numbers of *jaebul* appear to mimic each other's investment activities. The Korean financial system is not efficient; payment services are provided at high cost. The new firms that might provide the stimulus for continued rapid growth are penalized by having to pay exceptionally high interest rates. And financial decisions are not transparent.

Institutional Reform in the Korean Financial System

The objective of institutional reform in the Korean financial system is to develop a set of banks and related financial institutions that will lead to a more efficient allocation of credit and to do so at a significantly lower cost.

Four issues are central to financial reform and restructuring in Korea. One is whether Korean financial institutions should be specialized or universal—whether commercial banks should underwrite securities, sell insurance, and manage the retirement funds of households. A second issue is the scope of government intervention in the credit allocation process; one aspect of this matter is the scope of insurance on bank deposits, and another is the use of government funds to enhance the capital of banks and other financial intermediaries. A third issue involves the role of government in providing guidance to banks in the allocation of credit. A fourth issue involves the boundary between commerce and finance, especially whether Korean industrial firms might own or effectively control financial institutions.

Korea might adopt a foreign model for its financial system, perhaps the U.S. model or the German or Japanese model; each model deals with the topics noted above. Should the financial system contain specialized types of institutions (commercial banks, trust banks, investment banks, pension funds, insurance companies, brokerage firms, and thrift banks) as in the United States and Japan, or universal-type institutions as in Germany? Should the number of firms in each of these sectors be a handful, say, three to five, or should there be as many firms as is feasible, given the desire to achieve economies of scale in the various production processes within banks? Should government agencies and political leaders continue to intervene directly in the allocation of credit as in Japan, or should they take a hands-off attitude toward the credit decisions of banks and other financial firms, as in the United States and Germany? Should there be a barrier between finance and commerce as in the United States, or should industrial firms be allowed to own banks, or should banks be allowed to own industrial firms, as in Germany?

The financial systems in the United States, Germany, and Japan evolved in response to their own concerns and traditions. The U.S. financial system developed in response to regulations that reflected a distrust of large financial institutions; these regulations forestalled the development of a nationwide bank and maintained high barriers between different types of financial institutions, as well as between commerce and finance. The German system of universal banks was developed to facilitate the accumulation of funds for business finance more than a century ago. The Japanese financial system evolved as part of the development of *zaibatsu*; industrial firms would have a house bank, much as in Germany.

The traditional distinctions among the financial systems in the United States, Germany, and Japan are being partially eroded by financial liberalization or deregulation. Financial liberalization has been extensive in many countries in the 1980s, especially in the United States and, to a lesser extent, in Germany and Japan. The factor that motivated liberalization in many different countries was that rapid growth in new financial instruments led investors to move funds from the commercial banks, largely because various regulations became much more expensive in a period of increasing inflation, so that interest rates paid by banks on various deposit liabilities declined relative to interest rates on money market financial instruments. Interest rates tend to increase during a period of inflation. The United States and most other countries had interest rate ceilings on bank deposits; as money market interest rates began to increase relative to these interest rate ceilings, some owners of bank deposits found it financially attractive to shift funds to nonregulated investments, including Eurodollar deposits and money market funds.

The implicit tax associated with non-interest-bearing reserve requirements increased during a period of inflation; as a result, the interest rates banks could pay on deposits were increasing less rapidly than the interest rates on money market funds and on deposits in offshore banks.

Much of the motivation for deregulation of interest rate ceilings in the United States and in many other countries was to reduce the increasing competitive disadvantage of banks relative to nonregulated financial institutions. The reduction of reserve requirements was motivated by this same concern.

Within the United States, financial liberalization also has involved relaxation of two traditional forms of regulation. One is the relaxation of geographic restrictions against branching of banks across state lines, which initially involved permitting banks headquartered in one state to acquire failing (or failed) commercial banks and failing (or failed) savings and loan associations headquartered in other states. Many states now permit banks headquartered in one state to acquire banks headquartered in other countries through their holding companies. And it seems likely that banks will be able to expand across state lines by branching as well as through holding companies.

The consensus is that there will be significant consolidation of banks in the United States; however, even after this process of consolidation is completed, there will remain at least several thousand or more banks. There will be a few large money-center banks, a handful of super-regional banks, and large numbers of regional and community banks.

The second form of financial deregulation in the United States involves the relaxation of the regulations that distinguish commercial banks, investment banks, savings and loan associations, and insurance companies from each other. Traditionally, each type of institution was distinguished by the uniqueness of one of its liabilities: only commercial banks could issue checkable deposits, only investment banks could underwrite securities, and so on. Now, the height of the barriers that distinguish the liabilities and activities of each type of institution is being reduced; a few commercial banks are becoming more like investment banks, and the deposit liabilities of saving and loan associations seem increasingly similar to the deposit liabilities of commercial banks. The U.S. Treasury and the Federal Reserve have recommended that commercial banks be allowed to sell insurance and that industrial firms be allowed to own banks.

The liberalization of geographic and product line restrictions on the expansion of U.S. banks means that those banks will become more nearly like financial department stores and will approach the universal banks of Germany. The German banking system appears dominated by three large banks, which perform functions of commercial banking, investment banking, trust banking, and investment banking. In addition, there are many smaller banks and some state-owned banks. These banks frequently own and control sufficient shares to have effective control in individual industrial firms.

Financial liberalization has been extensive in Japan, primarily with respect to relaxation of interest rate ceilings. Deregulation has been less extensive than in the United States with respect to product lines of the different types of Japanese financial institutions. Since many Japanese life insurance companies and trust banks are already grouped around banks in the *keiretsu* system, the likelihood of extensive competition between banks and life insurance companies seems less extensive in Japan than in the United States. Similarly, the likelihood that the boundaries between banks and brokerage firms will decline seems modest. The Japanese have also permitted foreign investment banks to enter the Japanese market and to acquire seats on the Tokyo Stock Exchange.

The financial systems in the United States, Germany, and Japan are evolving in such a way that they increasingly resemble each other, despite their very different origins. Most of the change reflects the increasing consolidation of banks in the United States, both within states and metropolitan areas and across state lines. Some of the change involves the relaxation of the boundaries between different types of financial institutions in the United States. Still, there will remain significant differences among these systems in terms of the range of products banks can sell; the U.S. system is likely to remain more decentralized than the German and Japanese systems.

The Korean financial system resembles the U.S. system in the formal sense of strong distinctions among different types of financial institutions. The Korean system resembles the German and Japanese systems in that the major Korean banks branch out on a nationwide basis. Moreover, the Korean system is similar to the German and Japanese systems in that the boundary between finance and commerce or industry is modest; however, the Korean system differs from both Japanese and German systems in that the *jaebul* have captured—or nearly captured—major financial firms as a way to enhance their access to more credit. The Korean system resembles the Japanese system and differs sharply from the German system in the extensive scope of government involvement in the credit allocation system; indeed, the involvement of Korean authorities in these decisions seems much more extensive than the involvement of Japanese government authorities.

Changes in institutional arrangements in the Korean financial system should be responsive to changes in financial technology, the increasing integration of national financial markets, changes in the regulatory environment in various foreign countries, and the pace of the movement to a more pluralistic society in Korea. Moreover, these changes in Korean financial arrangements must be consistent with changes in the macroeconomic environment in Korea, which is likely to feature a reduction in the rate of economic growth as a result of both the aging of the Korean population and the reduction of the excess supply of labor in agriculture.[8]

As world financial markets become increasingly integrated, Korea's financial institutions must become increasingly efficient or else their market share of transactions with Korean savers and borrowers will decline—and Korean institutions now seem far from efficient in managing the payments process and skillful in credit analysis and risk evaluation. The competitive disadvantage of Korean banks relative to banks headquartered in the United States, Japan, and other industrial countries is not likely to decline significantly as long as the "heavy bureaucratic hand" of the government is involved in the credit allocation decisions of commercial banks and as long as bank deposits are fully insured by the government.

Korea is under increased pressure to open its financial markets to foreign firms. The U.S. tolerance for asymmetric policies—that foreign financial institutions have much less favored access to the Korean market than Korean institutions have to various foreign markets—is likely to decline as per capita incomes in Korea increase.

The pattern of institutional reform of the financial system begins with both the recent history of Korean institutions and the value structures of the Korean people. These institutions were, until relatively recently (as time goes for financial institutions), under government ownership, and subsequently under government control even after having been privatized. Indeed, for many purposes the banks remain extensions of the Ministry of Finance because credit allocation is responsive to government fiat. Commercial banks, and perhaps other types of financial institutions, benefit from implicit government insurance of their liabilities. Some of the waste in the Korean economy comes from the centralization of decision making about allocation of credit among a small number of politicians and government officials, who almost certainly have not been especially sensitive to the impacts of their decisions on the operation of a market economy.

The move to a more efficient financial system in Korea is likely to be slow in the absence of a move toward greater pluralism in Korea. The number of independent centers of decision making has been modest, in part because authority and hierarchy have high rank in the value structure in Korea and in part because many institutions were inherited from the Japanese. Decisions are essentially made top-down, with modest input from the bottom (in contrast to the Japanese tradition of a bottom-up approach).

The argument for increased pluralism in Korea suggests maintaining four or five types of financial institutions and prohibiting joint ownership or control of different types of institutions; the Korean economy is sufficiently large and robust to support eight or ten firms of each type of institution. The gains to efficiency from competition among eight or ten firms—including several foreign firms operating through joint ventures with Korean partners—is likely to be significantly greater than the gains to efficiency from permitting or facilitating mergers in the belief that there are significant economies of scale or scope from somewhat larger institutions.

The basic social argument for universal-type financial institutions is that there are significant economies of scope from permitting individual firms to sell many types of products—bank deposits, life insurance policies, mutual funds, and retirement annuities. The evidence for economies of scope is modest. Many traditional department stores, which developed because they offered significant economies of scope, are losing market shares to specialty stores; specialty stores carry a much larger range of goods of each particular type than the department store. Moreover, the scope of vertical integration in many firms appears to be declining. These observations are not Korea-specific; but in the absence of data suggesting significant scope economies, there is a strong case for a regulatory framework which prohibits banks from selling insurance and retirement annuities and which prohibits insurance companies from selling bank deposits.

The cost to the Korean economy of following the German model is that the development of universal institutions would reduce the number of centers of independent decision making, since the managers of each of the major divisions of a universal institution would be much more severely constrained in their decisions than the managers of independent firms. The rationale is that the efficiency in the allocation of credit would be enhanced by a large number of competitors; the smaller the number of firms, the less extensive the scope of competition.

The case for maintaining significant barriers between commerce and finance is especially strong in Korea; otherwise industrial firms will capture financial firms and use the funds from the financial firms as a way to circumvent the financial markets.

The Korean financial system is well positioned to enhance its efficiency by relatively few changes. The single most important change is the elimination of interest rate ceilings on deposits and on loans, much as in the United States and Japan. This policy change should lead—perhaps slowly—to the recognition that Korean bank managers are no longer civil servants and instead should become responsible for their own pricing and credit decisions.

A reduction in the scope of interest rate ceilings on bank deposits and bank loans is the most important measure to enhance the efficiency of the credit allocation process; these ceilings might be raised gradually, perhaps over a period of two or three years, as in Japan in the early 1980s, so as to ease the impact of the reduction of implicit interest rate subsidies on the borrowers.[9]

The principle that interest rate regulations should be gradually relaxed and then eliminated would be separate from the decision about the timetable for the relaxation of these ceilings. The Korean government should adopt formal insurance on bank deposits and a deposit insurance fund should be established. Banks should be charged a premium to insure deposits. The principle of coinsurance might be followed; small deposits might be insured to 90 percent of their value and larger deposits should be insured for lesser amounts. Some banks might wish to sell only uninsured deposits, and they should be allowed to do so. The paradox is that this change would reduce the implicit 100 percent deposit insurance that now characterizes the Korean banking system.

To the extent that government authorities believe that particular types of investment activities should receive more credit (or credit on more favorable terms) than they would under a competitive market system, the government should rely on existing government credit agencies or establish new ones.

The lessons of Japan and Taiwan suggest that the rate of economic growth is likely to decline in Korea within the next five to ten years because of a decline in the growth of the labor force and the difficulties in expanding Korean exports. At that time, Korea is likely to develop a larger current-account surplus, since household saving will then be very high relative to domestic investment opportunities, assuming that Korean products remain price-competitive. Korean investors will seek the higher returns on foreign investments. As Korean funds flow abroad, the agents for these flows will normally be Korean financial institutions. These institutions are relatively inefficient on an international scale because they have been so extensively protected in their domestic markets.

The unification of the two Koreas would greatly prolong the period of rapid Korean growth, since there is a large excess supply of labor in North Korea. The differences in the levels of per capita income, plant and equipment, and infrastructure are extremely large (almost certainly larger than the differences between the two Germanys); the implication is that the investment requirements would be extensive and would significantly delay the date when Korea would develop a trade surplus.

Conclusion

The central objective of financial reform in Korea is to secure a significant improvement in the allocation of credit, and hence in the efficiency of investment. The dominant problem in the past in the allocation of credit in Korea has arisen from its hierarchical and authoritarian tradition; credit allocation decisions have been centralized, and those making these decisions have had neither the background nor the competence to make these decisions in a general equilibrium framework.

Many of the problems of the Korean financial sector can be traced to the combination of interest rate ceilings and government ownership and subsequent control of the commercial banks. Interest rates on loans were set at levels substantially below the levels that would clear the credit market, with the consequence that the demand for credit exceeded the supply. Credit rationing was extensive. Some firms profited by borrowing from the commercial banks at these preferential rates and then diverting funds to the curb market. Some firms made "side payments" to bank credit officers to obtain more credit; in effect, they shared some of the "economic rents" with the individual lending officers in the banks. The subsidy inherent in these below-market interest rates enabled inefficient firms to expand and compete. And a major consequence was that the level of investment in plant and equipment in certain industries was too high, while some less established firms that may have had more promising prospects received less credit than they would have if credit had been allocated on the basis of prospective returns.

Because credit has been allocated in response to administrative guidance, there has been little incentive for lending officers to develop responsibility for credit decisions.

The single most important measure to achieve the more efficient allocation of credit is the elimination of ceilings on interest rates on bank deposits and bank loans, a reform similar to the reforms adopted by the United States and Japan in the 1970s and 1980s. Individual banks would be able to compete for deposits on the basis of interest rates and would then become much more sensitive to the credit standing of individual borrowers.

Insurance for bank deposits should be formalized with the establishment of a deposit insurance fund based on the principal of coinsurance.

There are powerful reasons for maintaining strong barriers between different types of financial institutions and of ensuring no common ownership or control among commercial banks, insurance companies, and investment banks. Similarly, there are strong arguments for maintaining high barriers between finance and commerce and of developing measures to ensure that industrial firms do not own or control financial firms.

NOTES

1. Thus per capita income is $13,645, while per capita income is $5,682.
2. The paradox of the apparent overvaluation of the Japanese yen is that Japan is a large capital exporter; Japanese purchases of U.S. dollar and other foreign securities lead to a lower foreign exchange value of the yen.
3. A nontrival part of the increase in income results fom the "gains from trade"—that is, the shift of productive resources from the production of import-competing goods to the production of goods; the foreign exchange earned was used to finance the purchase of imports.
4. The sales of thirty *jaebul*, as a ballpark estimate, are about 75–80 percent of Korean national income. The sales of the top four—Samsung, Hyundai, Lucky-Goldstar, and Daewoo—approximate one-half of the Korean GNP, and those of the top ten approximate two-thirds of Korean GNP. (Sales and GNP are apples and oranges; the more apropriate calculation would involve corporate value added and GNP, and the ratios of value added to sales might be 20–30 percent—which would mean that the value added by the top 30 was 25 percent of national income, still an impressively large measure of industrial concentration.) There is little evidence of a large successful Korean independent business firm, say, a counterpart to Sony or Honda in Japan, which has not gone the conglomerate route.

   These *jaebul* are like ministates or a manorial system, with extensive vertical integration. Within each *jaebul* there is an implicit capital market, as credit is allocated among the various constituent firms; since money is fungible, the firms within a *jaebul* which receive the credits from the banks are not necessarily the firms that increase their investment 5. The assertion is made that there is an effective capital market within each conglomerate. Perhaps, but it would be nice to know the evidence.
6. One frequent complaint in Korea, as in other nearby countries, involves the high price of housing; the ratio of house prices to income appears to be three to four times that of other countries with relatively high ratios of population to income. One explanation for high housing prices is that the real returns on bank deposits and other fixed-price assets have been relatively low.

7. The statement is that bank credit officers "live well for their incomes."

8. Both of these arguments, and many others, will have to be modified to cope with the eventual consolidation of North Korea and South Korea, which will significantly prolong the period of an excess supply of labor.

9. From time to time, government authorities may conclude that the achievement of a worthy economic objective will be enhanced if particular firms are subsidized. These firms might be subsidized directly from fiscal revenues, or from a government-owned credit agency.

REFERENCES

Amsden, Alice H. 1989. *Asia's Next Giant: South Korea and Late Industrialization.* New York: Oxford University Press.

Bagchi, Amiya Kumar. 1987. *Public Intervention and Industrial Restructuring in China, India and the Republic of Korea.* New Delhi: International Labor Organization.

Cho, Lee-Jay, and Yoon Hyung Kim, eds. 1991. *Economic Development in the Republic of Korea: A Policy Perspective.* Honolulu: East West Center.

Emery, Robert F. 1991. *The Money Markets of Developing East Asia.* New York: Praeger.

Euh, Yoon-Dae, and James C. Banker. 1990. *The Korean Banking System and Foreign Influence.* London: Routledge.

Kuznets, Paul W. 1977. *Economic Growth and Structure in the Republic of Korea.* New Haven: Yale University Press.

Lau, Lawrence J., ed. 1990. *Models of Development.* Rev. ed. San Francisco: ICS Press.

McKinnon, Ronald I., and Donald J. Mathieson. 1981. *How to Manage a Repressed Economy.* Essays in International Finance, no. 145. Princeton: Princeton University Press.

Song, Byung-Nak. 1990. *The Rise of the Korean Economy.* New York: Oxford University Press.

Woo, Jung-En. 1991. *Race to the Swift.* New York: Columbia University Press.

PART V

The System of Land Ownership and Use

Chapter 12

Korean Land Ownership and Use

Jin Soon Lee
Soongsil University

Introduction

Korea has suffered from cyclical land speculation since the mid-1960s, and the land problem may now be the most serious problem confronting the nation. The Korean people, like the Japanese as described in Hanayama (1986), have created three myths about urban land: the myth of urban land shortage, the myth of continuous increases in land prices, and the myth of the futility of land policies. These myths have so dominated Korean thinking that land seems to have acquired some supernatural power to bring large fortunes to those who possess it. People are willing to buy land at an inflated price because they expect to sell it later at an even more highly inflated price.

The current economic crisis in Korea may be deeply rooted in the land problem. Rapidly rising land values have attracted savings away from productive forms of investment. Since land has been the most secure and profitable investment, it has attracted money and entrepreneurial skills that would otherwise have been devoted to private savings because home ownership (the objective of most private savings in the past) is now beyond the means of most workers. Astronomical land prices could sabotage many government projects for regional development; they may reach a level that deters the building of roads, bridges, and public housing.

The land problem in Korea has, however, rarely been analyzed by economists. The study of land and the land market encompasses various disciplines, ranging from economics and finance to planning, real estate, and geography. Whereas professionals in regional and urban planning have been more concerned with problems relating to the allocation of land according to the type of use, economists have been mainly interested in the determination of prices in the land market. Before the nineteenth century, land market analysis was confined to the agricultural land market. The subsequent emergence of capital and labor as more important factors of production in industrialized societies relegated land to the background. Furthermore, the fact that land has some characteristics in common with capital—

such as durability and heterogeneity—led to the belief among economists that land is synonymous with capital and that therefore no separate theory of the land market is required. Many economists (e.g., Mills and Song 1979) believe that land speculation can keep prices above equilibrium for only short periods, and that speculation is likely to make land prices more (rather than less) stable. They also tend to believe that land speculation does not create problems in terms of either equity or efficiency. This view, however, may be erroneous, as argued by Henry George (1946) and his adherents.

My main purpose in this chapter is to examine two closely related issues—one theoretical, the other policy-oriented. Although land value theory is still a controversial subject among economists, I attempt to examine it from the perspective of the Korean phenomenon of cyclical land speculation. I also consider another theoretical issue—George's hypothesis on the cause of economic recession—in conjunction with the historical data on Korea. Finally, I investigate policy solutions to land problems.

Theoretical Background

Unique Characteristics of Land

Land is indispensable to human life. People have always been dependent on land for life and livelihood. The human being is a land animal, who can live only on and from land and can use other natural resources necessary to life (such as air, sunshine, and water) only in conjunction with land. Land is required for housing and land is essential for the modern factory or office building just as it is for the traditional farm.

Modern economists have largely ignored the distinction between land and capital. Although the production function was defined by classical economists in terms of three factors—land, labor, and capital—it was subsequently simplified to include only capital and labor. Reflecting the diminishing importance of land in the dynamic process of urban-based industrial production, land was subsumed into the concept of capital, and its unique characteristics were thereby masked or effaced. This change consequently permitted limited numbers of land speculators to exercise a disproportionate influence over the economy.

Economic theory argues that speculation serves a useful economic purpose, since speculators bear risks not borne by other agents in the market. The theory also asserts that speculation does not affect long-run price levels and that it in fact speeds up the adjustment to long-run equilibrium and dampens the oscillations of adjustment. Ultimately, the price is determined by user demand and by nonspeculative supply. These notions have, however, developed largely from studies of speculation in markets other than the land market—notably the foreign exchange markets and stock exchanges. The arguments against this conventional view were developed mainly by George and his followers—W. D. Carter (1982) and Fred Harrison (1983)—who clarified the unique characteristics of land relative to capital. Their views are summarized in the following paragraphs.

Essentially, according to this view land is fixed in quantity, whereas capital may be increased without limit, since capital is the product of human labor. Because of this difference, speculation in products (including capital) tends to stimulate production, whereas speculation in land tends to check production. Speculation in products tends to increase the demand for, and thus the price of, products. The price increase induces more production, which increases the supply and tends to lower the price again. Throughout this cycle there is a stimulating effect on production. Speculation in land also tends to increase the demand for land and thereby increases its price. However, since the supply of land is fixed, an increasing scarcity of land develops. Land prices rise beyond the level at which labor and capital can profitably engage in production. The inevitable result is to check production.

Speculation, whether in land or in stocks, is a risky activity; however, speculation in land tends to have the opposite effect on the economy of speculation in stock. When speculation runs high primarily near the peak of the land value cycle, applications for credit to buy land push up the rate of interest. It then becomes more difficult to borrow in order to finance the development and manufacture of new capital, which creates new jobs and wealth. Speculation in share prices on the stock exchange in the hope of capital gains, on the other hand, reduces the cost of financing to firms, thereby directly encouraging investment.

Land, unlike capital, is not perishable; therefore the land value speculation bubble can be sustained whereas capital value speculation cannot. The economic influence acquired by those who buy land depends crucially on the unique characteristics of land. The time frames are different in the land and capital markets. Land can be left idle for long periods because it is not perishable. Land is far less vulnerable to time pressures than are labor and capital. Agricultural land can renew itself, thereby retaining its value; thus owners need not capitalize their assets for long periods. Land tends to retain its value over time better than capital. Capital in the form of machines and buildings depreciates and must therefore pay for itself within a limited period, during which the capitalist cannot avoid the costs of maintenance. This cannot be avoided by transforming capital into cash, for unless the money is employed, by being lent to others, it either depreciates in value as a result of inflation or does not earn an income (in which case it might as well be used for consumption).

Furthermore, there is a distinct difference in the ability to finance loans originally taken out to buy land or accumulate stocks. Except during deep recessions, banks continue to lend money for purchases of land, even (or rather, especially) during uncertain times. This makes it possible to refinance loans used to buy land, which in turn enables the speculator to hold out for better prices. A land speculation bubble can be sustained, but credit to help finance inventories is much more difficult to obtain. The need to finance inventories, therefore, tends to prevent stock accumulation far more regularly than does land investment.

Thus, we begin to see that land speculation is a unique economic phenomenon. Land speculators are able to exert disproportionate influence over the economy by playing a passive, wait-and-see game which can yield enormous fortunes for shrewd dealers who, as land monopolists, do not contribute anything to the wealth of the nation. This economic influence in effect enables land speculators to create economic disadvantages for the active agents of the wealth-creating process: the workers and their accumulated savings (capital).

Land speculation is a two-dimensional activity. It is spatial, since it entails the acquisition of control over a clearly defined piece of territory, such as land on the fringe of an urban area. It is also temporal in that purchases today are calculated to provide financial gain through resale in the future. Thus the dealer has to be willing and able to hold onto land for some time, then sell when he calculates that prices have reached their most attractive levels.

Land speculation is an investment in an asset that yields an extremely high rate of return accompanied by a relatively low degree of risk. In this respect, it contrasts with speculation in other areas, such as security markets, where the risk of loss is much greater. For building an asset portfolio in a high-growth economy, land speculation offers many attractive opportunities.

Land Value Theory

Land has a dual character. It is an input in the production of all goods and services, and it is an asset for saving. Corresponding to this dual character, land provides two closely related types of income streams to the owner—income (e.g., rent) and capital gains. We assume that a "speculator" is a person who buys and sells land for the sake of an anticipated capital gain. Speculators may also use land. Homeowners are typically speculators in part, as are farmers and the owners of woodlands and pastures.

Classical economics focused on the first character of land—as an input in production. Rent, which is the price of land services, is determined by supply and demand in the rental market. The function of rent is to allocate land services to valuable uses. Static efficiency can be ensured by a competitive rental market.

According to classical economics, the land price is the present value of the anticipated future rents from the land, discounted at an appropriate interest rate. If R_t is the rent anticipated on a plot in year t and i is the interest rate, then the price of the plot in the year zero, P_0, is given by

$$P_0 = \sum_{t=0}^{\infty} \frac{R_t}{(1+i)^t} \qquad (1)$$

If the anticipated rent R_t is a constant, this formula can be simplified to $P_0 = R/i$. For example, if the annual rent of a plot were 100 and the interest rate were 10 percent, then the price of the plot would be 1,000. It is sometimes observed that land values are very high relative to land rents at the time. In rapidly developing countries, the productivity of land and other inputs increases rapidly. Anticipated future increases in the land's productivity become capitalized in the land price, and the price becomes large relative to the current rent. If the annual growth rate of rent is g, then the price of the plot in year zero, P_0, becomes $P_0 = R/(i-g)$.

Land close to an urban center is the most valuable of all—usually one or two orders of magnitude more valuable than agricultural land. While urbanization proceeds and cities grow, high land values spread beyond the urban centers. Thus, high and rising land values are always associated with rapid urbanization. The extraordinarily high productivity of urban land arises from its proximity to related economic activities. Land in a central business district is extremely valuable because it is within walking distance of an enormous range of densely packed and related activities. The closest surrounding residential land is valuable because it provides access to central employment and shopping at low transportation costs.

George (1946) pointed out, however, that the story does not end there. In a rapidly growing economy, where the swift and steady increase of rent lends credence to calculations of further increase, the confident expectation of increased prices produces a tendency for the landowner to withhold land from use in the expectation of higher prices. This confident expectation of the future enhancement of land values leads to speculation. In societies such as Korea and Japan, this mechanism operates with tremendous influence on the economy.

> The same phenomenon may be observed in every rapidly growing city. If land of superior quality in terms of location were always fully used before resorting to land of inferior quality, no vacant lots would be left as the city grows. Nor could we find miserable shanties in the midst of costly buildings. These lots, some of them extremely valuable, are withheld from use—or from the full use to which they might be put—because their owners, not being able to or not wishing to improve them, prefer, in expectation of upward movement in land values, to hold them for a higher rate than could now be obtained from those willing to improve them. And, in consequences of this land being withheld from use, or from the full use of which it is capable, the margin of the city is pushed away even further from the center.
>
> When we reach the limits of the growing city—that is, the actual margin of building, which coincides with the margin of cultivation in agriculture—we do not find the land purchasable at its agricultural-purpose value, as it would be were rent determined simply by present requirements. Instead, we find that, for a long distance beyond the city, the land bears a speculative value, based on the belief that it will be required in the future for urban purposes. To reach the point at which land can be purchased at a price not based upon urban rent, we must go very far beyond the actual margin of urban use. (George 1946:257)

As a result, land speculation spreads outward from the city center, eventually encompassing the countryside. Under these circumstances, land becomes an asset for saving rather than an input of production. To the landowner, expected capital gain from land becomes more important than rent.

In this situation, the demand for land is determined by investors' portfolio behavior, and the land price is determined in the asset market. Let the current price of land be P, rent R, the interest rate i, and the expected capital gain ΔP. In the assets market, without tax and uncertainty,

$$i = \frac{R}{P} + \frac{\Delta P}{P} \tag{2}$$

From equation 2, it is simple to derive

$$P = \frac{R}{1+i} + \frac{P_t}{1+i} \tag{3}$$

where P_t represents the expected land price in the next period. Equation 3 implies that the current price of land depends on the expected price of land in the future.

Land Speculation and Economic Recession

George offered land speculation as a possible explanation for cyclical recessions. Land speculation, he asserted, was not the only cause of depressions, but it was "the great initiatory cause."

Land speculation operates at two different levels of intensity. Speculation contributes to depressions by enabling landowners to demand prices that are extraordinarily high: in effect, the elevated land prices demand a part of tomorrow's output today. The effect is to milk the returns to capital and labor. But this can be tolerated only up to a point, beyond which it becomes uneconomic to employ either capital or labor, and unemployment ensues. Second, rapidly rising prices enable speculators to hold land idle in the expectation of future capital gains—a wait-and-see strategy. As a result, scarce land is withheld from production—an action that prevents new employment—and as a consequence of the contraction in supply the level of rents of land in use is pushed up. This process has the effect of bankrupting some firms that would otherwise be profitable and competitive.

George used largely impressionistic evidence to support his theory, but Hoyt (1950) discovered a regular 18-year cycle in U.S. historical data between 1818 and 1929, with close correlation between the trends in land values and in the business cycle.

We expect to see a rise in land values, for as national income increases, so does the surplus, or economic rents. Income depends on the functioning of the labor and capital markets, and a downturn in national income results in a drop in land values. This is the popular view. Harrison (1983), however, found in Hoyt's data that the peak in land values is reached 12 to 14 months before the economic recession; that is, the downturn in land values precedes the decline in general economic prosperity. Harrison postulated a transmission mechanism by which antecedent behavior in the land market is diffused into the whole economy. In the construction industry, if the land costs too much because of speculation, construction is curtailed, thereby decreasing the activity throughout the economy.

Evolution of Land Problems in Korea

Current Status of National Land Use

Korea is an extremely crowded country, with a total land area of about 99,222 square kilometers and a population of 42 million people. The population density of more than 427 people per square kilometer is greater than that of any other relatively populous country (i.e., with at least four million people), except for Bangladesh and Taiwan. Korea, like Japan, is mountainous and only about one-fifth of its land is suitable for agriculture or urban uses. By contrast, Belgium and the Netherlands have comparable population densities but flat terrain, and most land there is suitable for agriculture or urban uses.

Land in Korea can be divided into four categories. Forested land occupies 66.2 percent of the total land area, agriculture land 22.6 percent, and land for other nonurban uses (including water surfaces) 7.7 percent. This leaves only about 4,000 square kilometers (4.0 percent) for urban uses such as residential, industrial, and public purposes (including roads, parks, and schools). This economically valuable land can be divided according to use: 1.8 percent, residential; 0.2 percent, industrial; and 2.0 percent, public use (as of 1987, KRIHS 1988).

Land Systems

Basically, the most efficient use of land can be realized through the mechanism of the competitive free market. However, such reliance on the free market becomes inefficient in circumstances where public goods and externalities play an important role. The free competitive market's function for dynamic efficiency in land use is unreliable, especially where speculation is involved. These market failures in land use provide a rationale for government intervention in the land market.

"Land system" as used in this chapter means a series of laws for government intervention in the private ownership of land, including limitations on exercising the right to use land, taxation on the right to earn from land, and expropriation of the right to dispose of land. Remarkable progress has been made since 1961 in the institutional arrangements for the control of land use in Korea. Various laws necessary for the development of cities, regions, and public lands have been enacted. The City Planning Law was enacted in 1962 to accommodate urbanization in a planned and orderly manner, and the National Land Use Planning Act was promulgated in 1963 for the purpose of advancing planned land use throughout the country. The first National Land Use Plan, implemented from 1972 to 1982, extended to the entire country the restrictions on land use that were already applicable to urban areas.

A reasonable land use plan is an indispensable prerequisite to land policy. Its purpose is to control the use of land; that is, the government prohibits specified forms of land use within designated areas. In this way, land use can be limited to a certain extent. On the other hand, neither the City Planning Law nor the National Land Use Planning Act has the power to positively encourage specific forms of land use. Because the system of land use control cannot advance the conversion of forestland and farmland into urban land, it cannot effectively control land prices. The National Land Use Planning Act provides for a system of designated areas where land prices are controlled. But it is unrealistic to designate as controlled areas all the suburban zones where demand for land is strong. Even if such an area were designated, there would be widespread black marketeering.

While control over land use may deter undesirable uses of land, land expropriation can result in desirable uses. The Eminent Domain Law was enacted in 1962 mainly to facilitate the construction of industrial sites, and the Land Readjustment Project Law was passed in 1966 to promote urban land development. In the case of eminent domain, private land ownership is terminated with compensation paid in exchange, while a land readjustment project offers substitute land in exchange for the termination of private land ownership.

Various kinds of taxes are imposed on land. The acquisition tax is imposed on newly acquired land. The tax base is the declared price of land, and the basic rate is 2 percent (for golf courses, high-cost residences, and corporate land used for nonbusiness purposes, the rate is 15 percent). A registration tax is also imposed. The tax base is the declared value of the land as registered by the owner. But in cases where the tax base is not reported or the value at the time of acquisition is less than the "standard value" determined by the government each year, the standard value at the time of registration is deemed to be the tax base. In actual practice, the standard value usually serves as the tax base. The basic registration tax rate is 3 percent, but a preferential tax rate of 1 percent is applied to farmland. The heavy taxation on land transactions has been criticized as disruptive to the smooth functioning of the land market.

Until 1990, a property tax was imposed annually on the land owners listed in the land tax registers. The property tax base was the current value of the land, and the tax rate ranged from 0.1 percent for farmland and woodlands to 5 percent for land used for golf courses and high-cost places of amusement. A progressive rate, depending on the area and ranging from 0.3 to 5.0 percent, was applied to household lots. In addition, an excessive landholding tax was imposed on individuals and corporations in cases where land was not used directly for the respective owners' business purposes. These two taxes were superseded in 1990 by the Global Land Value Tax.

As a type of capital gains tax, the Temporary Antispeculation Tax on Real Estate was enacted in 1969 to curb land speculation along the route of the Seoul–Pusan Expressway, which was planned in 1969 and completed in 1970. This tax was incorporated into the income tax in 1975, and subsequently the real estate capital gains tax has been subject to frequent revisions. The tax base in the current tax system is real capital gain—that is, the transfer amount, less necessary expenses (including those for land improvement and transfer), less appreciation at the rate of increase of the wholesale price index, less a deduction in the amount of 1.5 million won. The deduction and the appreciation, however, do not apply to cases where the land has been held for less than two years or held without registration. In cases of long-term holding, a special deduction is applicable: 10 percent of the capital gain can be deducted for land held between five and ten years and 30 percent for land held more than ten years. Progressive tax rates from 40 to 60 percent are applied to taxable capital gains.

The capital gains of a corporation are included in the ordinary taxable income subject to the corporate tax, then the Additional Capital Gains tax is specially assessed and added to the amount of the ordinary corporate tax. Consequently, the capital gains of a corporation from land acquired for nonbusiness purposes is subject to double taxation. The tax base is defined similarly to individual income tax, and the tax rate is 25 percent.

The inheritance tax on land is levied on the legal heir of the deceased, and the tax calculations area based on the total estimated value of the inherited land less deductions, debt, funeral expenses, and public imposts. Various deductions are allowed: a basic deduction in the amount of 10 million won, a personal deduction of 40 million won for a spouse, and a 10 million won deduction for each child. A larger deduction in the amount of 110 million won is allowed for farmland, grassland, and forestland. A progressive rate scheme, ranging from 5 to 55 percent, is applied to the tax base defined.

Trends in Land Values

Since the mid-1960s, the rapid increase of land prices has emerged as a serious economic, social, and political problem in Korea. As economic development plans were successful, industrialization proceeded rapidly. The resulting rapid urbanization has caused the demand for land for urban uses such as industrial sites, residential sites, and public sites to increase quickly; thus, land prices have risen dramatically around industrial complexes and in the cities and their surrounding areas, where there is heavy pressure for development.

It is not possible to construct aggregate land price indexes for all Korean land. But the Korea Appraisal Board has conducted land price surveys in urban areas since the 1960s, and the Ministry of Construction has conducted land price surveys across the country since 1975. The rate of increase in land prices and other major economic indicators for Korea's twelve largest cities are presented in Table 12.1 for the period 1963–89. The consumer price index and the growth rate of GNP are presented for comparison. Land prices have risen rapidly indeed. Land prices in Korea's largest twelve cities in this period increased by 618 times, whereas GNP in current prices increased by 386 times. This represents a compounded average annual growth rate of 23.8 percent.

Part of this extraordinary gain is, of course, due to inflation. In 1989 the wholesale price index was about 18.4 times its 1963 level, representing an average compounded inflation rate of 10.7 percent. But these data imply that the average real rate of return on landholding was 13.1 percent in urban Korea during the 27-year period. This return is in addition to annual rents paid for use of the land.

TABLE 12.1
Annual percentage increase of land prices, GNP, and wholesale prices, 1963–1989

	Major cities land price	GNP growth	WPI	CPI	Nominal GNP	Urbanization (% of total population)	Money supply (M2)	Permitted floor area in building construction
1963	na	9.1	20.5	na	41.4	40.0	7.4	18.5
1964	50.0	9.6	35.0	na	42.4	41.0	14.8	21.6
1965	35.3	5.8	9.6	na	12.5	41.0	52.7	24.0
1966	41.4	12.7	8.8	11.6	28.7	42.0	61.7	15.8
1967	43.6	6.6	6.8	10.7	23.5	44.0	61.7	30.6
1968	48.5	11.3	3.1	10.8	29.0	45.0	72.0	31.1
1969	80.7	13.8	6.5	12.3	30.4	47.0	61.4	24.0
1970	29.7	7.6	9.1	15.4	24.5	50.0	27.4	12.7
1971	33.4	9.1	10.6	14.0	22.7	50.0	20.8	–10.8
1972	7.5	5.3	12.1	11.7	22.6	52.0	33.8	–9.5
1973	5.8	14.0	6.7	3.0	28.2	54.0	36.4	90.5
1974	18.7	8.5	42.3	24.3	41.2	56.0	24.0	1.9
1975	25.5	6.8	26.5	25.4	33.1	57.0	28.2	9.1
1976	24.9	13.4	12.2	15.3	37.3	59.0	33.5	–2.4
1977	50.0	10.7	9.0	10.0	28.3	61.0	39.7	24.2
1978	79.1	11.0	11.6	14.5	35.0	63.0	35.0	37.9
1979	22.0	7.0	18.8	18.2	28.4	65.0	24.6	–10.8
1980	17.0	–4.8	38.9	28.7	19.3	68.0	26.9	–6.5
1981	7.1	5.9	18.8	21.6	23.9	69.0	25.0	–19.0
1982	5.6	7.2	4.4	7.1	14.6	70.0	27.0	42.9
1983	31.7	12.6	0.2	3.4	18.3	72.0	15.2	33.2
1984	21.6	9.3	0.8	2.3	13.5	73.0	7.7	–0.3
1985	7.8	7.0	0.9	2.5	11.4	74.0	15.6	–3.4
1986	6.4	12.9	–1.5	2.8	16.0	75.2	18.4	13.9
1987	13.9	12.8	0.5	3.0	16.7	na	19.1	10.2
1988	29.8	12.2	2.7	7.1	17.0	na	21.5	24.6
1989	30.5	6.5	1.1	5.2	11.0	na	11.8	17.7

Source: EPB, *Korea Statistical Yearbook* (various years); EPB, *Monthly Economic Statistics* (various issues); Ministry of Construction, "Change Rate of Land Prices" (various issues); Korea Appraisal Board, "Survey of Market Prices of Land" (various issues).

na = not available.

TABLE 12.2
Land values and business cycles, 1969–1988

Peaks land price increases	Building cycle peaks in	Economic recessions in
1969	1969	1970
1978	1978	1979
1983	1982	1984
1988	1988	1989

The implication is that holding urban land must have been one of the most profitable investments in Korea during the period of rapid growth.

The Korean economy has experienced three ten-year land speculation cycles since 1962. The annual increase in land prices for the major cities and the annual growth of GNP at current prices are presented in Figure 12.1. The differences between these two rates and the annual increase in land prices and the consumer price indexes for all cities are presented in Figure 12.2. The Korean experience of land speculation shown in Figure 12.1 seems to support George's hypothesis on the cause of recession, as illustrated in Table 12.2. Figures 12.1 and 12.2 show that the period 1962–89 can be divided into three periods: 1962–69, 1970–78, and 1979–89.

First Phase, 1962–69 During the first period, the annual increase rate of land prices was about 35 percent. Moreover, the difference between this increase and that of the consumer price index was greater than 25 percent. The increase in land prices was much higher than the growth of GNP at current prices in every year. Since the annual price rise of 35 percent or more was much higher than the average commercial bank interest rate, real estate was generally accepted as the most profitable investment whenever surplus funds were available. During this period, the myth of profit-bearing land became deeply rooted in the thinking of Koreans, and a fetishism about land dominated the Korean mentality. The big companies, like their Japanese counterparts, searched for land more because of this fetishism than because of actual need.

The entry of the Korean economy into the high-growth stage in the mid-1960s witnessed the movement of the labor force from primary to secondary and tertiary industries. This interindustrial labor force movement gave rise at the same time to an interregional population migration. There was a continuous and intensive population influx into the Seoul and Pusan areas. Rapid urbanization was accelerated by the rapid growth of GNP, particularly as a result of the urban-oriented manufacturing and service sectors, which are relatively labor-intensive. The urban share of the population soared from 36 percent in 1960 to 50 percent in 1970. Rapid urbanization had a strong impact on the demand for land in urban areas. Land prices in urban areas rose rapidly, but land prices in rural areas fell in real terms.

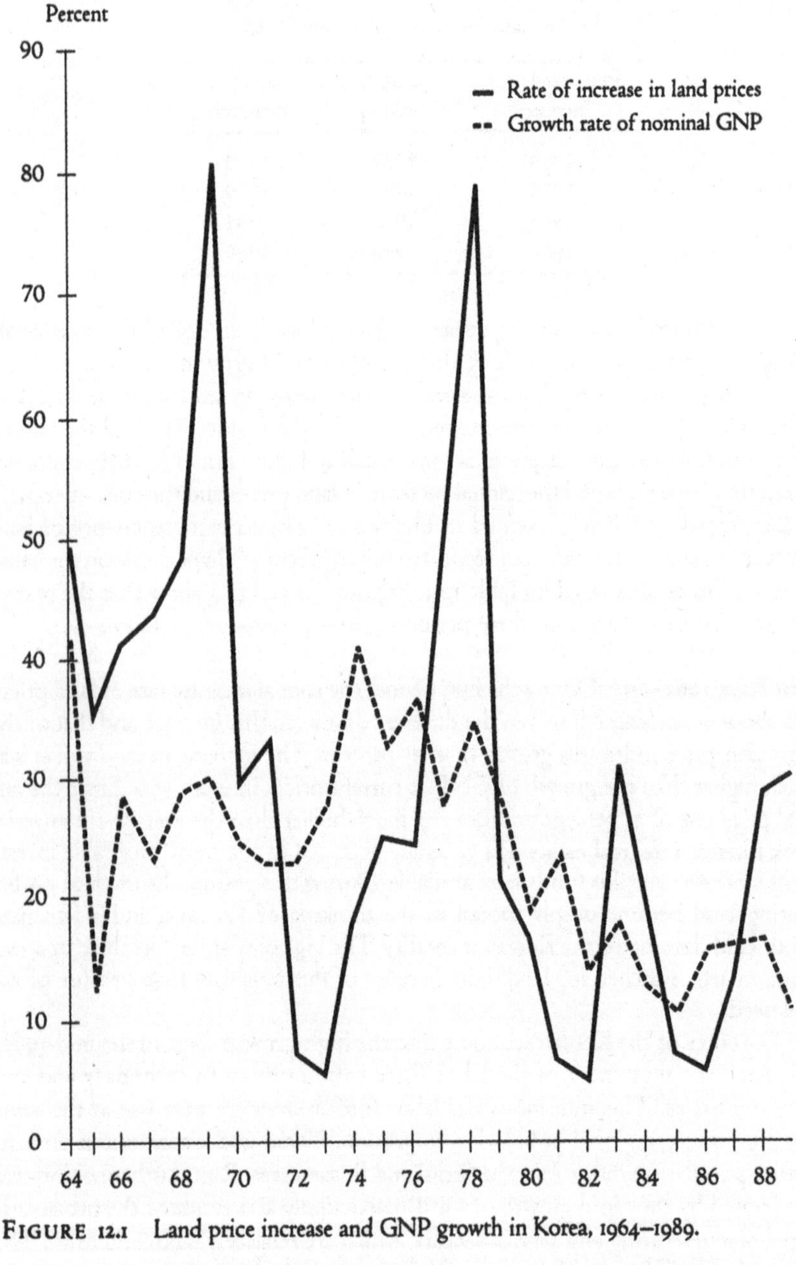

FIGURE 12.1 Land price increase and GNP growth in Korea, 1964–1989.

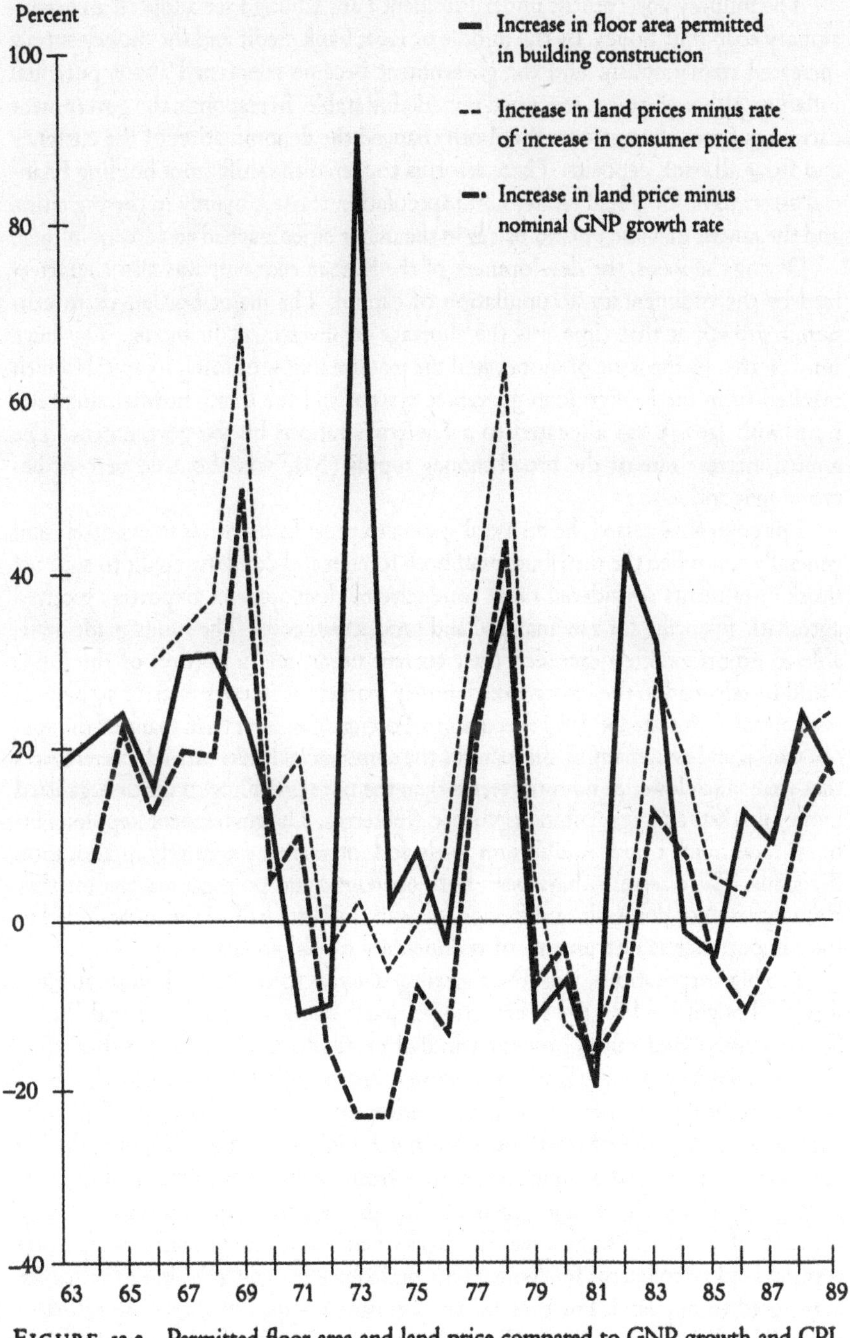

FIGURE 12.2 Permitted floor area and land price compared to GNP growth and CPI, 1963–1989.

The military government under President Park Chung Hee adopted an expansionary economic policy. By the middle of 1962, bank credit and the money supply increased tremendously, and the government became concerned about potential inflation, although prices remained remarkably stable. In response, the government carried out monetary reform that both changed the denomination of the currency and froze all bank deposits. These reforms triggered the shift from holding financial assets to holding real estate. Land speculation started, mainly in the big cities, and the rate of increase in land prices in the major cities reached 50 percent in 1964.

During the 1960s, the development of the Korean economy was also characterized by the rudimentary accumulation of capital. The major bottleneck to economic growth at that time was the shortage of investment financing. The huge fund created by the issue of money and the massive inflow of foreign capital (which resulted from the foreign loan guarantee system and the treaty normalizing relations with Japan) was allocated to a few corporations by the government. The annual increase rate of the broad money supply (M2) was about 60 percent between 1965 and 1970.

The government used the financial system to provide incentives to exporters and generally controlled the distribution of both foreign and domestic credit to support those investments considered most conducive to development. Exporters received automatic financing for raw material and production costs. The funds made available to exporters often exceeded their current needs, and a portion of the funds could be reloaned in the unorganized money markets at interest rates of 30 percent per annum, or invested in land speculation. Foreign loans, the term loans of the special banks, and even many of the loans of the commercial banks carried interest rates that were much lower in nominal terms than the rates prevailing in the unorganized money markets and were often negative in real terms. The government kept loan interest rates much below equilibrium levels and intervened extensively in allocation decisions. There seem to have been both economic and political reasons for this. Rapid growth of domestic and foreign loans in the latter half of the 1960s added to their importance as instruments of rudimentary capital accumulation.

The big corporations, with their privileged access to credit, both domestic and foreign, bought land on the urban fringes, particularly around Seoul and Pusan. Rapidly rising land values brought windfall profits to landowners in urban areas and attracted savings away from productive investment. Land speculation has been an important link in the capital accumulation process since the 1960s. Since the annual percentage rise of land prices was much higher than the bank rate, the big corporations borrowed as much as possible from banks to buy land, and they expected large profits. The larger the landholdings, the greater the guarantee of large future profits. At the same time, the banks had a traditional preference for accepting land as collateral for loans. This preference made it possible to refinance loans used to buy land. For these reasons, private companies spared no effort in expanding their landholdings. Consequently, speculation-based demand invited more speculation, and the ever-increasing demand surpassed the limited supply of urban land, causing prices to skyrocket.

Land prices in the major cities increased by more than 40 percent during the second half of the 1960s. The land speculation peak in 1969 was initially caused by the announcement of construction plans for the Seoul–Pusan Expressway and the development plan for the southern part of Seoul. The government adopted the Antispeculation Tax in Real Estate in 1967, which was a kind of capital gains tax on real estate. This law, however, was not as effective as expected.

Second Phase, 1970–78 Korea experienced an economic downturn in 1970, before the oil crisis struck in 1973. Land speculators were caught in the classic squeeze of having to finance the large loans they had taken out to buy land. The bubble of inflated land prices burst, and the big corporations were on the verge of insolvency. The interest rate in the unorganized money markets had become unsupportably high due to excessive borrowing for purposes such as speculation in land.

Korean landowners, like their counterparts in Japan who were rescued by government and central bank "lifeboat" operations, were effectively insured against the costs of their own economic excesses. Land values were held buoyant, instead of becoming the most seriously depressed of all factor prices.

As predicted by Goerge's theory, the peak in the increase in land prices in 1969 was followed by economic recession. The economic growth rate was 7.6 percent in 1970, much lower than the 13.8 percent rate of 1969. Monetary expansion and the increase in the consumer price index slowed during the early 1970s. Also, land price increases in urban areas had dropped to 7.5 percent in 1972 and 5.8 percent in 1974. The government came forth in the summer of 1972 with the August 3 Emergency Measures, which provided relief to large business interests at the expense of the unorganized money market. The government also tried to promote the development of the securities markets and finance companies. In 1973 the government initiated an aggressive approach by requiring certain companies, identified by the Ministry of Finance, to go public. The stock market boomed in both 1972 and 1973. During that period, securities and short-term bills were probably competitive with urban land as an alternative to investors.

During the 1970s the emphasis of industrialization policy was switched to the promotion of heavy industry. The southeastern coastal region emerged as the major growth area during this period, and the rate of growth of Seoul was outstripped by that of several cities in the region (such as Ulsan, Masan, and Pohang), where the government constructed ports and other infrastructure.

Land speculation boomed again in the late 1970s. Land prices in major cities increased 50 percent in 1977 and 79 percent 1978. In Seoul they increased by 136 percent in 1978. Speculation in apartments emerged at this time. Land speculation began to spread beyond the southeastern coastal region.

The national land price increased by 34 percent in 1977 and by 50 percent in 1978. Land speculation during the period was triggered by a sharp increase in the money supply, resulting from domestic money creation to support heavy industry as well as the inflow of foreign exchange from the Middle East construction boom. The government adopted the August 8 measure in 1978, which raised tax rates on capital gains from real estate.

Third Phase, 1979–89 The so-called miracle economy was unable to avoid the distress of the late 1970s, which was officially attributed to the OPEC oil price explosion. Again, the land speculation peak in 1978 was followed by economic recession. Therefore, with the slump in construction that occurred a full 12 months before the oil price rise, the Korean economy was destined for a recession of severe proportions regardless of the decisions taken by the oil sheikhs. The economic growth rate slowed from 13.8 percent in 1978 to 7.6 percent in 1979, and the Korean economy experienced negative economic growth in 1980. Urban land prices fell in real terms by 11.7 percent in 1980, 14.5 percent in 1981, and 1.4 percent in 1982.

Noting that land prices were already extraordinarily high in the big cities, the government correctly predicted that a rise in land prices would make it difficult for people to own detached houses. The declining demand associated with high prices was in turn linked to a downturn in the building industry. Expansion of housing investment is necessary to provide demand for stable economic growth.

In the early 1980s, efforts were made to boost the overall economy by stimulating the housing industry through legislation, such as the June 26, January 4, May 18, and June 28 measures. The mixture of tax policies and large-scale public investment in housing (designed to restimulate the depressed economy) ensured a premature recovery of land prices, which started accelerating upward again. Land speculation came to the fore again around late 1982. Land prices in the major cities increased by 28.3 percent and those in Seoul rose by 54.3 percent in real terms in 1983.

A series of speculation control measures were again adopted, including the December 22 Speculation Control Measure at the end of 1982; the February 16 measure in 1983; the Notice of Specially Designated Areas in February and March 1983; implementation of bond bidding for apartment houses in 1983; and the April 18 Overall Land and House Measure and Land Transaction Report System for the Daeduk Research Complex in Choongchung Nam-do Province in 1985.

There was a decline in land speculation between 1984 and 1987; land prices in urban areas remained stable but rents rose rapidly, preparing the way for further land speculation in 1988. The rapid growth of exports and the large foreign trade surplus between 1986 and 1988 caused a large amount of foreign currency to flow suddenly into Korea, thereby causing excessive liquidity in the Korean money market. This excessive liquidity triggered a renewed round of land speculation around 1988 that was accelerated by the government's development plan for the southwestern region of the country and by the Olympic Games in Seoul. The increase in land prices in urban areas was 30 percent in both 1988 and 1989. This most recent bout of land speculation has spread across the entire country. The national average increase in land prices has been higher than any registered in urban areas since 1986. In particular, land speculation has centered around the southwestern coastal region, which is expected to be developed as a new industrial site. The government adopted the August 10 measure to control land speculation in 1988, but the land speculation boom continued until mid-1989.

National Land Values

The Korea Land Development Corporation estimated the market value of land in Korea as of October 1988 (Table 12.3). Nonmarketable lands such as streams, lakes, rivers, roads, and parks are excluded from this estimate. A total of 14,038 plots were drawn by the multistage stratified random sampling method according to category of use and administrative district. Each sample was evaluated using the market data approach, which was then used to calculate total land values by multiplying sample average land values by total land area in each category.

The market value of Korea's land was estimated to be 936,931 billion won in August 1988. By comparison, Korea's 1988 GNP was 123,579 billion won. Thus Korea's total land value was about 7.58 times annual GNP. A comparable estimate for the United States concludes that the market value of U.S. land was 0.7 times the U.S. GNP. Land value in the United Kingdom was estimated to be double the annual GNP. Land in Japan was worth about 6.5 times annual GNP in 1988.[1]

Land values in relation to GNP vary greatly among countries. An explanation for these differences is the relative scarcity of land. Korea and Japan are densely populated countries, whereas the United States is among the most land-rich of industrialized countries. But this cannot be the entire explanation. It is reasonable to assume that U.S. land rents are capitalized into land values at an interest rate of about 10 percent. That assumption and the fact that land values are about 70 percent of GNP imply that a constant land rent would be about 7 percent of GNP according to equation 1. This number is very close to the best estimate of the rate of capitalization of land rents in the United States.

Ten percent is a low interest rate to assume for capitalizing land rents in Japan and Korea. Even that low rate would imply that land rents are 76 percent of GNP in Korea and about 65 percent in Japan. It is not possible to check this against the GNP accounts because land rents are not reported separately from other GNP components. But the Japanese figure of 65 percent of GNP exceeds the percentage of all property income in GNP, and a large proportion of property income is clearly derived from produced capital. The Korean figure is even higher than the percentage of all property income in Korean GNP, but it seems very unlikely that land rents are as much as 76 percent of Korean GNP. A possible resolution of this paradox may be that the forecasted rapid future growth of land rents has been capitalized into land values in Japan and Korea. This could cause land values to be

Table 12.3
Land values by category and area, 1988

	Total area (km^2)	Average price (10^3 won/m^2)	Total land value (10^9 won)
Residential	1,485 (1.6)	261.42	388,354 (41.5)
Commercial	170 (0.2)	924.34	156,721 (16.7)
Industrial	452 (0.5)	105.84	47,886 (5.1)
Forest	8,215 (8.9)	15.52	127,520 (13.6)
Nonurban	81,901 (88.8)	2.64	216,448 (23.1)
Total	92,223	10.16	936,931
Residential	596	499.39	297,846
Commercial	66	1,438.84	95,582
Industrial	131	243.84	31,875
Forest	1,448	42.88	62,109
Nonurban	75	14.09	1,058
Six big cities	2,317 (2.4)	210.82	488,470 (52.1)
Residential	479	161.40	72,110
Commercial	63	88.16	52,101
Industrial	225	57.05	12,904
Forest	2,658	16.47	41,932
Nonurban	1,142	6.60	7,536
Medium and small cities	4,567 (5.1)	43.99	186,585 (19.9)
Residential	410	44.82	18,397
Commercial	41	222.57	9,038
Industrial	96	32.26	3,106
Forest	4,108	5.72	23,478
Nonurban	80,684	2.58	207,853
Rural area	85,339 (92.5)	3.07	261,874 (28.0)

Source: Korea Land Development Corporation (1989).

high relative to land rents. Thus, the expectation of continued rapid economic growth can be an important explanation of the high ratio of land values to GNP in Korea and Japan. But even this cannot be the entire explanation. It may be that classical economic theory on land price is not applicable to Korea and Japan. Are people in Korea and Japan irrational in expecting such high future land rents?

In Korea, as elsewhere, urban land prices are much higher than rural land prices. The data in Table 12.3 imply that urban land in Korea's six largest cities is on average worth 69 times as much as rural land. In fact, of total land the 2.4 percent that is in urban areas accounts for more than 52 percent of total land value. One reason for this is that, in urban activities, structures and other improvements can be substituted for land much more easily than in agriculture and other rural activities.

Table 12.3 also shows that the average price of residential land in the six largest cities was 499,000 won per square kilometer (US$3 million per acre). This is certainly much higher than the average price of urban residential land in the United States. A traditional Korean single-family urban home might be on a plot of about 50 pyong (1 pyong = 3.31 m^2). The value of such a plot was about 83 million won ($120,000) in 1988. This compares with an average wage income of about 5.4 million won in the six largest cities. The figures imply that the value of a residential plot is equal to about 15 years of wage income and 45 years of average savings, assuming that the average propensity to save is one-third.

Concentration of Land Ownership

In most Western societies, land is more equitably distributed than any other important asset. The same was true in Korea until the early 1960s, when most farmland was in the hands of owner-operators as a result of land reforms carried out during the previous decade. Most housing in the early 1960s was owner-occupied, and land was more widely held by the populace than financial assets, including corporate assets. Under these conditions, rapid increases in land values had the effect of decreasing the concentration of wealth. The situation has, however, changed dramatically. Now the ownership of land in Korea is highly concentrated among a few wealthy owners.

Rapid increases in land values in the process of the cyclical land speculation have made the return on investment in land much higher than that on investment in securities, on profits from manufacturing enterprises, or on any other investment. Land has become the most profitable asset, rather than an input to production or for housing. But not everyone can make a large fortune from investment in land. A relatively large initial investment is often required to buy land. Moreover, successful speculation in land requires accurate information on the government's regional development plans. Thus, a few persons with access to the requisite funds and information—both of which have been controlled by the government—were able to make large fortunes from investment in land. Ordinary persons, however, could not gain access even to bank financing at low interest rates. The government has provided only minimal financing of mortgages. Bank financing has amounted to less than 5 percent of the value of homes purchased in urban areas. The extreme scarcity of bank financing for the purchase of dwellings has made it very difficult for families to buy their own homes.

Housing development has been largely left to private enterprise, which relies on its own financial resources. As a result, urban landlordism has become widespread. Urban landlords are potential land speculators who seek capital gains rather than rents. This process has accelerated in the course of cyclical land speculation since the mid-1960s. The increases in land values were mostly limited to a few big cities in the 1960s, but today they extend from one end of the country to the other. Much of the speculation involves land earmarked by the government for new towns and factory sites. The government's regional development plans have led to renewed speculation. Many people believe that politicians and the bureaucracy, who have access to information on regional development plans, are able to make large fortunes from the land booms. Many privileged companies and individuals have poured extensive funds into land speculation. As a result, much of the country's total land area is now owned by a few wealthy people.

Land ownership in Korea can be divided into three categories: 24.3 percent of land

Table 12.4
Distribution of land ownership by individuals, 1988

	Ownership category	% of total area	Area per person (m^2)
	Top 5%	65.2	86.7
I	Top 10%	76.9	51.1
II	10–20%	10.8	7.2
III	20–30%	5.4	3.6
IV	30–40%	3.2	2.1
V	40–50%	1.9	1.2
VI	50–60%	1.0	0.7
VII	60–70%	0.5	0.4
VIII	70–80%	0.3	0.2
IX	80–90%	0.2	0.1
X	90–100%	0.0	0.04
All owners		100.0	6.7

Source: KRIHS (1988).

Table 12.5
Distribution of land ownership by category of use, 1988

	% of total land area owned by		
	Top 5% of owners	Top 20% of owners	Top 40% of owners
Residential	59.7	72.5	11.5
Industrial	35.1	53.1	na
Dry field agriculture	29.5	69.8	1.6
Paddy fields	31.9	72.7	0.4
Forest	84.1	97.7	0.1
Miscellaneous	61.3	85.7	1.9
Other uses	64.8	81.4	4.8
Total land area	65.2	87.6	1.0

Source: KRIHS (1988). na = not available.

Table 12.6

Distribution of land ownership by city, 1988

City	% of total land area owned by: Top 5% of owners	Top 10% of owners
Seoul	57.7	65.9
Pusan	72.3	81.4
Taegu	72.6	82.4
Inchon	64.2	77.8
Kwangju	55.7	69.4
Taejon	65.1	76.4
Total land area in Korea	65.2	76.9

Source: KRIHS (1988).

Table 12.7

Capital gains from land, 1975–1989

	Increase in land values (%)	Capital gains (10^{12} won) (1)	GNP (10^{12} current won) (2)	Ratio (½)
1975	27.0	24.9	10.1	2.5
1976	26.6	31.2	13.8	2.3
1977	33.6	49.8	17.7	2.8
1978	49.0	97.1	23.9	4.1
1979	16.6	49.1	30.7	1.1
1980	11.7	40.3	36.7	1.1
1981	7.5	28.8	45.2	0.6
1982	5.4	22.3	52.2	0.4
1983	18.5	80.7	61.7	1.3
1984	13.2	68.1	70.1	1.0
1985	7.0	41.0	78.1	0.5
1986	7.3	45.6	90.5	0.5
1987	14.7	98.7	105.6	0.9
1988	27.5	211.1	123.6	1.7
1989	30.5	299.4	137.1	2.2

Source: Korea Land Development Corporation (1989), and Ministry of Construction, "Change Rate of Land Prices" (various issues).

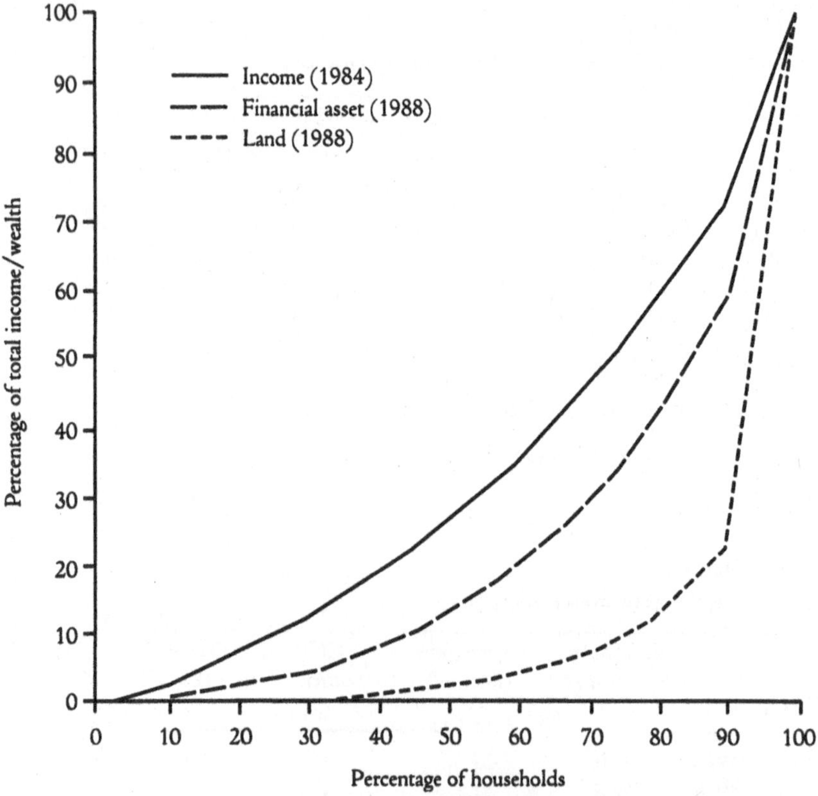

FIGURE 12.3 Lorentz curves (adapted from Kang 1989).

is owned by the public sector, 4.1 percent by corporations, and the remaining 66.1 percent by individuals (10,801,000 persons). In 1988 the top 5 percent of all landowners owned 65.2 percent of the total area owned by individuals, and the top 10 percent owned 76.9 percent (Table 12.4). In particular, the concentration of land ownership is strong in residential/commercial land and forestland that is expected to be developed for urban uses. Thus, recent land speculation has concentrated on these lands. As shown in Table 12.5, the top 5 percent of landowners account for 84.1 percent of the total forest area and for 59.7 percent of the residential and commercial area. Table 12.6 shows that land ownership by the top 10 percent ranges from 66 to 82 percent of the total urban area in each of the six largest cities. This implies that land ownership is more concentrated in urban areas, where land prices are higher.

Most households in the big cities do not own any land at all. Only 28.1 percent of households in Seoul own land. The share of households that own land is 33.1 percent in Pusan, 38.3 percent in Taegu, 30.1 percent in Inchon, and 69.7 percent in Kwangju. The Gini coefficient of the distribution of the landownership in the big cities is 0.911 in Seoul, 0.946 in Pusan, 0.937 in Inchon, and 0.838 in Kwangju

(KRIHS 1988). Figure 12.3 shows that land ownership is much more concentrated than is the ownership of financial assets or the distribution of income in Korea. Thus, rapidly rising land values since the 1960s have caused income distribution to become more unequal in Korea. Large fortunes from land speculation resulted in a large portion of social wealth being placed in the hands of a few landowners, who do not contribute anything to the wealth of the nation.

Tremendous amounts of wealth have been transferred to a few landowners from the active agents of the wealth-creating process—the workers and their current and future accumulated savings—in the form of capital gains. Table 12.7 presents annual capital gains from land due to the increase in land prices, based on the total marketable land value shown above and the increase in national land prices estimated by the Ministry of Construction. Table 12.7 also shows the ratio of capital gains to GNP in current prices. In the most recent phase of the land speculation cycle (1979–88), the ratio was 0.98 on average, indicating that a few landowners have milked the savings of persons who need homes or factory sites to an extent almost equivalent to the annual GNP.

Evolution of Land Problems in Japan

Despite its formidable economic growth, Japan has one of the worse-housed populations in the industrialized world. People live in wooden structures, cramped for want of space. During the past few decades, the housing situation of the Japanese people—particularly the working class in major metropolitan areas—has not improved. It has, in fact, worsened. The most important reason for the poor housing situation in Japan is the rapid increase in land prices.

Japan is a crowded country. Its overall population density is 316 people per square kilometer. And Japan is even more crowded than this figure suggests: 61 percent of its land is mountainous. Only one-quarter of the country's land has slopes of less than 15 degrees. Both farms and cities are thus concentrated on the small amount of relatively flat land.

Japan is one of the world's most industrialized and urbanized countries. Since 1945 the urbanization of Japan has been among the fastest in the world: the urban population more than tripled during 1945–70. The proportion of Japanese living in cities rose from 28 percent in 1945 to 72.2 percent in 1972. The rate of urbanization has not been uniform across the country. After the outbreak of the Korean War, industrial growth was heavily concentrated in the largest cities along the Pacific Coastal Belt. Much of the growth of settlement was inevitably on the gently sloping and flat lands of the Kanton Plain and the other lowlands, which had traditionally been major areas of agriculture.

Trends in Land Values

Japanese land values have risen rapidly during the period of postwar economic growth. Under the influence of roaring inflation, the price of urban land escalated by a factor of 26 between 1945 and 1950. This, however, represented a loss in real value. During the same period, wholesale commodity prices rose by as much as 82 times. The adjustment in relative values occurred between 1951 and 1955. Land prices maintained their upward trend, but wholesale commodities and land were valued at 326 and 325, respectively, when compared with those of 1936. The market had returned to a state of prewar normality, and so 1955 has been used as the base year for comparing urban land price movements.

Figure 12.4 shows the increase in land prices and the growth of nominal GNP. Figure 12.5 shows the difference between the increase in land prices and the consumer price index. These figures show that the time span from 1956 to 1987 can be divided into four periods: 1956–61, 1962–71, 1972–81, and 1982–87 (Noguchi 1989:29–61).

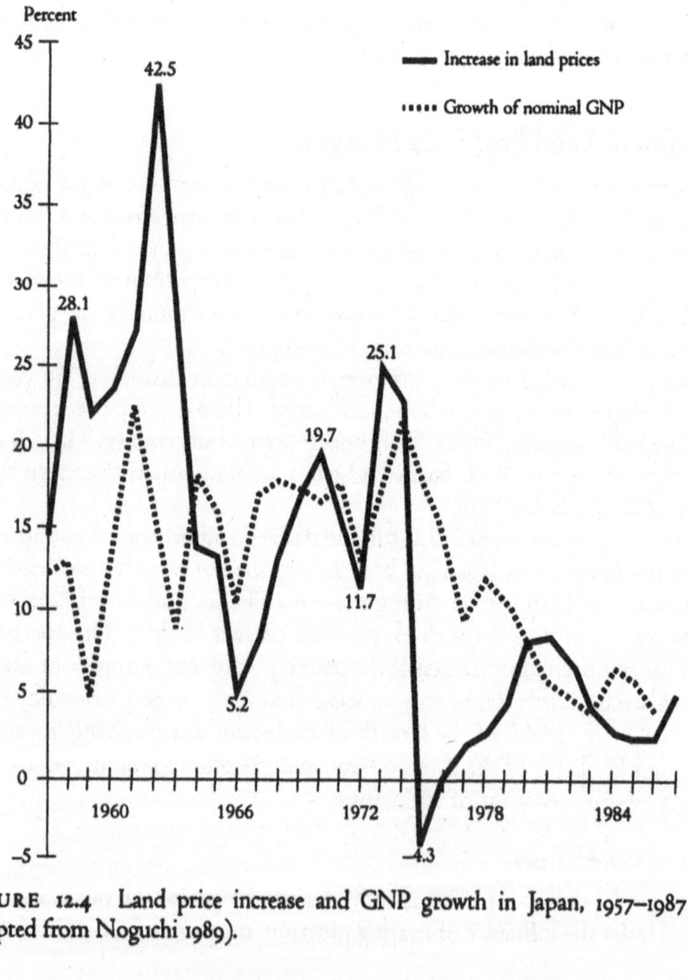

FIGURE 12.4 Land price increase and GNP growth in Japan, 1957–1987 (adapted from Noguchi 1989).

First Phase, 1956–62 During the first period, the annual increase in land prices was above 20 percent. Moreover, the difference between that rate and the consumer price index was greater than 20 percent, except in 1957. The increase in land prices was much higher than the growth rate of GNP at current prices every year.

The Japanese urban land market during this period was characterized by rapidly expanding demand for residential land but a low supply. Demand for residential land in the big cities increased mainly due to the massive population influx into the big cities from the rural areas.

The massive population migration into major cities from farm villages touched off a business boom after the outbreak of the Korean War which activated the

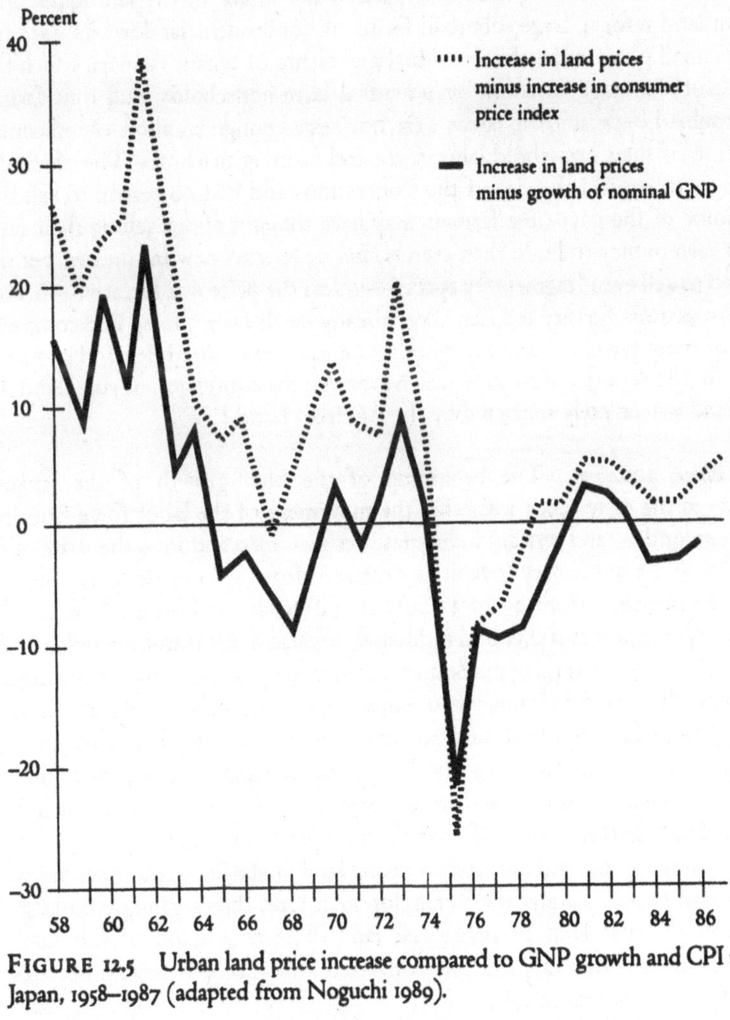

FIGURE 12.5 Urban land price increase compared to GNP growth and CPI in Japan, 1958–1987 (adapted from Noguchi 1989).

"miraculous recovery" of the Japanese economy. The net inflow of farm village population to three major cities during this period was above 400,000 every year. The average income of urban worker households surpassed the farm household income during the so-called Jinmu boom. The young workers from rural farm villages lacked the financial resources to buy land on which to build their own homes; they needed rental units. To meet the needs of these workers, wooden apartment houses were built. These apartments mushroomed throughout the late 1950s and the early 1960s (Hanayama 1986:25).

The demand for factory sites grew even more rapidly than did the demand for residential land in the urban areas during this period. Therefore, the increase in land prices for factory sites was greater than that for residential land. This tendency was reversed during the latter part of the 1960s. In the late 1940s under agrarian land reform, large suburban farms of nonresident landowners were split up into small plots under the individual ownership of tenant farmers, which thus decreased the average farm size of individual farm households. Full-time farmers were troubled because their farms were not large enough to allow the maximum utilization of their household labor force and farming machines. Therefore, they were eager to expand the size of their operations and had no reason to sell their land. Some of the part-time farmers may have thought about selling their farmland to earn money to build their own homes or to start new businesses, but they hesitated to sell even fragmentary spaces—unless the price was lucrative—because such transactions further reduced their already small farm plots. The competing needs for more farmland and for more residential land caused demand to further increase in the suburbs of major cities. Moreover, the conversion of rural land into urban land was severely restricted by the Agrarian Land Law.

Second Phase, 1962–71 The beginning of the high growth of the Japanese economy in the early 1960s witnessed the movement of the labor force from primary to secondary and tertiary industries. Between 1960 and 1970 the share of the total labor force in primary industries decreased from 33 to 19 percent, compared with share increases from 29 to 34 percent in tertiary industries. Not only resources-reliant heavy and chemical industries but also marketing-oriented factories sought sites close to the three major metropolitan areas. Because these growing sectors were located overwhelmingly in urban areas, population in urban areas also increased rapidly. During the second phase, strong demands for better houses were made by the tenants in the cheap wooden apartments and corporate rental houses who had migrated from the rural areas during the first period. Thus demand for residential land in the suburbs of major cities expanded rapidly.

The mounting demand for urban housing land finally led to the amendment of the Agrarian Land Law and the Redevelopment Law, thus legally permitting the conversion of rural land to residential land. The conversion of farmland to housing land increased rapidly. The converted area exceeded 20,000 hectares in 1961 and 30,000 hectares in 1964.

As a result, the supply of housing land expanded, the increase in urban land prices slowed, and the increase in agricultural land prices caught up with that of urban land. Between 1960 and 1971, the national average price of middle-grade paddy land rose sixfold, at a compounded annual rate of over 20 percent after 1967.

The rise in land prices, which far surpassed the increase in the prices of agricultural products or in the cost of living, hindered transactions in farmland. Farmers tended increasingly to retain their land as valuable property rather than as a factor of production. As a result, there was underuse of both farm labor and capital equipment. The explosive rise in rents and land values was not, however, paralleled by a similar rise in farm labor wages. In the absence of an adequate fiscal penalty on underused land, it was worth it to farmers to turn into part-time urban wage earners, sitting on their land in the expectation of future capital gains. Genuine full-time farmers had the lowest average per capita income. As in Korea in the 1960s, land was transformed into a source of profit of mythic proportions in Japan, and fetishism about land began to dominate the Japanese mentality. In summary, the second period was characterized by rapidly expanding demand for residential land in the big cities as well as a rapidly expanding supply of housing land through the conversion of agricultural land.

Third Phase, 1972–81 The third phase was characterized by dramatic changes in land prices and in the volume of rural-urban land conversion. The increase of land prices was again above 20 percent in 1972 and 1973. The volume of rural-urban land conversion reached 60,000 hectares in each of these years. This was caused by rapid growth in the demand for residential land due to land speculation and a dramatic increase in the availability of housing loans.

Land speculation boomed during 1972-73. Since the annual price rise of 20 percent or more was much higher than the average commercial bank interest rate, real estate was generally viewed as the most profitable investment whenever surplus funds were available. In those two years, companies and individuals poured 5–10 trillion yen (US$25–50 billion) into land speculation purchases. Private companies spared no effort in expanding the acreage of land in their possession. Consequently, speculation-based demand invited more speculation, causing demand to greatly surpass the limited supply of untapped land and thus bringing about skyrocketing land prices.

In 1972 and 1973 a large amount of foreign currency suddenly flowed into Japan from speculation in foreign exchange transactions conducted during the transition from the fixed exchange rate system to the floating system, thus causing excessive liquidity in the Japanese money market. In this context, the slogan "Building a New Japan" incited private enterprise to hunt for and buy land far from urban areas. Private enterprise at that time was said to have bought hundreds of thousands of hectares throughout the country.

The supply of residential building land peaked in 1971, then started on a downward course. Farmers, as the original owners of untapped land, preferred to hold land idle in the expectation of even greater capital gains in the future. In addition, farmers in need of cash could raise what they needed by selling lesser acreage because of the rise in land prices.

Japan's economy was declining in 1973, even before the oil crisis. The bubble of inflated land prices had burst. Land prices were extraordinarily high in the big cities, and people could not afford to buy residential land at the asking prices. Consequently, there was a downturn in the construction industry during the first quarter of 1973, and severe economic recession followed. The interest rate had become insupportably high due to excessive borrowing for such purposes as speculation in land. Output fell more heavily in Japan than in other industrialized economies. The real economic growth rate fell from 7.9 percent in 1973 to -1.4 percent in 1974. Real land prices in urban areas fell by 26.1 percent in 1974. The government, alarmed by the effects of land speculation, passed the Progressive Sales Tax on land transaction and the Special Land Retention Tax in 1973. The National Land Use Planning Act was enacted in 1974.

Large-scale public investment in housing and the central bank's expansion of the money supply (designed to restimulate the depressed economy) brought about a premature recovery of land prices, which started moving upward again in 1977. During the latter part of the 1970s housing construction increased, but the rural-to-urban land conversion continued to decrease. The average size of individual housing sites contracted. Land prices increases slowed during this period.

Fourth Phase, 1982–87 The fourth period can be characterized by two developments: the rapid rise in land prices that occurred mainly in the national capital, and the rapid rise in land prices initiated by the rise of commercial land prices. Between 1983 and 1988, the increase in land prices was 192.8 percent in Tokyo, 38 percent in Osaka, and less than 10 percent in rural areas. As described earlier, land speculation was initiated by the rising prices of factory sites in the 1950s and by the skyrocketing prices of residential land in the second and third periods (1962–1981).

As Japan's economy became internationalized and service-oriented, the demand for office space increased rapidly. This brought about sharp increases in commercial land prices in the central business districts. The rise in commercial land prices spread to residential land. Land speculation accelerated the increase in land prices in the metropolitan areas.

Land Use Planning and Control

Institutional arrangements for the control of land use in Japan have made remarkable progress. The City Planning Law was substantially revised in 1968. It prohibits land development without permission from the government (except under certain specified circumstances) and empowers local governments to encourage or discourage the growth of urban areas. Thus, the Japanese are now committed to government controls on the density and other characteristics of residential development and have enacted laws to segregate commercial, industrial, and residential land. The Agricultural Promotion Arrangement Law, which limits the conversion of farmland into residential land, was enacted in 1969.

The trend toward greater government control over land use in Japan was accelerated by the passage in May 1974 of the National Land Use Planning Act, which established land use plans and, perhaps most important, permits prefectural governments to establish control areas within which all land transactions require government permission and are subject to governmentally established price ceilings.

However, neither the National Land Use Planning Act nor the City Planning Law has the power to encourage specific forms of land use positively. These acts can therefore never effectively control land prices. The National Land Use Planning Act provides for a system of designated price control areas for the purpose of freezing land prices. This, however, could lead to widespread black marketeering.

Land expropriation by government can achieve desirable use. The Eminent Domain Law, however, is insufficient to control residential land prices in major urban areas because of the problem of just compensation.

There is no such thing as a society free of landlordism when the benefits of publicly created land values are privately appropriated. It is surprising that so little attention has been paid to taxation of unearned increments in land values in a country that is so concerned with land speculation. A policy of land value taxation was in fact successfully tried in Japan in the early decades of the Meiji Restoration (Harrison 1983:153–161). But land value taxation was not part of the land reform program after World War II.

The postwar reforms sought to eliminate the despised landlords by increasing the number of owner-occupants. But by merely transforming tenants into owners, the "reforms" succeeded only in consolidating the system of land oligopoly, with the privileges enjoyed by an enlarged class. When the fiscal system permits oligopolists to exploit the land market to their advantage, society becomes the tenant of the owner-occupants.

The Meiji land tax had been allowed to degenerate into a system that reinforced speculation. The Shoup Tax Reform Committee combined the land tax and house taxes with the depreciable assets tax and named them the property tax. It is now called real property tax, and its rate has decreased to 1.4 percent, with 0.7 percent upward allowance at the discretion of every municipality. Real property was assessed on the principle of appraisal by market value. The only exception was farmland, which had been subject to taxation on the basis of legally fictitious prices since 1949.

The revision of the Local Taxes Law in 1964 applied the rule of appraisal by market value to farmland and standardized the diverse criteria among municipalities for the assessment of land. The assessed land value at that time was said to be around one-quarter of actual transaction prices for farmland and woodland and around one-sixth for residential land. Farmers' organizations and the opposition parties, however, launched a resolute campaign against such radical tax increases, which led to a partial revision of the Local Taxes Law. Thus, the real property tax has been virtually invalid insofar as farmland is concerned. Farmland on which urban-based families and industries relied for expansion was taxed at only 0.5–1 percent of the rate on residential land. The incentive, then, was for farmland owners to keep their land ostensibly in agricultural use, while their properties appreciated in value.

The Japanese government continued the conventional one-half tax on capital gains—taxing only one-half of the total capital gains in the year when the gains accrued. In response to the land speculation boom in the late 1960s, the proportional tax was imposed on capital gains apart from the other income during the period 1969–75. The tax rate was 10 percent with 5 percent added every other year after 1971. The mushrooming of the land-based nouveaux riches led the government in 1976 to adopt a tax rate of 20 percent on the taxable amount of capital gains of 20 million yen or less, while applying the ordinary progressive tax rate on three-quarters of the amount exceeding 20 million yen. Since 1979, however, the ordinary progressive tax rate has been applied only on one-half of that excess amount.

Comparison of Land Problems in Korea and Japan

There are many similarities in the experiences of Korea and Japan in land problems. Both are extremely crowded mountainous countries. The land system in Korea is very similar to that of Japan. Taxation of unearned increments in land value has not been successful in either country, so most of the benefits of publicly created land value are privately appropriated. Both countries experienced cyclical land speculation during the rapid economic growth period.

There are some striking differences as well. Despite the Japanese tradition of strong, centralized authority, the role of government has been to encourage, rather than direct, the changes that have affected land use. Comprehensive national land development plans and the National Capital Region Development Plan have spelled out government hopes for some dispersal of land development. However, action to achieve this goal has been limited largely to the improvement of infrastructure in the slower growing areas and the offer of subsidies to firms moving to those areas. In contrast, the Korean government exercises direct control over the changes in land use. It has regulated development of new areas on the urban fringe and has been slow in approving new sites. The conversion of land use is strictly controlled. The public sector has initiated residential land development through the government acquisition of private land since 1980. Direct action by the Korean government to control the spatial pattern of development resulted in a high degree of concentration of economic activity in the two largest cities and along the axis linking them.

There also appears to be a major difference between Korea and Japan in the distribution of land ownership. Much of the land on the urban fringe is owned by farmers in Japan. Japanese farmers have been reluctant to sell their farmland, though they cannot or do not wish to fully exploit it agriculturally. Japanese farmers can earn income by turning into part-time urban wage earners. Much of the farmland on the urban fringe in Korea, however, is owned by speculators. Korean farmers have no choice but to sell their farmland, because there are few opportunities for part-time jobs for farmers. The distribution of land ownership appears to be much more concentrated in Korea than in Japan. Thus, land speculation affects income distribution in Korea more seriously than in Japan.

Proposals for Institutional Reform

Cyclical land speculation in Korea accelerated the rudimentary accumulation of capital and thus functioned as a catalyst to rapid economic growth in the early stages of economic development in the 1960s and 1970s. The large corporations, which had access to credit allocated by the government at low interest rates, bought land on the urban fringes, and rapidly rising land values brought windfall capital gains to the corporations. Cyclical land speculation as well as inflationary money creation promoted the concentration of social wealth in a group of large corporations. This helped overcome the major bottleneck to economic growth at that time—the shortage of capital. On the other hand, the rapid rise in home prices, due to the rapid rise in land prices, forced people in urban areas to save more of their incomes to buy homes and thus promoted private savings. Therefore the cyclical land speculation of the 1960s and 1970s may be viewed as an important mechanism for rapid economic growth in Korea.

The situation has changed dramatically, however, and the shortage of capital is no longer a major constraint to economic growth. Instead, extreme centralization of capital has created a variety of economic and social problems. The legitimization crisis—the most fundamental problem confronting Korea—is deeply rooted in the inequality of wealth distribution and particularly in the extreme concentration of land ownership. Land value is always a socially created value and never the result of action by the landowner. The land value in urban areas does not rise until a city is formed and (unlike other values) increases with the growth of the community and public investments. Most Koreans feel that it is not fair that a minority of land oligopolists have exclusively appropriated the socially created value. Koreans resent paying high prices for land, especially because no resources have been devoted to the production of land. Land is a natural resource, yet land prices have become so high that ordinary people are unable to afford decent housing. The prospect of achieving home ownership, which has been the greatest incentive for private saving and hard work, has been withdrawn from most workers. The work-and-saving incentive has suffered seriously from recent land speculation. As a result, the legitimacy of government economic policies has been brought into doubt. In the extreme, even the free market system has been blamed, and the legitimacy of wealth is in doubt. The legitimization crisis as well as the economic crisis cannot be overcome without solving the land problem in Korea. The land oligopoly, and not the free market, must accept the blame for the worsening housing conditions of the working class in major metropolitan areas.

The concentration of wealth is a necessary precondition for the development of the capitalist mode of production. But the land oligopoly, as Henry George noted, is not a necessary condition for the capitalist mode of production. Capitalism entails the accumulation of wealth based on the provision of goods and services to consumers. It is a two-way exchange: consumers produce wealth in order to consume (that is, by exchanging the wealth with others). The emergence of a land oligopoly undermines this creative process because the latter is a one-way relationship. The land oligopolist secures legal title to the resources of nature and then claims a portion of the wealth created by others in return for nothing more than the permission to use land. In essence, this is the economics of the bandit sanctioned by law. The land oligopolist per se does not contribute to production; he is therefore an anomalous feature within an otherwise efficient system. This ownership of land, in turn, creates another problem: market failure in the dynamic allocation of land as a scarce input to production. If the government levies a tax on the increase in the value of land, mainly due to economic progress and public investment, and spends the money on socially necessary projects, there is no need to interfere with either liberties or property rights. But let us examine more closely the cause of land speculation in Korea to find a more concrete solution.

Causes of Land Speculation

One of the most significant legacies of the cyclical land speculation is the myth that land prices will inevitably continue to rise. Because of this myth, people (particularly large entrepreneurs not even in the real estate trade) tried to buy as much land as they could. This belief also led landowners to expect greater economic advantages from holding land and then selling it. Consequently, land prices rose and demand for land increased while supply slowed. A rise in land prices in one area touched off more price increases in other areas, thus causing this myth to become an even more deeply rooted belief. The Koreans applied the myth to all land and believed that all land prices would continue rising, regardless of location. Moreover, the Korean people seem to have lost faith in any land policy the government might propose. Their distrust of land policy involves the myth that land policy is completely futile, along with the myths of land shortage and the inevitable rise in land prices. It is crucial that the causes of land speculation are analyzed scientifically and that a viable land policy is shown to exist, so that myths can be abandoned.

Land is an extremely valuable resource in a crowded, rapidly developing and urbanizing country like Korea, and its price can be correspondingly high. It is therefore important that it be used efficiently. Market-clearing prices under circumstances without land speculation are parameters in ensuring that land is devoted to its most valuable use. The essence of the land problem is not high land value but land speculation. High land value is a signal to use land intensively as a scarce resource. Land speculation results in market failure, both in inefficiency and equity. Astronomical land prices, for example, would sabotage the government's projects for regional development. Since the 1960s, land prices have increased so rapidly that the cost of buying a home has risen beyond the reach of most family budgets, even those of white collar workers. The relative scarcity of land cannot entirely explain the astronomically high land values in Korea. It is also worth noting that residential and commercial sites account for only 2 percent and factory sites a mere 0.2 percent of the total land area in Korea. The shortage of land for these purposes has regularly served as a trigger for land speculation. Furthermore, about half of Korea's forested lands have slopes of less than 15 degrees, and it is feasible to convert such land to urban uses.

The basic reason for the rapid increase in land prices is a demand from industrialization and urbanization while the supply of land for urban uses has been restricted. Although the stock of land with potential for conversion to urban uses is large, actual conversion has been limited. Thus, the urban land supply has not been able to catch up with the rising demand. Land speculation emerges when demand for land increases rapidly and the supply cannot meet it. Land has therefore become an asset—indeed, the most profitable asset—rather than a factor of production. In the second half of the 1960s and in 1978 and 1979—the periods when land speculation was most intense—land price increases were in the range of 50 to 80 percent. As prices rapidly increased in the land market, it was natural that the expected rate of return on real estate was far higher than the prevailing interest rate, the rate of profit in manufacturing enterprises, or the rate of return on securities. Expectation of such increases led to land speculation, which in turn accelerated the rise of land prices for urban uses in two ways. The land speculation booms created speculative demand for land, causing the demand curve to be shifted upward. At the same time, land speculation brought about a contraction in the effective supply of land. Land owners preferred to hold land idle in the expectation of even greater capital gains, thus causing an upward shift in the supply curve. This vicious circle caused the land situation to deteriorate even further.

Over the past thirty years, Korea has undergone a rapid transition from an agriculture-based economy to a modern industrial society. This process has been accompanied by a major shift in population from rural to urban areas. In 1960 just over a quarter of the population lived in six large cities. Today almost three-quarters of the populace are urban dwellers. Moreover, Korea's development has been characterized by a high degree of concentration of population and economic activity in the two largest cities—Seoul and Pusan—and along the axis linking them which extends the entire length of the country and includes the cities of Taegu, Inchon, and Taejon.

The process of rapid urbanization has been accompanied by rapid growth in the demands on the limited areas available for urban uses, including the demand for industrial and residential sites and land for roads, schools, and other public amenities. Thus, the discrepancy between demand and supply accounts for the initial increase in land prices. Various public investments in construction (of industrial sites, roads, and the development of cities, etc.) create development profits in the form of increases in land prices within the area under development and in its environs. Such a rapid increase in land prices and creation of development profits generated by public investment become potential factors in speculation. When other economic factors, including monetary expansion and inflation, are added, speculation begins to appear.

When the fiscal system permits a few landowners to exploit the land market to their advantage, the benefits of public created land values are privately appropriated. This has been characteristic of development in Korea since the late 1960s. The hard work of employees and the entrepreneurial skills of management suffered an unwarranted setback with the collapse induced by the land speculation booms. The government, alarmed by the effects of this speculation on the rest of the economy, attempted to resolve the problem through legislation. However, the 1968 antispeculation tax on land transactions was enacted and enforced after the proverbial horse had bolted, since land prices started coming down in the next year.

Despite legislative efforts, the system of land taxation has continued to reinforce speculation and the inequitable distribution of land. Urban families and industries rely for expansion on a relatively scarce amount of land in an exceedingly mountainous country. Yet urban land has been taxed at only 0.02 percent of the market value of the land. The incentive, then, is for landowners to keep their land while their properties appreciate inexorably in value. Then, those who mistimed their sales—having failed to dispose of properties before the peak of the cycle—are encouraged to hold onto their land because of the real estate capital gains tax. Why sell (if there is no fiscal inducement to do so, whatever the demands of the market) when you can postpone the transaction into the future, when the tax may be removed?

Furthermore, the national government exercises strict control over the conversion of land from rural to urban uses. As urban areas grow and decentralize, land must be converted from rural to urban uses. It is inevitable that governments become involved in this process because of the need to provide infrastructure in the form of roads, schools, sanitary facilities, and so on. The government, however, has regulated development of new areas on the urban fringe, and the slowness in approving new sites has contributed to the shortage and high price of housing sites.

The main government program for rural-to-urban land conversion through the late 1970s was the Land Readjustment Project (LRP). Under this program, undeveloped sites near the urban fringe were designated as development sites. Development sites could have been chosen by an 80 percent vote of the landowners, but mostly they were designated by either the city government, the national government, or the Korea Housing Corporation. The essential feature of the LRP was that public sector infrastructure costs were financed by a project-specific tax. This tax was paid in the form of a portion of the land under development (usually about half of each site), which was transferred to government ownership.

The LRP was used extensively during the period of rapid urbanization until the late 1970s. The fact that inclusion in a project caused land values to rise substantially made the program viable. From the perspective of the landowners, the 50 percent of the land they retained was worth considerably more after the installation of the infrastructure than the entire site had been worth before it was designated for development.

In Korea, for the most part, it is not legal to develop land for urban uses without being included in an LRP. Thus, one reason that inclusion in a project raises land values is that infrastructure is supplied; another reason is that development permission is itself scarce and therefore valuable. William A. Doebele (1982) was concerned that land in readjustment projects would become so valuable that low-income housing could not be built on it. Korean land values rose by more than the value of the infrastructure because development land was kept scarce by permitting too few projects. One consequence has been the frequent, rapid rise in land prices and subsequent land speculation around the project. Another drawback of the LRP was that it deterred high-density use of scarce urban land. Single detached housing lot development prevailed, and it was very difficult to get large-scale lots for multifamily higher-density housing development.

Since 1980, the government-initiated residential land development method has replaced the LRP for purposes of urban development. The nature of so-called public (or government-led) development is to acquire land from landowners by block purchase. Development plans are formulated by public institutions, such as the Korea Land Development Corporation, and development takes place accordingly. Once lots are subdivided and partitioned, they are either sold or leased to actual demanders. It is a genuinely holistic approach. In 1986, 80 percent of large-scale urban development was undertaken according to this development technique (Figure 12.6). When compared to the LRP method, the holistic residential land development method has several advantages. First, it allows for an ideal type of development plan, and such a plan can be implemented effectively. Second, individual lots can be sold at relatively low prices to the demanders. Third, the method is efficient, given the fact that it takes only three to five years on average for completion—in contrast to LRPs, which often take more than ten years.

The most serious problem with the new method is related to public acquisition of private land. The difference in land prices before and after the project (i.e., development profit) is substantial. The original landowners do not feel justly compensated for their properties and therefore resist the proposed development. Table 12.8 shows how the development profits are distributed by each method. This suggests again that it is necessary that development benefits, both within and outside the project area, be appropriated socially by the capital gains tax for smoother development.

Misdirected Land Policy

Real estate speculation reemerged and land prices soared again in 1988 and 1989. Previously, price increases tended to be concentrated in a few large cities, but now the entire country is affected by them. Much of the speculation involves land earmarked for new development. The cost of buying a home in the large cities rose

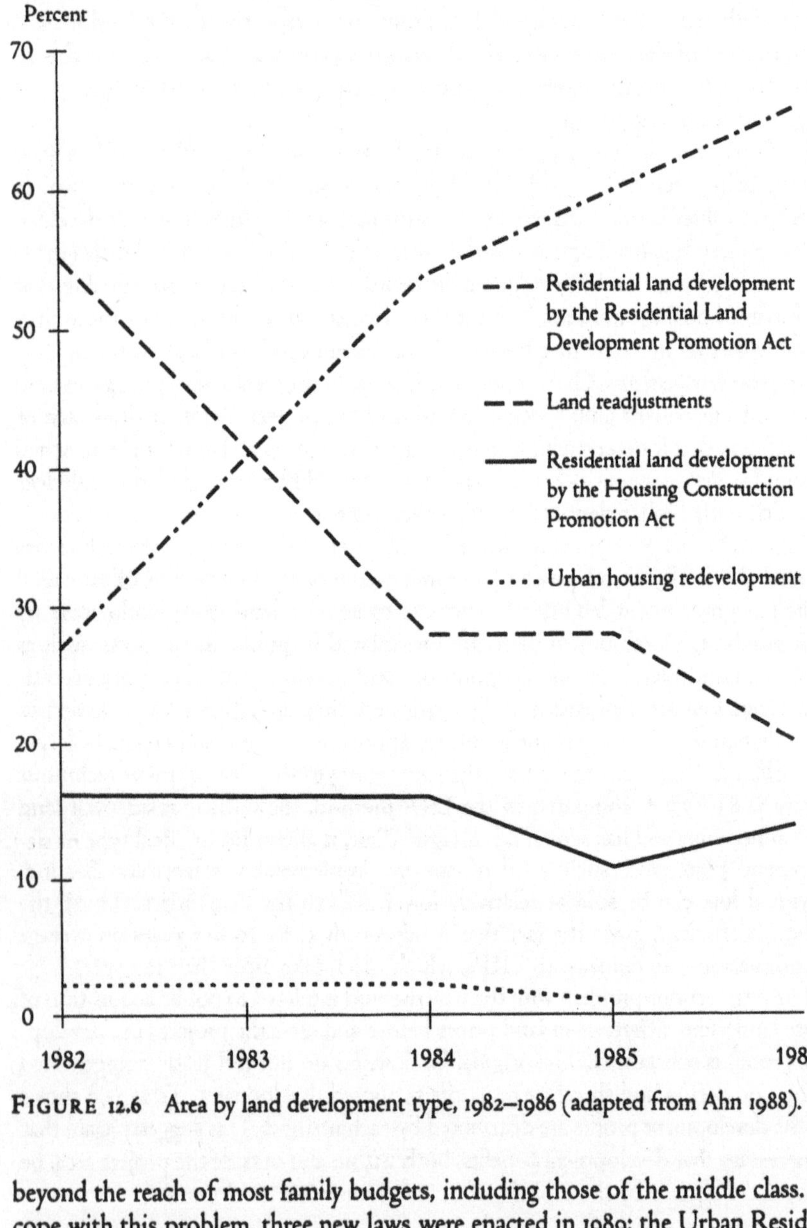

FIGURE 12.6 Area by land development type, 1982–1986 (adapted from Ahn 1988).

beyond the reach of most family budgets, including those of the middle class. To cope with this problem, three new laws were enacted in 1989: the Urban Residential Land Ceiling Act, aimed at regulating residential land held for speculative purposes; the Development Charge Act, which levies a 50 percent charge on betterment profit; and the Abnormal Capital Gains Tax Act, which assesses unused land in cases where the land price increases at rates higher than the national average on an accrual basis. In fact, however, these three acts can be regarded as modifications

Table 12.8
Profit distribution by land development type (percentage)

Participant	Land readjustment	Housing lot development	Residential land development
Public	6.0	33.2	41.8
Developer	0.1	2.0	36.3
Government	5.9	31.2	5.5
Private	94.0	66.8	58.2
Original landowner	84.1	i	i
New land buyer	4.1	38.8	16.6
Builder	0.7	3.8	4.5
New house builder	5.1	24.2	37.1

Source: Korea Land Development Corporation (1989).
i = inapplicable.

of the existing Global Land Value Tax and the Real Estate Capital Gains Tax to provide a means of imposing a heavier tax on specific tax bases. The essence of the Urban Residential Land Ceiling Act is to impose a 6 percent tax on residential land holdings above the ceiling (300 pyong) in the six largest cities. The Development Charge Act is a modification of the real estate capital gains tax imposed on developers only. The Abnormal Capital Gains Tax is a modification of the real estate capital gains tax imposed on unused land only. The crucial drawback of these three acts is the narrowness of the tax bases. The acts cannot provide an effective means of curbing land speculation if the fact that the recent land speculation has affected the entire country is taken into consideration. In particular, much of the recent land speculation involves woodland and farmland around new development areas, most of which are not covered by any of these acts.

Furthermore, the Urban Residential Land Ceiling Act and the Development Charge Act will restrain the conversion of rural land to urban uses, thus limiting the supply of urban residential land. The woodland or farmland in urban fringe areas will be converted into residential land as urbanization proceeds. Under the provisions of the Global Land Value Tax, farmland and woodland are subject to a tax rate of 0.1 percent, while residential land is subject to a progressive rate scheme ranging from 0.3 to 5.0 percent. Moreover, the residential land area beyond the ceiling is again subject to a 6 percent tax rate under the Urban Residential Land Ceiling Act. A landowner thus faces far higher tax rates (more than sixty-fold) if he converts his farmland or woodland into a tract of residential land with an area exceeding the fixed ceiling. It is therefore natural to expect that he will be reluctant to convert. As a result, the increase in residential land prices will accelerate due to the shortage. The prices of woodland and farmland on the urban fringe will rise, too, due to expected capital gain from future conversion. A similar mechanism works under the Development Charge Act. A developer who owns a huge area in the urban fringe, rather than developing his land for urban uses, will take a wait-and-see strategy to avoid the development charge.

The Abnormal Capital Gains Tax works against the equity principle. The tax will be imposed periodically with a 50 percent tax rate on capital gains, but only if the price of unused land increases at rates higher than the national average. In fact, the tax base is quite narrow: land held for business purposes is exempted, including golf courses and parking lots as well as farmland, pasture land, and factory sites. It is inequitable to levy a capital gains tax only on land held for nonbusiness purposes, because there is no difference with respect to capital gains accrued between land held for business purposes and that held for nonbusiness, due to the character of land. Most of the land oligopolists, including big corporations and related persons, can easily avoid the tax by disguising the use of their land as though it were for business purposes. Only the small landowners, mainly from the middle class, will be subject to the tax, since they cannot afford to use their land for business purposes. As a result, the concentration of land ownership will be accelerated by this act. Broadening the tax base is thus a crucial step necessary in land taxation to curb land speculation and to improve the equity of the tax system in Korea.

Alternatives for Reform

To dampen land speculation, it is necessary to both decrease speculative demand and increase the supply of urban land. To decrease speculative demand for land, it is necessary to induce a shift in investment portfolio composition from land to other socially productive assets. The rates of return on land have been much higher than those on such assets as securities. Thus, the relative advantage of land should be eliminated, and this objective can be achieved through taxation.

There are two types of taxes imposed on land, corresponding to the dual character of land: a land value tax (property tax) is imposed on rent, and a capital gains tax is imposed on capital gains. The two are closely related. Almost all countries impose a tax on land value. Taxation of land and structures is the main source of local government revenue in the United States and, to a lesser extent, in other English-speaking countries. In the United States, annual urban real estate taxes are typically in the range of 2 to 4 percent of the market value of land and structures, or an average of about 25 percent of land rent.

Land taxation is an efficient source of government revenue, because land is a nonproduced input and taxation therefore does not reduce its supply or affect its gross value or rent. Some economists, for example Henry George, believe that land taxes should be as high as annual land rents, but this is certainly unwise. Resources must be devoted to finding the most valuable use of land, and no one would commit those resources if all the resulting rent were taxed away. But land taxes can presumably be a substantial fraction of annual rent without loss of efficiency. Taxation of structures is always distorting to some degree, although there is much controversy about the magnitude of the resource misallocation it causes. Equity aspects of land taxation are even more attractive. Since assets are being held more in land than in any other form by the small number of wealthy Koreans, taxation on land could be made more progressive than other forms of wealth taxation.

Existing property taxes in Korea, including the Vacant Land Tax, were superseded in 1990 by the Global Land Value Tax. The new legislation adopts the aggregate land value of an individual as the tax base. The land value tax is imposed on this base at progressive rates ranging from 0.3 to 5 percent. The enactment of this new land value tax represents considerable progress in the tax system, especially in view of the fact that most land is in the hands of a few wealthy persons.

Valuation is the most difficult problem in implementing a land value tax. A land value tax is a tax on a stock rather than on a flow, and stock must be evaluated each time the tax is collected. Land valuation is always a problem because the land market is not centralized or standardized. An efficient valuation service is important. But the authorities in Korea have deliberately undervalued the land, and the land tax has thus become negligible. The valuation of land for tax purposes was on average below 20 percent of the market value in 1988. To improve this situation, the government decided to announce a standardized land price for the entire nation beginning in 1990. The tax rate is so low, however, that the effective tax rate is still 0.08 percent, for example, for the owner of land with a real market value of 0.5 billion won. The nominal tax rate should be raised so that annual land taxes collected from the top 5 percent of the landowners are in the range of 1 to 2 percent of the market value of the land. The land value tax alone, however, may not be sufficient to curb speculation. It can be shown that the dampening effect of the land valuation tax will diminish rapidly in areas where the expected capital gain is higher.

Korea appears to have a commendable approach to the taxation of capital gains when compared with most industrialized countries. Korea's real estate capital gains tax rate is very high. In reality, however, this tax is simply a "paper tiger," since the tax base has been eroded severely through extreme undervaluation and wide loopholes in the law. Tax revenues from the real estate capital gains tax have been very small relative to the huge capital gains in each year. As a proportion of total internal tax revenue, even at the peaks of the land speculation cycle, these revenues amounted to only 1.5 percent (34 billion won) in 1983. The Korean government adopted cyclical control and relief measures, mainly through frequent revision of the capital gains tax law. In response to the surge in speculative buying of real estate, the government moved toward harsh tax treatment of capital gains on transactions in real estate. But in response to economic recessions, the government relaxed the tax treatment of capital gains.

An antispeculation tax was enacted in 1967. It applied only to Seoul, Pusan, and other areas that might subsequently be specified by presidential decree. The provisions of this tax were incorporated into the income tax system in 1975. Capital gains taxes exist as a supplemental tax to bolster the global income tax. Indeed, capital gains fall within a broad definition of income and should be considered as part of the global income tax base. The capital gains tax imposes a 40–60 percent tax on capital gains on real property. The tax is calculated on sales price less purchase price, less capital improvements, less appreciation at the rate of increase of the wholesale price index. Thus, the law basically taxes only real and not nominal capital gains. Basing the tax on real rather than monetary capital gains represents a degree of economic sophistication that is rare among governments.

By international standards, Korea's schedular progressive real estate capital gains tax rate is unusually onerous. Among OECD countries with a schedular capital gains tax, only Denmark begins to approach the Korean level of tax rates, with a flat tax of 50 percent on all capital gains. But in Denmark the cost of real property is indexed according to the length of ownership and other adjustments. In other countries the rate varies, from 10 percent in Portugal to 40 percent in Switzerland. The tax in Korea may reach as high as 89.25 percent on short-term gains (if the defense surtax is included) and 96 percent on gains on unregistered property.

It is unlikely that the stiffening of this tax rate has had a psychological impact on the real estate market, dampening the impetus for speculation. On the other hand, the imposition of such an extremely high tax rate may have led many landowners to defer the sale of land in the hope that it will ultimately be reduced. At the minimum, it may lead speculators to hold land for two years in order to take advantage of the lower rates imposed on long-term owners. The higher tax rates are likely to stimulate tax evasion efforts. This may lead to a shift in the focus of speculators toward types of land and buildings for which tax evasion is easier. This has already happened in Korea, because wide loopholes in the law still exist.

In fact, the capital gains tax on land sales has affected but few persons, mainly because many who should come within the tax network avoid taxes and partly because the existence of anonymous financial assets makes it difficult for tax authorities to cross-check real estate transactions and ownership. Tax loopholes have widened mainly in the recession periods, for example, in the early 1970s and 1980s. The most serious drawback of the real estate capital gains tax is that exemptions and preferential taxation have been widely permitted. The exemption of gains on the sale of personal residences is permitted in most countries. Only in Korea, however, have exemptions been allowed on capital gains from the sale of forestland, pastures, factory sites, farmland, and reclaimed land. Although certain conditions are imposed on such exemptions, they can be easily satisfied.

The variety of exemptions render it virtually impossible for administrators to verify whether a realized capital gain is taxable. Nor can underdeclaration be checked, because the cross-checking mechanism is weakened by various exemptions. As a result, the real estate capital gains tax has never been effective. Thus, tax loopholes are so wide that land speculators avoid capital gains tax without difficulty. The most important step the government can take is to close all loopholes.

Another important drawback of the tax is caused by the lock-in effect, which is an undesirable consequence of taxing capital gains on a realization basis. The tax system has a built-in incentive for postponing realization, since the owner of any land that has increased in value will benefit from a virtually interest-free loan on the tax payment by postponing the payment of taxes. This incentive reduces the supply of marketed land, thereby tending to raise prices, and the tax is shifted to the buyer. To avoid this problem, it is necessary to tax capital gains on an accrual basis rather than on realization. Taxation on an accrual basis, however, might force landowners to sell land prematurely to obtain the money needed to pay the tax (thus creating a liquidity problem). For this reason, the best course would be to limit the regular tax levy to the amount of *interest* on the accrual capital gain, and then, at the realization, the capital gain itself could be taxed.

Capital gains tax on assets must encompass large gifts and bequests. Otherwise, a valuable estate could pass from generation to generation without ever paying capital gains tax. Capital gains are completely exempt from income tax, which encourages the lock-in effect as an asset-owner approaches the later years of his life. Because the present system for collection of estate and inheritance duties operates inadequately, it is all the more necessary to make gifts and bequests liable to capital gains tax.

At the corporate level, the taxes on gains arising from real estate transactions are doubled by means of the Additional Capital Gains Tax, but without permitting any matching offset of real estate losses with gains. In fact, however, more loopholes are available to corporations than to individuals. Corporations are exempt from accrued gains arising from voluntary revaluation of business assets (under the Asset Revaluation Law) and are taxed at a substantially more preferential rate. The Assets Revaluation Tax Law provides potential tax benefits—a very preferential 3 percent rate and eligibility for increased capital deductions. Furthermore, various exemptions of the capital gains tax are permitted to corporations. The tax revenue from the Additional Capital Gains Tax imposed on corporations has been negligible, although the big corporations are generally believed to have led the land speculation. To reform the system, it will also be important to abolish all exemptions and the preferential treatment of capital gains.

On the supply side, one of the most important steps the government could take would be to relax controls on land use conversion. The supply of land suitable for development is limited by greenbelt areas, where development is not allowed. If some of the land currently zoned as agricultural land or a greenbelt were released for development, downward pressure would be exerted on land prices. If there is little scope for expanding the supply of urban land, it will be necessary to develop satellite cities outside the greenbelt areas. It may eventually be necessary to disperse industry and settlement across the country. The Second Comprehensive National Land Development Plan has spelled out government hopes for some such dispersal.

Land is a very scarce resource in Korea, and the price of land is accordingly high. If land is expensive, other inputs are substituted. In manufacturing, a tall factory building can be built on a small plot. For residences, high-rise apartments on small plots are preferred. But Korea's government has imposed severe controls on the height and density of buildings. This policy may have been mechanically copied from the Japanese policy. After the Kanto earthquake and fire of 1923, severe controls were imposed on the height and density of buildings in Tokyo. The Korean peninsula, however, is not earthquake-prone. Real construction costs have fallen since the late 1960s, as the construction industry has become more productive. But urbanization and land speculation have forced land values up, so scarce urban land must be used more intensively. If government controls on the height and density of buildings were relaxed, the effective supply of urban land could be increased. The high-rise apartment solution of the 1950s and the 1960s proved to be a disaster in some ways in the United Kingdom and the United States. But the average height of all Korea's buildings, even in Seoul, is a mere 2.8 meters.

Concluding Remarks

The essence of the land problem in Korea is land speculation. Land speculation has resulted in market failure, in both efficiency and equity. The cyclical land speculation booms in Korea have been based on three myths about urban land: the myth of land shortage, the myth of continuous increases in land prices, and the myth of the futility of land policies. The basic reasons for rapid increases in land prices in Korea are the rapidity with which the demand for urban uses has grown, the limitations placed by the government on rural-to-urban land conversion, and the private appropriation of socially created land value. I have argued that a viable and fairly simple land policy does exist and can be used to dispel the three myths. To dampen the speculative demand for land and to appropriate socially the increases in the value of land, the effective tax rate of the Global Land Value Tax should be raised, and all loopholes in the Real Estate Capital Gains Tax should be closed. Also, the land use control system should be reformed to promote rural-to-urban land conversion.

Further research is clearly needed. The conclusions presented here are hypothetical and should be examined rigorously. In the first place, there is no unified land speculation theory. Two opposing views—neoclassical and Georgian—are still in use simultaneously. A more demanding theoretical model should be developed to explore the nature and effects of land speculation on the economy. Another theoretical issue that must be closely investigated is which type of tax (land value or capital gains) is the more effective means of curbing land speculation. Ever since Henry George formulated his theory, it has been believed that the land value tax is the better policy instrument. But the Georgian view is not fully supported by typical portfolio theory and has remained controversial.

In this chapter I have implicitly assumed that land markets in Korea (in particular the urban fringe land market) are competitive, even though land ownership has become highly concentrated. In fact, the market power of large landowners in some localities is an important issue that needs to be investigated empirically. The astronomical land prices in Korea which throw suspicion on classical land value theory may be a result of both land speculation and the land oligopolists' market power. Individuals owning a sizable share of the supply of urban fringe land can intentionally withhold part of their land to drive prices up. Markusen and Scheffman (1977) showed that concentrated ownership always confers potential market power on the large landowners, and they demonstrated the existence of leapfrogging. In the case of urban areas in Korea, an empirical question remains: is there in fact sufficient ownership concentration to demonstrate the existence of significant market power? Finally, the historical experiences of other countries with respect to land speculation and policies to curb it should be more closely examined. Such a study, taking a comparative cross-country approach, would be helpful in formulating viable institutional reforms.

NOTES

1. U.S. data are drawn from Mills and Song (1979) and Japanese data from the *National Account Yearbook*. Estimates for the United Kingdom were calculated for the author by a British government official.

REFERENCES

Ahn, Kun Hyuck. 1988. "Korean Experience in Urban Development." Unpublished report. Korea Research Institute for Human Settlements, Seoul.

Carter, W. D. 1982. "An Introduction to Henry George." In R. W. Lindholm and A. D. Lynn (eds.), *Land Value Taxation*. Madison: University of Wisconsin Press.

Doebele, William A. 1982. *Land Readjustment*. Lexington, Mass.: Lexington Books.

Economic Planning Board (EPB). Various years. *Korea Statistical Yearbook*. Seoul.

Economic Planning Board (EPB). Various issues. *Monthly Economic Statistics*. Seoul.

George, Henry. 1946 [1879]. *Progress and Poverty*. 15th ed. New York: Robert Schalkenbach Foundation.

Hanayama, Y. 1986. *Land Markets and Land Policy in a Metropolitan Area: A Case of Study of Tokyo*. Boston: Oelgeschlarger, Gunn, and Hain.

Harrison, Fred. 1983. *The Power in Land*. London: Shepheard-Walwyn.

Hoyt, H. 1950. "The Urban Real Estate Cycle: Performances and Prospects." *ULI Technical Bulletin*, no. 38.

Kang, B. K. 1989. "The Effect of Economic Policies on Income Distribution in Korea." Ph.D. diss., Hanyang University, Seoul.

Kim, Hyun Sik. 1988. "Land Use Planning and Policies in Korea." Unpublished report. Korea Research Institute for Human Settlements, Seoul.

Korea Appraisal Board. Various issues. "Survey of Market Prices of Land" (in Korean). Seoul.

Korea Land Development Corporation. 1989. *A Study of Improved Residential Land Development Methods* (in Korean). Seoul.

Korean Research Institute for Human Settlements (KRIHS). 1988. *The Final Report of the Research Committee for Public Control of Land* (in Korean). Seoul.

Markusen, James R., and David T. Scheffman. 1977. *Speculation and Monopoly in Urban Development: Analytical Foundations with Evidence for Toronto*. Toronto: University of Toronto Press.

Mills, Edwin S., and B. Song. 1979. *Urbanization and Urban Problems*. Cambridge: Harvard University Press.

Ministry of Construction, Republic of Korea. Various issues. "Change Rate of Land Prices" (in Korean). Seoul.

Noguchi, Yukio. 1989. *Land Economics* (in Japanese). Tokyo: Nippon Economic Daily Newspaper Company.

CHAPTER 13

The "Land Problem" in Korea

Jae-Young Son
Korea Development Institute

Introduction

Korea has gone through industrialization and urbanization in a relatively short time. Perhaps it was inevitable that the population of once more or less equal poverty has become stratified into various socioeconomic classes, and issues of income and wealth distribution have emerged as the focal point of social conflict. If it does not address the issue of distribution of economic resources, Korea will have difficulties meeting the present challenge of entering the ranks of advanced industrialized countries.

Among the factors contributing to uneven distribution of economic resources is the "land problem." As the price of land has been rapidly rising, landowners have reaped windfall gains that have aggravated the inequity in income and wealth distribution. But the land problem is not confined to the distribution of windfall profits: higher land prices mean higher housing prices, higher production costs for firms, and a greater fiscal drain on governments to build roads, dams, ports, and airports.

A major culprit behind the rising cost of housing, the bottleneck in the development of infrastructure, and economic recession and inflation is said to be the rapidly increasing price of land. The evils of high land prices are not, however, as self-evident as most people assume. One may argue that the high price of land is not all that bad. As long as the market is functioning properly, a high price reflects the scarcity of land and indicates to all current and potential users that they should economize on land. Without concrete evidence of market failure, any effort to curb the land price increase may entail inefficiency in resource allocation. In the formulation of any policy, however, the perception of a problem and its causes may be more important than the actual facts surrounding the problem. There is no doubt that Korean policymakers are under pressure to prevent the land price increase, or at least to slow its pace.

The second problem is closely related to the first. For a clever investor who had bought the right parcel of land at the right time, the returns were enormous. Since the early 1970s, more and more Koreans have engaged in property speculation. In reaping large gains from property transactions, people may have less motivation to save or engage in other productive activities. Some speculative activities are illegal since they involve tax evasion and the violation of regulations governing property transactions. Even legitimate speculation inflates demand for land and hence causes more rapid increases in prices. Thus, on the one hand, there exist a small number of people making a great deal of money through property speculation; on the other hand, a large number of people cannot afford decent housing. The alienation felt by the latter, who of course do not have the means to join the speculative frenzy, exerts great pressure on policymakers to do something. Otherwise, this frustration of the masses could lead to social unrest.

The government set up the Land Gongkaenyum Study Committee[1] in 1989 to formulate new policy measures, which were aimed at solving the land problem, and introduced the residential landownership limit, the development gains charge, and the excess land profits tax, based in part on the committee's report. At the same time, the comprehensive land tax, a new system of land assessment, reinforced transaction regulations, and the compulsory registration of land transactions were enacted. These pieces of legislation were supplemented by occasional administrative decrees, such as the one announced on 8 May 1990, when the land problem seemed to escalate.

Still, skepticism remains, and some question whether the decades-old problem can really be solved. Others doubt the earnestness of the government or the compliance of large conglomerates which, they claim, are major actors in property speculation.

Increases in Land Prices and Related Problems

Official publication of the land price index began in 1975 with October 1974 as the base. The data series contains price indices and the rates of increase of various types of land and locations, but the price level is not available. With little information on the characteristics of all land parcels in the nation, the aggregation procedure utilizes assumptions of dubious quality.[2] Still, these official figures are used in this chapter for lack of an alternative.

During the fifteen-and-a-half-year period since October 1974, land prices increased by 14.3 times for the nation as a whole (Table 13.1). The price rise for Seoul was much higher, rising 29 times. In the same period, the consumer price index increased by 4.8 times, the wholesale price index by 3.7 times, real GNP by 3.6 times, M2 by 26.1 times, and the stock price index by 10.9 times (see Chapter 12, Table 12.1). Thus, it is evident that land prices increased more swiftly than most other economic indicators. Figure 13.1 shows that, among regions, major cities had higher rates of land price increases than other cities and rural areas. By type of land, all categories showed similar trends.

Table 13.1
Land price indices and other economic variables

	Land price[b]		Real	Stock
Year[a]	Nation	Seoul	GNP	price[c]
1974	100	100	100	100
1975	127	132	105	111
1976	161	153	119	136
1977	215	201	130	158
1978	329	474	145	200
1979	373	505	160	168
1980	414	599	160	151
1981	429	612	166	176
1982	444	656	177	170
1983	527	1,035	202	170
1984	596	1,276	224	184
1985	638	1,380	239	194
1986	685	1,431	271	317
1987	761	1,499	309	582
1988	968	1,878	352	966
1989	1,286	2,523	373	1,280
1990	1,431	2,901	na	1,094

Source: Ministry of Construction (various issues); Economic Planning Board (various issues).

[a]October each year, except April 1990.

[b]Official publication of the land price index corrected to account for missing periods (October–December 1986) and inconsistencies (1980).

[c]Year average.

The Causes of Land Price Increases

There are a multitude of possible explanations for rapid land price increases, but few scientific investigations have been directed at the problem. Some of the popular explanations are listed here, along with discussions of their plausibility and implications.

Urbanization and Industrialization Korea experienced one of the world's most rapid industrializations during the past three decades, radically transforming a traditional, rural, agriculture-based socioeconomic structure into a modern industrial economy centered around urban areas. Industrialization and the consequent

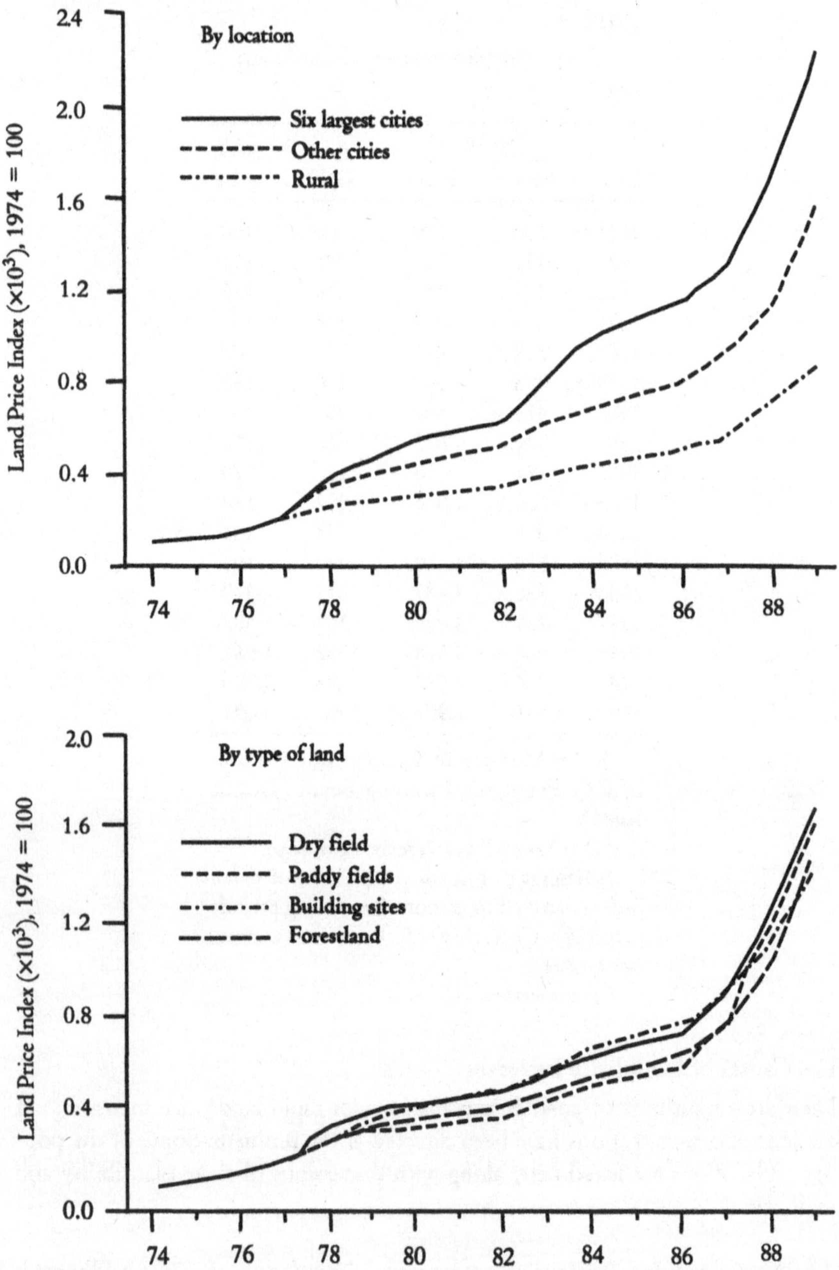

FIGURE 13.1 Land price increase by location and type of land.

urbanization created a disproportionate demand for different types of land in various locations. Demand for potential sites for housing, manufacturing, services, and recreational facilities expanded rapidly while that for agriculture and forest land may not have increased at all. In most cases, the supply of land with good accessibility and desirable environs was limited in the short run and competition to occupy such land was stiff.

Development and conversion of agricultural land, redevelopment of low-density developed areas, and land reclamation constitute new supply of urban land. When the supply of a certain type of land falls short of demand for it, the price naturally rises. Conceptually, we can identify two distinct aspects of land price increases. Following Rosen's (1974) framework, a parcel of land can be viewed as a heterogeneous good with a quality dimension represented by a vector of characteristics such as regulatory variables, location, size, shape, accessibility, and condition of the environs:

$$L = (l_1, l_2, \ldots, l_k)$$

The market price of each parcel occurs at the intersection of the functions representing bids by would-be purchasers and offers by sellers, both of which depend on the characteristics of that land parcel. The market clearing price thus obtained is a function of the characteristics vector:

$$P = P(l_1, l_2, \ldots, l_k)$$

A new road that increases accessibility, concentration of people that improves prospects for commercial success, a change in zoning that allows high-density development, and other such changes that accompany increasing urban activity will alter the components of the quality factor—in other words, development, whether it is due to investment by the owner or by others—enhances the quality of the land. An important aspect of price increase is this quality change, which undoubtedly accounts for much of the increase in Korean land prices. Price increases caused by development will continue and should not be constrained. Any attempt at constraining them will either discourage development or keep land from being put to its best possible use.

It is also possible, however, that the price function itself has shifted upward over the years because increasing demand for urban land could not be satisfied by the new supply. Rosen's framework, although successful in explaining price differentials among land parcels of different qualities, is not adequate for describing movements of the aggregate land price index. Hence, an ordinary demand and supply relationship that abstracts the quality dimension would be more appropriate. Considering the development and redevelopment of land, it can be postulated that the supply curve of urban land is upward sloping, although its short-run price elasticity will be low.[3] The demand for land is determined by two properties of land: as an input in the production process, demand depends on land's marginal productivity; as an asset, demand depends on both future returns and risks.

The productivity of land increases with the introduction of new production methods, the concentration of people and industries in cities, improved accessibility, and the creation of new demand. Such changes shift the demand curve upward, raising the price for any given supply curve. The productivity of land derived from present and future use may not explain the entire price increase, since continuous price hikes compel more people to view land as a profitable asset. The demand for land is thus influenced by expected capital gains, and the expectation of high returns shifts the demand curve upward. On the supply side, a high expected future price has a mixed effect: new development and redevelopment will expand, but owners of improved or unimproved land with high development potential may hesitate at selling their holdings if the cost of postponing the sale is lower than the expected gain; that is, their demand for land as an asset justifies holding it, even if the demand for land as an input does not.

Land price increases due to such an imbalance between supply and demand encourage more development and redevelopment, but this is restricted by land use regulations. Such regulation is a necessary complement to the functioning of the market, since the way a parcel of land is used has an externality effect on adjacent parcels. But if such regulation is inflexible, it may keep the market from satisfying excess demand by development.

Whether we adopt Rosen's disaggregated land market model of the supply-demand approach or not, speculation is an integral part of market adjustment. Sensing future changes in their favor, speculators buy land at a higher price and, in many cases, do not put land into use until a more profitable development possibility ripens. If the prediction turns out to be correct, speculators are rewarded for taking risks; if not, they suffer losses. From a broader point of view, by keeping land from being developed prematurely, speculators secure its long-run optimal allocation. Without such speculation, land is likely to become entangled with the interests of too many parties, which can hinder its optimal use when the time comes (See Lindeman 1976). Speculation has its role in a well-functioning market.

Speculation In cases where rapid land price increases have caused much confusion and distribution problems, many people believe that the idle holding of valuable land, particularly in newly developing urban fringes, is detrimental. More articulate proponents of such a view frequently refer to writings of Henry George to describe, analyze, and remedy the problem. Setting aside ethical judgments, however, much of the Georgian argument can be embraced by neoclassical economic thinking, like that described in the previous section. The question remains whether speculation pushes up land prices, which in turn invites more speculation, until finally the real estate sector can no longer support the elevated prices. If this is so, the market is failing and government intervention is necessary to reinstate efficiency. In theory, land, as is the case for any other means of storing wealth, has the potential to become an object of speculative binge buying that may continue to raise prices until the entire bubble suddenly bursts. Whether land prices in Korea are subject to such a danger is a question that should be answered through empirical evidence. Unfortunately, few systematic analyses of the question are available, and one can only quote some arguments for and against the bubble theory.

To support this argument, some researchers observe that the ratio of imputed rent of all land to GNP is unreasonable high.[4] But many others feel that two to three decades is too long for a bubble to be sustained. In the 1960s people believed that the price of land was rising too fast, but in retrospect the price level was still very low. The same thing may be happening now, since land prices in Korea are still considered lower than those for similar types of land in the advanced industrialized countries. Furthermore, the prices of different types of land show remarkable correspondence to the characteristics of that land. For various purposes, researchers have estimated hedonic price equations, regressing the price on the characteristics of land.[5] In most cases, the fit is very good, with R^2 frequently exceeding .9. If the land price were rising because of indiscriminate speculation, such results would be hard to come by.

Although the issue of the price bubble must await further analysis, the conjecture here is that intervention in the land market is not necessary on efficiency grounds, with the exception of the externality problem that justifies land use regulations. This opinion implies that antispeculation measures are not needed as supplements to the price mechanism. This should not be interpreted, however, as a denial of the need for land policy reforms. As I discuss later, land price increases have rapidly contributed to the inequality of income and wealth distribution, and the government must act to correct the situation by taxing capital gains more effectively as well as instituting other measures.

Macroeconomic Factors Since land is an important form of wealth, macroeconomic variables that affect the size and composition of wealth influence land prices. We can illustrate this point by adding land to a simple asset market equilibrium condition. Assume that households hold real wealth (W) as equities and bonds (V), money (M), and land (L):

$$W = \frac{(V + M + p_L L)}{p}$$

where p_L is the unit price of land and p is the price level. By Walras' Law, the asset market equilibrium is characterized by two conditions:

$$\frac{M}{p} = \frac{M_D}{p} = m(r, \pi, Y, W)$$

$$\frac{p_L L}{p} = \frac{(p_L L)_D}{p} = l(r, \pi, Y, W)$$

where subscript D stands for demand, r for the real interest rate, π for the expected rate of general price increase, Y for the aggregate output, W for real wealth, and m

and l for demand functions for real money and land. By incorporating these equations into the full-scale macroeconomic model, we can analyze the effects of exogenous changes on land price. For a simple example, assume that the demand for real wealth is fixed, and for greater simplicity assume that the ties between the real and monetary sectors are severed, that is, r and Y do not change as a result of changes in M. Then, a unit increase in M causes p to rise by p/M, which in turn increases $p_L L$ by $p_L L/M$. As L is more or less fixed, most of the change in $p_L L$ is achieved by a change in p_L. An increase in the money supply thus raises land prices.

Though by no means a serious attempt to analyze reality, this example suggests that any macroeconomic condition that affects the size and composition of wealth has an influence on land prices. The exceptionally rapid increases in land prices in the late 1970s and 1980s are most likely related to the excess liquidity resulting from the overseas construction market boom and enormous trade surpluses, respectively. The policy implication of the argument is that unstable macroeconomic conditions may render microeconomic policies futile in achieving land policy goals such as land price stability.

Concentration of Ownership One of the most striking findings by the Land Gongkaenyum Study Committee was the extreme concentration of land ownership in Korea. In 1988 the top 5 percent of landowners held 65.2 percent of all land area owned by individuals (KRIHS 1989, and see Chapter 12, Table 12.4). The degree of concentration probably exceeded even the most pessimistic of previous estimates and was far more extreme than any indicators of income distribution. I discuss the implications of concentrated land ownership on distribution issues later, but another important question is if such an extreme concentration would affect the prices and the functioning of the land market.

If the owners of land are exercising market power, the market cannot be relied on to achieve optimal resource allocation. But no evidence suggests explicit or implicit collusion among landowners. Despite a high concentration of land ownership, landowners seem to act as atomistic individuals in a competitive market. They do not sell land when waiting seems more profitable, and they bargain for the best price when they decide to sell. If a particular parcel of land is not easily substituted by another, its owner has a stronger bargaining position and may enjoy a more rapidly rising price. Also, more landowners may hold on longer for better deals, since the cost of holding land is low. This behavior would, however, be the same even if land ownership were less concentrated.

The Effects of Land Price Increases

The price of land, an essential input for most production processes and an important form of wealth, has numerous and varied effects on the economy. Policy responses should reflect the different causes and effects of price increases, and as discussed in the previous section no convincing reasons can be found for the intervention in the allocation of land through the price mechanism. But land price increases can still bring about results that the country finds undesirable. The government should focus on alleviating the pain of land price increases rather than attempting to meddle with the workings of the land market.

Housing Problems There is no doubt that housing prices are affected by land prices, and the former have also increased significantly over the years (Table 13.2). The rise in housing costs was especially rapid in 1989 and 1990 and led to the suicides of some desperate families who could no longer afford the high rents. Even for middle-class families, the prospect of owning a home was becoming little more

TABLE 13.2
Quarterly increase in housing prices and rents

	Country		Seoul	
Quarter	Housing price	Rent[a]	Housing price	Rent[a]
1986				
2	–1.6	1.7	–2.0	2.0
3	–0.2	1.6	–0.3	2.1
4	–1.0	–1.8	–0.2	4.8
1987				
1	–0.2	4.0	0.7	5.8
2	0.1	4.3	–0.7	3.6
3	4.2	5.4	2.2	4.1
4	3.0	4.2	1.4	3.4
Year	7.2	19.2	2.1	18.0
1988				
1	6.1	9.5	5.3	11.1
2	3.6	4.7	1.9	1.8
3	3.1	2.2	2.4	1.4
4	–0.3	–2.9	–0.7	–6.0
Year	13.1	13.8	9.1	7.9
1989				
1	7.2	7.8	10.3	12.0
2	5.1	4.7	4.2	4.3
3	0.0	2.4	0.0	5.2
4	1.7	1.7	1.5	0.7
Year	14.6	17.6	16.6	23.7
1990				
1	8.3	17.5	9.9	21.9

Source: Korea Housing Bank, "Monthly Economic Review," each month.

[a]Chonsei rents.

than a dream. In the emotionally charged discussions on housing problems, major blame was reserved for the high price of land.

This view was probably accurate, although housing prices are affected by various additional factors. The question is whether any changes in land policy would improve the situation. First, the government might set a ceiling on land prices.[6] Such regulation, however, may hinder the optimal allocation of land and cannot be effectively enforced. Even if an effective measure can be found, the main beneficiaries would be the middle-class to higher-income families who can afford to buy houses. Second, land supply can be expanded by easing the regulations pertaining to development, redevelopment, and land use. Policies oriented in such a direction may be costly in terms of other policy goals, but it seems that circumstances may necessitate this choice. The price of land for housing rises mainly because there is excess demand, and land policy changes can alleviate the housing problem by removing the bottlenecks to increase the land supply.

It is doubtful, however, that land policy alone can solve the housing problem. For instance, low-income households could not afford to purchase a housing unit even if there were relatively low land prices. If society desires stable housing conditions for all, housing policies designed to meet the specific needs of various target populations are required. In Korea, expanding the supply of public sector rental units for low-income households and establishing a system of housing finance for middle-class households are but two of the urgently needed housing policy measures.

Economic Recession Henry George argued that speculation, by keeping good land out of production and extending the margin of production to poorer land, accelerates the tendency for land prices to increase and makes labor and capital less productive. In the extreme case, speculation raises land prices so high that labor and capital cannot engage in production. This obstructs normal economic development and can result in recession and widespread poverty.

According to several authors (e.g., Lee 1990; Hwang 1985; Lim 1985), the following conditions can be applied to Korea. First, high land prices hinder construction activities with a resulting loss of production in that sector. The government cannot afford the high cost of building infrastructure, and the lack of infrastructure becomes a bottleneck for industrial development. Manufacturing firms suffer from an increase in costs and may lose international competitiveness. In addition, inflation may be triggered.

Second, land speculation becomes an undesirable component of capital accumulation. For instance, large corporations, exploiting their easy access to bank credit and information on development plans, expand their landholdings, with virtually guaranteed large capital gains. In rare cases when the speculative bubble bursts, the government has to rescue these firms with infusions of new credit and other assistance, because it is unable to risk the mass bankruptcy of major corporations.

Finally, despite regulations on the use of bank credit (see below), large corporations utilize it to purchase land, since the expected return from land is higher than the prevailing interest rates. For smaller or new firms, which generally only have access to informed credit markets where they must pay higher interest rates, the situation gets worse.[7]

Some of these arguments apparently hold true, some are exaggerated, but more are backed by solid evidence.[8] Although evidence is not yet available, it would be an overstatement to view recession as solely caused by land speculation and price increases. The Georgian proposal for reform is, however, meaningful in correcting a less grand but more urgent problem of land price increase, namely, the distribution problem.

Distribution Problems There have been attempts to estimate the total value of national land and capital gains arising from land price increases. One such study by Son (1990) starts with the aggregate property tax base in 1985, divides it by the average assessment ratio to obtain market value, and by using the rate of price increase for each type of land calculates total land value in subsequent years. Another approach uses sample survey data to calculate the unit value of land for different types and locations, which is then multiplied by the total area of land in each category.[9] Both approaches have limitations, and the results vary considerably: the total land value in 1988 by the former approach was 216 trillion won; according to the latter, it was valued at more than four times as much—937 trillion won (at the time US$1.00 was worth approximately 700 won).[10]

The more conservative of the two approaches is shown in Table 13.3. The table also lists the capital gains from land. When compared to GNP and other aggregate variables, the capital gains are indeed large: in 1988 they were 55 percent of GNP, 60 percent of disposable income, 135 percent of employee compensations, and 303 percent of central government expenditures. The more interesting issue is how the capital gains are distributed by ownership classes. Table 13.4 groups the capital gains by ownership category: corporations account for about 10 percent of the capital gains, while the rest accrues to individuals. In 1988 corporations reaped a total of 5.8 trillion won of windfall gains from land, while individuals earned 62.1 trillion won. Among individual landowners, an average owner in the top 5 percent bracket received capital gains of 75 million won (US$107,000), while typical landowners in the top 10 percent bracket gained 44 million won ($63,000). When compared with the Korean capital GNP of $4,127 in that year, the amount of capital gains is very high, and it is easy to understand the intensity of emotions surrounding issues related to land. Korea has suffered aggravated labor relations since 1987, but this conflict over the distribution of production may have been pointless: without addressing the source of the large windfall profits from land, it is futile to argue about income distribution. The capital gains computed above, of course, are not on a realization base, and 1988 was a year with an unusually high rise in land prices. These facts cannot, however, alter the conclusion of the analysis fundamentally. I argued earlier in this chapter that a certain amount of the land price increase is inevitable and should not be

TABLE 13.3
Total value of and capital gains from privately owned land (billion won)

	1985	1986	1987	1988
Total value of privately owned land	158,163.0	169,086.0	181,428.0	216,234.0
(1) Capital gains	10,923.0	12,341.6	34,806.6	67,902.0
(2) GNP	78,088.4	90,543.9	105,629.8	123,579.2
(1)/(2)	14.0%	13.6%	33.05	54.9%
(3) Disposable income	71,122.5	82,696.4	96,378.9	112,404.5
(1)/(3)	15.4%	14.9%	36.1%	60.4%
(4) Employee compensation	31,968.9	36,259.0	42,911.5	50,139.8
(1)/(4)	34.2%	34.0%	81.1%	135.4%
(5) Central government expenditure	13,585.0	15,310.3	17,488.3	22,402.4
(1)/(5)	80.4%	80.6%	199.0%	303.1%

Source: Son (1990).

TABLE 13.4
Distribution of capital gains from land among ownership classes (billion won)

	1985	1986	1987	1988
Total capital gains	10,923.0	12,341.6	34,806.6	67,902.0
Corporations	1,080.8	1,319.5	3,471.2	5,770.5
Individuals	9,842.2	11,022.1	31,335.4	62,131.5
Top 5% (0.5 million people)	6,417.1	7,186.4	20,430.7	40,509.7
Top 10% (1.1 million people)	7,568.7	8,476.0	24,096.9	47,779.1
Top 25% (2.7 million people)	8,936.7	10,008.1	28,452.5	56,415.4

Source: Son (1990).

tampered with, except that government can and should take measures to facilitate development, namely, to increase land supply. Even with increased supply, land prices will rise as the economy grows; thus, recapturing windfall gains by taxation and other measures is the most urgently needed reform in Korean land policy.[11]

Reform of Land Taxation

Land Taxes in Korea

Two main directions for solving the problems associated with land have been identified thus far: minimizing the ill effects of land price increases on income and wealth distribution by taxing capital gains, and expanding the supply of urban land by facilitating land development. In this section I examine current land taxes, identify the problems, and propose policy reforms in turn. Table 13.5 shows the classification of Korean land taxes by two criteria: level of government with power to tax, and action subject to taxation. It should be understood that government in Korea is highly centralized. Even for taxes labeled as local, tax codes that define tax bases, rate structures, exemptions and reductions, and related procedures are established by the central government.[12] Local governments have little if any authority in these matters. For instance, they cannot raise the property tax rate to finance improvements to schools.

In many countries, a piece of real estate is taxed as a whole; building and land are assessed together for tax purposes. Since land is a natural resource and buildings are a result of human effort, George and his followers argued strongly against taxes on buildings and advocated taxes on land, and only on land. It should be pointed out that most Korean local taxes distinguish between land and buildings. The distinction apparently was not compelled by the Georgian spirit, since buildings are also taxed frequently by the same taxes listed in Table 13.5, possibly at higher rates.

National Taxes Most of the national taxes listed in Table 13.5 are not specifically targeted at land, but they are relevant to the discussion since land is frequently an important asset. These taxes are imposed mainly on income generated from acquisition, holding and renting, and sale of property and other assets.

The inheritance tax is regarded as important for income and wealth redistribution and thus has rates higher than the ordinary income tax. It is imposed on the heirs of any form of wealth inherited within one year of the death of the deceased. The rate structure is progressive in fifteen brackets: from 7 percent for under one million won to the top bracket rate of 60 percent for over 500 million won. Once the amount of tax is determined, the tax is divided among the heirs depending on their shares of the inheritance.

The statutory basis of the gift tax is given by the Inheritance Tax Law, since it supplements the inheritance tax by discouraging the transfer of wealth before death. The rates of the gift tax are even higher than those of the inheritance tax: from 7 percent for under 500,000 won to 67 percent for the top bracket of over 200 million won (fourteen brackets).

The transfer income tax is a component of taxes on an individual's income. When a person makes a profit by selling a property, but not as a construction company, the income is classified as transfer income and is taxed separately from other income. This tax has been a major deterrent to land and apartment speculation and incorporates many complicated rules that make the tax harsh on speculators while protecting those with honorable intents. At the same time, farmers who have tilled their land for eight or more years and households that own one

TABLE 13.5
Korean land taxes

Imposed on	National taxes[a]	Local taxes[b]
Acquisition	Inheritance tax	Acquisition tax
	Gift tax	Registration tax
Holding	Income tax[c]	Comprehensive land tax
	Corporate income tax[c]	City planning tax
	Excess land profits tax	
Transfer	Transfer income tax	
	Special surtax on corporate income tax	
	Corporate income tax	

[a]Stamp tax and defense tax are surcharged.
[b]Defense tax is surcharged.
[c]Imposed on rental income.

residence are not taxed. Tax rates are higher for properties owned for less than two years or transferred without proper registration, which is in effect a notice to the tax authority. Since rapid turnovers of property with tax evasion are the most flagrant form of property speculation, this tax has been feared by speculators. The tax base is the transfer income, which is essentially the difference between prices sold and bought.[13] With the revision of the tax law in 1988, the tax rate is now progressive with five brackets: 40 percent for under 30 million won to 60 percent for over 500 million won.[14] The low rate of 30 percent for a modest residence owned for over two years and the high rate of 75 percent for an unregistered sale remain in effect, but the rate for a property owned for less than two years has increased to 60 percent.

A special surtax of the corporate income tax is the corporate counterpart to the individual's transfer income tax. When a property is sold by a corporation that is not in the business of real estate development, the income from the sale is first added to all other income of the company and is subject to corporate income tax as well as the special surtax. Thus, any profit from a property sale is double taxed.[15] The calculation of the tax base is similar to that for the transfer income tax, and the tax rate is 25 percent for ordinary cases and 35 percent for unregistered sales. Combined with corporate income tax, a corporation's gross tax burden on a property sale is similar to that of an individual. This tax is intended to discourage property speculation by corporations, and the selective exemption rules help to achieve this goal. Pasture land is exempt if the business has been in operation for five or more years and if the purpose of the sale is to move the ranch to another location. A business property in other industries must have been in use for two or more years, and the revenue from the sale must go into new business capital. In both cases, the firm must have used the property for its own business. For instance, any farmland that is sold by a nonfarming corporation is subject to the tax.

Apart from provisions specified in individual tax codes, a separate law, the Tax Reduction and Exemption Regulatory Law, specifies other cases for reduction and exemption of the transfer income tax and the special surtax of corporate income tax. This law lists activities deemed desirable and in need of encouragement and specifies to what extent the taxes are to be reduced.[16]

A new addition to national land taxes is the excess profits tax on land, which was introduced as part of Gongkaenyum legislation. It intends to recapture windfall gains on an accrual basis, but by taxing only idle land or excess landholdings it is more of an antispeculation measure. For each three-year taxation cycle, the National Tax Bureau announces the normal rate of land price increase, which is the greater of the national average land price increase and the interest rate on a savings account, and any gain above this rate is subject to the 50 percent tax. To avoid double taxation, the transfer income tax is reduced by a certain percentage of the excess profits tax on land depending on the length of time between payment of the two taxes.

Local Taxes Most local land taxes are imposed on the acquisition or holding of land as a form of wealth. The acquisition tax is imposed on expenditures for acquiring land, buildings, vehicles, ships, and in some instances stocks, when they are transferred to a new owner (transfer acquisition) or when they are first built (original acquisition). The acquisition need not involve monetary or other compensation to be subject to the tax. Since land is not a producible good, the acquisition tax on land applies mostly to its purchase.[17]

For most property, the tax rate is 2 percent of the acquisition price and expenses. This tax, paid together with a 3 percent registration tax, is a burden to land buyers and bears an unmistakable resemblance to the Japanese land tax system. Perhaps because of the high tax rate, the acquisition tax is used to pursue various policy goals. For example, a company that acquires land in order to move its factory from Seoul, Pusan, or Taegu to other areas is not taxed. On the other hand, luxury properties (e.g., resorts, golf courses, luxury residences), a corporation's excess property holdings, and an individual's landholdings deemed to be speculative are taxed at a punitive 15 percent. The tax code is quite complicated, with definitions of excess property holdings.

In the late 1980s, a broad consensus that increasing costs of holding land should supplement the transfer income tax emerged. The most simple of such measures would be a uniform increase in the property tax rate, but this would find resistance from many landowners who consider themselves innocent of speculation. Hence, it was thought necessary to protect most small landowners while taxing large landowners heavily. The comprehensive land tax was conceived as such a tax. It would sum up the value of all landholdings of an individual or corporation and apply progressive tax rates.[18] Compared with the uniform increase in the property tax rate, its main disadvantage is the complicated summing-up procedure, while its greatest merit is its broad political appeal. A progressive rate structure is certainly not desirable in terms of neutrality (activities requiring a large land input would be discouraged), horizontal equity (two taxpayers with equal wealth of different compositions would have different burdens), administrative costs (adding up the values of an owner's nationwide landholdings requires an expensive system of record keeping and computation), and fiscal autonomy of local governments (the assessment standards and tax rates must be identical around the country), but the concept was deemed to be inevitable as one of the few feasible means of selectively increasing the landholding tax on large landowners.

The original idea of the comprehensive land tax aroused criticism for two very different reasons. The speculation fighters argued that "obviously" speculative landholdings might not be taxed heavily enough.[19] They also opposed scrapping the high property tax rate on luxury properties. A second view, representing the landowners' interests, contended that land used for productive purposes should not be penalized by higher taxes.[20] The final outcome of the controversy is a peculiar compromise of the three ideas: the first advocating the indiscriminate aggregation of all landholdings, the second intent on penalizing obvious speculative holdings, and the third opposing any tax increase for nonspeculative landholdings. The land tax rate structure includes three fixed rates and two progressive rates, as shown in Table 13.6. The fixed rates for factory sites and farmland and the high rate for luxury land are the same as under the earlier property tax system, but now residential land, commercial land, and suspected speculative landholdings are all subject to the progressive rate.

Although the first progressive rate, which applies to speculative land as well as to residential land, ranges from 0.2 to 5 percent in nine brackets, it reaches 1 per-

TABLE 13.6
Rate structure of comprehensive land tax

Classification	Land type	Brackets	Tax rate (%)
Fixed rates	Factory site	—	0.3
	Farmland tilled by owner	—	0.1
	Luxury property	—	5.0
Progressive rates	Speculative land and residential land	9	0.2–5.0
	Commercial land	9	0.3–2.0

cent only when the assessed value is as high as 500 million won, or a market value of 833 million won.[21] Thus the first progressive rate is a penalty only on the truly large landholders. The second progressive rate, ranging from 0.3 to 2 percent in nine brackets, is applied to commercial building sites that usually occupy expensive land in downtown areas. Again, the progressivity is very mild: the rate reaches 1 percent only for land assessed at 10 billion won. Even if the parcel is a building site, part of it may be subject to the first progressive rate when the density of its use is under a certain ratio.[22] Land is determined to be speculative by complicated rules similar to those for the acquisitions tax. The comprehensive land tax has become very similar to the excess landholding tax it replaced.

Applying progressive rates is possible only when the information on ownership of all land is computerized nationwide. After five years of preparation, the Ministry of Home Affairs currently runs a computerized land ownership record system and determines the amount of tax for each individual. The amount of tax owed is then divided in proportion to land values among localities in which the owner holds land, and each local government is responsible for collecting its share.

Land Tax Revenues Most land-related national taxes are imposed on total income, and statistics do not exist on how land is taxed in isolation from other income sources. As a result, I do not attempt to estimate revenues generated from land only.

On the other hand, local tax statistics usually distinguish sources of revenue (Table 13.7). In 1988 the five types of local land tax (acquisition tax, registration tax, property tax, excess landholding tax, and city planning tax) collected brought in 815 billion won, which accounted for a mere 7.9 percent of the total local government budget but 26.3 percent of all local tax revenues. This means that local land taxes are important among local tax but not so in the budget. This is explained by the fact that central government subsidies contribute a large part of the local government budget.

Table 13.7 also shows that the part of the land taxes related to the antispeculation goal is generally small and fluctuates widely. This may come as a surprise, considering all the elaborate standards in tax codes as to whether a landholding is speculative or not. The most plausible explanation is that local governments are not capable of enforcing the complicated rules on a constant basis. Only when speculation becomes a serious problem do they make a special effort at enforcement.

Issues in Korean Land Taxation

Assessment In the preceding discussions the government's ability to discover the actual value of land was not questioned. However, at the core of the problems involving land taxes is the issue of assessment. For the purpose of local taxation, local government officials are supposed to assess the unit value of each land parcel

TABLE 13.7 Local land tax revenues (million won, and percentage)

			Acquisition tax			Property tax[a]		
	1 Total local government expenditure	2 Total local tax revenue (2/1)	3 Total (3/2)	4 From land (4/3)	5 From corporations' excess land (5/4)	6 Total (6/2)	7 From land (7/6)	8 From corporations' excess/vacant land (8/7)
1979	2,311,917	599,199 (25.9)	135,037 (22.5)	42,299 (31.3)	1,044 (2.5)	81,593 (13.6)	81,551 (99.9)	—
1980	2,884,726	767,691 (26.6)	162,952 (21.2)	59,495 (36.5)	11,688 (19.6)	119,412 (15.6)	73,057 (61.2)	11,395 (15.6)
1981	3,629,014	914,372 (25.2)	179,769 (19.7)	62,885 (35.0)	2,827 (4.5)	152,679 (16.7)	94,093 (62.2)	15,473 (16.4)
1982	4,308,470	1,119,206 (26.0)	215,508 (19.3)	75,898 (35.2)	1,590 (2.1)	172,787 (15.4)	101,211 (58.6)	14,711 (14.5)
1983	5,293,524	1,397,167 (26.4)	307,767 (22.0)	112,720 (36.6)	2,198 (2.0)	194,753 (13.9)	108,149 (55.5)	10,955 (10.1)
1984	6,216,767	1,508,354 (24.3)	337,526 (22.4)	115,474 (34.2)	2,181 (2.2)	210,419 (14.4)	117,035 (55.4)	10,900 (8.7)
1985	6,785,007	1,654,635 (24.4)	356,318 (21.5)	121,868 (34.2)	2,727 (2.2)	237,460 (14.4)	131,464 (55.4)	11,498 (8.7)
1986	7,604,131	1,809,753 (23.8)	371,185 (20.5)	122,833 (33.1)	3,226 (2.6)	265,793 (14.7)	145,783 (54.8)	19,685 (18.5)
1987	9,351,672	2,192,323 (23.4)	406,934 (18.6)	150,973 (37.1)	4,410 (2.9)	277,030 (12.6)	152,236 (55.0)	18,071 (11.9)
1988	10,289,632[b]	3,099,969 (30.1)	640,987 (20.7)	235,671 (36.8)	5,587 (2.4)	306,860 (9.9)	158,927 (51.8)	13,040 (8.2)

Source: Ministry of Home Affairs, "Yearbook of Local Taxation," each year.

[a]Includes excess landholding tax revenue in 1988.

[b]Budget in 1988.

every year and set the Current Standard Value for Taxation (CSVT), which is then written on the official record of the parcel. As long as taxpayers do not find reasons to be upset (i.e., as long as the properties are undervalued), local governments do not bother to come up with an accurate assessment. The major part of the local government budget does, after all, come from the central government.

Even when land prices increase rapidly, the CSVT is raised only slightly. Nationwide, the CSVT in 1988 was 32.9 percent of the real price, according to the Ministry of Home Affairs, a figure that many feel is an overestimation. As has been shown, tax rates are quite low, but the discrepancy between the market value and the assessed value makes the tax insignificant to landowners and renders land taxation ineffective in achieving any policy goals. Another worrisome aspect is that the gap is greater in urban areas with high land prices and in areas frequented by speculators whose activities boost up land prices; in other words, the wealthy pay relatively less tax.

To calculate the tax base of the transfer income tax, the National Tax Bureau has employed a scheme to narrow the gap between assessed value and the sales price. In large cities and other areas where speculation is feared, the bureau announces factors that are multiplied by the CSVT to produce a value used in taxation.[23] Since the gap between the CSVT and the real price varies by land parcel, multiplication ratios are usually low enough not to overvalue too many land parcels; with the multiplication, the price used for the transfer income tax is considered to be less than 80 percent of the real price on average. The most important problem with this scheme, of course, is the inequity between the treatment of land subject to the multiplication rule and land not subject to it.

These problems of assessment were recognized, and after an intense political debate the Ministry of Construction managed to pass a law in 1989 to improve land assessment. Under the provisions of the new law, a sample of about 300,000 parcels is evaluated by licensed appraisers each year, and the rest of the 24 million parcels subject to landholding taxes nationwide are assessed by land price tables.[24] Each land price table is based on a multiple regression analysis of a particular land market, and nonexpert civil servants need to look at only one table to assess all the parcels in that market. An example is shown in Figure 13.2. Assessment of all privately held land was completed in the summer of 1990, and from early 1991 the transfer income tax, inheritance tax, and gift tax were imposed on that base. For the comprehensive land tax, the assessment ratio will be raised gradually to 60 percent by 1994. This change in assessment will have a far more substantial impact than any proposed changes in tax laws.

The Land Information Management System The difficulties intrinsic to land assessment are only part of a broader problem. Currently, two official records exist for each parcel of land. One is kept by the local government and shows the name, national identification card number and address of the owner, Gimok (type of land),

Distance from City Hall							
Assessed lot	0.1 km	0.3 km	0.6 km	1.0 km	1.5 km	3.0 km	>3.0 km
Standard lot							
0.1 km	1.00	0.62	0.46	0.37	0.31	0.23	0.18
0.3 km	1.61	1.00	0.74	0.59	0.50	0.37	0.40
0.6 km	2.17	1.35	1.00	0.80	0.67	0.50	0.40
1.0 km	2.70	1.68	1.25	1.00	0.84	0.62	0.50
1.5 km	3.22	2.00	1.49	1.19	1.00	0.74	0.59
3.0 km	4.35	2.70	2.00	1.61	1.35	1.00	0.80
Over 3.0 km	5.42	3.37	2.50	2.00	1.68	1.25	1.00

Distance from subway station							
Assessed lot	0.1 km	0.3 km	0.6 km	1.0 km	1.5 km	2.0 km	>2.0 km
Standard lot							
0.1 km	1.00	0.92	0.88	0.84	0.82	0.80	0.78
0.3 km	1.09	1.00	0.95	0.91	0.89	0.87	0.84
0.6 km	1.14	1.05	1.00	0.96	0.93	0.91	0.89
1.0 km	1.19	1.09	1.04	1.00	0.97	0.95	0.92
1.5 km	1.22	1.13	1.07	1.03	1.00	0.98	0.95
2.0 km	1.25	1.15	1.09	1.05	1.02	1.00	0.97
Over 2.0 km	1.29	1.19	1.13	1.09	1.05	1.03	1.00

Area designation (zoning)			
Assessed lot	Residential	Commercial	Green zone
Standard lot			
Residential	1.00	1.22	0.78
Commercial	0.82	1.00	0.64
Green zone	1.28	1.56	1.00

FIGURE 13.2 (continued p. 425) An example of a land price table (Chongro-gu, Seoul). The standard lot is appraised by licensed appraisers, and the assessed lot is assessed by using the price of a similar standard lot and the land price table (Korea Land Development Corporation 1989a).

location, CSVT, and size of the parcel. This record, computerized nationwide, is used for taxation and other administrative purposes. The other, kept by the judicial court, shows various property rights related to the parcel and concerned individuals. Registering ownership and other property rights in this record, on payment of a registration tax, is a protection against possible legal troubles.

The problem is that one or both of the records frequently contain defective information, and they may conflict with each other. For instance, in the records for

Actual Use				
Assessed lot	Residential	Commercial	Mixed	Undeveloped
Standard lot				
Residential	1.00	2.00	1.45	0.43
Commercial	0.50	1.00	0.73	0.21
Mixed	0.69	1.38	1.00	0.29
Undeveloped	2.35	4.70	3.41	1.00

Road condition				
Assessed lot	Six-lane & over	Four-lane	Two-lane	Below two-lane
Standard lot				
Six-lane & over	1.00	0.35	0.27	0.23
Four-lane	2.82	1.00	0.76	0.66
Two-lane	3.72	1.32	1.00	0.87
Below two-lane	4.28	1.52	1.15	1.00

Topography		
Assessed lot	Plain	Sloped
Standard lot		
Plain	1.00	0.79
Sloped	1.26	1.00

FIGURE 13.2 *(continued)*

the 10 million parcels held by individuals, over 3 million do not contain the identification number of the owner, who probably died before the introduction of national ID numbers. In the records of some parcels, the owner's name is omitted, while a building may stand on land classified as a rice paddy, and vice versa. An owner in one record may be different from the owner in the other, and neither of them may be the true owner of the parcel of land. In short, official records do not contain all the relevant information necessary to enforce tax codes and other regulations.

Official records are not accurate in part because of the legal system governing property transactions. When one buys or sells a property, he or she is supposed to register the change in ownership and pay the appropriate taxes. However, even if the proper procedure is not followed, the contract is still valid and the transaction is legally protected. A speculator who intends to evade taxes simply skips registration of the transaction but can legitimately sell the property to another person. In some cases, a purchase is disguised as a loan for which the property is offered as collateral. The buyer essentially acquires full property rights, but the title of the land need not be transferred. High rates for the acquisition tax and the registration tax do not, of course, encourage registration.

The National Assembly passed the Compulsory Property Registration Law in July 1990 which makes nonregistration a criminal offense. This law will deter major forms of tax evasion, enhancing the effectiveness of land taxes. But the majority of lawyers think that unregistered transactions are valid, regardless of the new law.

Tax on Landholding versus Transfer Right or wrong, speculation has been perceived as a major culprit in the rapid increase in land prices, and the transfer income tax has been used to combat it. Whenever speculation is suspected in a certain area, the National Tax Bureau designates that area as a "special zone" and declares a multiplication ratio. As the transfer income tax rate suddenly shoots up, a task force of tax agents is sent to the area to seek out tax evaders.

The increased tax burden and the risk of being caught have certainly deterred speculators, but there is an undesirable aspect to taxing only realized capital gains. A landowner is less motivated to sell the land when the gain is reduced, especially since most Koreans believe that land sales should be extremely lucrative. Most experts agree that, when the transfer tax burden increases, the supply of land tends to decrease.[25] Reduced supply means a higher price at a given level of demand, although no one has sorted out whether the transfer income tax has deterred increases in land prices by suppressing speculation or accelerated price increases by reducing supply. Additionally, a transfer tax whose rate is too high may impede the efficiency of the market. In an extreme case, if the transfer income tax rate is 100 percent, a landowner will not bother to find the highest bidder, much less sell the land at all as long as the price offered guarantees a net gain of zero. This behavior by the seller allows low-productivity users to occupy land; thus, rice paddies may pop up in the middle of major cities.

Since the transfer income tax rate cannot be too high, a holding tax should supplement it to recapture capital gains from land.[26] This argument should not, however, be interpreted as advocating the introduction of a tax to recapture windfall gains on an accrual basis. At least two countries, Taiwan and Great Britain, have tried such taxes, with both attempts failing: Great Britain abolished its land development tax and Taiwan enforces its land value increment tax only at the time of sale. The lesson of these examples is that, since recapturing windfall gains on an accrual basis is extremely difficult, a tax on the sale of land should be used as the primary means of taking away capital gains, and landholding tax supplementary to it should not be directly tied to capital gains in each tax cycle. Moreover, the ratio of the capital gains paid as tax should be reasonable. My opinion is that an effective rate of 50 percent on capital gains is the maximum for a tax on a sales transaction, while 1 percent of land value should be the maximum for tax on landholding.[27] Higher rates would prompt intense efforts for tax evasion, which in turn would distort the whole system.

Land Taxes as a Deterrent to Speculation The comprehensive land tax, the acquisition tax, the transfer income tax, the special surtax on corporate income tax, and the excess profits tax on land all make the distinction between speculative and nonspeculative land in provisions on exemptions, reductions, and tax rates. These taxes and other regulations listed in Table 13.8 are designed to be antispeculation measures, based on the belief that the distinction between speculative and nonspeculative holding of land is possible and that discrimination against speculative landholding is desirable. Land taxes are viewed more as a means of fighting speculation than as a source of revenue.

The success of such an intention depends on the government's ability to sort out which land is held speculatively and which is not. This task is extremely difficult, considering the diversity of land users and their activities, and any codified classification rules, however sophisticated they may be, is bound to be arbitrary. Such complicated rules contained in the Korean tax codes raise several serious issues.

First, as discussed earlier, one can question whether any discrimination against supposedly speculative landholding promotes efficiency in the long run. Second, if the distinction can be successfully made, it is not clear why a progressive rate structure should be applied, as with the comprehensive land tax, instead of a uniformly

TABLE 13.8
Penalties on speculative land

Taxation	Acquisition tax	7.5 times the normal rate of 2%
	Comprehensive land tax	Subject to progressive rate (0.2%–5%)
	Transfer income tax	No exemption or reduction applied
	Special surtax on corporate income tax	Higher rates for short-term turnover (60%) and unregistered transaction (75%)
	Corporate income tax	Deduction of interest payments equivalent to the land value not allowed
	Excess profits tax on land	Subject to taxation
Regulation	Land transaction report and permit	Transaction not allowed
	Bank credit regulation	Acquisition not allowed; penalty on acquisition without reporting or approval (19% interest rate or denial of new credit)
	Idle land designation	Recommendation or advice on land use expropriation
	Order of sale	Forced sale of excessive factory site

high rate, or why taxes should be used at all instead of an outright ban on such landholding. Third, administrative costs are too high to allow effective application of the classification rules to all land parcels. For instance, even if the Ministry of Home Affairs has developed a computerized land record system, it does not contain all of the information necessary to determine the excess landholdings defined by the local tax law. For each land parcel, local government officials must actually go out to examine the land (sometimes more than once), divide it into parts that are excessive and those that are not, and then calculate the value of excess land. Finally, as the tax codes become more complicated, greater personal judgment is required of tax officials, raising the possibility of corruption and the failure of the policy objective.

In fact, since ways to avoid the unfavorable designation of speculative land are well known and widely practiced, the task of selectively penalizing such land has degenerated into a process of justifying tax loopholes for land put into productive use. For such theoretical and practical reasons, I suggest that it is time to admit an inability to distinguish between land that is speculatively held or traded and that which is not.

Reform Proposals for Korean Land Taxation

The intention to suppress speculation not only complicates the tax system, rendering it more difficult to enforce, but also provides a tax loophole. Discarding this objective would dramatically simplify the tax system, reducing tax evasion and the possibility of corruption.

Under a comprehensive land tax, all of an owner's landholdings should be indiscriminately added up and a single progressive rate structure applied to the total. The acquisition tax should not make any distinction, either. As for the transfer income tax and the special surtax on corporate income, exemptions and reductions should be given to a much smaller number of cases than the present tax laws allow.

Tax reductions and exemptions should be limited. Special treatment should be confined to cases in which double taxation arises, as in the case of construction companies that build and sell apartment housing, or when proceeds of land sales go to the purchase of other pieces of land as in the move from one residence to another. In the latter case, there should be an upper limit to the exemption.

Public corporations and educational, religious, and other entities should be favorably treated, but 100 percent exemptions should not be given to any organization, possibly not even to the national government in the case of local taxes.

The tax on landholding should be raised, with a concomitant reduction in the tax on transactions and acquisitions. The effective rate of the acquisition tax should be reduced to under 1 percent and the rate of transfer income tax should be decreased to under 50 percent. In addition, the single progressive rate structure of the comprehensive land tax should be between 0.2 and 2 percent with more rapid progressivity, making the average effective tax rate among large landowners around 1 percent and among small landowners around 0.5 percent.

Assessment must correctly reflect the market price of land. The policy orientation currently pursued by the government is in the right direction, and the new assessment system explained in this chapter would ameliorate the present situation. However, the performance of local governments in this context shows that they may not be relied on for technical expertise. Also, room still remains for error, since local governments and local National Tax Bureau offices have separate powers of assessment—the former for local taxes and the latter for national taxes. It is desirable to set up a new institution responsible for the appraisal and assessment of all land that will supply information for other administrative functions. This institution should also manage all land-related information and make land registration records public and legally binding.

For taxes imposed on land acquisition or transfer, a certain degree of discretion should be given to taxpayers as to whether they pay taxes according to the official assessment or to the price actually declared in the sales contract. If the actual price is preferred, it must be recorded and used in the taxation of the next transaction. The other land taxes should be levied on the basis of the assessments, with the exception of the landholding taxes, which should discount the assessment by a certain proportion for the time being, since the new assessment may dramatically increase the tax burden overnight. As the precision of assessment improves and as landowners grow accustomed to higher landholding taxes, the discount should be reduced.

The functioning of the assessment system depends critically on licensed appraisers. Currently, approximately 1,000 appraisers are overburdened with responsibility for some 300,000 parcels of land to be assessed in annual government assignments and for other public and private sector businesses. Although the appraisers prefer to maintain strict entry requirements, the number of appraisers should be increased more rapidly. Also, measures must be introduced to improve the quality of appraisals.

Effort and resources should be devoted to improving the land-related record system. Issues to be considered include the synthesis of the two types of records into a single system correctly representing all related information, computerization of the information on a broader scale (linked to the national identification card and household database, as well as to building records), and a land census that updates necessary information once and for all.

Since the excess profits tax on land has met intense tax resistance, it should be imposed on only a small number of parcels. In the worst case, efforts to relieve tax burdens may distort the assessment system. Repeal of the tax should be seriously considered.

Reform of Regulations on Land

Regulations on Land Ownership

The progressive rate structure of the comprehensive land tax is an indirect regulation on large land ownership, but a direct measure was introduced by the Residential Land Ownership Law in 1989 as part of the Gongkaenyum legislation.

Compared to limits on land for other uses, setting a limit on the amount of residential land a household could own was politically popular and thought to be less obstructive to normal economic activities.

Under the provisions of the law, an individual can own up to 200 pyong (approx. 660 m^2) of residential land in the six major cities, 300 pyong in other cities, and 400 pyong in rural areas.[28] A corporation is not allowed in principle to hold residential land except to construct nonresidential buildings or for some other purposes by obtaining a permit from the local government. Acquisition of land above the limit is not allowed, and current holdings larger than the limit must be disposed of within two years (smaller parcels are not subject to this regulation). Otherwise, the excess ownership charge is levied, the rates of which are 4 percent for the first two years and 7 percent afterward in the case of built-up land, and 6 and 11 percent, respectively, in the case of vacant land.

This measure is largely a political gesture meant to demonstrate the seriousness with which government is approaching the land problem. Reports of excess landholdings by owners and a field survey by local governments have not yet revealed the amount of land that will be put on the market due to this law, but the quantity will not be large enough to affect the price level. Furthermore, the hidden cost of this regulation could be high. Problems that could arise as a result of this law include large requirements for administrative resources,[29] the possibility of residential land being converted to nonresidential use rather than broadening the ownership base of residential land, and the disappearance of tennis courts, indoor golf ranges, and unregistered parking lots. It seems quite likely that a higher landholding tax for large landowners would have less disruptive effects.

Regulations on Land Transactions

The Land Transaction Reporting and Permit System The Ministry of Construction can designate a transaction contract reporting area if speculation is expected or in evidence. In such areas, 64 percent of the national territory in 1988, a transaction contract for land larger than a certain size must be reported to the local government, which may then recommend a change in the sales price or in the proposed use of land. If more rampant speculation is involved, the area is designated as a transaction contract regulatory area (9,287 km^2 in 1988), in which a contract is not legal without a permit.

These regulations on transactions were conceived to serve two purposes. The first is to control land price increases by recommending a downward adjustment of contract price or by denying a permit should the price be above a certain level. This goal is not being achieved since buyers and sellers report false prices rather than adjust the actual price. The second goal is to identify suspected speculative transactions. Local government officials make judgments in reviewing each contract for information on both the buyer's residency and the intended purpose of the purchase. One obvious indication is when an urban dweller is buying agricultural land in the remote countryside. But such a transaction is already prohibited by other laws which have long been ineffective.[30] The transaction reporting and permit system is thus redundant and will remain ineffective while failing to correct the causes of the old regulation's deficiencies.

With false reporting and no effective means to enforce contract change recommendations, the land transaction reporting requirements have become an irrelevant nuisance both to parties engaged in transactions and to local government officials. In addition, the land transaction permit cannot affect the price of land, although it makes speculators more cautious in spite of the frequent use of legal and administrative loopholes to evade the regulations.

These regulations are, then, largely ineffective and redundant. In particular, efforts at controlling the market price are an abject failure. Resorting to psychological pressure on speculators without altering the expected returns does not seem appropriate.

Credit Regulation on Land Purchase It is popularly believed that large corporations engage in or, worse yet, initiate property speculation by using their network of information and easy access to bank loans. Two major groups of culprits are the powerful conglomerates and financial institutions. In an economy with a perpetual credit shortage, access to large bank loans and loan guarantees is considered a privilege given only to productive investments, and diverting this precious fund into property speculation is considered immoral, inefficient, and iniquitous. Provisions of the Bank Credit Regulatory Ordinance and regulations on the operations of financial institutions define when credit can and cannot be given, specify procedures for reporting and approving property purchases, state penalties for not following proper procedures, and in the case of financial institutions set limits on property holding.

As for financial institutions like banks, security firms, and insurance companies, each corresponding supervisory authority sets a limit on property holding. For instance, banks can own properties valued up to 100 percent of their capital, security firms 50 percent of the capital, insurance firms 15 percent of their assets, and so on. Since the authorities supervising financial institutions are government regulators, the standards should be enforced strictly, but the property holdings of most financial institutions are currently far lower than the limit, since most branches rent rather than own space.

Large conglomerates are prominent beneficiaries of bank credit, and the ordinance stipulates that conglomerates with 150 billion won or more in loans and loan guarantees must report property transactions to their main banks. If the property is classified as having no business purposes (i.e., as being speculative), the purchase is not approved,[31] and noncompliance can result in higher interest rates and denial of further credit as a penalty. If the land is indeed for business purposes, the conglomerate has to raise a certain proportion of the funds needed for the purchase by selling off other properties and nonessential businesses.

Banks have not effectively enforced this regulation. One reason is that banks, under almost complete control of the Ministry of Finance, cannot be too harsh on conglomerate customers who may mobilize support from the higher strata of the political structure. A more fundamental reason is that banks do not consider themselves land policy instruments. Their primary concern is the stability of the credit, not property speculation, and strictly enforcing the ordinance does not seem to be their responsibility, especially with the high cost of implementation. Large conglomerates have thus acquired land at will.

In response to a mounting mistrust of government and large conglomerates, on 8 May 1990 the government decreed that 49 large conglomerates could not acquire properties and had to sell those with no business purpose and that the National Tax Bureau would examine property holdings to ensure compliance. Also, properties acquired through a third-party title had to be reregistered with actual owners. Some contents of the decree are on dubious legal ground, but others simply confirm the existing laws and ordinances. Of the many controversies surrounding the decree, the most important is the dispute between the conglomerates and the National Tax Bureau as to which land is for business purposes and which is speculative. Considering that statutory codes have long been established on that issue, it is surprising that such a dispute would arise at all. The existence of this problem confirms the claim that complicated rules on classifying speculative land are beyond day-to-day administrative capacity and consequently serve as a loophole in land taxation.

Regulations on Land Use and Development

Land Use Regulations Prior to the enactment of the National Land Use and Management Law in 1972, land use planning was implemented only in Seoul under the 1964 City Planning Law. The National Land Use and Management Law initiated land use planning nationwide, and it became a basic law for all land development, planning, and regulation. The law classifies the nation's land into ten areas, as shown in Table 13.9. In each area, landowners are to use the land to fit the designated purpose, and local governments and other government agencies are to grant permits or approvals in accordance with the provisions of law and to establish and implement land use plans.

One of the ten areas designed by law is the urban areas, governed by the City Planning Law. The City Planning Law classifies urban areas into four basic areas, as shown in Table 13.10. The four basic areas are also subject to other designation criteria (which create fourteen districts and four special areas) overlapping the basic areas. For each designation, land use and construction activities are regulated by the City Planning Law and the Building Regulation Law. Among the regulations imposed by the two laws, the most severe restriction applies to the development of the greenbelts.

TABLE 13.9
National Land Use and Management Law

Area: objectives	Prohibited	%[a]
Settlement: current or likely residents' collective living site outside the urban area	Environment-polluting plants, storage facilities of oil and ammunition	0.8
Arable: paddyfield, dry field, orchard, and livestock feeding industry	Use unrelated to agricultural and livestock industries	24.4
Forest preservation: protection of timber, seed gathering, and environment	Use unrelated to forestation	46.5
Industrial: industrial facilities and related activities	Use unrelated to industrial facilities and construction	0.6
Natural environment preservation: protection of natural beauty, water resources, historic sites	Any obstacles to this objective	5.4
Tourism and resort: planned or concentrated tourist facilities	Use unrelated to tourism and resort purposes	0.2
Fishery resource: preservation of fishery resources and protection of coastlines	Any obstacles to this objective	0.6
Development promotion: saved for future development (e.g., farming, industrial)	Use of area that may hinder future development	2.4
Reserved: not designated for special purpose		0.02
Urban	Specified in the City Planning Law	12.9

Source: H. S. Kim (1989); Ministry of Construction (1989).

[a]Percent of total national land. As of 1989, 93.3 percent of total national land (99,237 km^2) had area designation.

The first greenbelt was established around Seoul in 1971 and later around thirteen other major urban areas to restrict urban sprawl, to preserve land for agricultural and recreational use, and to check land speculation on urban fringes. The policy on greenbelts, currently 5.4 percent of the national territory, is one of few consistently and strictly enforced regulations and has a positive effect on preserving open spaces around major cities.[32]

Since the mid-1960s, concentration of population and industries in Seoul has raised concern about urban overcrowding and unbalanced development among regions; therefore, decentralization of population and industries within the capital region as well as dispersal to other regions has been a major goal of regional policies. The National Comprehensive Development Plan established under the provision of the National Land Use and Management Law is one of the instruments for interregional dispersal, while the Growth Control and Management Plan for the capital region under the Capital Regional Planning Law (1982) is for

Table 13.10
City Planning Law

Area: objectives	Prohibited	%[a]
Residential: protect comfortable and sound living environment	Construction that hinders peaceful living	10.9
Commercial: promote business activities	Obstacles to business activities, danger of fire and sanitary problems	1.3
Industrial: promote manufacturing activities	Construction that hinders the establishment of industries	3.4
Green zone: protect open space[b]	High-density development	80.3

Source: H. S. Kim (1989); Ministry of Construction (1989).

[a]Percent of total urban area. As of 1989, 95.9 percent of total urban area (541 urbanized areas, 13,606.6 km^2) had area designation.

[b]Green zone is mostly parks, farmland, and forestland within the urban areas and should not be confused with the greenbelt. Part of the green zone may be in the greenbelt, but not necessarily so.

intraregional decentralization. This latter plan divides the capital region into five subregions depending on different management goals (Table 13.11).[33]

Other legal constraints restrict development in addition to the aforementioned basic laws for land use regulation and the plans drawn up under the provisions of such laws. By one account there are 72 laws that restrict development for specific policy goals, including the preservation of farm and forestland, environmental protection, reservation of land for future housing and industrial development, and deterrence of development in the vicinity of military facilities (H. S. Kim 1989). Table 13.12 contains some of the major regulations.

Development Methods Planners, legal experts, economists, civil servants, and developers may raise very difficult issues about the system of land use regulations, but there is no denying that the complicated and overlapping system has severely restricted land development by the private sector. As demand for more urban land expanded, the government had to institutionalize new development methods, thereby increasing the role of the public sector.

Ahn (1989) counts eleven different development methods. The most important element of each method is the manner in which land is acquired. Land purchase type developments allow developers to buy land at the market price or, if necessary, to expropriate the land at the price set by the government. In land reallotment type developments, landowners retain the title during the development. Residential land development that occurs under the Residential Land Development Promotion Law (1980) is typical of land purchase type development, whereas land readjustment projects are typical of land reallotment type development. Table 13.13 shows that until the 1970s land readjustment was the main

Table 13.11
Growth management subregions in the capital region

Subregion: major cities and towns	Growth management strategies and programs
I. Restricted development subregion: Seoul, Euijongbu, Kuri, Wondang	Dispersal, decongestion, and decentralization 1. Denial of new factory construction 2. Relocation of pollution-generating manufacturing establishments 3. Dispersal of population and control of in-migration 4. Selective dispersal of educational facilities
II. Controlled development subregion: Inchon, Suwon, Anyang, Banwol	Control of population growth and avoidance of urban sprawl 1. Limitations on new factory construction 2. Accommodation of some of the displaced industries from Seoul 3. Promotion of orderly land uses 4. Control of development density with the aid of the greenbelt
III. Encouraged development subregion: Pyongtaek, Anjung, Ansung	Intensive development 1. New town developments such as campus towns 2. Expansion of existing cities and towns as growth centers 3. Development of industrial estate in Ahsan Bay 4. Minimization of pollution problem and of loss of agricultural land 5. Promotion of light and clean industries inland
IV. Environmental protection subregion: Gapyong, Yangpyong, Yoju	Preservation, conservation, and protection 1. Prevention of pollution in the upper Han River basin to maintain water quality 2. Water resources development 3. Natural resources preservation and promotion of recreational activities 4. Promotion of dairy and vegetable farming, including commercial crops
V. Special development subregion: Gangwha, Munsan, Dongduchon, Pochon	Reserved for future development 1. Buffer for national defense 2. Limited development of agro-industries 3. Conservation of forestry and other natural resources 4. Promotion of livestock farming

Source: Kwon (1987).

TABLE 13.12

Regulations on land use and development for specific policy goals

Policy goal	Designation	Area[a] (km²)
To prevent urban sprawl	Greenbelt	5,397.10
To preserve farmland	Absolute farmland	13,618.55
	General farmland	7,760.92
	Farmland development promotion area	141.57
To preserve forest land	Preservation forest land	51,920.87
	General forest land	12,854.02
To reserve land for industrial development	Industrial base development area	606.70
	Industrial development promotion district	52.65
	Inducement area	19.14
	Power plant construction district	48.82
To preserve environment	Parks	7,385.40
	Drinking water protection district	1,307.00
	Historic site protection district	908.94
	Natural habitat preservation district	—
To develop tourism resources	Tourism area	304.29
Other	Pasture land development district	890.00
	Housing land development reservation district	96.82
	Graveyard development district	54.82
	Rural industrial district	17.02
	Hot springs district	39.20

Source: Ministry of Construction (1989).
[a]As of 1988.

development method, but since the enactment of the Residential Land Development Promotion Law the land purchase type has become the major development instrument.

With the land readjustment method, a project is financed by selling a portion of the improved land. That local governments can install infrastructure and acquire land for public use without any budget requirements and that landowners can still obtain significant development gains are reasons for the popularity of the method. However, these advantages may also act as drawbacks. Ahn (1989) points out that the quality of the residential environment can easily deteriorate, since

Table 13.13
Land readjustments and land purchase type developments (1,000 m² and percentage)

	1962–66	1967–71	1972–76	1977–81	1982–86	Total
Land purchase	1,112	3,017	2,735	10,471	54,668	72,003
	(4.6)	(15.8)	(3.3)	(13.3)	(63.9)	(15.6)
Land readjustment	23,003	187,879	79,685	64,494	30,935	390,261
	(95.4)	(84.2)	(96.7)	(86.7)	(36.1)	(84.4)
Total	24,115	190,896	82,685	78,965	85,603	462,264

Source: Ahn (1989).

neither concrete regulations with regard to future subdivision nor any detailed design guidelines exist. Moreover, poor tenants in the project area are not compensated, and a rise in land prices and speculation in and around the project area has been a problem. These are two main reasons why the government switched to the land purchase type development method in the 1980s.

With the land purchase type development method, usually called public development, the developer acquires, or expropriates if necessary, all the land in the project area before the start of the project. Local governments and public corporations under the authority of the central government, such as the Korea Land Development Corporation, the Korea Housing Corporation, and the Korea Water Resources Corporation (formerly the Industrial Site and Water Resources Corporation), can be the developer in public development projects, a role entailing the formulation and implementation of development plans and the consequent sale of the improved lands.

The public development method became popular since huge windfall profits are reaped by public entities. Also, improved land can be sold at a relatively low price to the final demanders, and speculation, at least in the project area, is contained. This method also allows for a comprehensive development plan that can be implemented efficiently; it takes from three to five years on average to complete a public development project, whereas a land readjustment project often takes more than ten years. But this method has its share of drawbacks. Compensation to landowners is based on the preproject appraisal, which is naturally far below the price of land after development. Landowners feel that they are not justly compensated, especially when the land is expropriated. Tenants without property ownership receive some compensation, but it is not always sufficient for relocating elsewhere. In addition, most projects are implemented by corporations under the central government, since local governments lack the necessary expertise and start-up funds. In some cases, conflicts arise between the developer and the local government because the developer is not sensitive to local needs and conditions.

Problems of Land Use and Development Regulations Since regulations on land use and development are complicated and sometimes overlapping, they also are inflexible and cannot accommodate the expanding demand for various types of urban land. Also, central government ministries have the authority to make most of the important decisions on the establishment and change of the area designation and on plans for development and implementation. Local governments and the private sector find it extremely difficult to initiate major development projects. Such difficulties arise for several reasons.

First, there are various conflicting policy goals. For instance, Korea suffered a chronic shortage of rice until the 1970s, and expenditure for imported rice was a significant drain on foreign currency reserves. It was thought necessary to restrict farmland conversion, and such intentions were institutionalized by laws to that effect. Even after self-sufficiency in rice had been achieved, the restriction on farmland conversion remained. Recently, environmental protection emerged as an important policy direction. Balanced regional development is another important consideration that restricts land development in the capital region. These policy objectives all conflict with the goal of adequately developing and supplying urban land to match the timing and location of demand. This is not to say that all other policy goals except those that increase the urban land supply should be ignored; rather, it is to suggest that development would be facilitated if the government were to abandon those policy goals that are obsolete or ineffectively enforced.

Second, even though most experts, including central government officials, agree that much of the regulatory power should be delegated or transferred to the local government level, they are not sure if local governments are capable of setting up and implementing land use and development plans. Lack of planning expertise and a shortage of financial resources are major concerns. But regardless of the state of readiness, local autonomy will be reinstated in the near future and a significant delegation or transfer of power will be inevitable.

Third, the possibility of charges of corruption as a result of development gains is certainly an important factor in the inflexibility of land use plans and the concentration of power in central government ministries. With little assurance that development gains will be recaptured, area designation is established and managed with extreme conservatism, and development permits are rarely given to private entities.

Having tried various measures for recapturing windfall gains with little success, the government introduced the development gains charge as part of Gongkaenyum legislation. The law stipulates that 50 percent of land price increases above the investment put into development be paid to the government. Twenty-six specific development projects stated in the enforcement ordinance are subject to this charge when project size exceeds 3,300 m^2, with development gains for large projects determined by licensed appraisers. Public developers are partially or wholly exempt from the charge. The effect of this charge is expected to be mixed: on the one hand, it can diminish incentives to develop land by cutting down on development gains, but on the other hand, instituting due process will free government officials from fear of suspicion related to the huge windfall gains.

Even under the circumstances described above, one may raise the question of whether the current system of land use regulation is well formulated or implemented. I do not deal with the issue in detail; but from a planner's point of view, two curious omissions in the system are subdivision control and performance criteria. These problems seem to be related to the lack of planning expertise in local governments.[34]

An important consequence of the regulations on land use and development and of institutionalized development methods is that most large-scale development projects are conducted by the public sector, in particular, by the three public corporations mentioned earlier. They have increased their role as legally designated developers under various laws and enforcement ordinances in housing site and industrial base development. Local governments have the same legal status, but with the exception of the largest cities like Seoul and Pusan they do not have the necessary technical expertise and financial resources.[35] At present, local development corporations or task forces are set up at the provincial level. It will take time and experience in completing many small projects to acquire technical expertise. Even then, they will have to learn to raise start-up funds in cooperation with the private sector before they can compete with corporations established by the central government.

Reform Proposals for Regulations on Land

- The residential land ownership limit has dubious benefits with high social costs. The excess land ownership charge overlaps with the excess profits tax on land and other taxes and regulations in punishing owners of idle land. As the effective tax burdens of large land owners increase, the repeal of the law should be cautiously considered.
- The limit on farmland ownership hinders the enlargement of farm size to accommodate mechanization and corporate farming. This limit should be removed.
- It is not possible to control the price of land by regulations on transactions. The land transaction reporting and permit system has been useful only in jailing suspected speculators. With the introduction of the compulsory registration of land transactions, the system becomes redundant. The system should be repealed.
- A qualification review for buying farmland and forestland must be supplemented by a follow-up check on whether the buyer is actually farming or is engaged in a forestation effort.
- Efforts to keep large conglomerates from land speculation are necessary, since the companies benefit from easy access to bank credit. However, bank credit regulation does not seem to be a solution. I propose that at least one reevaluation

of corporate land be compulsory within a certain period of time (say, three years), and any capital gains be taxed as income. Deferred payment, possibly until the sale of land or a major share of stocks, and payment in land should be allowed to relieve possible cash flow problems, and deduction of this tax from transfer income should be allowed when the firm sells the land later. Coupled with the comprehensive land tax, this tax would significantly increase the cost of holding land, and corporations would have an incentive to economize on their holdings. Many would choose to locate in less-developed regions where land prices remain low.

People with different expertise will have different opinions on the regulation of land use and development. Although detailed discussion of the issue is beyond the scope of this chapter, the main directions for reform can be mentioned.

- Much of the authority to establish and change a land's area designation must be delegated or transferred to local governments. The role of the central government should be confined to setting broad guidelines for planning, coordinating local government plans, assisting in the improvement of local government planning capacity, and supervising the recapture of windfall gains.
- Developers other than central government corporations should be encouraged to enter the development process. Currently, only the largest cities are capable of handling their own development projects, but more local governments should be able to develop land to meet the local need for improved land. Due to their lack of technical expertise and start-up funds, it would be inevitable for local governments to cooperate with the private sector. Eventually, private developers should be allowed to execute their own development plans, but only after a concrete system for recapturing development gains has been established.
- The contents of land use regulations should be more accommodating to development. Development should not be deterred for obsolete policy goals, and overlapping regulations should be simplified.

Conclusion

Korea has experienced rapid land price increases, although the price hikes have not come at a steady pace. One or two years of frantic rise were followed by several years of lull. During periodic land price crises, the government strengthens existing anti-speculation measures or introduces new ones, but efforts usually fade with price stabilization. The most recent sharp price increase came around early 1987 with the expansion of the money supply related to the trade surplus. This increase also received the government's usual attention, but with an unprecedented sincerity.

The change in the government's attitude toward property price increases and speculation is explained by changes in the political situation. This government was the first to be democratically elected since the early 1970s and thus must carefully listen to the voices of ordinary people who are fed up with prohibitively high housing prices and the speculative income of a small circle of people to which they do not belong. Unless the land problem is handled carefully, the resentment of the masses could become uncontrollable, and the possibility of extreme social conflict cannot be ruled out.

Since the summer of 1988, the government has launched an all-out attack on housing and land problems. Some of the government-initiated reform measures are undoubtedly essential in solving land problems, but other measures will beget yet more difficulties. Moreover, many needed measures have not been proposed at all.

Taxation's capacity as a device to recapture windfall gains has not yet been explored fully. If the transfer income tax combined with higher landholding taxes can be effectively administered, a large part of the distribution problem could be solved. To this end, the tax system must be simplified by discarding classification rules about speculative land which are virtually impossible to implement.

Substantial expansion of the land supply is necessary, and the nation has plenty of undeveloped land. By allowing local governments more authority in the planning and implementation of development projects and by refining current regulations on land use and development, the central government will be able to satisfy the increasing demand for improved land.

Without combining and initiating these critical reform measures, the land problem will persist for a long time, while more trivial reforms will come and go through the land price cycle.

NOTES

This chapter reviews Korean land market and institutional arrangements as of 1990 and does not attempt to address changes, some radical, since that time.

1. Literally, "Land Gongkaenyum" is translated as public control of land, meaning that society has the right to restrict ownership, use, and disposition of land held by individuals.

2. For instance, the national rate of land price increase is calculated as a simple average of the rates of provinces, which in turn are a simple average of lower administrative units. A more elaborate index would incorporate different weights for different types of land and locations.

3. This claim contradicts the conventional treatment of land supply as having zero price elasticity. Even if total land in a country is fixed, the supply of a particular type of land is not. New developments respond to price signals, and the amount of land put on the market by the current owners also depends on the price. See KRIHS (1989), Neutz (1987), and Evans (1983) for related discussions.

4. See Lee (1990). This conclusion can, however, be changed by adopting different price estimates and allowing for productivity increases.

5. They include studies to measure the size of development gains (KRIHS 1983) and to devise land price tables that would allow easy appraisal even for civil servants with no expertise on the subject (KLDC 1989a, 1989b).

6. An example is the currently implemented land transaction report and permit system, discussed later in this chapter.

7. The interest rate in the informal money market is sensitive to market conditions but is usually about 1.5–2.5 times that of bank loans.

8. I am currently engaged in a study that adopts the Granger causality concept to examine statistically pairwise links between land price increases and other variables, including inflation, private and public construction activities, real production, interest rates, and international competitiveness. Preliminary results indicate that land price is strongly affected by the measure of liquidity in the economy, and in turn land price affects price level.

9. Lee (1990) states that the Korea Land Development Corporation conducted the study, but this has not been formally reported in any publication.

10. The first approach is sensitive to the choice of assessment ratio, which is known to have wide variations. The author's estimate, quoted in this paper, sets the figure at 35 percent, but a more realistic figure may be close to 15 percent. If this is indeed the case, the amount of capital gains is much larger than shown in Table 13.3, but this only strengthens the arguments here. The second approach is risky since there is little information about the characteristics of the land population (i.e., all land parcels in the country), and it is difficult to give weights to particular sample points.

    Part of the difference between these assessments is explained by the different scope of the estimates. The first estimate is the value of land subject to property tax, while the latter estimate is of all land including government holdings.

11. One of the possible remedies to the ill effect of land price increases on land distribution is expanding the ownership base; if all people owned land equally, then land prices would not skew the income distribution. Since there seems to be no feasible method for achieving this goal, as such a state would not optimize resource use, I do not dwell on this proposal. It is worth mentioning that some analysts strongly argue for nationalizing land ownership (e.g., Lim 1985). I suggest that nationalization in any form is costly without definite benefits (see Son 1990 for detailed discussions).

12. They are local taxes in that they are assessed, levied, and collected by the local governments, and their revenue finances local government functions.

13. In the calculation of the tax base, the expenses for improving the property, the increase in the wholesale price index, a fixed amount per year, and possibly a family allowance are deducted. Some deductions are not available for suspected speculators.

14. The tax rates used to be 50 percent for a property owned for less than two years and 40 percent for one owned for more than two years. For a modest residence (floor space 85 m^2 or less), the rate was 30 percent with a two-year residency requirement.

15. Public corporations with a duty to supply land (Korea Land Development Corporation) or housing (Korea Housing Corporation), farming companies that have cultivated the land for eight or more years, religious bodies that use the land for their own needs, and several other kinds of corporations are exempt from the surtax.

16. For population dispersion and balanced development of the national territory, companies moving factories out of the six major cities (or headquarters out of the Seoul metropolitan area) to other parts of the country receive exemption. When land is transferred to qualified housing contractors as building sites for small homes or to governments for public works, and when a private school makes the sales to fund educational purposes, the transfers are also exempt from taxes. Several other activities of specified developers empowered by statutes are also fully or partially exempt.

17. However, an interesting exception, the deemed acquisition, exists. Every parcel of land belongs to one of twenty-four official classes of land (Gimok). Depending on the label attached to the parcel, the range of its use is restricted. All other things being equal, it is natural that a potential building site is more expensive than farmland. When land changes the Gimok, and its price increases as a result, the acquisition tax is imposed on the increase even without a transaction.

18. The progressive rate structure was introduced by the excess landholding tax in 1987, but the difference is that the excess landholding tax was intended to punish speculators and applied progressive rates only to land presumed to be speculative holdings. In contrast, the comprehensive land tax was aimed at broadening the tax base to discourage landholdings above a level that would be determined by the rate structure.

19. Example of such land are farmland held by urban dwellers, forestland with no forestation efforts put in, residential land held by nonresidential landlords, and various kinds of land held by corporations but not used for any apparent business activity.

20. Under the progressive tax rate structure, building owners in the downtown areas of major cities, heavy industry with large requirements for land input, dairy farms which need large pasture land, and so forth will see a sharp rise in tax burden. Subscribers to this view assert that, since they are using land productively, a penalty for accidentally holding highly valued land is not justifiable.

21. I convert the assessed value to the market value by dividing the former by 0.6, since the government plans to raise the assessment ratio to 60 percent by 1994.

22. It is intended to be a penalty for underutilizing land, but the tax burden can decrease, since it will be calculated from the low bracket rates.

23. For instance, if the CSVT is 10,000 won for a unit of land and the multiplication ratio is 5, the National Tax Bureau assumes that the real unit price of land is 50,000 won. In 1989 the area covered by such a rule was 43.5 percent of all land (M. S. Kim 1989)

24. See KLDC (1989a) for a comprehensive explanation of how the land price tables are made and used. KLDC (1989b) contains over 250 land price table corresponding to each jurisdiction of local government.

25. See KRIHS (1989), Kim, Jang, and Kim (1989), and M. S. Kim (1989) for a sample of arguments for the so-called lock-in effect of the capital gains tax.

26. Also, raising the landholding tax would urge the landowner to give up land of which he or she cannot make profitable use even in the long run. Introduction of a comprehensive land tax is in part motivated by such reasoning. As described earlier, its tax rates are probably too low to make any substantial impact.

27. A calculation shows that, at the rate of land price increases in the period 1974–87, the transfer income tax with an effective rate of 50 percent coupled with a 1.7 percent landholding tax could have recaptured 75 percent of capital gains in Seoul. With the same transfer income tax rate and the goal of recapturing capital gains, the landholding tax would be 1.0 percent for the nation (Land Gongkaenyum Study Committee 1989). While apparently a reasonable burden, these landholding tax rates are 10 to 20 times that of the present effective rate.

28. The enforcement ordinance stipulates that only land in the six major cities is subject to the limit for the time being.

29. The computerized land records contain information about current use (Gimok), but "building site" is not differentiated into commercial or residential categories. Thus, a field survey of each parcel is needed to enforce the law, and a new, additional, nationwide recordkeeping system is required.

30. Proclaiming the land-to-the-tiller principle, the Land Reform Law (1950) redistributed agricultural land to farmers and prohibited farmland ownership to nonfarmers. Local committees of farmers are supposed to decide on the credentials of prospective buyers, but the committee review is largely ineffective since farmers prefer the higher prices offered by urban dwellers. Recently the government introduced a similar measure for forestland, mandating a forestation plan as a precondition to purchase.

31. For the classification of land, standards similar to those of local tax laws are used.

32. However, the cost is high. Kwon (1987) identifies major problems as including the following: residents and landowners in greenbelts suffering losses without compensation for relative declines in land prices and restrictions on development; rigid regulations and confusion over implementation, resulting in no development at all even for open-air recreation facilities; high costs for protection of greenbelts in local growth centers that inhibit their role in national development plans. In addition, demand pressures on other land in the city are accelerating.

33. "The basic strategy is to reserve the Special Development and Environmental Protection Subregions as open space for future use and to develop extensively the southwestern part of the Capital Region to absorb the population and industry dispersed from the Restricted and Controlled Development Subregions" (Kwon 1987).

34. With subdivision control, local governments can regulate the size and shape of a lot and its accessibility and negotiate with the developer for the provision of public utilities. An industrial facility classified as a manufacturing site by purely economic standards is regulated in more or less the same way whether or not it produces pollution or any other public nuisance. Performance standards instead evaluate various locational qualifications of the activity for admissions to a particular use zone. Both techniques would require a substantial refinement in the present state of urban planning in Korea (H. S. Kim 1989).

35. In early 1989 the president gave instructions that some of the public projects being planned by the Korea Land Development Corporation and others under the Ministry of Construction be transferred to local governments or to corporations set up by them. It was supposed that such measures would satisfy local needs better and raise extra revenue for local governments. Many of these projects were later returned to the original developers because local governments were not capable of handling the projects.

REFERENCES

Ahn, Kun-hyuck. 1989. "Korean Experience in Urban Development." In *Training Course on Human Settlement Planning*. Seoul: Korea Research Institute for Human Settlement (May).

Economic Planning Board (EPB). Various years. *Monthly Economic Statistics*. Seoul.

Evans, Alan C. 1983. "The Determination of the Price of Land." *Urban Studies* 20:119–129.

Hwang, Myung-chan. 1985. "The Directions for Land Policies." In Myung-chan Hwang (ed.), *Studies on Land Policy* (in Korean). Seoul: Kyung young moon whawon.

Kim, Hyun-sik. 1989. "Land Use Planning and Policies in Korea." In *Training Course on Human Settlement Planning*. Seoul: Korea Research Institute for Human Settlement (May).

Kim, Myung-sook. 1989. "The Capital Gains Tax and the Lock-in Effect in Korea." *Korean Development Review* 4:2–22.

Kim, W. T., D. H. Jang, and K. S. Kim. 1989. "On the Effectiveness of Capital Gains Tax as a Stabilizer of Real Estate Prices." Paper presented at the Seminar on Socioeconomic Policies, Socioeconomic Policy Institute, Seoul (June).

Korea Land Development Corporation (KLDC). 1989a. *A Study on Land Assessment Tables and Their Use* (in Korean). Seoul.

Korea Land Development Corporation (KLDC). 1989b. *Land Assessment Tables* (in Korean). Seoul.

Korea Research Institute for Human Settlement (KRIHS). 1983. *A Study on Recapturing Development Gains and Compensating for Developing Losses* (in Korean). Seoul.

Korean Research Institute for Human Settlement (KRIHS). 1989. *A Study on Land Taxation* (in Korean). Seoul.

Kwon, Won-Yong. 1987. "Population Decentralization from Seoul and Regional Development Policy." In H. Richardson and M. C. Hwang (eds.), *Urban and Regional Policy in Korea and International Experiences*. Seoul: Kon-Kuk University Press.

Land Gongkaenyum Study Committee. 1989. *Report of the Land Gongkaenyum Study Committee* (in Korean). Seoul.

Lee, Jin-soon. 1990. "System of Land Ownership and Use." Paper presented at the workshop on Comparative Analysis of Development Policies in China, Japan, and Korea, Korea Development Institute–East-West Center (May).

Lim, Jong-cheol. 1985. "Whose Land Is It?" In Myung-chan Hwang (ed.), *Studies on Land Policy* (in Korean). Seoul: Kyung young moon whawon.

Lindeman, Bruce. 1976. "Anatomy of Land Speculation." *AIP Journal*, 142–152.

Ministry of Construction, ROK. 1989. *Annual Report on National Land Use*. Seoul.

Ministry of Construction, ROK. Various issues. "Change Rate of Land Prices." Seoul.

Neutz, Max. 1987. "The Supply of Land for a Particular Use." *Urban Studies* 24:379–388.

Rosen, Shirwin. 1974. " Hedonic Prices and Implicit Markets: Product Differentiation in Pure Competition." *Journal of Political Economy* 82 (Jan./Feb.).

Son, Jae-young. 1990. "Economic Analysis of the Land Problem and Policy Alternatives." KDI Policy Analysis series 90-01 (January).

Chapter 14

More Land at Lower Prices: The Deregulation Alternative

Michael L. Hoffman and Raymond J. Struyk
The Urban Institute

Introduction

The question of land—its price and its effect on the affordability of housing—has recently been attracting popular, governmental, and scholarly attention in many countries. This is true in Korea as well, but there this high level of attention has existed for several decades and has included substantial governmental efforts to address the issues. Thus, Korea presents a situation where a large body of experience can be analyzed, and lessons articulated, which we hope serve as a basis for discussions on change and reform.

In Korea, as elsewhere, much of the government's policy agenda, and much of the scholarly research agenda as well, has been shaped by several widely held propositions: the absolute amount of available land is small; land prices have been rising at unreasonably fast rates and their level is much too high; land speculation is widespread and detrimental to sound development; and land ownership is concentrated in the hands of a small group of actors. Like all such propositions, there is some truth in some of these, but over time they all become overstated and overused, fueling popular discontent and encouraging quick, simplistic political responses. Further, such widely held beliefs obscure the complexity of the land problem, hinder dispassionate analysis, and limit politicians' ability and will to make the hard tradeoffs and decisions that any solution will require (see Clifford 1989a, 1989b, and 1991 for an account of recent events).

Much of the response of the Korean government to the problem of high land prices and limited supply has been a mixture of demand-side measures—taxation of profits, price ceilings, and so on—combined with attempts to increase supply through a greater public role in the provision of land for development. This approach has not only responded to public concerns but also been consistent with the government's overall philosophy regarding the Korean political economy (see Y. H. Kim 1990). Unfortunately, early signs that this approach was not working to solve land development problems were met only with variations on the previous themes rather than a broad reassessment of the nature of the approach. Thus, different taxes were added, more restrictions were placed on land uses, and new public supply mechanisms were layered on top of old.

Today, Korea finds itself with underinvestment in the urban sector as a whole and housing in particular, house purchase has become unaffordable to a large sector of the population, and the land problem is affecting the country's economic and political growth and development. In Chapters 12 amd 13, Jin Soon Lee and Jae-Young Son describe in considerable detail the nature and dimensions of land development in Korea; here we build on their foundation and explore the institutional questions affecting land supply and development. In particular, we assess the impact of the regulatory framework and focus on modifications and reforms that could facilitate land provision. In doing this we are aware that changes in the land regulation system are only part of a broader economic picture, and we agree with Renaud's analysis that in the past "extended periods of financial repression and the scarcity of mortgage lending have generated significant distortions in the output of the Korean housing sector" (1989:3). But we would add that removing or liberalizing land supply constraints is a key part of the solution.

We begin with a brief review of the quantitative supply of urban residential land in order to illustrate how quickly land is being consumed by urbanization and residential development and what the limits might be in the future. We then look at Korea from an international perspective, contrasting the Korean experience with that of the United States, Germany, and Japan in terms of land supply, housing prices, household income, and finally the responsiveness of the housing supply. We then review the Korean regulatory framework and conclude with an analysis linked to reform measures.

Urban Land Supply in Korea: The Quantitative Dimension

In this section we briefly review the provision of land for urban and especially residential use in Korea. We do this in order to sketch the physical setting for the discussion that follows as well as to answer several questions: What share of the country is urbanized? How rapidly is this urbanization proceeding? How does this urbanization compare to the rate of household formation?

In gross terms, and varying slightly with the data source and definitions, we find that urban land use[1] in Korea was slightly more than 2 percent of the nation's land area in 1990. In areal terms, such land uses increased at an annual average of 28 square kilometers a year, or 0.03 percent of the land base during the 1985–90 period (Korea, Ministry of Home Affairs, 1985, 1990). Other sources, taking a broader definition of urban use, give estimates as high as 4.5 percent of the national land base; but even with the higher figures the actual share of the nation's land resource base annually consumed by urbanization is minimal.

While this gross land use pattern is informative, a closer appraisal of land provision can be gained by comparing the growth in residential land supply to the growth in households over the past two decades (Figure 14.1). For the nation as a whole, the rate of growth for residential land supply paralleled that of household formation in the 1970s, but in the 1980s a marked difference appeared with land supply growing at a slower rate. For Seoul, households grew at a faster rate throughout the period, but that rate appears to have slowed in the late 1980s. Thus, although land is available, it appears not to have been entering the development process at rates comparable to household formation or the potential demand.

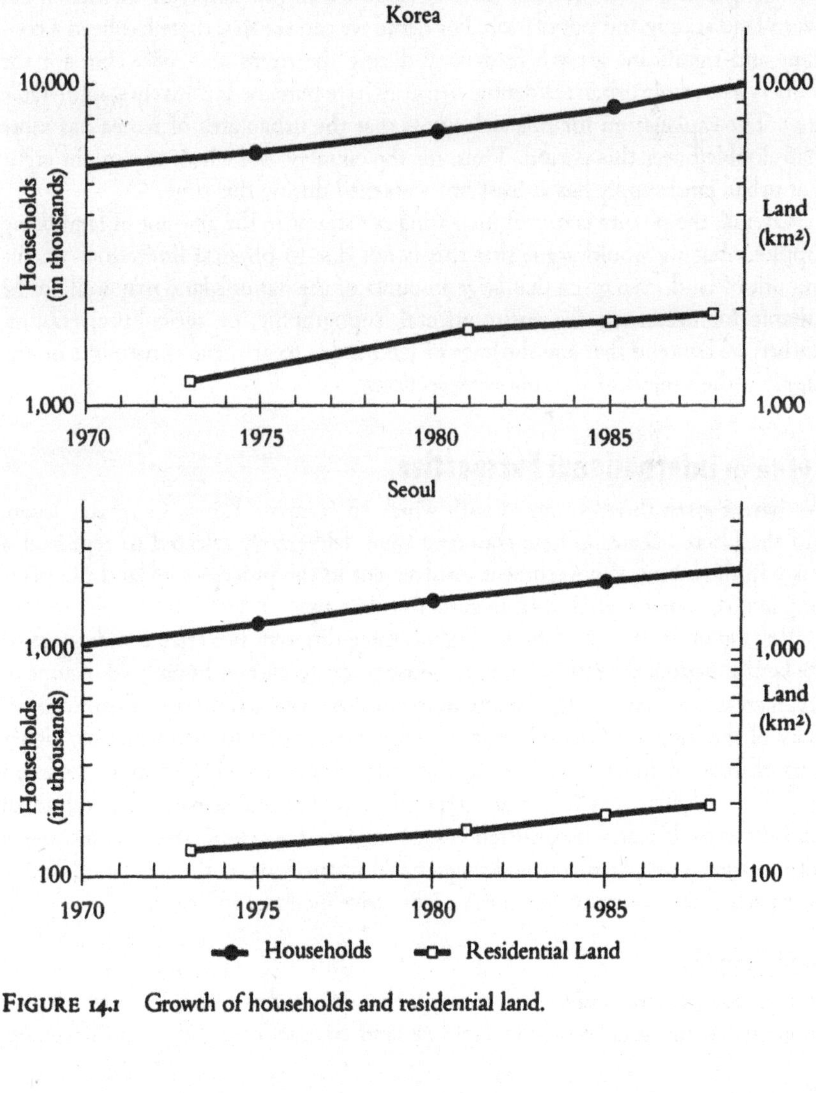

FIGURE 14.1 Growth of households and residential land.

TABLE 14.1
Gross residential density (persons/km²)

Year	Seoul	All cities
1973	10,030	3,650
1981	13,837	3,835
1985	15,944	3,828
1988	17,003	3,538

Source: Authors' calculations.

Changes in gross residential density also give an indication of the match between land supply and population. For Seoul we can see that there has been a constant and significant growth in density during the 1970s and 1980s, but for the country as a whole urban residential densities have remained relatively stable (Table 14.1). The explanation for this stability is that the urban area of Korea has more than doubled over this period. Thus, for the country as a whole one might argue that urban land supply has at least not worsened during this time.

Overall, the picture is one of increasing constraint in the amount of land being supplied, but we would argue that this is not due to physical limitations on the amount of land, even given that large amounts of the nation's land may well not be suitable for urban use for environmental, topographic, or agricultural reasons. Rather, we contend that any shortage of land is due to artificial constraints on the supply—the subject of the following sections.

Korea in International Perspective

We have chosen three countries with which to compare Korea: Germany, Japan, and the United States. These countries were deliberately selected to represent a range in the extent of government involvement in the processes of land use planning and conversion of land from rural to urban uses.

Relying on secondary data, we look at three different but related indicators of the land situation: the ratio of average house prices to average household income in urban areas, the trends in land prices in recent years, and estimates of the price elasticity of the supply of urban housing. Higher house price to income ratios, higher rates of inflation in land prices, and lower price elasticities all signal restrictions on the ability of suppliers to readily respond to household demand for additional housing units. If Korea is consistently identified in these comparisons as a country with restricted supply, this would suggest that restrictions on the supply side are at least partially the cause of the extreme land price increases in Korea.

Land Supply

Briefly, Japan, Korea, and Germany are all characterized as countries in which government has immense power to regulate land transactions; the main differences among them may be in the efficiency with which these duties are discharged and the relation among the effects of these regulations, tax laws, and monetary policy in each country. The United States stands in stark contrast with, on average, relatively little government intervention.

As recounted in Chapter 12, in Japan there has been a steady expansion over the past twenty years in the powers provided to regional governments over land use planning and control. The 1974 National Land Use Act, for example, permits these governments to establish control areas within which all land transactions require government permission and are subject to government-established price ceilings. Beyond the formidable local controls, administration of the Agricultural Law of 1952 (amended several times, notably in 1969) has strictly limited the volume of land converted from agricultural to residential land. Similarly, the provisions of the Building Standards Law and regulations on residential development passed by local government have limited the efficient use of land.

These restrictions on the urbanization of land have been exacerbated by other provisions which together have contributed to land price inflation (Noguchi 1990; Ito 1990). These include easy monetary policy during key periods (especially during the recent land price surges in Tokyo of 1986 and 1987), very low property tax rates which encourage land hoarding, undervaluation of inherited land (until recently changed), and a land lease law that gives occupants very strong rights and thereby encourages landowners to keep land unoccupied and undeveloped.

The situation in Korea has been substantially discussed in Chapter 12 and 13. J.H. Cho (1990) gives some additional details on government's pervasive role in the land urbanization process. Perhaps most striking is the absolute primacy of municipal governments and two government corporations (KHNC and the Korea Land Development Corporation [KLDC]) in acquiring and servicing land. The lack of really any role for private developers is remarkable. This arrangement coupled with the highly centralized administrative decision procedures governing land conversion appears to make a lethargic supply response nearly inevitable.[2] However, it may well be that this already difficult situation is made even worse by price controls on new apartments, which makes new developments more difficult to structure profitably in light of the land costs and, as Renaud (1989) has pointed out, extended periods of financial repression and little mortgage lending; the net effect is lower production and greater excess demand.

The situation in Germany is somewhat different.[3] It is characterized by highly decentralized decision making within a system of heavy government regulation. Assuring the provision of the appropriate quantity of new urban land is a task of the municipal government, operating within general federal government laws. Municipalities prepare and update master plans through an elaborate process that includes substantial consultation with the public. Many municipalities purchase land well in advance of urbanization needs; at times they make use of their powers of expropriation to do so. The municipality then undertakes to ensure that land is converted (provided with the necessary urban services) at the appropriate time, either by acting as its own developer or permitting private entities to carry out this function—that is, a private developer receives permission to develop a subdivision within the master plan. The comprehensiveness of the planning process and the powers of local governments in these areas should not be underestimated. In brief, an adequate provision of land depends very heavily on the efficiency of the local bureaucracy. Note also that the German economy has been carefully managed to keep inflation at low levels and to restrict undue growth in the money supply; moreover, investment opportunities besides real estate are abundant.

The United States is similar to Germany in the extent of local control over land planning. It differs from Germany, however, in that in the United States there is no structure of federal law establishing the overall framework; rather, land issues fall under the legal jurisdiction of the states. In the main, local governments have enormous latitude in permitting development; indeed, until the past ten or fifteen years development was viewed as a sign of a prosperous community and was encouraged by local governments. Planning in many communities was limited, and approved plans were subject to fairly easy modification. Developers received approval for their plans quickly compared with the experiences in Europe or Japan.

More recently, the situation in the United States has become rather complex, with many communities and some states dramatically increasing the comprehensiveness and detail of the planning process and being more assiduous in their administration of the plans. Tough zoning provisions and growth controls are now common in the cities on both the Pacific and Atlantic coasts but remain exceptional for cities in the remainder of the country. The general view is that, where growth controls are being implemented, they are raising the price of housing and possibly leading to inefficient land use.[4] In looking at data on the United States as a whole, the sharp variance among regions should be kept in mind.

House Prices and Income

Renaud (1991) and others argue that the ratio of the average house price to the average household income in urban areas is a good summary indicator of a housing market's performance; higher ratios generally signal some sort of bottleneck in the supply of housing. Typically, these supply bottlenecks result from inefficiencies in the development of serviced land; stated alternatively, binding constraints are seldom in effect on the supply of structures. Having said this, the interpretation of differences in this ratio across countries must be undertaken with some caution, because there may be systematic differences in dwelling quality and unit size (reflecting both differences in tastes and preferences and the price of housing relative to other goods and services) accounting for some of the variation. That is, prices in this ratio are not for a constant quality unit across countries.

TABLE 14.2
Housing price income ratios: Selected countries

Country	Ratio	Country	Ratio
Korea		Australia	4.0
Seoul	6.0	Canada	4.8
Pusan	5.5	France	2.8
Small cities (average)	4.5	Netherlands	2.4
Japan	6.6	Sweden	1.8
Germany	3.8	United Kingdom	3.7
United States	2.8		

Source: Renaud (1991: tabs. 1 and 2).

Table 14.2 provides data on this ratio for several countries in recent years. Of the countries included in the table, Korea and Japan have ratios at the top of the range, Germany is in the middle, and the United States is near the bottom. We had anticipated a higher ratio for Germany, based on the elaborate planning by and active intervention of local governments in the urbanization process. That the ratio is fairly low suggests that, although local government intervention is substantial, the outcome is nevertheless reasonably efficient.

Trends in Land Prices

The house price-to-income ratios give an indication of the efficiency of the supply side in a country at a given time, but at any time they may also be influenced by surges in demand and other factors.[5] Therefore, we complement the ratios just presented with data on recent trends in land prices for the four countries included in the analysis.

We assembled data on land prices from a variety of sources for three of the countries. For the United States a suitable series for land prices was not available. In this case we have used the index on constant quality new homes, under the assumption that, particularly after deflation by a general price index, the price trend is related to the trend in land prices. The length of the price series varies among countries, with all including part or all of the 1980s. The shortest series is for Tokyo and Osaka in Japan (1983–90), owing to inconsistencies identified among several series that we located for other periods.[6] The series for the other countries all extend well into the 1970s.

Figure 14.2 shows the trend in nominal and real land prices in the four countries. All figures have been converted to a 1985 base year and real land prices are defined as nominal prices divided by the consumer price index. The figure shows clearly the jump in land prices in the second half of the 1980s in Korea and Japan relative to Germany and the United States. It also demonstrates that real land prices in the United States and Germany have been very stable over time, whereas they have taken upward jumps in Korea from time to time and in Japan in the 1980s.

As suggested earlier, the price patterns observed are consistent with a story of restrictions on the supply of land exacerbated by other factors such as macroeconomic easy-money policy. The information on trends in regional house prices in the United States shown in Figures 14.3 and 14.4 adds some support for this hypothesis. Figure 14.3 displays the trend in the price of constant quality new homes in the Northeast and Midwest regions, and Figure 14.4 gives the trend in the ratio of house prices to mean family incomes in these regions; in effect it controls for housing price increases being matched by income increases. We selected these two regions because they offer a strong contrast in terms of growth controls: jurisdictions in the Northeast have over the past decade or longer added increasingly restrictive growth controls and environment-preserving requirements for new housing development; in contrast, local governments in the Midwest region have remained relatively pro-growth.[7] Hence, the differences in price developments between the two areas are a loosely controlled experiment on the impact on housing prices of supply-side restrictions.

The figures illustrate a significant surge in house prices in the Northeast compared to the Midwest during the mid-1980s. The difference disappeared, however, when the "Massachusetts Miracle" of economic growth collapsed in 1988–89. The very sharp decline in housing demand in the Northeast sent house prices falling, as shown in the figure. Thus it is too early to ascertain the prolonged effect of the growth restrictions on development.

Responsiveness of Housing Supply

The final comparative data to be presented are on the price elasticity of the supply of housing. Fundamental to increasing the housing supply are increases in the volume of urbanized land. Obviously, the lower the degree of supply responsiveness to a demand shock, the greater the price increase. Our working hypothesis is that low responsiveness is the fundamental explanation for land price inflation in Korea.

Analysts at the World Bank (1988:88) report a price elasticity of housing supply of about 1.0 for Korea. Using the same analytic approach, these authors also estimate an elasticity of 22 for the United States. This very high U.S. elasticity is consistent with Follain's (1979) earlier estimate of an essentially infinitely elastic long-run supply curve. These differences speak for themselves.

Conclusions

The general, if highly simplified, picture that emerges from comparing the Korean situation with that of several other countries is one of restrictions in the supply of land being a fundamental factor in driving land price increases. A more general review of the patterns of land price increases rightly brings in other factors, including macroeconomic developments which, by driving demand increases, produce inflationary bubbles.[8] In his review of sharply contrasting patterns of housing price increases in individual metropolitan areas in the United States, Case (1990) conjectures that the existence and amplitude of such bubbles is related to the presence and

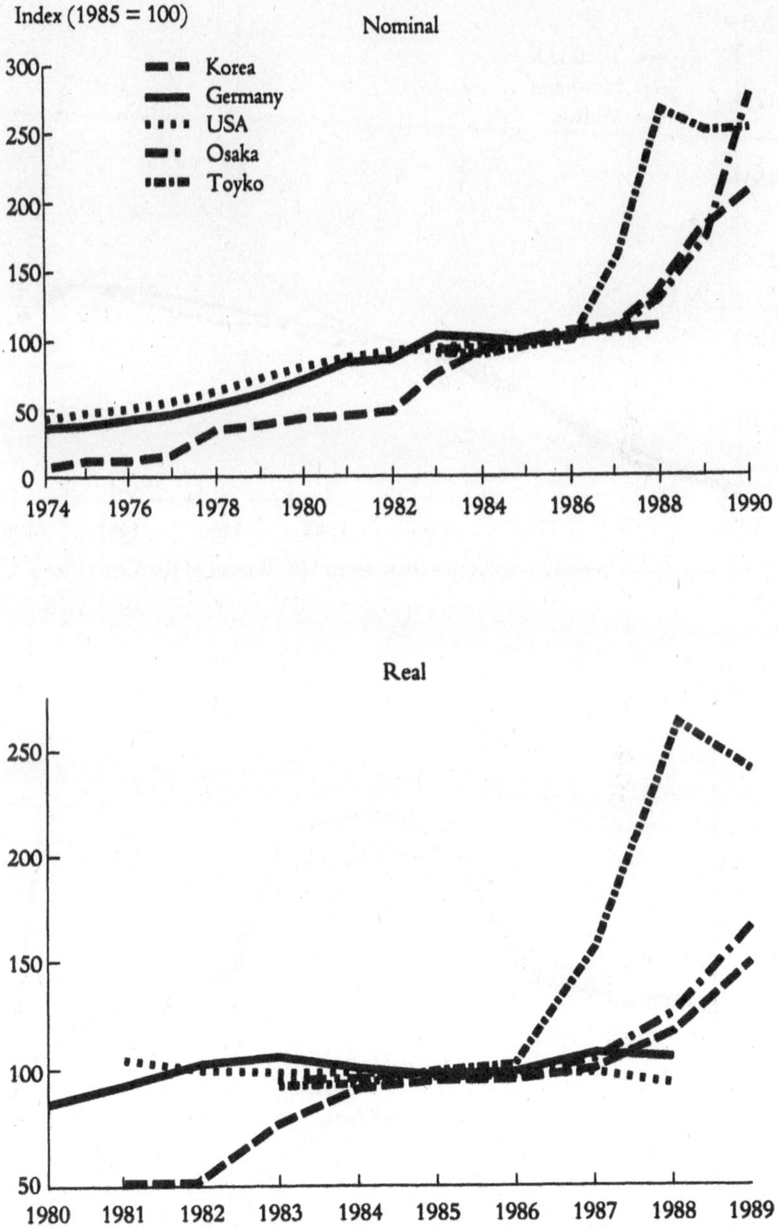

FIGURE 14.2 Nominal and real land prices (Son 1990:tab. 1; Noguchi 1990:tab. 2; *Statistiches Jahrbuch* 1990:538, 1985:507, 1981:498, 1974:447; and U.S Bureau of the Census 1989).

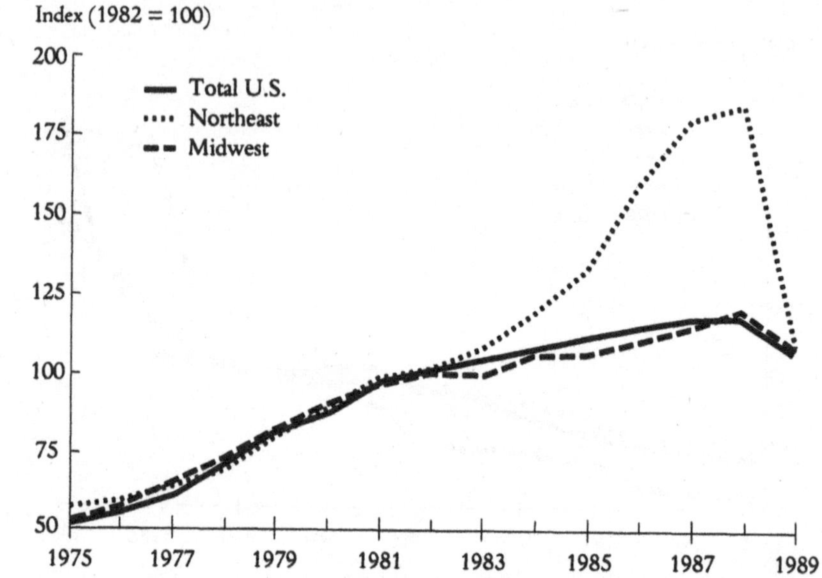

FIGURE 14.3 U.S. housing price index (data from U.S. Bureau of the Census 1989, C-27 series).

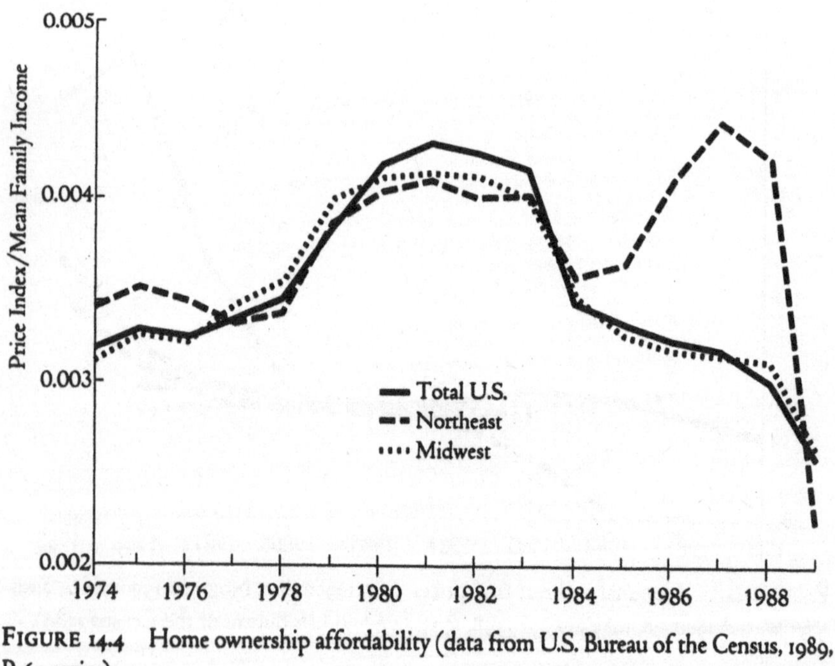

FIGURE 14.4 Home ownership affordability (data from U.S. Bureau of the Census, 1989, P-60 series).

strength of growth restrictions. The greater such restrictions, the greater the likelihood of bubbles and the greater their amplitude. The recent sharp declines in land prices in Korea and Japan provide dramatic evidence of the dislocations on the overall economy such "bubble bursts" can cause. If land price bubbles are strongly related to land supply restrictions, the path to reducing the severity of land inflation bubbles in Korea leads through increasing land supply responsiveness. In the balance of this chapter we deal with ways supply responsiveness might be improved.

The Regulatory Framework of Land Supply

In general, Korean laws and regulations affecting land supply can be placed in three groups: those that create institutions and procedures for the public acquisition and development of land; those that control the conversion and use of land; and those that affect private sector ownership and transfer. A list of the various laws is found in Table 14.3. This listing of laws and regulations is not comprehensive—by one count there are 72 laws that restrict development (see Chapter 13). It is provided to illustrate the level of regulatory attention land issues have received. It should be noted that after a period of intense activity in the 1970s there was a break in the 1980s that corresponded roughly to the period when real estate activity lessened somewhat. But then in 1989, perhaps in response to public unrest, a new effort was

Table 14.3
Major laws affecting land supply

Act	Purpose
Urban Planning Law (1962)	Regulation of housing development
Eminent Domain Law (1962)	Compulsory land acquisition
National Land Use Planning Law (1963)	Regional land use planning
Land Readjustment Law (1966)	Land readjustment; provision of infrastructure
National Land Use and Management Law (1972)	Designation of land use areas
Industrial Base Development Promotion Act (1973)	Provision of land for industry
Land Banking Law (1974)	Establishment of Land Bank
Law on Public Land Acquisition (1975)	Purchase of land by negotiation
Urban Redevelopment Law (1976)	Development of high-density commercial areas
Housing Construction Promotion Act (1977)	Public housing construction
Korea Land Development Corp. Law (KLDC) (1978)	Established KLDC
Residential Land Development Promotion Act (1980)	Low-cost residential land supply
Land Transaction Permit and Reporting Laws (1989)	Requires permit for and reporting of land transactions in designated areas
Urban Residential Land Ceiling Act (1989)	Regulation of land held for speculation
Development Charge Act (1989)	50 percent charge on betterment value
Abnormal Capital Gains Tax Act (1989)	Taxes unused land with high value increase

begun with a series of laws aimed at further controlling speculation and concentration of ownership.

Mechanisms for Public Supply

The government of Korea has created several public agencies and administrative procedures for land provision, and almost all development takes place through these paths as opposed to the private sector. Different writers list anywhere from six to eleven different land development paths, but the two main methods have been land readjustment and public purchase and development. Together these methods accounted for approximately 85 percent of the land area developed during the 1982–88 period, with the balance being housing lot development under the Urban Planning Law of 1962, also a public development method. Figure 14.5 shows the relative shares of the two major methods from 1962 through 1988; most noticeable is the shift from land readjustment to public purchase and development in the early 1980s.[9] In part, the land readjustment process had been criticized for contributing to land price increases and speculation in and around project areas (Cho 1990:14; Doebele 1982), and also because the process was extremely lengthy and cumbersome, with some analysts stating that such projects often took more than ten years to complete.

The main method replacing the land readjustment process was direct public purchase and redevelopment authorized under the Residential Land Development Promotion Law of 1980. Here the developer (the local government or a public corporation) either purchases the land at a fixed price or expropriates the land and develops or services the land according to a comprehensive development plan. Most such projects have been implemented by public corporations under the control of the central government because local governments appear to lack the expertise and initial capital. More interesting, the shift from land readjustment to public purchase and development resulted in a corresponding shift in capital gains from the original landowners to the developer and to a lesser extent to the final consumer (Cho 1990:19–20).

Regulations on the Conversion and Use of Land

Beginning in 1972 with the enactment of the National Land Use and Management Law, Korea instituted land use planning and management procedures across the country, dividing the national territory into ten areas: agriculture, forest, human settlement, and so forth. Local government and other government agencies grant development permits for proposed uses that are in conformance with the law and pertinent regulations. Within the areas designated for urban use, the Urban Planning Law also applies, and additionally there are fourteen other districts and special areas that overlap the basic land use categories (see Chapter 13 and Cho 1990:11–12). Among the urban land use categories, the greenbelt area is of particular importance; it currently is in effect around fourteen major urban areas and includes over 5 percent of the nation's land.

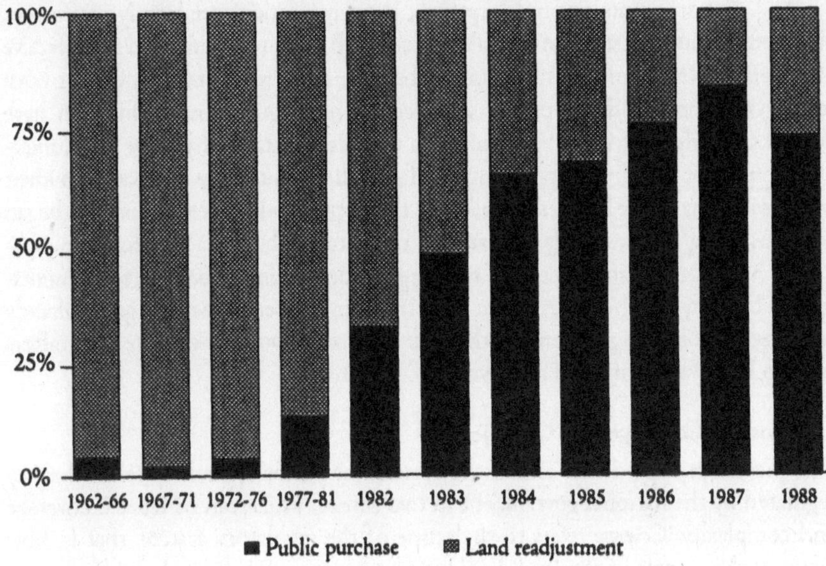

FIGURE 14.5 Major paths for residential land supply by development path (adapted from Cho 1990).

Without going into more detail, it can be said that these regulations tightly constrain and often prohibit urban development on an immense portion of Korea's land; for example, forest, agricultural, and environmental protection areas amount to approximately 75 percent of the total national land area. And it should be remembered that, even where development is permitted, these laws carry high administrative costs for permits, licenses, and so on—costs borne by both the developer and the public at large. As a whole, the government has created a vast network of complicated and often overlapping regulations which heavily impacts all efforts to supply land.

Price Control and Antispeculation Measures

A third general area of regulation involves government's attempt to control speculation and concentration of land ownership. Some of the more recent efforts in this area have included taxation measures, limits on the amount of land a party can own, and reporting and permitting of private land transactions (see Table 14.3). The reporting and permitting system regulations permit the Ministry of Construction to designate a transaction contract report area if speculation is expected or in evidence. Once an area has been so designated, contracts larger than a specified size must be reported to the local government, which may then recommend a change in the sale price or use of land. If more severe land speculation is involved, the area may be designated a transaction regulatory area where a contract for the sale of land is not legal without a permit.

As J. Y. Son points out in Chapter 13, these regulations are largely ineffective, since buyers and sellers report a false price; with false reporting and no effective enforcement, the regulations have simply become an "irrelevant nuisance" for both local government and the parties involved. Other regulations in this vein have proved similarly ineffective. For example, a 1990 decree stated that large conglomerates could not acquire property and had to sell landholdings unrelated to their business. Many of the businesses balked at the decree, and numerous disputes began over classifying various lands as related or unrelated to business (Clifford 1991). As others have noted, enforcement of such regulations is simply beyond the administrative capacity of the government and in many respects involves goals already addressed by other regulations. In the end, one has to wonder whether the drafters of such laws wanted more than a symbolic gesture.

Conclusion: Coverage and Complexity

The picture presented here is that the Korean land development system is heavily regulated by the national government in two senses, which can be labeled coverage and complexity. *Coverage* refers to the scope of the regulatory system, that is, how many of the aspects of the land development process are regulated and how many are left to the market. *Complexity* refers to how many regulatory actions—permits, approvals, licenses—are required both to achieve that coverage and to develop land.

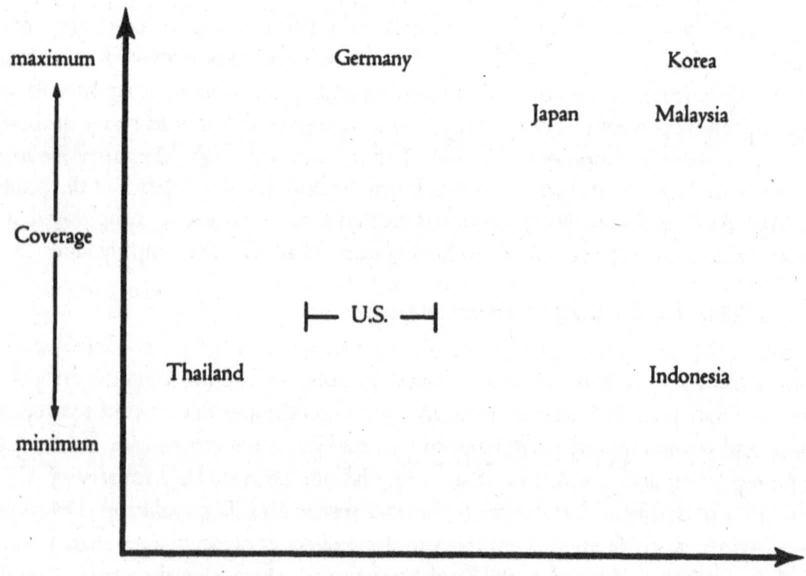

FIGURE 14.6 Extent of regulation.

As a simple example of this distinction, it is possible to imagine a system with very comprehensive coverage but minimal complexity: the government decides about all aspects of proposed development, but it does so on the basis of one permit. Alternatively, coverage may be limited but the number of approvals extreme. The application of this distinction to different countries is illustrated in Figure 14.6.

Germany and other similar states have fairly comprehensive regulatory systems, but the regulatory burden is not unduly excessive. Indonesia, on the other hand, is an example of a country where the amount of regulation is excessive but the comprehensiveness of such regulation limited. The United States has a moderate amount of regulation in both senses, although as pointed out this varies significantly within the country. Finally, we would argue that Korea is a case of excess regulation in terms of both comprehensiveness and complexity.

The reason for emphasizing this distinction is that each of these aspects of regulation raises different concerns from the perspective of reform. Coverage raises questions of policy goals and the rationale for regulation; complexity raises questions of cost, delay, and efficiency.

Reforming the System

Although the idea of reforming and removing regulations in order to facilitate land supply has become a recognized policy solution (see World Bank 1989; Dowall 1990; Struyk, Hoffman, and Katsura 1990), the idea of less regulation must still be analyzed with a view toward understanding what is meant by "less" and where and how improvements can be made.

Steps to Lessen Complexity

One of the clearest, easiest, and least political methods for increasing land supply and lowering land prices is to lessen the complexity of the regulatory system. This can be approached in several ways: eliminating redundancy; streamlining administrative procedures; clarifying standards for approval or denial; combining different application and approval processes; removing ineffective, unenforceable, and outdated provisions. We suggest that such activity could begin immediately. It would involve a simple but detailed inventory of all the regulatory steps and processes, followed by a review of these steps, and would lead to specific recommendations to lessen the complexity of the process. For example, a "one-stop" combined approval process system, where one office processes all the required permits and approvals, could be put into effect.

The importance of this simplification is twofold: it would lessen the amount of time required to develop land, and, more important, it would lower costs. Lengthy processing times and complicated applications and permitting processes all impose direct costs on the developer and the public. Recent work in other countries has indicated that these costs can be surprisingly high: it is estimated that in Indonesia they add one-third or more to the price of land (Struyk, Hoffman, and Katsura 1990; Hoffman, Ferguson, and Rerimassie 1991). And the Indonesian regulatory system, while complex, is less complex than the Korean. Making permitting processes more efficient need not lessen the legitimate interests of the government in guiding development; rather, it would permit government to fulfill its role in a more effective manner.

Another dimension to the simplification of the system is the decentralization of decision making. In many countries, land use and development decisions are viewed as appropriate matters for local government, although it is recognized that there are some special—but limited—cases where national interests are involved. One of the most salient aspects of the U.S. system is the strong role of local government in guiding or regulating land development. Although the U.S. system has it problems (e.g., environmental degradation, inefficient land use patterns), these are not noticeably worse than those in countries with much more centralized systems. On the other hand, this more decentralized approach in the United States has helped to create a system in which land speculation and wildly rising land prices are not major problems and land supply proceeds with reasonable efficiency.

If there is a sincere interest in increasing land supply, then the government needs to take a hard look at the necessity of having so much of the approval system tied to decisions at the national level. Rather, the assumption should be that such decisions are a local matter unless there is a demonstrable need for national attention.

Improvements in this direction, however, require attention to the capacity of local government officials and staff in several ways. Such staff must be able to understand the technical issues involved, they must have the administrative and logistical capacity to cope with the increased workload such decentralization would bring, and they need adequate implementation and enforcement capacity, that is, the ability to determine if procedures are being complied with or otherwise working properly, and to correct matters if they are not.

In sum, we have argued that improvements can be made in land supply through lessening the complexity of the current regulatory system, and that this should include improvements in the efficiency of existing structures as well as decentralizing decision-making responsibilities in concert with efforts to upgrade the capabilities of local government.

Steps to Narrow Coverage

The second area for consideration is politically more difficult, since it involves decisions about the scope of the public or community interest—or in other words, which aspects of land development should be regulated and which should not. The general Korean approach appears to be that, if land development is to be consistent with national goals, all aspects of the process must be regulated. In opposition, we argue that a clear understanding of which goals are critical and which are merely desirable or ideal leads to a narrower view of the need for regulation. Further, there may well be regulations that address no current goals. In other words, a thorough review of the regulatory system should be undertaken with the objective of establishing whether all the existing regulations are aimed at some legitimately established goal. It is our impression that most land use regulatory systems contain controls that have outlived their purpose and utility.

Another aspect of this is the question of tradeoffs. To focus on Korea's system of land use planning as one example, we suggest that, however worthy comprehensive land use planning may be, it is also worthwhile to consider such planning and zoning as a tradeoff with land supply: the more thorough the planning and use regulation, the more constrained the supply and the higher the price of land (see, e.g., Brueckner 1991). This is not a suggestion that land use planning be eliminated, but rather that consideration be given to balancing the degree of planning regulation with its impact on the cost of development. This in turn means that an assessment must be made of the purpose or rationale of planning and land use efforts and not simply a decision that all the land in the country needs strict and comprehensive use regulation.

State and Market as Paths of Land Supply

The above comments all look to the question of improving the existing regulatory system, of making it more rational and efficient. However, these actions sidestep the central question of public versus private (government versus market) supply of land. We would characterize this, not as a question of philosophy or politics, but rather as a practical matter. Supply of land through administrative mechanisms and public or quasi-public institutions as is being attempted in Korea is supply of land by regulation. As we discussed above, the intrinsic nature of regulations in mixed economies is that they limit supplies and drive up prices.

In Korea everyone has recognized the need for increased supply of land, but there is a marked resistance to supporting and encouraging the cheapest and easiest method to accomplish this: the market. One imagines that the response to this suggestion is that less regulation, or greater reliance on market forces, means more speculation, greater concentration of ownership, and higher land prices. But that is the irony. This is a description of what has followed each effort to regulate land in Korea, and a description of what exists now with one of the most highly regulated land systems in the world. We suggest that it is time to consider the alternative.

NOTES

We thank Barbara Haupt and Robin Rose for capable assistance in assembling data used in this chapter for Japan, Germany, and the United States.

1. This is residential, commercial, and industrial land, not land in cities or other administrative divisions. The total land area of Korea is approximately 99,200 square kilometers.

2. Cogent observations on the current situation are also provided in a research outline prepared in 1991 by Jae-Young Son and shared with us.

3. This section draw heavily on Pflaumer (1990).

4. See, for example, Black and Hoben (1985), Fischel (1990), Chinitz (1990), and Advisory Commission on Regulatory Reform to Affordable Housing (1991).

5. In fact, we did construct ratios of the index in land prices to the index for manufacturing wages for each of the four countries for several years in the 1980s. The wage index is being used as a proxy for household income. Interestingly, these ratios were quite stable over the periods for which we were able to compute them. Note that for the United States we employed the constant quality house price index rather than a land price index.

6. See J. S. Lee (1990) for a longer time series for overall urban land prices. Interestingly, this series shows a downward drift in the *rate of increase* above inflation between 1964 and the mid-1980s when it again increased. Nevertheless, with the exception of two episodes, land prices increased faster than the consumer price index over the period 1958–87.

7. Jurisdictions in states on the west coast have been even more aggressive in terms of development controls. As defined by the census, however, the West Region includes thirteen states, most of which are noncoastal and many of which are more like the Midwest in their policies than like the coastal states.

8. See Chapter 13 and, for a parallel discussion on the situation in Japan, Noguchi (1990).

9. Although the land readjustment process could by carried out by either local authorities or groups of private landowners, in most cases it was the local authorities that undertook the work.

REFERENCES

Advisory Commission on Regulatory Reform to Affordable Housing. 1991. *"Not in My Back Yard": Removing Barriers to Affordable Housing.* Washington, D.C.: U.S. Department of Housing and Urban Development.

Black, T. J., and J. E. Hoben. 1985. "Land Price Inflation and Affordable Housing." *Urban Geography* 6 (1):27–47.

Brueckner, Jan K. 1991. "Growth Controls and Land Values." *Land Economics* 66(3):237–248.

Case, Karl E. 1990. "Single Family Home Prices in the United States: 1950–1990." Paper Presented at the Joint Meeting of the National Bureau of Economic Research and Japan Center for Economic Research on the Economics of Housing in Japan and the United States, Cambridge.

Chinitz, B. 1990. "Growth Management: Good for the Town, Bad for the Nation?" *American Planning Association Journal,* winter, 3–8.

Cho, Joo Hyun. 1990. "Evolution of Residential Land Development Policies in Korea." Paper Presented at the International Conference on Korean Housing Policies, Seoul.

Clifford, Mark. 1989a. "Through the Roof." *Far Eastern Economic Review*, June 8, 102–103.

Clifford, Mark. 1989b. "Landed in Trouble." *Far Eastern Economic Review*, September 14, 72.

Clifford, Mark. 1991. "Loans or Land." *Far Eastern Economic Review*, May 16, 73–74.

Doebele, William A. 1982. "Reshaping Land Readjustment to Serve the Needs of Lower-Income Groups." In William A. Doebele (ed.), *Land Readjustment: A Different Approach to Financing Urbanization*. Lexington, Mass.: D.C. Heath.

Dowall, David E. 1990. "Less Is More: The Benefits of Minimal Land Development Regulation." Paper Prepared for the Workshop on Regularizing the Informal Land Development Process, Sponsored by the Office of Housing and Urban Programs, U.S. Agency for International Development, November 1.

Fischel, William A. 1990. *Do Growth Controls Matter?* Cambridge: Lincoln Institute of Land Policy.

Follain, J. 1979. "The Price Elasticity of the Long-Run Supply of New Housing Construction." *Land Economics* 55(2):190–199.

Hoffman, Michael, Bruce Ferguson, and Robert Rerimassie. 1991. "Modernizing Land Administration in Indonesia." Washington, D.C.: Urban Institute.

Ito, Takatoshi. 1990. "Tax System and Public Policy." Paper Presented at the Joint Meeting of the National Bureau of Economic Research and Japan Center for Economic Research on the Economics of Housing in Japan and the United States, Cambridge.

Kim, Yoon Hyung. 1990. "An Introduction to the Korean Model of Political Economy." Mimeo. East-West Population Institute, East-West Center, Honolulu.

Korea, Ministry of Home Affairs. 1985, 1990. *Municipal Yearbook*. Seoul.

Lee, Jin Soon. 1990. "System of Land Ownership and Use." Mimeo. East-West Population Institute, East-West Center, Honolulu.

Noguchi, Yukio. 1990. "Land Problem in Japan." Paper Presented at the Joint Meeting of the National Bureau of Economic Research and Japan Center for Economic Research on the Economics of Housing in Japan and the United States, Cambridge.

Pflaumer, H. 1990. "Building Land in the Federal Republic of Germany." In *Third International Shelter Conference*. Washington, D.C.: National Association of Realtors.

Renaud, B. 1989. "Compounding Financial Repression with Rigid Urban Regulations: Lesson of the Korean Housing Market." *Review of Urban and Regional Development Studies* 1(1):3–22.

Renaud, B. 1991. "Affordability, Price-Income Ratio and Housing Performance: An International Comparison." Washington, D.C.: World Bank.

Son, Jae-Young. 1990. "Analysis of and Reform Proposals for the 'Land Problem' in Korea." Mimeo. East-West Population Institute, East-West Center, Honolulu.

Statistiches Jahrbuch. 1974, 1981, 1985, 1990. Wiesbaden: Government Printing Office.

Struyk, Raymond, Michael Hoffman, and Harold Katsura. 1990. *The Market for Shelter in Urban Indonesia*. Washington, D.C.: Urban Institute Press.

U.S. Bureau of the Census. 1989. *Price Index of New One-Family Homes Sold*. Series C27. Washington, D.C.: U.S. Government Printing Office.

World Bank. 1988 *Malaysia, The Housing Sector: Getting the Incentives Right*. IBRD Report no. 7929-MA. Washington, D.C.

PART VI

The Relationship between Business Ownership and Management

Chapter 15

Ownership-Management Relations in Korean Business

Kyu Uck Lee
Korea Development Institute

Introduction

The relationship between corporate ownership and management has become a major issue in economics and management science as modern capitalism, especially in the United States, has increasingly become dominated by "modern corporations" characterized by a wide dispersion of ownership and "the divorce of ownership from control."[1] In contrast, mainstream microeconomic theory has postulated "a classical capitalist firm" run by an owner-manager.[2] Thus, the problem of agency may arise in a modern corporation, even though it does not exist, by definition, in a classical firm.[3] A parallel difference appears between neoclassical theory and the managerial theory of the firm: the former postulates that a typical firm pursues simple profit maximization; the latter argues that a modern corporation is motivated by a complex objective such as constrained revenue or growth maximization. Many theoretical and empirical works address the issue of whether such a difference really exists, and whether and how it matters.[4]

For the purposes of this chapter, however, I am not concerned with which methodological approach is more appropriate for analyzing the internal structure of a firm. Nor do I seek to generalize from an outsider's viewpoint about how ownership-management relations have evolved historically in the capitalist system. Instead, I review the institutional and economic environment that has shaped corporate growth in Korea and offer some related insights for future policy direction concerning the deconcentration of corporate ownership. In so doing, I consider the lessons of the Japanese experience as well.[5]

One of the reasons for this approach is that corporate ownership is still very much concentrated and ownership-management relations relatively unchanged in Korea. It may be more worthwhile, then, to focus on the specific peculiarities of the current state of corporate structure in Korea. Therefore the analysis is framed in the context of "business groups" and their economic power in Korea. These groups are, and will remain, a predominant characteristic of Korean capitalism, in both its successes and failures.

Business Groups and Economic Power in Korea

The Significance of the Concentration of Economic Power

Since economic power is based on the organized ownership of economic resources, and the most important economic organization in a modern economy is the firm, the concentration of economic power takes the form of a few firms owning a substantial portion of resources in a distinct sector or in the whole of an economy. It is well known that a monopolistic or oligopolistic firm generally impairs allocative efficiency by eliminating free competition. At the same time, to the extent that these firms are controlled by a few individuals, they may manipulate resource allocation for the entire economy. In this respect, in practical terms, the issue of whether those who run the firms are owner-managers or salaried managers is not important.

The concentration of economic power has been a critical economic issue in Korea. This has been observed not only in Korea but also in many other countries throughout history. Some salient examples include trusts in the United States, *Konzerne* in Germany, and *zaibatsu* in Japan in the first half of this century. Given this historical precedent, the concentration of economic power would appear to be an inevitable stage all capitalist systems must undergo at one time or another; therefore, continued development of the Korean economy necessitates coping with this problem. The concentration of economic power is ironic in that it is a historical product of the free market system itself. The principles of free competition and free enterprise constituted the foundation of modern economic society in Western Europe, and the underlying legal principles were the guarantors of human rights, property rights, and the freedom to enter contracts. Free competition was upheld in the belief that it leads to optimal resource allocation, and thereby maximal materialistic growth, and contributes to the preservation of a democratic political and social system. As the size of firms became larger due to rising economies of scale embodied in mass production technology, the discrepancy in size among firms became more visible. The economic principle of natural selection, or survival of the fittest, prevailed; eventually a few big firms preempted scarce resources and market opportunities, leading to the concentration of economic power.

Though it was supposed to preserve free competition, the free market system gave rise to its antithesis—the concentration of economic power. Inevitably, the issue of the concentration of economic power is tinged with ideology. It is not an exaggeration to state that the difficulty of solving this issue lies in ideological differences, regardless of the era or the country in question.

As Berle and Means (1932) suggested, the centripetal force toward market concentration can be balanced against the centrifugal force away from the concentration of corporate ownership. They argued that such a balance would enable modern corporations to grow with their ownership separate from their management. Yet this may merely be one of many possible solutions, and different countries may require the application of different solutions. In any case, what is most important and most difficult is to find a solution based on the consensus among the citizenry in a country.

The concentration of economic power in Korea can be summarily represented by the *jaebul*—the conglomerate business groups, the majority of whose component firms are monopolistic or oligopolistic in their respective markets, owned and controlled by particular individuals or their close family members. Hence, the *jaebul* are characterized both by market concentration and by a concentration of ownership. This peculiarity distinguishes them from analogous business groups in other countries.

Historically, the concentration of economic power began with the advent of large monopolistic firms. There have been three different approaches to the issue of "monopoly capitalism." The first is communism, which has recently lost almost all its persuasive power, even among its previously adamant followers. The second is fascism, which collapsed in World War II. The third is the self-cleansing of capitalism itself. In most of the major capitalistic countries, laws have been introduced to deal with the issue of monopoly, and the ownership of big firms has been steadily dispersed. All in all, revised capitalism appears to be the ultimate victor in the competition among economic systems. Western capitalism has evolved in line with political democracy, which was secured through the struggle for civil rights on the basis of free and fair competition among individual economic agents. Western governments have exercised their public authority adequately to deal with many problems, including the concentration of economic power, and this has contributed to the preservation of the fundamental vitality and value system of capitalism.

This has not been the case in Korea, however. Western capitalism and democratic political institutions were introduced in Korea only at independence, whereas paternalistic bureaucracy and communitarianism had dominated the country for centuries. Moreover, a combination of capitalism *and* democracy could not be reached effectively as the country first fought the Korean War and later set the national goal of economic development under the direct supervision of the government. Economic activity in the private sector was directed more by the will of the government than by individual choice. Consequently, government intervention in the private sector became ubiquitous. Korean firms were not capitalist in the true sense of the word. Therefore, the concentration of economic power that occurred in Korea was not necessarily a product of the market system. This may lead to a characterization of the concentration of economic power as a product of an inequality of economic opportunity stemming from the close government-business relationship.

It cannot be denied that Korea has made economic development its primary national goal and has tended to justify all economic consequences under the pretext of economic efficiency. Currently, however, the desire of the general public for greater economic equity can no longer be disregarded, and equity is ultimately necessary in attaining efficiency over the long run. The issue of concentration of economic power and the proper ownership-management relationship should be viewed with this crucial issue in mind.

The Major Characteristics of Business Groups

Relative Size In measuring economic power, one may use either a stock variable such as fixed assets, production capacity, or employment, or a flow variable such as production, shipments, value added, or profits. Since each of these measures has different properties, analysis of statistics must be done with care. Bearing in mind these difficulties, I analyze the 30 largest business groups in terms of manufacturing shipments in 1987.[6]

The relative sizes of business groups are shown in Table 15.1. In 1987 the share of the 30 largest groups in the manufacturing sector reached 17.6 percent in terms of employment and 37.3 percent in terms of the value of shipments. The striking difference between their shares of shipments and employment may be caused by their capital-intensive methods of production and their market power to manipulate commodity prices to some extent. Recently, their share of total shipments has tended to increase, while that of total employment has generally decreased. It should also be pointed out that the share of total shipments of the top five business groups (Lucky Goldstar, Hyundai, Samsung, Sunkyung, and Daewoo) has substantially risen, whereas that of the remaining groups has decreased. In other words, even among business groups a dual structure has emerged.

Growth In the rapidly diversifying Korean economy, business groups cannot expand sufficiently if they merely rely on internal growth. Additionally, they must acquire existing firms and establish new ones. On the average in 1970, the top 30

TABLE 15.1
Relative position of business groups in the manufacturing sector (percentage)

	Employment			Shipments		
	1977	1982	1987	1977	1982	1987
Top 5	9.1	8.4	9.9	15.7	22.6	22.0
Top 10	12.5	12.2	11.9	21.2	30.2	28.2
Top 20	17.4	16.0	15.1	29.3	36.6	33.9
Top 30	20.5	18.6	17.6	34.1	40.7	37.3

business groups owned 4.2 subsidiaries each, but this number jumped to 14.3 in 1979. It is worth noting that the number of new establishments (202) was far greater than the number of acquisitions (135) during this period.

Generally speaking, if a business group seeks to enter a new market, it is more advantageous for it to establish a new firm than to acquire an existing one, because of the business group's superior technology, management, manpower, and financial resources. Additionally, since new markets emerge as an economy develops, there is a need for the establishment of new firms to enter them. During the period 1970–79, the total number of manufacturing firms increased 1.3 times, whereas the number of subsidiaries of the 30 largest business groups increased 3.4 times. The *jaebul* issue has arisen, in part, as a result of this unbalanced growth among firms.

Due to the recession in the late 1970s and the consequent rationalization of business groups, the number of their divestitures surpassed the number of their new entries in the early 1980s, and business groups ended up with an average of 13.4 subsidiaries in 1982. In other words, for business groups the 1970s was an expansionary period and the early 1980s was a time of consolidation. In the mid-1980s, however, they took over many failing firms and public enterprises and also began to establish new firms for industrial restructuring. Consequently, the average of subsidiaries for the 30 business groups increased again to 17.1 in 1989.

Diversification and Competition The distribution of the subsidiaries of the 30 largest business groups by two-digit industrial classification codes in 1987 is shown in Table 15.2. It is apparent in the table that most of the subsidiaries are in the heavy and chemical industries, textiles and apparel, and food and beverages. The five

TABLE 15.2
Number of subsidiaries by industry, 1987

	Industries								
	31	32	33	34	35	36	37	38	39
Top 5	2	10	2	4	12	4	5	57	1
Top 10	3	18	3	6	21	6	15	74	1
Top 20	27	22	3	13	42	10	20	90	1
Top 30	32	39	4	14	55	14	23	99	2

Note: The nomenclature here follows the Korean Standard Industrial Classification (KSIC). 31: food and beverages, and tobacco; 32: textile, wearing apparel, and leather; 33: wood and wood products; 34: paper and paper products, printing, and publishing; 35: chemicals and petroleum, coal, rubber, and plastic products; 36: nonmetallic mineral products; 37: basic metals; 38: fabricated metal products, machinery, and equipment; 39: others.

largest business groups have many subsidiaries concentrated in fabricated metal products and machinery and transportation equipment, whereas the 30 top business groups as a whole show a relatively even distribution of subsidiaries throughout the industries.

As the diversification of business groups has proceeded, the number of markets entered has also greatly increased. In particular, groups have participated heavily and simultaneously in industries with large market size and strong growth potential. Consequently, competition among business groups themselves has intensified. Considering only the top 20 business groups, for lack of time series data, Table 15.3 shows that the number of commodity markets they participated in has increased from 292 in 1974 to 587 in 1982 and to 739 in 1987.[7] Nevertheless, the percentage of markets in which only a single business group participated has decreased from 76.7 percent in 1974 to 59.3 percent in 1987.

Market Position A fundamental source of the economic power of the large business groups is their positions in individual commodity markets. In 1987 the top 30 business groups competed in selling 1,499 commodities in 837 different markets. Their market positions are summarized in Table 15.4. In 103 markets, a single business group had a monopolistic share of more than 80 percent and in 232 markets a dominant share of 40–60 percent. If we consider only the ranking of their market shares, the number of markets in which a single business group was ranked third or higher was 941, or 62.3 percent of the total cumulative number of markets in which they participated. Such a dominant market position is most visible for the top five business groups, but it holds true for the others as well.

Expansion into the Financial Sector Almost all Korean business groups have their roots in the manufacturing sector, but many have recently expanded their activities into the financial sector as well, including banking, insurance, and stock brokerage services. It may be said, therefore, that industrial capital is at least partially being coupled with financial capital. Nevertheless, Korean business groups are not like the prewar Japanese *zaibatsu* in two ways: Korea's previously nationalized commercial banks were privatized only in 1981, and no single legally acknowledged "identical person" was allowed to own more than 8 percent of any nationwide commercial bank's total stock. In other words, Korean business groups could only become oligopolistic shareholders of these commercial banks. By contrast, there is no legal ceiling to the ownership of local banks, and each is practically controlled by a single business group. Currently, 11 of 27 stock brokerage companies are owned by individual business groups, and the same is generally true of life insurance companies. In all, 30 business groups own a total of 47 financial institutions.

Concentrated Ownership The Korean *jaebul* have yet another characteristic—the concentration of ownership. There are several ways for an individual to control a business group. The most obvious is to hold a majority share of each component

TABLE 15.3
Competition among business groups

Number competing	Number of markets (%) 1974	1982	1987
1	224 (76.7)	366 (62.4)	438 (59.3)
2	51 (17.5)	24 (21.1)	182 (24.6)
3	15 (5.1)	67 (11.4)	63 (8.5)
4	2 (0.2)	30 (5.1)	56 (7.6)

TABLE 15.4
Market positions of 30 largest business groups

	Market shares (%)					Ranking of market shares			
	0–20	20–40	40–60	60–80	80–100	1st	2d	3d	4th+
Top 5	345	141	82	28	42	224	133	68	223
Top 10	494	186	98	47	64	295	177	104	313
Top 20	738	250	136	69	94	410	256	141	449
Top 30	873	291	151	81	103	475	296	170	558

firm, but this method is limited by its high capital requirements. The second is a pyramid-like control of firms through a holding company, which is forbidden in most countries. In Korea the Act on Monopoly Regulation and Fair Trade of 1980 (hereafter, the Antimonopoly Act) was revised in 1986 to include a new clause to the same effect.

A more general method of control is intercompany shareholding, which can take either one or all of the direct, radial, circular, or matrix forms of shareholding (see Lee and Lee 1990). Among these, direct cross-ownership between a parent and a daughter company is prohibited by the 1986 amendment to the Antimonopoly Act. At any rate, this method has had limited or little application in consolidating a large number of firms into a single business group, and indeed it was used rarely even before it was legally prohibited.

It is extremely difficult to disentangle the complicated web of cross-ownership that can constitute a business group. In an attempt to restrict intercompany shareholding, therefore, the amended Antimonopoly Act stipulates that any subsidiary of a business group beyond a specific size may neither obtain nor hold shares of the other domestic firms in excess of 40 percent of its net assets.[8] In 1984 when no such restriction existed, the average intercompany shareholding ratio for the 30 largest business groups was 46.5 percent. Specifically, this ratio was 50.9 percent for the top bracket (1–10) of business groups, 41.8 percent for the second (11–20), and 26.3 percent for the third (21–30). The larger the size of the business groups, the higher the average ratio of intercompany shareholding.

With the enforcement of the amended Antimonopoly Act, however, business groups have taken various measures such as increasing the issue of shares in the stock market and augmenting internal reserves to adjust to the new restrictions. Such measures are optimal for business groups that do not want to divest substantially from their subsidiaries but still wish to meet the legal requirements. Consequently, their capital bases have expanded and their ownership has dispersed, at least to some extent. It is possible that some imprudent investment in other firms that might otherwise have been better employed could have been discouraged. The Antimonopoly Act may be said to be effective in this respect, since in 1989, when the grace period was still in effect, the average ratio of intercompany shareholding decreased substantially to 31.5 percent. It should be an interesting research topic to investigate how these business groups will realign their ownership structure in response to this act.[9]

As mentioned earlier, subsidiaries of business groups are owned by particular individual shareholders and other firms they control. However effective the Antimonopoly Act may be so far in dissipating the concentrated ownership of business groups, it remains true that generally a particular individual still holds a controlling share in his business group. For example, Table 15.5 shows that, in the case of the top 10 business groups, an average of 46.4 percent of total company shares are owned by particular individual shareholders and the firms they control. At the same time, less than 30 percent of their subsidiaries have gone public in the stock market and account for less than 60 percent of business groups' total equity, on average. It can therefore be said that the *jaebul* still maintain quite a closed ownership structure.

Sources and Effects of the Economic Power of the *Jaebul*

Genesis and Growth Since economic power became most concentrated during the process of economic development, one must examine the relationship between economic development and entrepreneurship to discover the source of such concentration. One economic theory suggests that, if labor contracts have not been completely specified, the production function not well understood, and the market for certain factors of production not fully established, then entrepreneurship becomes critical in determining the success or failure of a firm's operation.[10] Such a situation usually prevails in the early stages of economic development, and therefore an entrepreneur must fill the gaps inherent in the market in addition to performing the customary managerial function of coordinating intermarket activity. A particularly important role of entrepreneurship in economic development is obtaining and utilizing factors of production that are not fully transacted in the market. One extreme example is mobilizing political influence to expedite

Table 15.5
Ownership structure of 10 largest business groups

	Shareholding ratio		Open/closed	
	An individual	Subsidiaries	No. of firms	Equity
Top 5	13.7%	35.7%	56/187 (29.9%)	56.6%
Top 10	14.7%	31.7%	139/514 (27.0%)	56.3%

loans from banks. Similarly, the entrepreneur must have the ability to obtain and utilize the minimum amount of inputs required for the operation of the firm.

It cannot be denied that entrepreneurship of this sort is a scarce resource in a developing economy with an immature market system. Entrepreneurship becomes even more valuable as the target rate of economic growth is raised, because demand for the "gap-filling" and "input-completing" functions also increases. Although entrepreneurship is essential for business activity, its supply is not elastic. Nor is it a service that is transacted in the market. Moreover, it is not exhausted easily, despite repeated use. Because of these peculiarities, economic power is bound to be concentrated in the hands of a few entrepreneurs and their business groups up to a certain stage of economic development.

Of course, the relative importance of the various aspects of entrepreneurship is determined by the entire economic and social structure of an individual country (see Casson 1982). Furthermore, whether the exercise of entrepreneurship is compatible with social mores is a different issue entirely. Entrepreneurship itself is free of value judgment, but the way it manifests itself is determined by the modus operandi of a specific economy. It follows that, as far as the informal sector dominates an economy, entrepreneurship tends to be scorned by the general public. This element evidently accounts for the general antipathy toward the *jaebul* in Korea.

The concentration of economic power can also be traced to the diversification of business groups. Since the ability to produce capital goods is extremely limited in a developing economy, economic development is dependent on the simple transmission of advanced technology. This technological dependence tends to push the domestic market structure toward monopoly or oligopoly (Merhav 1969). Concurrently, although the general income level rises with economic development, the "demonstration effect" will tend to extend the scope of consumption, leading to a proportionately smaller market size for individual commodities. Once advanced technology originally conceived for mass production is introduced into a small developing economy, the market naturally becomes monopolistic or highly oligopolistic as a result of the economies of scale embodied in such technology. Technological dependence also reduces the "multiplier effect" in the technology-importing economy. Since the increment in domestic production and employment induced by greater investment decreases as the share of imports in total investment expenditure grows, the expansion of the domestic market is constrained by such a "leakage" of the benefits of the multiplier effect. Consequently, technological dependence helps create and maintain a monopoly or oligopoly in a developing economy.

This tendency was quite apparent in the early stages of economic development in Korea. While better manpower and physical resources were concentrated within monopolistic and oligopolistic firms, various structural and institutional barriers also protected these firms' initial monopolistic market enclaves. This gave rise to the formation of business groups through diversification. The early monopolists and oligopolists expanded into markets to make use of their excess capacity in manpower and capital, which had accumulated as competitive pressures were eliminated in their already existing markets.[11] Diversification accelerated as the demand for existing goods became less elastic, factors of production less specialized, and the excess capacity of firms larger; these are all characteristics of a developing economy.

In a developing economy, a firm initially manufactures goods that can benefit from mass production. As the opportunities for primary expansion diminish in these markets, the firm gradually diversifies into smaller markets. In this process of diversification, firms that initially did not compete with one another eventually become competitors. In fact, in the second half of the 1970s many Korean business groups moved simultaneously into overseas construction, financial services, and the heavy and chemical industries, though this was done partially at the urging of the government.

The government was also largely responsible for the concentration of economic power in Korea. Because strategic industries emphasized by the government required huge inputs of technology, capital, manpower, and organization, the *jaebul* were favored over other firms. It was then natural that the benefits of the tax, credit, and trade policies should accrue primarily to these business groups. In other words, the growth of business groups through diversification, attributable to the original advantages provided by their business capabilities, was further aided by the growth-first policy of the Korean government.

The government policy toward financially failing firms gave another boost to business groups. If a big firm on the brink of bankruptcy or under the managerial supervision of loan-providing banks were actually to go bankrupt, serious economic, social, and political repercussions would follow, including the proliferation of unliquidated bank loans and other debts, mass unemployment, and social unrest. To prevent such an unfavorable outcome, the Korean government typically exhorted the *jaebul* to take over such firms; in return, it usually provided so-called rescue loans and priority in granting licenses. This might not have been desirable from the short-run financial viewpoint of the *jaebul*, but it eventually increased the size of these groups.

So far, I have examined the real causes of the concentration of economic power in Korea. The concentration of ownership—the other side of the issue—has resulted to a great extent from the peculiarities of the Korean financial environment. The rapid growth of large business groups requires a tremendous amount of capital. In general, a firm can raise funds by tapping internal reserves, issuing stocks, or borrowing. In an economy where the general income level is low, inflation is rampant, and other profitable speculative investment opportunities exist, it is extremely difficult for a firm to raise its required capital by issuing stocks to the general public. Furthermore, only rarely are the internal reserves of a firm sufficient to finance new investment projects, especially in capital-intensive industries. Hence, such rapid economic growth with a weak capital base makes it inevitable that firms will be highly dependent on external financing. Because of this financing method, the ownership of business groups was not dispersed in the course of their growth; the concentration of ownership was accelerated by the intercompany shareholding practice mentioned earlier.

In addition, the loan policies of banks provided an incentive for intercompany shareholding. To deal with the chronic excess demand for funds, the banks relied on a rationing system that allocated total available funds in proportion to the amount of capital held by each potential recipient. Under this system, business groups connected through intercompany shareholding had better access to bank loans, because the capital of an individual subsidiary firm could thereby be fictitiously increased. A subsidiary of a business group thus had stronger bargaining power than an independent firm of the same real size. This may be an additional factor in explaining the relatively rapid growth of business groups compared to other firms.

Consequences of the Concentration of Economic Power The consequences of the concentration of economic power depend on the way this concentration has developed, the extent to which economic powers have been exercised, and the value system of the society at large. In addition, it is important not to confuse the issues of a noncompetitive market structure with that of economic power, even though most subsidiaries of the large business groups are monopolists or oligopolists in their respective markets, and whether a firm is a subsidiary of a business group or an independent company matters little as far as the economic effects of monopoly are concerned. Therefore, I largely disregard monopoly-specific issues in analytically assessing the performance of the business groups. It goes without saying, however, that antimonopoly measures must be included when an overall policy package to deal with business groups is considered.

The primary advantage enjoyed by the *jaebul* lies in synergy, or the economies of scope inherent in multiproduct activities (see K. U. Lee 1989). As pointed out earlier, entrepreneurship is an important factor, especially in the early stages of economic development. Business groups can more easily obtain the capital, technology, and managerial resources required to transform an idea into an innovation and an economic opportunity into an actual investment and production decision; in this respect, they are able to make better use of entrepreneurship.[12] In Korea, this was particularly relevant for the export drive and industrial restructuring of the past couple of decades. The participation of business groups in several different markets facilitates the flow of information, reducing uncertainty in decision making on investment and production. At the same time, diversification disperses risk and stabilizes the rate of return on investment for business groups. This may ultimately increase the incentive to invest in the economy as a whole.

The advantages the *jaebul* enjoy may, however, be disadvantageous to other independent firms. For instance, though vertical integration on the part of a business group tends to enhance its internal efficiency, it concurrently reduces the size of the market for other firms that had previously supplied this business group and consequently decreases the number of independent firms that can attain the "minimum efficient scale." Unless a specific functional form can be used to represent the social welfare criterion, the net welfare effect of such an internalization cannot be calculated. In any case, the very fact that some firms are eliminated from the market raises a distribution issue. If the improved internal efficiency contributes only to the private interests of the *jaebul*, the problem becomes even worse.

Compared to an independent firm, a subsidiary of a business group has greater bargaining power and a better market position in product markets and even greater power in factor markets. The advantages to be had in obtaining bank loans as a result of the artificial inflation of the subsidiary's capital base, through its connection with the entire group, have already been mentioned. Even if a subsidiary is not connected to its sister companies through intercompany shareholding, it can take advantage of the creditworthiness of the entire business group and also profit from the group's personal contacts. A subsidiary is, likewise, in a better position to attract high-quality manpower than an independent firm—especially a small or medium-sized company—because it can offer more social prestige, job security, and the potential for lifetime earnings, all of which may be credited to the large size of the business group as a whole. Furthermore, synergy in advertising and other marketing activities of each business group induces more consumers to purchase the products of the group's individual subsidiaries. All these factors help a large business group eliminate smaller independent competitors from the markets of its subsidiaries.

The managerial objective of a business group can generally be summarized as "diversification." In the pursuit of such a strategy, however, a business group may sometimes enter markets that are already efficiently serviced by small- and medium-sized firms and drive these firms out of business. Of course, this possibility is even greater if a business group is also more efficient in real terms. I do not pass judgment on such cases here, but there are unfair business practices used specifically by such large business groups: market foreclosures, price squeezes, reciprocal dealings, cross-subsidization, mutual forbearance, and the prevention of potential competition, for example, through the "toehold effect."[13]

Another negative effect often observed in the past is the chain bankruptcy of an entire business group triggered by the financial failure of a subsidiary firm through intercompany shareholding. As mentioned earlier, this financial interdependence tends to build a high "exit barrier," and scarce economic resources are often inefficiently diverted to rescue a subsidiary from bankruptcy.[14] Bankruptcy can occur in any firm, but it is far more dangerous in the case of one in the *jaebul*.

In a similar vein, laborers in individual subsidiaries of a business group tend to regard their labor-related issues as part of the overall labor relations of the business group rather than something specific to their own firms. For example, although a particular subsidiary firm cannot justify an increase in wage rates, its laborers may demand it when other subsidiaries of the same business group raise their wage rates. Sometimes, a strike in one subsidiary may trigger a wave of labor disputes across all firms within the same business group. This umbrella effect of group-wide labor relations may render "industrial peace" more fragile and the settlement of labor disputes more difficult.

The negative image of the *jaebul* in Korea is generally attributed to the inequality of economic opportunities among firms, as well as to the general perception of their concentration of ownership and large size. Granted that an unequal distribution of ownership is inevitable in every free market economy, the most fundamental reason this is raised as a critical issue in Korea is that the process of capital accumulation itself has not yet been fully justified in the eyes of the general public. It cannot be denied that the general public believes that most business groups have accumulated monopoly profits at the expense of consumers and other smaller firms through the help of loans, both domestic and foreign, and the protection of the government. It is also widely believed that the *jaebul* have invested their profits in unproductive sectors, such as real estate, and have influenced government policy to promote private interests.

These negative general perceptions—notwithstanding the issue of whether they are justified—have fomented social tension, raised distrust and doubts about the "capitalist" economic system, and further contributed to the perception of economic immorality among some segments of Korean society. The concentration of economic power in Korea has evolved into an issue with political and social ramifications transcending the simple economic sphere; as a result, value judgments are becoming intertwined with objective facts, rendering the whole issue all the more difficult to solve.

Prewar *Zaibatsu* and Postwar Business Groups in Japan

Zaibatsu before 1945

One of the main features of the prewar Japanese economy was the predominant position of the *zaibatsu*. "*Zaibatsu*" is a political expression referring to an estate of great wealth and, by inference, to the source of this wealth—the combine. "Combine," in turn, refers to a complex of corporations displaying a unified business strategy arising primarily out of an ownership base. The combine was

Table 15.6
The role of the *zaibatsu* in terms of paid-up capital, 1945

Industry	The Big Four[a]	The Other Six[b]	The Ten
	% of national total		
Financial industry	49.7	3.3	53.0
Banking	48.0	2.4	50.4
Trust	85.4	–	85.4
Insurance	51.2	9.1	60.3
Heavy industry	32.4	16.6	49.0
Mining	28.3	22.2	50.5
Metal mfg.	26.4	15.4	41.8
Machine tool	46.2	21.7	67.9
Shipbuilding	5.0	7.5	12.5
Chemical	31.4	7.1	38.5
Light industry	10.7	6.1	16.8
Paper	4.5	0.2	4.7
Ceramics (incl. cement)	28.4	27.4	55.8
Textiles	17.4	1.4	18.8
Agr., forestry, food	2.7	7.7	10.4
Marine products	9.7	6.5	16.2
Miscellaneous			
Others	12.9	2.6	15.5
Electric power, gas	0.5	0.03	0.5
Land transport	4.9	0.7	5.6
Marine transport	60.8	0.6	61.4
Real estate,	22.7	6.7	29.4
Commerce & trade	13.6	6.7	20.3
Combined	4.5	10.7	35.2

Source: Holding Company Liquidation Commission.
[a]The Big Four: Mitsui, Mitsubishi, Sumitomo, and Yasuda.
[b]The Other Six: Aikawa, Asano, Furukawa, Okura, Nakashima, and Nomura.

usually directed by a "holding company." In Japanese usage, not all combines, only family-dominated combines, were considered to be *zaibatsu* (Hadley 1970). Among the largest *zaibatsu*, Mitsui and Sumitomo had long histories, dating back 300 years, when they were key Tokugawa merchant houses. In the beginning of the Meiji period (1868–1912), new *zaibatsu* such as Mitsubishi, Yasuda, and Furukawa were formed. *Zaibatsu* then rapidly flourished, playing a strategic role in Japan's economic modernization at the behest of the Japanese government.

Beginning as "political merchants," they quickly grew by taking over government-run businesses. They began to take the shape of *zaibatsu* in the current sense of the word around the time of World War I in the later Taisho period (1912–26). At this stage, Mitsui and Mitsubishi diversified their businesses beyond production and distribution, transforming their first-line businesses into joint stock companies and then establishing holding companies to control them. As the *zaibatsu* expanded, they also began to exercise political power. In particular, as the center of political influence moved away from political parties toward the military after the so-called Manchu incident in 1932, the giant *zaibatsu* and the military congregated into a single ruling entity, which governed Japan at war during the first phase of the Showa (1927–89), which lasted until 1945. Table 15.6 shows the extent of *zaibatsu* control over the Japanese economy at the end World War II. Some salient characteristics of the prewar *zaibatsu* can be summarized as follows:

- The *zaibatsu* operated in a feudalistic mode under the monopolistic control of a few members of a family. This characteristic was not compatible with modern corporate management practice.
- The internal control mechanism of the zaibatsu took the form of a pyramid, with the top holding company (*zaibatsuhonsha*) hierarchically controlling layers of companies—subsidiary companies (*chokkeikaisha*), affiliated companies (*kokaisha*), and related companies (*mogokaisha*).
- The *zaibatsu* did business in almost every industry. In those industries they dominated, other firms were subject to their control or remained only marginal.
- The *zaibatsu* controlled not only the manufacturing sector but also the financial sector. They owned banks, trust companies, insurance companies, and other financial institutions, which served as their major sources of capital and their principal means of controlling other firms.

Dissolution of the *Zaibatsu* after the War

Shortly after war's end, the American Mission on Japanese Combines summed up the consequences of the existence of the prewar *zaibatsu* this way:

> Reviewing the adverse effects of the *zaibatsu* from a broad perspective, their extreme concentration of industrial control prolonged the existence of semifeudalistic labor relations, lowering the wage. At the same time, they deterred independent entrepreneurs from launching businesses and prevented the rise of a middle class. Since there was no middle class, there was no economic basis for individuals to become independent. Consequently, there was no countervailing power to deploy against the military establishment nor could a democratic or humanistic national mood develop. Moreover, because of the low wages and accumulated profits brought about by the economic control of the privileged *zaibatsu*, the domestic market could not expand. This made commodity exports all the more important for Japan, and eventually led her to an imperialistic war. (Koseitorihikiiinkai 1977, my translation)

The American government, as the occupying force after World War II, decided to dissolve the *zaibatsu* in the belief that as long as they continued to exist Japan would remain firmly under their control. In September 1945, the American government adopted a basic policy line for the management of the Japanese economy: demilitarization, economic democratization, and the preservation of the peacetime economy. In November 1945, the program for economic democratization was further spelled out as a combination of land reform, the legislation of the Labor Union Act, and industrial democratization. "Industrial democratization" specifically included two types of method. The first consisted of adopting temporary measures to eliminate anticompetitive institutions, such as the dissolution of the combines, deconcentration of economic power, and the removal of private cartels. The second entailed enforcing the Law for the Prohibition of Monopoly and the Establishment of Fair Trade, enacted in 1947. To carry out the dissolution of the combines, in 1946 the Supreme Command of the Allied Powers (SCAP) established the Holding Company Liquidation Commission (HCLC), which was empowered to enforce specific programs for the dissolution of holding companies, the removal of *zaibatsu* families from corporate managerial posts, the dispersion of the ownership of corporate securities, and the elimination of an excessive concentration of economic power.

As the first step toward combine dissolution, the HCLC stipulated that securities held by 83 holding companies and 56 *zaibatsu* family members be transferred to the commission itself, which sold the securities to new owners with nominal compensation to the former owners. The *zaibatsu* family members were also banished from high-ranking managerial positions and banned from reemployment. The total amount of securities transferred to the HCLC comprised 42 percent of the total paid-in capital of all Japanese joint stock companies in 1946. In those days, however, the Japanese public was not in a position to absorb to any significant degree the securities released by *zaibatsu* due to the country's low income level and shortage of food. Thus, in practice, a large amount of the securities eventually found their way back to their original owners. One may therefore term the outcome of the measure "the confusion of ownership" rather than "the dispersion of ownership" (Misonou 1987).

To sever the ownership linkage between firms, the HCLC designated a total of 2,843 companies, including "restricted concerns" (*seigenkaisha*), and their subsidiaries and affiliates and prohibited their directors from acquiring the securities or bonds of other companies or from forming interlocking directorships with other companies. In addition, restricted concerns and their subsidiaries and affiliates sharing the company titles and trademarks of the top holding companies of Mitsui, Mitsubishi, and Sumitomo were banned from using them further.

Having taken measures to sever the capital and human linkage within the *zaibatsu*, it also became necessary to prevent the individual firms, which formerly belonged to the *zaibatsu* but were made independent by combine dissolution, from establishing new monopolies. With a view to reorganizing the giant firms, especially the large-scale multiplant companies, the Act for the Elimination of the Excessive Concentration of Economic Power was enacted in 1947.[15] Pursuant to this act, the HCLC designated a total of 325 companies for reorganization, including 257 companies from the mining and manufacturing sectors and 68 companies from the distribution and services sectors. Before this measure was put fully into effect, however, the Korean War broke out and the American government changed its policy toward Japan. Faced with the growing threat of communist aggression, the United States decided to regard Japan as the frontline of the free world. This made an early rehabilitation of Japanese industry desirable from the standpoint of American foreign policy. Consequently, the original intent of the deconcentration measures was attenuated and eventually only 18 companies were subject to divestiture and reorganization. In addition, restricted concerns were again allowed to use the company titles and trademarks of their former holding companies.

The Consequences of Combine Dissolution

The anti-*zaibatsu* policy had a far-reaching effect on the Japanese economy. The dissolution of the giant *zaibatsu* proved quite instrumental in imbuing the Japanese economy with a new vitality. The extremely closed nature of the *zaibatsu*—particularly the hierarchical control of multilayered companies by holding companies owned by *zaibatsu* families—became outmoded as the Japanese economy developed. The concentration of ownership and control in the *zaibatsu* occurred under the conditions of the prewar economy, in which the distribution of income was extremely skewed and, therefore, public participation in the stock market quite limited.

Since the early Showa period, however, the general criticism of the *zaibatsu* intensified, and some of the *zaibatsu* companies went public, at least partially, in the stock market and at the same time attempted a separation of ownership and management. Moreover, because the *zaibatsu* had expanded into the defense industry during the wartime era, they had to draw on special banks such as Kogyogingko, as well as on non-*zaibatsu* banks to meet their increasing capital requirements. So the self-financing capacity of the *zaibatsu* through their own subsidiary banks and financial institutions became insufficient, and this served to weaken the closed nature of the *zaibatsu*. Hence, one may say that the postwar dissolution of the combines merely accelerated this process of *zaibatsu* disintegration.

The most striking effect of combine dissolution can be found in the abrupt rejuvenation of management, due to the limitation of hereditary owner-managers and traditional managers. The emergency of nonowner managers infused a competitive spirit and positive attitude into corporate management in the postwar era. These young managers began to make independent decisions, free from the control of holding companies. It may not be an exaggeration to say that the increase in private capital investment, which led to the rapid postwar economic growth, could not have been realized without such a drastic managerial transformation.

In the course of time, nevertheless, the individual firms that were made independent from *zaibatsu* control formed a new horizontal relationship. In this respect, it must be pointed out that the SCAP did not institute any deconcentration or dissolution measures whatsoever for banks in Japan. In retrospect, this policy left open the possibility that the *zaibatsu* would soon be regrouped into *kigyo shudan* (business groups) under the initiatives of the banks. In effect, combine dissolution contributed to the reshaping of the closed prewar *zaibatsu* into open postwar business groups by providing them with an incentive to modernize and rationalize their outmoded organizational forms and functions.

The Fair Trade Commission of Japan assessed the overall effects of postwar antimonopoly policies as follows:

> A series of antimonopoly policy measures enforced during the early postwar period made not only firms but also industrial and market structures more competitive, eventually making competition a major feature of the Japanese economy. Consequently, these policies' effects became widely visible and, combined with the success of other economic policies, laid the foundation for the continued development of the Japanese economy. At the same time, the competitive structure of the Japanese economy was not affected much by subsequent industrial policies, which by nature had a tendency to restrict competition. The introduction of the competitive system gave rise to the founding and growth of new firms like Sony and Honda, as well as to active capital investment and technological innovation in the fields of iron and steel, petrochemicals, electronics, and automobiles. Combined with the attenuation of the dual structure of large and small firms and the benefits of land reform and labor-related laws, the competitive system also influenced the Japanese economy extensively and dynamically, enlarging the domestic market and increasing the independence and responsibility of corporate managers. (Koseitorihikiiikai 1977, my translation)

Postwar Business Groups

The large postwar Japanese business groups can be classified into two general categories: Mitsubishi, Mitsui, and Sumitomo are reorganized groupings of the prewar *zaibatsu*; Fuyou, Taiichi Kangin, and Sanwa are new groupings centered around big banks and comprise subsidiaries of smaller prewar *zaibatsu*. In addition to these six groups, other smaller independent business groups came into being somewhat later; these include Shinnitetsu, Toyota, Nissan, and Hitachi, which are based in the manufacturing sector, and Tokyu and Seibu in the distribution and services sector. Although some of the business groups appear to be outgrowths of the prewar *zaibatsu*, they are functional groupings based on synergy (Aoki et al. 1986).

In fact, large firms that became independent through the dissolution of the combines attained business integration in two ways. First, they established vertical relationships with small firms through subsidiarization (*keiretsuda*). Second, they formed horizontal linkages with other large firms through intercompany shareholding. These horizontal linkages grew into the "Presidents' Clubs" (*shachoukai*), whose members were presidents of large core companies of business groups.[16] As mentioned earlier, in contrast to the prewar *zaibatsu*, postwar business groups depended on banks, since the shortage of capital was the most formidable bottleneck to the postwar industrial reconstruction of Japan.

In the early 1950s when business groups began forming, the prewar industrial structure, based primarily on mining and light industries, was fundamentally transformed by new technologies. The implication was that business groups would inevitably be reshaped under a new industrial structure. New industries such as synthetic fibers, petrochemicals, home electronics, and automobiles began to flourish, leading to a rapid increase in private investment in the heavy and chemical industries in general. In response to these industrial changes, the internal structure of the business groups was reorganized as well. Light industries and mining industries such as coal and nonferrous metals lost their predominant positions in business groups, replaced by the petrochemical and electrical and electronic machinery industry. At the same time, large-scale independent firms tended to grow faster than business groups.

After the recession of 1965, the Japanese economy resumed its rapid growth, but this was merely an extension of early expansion, since the industrial structure remained dominated by the same heavy and chemical industries. Under these circumstances, business groups restructured their internal organization and regained their dominance over the large-scale independent firms. It was during this period that Fuyou, Taiichi Kangin, and Sanwa grew out of the embryonic stage and became full-fledged business groups. In those days, there were several large-scale mergers between independent firms, most of them in response to the growing strength of the business groups. On the other hand, business groups steadily merged and acquired independent firms to consummate their vertical integration. The liberalization of access to capital since 1967 further accelerated industrial restructuring and business groupings. As a protective measure against acquisition by foreign capital, the degree of intercompany shareholding increased rapidly.

When the formation of the business groups is examined, it is necessary to take into account the characteristics of the industrial structure as an essential determinant of the nature of the constituent organizations and their functions. The prewar *zaibatsu* were characterized by the availability of commercial capital, because for them to perform their monopolistic function effectively in an industrial structure dominated by light industries, especially textiles and fiber, commercial capital was important in controlling the distribution sector. In contrast, the postwar business groups came into being because the successful expansion of businesses in the course of industrial upgrading centered around heavy and chemical industries and required the mobilization of a huge amount of capital that secured a market through the formation of a self-sufficient and diversified organization comprising banks, trading companies, and firms in various industrial fields.

In 1987 the number of nonfinancial member companies of the Presidents' Clubs of six major business groups was 163, corresponding to 0.006 percent of all nonfinancial corporations (1,929,754) in Japan. But this number belies their substantial presence in the Japanese economy. They accounted for 13.28 percent of total assets, 14.68 percent of the value of shipments, and 15.19 percent of total paid-in capital of all nonfinancial corporations.[17] As indicated by these figures, the six business groups exerted a strong influence on the Japanese economy, comparable to that of the prewar *zaibatsu*. This is further evidenced by the fact that in 1987, of the top 100 nonfinancial companies in terms of total assets, 54 were member companies of the six business groups. The main characteristics of business groups can be described as follows:

- Large firms within a business group are related organizationally by mutually holding each other's shares. For a business group as a whole, such intercompany shareholding takes a circular form.
- As indicated earlier, each business group has a Presidents' Club. Each president represents the combined shares of fellow member companies that his company holds. Therefore, this club practically acts as the board of large shareholders.
- As member companies of a business group form joint ventures, they may establish a community of interest.
- Large city banks are holders of major shares in business groups, and hence they form the core of the nexus of intercompany shareholdings. At the same time, they also serve as financial intermediaries within their business groups, catering to the capital requirements of other member companies.
- In addition to banks and general trading companies, business groups have subsidiaries in a significant number of industries. They do not constitute a mere conglomerate but contain a comprehensive industrial complex, often called a "one-setism."

Clearly, *zaibatsu* and business groups are distinguished by several features. There exists a difference in the control mechanism at the top of each type of organization. Whereas the *zaibatsu* had a one-sided vertical ownership structure stemming from top holding companies, business groups are owned by their subsidiaries through intercompany shareholding. In line with this change in the ownership structure, the internal managerial structure also moved from top-down hierarchical control to mutual control by the Presidents' Club. In a similar vein, the *zaibatsu* were controlled by particular families based on their ownership, whereas business groups are represented by Presidents' Clubs, consisting of salaried top managers, whose power originates from the ownership of their companies. And, as mentioned earlier, banks have greater power in business groups than in *zaibatsu*; the financial resources of the *zaibatsu* were maintained by their holding companies, but in business groups they rest in their member banks.

In sum, the fundamental difference between *zaibatsu* and business groups lies in the nature of their ownership structure, and this structure is the key element toward understanding why their economic power has had different effects and why they are perceived differently by the Japanese general public. This concluding observation has an important implication for those in Korea groping for a policy to deal with the *jaebul*. Ultimately, the issue of ownership is at the heart of the matter.

Basic Policy toward the Deconcentration of Economic Power

Overview of Previous Policies for Deconcentration

Even before the enactment of the Antimonopoly Act, the Korean government had attempted to take measures to deconcentrate economic power, either directly or indirectly. An earlier effort was the May 29 measures of 1974, which purported to induce large *jaebul* into going public on an extensive scale while simultaneously improving their financial structure. Another notable attempt was the September 27 measures of 1980, which aimed at preventing the corporate liquidation system, limiting real estate holdings by companies, minimizing rescue loans, and tightening supervision on bank loans. However, these measures were terminated prematurely without any visible results, due ostensibly to changes in the economic environment or to inadequate administrative support.

Later, the government continued to take similar measures sporadically, such as exertion of special control over loans to large corporations, limitations on bank ownership of large business groups, inducements to offer more corporate securities in the stock market, more effective tax-collecting administration, and the introduction of greater competition from both domestic and foreign markets. These various measures were implemented at different points in time with different intensities. As one might assume, not much could be expected from such a poorly coordinated policy. There were certain cases, on the contrary, in which some business groups even benefited from the government policy for industrial rationalization.

The first serious attempt to deal with the *jaebul* issue through a legal institution was in the Antimonopoly Act. When this act was legislated in 1980, there was only one mention of the prevention of excessive concentration of economic power as one of the purposes of the act. The main body of the act stipulated the standard clauses against monopolization through business combinations such as mergers and acquisitions. In this act, "the establishment of a new firm" was listed as a form of business combination, a peculiarity of the Korean Antimonopoly Act, but it was understood from a practical viewpoint that "conglomerization"—the quintessence of every *jaebul*—was left largely intact.

As pointed out earlier, a direct and specific restriction on business groups was introduced into the Antimonopoly Act by its first and second amendments in 1986 and 1990, respectively. Under these amendments, holding companies are prohibited and subsidiaries of the same business group are not allowed to invest directly in each other. In practice, the limit imposed on subsidiaries of business groups imposes a stronger constraint, restricting their total investment in other companies to less than 40 percent of their net assets. This stipulation is also applied to banks and insurance companies, which are also considered subsidiaries of business groups. Furthermore, they are not allowed to exercise their voting rights in their domestic subsidiaries.

Since the amended Antimonopoly Act was enforced in 1987, the restriction on investments by subsidiaries of business groups has actually had some effect. For effective control of the *jaebul*, however, it is necessary to mobilize simultaneously other policy tools, including taxation and credit rationing, since the entire *jaebul* issue is a complex one hinging on various aspects of economic policy. It should also be noted that the restriction on the investments by subsidiaries mentioned above does not cover the absolute amount of investment itself, only the investment ratio in terms of net assets. Consequently, the absolute size of subsidiaries or business groups may even increase as a response to the restriction, since they can always justify the amount of their current investment simply by enlarging their net assets. Though this new legal measure evidently improves the financial structure of the companies concerned and serves to dissipate their ownership to some extent, it appears to fall short of deconcentrating ownership of business groups in any significant way.

How to Interpret the Concentration of Economic Power

Before attempting to suggest a few basic policy directions for the deconcentration of economic power, I briefly discuss my position in interpreting this issue. A policy designed with the purpose of deconcentration requires a careful evaluation of the effects of the concentration of economic power and ultimately depends on a study of the evolution and nationwide ramifications of such concentration.

In contrast to socialism and libertarianism, I uphold an evolutionary view that the essence of capitalism can be preserved as long as the negative effects that arise in the course of its evolution are dealt with appropriately. Although the concentration of economic power seems inherent in the capitalist system, it can be neutralized and may even be utilized as a catalyst for the self-propulsion of capitalism. This can be brought about by striking a proper balance between the size of a firm as a single entity and its internal structure of ownership.

In other words, the basic tenet of the deconcentration policy must be to induce a synergy between efficiency and equity. To the extent that business groups emerge partly as an optimal response to market conditions, it may be desirable to acknowledge and preserve competitive forces and their efficient outcomes, while eliminating their unfavorable side effects. The issue of equity should first be approached by guaranteeing equitable economic opportunities and justice in economic activities, and should these measures prove insufficient, other policy means may need to be introduced. In this respect, one must also bear in mind that an improvement in equity leads in turn to an increase in overall economic efficiency through its boost in individuals' motivation and toward a cooperative social atmosphere. At the same time, equity requires, not merely a quantitive redistribution, but also a certain code of conduct on the part of all economic agents, including the government itself.

Once the linkages among subsidiaries of business groups are severed and their ownership is dispersed among the public, business groups will simply cease to exist. Moreover, the more perfect the individual market transactions and the more effective the administration of taxation and antimonopoly are, the less will be the synergistic effect of networking for the firms involved. At any rate, the decision as to whether a firm should perform a particular activity independently in the market or within an organization, and in the latter case whether it is to be made within a "hard" hierarchy or a "soft" network, will be determined by the preferences of all firms concerned and their owners responding rationally to economic conditions. To illustrate this point, when the original owners of a business group are replaced by their heirs, these descendants may either collectively maintain the original shape of the business group by sharing its ownership or exchange their controlling rights among themselves, allowing each full power over certain individual firms. From this viewpoint, business groups in their pursuit of economic rationality cannot be said to last indefinitely; however, they can always be reorganized to varying extents and in different forms.

Judging from their size and capabilities, business groups now existing in Korea are expected to continue to grow on their own. At the same time, the adverse effects of their growth may not be countered sufficiently by market forces alone. Moreover, nonmarket causes may underlie these adverse effects as well. Therefore, government intervention to cope with the concentration of economic power appears to be justified. Since the execution of government policy always involves a strong possibility of "government failure" and consequently may even aggravate the situation, careful attention must be paid to the necessity and sufficiency of government intervention. This is all the more important given the very distinct and powerful interest group against such policy and the concurrent difficulties in forming a social coalition to support a policy having a universal, invisible, and long-run effect. All these factors must be duly considered for a relevant and effective policy to be formulated.

The Basic Policy Lines for Deconcentration

The Accelerated Dispersion of Ownership As implied by the discussion thus far, the core of the *jaebul* issue cannot be remedied until the ownership of business groups is shared widely by the general public. In pursuing this goal, however, the pace of ownership deconcentration must be tuned to many factors, including the level and distribution of personal income, the financial structure of corporations, the sense of managerial responsibility, and the conditions in the stock market.

A once-and-for-all dispersion of ownership as witnessed in postwar Japan may result in concealed ownership or a zero-sum redistribution among well-off individuals, including large shareholders of business groups. In its stead, therefore, the goal must be attained through comprehensive and long-lasting efforts. In the past, the majority of the *jaebul* did not seek to go public in the stock market, and the government was not eager enough to enforce the Act for Promoting the Public Offering of Corporate Securities. It is therefore recommended that the government impose strong measures, such as restraint on bank credit and the issue of bonds, on companies that resist going public even though they meet legal requirements.

To prevent *jaebul* monopolistic control of the banking industry, the Banking Act should be amended to narrowly redefine "the legally acknowledged identical person"; to further reduce the limit on *jaebul* ownership of commercial banks; and to introduce a similar limit for regional banks that have been heretofore immune from such control. It is also desirable for the dispersion of ownership to induce firms to repay their bank loans by mobilizing capital in the stock market.

I have argued that the synergistic effect expected from business groups does not require a strong financial linkage between firms, while intercompany shareholdings may entail various adverse effects. Therefore, the limit on investment by subsidiaries of business groups should be lowered further. Nevertheless, this recommendation does not nullify the lesson of the Japanese experience that, as a safety valve after capital liberalization, intercompany shareholding may be promoted to the minimal extent necessary as a means of protecting domestic firms against potential takeovers by foreign capital.

The Strong Pro-Competition Policy The concentration of economic power may be inevitable, as long as a discrepancy in entrepreneurial capabilities among individuals exists. At the same time, it cannot be denied that diversification of business activities, often criticized as a prime sin of the *jaebul*, is, at least partially, a natural manifestation of profit-seeking and risk-dispersing motives. Therefore, public policy toward business groups needs to tread the line between discouraging their inefficient or anticompetitive diversification and respecting bona fide entrepreneurship. The most effective means for this may be to expose them to competitive pressures. Faced with tight competition, no firm has recourse but to shed itself of excess capacity in organization and inefficient management. In this respect, pro-competition policy such as removing entry barriers to firms from home and abroad is both fundamental and necessary.

Similar to competitive pressure, the countervailing power of consumers, labor unions, and small and medium-sized firms can check the abuses of the economic power of the *jaebul*. Consumers, especially when they are organized, can put pressure on the *jaebul* from without, while labor unions can do so from within. Small and medium-sized firms, insofar as they are efficient and able to compete effectively with large firms, can work against the inefficient expansion of business groups. Proper attention should be paid to the strengthening of such countervailing power. This attention is all the more important, not only because it does not require direct government intervention in the market mechanism, but because it serves to enhance democracy by bringing about a more equitable distribution of economic power.

It is sometimes suggested that the government make it mandatory for the *jaebul* to curtail their scope of diversification and focus on a few narrowly defined business fields. Notwithstanding the practical need for specialization of business groups, government coercion of the *jaebul* to select a predetermined set of specialization areas would violate the functioning of the free market mechanism. This statement should not be construed as unconditional support for laissez-faire policies, however. I merely want to draw the line between areas left to the proper working of the market mechanism and those left to the appropriate policy intervention of the government.

What is needed for firms in the ever-changing world is not blind adherence to the same old market but flexible adjustment, resulting at times in diversification across different markets or in a focusing on a niche in the firm's traditional market. The characteristics of a firm are defined not by the nature of its products but by that of its managerial resources. Even among firms in the same market, therefore, the pattern of adjustment in terms of both internal reorganization and the product mix is different when market conditions change. It is thus a matter of course that the government does not interfere in the decisions of private firms, providing instead competitive incentives for the self-specialization of firms. Moreover, in line with the rapid growth of an "information industry," boundaries between industries are disappearing, leading to their "fusion" (see Lee 1989). The ramifications of specialization should also be reinterpreted from this viewpoint.

The Role of Business Groups in High-Technology Industries An argument raised frequently against deconcentration is that, since high-technology industries require a huge amount of investment in physical assets as well as human capital, business groups are indispensable in their development. Although I acknowledge the capital requirements for developing high technology, it does not follow necessarily that the *jaebul* should be exempt from control altogether. First, as the capital market matures, more capital can be mobilized outside the firm. Second, there is always the possibility of joint research and development by independent firms as an alternative to collective investment by a single business group. Third, and most important, even if there is a need for large corporate size, the concentration of corporate ownership is not justified.

What is essential for our purposes is to grasp the rationale for business groups from the perspective of high technology. The most conspicuous characteristic of recent technological innovation is that it does not allow monopolies based on commercialization of new technologies to be maintained for long. Whereas a high market share implies strong market power in capital-intensive industries, such as iron and steel, nonferrous metals, and petrochemicals, market share does not carry much weight in high-technology industries where existing technologies become rapidly obsolete. In these highly competitive industries, the best means to a firm's survival is simply continuous Schumpeterian "creative destruction."

As the competition for new technologies intensifies on a global scale, the mere size of a corporation quickly loses its meaning. It cannot be predicted easily whether business groups will experience synergy in developing high technologies and, if so, how they will be effectively restructured. These questions could form an agenda for future research. In this context, however, one can refer to the recent Japanese experience that joint research and development by independent firms has contributed more to technological breakthroughs than collective efforts by subsidiaries within business groups. Though it is possible to accept the argument that, in light of various current market conditions prevailing in Korea, the *jaebul* should play an important role in high-technology industries, it is necessary to recall that "real" economies of scale can be achieved without the concentrated ownership of business groups. The "high technology" argument in favor of the *jaebul* seems to reflect the personal inclination of their owners, who do not wish to share their sphere of influence or industrial empire with others. This assessment, if based on fact, has a far-reaching implication for ownership-management relations in Korea and leads to the final point of this analysis.

The Improvement of Social Accountability and Commercial Morality Since the amended Antimonopoly Act was enforced in 1987, there has been strong public pressure to contain the size of business groups and to regulate their business conduct. This seems to have been amplified by the new movement toward political and economic democracy. Recently, the government introduced strict sanctions against excessive *jaebul* landholdings, which may be better than no action. However, insofar as the *jaebul* issue represents, in a nutshell, the whole array of problems inherent in Korean society, such a piecemeal approach may be able to remedy only some of the surfacing problems.

The Korean people have a strong desire for economic justice, and the government's most fundamental task is to let the general public understand correctly the essence of capitalism and to establish an economic order in which efficiency is harmonized with equity. This is essential not only for building a national consensus in the southern part of Korea but also for preparing for the eventual reunification of the two diametrically opposed systems on the Korean peninsula. The *jaebul* issue, or for that matter the issue of ownership-management relations, must be addressed in the context of this long-term perspective.

Considering the fact that the popularly critical assessment of the *jaebul* can be ascribed to the unequal distribution of wealth, the unproductive and speculative utilization of such wealth, and the unfairness and injustice perpetrated in the course of its accumulation, the *jaebul* issue cannot be resolved by the mere dispersion of the ownership of business groups. More fundamentally, Korea must firmly establish a new economic order throughout the whole society, aimed at eradicating the roots of the problem. First of all, tax collection should be administered strictly and neutrally while concomitantly eliminating "quasi-taxes." Government regulations on business licenses and banking practices should also be reformed to prevent collusion between business and government. At the same time, a real-name system should be introduced to transactions of financial assets and real estate, which should assist in uprooting the underground economy and increasing justice in ordinary economic activities. Only then can the issue of ownership-management relations be discussed in a different context.

Last but not least, the particular importance attached to the commercial morality or economic ethics of the *jaebul* must be emphasized. Basically, as far as the profit motive of private firms is considered legitimate in the capitalist system, their performance can be regulated only by legal and social constraints binding their activities. Therefore, it is more logical to set up appropriate constraints than to rely on moral persuasion if a "fair" business performance is desired (see Lee 1988). However, a perfect system of such constraints cannot be established, nor can all individuals be forced to abide by such rules. This is where economic ethics come into the picture. Economic ethics should be emphasized more for the *jaebul* in light of their past evolutionary process and potential. Insofar as the "invisible hand" may not function fully without a modicum of commercial morality adhered to by each economic agent, any economic policy will be neutralized similarly if business groups do not recognize their social responsibilities: the more imperfect the market mechanism and the more uneven the distribution of market power, the greater the value and importance of economic ethics. This must be true especially of *jaebul* attitudes toward the dispersion of their ownership and the consequent separation of ownership from management.

NOTES

1. The seminal work dealing explicitly with this issue is Berle and Means (1932).
2. This term is used here in the sense of Alchian and Demsetz (1972).
3. One recent treatment of this problem can be found in Pratt and Zeckhauser (1985).
4. A survey of related literature can be found in most graduate-level textbooks on industrial organization; see, for example, Lee (1989).
5. Korea has experiences in common with Japan in the sense that capitalism was not an endogenous but an imported ideology in both countries. Differences may out-

weigh similarities, however, since the Japanese corporate system underwent a forced transformation after World War II. One may find copious literature on their past history, and some researchers have begun to explore the future evolution of the ownership structure of Japanese corporations. A recent work edited by Sougoukenkyukaihatsukikou (1985) presents the views of four different schools of thought on this point.

6. The following statistical results are the summary of a more detailed analysis (Lee and Lee 1990).

7. It is always tricky and sometimes arbitrary to delineate boundaries of commodity markets. This chapter adopts, without any modification, the commodity categorization of the KSIC.

8. In the 1986 amendment to the Antimonopoly Act, banks and insurance companies that were considered subsidiaries of business groups were exempt from this restriction. They were required only to abstain from exercising their voting rights in the companies in which they had invested. In the 1990 amendment, however, these same banks and insurance companies were made subject to the restriction like other subsidiaries.

9. I am currently studying this issue. One of the tentative initial results is that, while previously core companies or large shareholders of individual business groups could be identified, it appears that they have dispersed shareholdings more equally among their subsidiaries today.

10. Leibenstein (1986) presented an early analysis of entrepreneurship in developing economies in this vein. Leff (1978) followed Leibenstein's approach in his treatment of "economic groups," the equivalent of "business groups" in my terminology.

11. Business groups can be analyzed in terms of a "multiproduct firm," originating from the concept of an "optimum firm" proposed by E. A. G. Robinson. For a summary of these concepts, see Lee (1989).

12. Kirzner (1973, 1979) elaborates on the "alertness to market opportunities" as a basic nature of entrepreneurship from the neo-Austrian viewpoint.

13. These are from standard terminology referred to in the American antitrust literature. Putting aside the pros and cons of the logic these terms seem to imply, one can find a fairly broad understanding of the meaning of these terms in Areeda and Turner (1978).

14. In contrast to entry barriers, there is only scanty literature on exit barriers. Caves and Porter (1976) offer the seminal treatment of this concept. One of their propositions relevant to this chapter is that entry barriers themselves constitute exit barriers.

15. In the title of this law, the phrase "the excessive concentration of economic power" was somewhat misleading in this context, since this law was aimed at the dissolution of individual monopolistic or highly oligopolistic firms, not business groups as a whole.

16. Since these "clubs" started rather informally, it is not always possible to determine when they were recognized officially. Their names, number of member companies,

and dates of formation follow: Mitsui, Second Thursday Club, 24 companies, October 1961; Mitsubishi, Mitsubishi Friday Club, 29 companies, around 1955; Sumitomo, White Waters Club, 20 companies, around 1951–52; Fuyou, Fuyou Club, 20 companies, January 1961; Sanwa, Third Wednesday Club, 44 companies, February 1967; Taiichi Kangin, Third Friday Club, 47 companies, January 1978.

17. Koseitorihikiiinkai (1989) provides a detailed statistical description of these business groups.

REFERENCES

Alchian, A., and H. Demsetz. 1972. "Production, Information Costs and Economic Organization." *American Economic Review* 62 (December).

Aoki, M., K. Koike, and I. Nakatani. 1986. *Nihon Kigyo no Keizaigakku* (The economics of the Japanese firm). Tokyo: TBS Britannica.

Areeda, P., and D. F. Turner. 1978. *Antitrust Law: An Analysis of Antitrust Principles and Their Application*. 5 vols. Boston: Little, Brown.

Berle, A. A., and G. C. Means. 1932. *The Modern Corporation and Private Property*. New York: Harcourt, Brace and World.

Casson, M. 1982. *The Entrepreneur: An Economic Theory*. Totowa, N.J.: Barnes and Noble.

Caves, R. E., and M. E. Porter. 1976. "Barriers to Exit." In R. T. Masson and R. P. Qualls (eds.), *Essays on Industrial Organization in Honor of Joe S. Bain*. Cambridge, Mass.: Ballinger.

Galbraith, J. K. 1984. *The Anatomy of Power*. London: Hamish Hamilton.

Hadley, E. M. 1970. *Antitrust in Japan*. Princeton: Princeton University Press.

Kirzner, I. 1973. *Competition and Entrepreneurship*. Chicago: University of Chicago Press.

Kirzner, I. 1979. *Perception, Opportunity, and Profit: Studies in the Theory of Entrepreneurship*. Chicago: University of Chicago Press.

Koseitorihikiiinkai (Fair Trade Commission). 1977. *Tokkusenkinshiiseisakku Sanjunenshi* (30 years of antimonopoly policy). Tokyo.

Koseitorihikiiinkai (Fair Trade Commission). 1989. *Kigyoshudan no Jittai ni Tsuite* (On the current situation of the six largest business groups). Tokyo.

Lee, K. U. 1988. "Sijangkikueu Nonriwa Yunri" (The logic and ethics of the market mechanism). *Korea Development Review* (Fall).

Lee, K. U. 1989. "Jungbohwawa Sanupjojik" (Informationalization and industrial organization). *Korea Development Review* (Fall).

Lee, K. U., and J. H. Lee. 1990. *Kiupjipdankwa Kyungjeryuk Jipchoong* (Business groups and economic power). Seoul: Korea Development Institute.

Lee, K. U., and C. H. Yoon. 1989. *Sanupjojik* (Industrial organization). Seoul: Bupmoonsa.

Leff, N. A. 1978. "Industrial Organization and Entrepreneurship in the Developing Country: The Economic Group." *Economic Development and Cultural Change* 26(4).

Leibenstein, H. 1968. "Entrepreneurship and Development." *American Economic Review* 58 (May).

Merhav, M. 1969. *Technological Dependence, Monopoly and Growth*. London: Pergamon.

Misonou, H. 1987. *Nihon no Tokusenkinshiseisakku to Sangyososikki* (Antimonopoly policy and industrial organization in Japan). Tokyo: Kode.

Okumura, H. 1983. *Shin Nihon no Rokkudai Kigyoshudan* (The new six largest business groups in Japan). Tokyo: Diamond.

Pratt, J. W., and R. J. Zeckhauser, eds. 1985. *Principals and Agents: The Structure of Business.* Cambridge: Harvard Business School Press.

Russell, B. 1938. *Power.* New York: Penguin.

Sogokenkyukaihatsukikou (National Institute for Research Advancement). 1985. *21 seiki no Nihon no Kabushikikaishazou* (The vision of the Japanese corporation in the 21st century). Tokyo.

CHAPTER 16

Big Business Groups in South Korea: Causation, Growth, and Policies

Leroy P. Jones
Boston University

Issues

What should government policy be toward big business groups (BBGs) in the 1990s? A decade ago I addressed the same question for the 1980s, framed as follows:

> A major feature of South Korea's high-growth period has been the rapid rise of *jaebul*.[1] This increasing concentration of economic power in a small number of hands has occurred largely
>
> . . . as a natural result of the economic growth process itself. Korea has modernized rapidly. Economic modernity means taking advantage of scale in technology, organization and marketing. Rapid growth means rapid structural change from small primitive production units to large, modern units. It also requires placing resources in the hands of those entrepreneurs who have proven themselves capable of survival in the international arena. The rapid rise in business concentration is thus merely one inescapable facet of Korea's transformation from a primitive economic structure to one which is modern and internationally competitive. If Korea is to
>
> . . . as the result of a circular political economy process. Economic size means economic power and influence on the government's resource allocation decisions. This in turn means greater size, greater power, and still greater influence. Most importantly, large groups have disproportionate access to large volumes of subsidized credit, allowing them to generate subsidized profits. These are then plowed back and, with the multiplier effect of a high debt-equity ratio, form the basis for still more credit, growth and profits. One result is economic inefficiency, as resources are diverted from more productive uses. In addition, there

> continue to grow, then this process must not be attenuated by the facile egalitarian notions which have contributed to stagnation and continued poverty in many LDCs. It is of course essential that efficient small and medium entrepreneurs be given the opportunity to grow, but this is already insured by existing policies and institutions. The fifth Five-Year Plan therefore need give no special attention to the *jaebul* problem.

> are detrimental social and political effects as income distribution is adversely affected and as economic power begets political power. It is therefore imperative that the Fifth Five-Year Plan redress this imbalance by allocating a larger share of resources to the non-*jaebul* sector and by enacting measures to control the negative consequences of existing concentrations of economic power. (Jones 1987:87–88)

Though the questions and analytics remain unchanged today, the dramatic changes during the transition decade of the 1980s lead to a rather different set of answers for the 1990s. Three sets of interdependent factors are primary: the external strength of the BBGs has shifted relative to the countervailing powers of both government and the market; the internal advantages of the BBGs have changed as first-generation entrepreneurs are replaced by second-generation family members and professional managers; and government policy toward BBGs has changed dramatically, most notably with regard to the credit market.

Relative Power of BBGs

The objective danger of BBGs is that the concentration of power will allow them to exert disproportionate influence and thus distort both economic and political decision making in their favor. The subjective danger is that popular perceptions of inequity will distort both economic and political decision making against the BBGs. These dangers in turn threaten to retard Korea's economic development by reducing international competitiveness and the nation's political development by encouraging power politics on the one hand and demagoguery on the other.

I deal with these problems more fully below. Here I simply note that the magnitude of both problems is a function of the relative power of the BBGs. This in turn depends on their economic size relative to the rest of the economy and their political power relative to the countervailing forces of the executive, legislative, and judicial branches of government.

Economic Power: Flows

Under the Park regime of the 1960s and 1970s, the BBGs grew far more rapidly than the rest of the economy. For example, from 1973 to 1978 the top 46 groups grew at a real annual rate of 24.2 percent per year while the economy as a whole was growing at 9.9 percent and the manufacturing sector at 17.2 percent (Jones and Sakong 1980, and Skong 1980; see line A in Figure 16.2). Though the resulting *level* of aggregate concentration was high relative to modern industrial democracies, it was not atypical of less developed countries (Jones 1987:101–107). The *trend*, however, was unprecedented and worrisome. Had this relative growth rate persisted, by 1991 the BBGs would have accounted for 73 percent of GDP. Such an outcome is of course impossible, so one could confidently predict a diminution of the BBG growth rate in the 1980s. Further, it was clear that it would be "necessary to adjust government policy to *accommodate* this change, if not to *precipitate* it" (Jones 1987:185). What has actually happened?

Seok Ki Kim Data Policymakers, academics, and journalists in Seoul are virtually unanimous in believing that the growth of BBGs continued unabated in the 1980s. Academics agree. Alice Amsden, in by far the best known English work on the Korean economy, states that under the Fifth Republic "big business grew even bigger and concentration increased further as a result of liberalization measures in Korea" (1989:137). Karl Fields agrees: "Liberalization efforts initiated by the Chun government have actually opened the way for the *chaebol* to increase their economic clout and financial autonomy" (1991:29). What evidence is available to support this conventional wisdom?

Consider first the Seok Ki Kim (1987) series (Figure 16.1), which gives sales of the top 10 BBGs as a share of GNP. This is of particular relevance because it is the source cited by both Amsden (1989) and Fields (1991) and it has been used by other authors as well.[2] Results are dramatic. In Amsden's words: "In 1984 the three largest *chaebol* alone accounted for a staggering 36 percent of national product in Korea" (1989:116). This is staggering indeed, but nothing compared to the results of extending the methodology. The same data set shows that 10 groups account for two-thirds of national product; since we know from other work that the next 30 or so groups produce half the output of the first 10, we are forced to conclude that something like the top 40 groups "account for" *all* of national product. It follows that agriculture, government, public enterprises, and small and medium private producers produce absolutely *nothing*. If you like this sort of logic, you will also believe that my itty-bitty wife is bigger than I because her body weight exceeds my bone weight. The point is that it is misleading, to put it gently, to compare the levels of net and gross figures.[3]

It is, however, a simple matter to legitimize the series by converting the denominator to economy-wide sales. This is also shown in Figure 16.1, and the differences are striking. The top 10 groups account for not 67 percent of the economy but "only" 21 percent. Even without the exaggeration, the BBG share remains extremely high by international standards. Even more impressive is the trend; over the entire 1974–1984 period, the BBG share increases at an annual

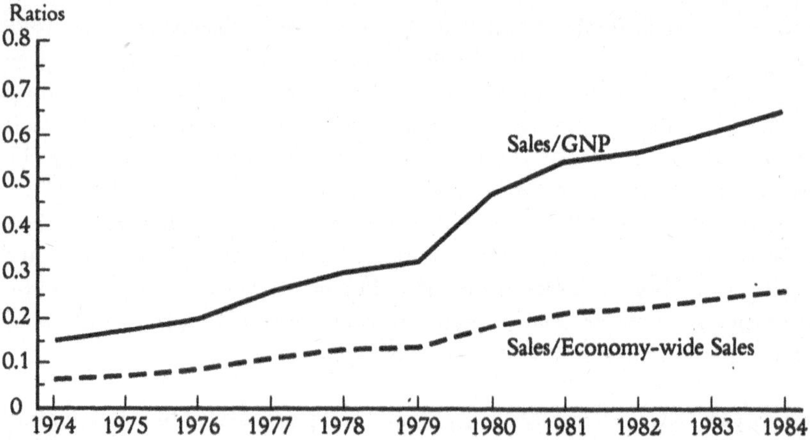

FIGURE 16.1 Sales of top 10 BBGs relative to GNP and economy-wide sales (see Table 16.1 for data and sources).

average compound rate of 15.9 percent. Note, however, the deceleration: from 1974 to 1981 the rate was 19.1 percent; thereafter, only 7.9 percent. In sum, the Kim data confirm the high rate of growth of the BBGs in the 1970s and suggest that it continued, but at a markedly reduced rate, in the early 1980s.

To see what happened in the later 1980s, we need to turn to four additional data sets. These are displayed, together with the two series described above, in Figure 16.2. None of the series are conceptually compatible: some compare sales, others value added; one is for manufacturing only, the others for the whole range of economic activity; and different numbers of groups are included. Nonetheless, taken as a whole, I think they allow some rather strong conclusions to be reached.

Kyu Uck Lee Data Consider first Kyu Uck Lee's series on manufacturing sales by the top 30 groups (line E in Figure 16.2). This is certainly the most reliable set in the series. It is based on a computer run on the Economic Planning Board's mining and manufacturing survey, so the BBG and economy figures are identical, not only in conception but in execution. Further, the series has been regularly updated for nearly a decade and is widely used and quoted, so the likelihood of bugs is low. Results are surprising: the BBG share peaked in 1982 and has declined slowly but steadily ever since (at a compound annual rate of –1.7 percent).

Shin Il Kang and Management Efficiency Institute Data Next consider the Shin Il Kang and Management Efficiency Research Institute series (lines D and E in Figure 16.2). These are conceptually identical in terms of the variable used, with both referring to sales across all sectors. One does include 50 groups and the other 53, but this is a minor difference reflecting only about a few percent of the total. As can be seen, the Kang series rises from 1980 to 1984 but stagnates thereafter. The

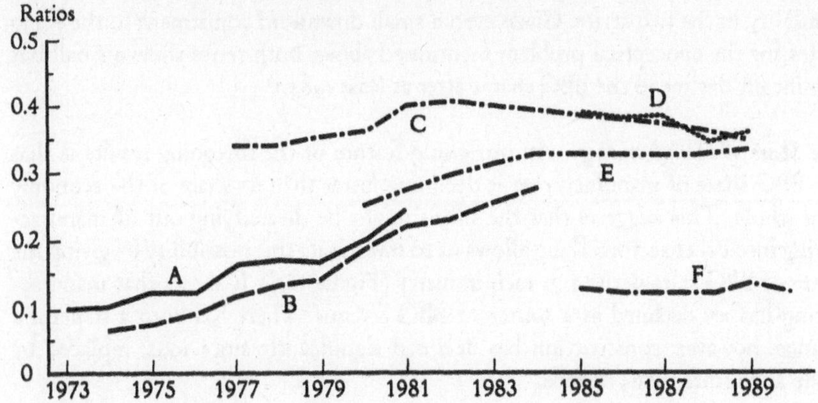

FIGURE 16.2 BBG share of the economy. (A) value added of top 46 groups over GNP; (B) sales by top 10 groups over economy-wide sales; (C) manufacturing shipments by top 30 groups over total manufacturing shipments; (D) sales by top 53 groups over economy-wide sales; (E) sales by top 50 groups over economy-wide sales; (F) nonfinancial net value added of top 50 groups over net national product (see Table 16.1 for data and sources).

shorter Management Efficiency Research Institute series shows a small but significant decline over its life from 1985 to 1990. The two do differ significantly both in level and in trend. This is presumably due partly to differences in execution in terms of data sources firm listings. There is, however, one subtle but important conceptual difference that explains part of the differences: Kang uses a *stable* set of firms and groups, taking the biggest 50 in 1989 and tracing the historic evolution of that fixed set; the Management Efficiency Research Institute, in marked contrast, uses a *constantly changing set*, taking the sales of the largest 50 groups in each year. For simplicity, assume that both used the same methods and had the same set of firms in 1990, and only one group was replaced in the set between 1989 and 1990. In 1989 the constantly changing set would show a higher level because the group it includes is larger (compared with the one in the stable set) in that year. Its growth rate across the two years would be correspondingly lower. This difference is exactly what we observe: the Management Efficiency Research Institute series is higher in earlier years and shows a lower growth rate, so that it converges with the Kang series over time. Which method is to be preferred? If, over a decade, one group rises from obscurity while another dies, and if one's growth is exactly offset by the other's decline, then what has happened to BBG power? Obviously, there has been no change in the BBG role, only a redistribution. Accordingly, the Management Efficiency Research Institute method is theoretically preferable. As to whether the magnitude of the difference is worth the cost of complicating the calculations, and whether this effect is strong enough to explain the difference in the two series, I am agnostic.

These differences notwithstanding, let us not forget the one fundamental similarity in the two series. Given even a small downward adjustment to the Kang series for the conceptual problem mentioned above, both series show a small but significant decline in the BBG shares after at least 1984.[4]

The Share of Manufacturing An intriguing feature of the foregoing results is that the BBG share of manufacturing is declining faster than its share of the economy as a whole. This suggests that the BBGs might be diversifying out of manufacturing into other sectors. Kang allows us to investigate this possibility by giving the share of BBG sales derived in each industry (Figure 16.3). It shows that manufacturing has *not* declined as a source of BBG revenue. There has been a structural change, however: construction has declined significantly since 1982, replaced by trade and (since 1986) finance.

Value Added versus Sales Data Now return to the remaining series in Figure 16.2, which are based on value added. Value added nets out intermediate inputs and thus nets out intercompany sales. Assume a group creates a trading company that markets all the group's output. Sales have doubled but value added and real economic activity are unchanged. Accordingly, national accounts use only value added in calculating national product, and a strong case can be made for doing the same when analyzing BBGs.

As shown in Figure 16.4, value added averages about 43 percent of sales for the economy, but there is high variance both across sectors (manufacturing is only around 0.25) and over time. In part this temporal variation is cyclical, with profits

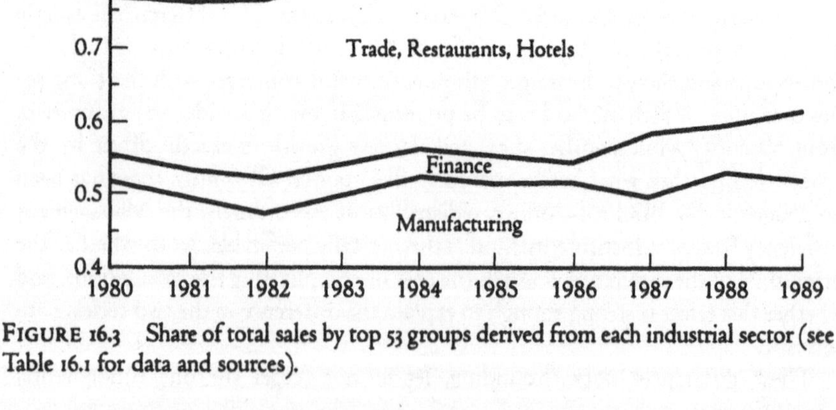

FIGURE 16.3 Share of total sales by top 53 groups derived from each industrial sector (see Table 16.1 for data and sources).

suffering more in recession than sales (see 1980), and in part there is a secular trend as some sectors become more intermediate intensive with development (see manufacturing) and as the sectoral mix changes. The BBGs, however, are not typical of the economy, being concentrated in the more intermediate intensive sectors.[5] Figure 16.5 compares BBG value added and sales shares for the two sources that report both. Note that the trends differ significantly, with at least the manufacturing gap widening over the limited time series. The magnitude of difference in the Management Efficiency Research Institute series is puzzling. What lies behind it is that their implicit value added to sales ratio for BBGs is only 0.14–0.15, compared with an economy-wide figure of about 0.43 (and 0.25 for manufacturing). Part of this is due to their using net (of depreciation) value added, but for the economy as a whole this amounts to only 4 or 5 percent, so that even if BBGs were twice as intermediate intensive, their figure would still only match that of economy-wide manufacturing. Until this low level is explained, I will treat their estimates with some caution. Most immediately, it means that one cannot link the otherwise comparable Jones and Sakong series to theirs and conclude that there has been a major drop in BBG value-added shares.

Two points emerge here. First, one cannot infer either the level or the trend in value added from sales data. Second, assuming that the Management Efficiency Research Institute data are internally consistent, we once again have a small but steady decline in the BBG share of economic activity from 1985 onwards.

Top Five Groups Kyu Uck Lee (Chapter 15 of this volume) has noted that there is a dual structure in the BBGs, with the top five groups quite different from the rest. This suggests the possibility that the very biggest groups might still be growing

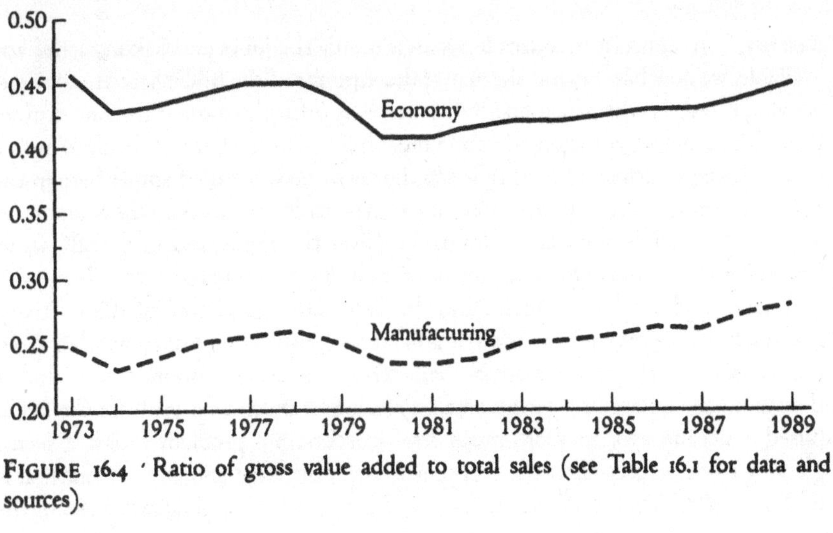

FIGURE 16.4 Ratio of gross value added to total sales (see Table 16.1 for data and sources).

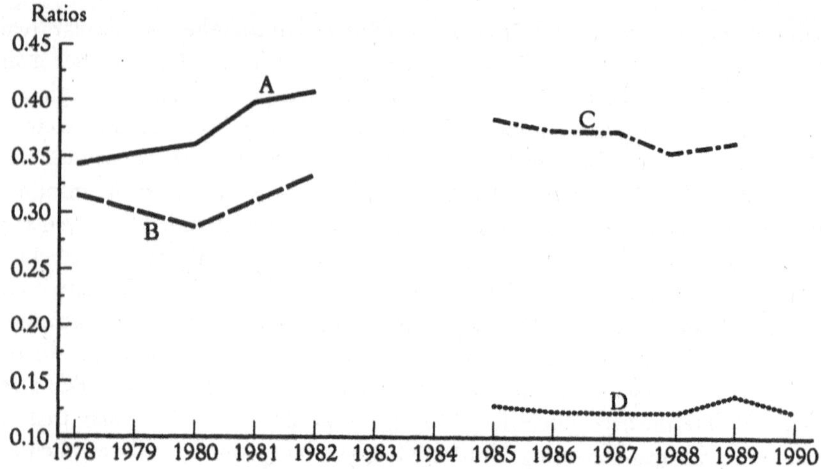

FIGURE 16.5 (A) manufacturing shipments and (B) value added of top 30 groups over corresponding variable for total manufacturing; (C) sales and (D) net value added of top 50 groups over corresponding economy-wide variable (see Table 16.1 for data and sources).

rapidly, with only the smaller firms' shrinkage making the set as a whole decline. Figure 16.6 investigates this possibility, displaying the share trends for the top five groups and the remaining groups for the three data sets that permit such a comparison in the 1980s. The dual structure is abundantly apparent in terms of levels, with the top five producing more than the remaining groups in each set. It is also apparent in the much greater growth of the top groups until the early 1980s. Since the early 1980s, however, the trend of the top groups is essentially identical to the remainder, that is, slightly downward.

Summary In contrast to a decade ago, when only the Jones and Sakong series was available, we now have several alternative descriptions of the BBG share of economic activity. However, their incompatibility makes it difficult to draw any fine distinctions. Nonetheless, at the broadest and most important level, it is difficult to escape a very strong conclusion: the BBGs rapid growth period ended somewhere in the 1982–84 period; thereafter, they grew at a somewhat lower rate than the economy as a whole. Two policy implications follow: (1) Given the importance of the BBG issue, it would seem advisable for someone in or around government to reconcile the various series and produce a careful and detailed statistical picture of BBG activity. Although many governments make it a habit of constructing policy without facts, this is emphatically not a Korean characteristic in other economic areas and it should not be allowed to persist here. (2) However much of a problem the BBGs posed a decade ago, they are much less an economic problem today; a sector growing 10–15 percent faster the economy is a very different animal from one that is declining, albeit slightly. What *has* increased in the 1980s is public awareness of the

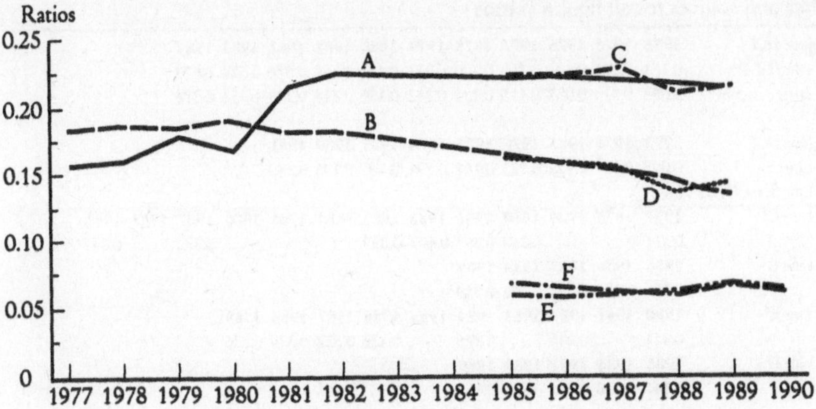

FIGURE 16.6 (A) manufacturing shipments by top five and (B) next 25 groups over total manufacturing; (C) sales by top five and (D) next 45 groups and (E) nonfinancial net value added by top five and (F) next 45 groups over corresponding economy-wide variable (see Table 16.1 for data and sources).

problem. This concern is not necessarily misplaced, for two reasons. Even if a problem is not getting worse, something may still need to be done. And even though income shares (a flow) may not be rising, wealth shares (a stock) may be.

Economic Power: Stocks

In many developing countries, especially in Latin America, the original source of capitalist accumulation is land, with surpluses therefrom reinvested to create commanding positions in industry. In Korea it may well be the reverse. I say "may" because only half the proposition is clear. It is undoubtedly the case that capitalist accumulation originated in industry in Korea. It is also abundantly clear that those profits have been in part reinvested in land at enormous profits to the BBGs and their owners. What is not so clear is how their share in real estate compares to their share in production. Are they earning immense profits in land speculation at the expense of other investors? Or are they merely making the same portfolio decisions as others and benefiting only proportionally to their share of national wealth? I know of no studies publicly available that shed any light on this subject.

More generally, the question of BBG economic power extends beyond the share of the BBG firms in income flows. On the one hand, one must also consider the accumulated stock of wealth (including real estate and financial instruments as well as firms). On the other hand, one must also consider the wealth of the families behind the groups. The relevant question is the level and trend of the wealth controlled by the families. It can certainly be argued that, although the primary source of BBG accumulation leveled off in the 1980s, their total accumulation continued to rise disproportionately because of their shares of real estate and financial instruments. In the absence of a single relevant set of data, however, one can make an

TABLE 16.1

Data and sources for all figures (ratios)

Figure 16.1	**1974**	**1975**	**1976**	**1977**	**1978**	**1979**	**1980**	**1981**	**1982**	**1983**	**1984**			
sales/GNP[1]	0.151	0.171	0.198	0.260	0.300	0.328	0.481	0.557	0.576	0.624	0.674			
sales/economy[2]	0.064	0.073	0.087	0.115	0.133	0.142	0.189	0.218	0.229	0.254	0.274			
Figure 16.2	**1973**	**1974**	**1975**	**1976**	**1977**	**1978**	**1979**	**1980**	**1981**					
Line A[3]	0.098	0.103	0.123	0.123	0.163	0.171	0.166	0.195	0.240					
Line B: see Figure 16.1														
Line C[4]	**1977**	**1978**	**1979**	**1980**	**1981**	**1982**	**1983**	**1984**	**1985**	**1986**	**1987**	**1988**	**1989**	
	0.341			0.360	0.397	0.407	0.399				0.373		0.347	
Line D[5]	**1985**	**1986**	**1987**	**1988**	**1989**									
	0.385	0.380	0.385	0.348	0.359									
Line E[6]	**1980**	**1981**	**1982**	**1983**	**1984**	**1985**	**1986**	**1987**	**1988**	**1989**				
	0.251		0.295		0.326		0.328	0.322	0.329	0.336				
Line F[7]	**1985**	**1986**	**1987**	**1988**	**1989**									
	0.142	0.136	0.135	0.136	0.152									
Figure 16.3[8]	**1980**	**1981**	**1982**	**1983**	**1984**	**1985**	**1986**	**1987**	**1988**	**1989**				
Ag/Fish/For	0.001		0.001		0.001		0.002	0.001	0.002	0.002				
Mining	0.002		0.002		0.002		0.002	0.002	0.002	0.002				
Manufacturing	0.521		0.475		0.520		0.508	0.486	0.524	0.510				
Elect/Gas/Water	0.000		0.000		0.000		0.001	0.000	0.002	0.002				
Construction	0.191		0.197		0.152		0.106	0.081	0.076	0.077				
Trade/Rest/Hotel	0.215		0.248		0.259		0.313	0.310	0.303	0.279				
Trans/Commun	0.041		0.037		0.034		0.040	0.038	0.037	0.035				
Finance (etc)	0.030		0.041		0.032		0.028	0.081	0.054	0.092				
Services: Pvt	0.000		0.000		0.001		0.001	0.001	0.001	0.001				
Total	0.999		0.999		0.999		0.998	0.999	0.998	0.998				
Figure 16.4[9]	**1973**	**1974**	**1975**	**1976**	**1977**	**1978**	**1979**	**1980**	**1981**	**1982**	**1983**	**1984**	**1985**	**1986**
Manufacturing	0.248	0.231	0.239	0.251	0.255	0.260	0.252	0.235	0.235	0.239	0.250	0.253	0.257	0.263
Economy	0.457	0.428	0.434	0.443	0.450	0.451	0.440	0.408	0.408	0.416	0.421	0.421	0.427	0.431
	1987	**1988**	**1989**											
Manufacturing	0.262	0.273	0.280											
Economy	0.430	0.440	0.451											
Figure 16.5	**1978**	**1979**	**1980**	**1981**	**1982**	**1983**	**1984**	**1985**	**1986**	**1987**	**1988**	**1989**		
Line A[10]	0.315	0.301	0.287	0.308	0.332									
Line B[10]	0.341	0.352	0.360	0.397	0.407									
Line C[11]								0.142	0.136	0.135	0.136	0.152		
Line D[11]								0.382	0.372	0.370	0.353	0.362		
Figure 16.6	**1977**	**1978**	**1979**	**1980**	**1981**	**1982**	**1983**	**1984**	**1985**	**1986**	**1987**	**1988**	**1989**	**1990**
Line A[12]	0.157	0.161	0.179	0.169	0.215	0.226	0.223	0.222	0.222	0.221	0.220	0.217	0.214	
Line B[12]	0.184	0.186	0.185	0.191	0.182	0.181	0.176	0.170	0.165	0.159	0.153	0.143	0.133	
Line C[13]									0.222	0.222	0.228	0.211	0.215	
Line D[13]									0.163	0.158	0.157	0.137	0.144	
Line E[14]									0.059	0.057	0.061	0.060	0.068	0.062
Line F[14]									0.067	0.065	0.060	0.061	0.066	0.060

1. *Variable:* Sales by top 10 groups over GNP.
   Source: Kim (1987), as reported in Amsden (1989:116).
2. *Variable:* Sales by top 10 groups over economy-wide sales.
   Source: Numerator as above, denominator from Bank of Korea, Economic Statistics Yearbook (various years).

Table 16.1 Notes (*continued*)

3. *Variable:* Value added of top 46 groups over GNP.
   Source: 1973–75: Jones and Sakong (1980:258–269), also gives methodology. 1975–78: Sakong (1980:2–3). 1978–81: unpublished update by Sakong Il.
4. *Variable:* Manufacturing shipments by top 30 groups over total manufacturing shipments.
   Source: 1977, 1982, and 1987: K.U. Lee (1990); other years from a variety of sources by the same author.
5. *Variable:* Sales by top 50 groups over economy-wide sales.
   Source: Numerator from Management Efficiency Research Institute (various years), denominator as in 2.
6. *Variable:* Sales by top 53 groups over economy-wide sales.
   Source: Numerator from Kang (1991), denominator as in 2.
7. *Variable:* Nonfinancial net value added of top 50 groups over net national product.
   Source: Numerator as in 5, denominator from same source as 2.
8. *Variable:* Share of total sales by top 53 groups derived from each industrial sector.
   Source: Same 6.
9. *Variable:* Ratio of gross value added to total sales.
   Source: Same as 2.
10. *Variable:* Manufacturing shipments and value added of top 30 groups over corresponding variable for total manufacturing.
    Source: Unpublished Economic Planning Board data, but apparently derived from 4.
11. *Variable:* Sales and net value added of top 50 groups over corresponding economy-wide variable.
    Source: Same as 5.
12. *Variable:* Manufacturing shipments by top five and next 25 groups over total manufacturing.
    Source: Same as 4.
13. *Variable:* Sales by top five and next 45 groups over corresponding economy-wide variable.
    Source: Same as 5.
14. *Variable:* Nonfinancial net value added by top five and next 45 groups over corresponding economy-wide variable.
    Source: Same as 5.

equally strong case for a declining share. Journalistic opinion certainly favors the growth hypothesis, but this version of conventional wisdom may be no better than the one that said (falsely) that the BBG share of economic activity continued to grow throughout the 1980s. Until someone does some serious research in a National Wealth Accounts framework, we simply have no idea.

Countervailing Forces

BBG behavior is constrained by both the invisible hand of the market and the visible hand of government. During the 1970s the literature stressed the role of market forces in explaining the Korean miracle. Jones and Sakong (1980) then detailed the pervasive interventionism of the Korean government in compensating for market imperfections. Though this notion was initially received with derision in some circles, it has since become widely accepted.[6] In fact, it has gone to the opposite extreme, with one widely read volume overemphasizing the government role relative to the market by arguing that government intervened to the extent of "getting relative prices wrong" (Amsden 1989: chap. 6). I would argue that what government often did was intervene to get prices right where the imperfectly developed market mechanism got them wrong. This is not the place to debate the precise balance of market and government forces in the 1970s and 1980s, but the following summary is necessary to understand the countervailing forces facing the BBGs in this period:

> Despite our emphasis on the role of government, Korea is in no sense a command economy. Rather, it is "mixed" both in terms of ownership and in the distribution of decision-making power.

> In Korea, [getting prices right] has by no means been eschewed, but it has been heavily supplemented by the illiberal compliance mechanisms of command and administrative discretion. Korea is thus interventionist in the broad sense of altering decisions of productive entities, but also in the narrower sense of using compulsion and discretion in doing so.
>
> Discretionary credit allocation is the fulcrum upon which partial mutuality[7] rests. The critical importance of credit to the enterprise, and its virtually complete control by the government, make this a powerful tool for ensuring private compliance with almost any command the government wishes to give. Government control of the banks is thus the single most important economic factor explaining the distinctly subordinate position of the private sector.
>
> Given economic growth as the legitimizing goal of the Park regime, there is a clear harmony of interest between government and business, and this is reflected in close working relationships of a sort that might be crudely characterized as "Korea, Inc." The analogy with "Japan, Inc." is misleading, however, in that the Korean government is clearly and unquestionably the dominant partner. (Jones and Sakong 1980:293–296).

What has happened to change this balance of power? During the 1980s, four major changes may be hypothesized to have altered the relative power of BBGs:

1. Market forces rose: Markets became steadily more perfect during the 1980s. Two areas are of particular importance. First, and most important, capital markets deepened with a host of new and perfected instruments available, and the availability of underpriced discretionary loans was substantially reduced. Second, domestic competition rose and tariff barriers were reduced, increasing competition with imports.

2. Union power rose: After 1987, the previously tame union movement went wild, unleashing a series of changes in labor relations that can only have harmed the BBGs.

3. Bureaucratic power declined: According to Y. H. Kim (see Chapter 2), after 1980 Korea "experienced a radical discontinuity in its civilian bureaucracy and especially in its economic cadres, with resulting discontinuities in economic policies. These developments, coupled with a new orientation in economic policy emphasizing a free market ideology, propelled the business leaders into the vacuum thus created, and private enterprise emerged with enhanced powers."

4. Popular democratic power rose: The introduction of democracy in 1987 increased the influence of BBGs on government because, though it had proved hard to buy bureaucrats, it was easier to buy politicians through campaign contributions.

The first two changes acted to reduce the relative power of the BBGs. The second two acted to increase the relative power of the BBGs, and I take their impact to be less then self-evident, though there may be considerable truth in one or both.

Conclusion

The conventional wisdom is wrong in asserting that aggregate concentration continued to increase during the 1980s. Available evidence strongly suggests that the BBG share of economic activity peaked somewhere in the 1981–84 period and, if anything, declined thereafter. It is certainly possible that their share of wealth continued to increase, but this is totally undocumented. It is even more possible that their relative power nonetheless increased because of a decline in the countervailing force of government.

As a foreign economic empiricist, I am in no position to evaluate the subtle workings of the Korean bureaucracy and political system. However, I would ask two questions of those better qualified. If the relative power of the BBGs rose relative to the government, (1) Why was their relative growth curtailed? It is possible to argue that, if the government had not been weakened, the BBG shares would have really taken a nose dive, but that case remains to be made. (2) Why did the government in the 1980s implement a series of anti-BBG polices when virtually none had been effectively implemented before?

Advantages of BBGs

Korea's high growth rate can be explained from many perspectives: export orientation, Confucian culture, correct price setting, intelligent government intervention, technological change, and so forth. The question is, Whatever it is that Korea did, why did the BBGs do it better? This is an old question. The new question is, Why do they no longer do it better?

Since it was first posed,[8] the old question has generated a lot of work, but not much consensus. The new question may help to solve the old, since it is variance in the dependent variable that allows us to infer causation by the independent variables. If we can figure out what stopped BBG relative growth, we can better understand what caused it in the first place. As befits a first quick cut at answering a new question, I focus on what seems to be the most obvious explanations, leaving it to later work to fill in the "howevers" and "in additions." I propose only two primary causal factors: entrepreneurship and credit.

Entrepreneurship

The simplest way to describe the entrepreneurial advantages of BBGs is as follows:

1. Entrepreneurship is the scarcest of the scarce factors constraining economic development; capital, after all, can be readily borrowed domestically or internationally by someone capable of putting it to work efficiently.

2. The distribution of entrepreneurial ability is highly skewed—just as a small percentage of athletes produce most of the points and a small fraction of the economics profession produces the bulk of the seminal articles.
3. A growth-maximizing strategy of development allocates capital to those who will use it to generate the highest rate of return.
4. A rapidly growing economy has allocated a disproportionate share of resources to a relatively small number of entrepreneurs best able to put them to productive use.

Fair enough, but is not this process subject to diminishing returns as increasing amounts of a variable factor (capital) are applied to a fixed factor (entrepreneurial ability)? The answer is "not necessarily." *Entrepreneurial* talent is required only at the margin to induce change. Ongoing inframarginal activity requires only *managerial* talent which can be hired as a variable factor. The entrepreneur starts one project, gets it running smoothly, turns it over to a subordinate, and moves on to a new project (Jones 1987:129).

What happened to change this advantage in the 1980s? The answer is regrettably but inevitably simple: age. Some entrepreneurs died, and the second generation is not the same as the first. Others just got old, and a 75-year-old entrepreneur is not the same as a 45-year-old. I can find no data on the age of the entrepreneurs, but Lee (1989:183) reports the founding dates of the twenty largest BBGs in 1986. Most were founded under the Rhee regime, with three earlier and four later. The average age of the groups is 34, and if the founders were typically 30 years of age at inception, then they would have averaged 64 years of age in 1986.

Aging is not confined to Korea. Alfred Chandler and Herman Daems (1974:5–7) identify a standard three-stage evolution of the capitalist enterprise. In the words of Jurgen Brockstedt:

> In the owner-managed enterprise, long-term strategic decision and tactical management decisions are taken by the owners (personal enterprise); in the intermediate stage (entrepreneurial enterprise), the tactical management decisions are taken by managers while entrepreneurial decisions on financial policy, the use of resources or the appointment of senior executives are taken by the founder or his family, that is, by the owners; the third and last stage is represented by the managerial enterprise, in which the capital is relatively widely distributed and salaried entrepreneurs with no significant ownership in the enterprise make the long-term as well as tactical decisions. (1984:242)

Korean BBGs are now in the midst of the very difficult transition from the second to third stage; some may not survive, and all but the nimblest are likely to suffer in the process.[9] Even if so, this can only be part of the story, for we must consider entry as well as exit. Where are this generation's Ju Yung Chungs and

Byung Chul Lees? I know of no work on this subject, but the answer probably runs something like this: they worked hard in primary and secondary schools, were admitted to a prestigious university, were hired by Chung or Lee and are now managers, not entrepreneurs. A further reason may be that credit—the traditional multiplier of entrepreneurial talent—is no longer available in the old way.

Privileged Access to Credit

By now it is widely recognized that credit markets are central to the early BBG phenomenon in Korea, so only a summary is required here.

Korean credit markets have been characterized by discretionary government allocation of underpriced capital to firms with extremely high debt–equity ratios.[10] BBGs received a disproportionate share of this underpriced resource in part because they had proven themselves best able to do the things government wanted done (be it exporting or building heavy and chemical industries), and in part because they were most adept at taking advantage of whatever profit-making opportunities existed in the economy, including exploiting market distortions. If this had negative consequences, they were not due to the BBGs but to government policy; if one BBG did not exploit the opportunities provided by underpriced capital, another would have, and thus replaced the first in the BBG set.[11]

There are, however, two socially undesirable features of the BBG role. First, their size and power may have allowed them to obtain a share of resources beyond those warranted on the grounds of their comparative advantage. Second, their conglomerate structure, coupled with the availability of capital, allowed some of the credit to be ultimately used for expansion into sectors not intended by the original government allocation—thereby promoting unfair competition with non-BBG businessmen whose capital costs were higher.

In sum, BBG growth in the 1960s and 1970s was indisputably fueled by access to underpriced credit. It is open to question how much of this was legitimate exploitation of government policies and how much was due to illegitimate influence and distortions via transfers to ostensibly nonsubsidized activities. What is not in question is that, had BBGs paid competitive rates, their growth would have been considerably slower than it was.

What happened in the 1980s was, I believe, simple: the BBGs had to rely increasingly on competitively priced credit, and their growth slowed as a result. Proving this is not so simple. The reader deserves a table showing the trend in the real cost of capital to BBGs or at least one showing the proportion of BBG funds derived from policy loans and other bank credits provided at less than competitive rates. The latter is certainly available at the Bank of Korea (BOK), and the former is accessible to a little grubbing around in the groups' financial statements, but neither is presently available. Instead, we must take a more indirect route of listing the changes that make this result a pretty good bet. There are two sets of such changes, one affecting the economy as a whole, and the other targeted at the

BBGs specifically. Financial developments in the economy as a whole during the 1980s are fully described by Sang-Woo Nam (1991), but the germane facts are as follows:

1. Policy loans declined as a share of domestic credit, from 47.3 percent in 1980 to 28.1 percent in 1991 (Nam 1991:19).
2. BBGs probably received a decreasing share of policy loans. This may be inferred from partial data (deposit money banks only) on a declining share of manufacturing in policy loans from 54.1 percent in 1980 to 42 percent in 1991 (Nam 1991:20). Further, the share of policy loans in manufacturing that went to small and medium industry rose.
3. The advantages of policy loans declined, as their rates were unified in 1982 and rates subsequently raised (Sakong 1993:chap. 4).
4. Financial deepening occurred with the introduction of a wide range of new instruments and institutions. Since these largely charged market rates, the role of underpriced credit declined. The M3/GNP ratio rose from 43 to 115 percent during the 1980s, but the M2/GNP ratio rose only from 32 to 41 percent (Nam 1991:14). Since most of the new instruments are included in M3 but not in M2, the extent of financial deepening is remarkable, and even more so when compared with the trend of previous decades.
5. Real interest rates rose. Regulated interest rates on general bank loans were −2 percent in 1979–81 but substantially positive throughout the 1980s (Nam 1991:11). More important, the real average cost of borrowing for manufacturing firms was substantially negative (up to −14.1 percent) during the 1970s, but substantially positive (up to +12.1 percent) during the 1980s (Nam 1991:12).
6. With the rise in the cost of borrowing, securities became more appealing as a source of funds, and debt–equity ratios fell for Korean firms in general (Nam 1991:22–24). Even more remarkable, debt–equity ratios of large firms, which had been up to double those of small and medium firms in the 1970s (Jones 1987:138), were slightly higher in the 1980s.[12]

In addition, certain measures were targeted directly at the BBGs:

7. BBGs received a decreasing share of underpriced bank credit. In 1984 the minister of finance announced a freeze on further credit allocations to BBGs. This draconian measure was soon modified, but since that time a BBG credit limitation of one form or another has been in place. As a result, the top 30 groups' share of all credits from commercial banks has declined from 26.3 percent in 1987 to 19.8 percent in 1990.[13] Comparable figures for the early 1980s are not

available (although the BOK has them), but one can safely assume that they were much higher. This may well be the single most critical policy change.

8. Concomitantly, a greater share of credit was allocated to small and medium-size enterprises.
9. To reduce BBGs' unfair advantage in the competition for credit, core companies were prohibited from guaranteeing the loans of subsidiaries.
10. To reduce the problem of pyramiding (debt in one firm used for equity in another, allowing more borrowing, and an explosion of the group debt–equity ratio), interlocking shareholdings were restricted.

In sum, the Korean financial system developed considerably during the 1980s, thus reducing sharply the market imperfections the BBGs had traditionally exploited. The scope of preferential credit was reduced, the benefits of such access were cut, and BBG access to those reduced benefits declined. Is it any wonder that the BBG growth rate declined?

This is not to say that perfection has been achieved with a level playing field in credit. Far from it. The trend, however, is impressive.

Other Markets

While credit is the key market in understanding BBG growth, other markets are relevant as well. It has already been noted that events in the other major factor market—labor—were deleterious to BBGs after 1987. Turning to product markets, we also have a story of enhanced competition and thereby reduced BBG advantage. Also as with credit, there is a mix of economy-wide and specific BBG policy at work. For manufacturing, we have a particularly good handle on what is going on, thanks to the ongoing work of Kyu Uck Lee, who I rely on heavily below. The more important factors would seem to be these:

1. Domestic competition has increased somewhat. In 1970, 36 percent of BBG manufacturing sales were made in competition with numerous domestic producers,[14] a figure that increased to 39 percent in 1977 and to 45 percent in 1989 (Lee n.d.:32). The change came solely at the expense of duopoly markets: sales shares in monopoly markets were unchanged and those in oligopoly markets actually rose.
2. The ability to exploit markets is not just a function of domestic competition, but also of competition with imports. As a result of trade liberalization, foreign competition may also have increased.[15] Consumer and producer goods did increase from 29.4 percent of total imports in 1980 to 43.4 percent in 1990 (NSO 1991:214–215), but the ratio of imports to GDP declined substantially and we do not know how competitive the imports were. To assess the true competitiveness of Korean manufacturing, we badly need calculations of industry concentration incorporating imports.

3. Various measures were taken to support small and medium-size enterprises. In addition to the requirement that such firms receive a minimum share of bank credit, there was a prohibition of BBG entry into designated markets. The number of markets so designated rose from 23 in 1979 to 103 in 1983 and 246 in 1989 (Lee n.d.:20–22). In contrast to some other fair trade provisions, this one seems to have had been enforced stringently: of 154 cases examined under the act, entry has been permitted in only four cases. In part as a result, the share of these smaller businesses in manufacturing value added grew from 31.7 percent in 1975 to 35.1 percent in 1980 and to 45 percent in 1989. The resulting acceleration in the annual compound relative growth rate of these firms is small but noticeable, from 2.1 percent in 1975–80 to 2.9 percent in 1980–89.
4. A host of other constraints were placed on market conduct by the Fair Trade Act of 1981 and strengthened by amendments in 1986 and 1990 (Lee n.d.:42–49). This legislation is generally regarded as having been considerably less effective than its authors intended (see Fields 1991:28–29), but it is clearly a step in the right direction.

Most of these changes are evolutionary and all seem unlikely to have been important enough to have had a major causal impact on BBG growth rates.

Overall, changes in the credit market and the aging of the entrepreneurs seem the most likely candidates for explaining the sharp drop in the BBG growth rates in the 1980s. Labor strife after 1987 also must have been significant. The impact of product market competition and fair trade regulation also needs to be considered, particularly as their impact will continue to accumulate.

Policy toward BBGs

The Korean philosophy of economic management may be described as follows: When the market works, let it; when it doesn't work, try to fix it; and until it can be fixed, intervene. Like many successful philosophies, this is sufficiently ambiguous (what does it mean to "work"?) to be endorsed by a rather broad spectrum of the economic policy elite. What separates the elite (and thereby policy regimes) is the degree of adherence to a fourth principle concerning the test of what "works": markets are innocent until proven guilty.

No such simple framework can encompass the variety of three decades of Korean economic policy, but it does provide a useful broad-brush characterization of the more important changes. In the early 1960s the underdeveloped state of Korean markets gave policymakers good reason to presume them guilty, and to good effect. By the late 1970s markets had evolved considerably—especially the export market with all its competitive consequences and the internal information market of the BBGs. Policymakers had also evolved, though at a slower rate, with the presumption of guilt having considerably less justification than in the 1960s.

The Fifth Republic brought in a new economic team who, judging the heavy and chemical industries episode harshly, reversed the presumption and assumed markets innocent. Some distinguished Korean observers see this as a marked discontinuity in economic policy (Kim 1990). The changes were indeed significant, but to a foreigner they look much more evolutionary than revolutionary. If one asks which government, anywhere in time or space, the Fifth Republic most resembled, it was Korea's Fourth Republic. Even if these "reform economists" or "liberalizers" can by no means be identified with the Chicago/Chile school, they nonetheless generated a certain backlash, and today in Seoul one detects a considerable rise in skepticism about the innocence of markets. How has this evolution of policy regimes been reflected in policies toward the BBGs?

The 1960s and 1970s One of the earliest acts of the Park regime was to intervene rather forcefully by throwing all the BBG leaders in jail in the "Illicit Wealth Accumulation Episode." Thereafter, BBGs were largely allowed to go about their business of accumulation as long as they recognized the government's supremacy and followed its "informal guidance." The one major exception was the May 29 Presidential Special Directives of 1974 and associated measures designed to get the BBGs to reduce their debt–equity ratios and go public (Jones and Sakong 1980:280–284). The measure is noteworthy, not because of its success, which was limited, but rather on the symbolic front, where it was important because for the first time the BBGs were identified as a collective target of policies designed to constrain their excesses. Further, on the operational front, it initiated the process of group-by-group credit data collection at the Bank of Korea and the Ministry of Finance. The dramatic story told by this data was partly responsible for both inducing and permitting the credit controls of the 1980s.

The 1980s The consensus view seems to be that government policy in the 1980s was ineffective in controlling BBG growth (Amsden 1989:137; Fields 1991:29). My view of policy in the 1980s is considerably more favorable. In part, no doubt, this is because my reading of the data is different and what I need to explain is a drop in the BBG growth rate. At a more subjective level, however, there has been a dramatic change in the orientation of government officials. In the late 1970s there were few policymakers operationally concerned with BBG issues. By 1984 it was easy to find people at the Economic Planning Board, the Ministry of Finance, the Bank of Korea, and the Blue House who were so concerned. By 1991 it is hard to find those who are *not* so concerned, if only because they want to influence BBG control measures under consideration by their peers. As tangible evidence of this change, consider the five-year plans. The first six plans make no mention of the BBGs. The Seventh Plan, however, devotes a substantial section to BBG policy.

For the 1980s, the most important BBG control policies have already been described. There was also a continuation of support policies. By far the most important in this regard was the "rationalization" of the mass of sick industries, which were the downside of the push for heavy and chemical industries. Because of the secrecy surrounding these policies, their importance is sometimes not fully appreciated, but they preoccupied policymaking in a variety of areas for much of the Fifth Republic.[16] Critics see this bail-out as evidence of capitulation to the rising power of the BBGs, but is it so different from the "too big to fail" bail-outs of banks in the United States? The episode was very much in keeping with the partial-mutuality tradition of previous decades: the government got the BBGs into the troubled industries and was obligated to get them out. Continuity of policy regimes was also apparent in the flip side of government control. Just as Shinjin was dismantled in the 1970s, so also was Kukje in the 1980s. You don't "get along" if you don't "go along."

To summarize the 1980s, return to the two quotations in the introduction to this chapter. There, the advantages of BBGs over alternative institutional forms of production are divided into two classes. The left-hand quote concerns the exploitation of efficiencies of scale, scope, and entrepreneurship, which create growth and jobs and make both the BBGs and the country better off. The right-hand quote refers to the exploitation of government and market imperfections that make the BBGs better off, but the country worse off. During the 1980s the government acted forcefully to control abuses, notably by controlling credit, while recognizing the advantages of BBGs by not allowing a chain reaction of bankruptcies to decimate the country's economic strength. BBG growth was restrained significantly, but the sector was hardly dismantled.

The foregoing principle—of minimizing disadvantages while maximizing advantages—serves as a guide to policy for the 1990s, a topic to which I now turn.

Credit Market Policy for the 1990s

As has already been emphasized, the most important source of socially undesirable BBG behavior is the credit market. The conventional view of this market's operation is summarized by Tibor Scitovsky in the context of the development of Taiwan and South Korea:

> For interest rates held below their natural level create excess demand for investable funds and so force the banks to ration credit. Credit rationing, however, usually favors large firms, the banks established customers, or those whom government wants to favor, and these are not always the ones who earn the highest rate of return on their investments. Accordingly, credit rationing by bank or government policy is likely to crowd out some high-return investments that would not be crowded out if the interest rate were the main factor limiting the demand for credit. In other words, rationing credit by interest rates instead of by bank managers and government officials is almost certain to raise the average return on the total volume of investment, thereby further accelerating growth. (Scitovsky 1986:149)

Permit me to exhibit ignorance of money and banking by espousing the following dissenting view:

1. Credit is seldom[17] given to the highest bidder, as willingness to pay is not necessarily an indicator of higher-yielding investment opportunities. If I am willing to pay 20 percent to your 15 percent, it may mean I have a better use for the funds; it may also mean that I am a financial fool, with exaggerated expectations of what I can accomplish, or desperate to keep my failing company afloat for just a few more months.
2. Credit could perhaps[18] be rationed by bankers who try to distinguish between high expected return and high expectations of a return; that is, they would evaluate the expected return on an applicant's project and compare it to the interest rate set by a demand curve established by those who have passed such a test.
3. Credit *is* rationed by bankers who evaluate the probability that the loan will be repaid. Having a good project is generally neither necessary nor sufficient to this end. What *is* sufficient is collateral or some other guarantee that the loan will be repaid even if this particular project goes belly up.

As evidence for the foregoing, (1) try getting a loan for a small business in the United States; or (2) examine the market's reallocation of Middle Eastern oil surpluses in the 1970s, which in part went to Latin American public enterprises, not because they had good uses for the funds, but because the international banks believed (incorrectly as it turned out) that the recipients' governments would repay the loans if the companies could not; or (3) examine the response of U.S. banks to reduced regulation in the 1980s, with the collateral value of real estate a major determinant of allocation.

The germane implication of this line of reasoning is straightforward: it is the unfettered credit market, not government, that necessarily "favors large firms and the banks' established customers." Governments can favor whomsoever they choose. In Korea in the 1960s and 1970s the government favored large firms but in the 1980s there was a shift toward smaller firms. A decade ago I suggested that in the 1980s, "administrative discretion needs to be exercised, not in the traditional pro-*jaebul* fashion, but with a tilt towards the excluded middle. . . . In part this means greater support for those institutions specializing in credit to the non-*jaebul* sector. . . . More importantly, it means increasing commercial bank support for this sector" (Jones 1987:188–189). This is precisely what has been accomplished by the policies described in the previous section.

What does this imply for policy in the 1990s? At a minimum, it means that the gains of the 1980s not be lost. There is room for concern on this score. In mid-1991 the government drastically altered its policy on commercial bank credit to the BBGs. Each group was encouraged to designate three core enterprises, for which the BBG credit limitation would be lifted. The ostensible goal of the policy was to encourage specialization, an argument whose merits are considered below. The danger is that this is very nearly equivalent to abolishing the credit limitation altogether. Funds are fungible and can be transferred throughout a group by a variety of mechanisms, including transfer pricing, dividend policy, intergroup lending, flexibility in accounts payable/receivable, cross-shareholding, and the simple reallocation of freed resources (which would otherwise have been used for the three core firms) to other firms in the group. This change is thus the strongest evidence I know of in support of those who believe that democratization has not weakened, but strengthened, BBG power. The policy should be reconsidered.

If the government tilt toward non-BBGs is to be maintained, how will it be implemented? At present, the credit control policy works because, despite the facade of privatization, the government continues to control the banks. There are many in the policy community who believe this control will need to be maintained as long as disequilibrium interest rates are maintained (Sakong 1993). Their arguments seem persuasive. However, a case can be made for continuing this control even longer, on two quite different grounds. First, if one wants to continue to tilt toward non-BBGs whereas even independent banks will tilt toward collateral-rich BBGs, then continued government intervention is necessary. Second, it is generally agreed that, with the government out, the BBGs will take over the commercial banks. A possible consequence is the ignition of a new spurt of BBG relative growth and conglomeration on the Japanese top-tier model. If this is deemed undesirable on sociopolitical grounds, then it is hard to think of a viable alternative to continued government control. Space limitations preclude a detailed treatment of this important issue here. Fortunately, such a discussion is provided by Sang-Woo Nam (1988, and see Chapter 10 of this volume). What does need additional emphasis, however, is the link between the banks' future and the issue of conglomerate structure.

Octopus, Lobster, and Shrimp Models

A major characteristic of Korean BBGs is their conglomerate structure; they are active in a wide range of industries, well beyond anything that can be explained by the traditional arguments for vertical integration (diversification from suppliers to users, and vice versa, to capture the technological interdependencies of sequential production processes; for details, see Jones 1987:133–138). I call this the octopus model, adopting the Korean journalistic appellation used to suggest tentacles grasping into all sectors of the economy.

Since at least the early 1980s, influential policymakers have argued that conglomeration is undesirable, stemming from illegitimate BBG advantages rather than real efficiencies.[19] Further, the spreading of capital and management over such a broad range dilutes the growth of their core firms, which are still small by international standards (Kang 1991). This in turn reduces Korea's international competitiveness by precluding the advantages of economies of scale. Accordingly, a series of policies have been adopted to encourage the BBGs to divest themselves of secondary and tertiary activities and to focus on a few core activities and such ancillary sectors as can be justified on the grounds of vertical integration.[20] I refer to this as the lobster model, reflecting a concentration of high-value, juicy morsels.

Insight into the ramifications of the choice between octopus and lobster models can be gained by considering the institutional organization of Japanese industry, whose top tier is remarkably sharply divided between the six largest *keiretsu*, which are octopuses, and the balance, which are lobsters. The top six—Mistubishi, Mitsui, Sumitomo, Fuyo (or Fuji), DKB (or Ikkan), and Sanwa—are larger by an order of magnitude (e.g., in terms of sales, the top group is less than twice as large as the sixth, but the sixth is more than four times as large as the seventh; Dodwell Marketing Consultants 1980:12–13); are highly diversified conglomerates as compared with the second tier, which produces a much narrower range of related products (Nippon Steel, Hitachi, Toyota, Nissan, Toyota, etc.); are horizontal affiliations of equals, linked loosely, partially, and nonexclusively through interlocking shareholdings, with Presidents Clubs as a dominant means of intergroup coordination (the second tier, in contrast, is vertically organized, with "one dominant parent corporation");[21] and all have a bank or banks as their "central organ."[22]

This is an extremely interesting set of characteristics, in part because one wonders whether the set is immutable. For example, is the central role of banks necessary for successful large-scale conglomeration? I do not know the answer to this question, but I suggest that it be pondered by those who favor the octopus model for Korea. For the moment, simply note that Japan's BBG structure encompasses not one model but two. There are six octopuses and a bunch of lobsters.

To complete the sea creature analogy, consider the shrimp. Taiwan, whose economic development has been so similar to Korea's in so many respects, differs dramatically on the dimension in question. Though it has realized technological economies of scale through an establishment size distribution not markedly different from Korea's, it has largely avoided the aggregation of these establishments into large groups as in Japan and Korea (see Jones 1987:138–144; Hamilton and Orru 1989:39–47).

The sides of the current policy debate may now be summarized:

- Some support the octopus model. Kyu Uck Lee (see Chapter 15) makes a positive case for the model of the top-tier Japanese business groups and implies that this would be an acceptable, if not laudable, outcome in Korea *if* ownership of the BBGs could be widely dispersed as in Japan.[23]
- Some support the lobster model. Given the mid-1991 shift in credit policy and continued government control of the commercial banks, this seems to be the view of the current dominant policy elite.
- Some support the shrimp model. Backers of Kim Dae Jung presumably fall in this category.

There are obvious sociopolitical elements in this debate, but on narrow economic grounds alone the question of comparative institutional advantage is a fascinating analytical topic, deserving considerable attention. Further, the equity issues may be as important as the efficiency issues. However, given time constraints, a finesse is in order.

Is the current regime or its successor likely to move dramatically toward a shrimp model? Most probably not, though they can and should continue the 1980s tilt in that direction. The choice is then between lobsters and octopuses. A good case can be made for either, but this is a second-order policy issue. The first-order policy question is, Who is better suited to decide the evolutionary path of Korea's BBGs, the government or the market? As long as other policies are adopted to minimize the tilt to the playing field, is there any market failure that will lead the BBGs to a socially undesirable point on the specialization-conglomeration continuum?

One argument might be that the government is better able to bear risk than are private firms, so that BBGs, in an effort to spread risk, will overdiversify from society's point of view. It would then follow that the government should subsidize specialization, much as it subsidized risky exports over less risky import substitution in an earlier time. But the theoretical underpinnings of this argument are shaky, and empirical verification of risk spreading as a critical BBG motive is lacking. In sum, until such time as someone comes up with a stronger market failure argument for intervention, the jury might be well advised to find markets innocent in this case.

Other Policies

In Chapter 15, Kyu Uck Lee makes a strong case for the social utility of hastening dispersal of BBG share ownership. Economic logic points in the same direction. Chandler and Daem's second-stage entrepreneurial capitalism is a viable form of business organization, as is the third stage of managerial capitalism. What is less viable is the intermediate transition stage in which less competent descendants control the groups. In long-run equilibrium, of course, the incompetent are weeded out through attrition, but in the meantime scarce national resources are wasted. What can be done to hasten this process? Viable policies include (1) *serious implementation of the inheritance laws.* One hopes that their intensive application to Chung Ju Young reflects the first step in a comprehensive policy rather than a punitive application of partial mutuality; (2) *extension of the real-name system to financial dealings.* This is a necessary precondition to implementing the inheritance laws. Application to real estate was a major accomplishment of the 1980s, but it is simply ludicrous that in a modern economy it remains impossible to identify the true owner of financial assets.

Two other sets of policies will be useful in further leveling the playing field. On the one hand there is competition policy via reduced restriction on both domestic entry and imports and traditional fair trade regulation. On the other hand, even with greater intramarket competition, attention is needed to control intermarket BBG abuses such as mutual restraint and horizontal and vertical predation. Here, however, nothing discontinuous need be done. It is only necessary to continue the evolutionary progress of the previous decade.

It is also important to avoid certain policies. In mid-1991 two policies being discussed in Seoul were the abolition of centralized recruiting and of the chairman's secretariat (or head office of the BBG). The goal is to reduce BBG advantages over non-BBGs, and this it would certainly do. The problem is that these policies reduce legitimate rather than illegitimate advantage and consequently harm economic efficiency. There are no market failures here, only legitimate economies of scope and scale. These markets are innocent and should be left alone.

Summary

The most important conclusion of this chapter follows from a little data grubbing, which strongly suggests that the rapid growth of BBGs relative to the Korean economy was halted somewhere between 1981 and 1984; thereafter, they grew at the same rate as the economy, or slightly more slowly. The primary causes of this reversal are hypothesized to be two: internal constraints on growth have been imposed, most noticeably those associated with the transition to second-generation management and the loss or diminution of the first generation's extraordinary entrepreneurial abilities; and external constraints on growth have been imposed, most importantly as government restrained privileged access to credit and moved toward market rates for unprivileged access. Other contributing factors included changing labor relations (after 1987), increased product market competition, and the operation of the fair trade laws.

Turning to policy prescriptions for the 1990s, a foreigner treads more warily. However, a case can be made that, if the gains of the 1980s are not to be reversed, then the policy to allow unlimited access to credit for selected BBG core firms should be reconsidered, and there seems to be no immediate viable alternative to continued government control of commercial banks. In addition, dispersion of BBG ownership should be hastened by more stringent enforcement of the inheritance laws and by extension of the real-name system to financial intermediaries, and competition policy and fair trade regulation should continue to evolve along the lines taken in the 1980s.

It is as important to know what to avoid as to know what to do. To avoid debilitating a real national asset and reducing Korea's international competitiveness, no other BBG control policies should be undertaken unless there is a clear case of market failure. Policies such as abolishing the chairman's secretariat or group recruiting attack legitimate sources of institutional comparative advantage and should not be tolerated.

In closing, let me put this discussion in comparative international perspective by assuming that it is early 1979 and a group of foreign experts on the Korean economy are called together and told: (1) President Park will be assassinated; (2) his successor will be forced from office by popular demonstrations and replaced via a democratic election; (3) the power of labor unions will soar; and (4) the credit advantages of BBGs will be curtailed and their growth rate cut in half.[24] With this foreknowledge, the experts are told to predict the real GNP growth rate for the 1980s.

Would any of them have come close to the right answer, which is that Korea would adapt and continue to chug along at its traditional, world-class 9–10 percent rate?[25] I know I would not have. There are many dimensions to this remarkable perseverance in the face of political change, but the germane one is that the BBGs went from a dominant, leading sector in the 1960s and 1970s to a normal one in the 1980s, and non-BBGs took up the slack. At the beginning of the 1980s I concluded: "There is substantial reason to believe that Korea is at a turning point in the evolution of her industrial structure and that increasing emphasis needs to be given to filling in the excluded middle. It remains to be ascertained how fast this can be accomplished without efficiency loss" (Jones 1987:192). It has now been ascertained that considerable progress could be made in only a decade, and there was no efficiency loss apparent in the economic growth rate. As always, problems remain, but from an international perspective what is impressive is how much has already been accomplished, and there are important lessons here for other countries. I look forward to returning in another decade and learning what the next lessons will be.

NOTES

1. Members of the big business community in Korea have come to feel that the Korean term is perjorative, so the BBG euphemism is adopted in this chapter.
2. Identical numbers are cited, though without attribution, in Lau (1986:9).
3. National product is a value-added measure, which is output net of intermediate inputs; bone weight is body weight net of tissue weight.
4. There is one other data set on BBG size which I do not treat in detail because it relies on different—and therefore perhaps incompatible—sources (including those above) for each of its four years (1975, 1980, 1983, and 1986). It is nonetheless quite consistent with the above results, showing rapid growth in the BBG's value-added share through 1983, with a slight decline from 1983 to 1986 (Zelle n.d.).
5. They may also well have a higher share of intergroup transactions, though I know of no evidence on this.
6. For articles stressing the role of the state, see Deyo (1987).
7. "Partial mutuality" refers to the government enforcement of its wishes by the threat

of withdrawing privileges previously conferred, or withholding future privileges; that is, the BBGs "get along by going along."

8. To my knowledge, in Jones and Sakong (1980:269–278).

9. By now there is quite a bit of work in English on BBG management. See the essays in Chung and Lee (1989) and Steers, Shin, and Ungson (1989); for specific treatment of the transition, see Fields (1991:14–16); also see Hattori (1984:121–142).

10. For a description of the discretionary allocation process, see Jones and Sakong (1980: chap. 4). For a description of the disequilibrium credit markets, see Cole and Park (1983).

11. For extensive elaboration on this and the following point, see Jones (1987:142–166).

12. At least for manufacturing (BOK 1991:93–94).

13. For loans covered by the Credit Control System, the figures declined from 23.8 to 16.8 percent. I regret that I am not at liberty to cite the source of this information, but it is pretty good.

14. As defined by a three-firm domestic concentration ratio of less than 0.60.

15. For details see Sakong (1993:chap. 4).

16. For an insider's view, see Sakong (1993).

17. This is not just a wishy-washy modifier to avoid saying "never." A common socioeconomic institution in Asia is housewives' investment clubs in which savings are pooled and allocated sequentially to members of the club. In one variant, the sequence is determined by willingness to pay the most to get the money first.

18. Though this is more properly accomplished by the equity market, not the debt market.

19. The major counterargument is based on the organizational economies of scope embodied in the founding entrepreneur. As these deteriorate with time, the argument against conglomeration is strengthened.

20. The latest is the abolition of the credit restriction for core firms, described above.

21. For the quote and a more elaborate description of organizational distinctions between the two groups, see Aoki (1984:7–15).

22. "Each group includes, as a rule, (at least) one city bank and one trust bank as members" (Aoki 1984:12); see also Nakatani (1984:231).

23. Lee does not distinguish between top and bottom tiers, but his description applies primarily to the top six.

24. Using the Jones and Sakong (1980) figures for 1973 to 1981, the BBGs' real growth rate was 19.7 percent compared with something in the 8–9 percent range threafter.

25. From 1981 to 1990 the real compound rate was exactly 10 percent. I omit the oil shock of 1979 from the question and the recession of 1980 from the answer. Factor them in if you like: the 1979–90 growth rate was 8.3 percent. Is this any less impressive?

REFERENCES

Amsden, Alice. 1989. *Asia's Next Giant: South Korea and Late Industrialization*. New York: Oxford University Press.

Aoki, Masahiko. 1984. "Aspects of the Japanese Firm." In Masahiko Aoki (ed.), *The Economic Analysis of the Japanese Firm*. Amsterdam: North Holland.

Bank of Korea (BOK). Various years. *Economic Statistics Yearbook. Seoul: BOK.*

Bank of Korea (BOK). 1991. *Financial Statements Analysis for 1990*. Seoul: BOK.

Brokstedt, Jurgen. 1984. "Family Enterprise in Germany." In Akio Okochi and Shigeaki Yasuoka (eds.), *Family Business in the Era of Industrial Growth*. Tokyo: University of Tokyo Press.

Chandler, Alfred, and Herman Daems. 1974. "Introduction: The Rise of Managerial Capitalism and Its Impact on Investment Strategy in the Western World and Japan." In Herman Daems and Herman van der Wee (eds.), *The Rise of Managerial Capitalism*. The Hague: Nijhoff.

Chung, Kae H., and Hak Chong Lee, eds. 1989. *Korean Managerial Dynamics*. New York: Praeger.

Cole, David, and Yung Chul Park. 1983. *Financial Development in Korea, 1945–1978*. Cambridge: Harvard University Press.

Deyo, Frederic C., ed. 1987. *The Political Economy of the New Asian Industrialization*. Ithaca: Cornell University Press.

Dodwell Marketing Consultants. 1980. *Industrial Groupings in Japan*. Tokyo: Dodwell.

Fields, Karl. 1991. "Developmental Capitalism and Industrial Organization: *Chaebol* and the State in Korea." Paper presented at the Conference on Political Authority and Economic Exchange in Korea, East-West Center, Honolulu, January 3–5. Tacoma: University of Puget Sound.

Hamilton, Gary G., and Marco Orru. 1989. "Oganizational Structure of East Asian Companies." In Kae H. Chung and Hak Chong Lee (eds.), *Korean Managerial Dynamics*. New York: Praeger.

Hattori, Tamio. 1984. "The Relationship between Zaibatsu and Family Structure: The Korean Case." In Akio Okochi and Shigeaki Yasuoka (eds.), *Family Business in the Era of Industrial Growth*. Tokyo: University of Tokyo Press.

Jones, Leroy. 1987. "*Jaebul* and the Concentration of Economic Power in Korean Development Issues, Evidence and the Alternatives." In Il Sakong (ed.), *Macroeconomic Policy and Industrial Development Issues*. Seoul: Korea Development Institute, 1987. Originally published as a World Bank report, 1980.

Jones, Leroy, and Sakong Il. 1980. *Government, Business and Entrepreneurship in Economic Development: The Korean Case*. Cambridge: Harvard University Press.

Kang, Shin Il. 1991. "Dae Gyu Mo Gi Up Jim Dan Ae Kyan Han Yon Ku" (Study of large conglomerate firms). Seoul: Korea Economic Research Institute.

Kim, Seok Ki. 1987. "Business Concentration and Government Policy: A Study of the Phenomenon of Business Groups in Korea, 1945–1985." Ph.D. diss., Harvard Business School, Boston.

Kim, Yoon Hyung. 1990. "An Introduction to the Korean Model of Political Economy." Mimeo. East-West Population Institute, East-West Center, Honolulu.

Lau, Lawrence J. 1986. "Introduction." In Lawrence J. Lau (ed.), *Models of Development: A Comparative Study of Economic Growth in South Korea and Taiwan*. San Francisco: ICS Press.

Lee, Kyu Uck. n.d. *Corporate Policies in Korea: With Special Reference to Competition Policy*. Seoul: Korea Development Institute.

Lee, Sang M. 1989. "Management Styles of Korean *Chaebols*." In Kae H. Chung and Hak Chong Lee (eds.), *Korean Managerial Dynamics*. New York: Praeger.

Management Efficiency Research Institute. Various years. *Korea's Fifty Major Groups*. Seoul: Management Efficiency Research Institute.

Nakatani, Iwao. 1984. "The Economic Role of Financial Corporate Grouping." In Masahiko Aoki (ed.), *The Economic Analysis of the Japanese Firm*. Amsterdam: North Holland.

Nam, Sang-Woo. 1988. "Readjustment of the Business Boundaries of Financial Intermediaries in Korea." KDI Working Paper, no. 8822 (December). Seoul: Korea Development Institute.

Nam, Sang-Woo. 1991. "Korea's Financial Reform since the Early 1980's." Seoul: Korea Development Institute.

National Statistical Office (NSO). 1991. *Major Statistics of Korean Economy: 1991*. Seoul: NSO.

Sakong, Il. 1980. "Kyng Jae Sung Jang Kwa Kyung Jae Ryug Jip Jung" (Economic growth and concentration of economic power). *Han Kook Kae Bal Yun Ku (Korea Development Review)*, March.

Sakong, Il. 1993. *Korea in the World Economy*. Washington: Institute for International Economics.

Scitovsky, Tibor. 1986. "Economic Development in Taiwan and South Korea." In Lawrence J. Lau (ed.), *Models of Development: A Comparative Study of Economic Growth in South Korea and Taiwan*. San Francisco: ICS Press.

Steers, Richard M., Shin Yoo Keun, and Gerardo R. Ungson. 1989. *The Chaebol: Korea's New Industrial Might*. New York: Harper Business.

Zelle, William. n.d. "Industrial Policy and Organizational Efficiency: The Korea *Chaebol* Examined." Research Program in East Asian Business and Development Working Paper Series, no. 30, University of California, Davis.

PART VII

TRADE AND INDUSTRIAL STRATEGY

Chapter 17

Industrial Policy and Trade Regimes

Kwang Suk Kim
Kyung Hee University

Introduction

As is widely known, the Republic of Korea has achieved rapid industrialization and growth since the early 1960s. From 1962 to 1990, Korea's GNP grew at an average annual rate of 9 percent, and per capita GNP increased more than six times, from about US$520 to $3,494 in 1985 constant prices. This GNP growth was led mainly by the manufacturing sector, which grew at an average annual rate of about 15 percent during the same period. The manufacturing sector's share in GNP more than doubled, increasing from 14 to 30 percent over the same period, whereas the agriculture-forestry-fishery sector's share declined sharply, from 37 to 9 percent.

Economic development prior to the early 1960s had been quite slow, if not stagnant, partly because of economic disruptions caused by the country's partition and the Korean War, and partly because of the inward-looking development strategy adopted in the postwar reconstruction period (1953–60). A massive amount of foreign assistance, particularly from the United States, was introduced to finance the postwar reconstruction and stabilization programs undertaken immediately after the armistice (1953). Although some success was achieved in stabilizing prices in the late 1950s, GNP grew by only 3.8 percent annually from 1953 to 1962; per capita GNP increased by a mere 1 percent per year.

Since 1962, Korea has sustained a high rate of GNP growth, except for the unusual year of 1980, in which real GNP declined by 5 percent. It is generally believed that Korea's sudden increase in output growth was due to the shift in development strategy that took place in the early 1960s. Although other economic and noneconomic factors that cannot be easily quantified were certainly involved, the shift from an inward-looking import-substitution strategy to an export-oriented industrialization strategy was an important factor in the acceleration of output growth. This shift of development strategy was quite effective in influencing the country's growth path because it accompanied a major reform in the system of industrial incentives.

Since the shift in development strategy, exports have undoubtedly acted as the engine of growth in Korea. The total volume of merchandise exports has expanded by about 23 percent annually since 1962, thereby stimulating the growth of the domestic economy. The exports of goods and nonfactor services jumped from a mere 5 percent of GNP in 1962 to 32 percent in 1990. Korea became the twelfth largest exporting country in the world in 1988–89.

Despite the rapid growth of exports, the country's current balance of goods and services was almost continuously in deficit until 1985, mainly because the country's imports had also been expanding rapidly since the early 1960s, starting from a much larger base than exports. The domestic excess demand, which was created to promote rapid industrialization and economic growth, was partly responsible for the expansion of imports. Because of this precarious balance-of-payments situation, the Korean government took a gradual and cautious approach to import liberalization. Even after export trade had been almost completely liberalized in the first half of the 1960s in line with the shift to an export-oriented industrialization strategy, a substantial step toward import liberalization was delayed until the late 1970s.

The country's current account balance turned to a large surplus beginning in 1986, owing mainly to the effective depreciation of the Korean won against major currencies and other favorable world trade conditions during 1986–88. This transition to a "surplus" economy increased foreign pressures on Korea, notably from the United States, to accelerate the opening of its domestic markets and made it almost impossible for Korea to justify a delay in opening its markets on the grounds of needing to balance its payments. In recent years, therefore, Korea has realized significant progress in opening its markets not only in the goods sector but also in the service sector. But this acceleration of market opening has brought about a new problem of industrial adjustment, particularly in the agricultural sector, in which Korea is least competitive in the face of imports from the United States and other countries.

Political liberalization since the 29 June 1987 declaration has been accompanied by a tremendous increase in labor disputes and resulted in a rapid rise in the wage cost of domestic industry. This rise in wage cost, combined with the appreciation of domestic currency since 1988, is hurting the international competitiveness of Korean industries, which has been largely dependent on the low wages of their workers. It now seems inevitable, therefore, that the domestic industries must undergo a structural adjustment to remain internationally competitive and to achieve a sustained high growth of the economy.

Against this general background of the Korean economy, in this chapter I analyze the evolution of Korea's industrial policy and trade regime during the period of rapid industrialization (1965–89), discuss emerging issues of Korea's industrial policy and trade regime, and finally present feasible institutional reform proposals for improving the industrial policy and trade regime in the 1990s and thereafter.

"Industrial policy" is a broad concept. Adams and Bollino (1983) interpret the term to include any measure, policy, or program that focuses directly on the supply side, thus eliminating such policies as those oriented primarily toward the stimulation of demand. The term may refer to general or nonselective industrial policies that aim at improving the resource allocation mechanism, investment environment, and technology, as well as to sector- and industry-specific policies. If this broad concept of industrial policy is used, trade policy and trade regimes are part of the industrial policy. For convenience, however, I separate the topic of trade regimes from the discussion of the evolution of Korea's industrial policy.

Evolution of Industrial Policy since the Early 1960s

Korea originally had an industrialization strategy based on import substitution but changed its import-substitution strategy to an export-oriented one in the early 1960s. The new strategy was introduced by the military government that came into power in 1961. Subsequently, the country's industrial policy has undergone many changes, although the main strategy of export orientation has remained unchanged.

Korean industrial policy has undergone three somewhat distinct phases over the period 1961–89. The first lasted only a short while, from 1961 to 1965, and was the transitional one in which major policy reforms were undertaken to institute an export-oriented industrialization strategy. In the second phase, which began in 1966 and continued through the end of the Park Chung Hee regime (1979), an export-oriented strategy was promoted in earnest to maximize output growth while maintaining excess demand in the economy. The period beginning in 1980 can be taken as the third phase, in which the government pursued the same export-oriented strategy while emphasizing domestic price stability and structural adjustment.

Transitional Phase, 1961–65

The industrial policy transition was actually begun during the period of political turmoil lasting from 1960 to 1963. Rhee's Liberal Party regime, which was overthrown by the student revolution of April 1960, was succeeded by the Chang Myun regime, but that regime was itself overthrown by a military coup in May 1961. The national economy was then managed by the military government for nearly three years until a nominal civilian government under President Park Chung Hee and the Democratic Republican Party emerged from the general election in early 1964. The military government initiated the economic policy shift from an emphasis on reconstruction and stabilization to a program of growth maximization through industrialization.

This policy shift reflected the changing conditions of the economy in the early 1960s. By around 1960 the country had almost completed the postwar reconstruction and the early stage of import-substitution industrialization. Domestic production could now replace the previous imports of nondurable consumer goods and the intermediate goods used in their manufacture. Both policymakers and the people were, however, frustrated by the country's poor economic growth. A growth strategy based on import substitution of machinery, consumer durables, and their intermediate product was found to be inappropriate owing to the small domestic market and the large capital requirements of ventures like these. Moreover, Korea's national resource endowment was so poor that a development strategy based on domestic resource utilization was inconceivable. Still another challenge to Korean policymakers was to find a source of foreign exchange for resolving the balance-of-payments difficulties arising from the phaseout of U.S. assistance programs. The availability of a well-motivated, low-wage labor force with a high educational level gave the country a comparative advantage in high-quality labor-intensive exports. The political leadership therefore decided to pursue a high rate of growth (Kim 1975).

The policy shift was reflected in the first formal five-year development plan (1962–66), adopted by the Korean government in 1961. The basic goal of the plan was to create the economic base for industrialization and self-sustained growth. To achieve this goal, the government decided to adopt the new strategy of export-oriented industrialization and growth. It then attempted various policy reforms, beginning with the exchange rate reform of early 1961, to create a system of incentives and the other economic conditions conducive to export-oriented industrialization. After the exchange rate reform, the military government undertook reforms in the currency, budget, tax systems, and foreign exchange control system in 1962. Some of these early attempts were unsuccessful or even deleterious because they were poorly designed or inconsistent with other policies. But the reform attempts indicated the government's interest in depending increasingly on domestic resources for industrialization. During 1961–63 the government started to take more effective measures to increase exports and restrict imports. Some institutional arrangements were also made to permit the introduction of foreign loans and direct investment into the country.

A package of policy reforms was developed to further strengthen the export-oriented industrialization strategy during 1964–65. The currency was devalued in May 1964 by almost 50 percent, from 130 to 255 won per U.S. dollar, and in March 1965 a unitary floating exchange rate was adopted. In September 1965, interest rates on both bank deposits and loans were raised sharply to increase voluntary private savings and discourage unproductive use of bank credit. By widening the gap between domestic interest rates and foreign rates, this interest rate reform greatly increased the business sector's incentive to borrow from abroad. These efforts to mobilize both domestic and foreign savings made a significantly higher ratio of investment to national income possible after 1965. A price stabilization program was again carried out during 1964–65 after a nearly four-year suspension. Along with these policy reforms, the government intensified incentives to exporters through various measures. Deliberate measures to liberalize import regimes were delayed, however, until the next phase.

As a result of the policy reforms, exports of labor-intensive manufactured goods began to increase rapidly during 1962–65, thereby making possible the rapid expansion of the country's manufacturing output and GNP beginning in 1963. Although gross fixed investment remained at around 11–15 percent of GNP until 1965, the government encouraged the rapid expansion of domestic output beginning in 1963, mainly by increasing the use of existing facilities that had not been fully operated because of a lack of domestic demand. Even in this transitional phase, the government emphasized investment in manufacturing and social overhead facilities, thus giving low priority to agricultural investment. It also maintained a policy of low grain prices for the purpose of price stabilization.

Export-Oriented Policy and Inflation, 1966–79

As a result of various policy reforms undertaken in the transitional phase, high output growth could be sustained by a continuous rapid expansion of exports in the second and third phases. In the second phase, most of the export-promotion measures adopted in the previous phase continued to be implemented. Although some modifications were made to accommodate the changing economic conditions, these modifications did not change the system of incentives significantly. For this reason, the rapid expansion of exports continued, greatly stimulating domestic production from the demand side. However, the government generally followed an expansionary monetary and fiscal policy to promote increased investment in manufacturing and related sectors. The result was a continuation of the demand-pull inflation, ranging around 7–10 percent except in the years of the first oil crisis, when it was higher.

Domestic inflation was harmful to domestic saving mobilization. In the latter half of the 1960s the government adopted high interest rates to mitigate the negative effect of inflation on domestic saving. Usually, however, the government followed the policy of encouraging foreign capital inflows (mainly in the form of loans) to fill up the domestic investment-saving gap rather than trying to maximize domestic saving mobilization. This policy turned out to spawn the serious foreign debt of the early 1980s.

Domestic inflation at a higher rate than that of Korea's major trading partners during this period made it difficult to maintain the exchange rate at a realistic level. The Korean won was therefore often overvalued in the nominal exchange rate. Beginning in 1965, however, the government could maintain an almost constant purchasing power parity (PPP)-adjusted, real effective exchange rate for exports[1] by adjusting the system of export incentives or undertaking an outright devaluation of the won when required. For this reason, rapid export expansion and high output growth could be sustained even under the inflationary condition in the economy.

But the country's current account balance was showing a chronic deficit due to the concurrent, rapid expansion of imports. It should be noted that the chronic balance-of-payments deficits in this phase were caused not only by the expansionary fiscal and monetary policy but also by the world oil crises in 1973–74 and 1979–80.

Although the export-oriented industrialization strategy was pursued throughout this phase, the chronic balance-of-payments deficits made it difficult to liberalize imports substantially. After an initial attempt to liberalize imports during 1965–67, the government nearly suspended the liberalization effort until 1978, when a gradual import liberalization program was again introduced.

During the second phase, the government's preferred manufacturing sectors changed significantly, reflecting the changing domestic and external conditions facing the Korean economy, even though the industrialization-first policy was continuously maintained. In the 1960s and the early 1970s, the government emphasized increased investment in the light industrial sectors, which were the producers of labor-intensive exports. Beginning around 1973, however, the government emphasis shifted to investment in more capital-intensive heavy and chemical industries.[2] The construction program of heavy and chemical industries was initiated for two reasons. First, it was considered necessary to diversify Korean export items into technology-intensive and capital-intensive products in view of both internal and external factors: the country's labor-intensive exports faced increasing import barriers imposed by the advanced countries beginning in the late 1960s, and the domestic wage/rental ratio was rising rapidly. Second, the U.S. foreign policy change unfavorable to Korea during the Carter administration prompted Korean policymakers to develop domestic defense industries for increasing the supply of military goods. Whatever the reasons, the construction of heavy and chemical industries was actively promoted by the government without a careful appraisal of each project's economic feasibility. This overly ambitious promotion of such industries led to problems of the so-called heavy and chemical industry adjustment and financially insolvent firms, which arose after 1979.

The government maintained the policy of low grain prices and generally neglected the development of agriculture until 1968. It switched to a policy of high rice prices in 1969 and initiated the Saemaul (New Community) movement in the early 1970s to increase agricultural production and income. Investment in the agricultural sector was increased in connection with the Saemaul movement. All in all, however, rapid industrialization and growth continued to be emphasized in the 1970s, although the government started to pay attention to agricultural development.

Export-Oriented Policy and Price Stability, 1980–90

Although the policy of export-oriented industrialization led to rapid economic growth, the chronic inflation which it also produced could not be immediately checked. In 1979–80, Korea had to shift the emphasis of its basic economic policy from growth maximization to price stability and structural adjustment while continuing to maintain its export-oriented industrialization strategy. This policy shift was considered inevitable in view of the domestic economic difficulties caused by the second world oil shock, as well as by the domestic political turmoil following President Park's assassination in October 1979. The economic conditions that made the policy shift inevitable require a brief discussion.

The high rate of commodity exports, which had previously stimulated the growth of the overall economy, decelerated, while import costs increased in response to the sharp rise in world oil prices that year. With the increase in export prices discounted, the volume of exports in 1979 actually declined by a small margin for the first time since the early 1960s. As a result, Korea's current account deficit jumped to an unusually high level in the same year. The GNP growth rate slowed substantially, from about 11 percent in the previous year to 7 percent. The situation was further aggravated in 1980. Although exports increased by nearly 10 percent in real terms after the devaluation of the Korean won in January, real GNP declined by nearly 5 percent, the largest negative figure since the end of the Korean War. The unemployment rate increased from 3.8 percent in 1979 to nearly 5 percent in 1980. Moreover, inflation measured in terms of the national wholesale price index accelerated from an average annual rate of about 10 percent during 1976–78 to about 29 percent in 1979–80.

This sudden economic recession and inflationary spiral was partly attributable to external factors, principally the second world oil crisis and the consequent recession in the Western industrialized countries. But it is generally accepted that domestic factors were also responsible. Inflationary pressures had been built into the domestic economy in the course of growth maximization through rapid industrialization over the previous decade. For this reason, the political upheaval after the October incident not only dampened industrial production but also set off the inflationary spiral. The sharp decline in agricultural output caused by unusually poor weather was also responsible for the negative growth of GNP in 1980. In addition, the misallocation of investable resources in connection with the government's promotion of heavy and chemical industries resulted in a sharp decline in capital utilization in those industries, while light industrial sectors faced some supply shortages.[3]

Faced with these external and internal factors, Korea shifted its economic policy direction to give priorities to price stabilization and structural adjustment. The new stability-first policy was promulgated in April 1979 in the form of a comprehensive economic stabilization program, which called for the tightening of fiscal and monetary policy management; readjustment of investment in heavy and chemical industry sectors; improvement of both the system of government price control and the distribution system for daily necessities, including agricultural and fishery products; and an institutional arrangement to control real estate speculation and to stabilize its prices (Nam 1984). The government implemented these difficult measures despite opposing economic pressures and the domestic political and social turmoil. From the second half of 1979 to 1982, it acted to avoid a serious economic recession while maintaining the basic direction of stabilization policy.

Accompanying the stabilization program were government efforts to undertake the structural adjustment necessitated by the previous policy of growth maximization. The government devalued the won currency in early 1980 to improve price competitiveness of Korean exports and undertook an institutional reform so that the exchange rate might be adjusted more flexibly by market forces. In late June 1982, however, the monetary authority drastically lowered the interest rates of financial institutions. To prevent a rapid hike in domestic wages, the government nearly froze the salary levels of its employees and concurrently restricted the labor union activities of private firms. These government policies were implemented with the objectives of minimizing upward pressures on domestic prices and of enhancing the international competitiveness of domestic industries by curtailing rises in domestic factor costs.

The firm implementation of the stabilization program, together with a minor decline in the world oil price beginning in 1981, brought about a gradual reduction in the annual rate of domestic inflation after 1980 to 0.2 percent by 1983. The current account deficit, which had peaked at US$5.3 billion in 1980, declined to $1.6 billion by 1983 and showed a steady decline thereafter. GNP, which had been seriously declining in 1980, began in 1981 to grow at a healthy rate. It was therefore obvious that the stabilization policy was a success as measured by macroeconomic indicators. In the course of implementing the stabilization program, however, the government had to undertake a difficult readjustment of investment in heavy and chemical industries. It also had to deal with the problem of financially insolvent firms which had been caused by overambitious investment in heavy and chemical industries and by competitive overexpansion of both shipping and overseas construction companies.

Although the economy achieved price stability beginning in 1983, the economic growth rate slowed somewhat in 1984–85 mainly because of economic recession in the industrialized countries. Beginning in 1986, however, the economy experienced a new takeoff and structural transformation, thanks to favorable external factors. The value of the U.S. dollar, which had been unusually strong in the previous years, fell and interest rates in world financial markets were lowered in accordance with an agreement reached at a meeting of finance ministers from five rich countries (the so-called G-5 Meeting) in September 1985. With the sharp decline in the world price of crude oil beginning in December 1985, the Korean economy had a "golden opportunity of three lows" (low oil price, low dollar value, and low interest rate). By effectively utilizing this opportunity, the country was able to rapidly expand its exports and attain a high (12 percent) rate of GNP growth for three consecutive years beginning in 1986. Unlike the experience of the 1960s and 1970s, the high growth was accompanied by domestic price stability and an improvement in the balance of payments. In fact, Korea registered a current account surplus (of US$4.6 billion) in 1986 for the first time in its economic history, thereby reversing its chronic balance-of-payments deficits, and achieved a continuous rise of the surplus, which reached approximately $14 billion by 1988.

On one hand, the continuous rise in the country's current account surplus led to increasing pressures from the United States and other industrialized countries to open up domestic markets, although Korea had been liberalizing its import regimes since 1978. The growing surplus also caused trade frictions with other advanced countries. On the other hand, it made sound domestic demand management difficult by rapidly expanding the money supply from the foreign sector.

The country's outstanding economic performance was mainly attributable to the gradual effective devaluation of the Korean won, which was made possible by delaying the appreciation of the won in relation to the U.S. dollar on world markets.[4] The domestic structural adjustment made in the first half of the 1980s was also helpful for generally improving economic performance. In 1988–89, however, the won currency had to be significantly appreciated to comply with U.S. pressures, thereby largely eliminating the price competitiveness of Korean exports, which had been based on the weak won. In addition, the strength of labor unions grew to the point that labor disputes increased drastically after the June 1987 declaration for democratization. As a result, the real wages of industrial workers began rising more rapidly than their productivity gains, thus increasing the unit wage costs of domestic industries. It may be said, therefore, that the "golden opportunity of three lows" had evaporated from the Korean economy by the end of 1988.

Evaluation

The shift of industrialization strategy from import substitution to export in the early 1960s was a wise choice for Korea, in view of its poor natural resource endowments and the export-oriented growth performance following the policy shift. Although the export-oriented strategy has generally remained in effect over the previous three decades, the government changed its basic policy direction for implementing that strategy in 1979–80 in the course of surmounting the economic difficulties caused by the second oil shock and the country's domestic political upheaval. In other words, the export-oriented strategy of the earlier period (1966–79), which had taken the form of a growth maximization policy through industrialization regardless of domestic inflation and other side effects, changed in the 1980s to an export-oriented strategy emphasizing domestic price stability and structural adjustment.

In retrospect, the policy of growth maximization through export-oriented industrialization during 1966–79 could work well because there were abundant supplies of the primary factors—labor, capital, and technology. Korea not only had a large pool of unemployed labor in the early 1960s but also experienced a rapid growth of its labor force since then. The country therefore did not experience any serious labor shortage in the course of its rapid industrialization. The relatively well-educated labor force could satisfy demands for various skill categories of workers created by the growth process. Moreover, the country could easily import foreign capital to augment the shortage of domestic capital. At this stage of development, technology was not yet a binding constraint on industrialization. Since the country was not yet near the world technology frontier, it could easily import the necessary technologies, together with capital goods. Under these circumstances the speed of industrialization could be determined solely by the demand factor, which in turn could be influenced by fiscal and monetary policy as well as by an export drive. In this sense, the expansionary fiscal and monetary policy and the export drive pursued by the government in the second phase were consistent with its primary objective of growth maximization through industrialization.

This policy paid off as far as the pace of industrialization and economic growth was concerned. But it caused several difficult side effects because the government neglected to deal effectively with economic issues not directly related to the attainment of the industrialization objective. Among those side effects were chronic inflation, repressed financial markets, chronic balance-of-payments deficits, an increasing gap in development between rural and urban areas, lags in social development programs, a visible inequality in the distribution of both income and wealth, and the concentration of population in the capital city of Seoul.

By the 1970s these problems started to be serious. The mounting foreign debt, which had resulted from the chronic deficits in the current account balance, became the most critical issue for macroeconomic management by 1979. Foreign debt, which was US$14.9 billion at the end of 1978, grew by almost 40 percent ($5.6 billion) in 1979 and was expected to increase more rapidly after 1979 mainly because of the effects of the second oil shock. The debt and the cost of servicing it were beginning to impose a major constraint on the country's growth. Although there were many other undesirable effects of inflation, the balance-of-payments deficits arising from the expansionary policy were so critical that the policy itself had to be replaced with a stability-first policy even if the country continued to follow an export-oriented industrialization strategy.

After the shift to the stability-first policy, the country could achieve both price stability and a current account surplus in the 1980s, as already explained. It could also attain a high growth of output during 1986–88 without inflation, partly owing to favorable external conditions. In addition, domestic saving increased rapidly, reaching approximately 35 percent of GNP by the late 1980s because price stability provided savers with higher incentives. The heavy and chemical industries, which had been problematic and subject to investment readjustment in the late 1970s and early 1980s, became important growth industries by 1986–88.

Still, the policy shift was accompanied by the difficult adjustments to the major legacies of the previous growth maximization policy. In fact, the government had to spend the first half of the 1980s dealing with the structural adjustment problems necessitated by the previous policy. The two most difficult were the readjustment of investment in heavy and chemical industries and the problem of the financially insolvent firms mainly in the heavy industry, shipping, and overseas construction sectors. Any policy to correct the other distortions created by the previous policy, such as the development gap between rural and urban areas or the inequitable distribution of income and wealth, had to be delayed until 1990.

The Korean experience with industrialization policy indicates, first, that an export-oriented industrialization strategy alone cannot assure the achievement of a current account balance, although it can bring about rapid export expansion and growth. An export-oriented strategy should be accompanied by a successful price stabilization policy in order to close the foreign trade gap; the reason is that it is difficult to maintain a realistic exchange rate, which is critically important for closing the foreign trade gap, when domestic prices are rising much faster than those of major trading partners. Second, the Korean experience shows that the transition from the inflationary, growth maximization policy to a stability-first policy requires a long period of painful adjustment if it is to succeed in transforming an inflationary economy into a growing economy with price stability. Finally, high growth of output does not necessarily require price inflation but can be sustained while price stability is maintained, as the country's experience of the 1980s demonstrates.

Trade Regimes and Liberalization, 1961–89

In the late 1950s, when the policy of import substitution was emphasized, the Korean government controlled imports so as to favor import-substitution industries. In addition to high tariff walls, it relied on quantitative restrictions (QRs) to control imports. Exports were usually discouraged by an overvalued exchange rate, the prevalence of inefficient industries, and the higher profitability of domestic sales relative to exports. A complex structure of multiple exchange rates was also developed to avoid balance-of-payments difficulties during this period. The shift of industrialization strategy from import substitution to exports, initiated in the early 1960s, therefore had to accompany substantial changes in the country's trade regimes. In changing the trade regimes to make them consistent with the new strategy of export promotion, the government first had to reform the system of export incentives. When the revised system of export incentives proved to be effective in actually increasing exports, the government then turned to gradually liberalizing import regimes.

Reforming Export Incentives

The first step toward reforming the system of export incentives was taken by devaluing the currency and attempting to reform the exchange rate. The won currency had been overvalued during most of the late 1950s because of the much higher rate of domestic inflation than that of major trading partners, and the currency overvaluation had been detrimental to export growth until the early 1960s despite the ad hoc measures taken by the government to offset disincentives to exporters. To pursue an export-oriented industrialization strategy, the government decided, appropriately, to change the exchange rate first so that the export disincentive effects of the currency overvaluation might be corrected.

A system of multiple exchange rates had emerged in the late 1950s through the various ad hoc measures taken to modify excess demand for imports and to offset disincentives to exporters. The government therefore attempted first to unify the exchange rate in 1961 by twice devaluing the currency. This attempt failed, however, mainly because of the military government's expansionary policy. To mitigate the continuing effects of currency overvaluation in the face of domestic inflation, in 1963 the government introduced a full-scale export-import link system under which the volume of nonaid imports was limited to the amount of export earnings. The result was a return to the multiple exchange rate system, since the market premium rates on export dollars became much higher than the official exchange rate in 1963–64. More significant in unifying the exchange rate, as well as in reforming the system of export incentives, was the exchange rate reform of 1964–65. The government devalued the currency very steeply by changing the official exchange rate from 130 to 255 won per U.S. dollar in May 1964, and it changed the existing system of a fixed exchange rate to a system of unified floating exchange rate in March 1965. Thereafter, the exchange rate was allowed to change gradually by market forces or by periodic government adjustments so that roughly the same real exchange rate might be maintained.

In addition to the exchange rate reform, other export incentives were greatly expanded during the transitional period of 1961–65. Those export incentives were (1) preferential export credit; (2) tariff exemptions on imports of raw materials for export production (drawback system); (3) indirect domestic tax exemptions on intermediate inputs used for export production and on export sales; (4) direct tax reduction on income earned from exports (abolished in 1973); (5) wastage allowances for raw materials imported for export production; (6) a system of linking import business to export performance; (7) tariff and indirect tax exemptions for domestic suppliers of intermediate goods used in export production; and (8) accelerated depreciation allowances for fixed assets of major export industries (Frank, Kim, and Westphal 1975:40–51). The preferential export credit became an especially important incentive for exporters after the interest rate reform of 1965, which had substantially widened the interest rate differential between export credit and ordinary bank loans.

With the exceptions of the preferential export credit and the direct tax reduction on export income, the various measures to increase incentives to exporters were intended mainly to ensure that Korean exporters, who must sell their products at world market prices, could purchase intermediate goods for export products at world market prices. In other words, most of the incentives served primarily to offset the disincentive effect on export the trade regime would otherwise have created. In any case, the incentives applied to all exporters on a nondiscriminatory basis.

After 1965, some adjustments to the export incentive system were made to accommodate changing economic conditions, although these adjustments did not significantly change the basic system. What was important was that the system of export incentives was adjusted to reduce net subsidies implicit in the system, thus reducing trade-distorting effects on the export side. For instance, the direct tax reduction on export income was dropped in 1973, and interest rate subsidies implicit in the preferential export credit significantly declined after 1972. With a more realistic official exchange rate in place after 1965, the value of net export subsidies per U.S. dollar of export could be gradually reduced over time.

Table 17.1 presents the estimated values of two different concepts of export subsidies per U.S. dollar of export for 1958–83. One is the concept of net export subsidies, including only the subsidies that may directly increase profit margins of exporters. These kinds of export subsidies include the exchange premium resulting from multiple exchange rates, direct cash subsidies, direct tax reductions, and interest rate preferences resulting from preferential export credit. The other concept is defined as the gross export subsidies, including indirect tax exemptions and tariff exemptions (for imports of intermediate goods for export production), in addition to net export subsidies.[5] Indirect tax exemptions and tariff exemptions are not considered to be genuine subsidies to exporters because they allow the exporters only to purchase their inputs at world prices and sell their products at competitive world market prices. They may, however, influence the business sector's decisions in regard to export versus import substitution. The ratio of net export subsidies to the official exchange rate is shown in column 10 of the table, whereas the ratio of gross subsidies to the exchange rate is presented in column 11.

Both ratios declined sharply between 1960 and 1965, reflecting the gradual abolishment of ad hoc export promotion measures after the exchange rate reform of 1964–65. After 1965, the two ratios not only remained at a much lower level but also showed less fluctuation, until the early 1980s. Since Korea has made no serious efforts to restrict the quantities of exports by means of export tariffs or QRs except during the war period,[6] the ratio of net export subsidies to the exchange rate may indicate the effect of the government's trade-distorting measures on the export side. In this sense, one minus the ratio may represent a rough measure of the degree of trade liberalization on the export side in Korea. The fact that the same ratio remained low beginning in 1965 indicates that Korea's export trade has been significantly liberalized since that year, in which the transition to an export-oriented policy was completed. Korea's export trade was also more liberal during 1972–81 than during the previous period (1965–71) and has been almost

TABLE 17.1 Estimated export subsidies for Korea, 1958–1983 (annual averages)

	Export subsidies calculated per U.S. dollar of export (won)									Ratio to exchange rate (%)	
	Official exchange rate (won/$) (1)	Direct cash subsidies (2)	Export dollar premium (3)	Direct tax reductions for exporters (4)	Interest rate preference for exporters (5)	Net export subsidies[a] (6 = 2 + 3 + 4 + 5)	Indirect tax exemptions for exporters (7)	Tariff rebates for exporters (8)	Gross export subsidies[a] (9 = 6 + 7 + 8)	Net export subsidies (10 = 6/1)	Gross export subsidies (11 = 9/1)
1958	50.0	0.0	64.0	–	1.2	65.2	–	–	65.2	130.4	130.4
1959	50.0	0.0	84.7	–	1.3	86.0	–	–	86.0	172.0	172.0
1960	62.5	0.0	83.9	–	1.2	85.1	–	–	85.1	136.2	136.2
1961	127.5	7.5	14.6	–	1.0	23.1	–	–	23.1	18.1	18.1
1962	130.0	10.3	–	0.6	0.9	11.8	5.1	4.7	21.6	9.1	16.6
1963	130.0	4.1	39.8	0.8	2.9	47.6	5.3	6.6	59.5	36.6	48.8
1964	214.3	2.9	39.7	0.7	6.0	49.3	7.6	10.1	67.0	23.0	31.3
1965	265.4	–	–	2.3	7.6	9.9	13.9	15.4	39.2	3.7	14.8
1966	271.3	–	–	2.3	10.3	12.5	17.8	21.3	51.6	4.6	19.0
1967	270.7	–	–	5.2	14.7	20.0	17.8	24.6	62.4	7.4	23.1
1968	276.6	–	–	3.0	15.2	18.2	19.9	39.6	77.7	6.6	28.1
1969	288.2	–	–	3.7	14.7	18.4	27.4	34.3	80.1	6.4	27.8
1970	310.7	–	–	3.5	17.3	20.8	27.0	40.4	38.1	6.7	28.4
1971	347.7	–	–	4.8	18.1	22.8	32.2	48.0	103.0	6.6	29.6
1972	391.8	–	–	1.9	10.5	12.5	26.4	66.3	105.2	3.2	26.9
1973	398.3	–	–	1.4	7.4	8.7	21.0	64.4	94.2	2.2	23.7
1974	407.0	–	–	–	8.6	8.6	22.5	55.1	86.3	2.1	21.2
1975	484.0	–	–	–	12.9	12.9	33.8	34.3	81.0	2.7	16.7
1976	484.0	–	–	–	12.3	12.3	33.6	35.9	81.8	2.5	16.9
1977	484.0	–	–	–	9.4	9.4	53.1	30.6	93.1	1.9	19.2
1978	484.0	–	–	–	11.0	11.0	53.6	30.0	94.6	2.3	19.5
1979	484.0	–	–	–	11.0	11.0	56.6	30.3	97.9	2.3	20.2
1980	618.5	–	–	–	20.6	20.6	74.6	36.4	131.6	3.3	21.3
1981	686.0	–	–	–	15.0	15.0	na	na	na	2.2	na
1982	737.7	–	–	–	3.0	3.0	na	na	na	0.4	na
1983	781.2	–	–	–	0.0	0.0	na	na	na	0.0	na

Source: Kim (1991).
[a]Totals may not add up due to rounding errors. na = not available.

completely liberalized since 1982, according to the ratio of net export subsidies to the exchange rate.

Import Regimes and Liberalization

In the late 1950s, imports were restricted by both high tariffs and QRs. Although a simple average tariff rate was as high as 30 percent, only a small proportion of importable items could be imported without prior government approval. The government controlled imports on the basis of the semiannual trade program, which usually listed the import-permissible items classified into two categories: automatic approval (AA) items and restricted items. In fact, the government relied mainly on the semiannual trade program to control imports quantitatively in the late 1950s. The reason was that tariffs were not effective in discouraging imports because domestic currency was almost always overvalued in the face of rapid domestic inflation. This kind of import regime remained nearly unchanged until the early 1960s, when the government started the transition of industrialization policy.

Korea's import regimes have undergone a gradual liberalization as the industrial policy has changed since the early 1960s. To show the long-term pattern of Korea's import liberalization since the early 1960s, Table 17.2 presents the overall degree of import liberalization estimated for the period 1960–88. The two main factors—the average legal tariff rate and the degree of import QRs—are taken into account in the estimation of the overall degree (Kim 1991).

First, the degree of import liberalization in terms of tariffs is estimated. For this purpose, the annual series of average legal tariff rates is calculated by adding the average rates of both the foreign exchange tax and special tariffs to the average legal rate of regular tariffs, both of which were imposed on imports on top of the regular tariffs during 1958–73 (see Kim 1991 for statistical data). The average legal rate of regular tariffs for 1960–85 is obtained by weighting legal rates on commodity groups by the value of domestic production in 1975 (column 1), whereas that for 1986–90 is extrapolated on the basis of a change in the simple average rate of legal tariffs for those years.

The average legal tariff rate may, however, have an upward bias in two respects. For one, this legal rate has been substantially higher than the average actual tariff rate because of the tariff exemptions and reductions granted for various purposes.[7] In addition, the average legal rate weighted by the value of domestic production may have an upward bias, since high protection on a sector tends to raise the nominal value of that sector's production above the level obtainable without such protection. For this reason, the average legal rate should be taken as an indicator of potential protection, reflecting the upper boundary of Korean tariff protection.

In any case, the annual series of the average legal tariff rate is inverted in percentage form to show the degree of import liberalization in terms of tariffs (column 3). This series indicates that the degree of import liberalization rises as the average rate of legal tariffs declines.

TABLE 17.2
Estimated import liberalization, 1960–1990 (percentage)

	Average rate of legal tariffs			Liberalization from QRs[a]		Overall liberalization	
	Regular[b] (1)	Total[c] (2)	Inverted rate[d] (3)	Trade program (4)	Trade + special laws (5)	Average of (3) and (4) (6)	Average of (3) and (5) (7)
1960	35.4	58.0	63.3	5.1	5.1	34.2	34.2
1961	35.4	36.0	73.5	4.1	4.1	38.8	38.8
1962	49.5	49.6	66.8	5.6	5.6	36.2	36.2
1963	49.5	49.5	68.3	0.4	0.4	34.4	34.4
1964	49.5	51.0	66.2	2.0	2.0	34.1	34.1
1965	49.5	52.7	65.5	6.0	6.0	35.8	35.8
1966	49.5	52.3	65.7	9.3	9.3	37.5	37.5
1967	49.5	52.6	65.5	60.4	52.4	63.0	59.0
1968	56.7	58.9	62.9	57.6	50.1	60.3	56.5
1969	56.7	58.3	63.2	55.1	47.1	59.2	55.2
1970	56.7	58.5	63.1	54.3	46.3	58.7	54.7
1971	56.7	57.9	63.3	55.0	47.0	59.2	55.2
1972	56.7	57.5	63.5	50.9	43.4	57.2	53.5
1973	48.1	48.2	67.5	52.1	44.7	59.8	56.1
1974	48.1	48.1	67.5	50.7	43.8	59.1	55.7
1975	48.1	48.1	67.5	49.1	41.6	58.3	54.7
1976	48.1	48.1	67.5	51.0	44.1	59.3	55.8
1977	41.3	41.3	70.8	49.9	40.8	60.4	55.8
1978	41.3	41.3	70.7	61.3	52.2	66.0	61.5
1979	34.4	34.4	74.4	67.6	56.2	71.0	65.3
1980	34.4	34.4	74.4	69.1	57.4	71.8	65.9
1981	34.4	34.4	74.4	74.4	60.7	74.4	67.6
1982	34.4	34.4	74.4	76.6	62.5	75.5	68.5
1983	34.4	34.4	74.4	80.4	66.6	77.8	70.5
1984	26.7	26.7	78.9	84.8	75.0	81.9	77.0
1985	26.4	26.4	79.1	87.7	78.2	83.4	78.7
1986	24.7	24.7	80.2	91.5	82.0	85.9	81.1
1987	23.9	23.9	80.7	93.6	84.1	87.2	82.4
1988	22.4	22.4	81.7	94.7	86.0	88.2	83.9
1989	15.7	15.7	86.4	95.5	86.7	91.0	86.6
1990	14.1	14.1	87.6	96.4	87.5	92.0	87.6

Source: Kim (1987:33).

[a]Represents the degree of import liberalization from QRs for the second half of each year in 1955–79, and that for the second half of the year indicated and the first half of the following year in 1980–90.

[b]Average rate of regular tariffs, weighted by the value of 1975 production.

[c]Includes the average foreign exchange tax rate and special tariff rate on imports in addition to the regular tariffs.

[d]1.0/[1.0 + value in column (2)].

For the degree of import liberalization from QRs, two different series are estimated. One is the degree of import liberalization based only on the semiannual or annual trade program without including the trade-restricting effects of special laws. For the period 1967–88, the degree represents the ratio of AA items to total commodity items, based on the United Nation's Standard International Trade Classification (SITC) or the Customs Cooperation Council Nomenclature (CCCN), as announced by the Ministry of Trade and Industry. For the period prior to 1967, an index of the number of AA items (with the first half of 1967 treated as 100) is estimated and used to extrapolate the degree for 1967–85.[8] The annual series so obtained for the entire period is shown in column 4 of Table 17.2.

The other series is the degree estimated by consolidating the trade-restricting effects of special laws with the QRs based only on the trade program (column 5). The only difference between the two series is therefore the trade-restricting effects of special laws on import liberalization. At this point, it should be noted that the special laws have provided for additional QRs since 1967 owing to the adoption of a new "negative-list system" of trade program in that year. The semiannual trade program had previously been formulated as a "positive-list system," under which only those items listed in the program could be imported with or without government approval. Under the new system, the trade program listed only those items whose import was prohibited or restricted, implying that all items not listed were AA items. As of the second half of 1985, for instance, there existed 33 trade-related special laws in total, but only the 11 special laws provided for the additional import QRs not consistent with the GATT rules, which needed to be consolidated with those based only on the trade program. The main objectives of most of the special laws are not to regulate foreign trade but to control the quantities and qualities or standards of the commodities supplied in the domestic market. Some of these laws, however, have been actually used as an additional instrument of trade restriction in Korea.[9]

Finally, the degree of import liberalization in terms of tariffs and the alternative figures representing the degree of import liberalization from QRs are simply averaged to obtain two alternative, overall degrees of liberalization—one using the degree of import liberalization based only on the trade program (column 6), and the other using the degree based on both the trade program and the special laws (column 7).

The two alternative degrees of import liberalization are shown in Figure 17.1 for visual comparison. From the figure, it can be seen that the overall degree including the effects of special laws was identical to the overall degree excluding them during 1960–66, as expected. During the latter period (1967–90), when the special laws provided for additional QRs on top of those based on the trade program, the overall degree consolidating the effects of the special laws was significantly lower than that excluding them. Still, the two degrees moved together.

It is clear from the two degrees that conscious efforts to liberalize imports were made in Korea during the two periods 1965–67 and 1978–90. For instance,

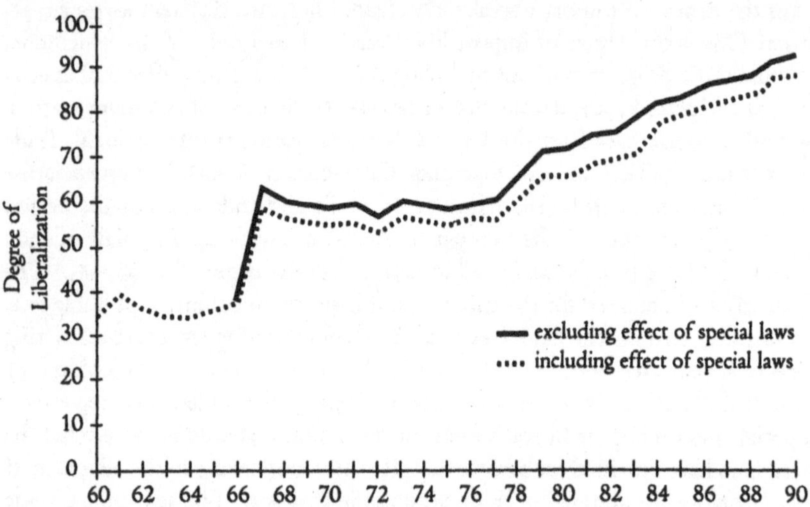

FIGURE 17.1 Import liberalization for Korea, 1960–1988, as tabulated in Table 17.2.

the overall degree of liberalization consolidating the effects of special laws, which had been only 34 percent in 1964, jumped to 59 percent by 1967, and then after about ten years of no change or minor deterioration rose again from 56 to 88 percent between 1977 and 1990. As can be seen from Table 17.2, the first episode of import liberalization consisted primarily of a loosening of QRs on imports, whereas the second episode took place in the form of both a loosening of QRs and a reduction of tariff barriers on imports. The first episode of import liberalization was not successful enough to assure continued progress in liberalization. In contrast, the second episode has been rather successful, since liberalization has continued, although slowly, and has provided the basis for continued liberalization even after 1990.

Evaluation of Trade Liberalization

The evolution of Korea's trade regimes discussed so far indicates that, although its export trade regimes were substantially reformed or liberalized in the transition phase of industrialization strategy (1961–65), the substantial liberalization of import regimes was delayed and undertaken cautiously in the second and the third phases. This type of sequencing in trade liberalization reflects the fact that Korean policymakers needed some confidence in export expansion before starting a cautious effort to liberalize imports, even after substantial completion of the system of export incentives consistent with export-oriented industrialization strategy. In addition, the precarious balance-of-payments situation until the second phase, which was largely attributable to the growth maximization policy, prevented earlier progress in import liberalization.

The system of export incentives established in the transition phase was clearly effective in increasing the country's exports, making rapid industrialization possible thereafter. The actual impact of import liberalization on the domestic economy has not been so visible, however, probably because the liberalization has been cautious and gradual. Neither of the two aforementioned liberalization episodes had any discernible negative impact on the growth rates of important macroeconomic variables for the country: GNP, employment, investment, exports, imports, or balance of payments. Although an analysis of the economic impact of import liberalization at the sectoral or industry-specific level would be more useful, such an analysis is theoretically complicated and practically difficult in the Korean context, given data availabilities. For this reason, I summarize the results of some previous studies at sectoral levels instead.

In an earlier study (Kim 1991), I attempted to estimate the actual imports of the specific commodity items liberalized from QRs during 1965–67 and 1978–79 and to compare them with annual aggregate imports. I found that those imports liberalized from QRs generally accelerated in the same year and the year following the liberalization. Although the imports of items liberalized in the first half of 1978 and in the same period of 1979 did not follow this tendency, the increase in imports of those items liberalized in other periods was generally much higher than the growth of aggregate imports in one or both of the first two years following liberalization.

A research report by the Korea Institute for Economics and Technology (KIET 1986) generally supports these findings, although it covers a different period, 1982–84. The KIET report discloses that imports of items liberalized from QRs generally show a higher rate of increase than the past trend during the period of six months to one year immediately following liberalization, but they taper off after that. The report concludes that over the entire period from the second half of 1982 to the first half of 1985 the loosening of QRs could not have contributed to the increase in imports above the level expected from the pattern of increases in the three years prior to liberalization.

The results of these two studies are actually related to the impact of the loosening of QRs by the trade program, not taking into account the changes in tariff rates and special-law QRs that might have replaced the QRs based only on the trade program. To examine the full impact of liberalization, one should measure the impact of change in the overall degree of import liberalization that consolidated the levels of all QRs (including special-law QRs) and tariffs. I conducted a correlation analysis (Kim 1988) by relating changes in sectoral degrees of liberalization (all QRs and tariffs consolidated) to changes in those sectors' major economic variables over the two periods of liberalization (1966–70 and 1975–85). The results indicate that import liberalization had some tendency to increase imports during the two periods, although the positive coefficient of correlation between the degrees of liberalization and the import ratios to domestic production at the

38 manufacturing sector levels for the earlier period was not high enough to have statistical significance. It seems that the liberalization clearly had some adverse effect on domestic production and employment during the earlier period but had no significant, direct effect during the latter period. There is no clear indication, however, that liberalization had any significant effect on domestic industrial productivity during both periods.

The Korean approach to liberalization clearly changed from one period to the next. Liberalization in the latter half of the 1960s was basically a one-stage approach, with a sudden jump in the degree of liberalization through the loosening of QRs in 1967 but no further progress thereafter; liberalization beginning in 1978 followed a gradual, multistage approach by using the system of "advance notices." It is also clear that Korea's level of industrialization progressed significantly between the two periods, with domestic manufacturing industries becoming more competitive internationally by the late 1970s and the 1980s than they had been in the earlier period. The fact that the country could maintain a more realistic exchange in the 1980s than in most of the earlier period was, of course, helpful for strengthening international competitiveness of domestic industries.

Issues and Policy Directions in the 1990s

Korea has been subject to strong foreign pressures, notably from the United States, to expedite import liberalization. In response to these pressures, the country has been more actively promoting liberalization in recent years than ever before. In fact, the government has already announced its intention to liberalize imports continuously in the future by further loosening QRs and cutting tariffs.

Import Injury Relief System Korea's trade liberalization is expected to increase to the level of advanced industrialized countries in the coming years. Export trade is already completely liberalized, except for the minor QRs implemented in connection with voluntary export restraint or orderly marketing arrangements imposed by advanced countries. The overall degree of import liberalization will rise further in the coming years because the average rate of tariffs will be reduced roughly to the level of industrialized countries and QRs, including special-law QRs, will be further loosened as proposed by the government in connection with the Uruguay Round of multilateral trade negotiations. It is likely, however, that further liberalization of agricultural imports will pose a much more difficult problem than that experienced in the past, because it must be accompanied by complementary measures to deal with structural adjustment problems in rural areas. In addition to trade liberalization, most of the country's service markets had begun to be opened to foreign access by the mid-1980s and are expected to be substantially opened in the future owing to strong pressures from the United States and the conclusion of the Uruguay Round.[10] Another area that will show rapid progress in liberalization in the 1990s is the regulation of foreign direct investment, which is not yet liberalized to the extent of trade liberalization.

The rapid opening of domestic markets to foreign competition is, however, giving rise to an increasing problem of industrial injuries from imports. So far, the problem has not been serious because the government has restricted imports injurious to domestic industries by claiming the GATT Article XVIII, Section B, waiver of the prohibition of QRs, which is normally granted to developing countries with balance-of-payments difficulties. Since Korea has graduated from the group of countries subject to this waiver, however, it is in urgent need of a system of relief from injurious imports consistent with the GATT rules. It seems that the system to deal with import injuries caused by unfair trade, including antidumping and countervailing duties, has already been well established in accordance with GATT rules. The system of relief from import injuries caused by fair trade, however, is not consistent with the GATT provisions and requires some modifications, specifically in the following directions.

First, the Korean tariffs for contingency import restrictions, which currently consist of the "emergency" duties (the Customs Law, Article 12) and the "adjustment" duties (Article 12-2), should be reformed by abolishing the adjustment duties, the purpose of which may also be served, if necessary, through the application of emergency duties. In addition, the contents of emergency duties as prescribed in the Customs Law should be revised to make them consistent with GATT Article XIX to avoid unnecessary trade friction with other countries.

Second, the system of investigating the effects of imports on domestic industries, which also provides relief from injurious imports through the imposition of import restrictions, seems to duplicate the function of temporary import restriction by the aforementioned emergency duties. The only difference between it and the emergency duties is that the system of investigating the effects of imports may use the instrument of QRs, in addition to tariffs, for necessary import restrictions. The system should be used as a device only for investigating the industrial injuries caused by increased imports associated with emergency duties, and should not be used as an additional instrument of temporary import restriction.

Third, the government may provide trade adjustment assistance for domestic industries, if necessary, by making use of the provisions of the Industrial Development Law, which permit government assistance for the rationalization of designated industries. But the law specifies two types of industries for designation as the subject of rationalization: promising infant industries and declining industries. It is suggested that the trade adjustment assistance based on the law be given mainly to the declining industries for the purpose of diverting them into new fields and promoting technological innovation.

Fourth, the function of the Ministry of Trade and Industry's Trade Commission seems to overlap that of the Ministry of Finance's Tariffs Deliberation Commission to a considerable extent. It is therefore suggested that a pan-governmental

Trade and Tariffs Commission be established to merge the two commissions. If this is not feasible under the current government organization, it will be desirable at least to redefine the two commissions' functions so as to reduce the extent of overlapping responsibilities.

Future of Industrial Policy Despite the rapid opening of the domestic market, the country's manufacturing output and exports will have to continue to grow rapidly to maintain sustained growth of GNP in the coming decade. In view of the country's progress in industrial deepening and recent developments in the labor market, the future growth industries within manufacturing should become the high-tech industries, for which the country may expect to gain a competitive edge by developing indigenous technologies. Such high-tech industries may include microelectronics; medical, optical, measurement, and controlling equipment; mechatronics; aerospace; fine chemicals; biotechnology; and new materials.[11] Due to the increased openness of the domestic economy, it may not be appropriate for the government to promote the development of such industries by utilizing the old instruments of import restrictions and tax concessions. What the government should do for the development of such industries is (1) provide direct and indirect support for research and development activities; (2) improve and allocate more resources to the national educational and training systems to increase the supply of high-quality scientists, engineers, and other skilled workers required both for research and development and for high-tech industries; and (3) provide special industrial zones to reduce the set-up costs of high-tech industries.

Since the high-tech industries are mostly of the processing type, in which scale economies are not as important as in the case of assembly-type industry, the development of a high-tech industry does not depend on the participation of a large business group. In this sense, the promotion of such industries will be consistent with the desirable policy of giving preference to small and medium-size industrial establishments on an equity basis. In any case, it is suggested that the government give preference in the allocation of financial resources for the future development of small and medium-size industries. In addition, future industrial policy should show an increased concern over the environmental aspects of industrial development, since rapid growth has so far been accompanied by a substantial deterioration in the quality of the country's environment.

Industrial Restructuring Industrial restructuring issues are expected to invite increasing attention from policymakers in the future, given both recent changes in the worldwide economic environment and the anticipated structural transformation of domestic industry. Although Korea had to deal with some industrial adjustment problems in the 1980s, many of them were not really structural but were instead related to excess capacities created by previous policy mistakes or resource misallocation. What appeared to be structural problems were also attributable to cyclical factors. The country therefore has not yet experienced many cases of declining (or sunset) industries caused by structural change and, for that reason, has had no satisfactory exit policy and no institution capable of managing such a policy. In the future, however, the need for industrial restructuring will emerge as an important issue, as evidenced by the signs of structural problems found in some small and medium-size industries.

Korea should establish a new exit policy and an institution to implement that policy in order to deal efficiently with anticipated industrial restructuring issues involving declining industries. The policy should not, however, follow past practice, in which the government was the only viable rescue agent. The role of the government should be limited to correcting market failures and alleviating social and economic shock by taking proper measures against unemployment problems arising from industrial restructuring. The restructuring problems should be solved by having the financial institutions involved play the role of rescue agent, as in the case of Japan. This implies that the establishment of a new restructuring policy will require a reform of the financial sector so that the financial institutions can accept primary responsibility for industrial restructuring.

Trade Friction Another issue that is becoming increasingly critical for Korea's industrial and trade policy is the government's policy for dealing with trade friction. Recent trade friction with the United States and other advanced countries has been mainly for one of two reasons: (1) too rapid expansion of exports to a certain trade partner, causing significant unemployment in that country; or (2) disagreement between two trade partners over the speed of domestic market opening for certain items exported by the major trade partner. Complete compliance with foreign pressure might easily solve trade friction, but it would lead to serious injuries to domestic industries not acceptable to the general public, not to mention the industries concerned. The government should therefore carefully prepare its policy or negotiation strategy to minimize domestic costs of adjustment involved in dealing with trade friction. The preparation of such a policy will require not only continuous in-depth research on the issues related to trade friction but also an administrative machinery for achieving consensus on the policy directions from government officials, private experts, and representatives of domestic industries. It seems that Korea's weakness so far has been in approaching such issues without having its policy or strategy worked out beforehand on the basis of some consensus from the government and other interested groups. Further research on the issues of trade friction, in collaboration with specialists in international relations, will also be needed to shed more light on trade negotiation practices, since any issue of trade friction should ultimately be resolved through negotiation with foreign partners.

NOTES

1. To calculate PPP-adjusted, real effective exchange rates for exports, one obtains a nominal effective exchange rate for exports by adding the amount of average export

subsidies per dollar to the official exchange rate, which is then deflated by the PPP index of Korea against its major trading partners. See Kim (1991) for the time series of PPP-adjusted exchange rates for exports.

2. In Korea, the phrase "heavy and chemical industries" is used to describe such industries as chemical and petroleum products, rubber products (tires and tubes), basic metals, primary metal products, machinery, and transport equipment.

3. See Kim (1981) for a detailed discussion of the domestic factors that caused the economic recession and inflationary spiral in 1979–80.

4. The foreign exchange rate of the Korean won used to be linked to the U.S. dollar.

5. Neither concept includes the effects of the aforementioned export incentive measures (5) through (8), since the subsidies implicit in such measures cannot be quantified consistently.

6. Even though semiannual, and more recently annual, trade programs listed export items to be restricted, such restrictions were mainly for the orderly marketing of indigenous products by Korean exporters, particularly in connection with the administration of the mandatory or voluntary export quotas imposed on Korea by industrialized countries (Kim 1991).

7. The average actual tariff rate was quite high until 1962 owing to the effect of the foreign exchange tax, but the actual rate generally ranged between 5 and 10 percent during 1963–85 (Kim 1991).

8. The ratio of AA items to total commodity items based on SITC or CCCN codes cannot be estimated for the period prior to 1967, since no consistent system of commodity classification was used during that period.

9. See Kim (1987) for a detailed description of import restriction by special laws in Korea.

10. Another area where U.S. pressure has probably had an important impact on the Korean economy is in protection of intellectual property rights. The Korean government established a full-fledged system for intellectual property rights in 1987 on the basis of a Korea-U.S. bilateral agreement reached in 1986. See Ministry of Trade and Industry (1989) for a description of the system.

11. See K. T. Lee (1989) for a detailed classification of high-tech industries.

REFERENCES

Adams, F. Gerard, and C. Andrea Bollino. 1983. "Meaning of Industrial Policy." In F. Gerard Adams and Lawrence R. Klein (eds.), *Industrial Policies for Growth and Competitiveness*. Lexington, Mass.: Lexington Books.

Frank, Charles R., Jr., Kwang Suk Kim, and Larry E. Westphal. 1975. *Foreign Trade Regimes and Economic Development: South Korea*. New York: National Bureau of Economic Research.

General Agreement on Tariffs and Trade (GATT). 1969. *Basic Instruments and Selected Documents*, Vol. 4: *Text of the General Agreement*. Geneva.

Industrial Development Council. 1987. *Industrial Policy Visions for Accommodating New Changes in Industrial Environment*. Seoul.

Kim, Kwang Suk. 1975. "Outward-Looking Industrialization Strategy: The Case of Korea." In Wongtack Hong and Anne O. Krueger (eds.), *Trade and Development in Korea*. Seoul: Korea Development Institute Press.

Kim, Kwang Suk. 1981. *Lessons from Korea's Industrialization Experience*. KDI monograph-no. 8105. Seoul: Korea Development Institute.

Kim, Kwang Suk. 1987. "The Nature of Trade Protection by Special Laws in Korea." Discussion Paper no. 87-01. Seoul: Graduate School of Business Administration, Kyung Hee University.

Kim, Kwang Suk. 1988. *Economic Impact of Import Liberalization and Industrial Adjustment Policy in Korea* (in Korean). Seoul: Korea Development Institute Press.

Kim, Kwang Suk. 1991. "Korea." In D. Papageorgian, M. Michaely, and A. M. Choksi (eds.), *Liberalizing Foreign Trade: Korea, the Philippines and Singapore*. Cambridge: Basil Blackwell.

Korea Institute for Economics and Technology (KIET). 1986. *Analysis of Effects of Import Liberalization* (in Korean). Seoul.

Lee, Kyung-Tae. 1989. *Development Strategies of High-Tech Infant Industries for an Open Economy:* Korea (in Korean). Seoul: Korea Institute for Economics and Technology.

Leipziger, Danny M. 1988. "Industrial Restructuring in Korea." *World Development* 16(1):121-135.

Ministry of Trade and Industry. 1989. *Free and Fair Trade: Korea's Record and Commitment*. Seoul.

Nam, Sang-Woo. 1984. "Integrated Economic Stabilization Program (1979)." Population Institute, East-West Center, Honolulu.

Presidential Consultative Commission for Economic Structural Adjustment. 1988. "Basic Framework for Achieving Advanced Economy" (in Korean). Seoul.

Young, Soo-gil. 1989 "Trade Policy Problems of the Republic of Korea and the Uruguay Round." KDI Working Paper no. 8913. Seoul: Korea Development Institute.

Chapter 18

Issues and Reforms in Korea's Industrial and Trade Policies

Seong Min Yoo
Korea Development Institute

Introduction

The philosophy behind industrial and trade policies in Korea has changed considerably over time. During the 1960s and 1970s, the government actively promoted targeted industries with deliberately designed industrial incentive schemes. In terms of trade policy, a system of strong export incentives consistent with Korea's export-led growth strategy was maintained during the period, while the liberalization of imports and foreign direct investment were kept to a minimum.

In the early 1980s, however, the government shifted to a more market-oriented approach, and the level of government support for industries as well as its intervention in the resource allocation of private firms gradually decreased. Instead, competition within industries has been more highly emphasized and encouraged. Furthermore, the barriers imposed on imports and foreign direct investment have been lowered to introduce more foreign competition. Partly because of foreign pressures to further open the market and partly as a result of policy reforms for efficiency gains, Korea has achieved considerable liberalization in its trade and investment policy regimes in recent years.

In spite of the progress achieved in the 1980s, recent changes in internal socioeconomic conditions and the external trading environment have made the old ways of doing business ineffective and impractical. Thus, the Korean government has been forced to reconsider its industrial and trade policies and to adopt reform measures where necessary. It is in this context that Kwang Suk Kim (Chapter 17 in this volume; see also K. S. Kim 1990:28–45) summarizes the following emerging industrial and trade developments and possible future policy directions.

1. The Korean market will be opened further to foreign exporters and investors, with the level of trade liberalization reaching that of advanced industrialized countries in the next few years. The country's service markets will also require

substantial opening in the near future. The agricultural sector, however, will continue to be the least open, since it will take some time for the complementary measures for dealing with structural adjustment in this sector to become effective.

2. Because the rapid opening of domestic markets to foreign competition may hurt indigenous industries, a system to provide relief to affected industries will have to be developed. Particular emphasis should be placed on designing a new system of relief from import damages caused by "fair" trade, since the current system is not consistent with GATT provisions.

3. Economic growth in the coming decade, as in the past, will be sustained by rapidly expanding production and exports in the manufacturing sector. Since high-technology industries will be the future growth industries within the manufacturing sector, the government should actively seek ways to promote development of these industries. Policies aimed toward the country's small and medium-sized industries should be geared to the needs of those high-technology industries.

4. Because the issue of industrial restructuring stems from causes more structural than cyclical or capacity-related, the government should establish both a new exit policy and an institution to implement it. But instead of following the past practice of serving as the ultimate risk bearer, the government should make the best use of a private-public division of labor in the process of restructuring.

Since these arguments are all straightforward, it is neither necessary nor relevant to create a new and different scenario on future economic development in Korea. It is relevant, however, to elaborate further on Kim's findings and identify issues that have been omitted or have received less attention in his study but are important nonetheless. Thus, my purposes in this chapter are to present a clearer picture of the Korean economy in the 1990s and then to discuss in further detail the directions of industrial and trade policies. Consequently, this study should serve as a complement to Kim's.

The Korean economy began a sharp downward slide in 1989. Korea's loss of economic dynamism was due mainly to a dramatic slowdown in export growth between 1988 and 1989—a decline in growth from 28 to 3 percent in dollar terms and from 15 to −7 percent in volume terms. Since 1989, Korea's economic performance has continued to worsen.

Two major factors account for Korea's recent sudden economic downturn: the wage increase, which has accelerated from single-digit rates to levels of 20 percent or more since late 1987, and the sharp appreciation of the won against the dollar in both 1988 and 1989. The wage hikes and the currency appreciation, however, seem desirable trends from a longer-term perspective if the Korean economy is to continue to grow rapidly. Therefore, an important question is, not how these trends could be reversed, but what the appropriate responses to these trends on the part of the Korean entrepreneurs and the government should be. It will be helpful if a clearer picture of the Korean economy in the coming decade is presented before answering this question.

Assuming that the future course of industrial development allows the Korean economy to fulfill its growth potential, the Korea Development Institute (KDI 1990) predicts that the economy will be able to grow 7.8 percent annually in the coming decade. As seen in Table 18.1, the growth of factor inputs will slow down as the economically active population begins to increase less rapidly. Thus, realizing the predicted level of growth in the coming decade will critically hinge on a 3.5–4.0 percent annual growth level of total factor productivity, which in turn requires the contribution of technological progress to increase from a rate of 1.0 percent during 1979–88 to 1.1–1.5 percent in 1988–2000.[1]

Accordingly, the appropriate response to the current "difficulties" of the Korean economy is to promote the upgrading of Korea's industries toward continued differentiation and diversification in favor of higher value-added goods. This approach will in turn require major changes in company management and government policies, which so far have been geared toward the promotion of assembly line production of a limited range of low value-added products that derive their competitive edge from cheap labor and economies of scale. To a great extent, companies and the government have also resisted wage increases and currency appreciation, which will only lead to larger and more abrupt changes later.

An international comparison of economic growth rates, as illustrated in Table 18.2, strongly suggests that it will be possible for the Korean economy to achieve 3.5–4.0 per-

Table 18.1
Sources of economic growth, 1970–2000 (percentage)

	1970–79	1979–88	1970–88	1988–2000
Actual growth	10.2	8.4	9.3	—
Cyclical factors	2.1	0.3	1.2	—
Potential growth	8.1	8.1	8.1	7.8
Factor Inputs	5.2	4.3	4.7	3.9
Labor	3.2	2.5	2.8	1.9
Capital	2.0	1.8	1.9	2.0
Total productivity	2.9	3.7	3.3	3.9
Resource reallocation	0.7	0.9	0.8	0.9
Scale economies	1.5	1.8	1.7	1.6
Technological progress	0.7	1.0	0.8	1.4

Source: KDI (1990).

Note: For the concept of potential growth rate and the estimation method employed, see Kim and Park (1985).

TABLE 18.2
International sources of economic growth (percentage)

	Japan 1953–71	U.S. 1948–69	France 1950–62	Italy 1950–62
Potential growth	8.81	4.00	4.70	5.60
Factor Inputs	3.95	2.09	1.24	1.66
Labor	1.85	1.30	0.45	0.96
Capital	2.10	0.79	0.79	0.70
Total productivity	4.86	1.91	3.46	3.94
Resource reallocation	0.95	0.30	0.95	1.42
Scale economies	1.94	0.42	1.00	1.22
Technological progress	1.97	1.19	1.51	1.30

Source: Denison and Chung (1976).

cent growth in total factor productivity in the coming decade. This level corresponds to what was achieved in European countries in their reconstruction period (1950–62), which in turn is much lower than that of Japan in its high-growth period (1953–71).

A question naturally arises about what the nature of the change in government policies to promote the upgrading of industries and to induce innovation in company management should be. In this chapter, I attempt to answer this by exploring the following related subjects: reforms toward advancing industrial restructuring; establishment of a new private-public relationship; and trade policy options consistent with Korea's growth path in the coming decade. I place particular emphasis on the first, since it deals with the most fundamental issues.

Reforms toward Advancing Industrial Restructuring

The international and domestic economic environments are changing rapidly. In addition to continued appreciation of the won and increases in domestic wages, trade liberalization will accelerate, providing foreign suppliers easier access to domestic markets. Rising protectionism abroad will also significantly affect the future of Korean industries.

In the long run, rapid technological change will be a driving force in fundamentally changing the way industries produce goods. The application of new technologies to traditional industries will change their factor proportions, affecting the pattern of international comparative advantage. All these elements will lead to inevitable industrial restructuring. The growth of various industries will vary significantly, and the number of declining industries will increase.

The issue of industrial restructuring is closely related to the most important task of the Korean economy, namely, the enhancement of Korea's national competitiveness. As Michael Porter (1990) argues, a nation's competitiveness depends on the capacity of its industries to innovate and upgrade.

The Future Course of Industrial Development in Korea

With continued economic growth, Korea's industrial structure will become similar to that of the developed countries, as shown in Table 18.3. It is important to note that the rate of increase in the share of the mining and manufacturing sectors will be smaller than in the past, as the industrial structure reaches maturity. Korea's employment structure is also expected to experience considerable change.

Rapid structural changes will also occur within the manufacturing sector. Because of the adjustment and advancement of the industrial structure in the manufacturing sector, the automobile, electronics, and machinery industries will continue to grow rapidly while the importance of the textile, food-processing, steel, and shipbuilding industries declines in relative terms (see Table 18.4).

Table 18.3
Changes in industrial structure

	1987		2000	
	% of GNP	% of emploment	% of GNP	% of employment
Agriculture, forestry, and fisheries	11.4	21.9	7.4	12.6
Mining and manufacturing	31.5	28.1	35.7	29.0
Social overhead and other services	57.1	50.0	57.9	57.5

Source: KDI (1987).

Table 18.4
Structural changes in the manufacturing sector (percentage)

	1984	2000
Machinery	11.5	15.8
Electronics	10.1	22.1
Automobiles	3 3	9 4
Shipbuilding	2.9	1.9
Petroleum chemicals	1.9	1.4
Fine chemicals	3.9	4.2
Iron and steel	6.7	5.4
Textiles	13.8	8.1
Processed food	9.2	5.4
Sports and leisure	2.5	2.2
Other manufacturing	34.1	23.9

Source: KDI (1987).

With this broad prospect for the future of industrial restructuring, a preferred scenario for Korea's continued industrial development can be summarized as follows.

Development of Capital Goods Industries Capital goods industries have grown rapidly since the drive to develop the heavy and chemical industries in the 1970s. Technological capability in the capital goods industries, however, has not seen much development, due to the past industrialization strategy of using imported machines to assemble imported parts.[2] Assembly-oriented industrial development has also been encouraged by the government's policy of export promotion: the government adopted a tariff structure in which higher protection is provided for finished products than for raw materials and parts.[3]

Within the machinery industry, general machinery is considered to be the most important since this branch of the industry supplies machines to other industries. But the general machinery industry in Korea is not well developed in terms of its relative share, as shown in Table 18.5. For example, machines used for the textile industry, a major export industry since the 1960s, are mostly imported. In other words, the competitiveness of the Korean textile industry is based on efficient processing technology, while investment technology is severely lacking.[4]

Capital goods industries are likely to expand rapidly in the future, for the following reasons. First, the development of finished goods industries such as textiles, automobiles, and electronics will induce development in upstream industries. Recent trends show that vertical integration of capital goods production by finished goods industries is increasing. This is so because the expansion of finished goods industries provides the economies of scale and demand necessary for the domestic production of capital goods. Second, technological capability in capital goods industries is improving fast. Royalty payments for advanced foreign technology and R&D expenditures in the capital goods industries are increasing. In addition, government support for industrial R&D is also rising. Third, the demand for

Table 18.5
International comparison of machinery industries (percentage)

	Korea 1984	Japan 1982	U.S. 1979	Germany 1982
General machinery	12.9	20.4	26.9	29.3
Fabricated metal	11.6	11.0	15.8	13.7
Electric machinery	37.9	32.3	18.5	24.4
Transportation equipment	35.3	33.7	33.0	29.1
Measuring, medical, optical	2.3	2.6	5.8	3.5

Source: KDI (1987).

automated capital goods will expand rapidly. As information technology begins to be applied to industries, demand for more automated machines and equipment will rise, which in turn will likely be met by domestic suppliers who can adapt better to the domestic production and working environments than foreign suppliers.

Growth of High-Technology Industries One of the distinctive characteristics of industrial development in the 1980s was the birth of the so-called high-technology industries. The computer, semiconductor, and communication equipment industries grew rapidly during this period. High-technology industries are of great interest to firms and government policymakers as a means of upgrading industries. In addition, there will be substantial spillover effects to related industries.[5] The rapid growth of technology-intensive industries will undoubtedly continue in the future (Table 18.6).

High-technology industries in Korea developed through participation in the process of international production specialization wherein foreign firms specialize in design and engineering while domestic firms take care of final production. This pattern of specialization is likely to continue in the near future. The development pattern of high-technology industries in Korea, therefore, differs vastly from that of advanced countries. In advanced countries, R&D is the major source of technological progress, and industries evolve according to the product life cycle—the introduction of new technology followed by the adaptation and dissemination of technology leading to a maturation stage.

The innovation process Korea experienced exhibits a different pattern. The acquisition of mature technology via formal and informal transfers of technology occurred first. In the initial stage, technological capability was limited to the production of output without a simultaneous capacity for investment. Therefore, the

Table 18.6
Prospects for high-technology industries

	Shares in world market (%)		Annual growth rate (%)	
	1987	2000	1988–94	1995–2000
Microelectronics	1.6	3.9	18.9	15.7
Mechatronics	0.9	4.2	34.0	25.0
New materials	1.2	3.8	38.1	30.5
Fine chemicals	2.0	4.3	11.8	10.8
Bioengineering	2.0	2.0	23.4	26.0
Optical fiber	0.6	4.7	40.7	35.5
Aviation	0.1	3.1	45.3	18.1
High-technology total	1.3	3.8	20.7	20.3

Source: KDI (1990).

gradual improvement and adaptation of imported technology raised the efficiency of production, and investment capability was concurrently cultivated. In this manner, gradual learning and adaptation of foreign technology has been far more important than revolutionary innovation.[6] In the near future, however, Korean firms should be able to acquire the abilities to develop new products and compete with leading foreign firms in certain segments of the market.

Advent of an Information Society Information and knowledge will be the bases of economic activities in an information society, the next stage in socioeconomic change after the industrial society. There are two principal features of the advent of the information society in Korea: the development of information industries and the application of information technologies in other industries.

An information society is realized to the extent that the collection, processing, and distribution of information comprise a large share of national value added. The value added created by the information industry (data communication, data processing, information networks, and information equipment) accounted for 3.9 percent of GNP in 1983 and for 7.6 percent in 1987. The industry's average annual growth rate during this period was approximately 30 percent, an indication of the industry's growing importance to the national economy (Lee 1989:17). The information industry will be at the forefront of economic growth in Korea, and information processing technology is expected to lead the expansion of the industry as a whole. The outlook for the industry predicts that the contribution of the industry's value added to GNP will increase from 5.9 percent in 1986 to 11.3 percent in 2001 (Lee 1989:10). Within the industry, the highest growth is expected in data processing, which is still in its infant stage in Korea.

The application of information technology in Korean industries has not been extensive compared to advanced industrialized countries. But rapid progress is expected in the future, for several reasons. The domestic information industry is developing quickly and will consequently be able to supply hardware and software suitable for the domestic environment. In addition, the rising wage rate will force firms to seek increased office and factory automation. Finally, the government is determined to promote the application of information technology.

Transition toward a Service-Oriented Economy One of the distinctive features of structural change in the future lies in the increase of service-related activities. At present, the service industry is often considered a residual part of the economy. In the future, however, service activities based on knowledge and experience will be an essential component of the value added in all industries.

In the advanced countries, the contribution of the service sector to GNP is higher than 60 percent. In Korea, the GNP share of the service sector should increase to 60 percent in 2010 from 55 percent in 1985 (Lee 1989:19). Faster growth is expected in sports and leisure, transportation, and environmental services.

Among services demanded by firms, rapid expansion is expected not only in the traditional service industries such as finance, distribution, advertising, and transportation but also in newer industries such as consulting, research and development, and marketing.

The share of service industries in GNP and the service component of manufacturing will increase for the following reasons. First, a rise in per capita income increases the demand for services. The income elasticity of services is supposedly greater than that of goods. Higher incomes will evoke greater demand for leisure-related services, financial and legal services, and other personal services. Second, the more sophisticated a country's industrial structure becomes, the greater the demand for service-related activities by firms. Firms will spend more on R&D, marketing, and after-sale services.

Policy Directions for Industrial Restructuring

The pattern of industrial development is expected to change in the future as suggested above. In the manufacturing sector, labor-intensive industries that rely on very simple technologies will be phased out gradually.[7] Meanwhile, industries with high labor productivity and value added should be expanded to accommodate higher wages.

To restructure industries, the labor and capital employed in declining industries should be shifted to growing industries. However, market mechanisms are not always sufficient in providing for the smooth reallocation of the factors of production. As a result, government assistance may be necessary to improve the mobility of the factors of production. The most important role of the government is to assist workers displaced from declining industries. The government should provide financial assistance for the retraining of workers so that they may find jobs in other industries. In the past, the government has tried to provide assistance to firms in declining industries; however, direct assistance to delay bankruptcies can lead to inefficiency. Thus, efforts should be made to keep government intervention in the restructuring process to a minimum. If the government intervenes excessively, as in the past, it will disrupt the efficient and fair operation of market mechanisms. Even when intervention is necessary for sociopolitical reasons, the entailed loss in economic efficiency should be minimized.

The policy toward sunrise industries must also be changed. In the 1960s and 1970s, the government directly interfered in the allocation of resources to accelerate the growth of leading sectors. Industries that exported or produced import substitutes were heavily promoted as a means of alleviating the chronic balance-of-payments deficits. In the 1980s, the extent of government intervention in the allocation of resources was gradually reduced to allow the market mechanism to function. Tax and financial incentives to promote strategic industries have gradually been phased out. Today, an increasing number of people insist that a more active government role is necessary in the development of high-technology industries in the belief that these industries will provide positive externalities that improve the productivity of all other industries. This group further believes that the government is responsible for the promotion of basic science to serve as the foundation for science-based industries. Naturally, it will be important for the government to espouse policies that promote the development of manpower and technology.

The government should, however, maintain the principle that industrial assistance should not be offered simply because industries are expected to grow in the future. Moreover, the government should not rely on policy instruments that restrict the potential entry of firms or raise barriers against imports. It should be emphasized that the government's most important role in industrial restructuring is to increase market efficiency.

Declining Industry Adjustment For declining industries, the policy should be one in which restructuring efforts are led by the private sector, with government intervention limited to minimizing the social costs incurred during the adjustment process. Until recently, the private sector has relied on and expected government support when making important business decisions to invest and restructure. Some firms, although cognizant of their inefficiency, make no effort to improve operations so that they can benefit from public intervention during the adjustment process. Such behavior acts as a drag on national productivity.

As internal and external economic environments change, declining industries will continue to emerge. Therefore, industries targeted for adjustment must be carefully selected. However, it is often difficult to judge which industries have passed the maturing stage and are actually declining. It is sometimes possible that an apparently declining industry can be saved through equipment replacement, automation, product differentiation, or the application of newer technology. Even among declining industries, firms employing sophisticated technology and rational management do exist. Industries selected as targets for adjustment should not be exceptional cases, but simply firms within industries that face declining competitiveness due to changing economic conditions.

Declining industries should be selected according to strict and objective criteria. Unfortunately, past industrial adjustment policies often llustrate an absence of such criteria.[8] Adjustment incentives, rather than reducing social inefficiencies, have delayed the bankruptcies of declining firms and sowed distrust between government and business. This is because incentives such as special loans and favorable tax treatment have been arbitrarily applied on an ad hoc basis. Instead, the following policy measures should be undertaken to address rising unemployment in declining industries. First, more public and private schools for specialized vocational training should be established and expanded, and greater financial and fiscal incentives should be provided for the purchase of equipment and facilities for such schools. Second, for localized areas of very high unemployment, employment opportunities should be created.

In offering public incentives to convert businesses, replace equipment, automate, differentiate products, and so forth, decisions should be made discretely, and when necessary should be offered on a limited and temporary basis. Emphasis should be placed on establishing and operating an institute to supply management and technology information and to facilitate overseas expansion of businesses. The availability of information can be increased by expanding the information functions of existing organizations, with necessary financial incentives provided by increasing the Industrial Development Fund.

To ease industrial adjustment, legal and institutional changes should also be made to reduce barriers to company transactions through mergers and acquisitions. Existing laws that provide incentives for industrial adjustment include the Industrial Development Law enacted in 1986[9] and the Tax Reduction Exemption Law, revised in 1985. These laws should be applied fairly and equitably. For this purpose, an inquiry commission should be established to gather the opinions of various interest groups and experts. New legislation to rationalize unemployment policies and resolve conflicts with the Fair Trade Law are also required. If these new policies to address declining industry adjustment are enacted, the following results can be expected. First, government failure can be reduced. The social cost of excessive financial support and continuous intervention to assist inefficient industries will be sharply decreased. Second, free competition and self-initiated adjustment by private firms will be promoted by having the scope of public intervention clearly defined in a way that promotes autonomy and competition. Third, such reform can reduce the social cost of industrial restructuring by enhancing factor mobility in both labor and capital. Retraining and job-creation programs for displaced workers, by reducing adjustment costs, will be particularly helpful in facilitating the transition process.

Restructuring the Agriculture, Forestry, and Fishery Industry Restructuring the agriculture, forestry, and fishery (AFF hereafter) industry to increase its competitiveness is crucial for its survival in the new environment of rapid industrialization and import liberalization. But there is serious skepticism about the feasibility of introducing innovations to the underdeveloped infrastructure of the AFF industry. Without a national consensus on practical means and a time schedule, agricultural policy will flounder in the midst of debate over policy alternatives. Furthermore, because of the lack of a coherent structural policy and insufficient investment in the upgrading of infrastructure, the AFF industry is still plagued by structural weaknesses. The vulnerability of the AFF industry to import liberalization also makes it particularly difficult to formulate a new agricultural policy.

Still, it should be clearly recognized that the restructuring of the AFF industry is a precondition for the successful achievement of the two basic goals of agricultural policy—the efficient production of food, and the provision of higher income and living standards for farmers. It is impossible for farmers to reach an income level comparable to that of urban wage earners without upgrading the presently underdeveloped infrastructure. This task cannot be achieved through short-term, temporary policies; it must be addressed through a consistent and determined long-term vision into the next decades. Thus, a gradual liberalization of agricultural imports is also required.[10]

Promotion of Technological Development The promotion of technological development will be crucial in the process of industrial restructuring. Since the expansion of the manufacturing sector will likely decelerate in the future, economic growth will be heavily dependent on gains in productivity, which in turn require continued technological progress.

Total R&D investment by the private sector and the government has been increasing rapidly. The share of government R&D investment in the national budget, however, has been stable over the period, while private R&D investment has increased rapidly.[11] An increase in the government's budgetary outlays for R&D investment could be justified in several ways. Research activities at the university level need to be strengthened through greater government assistance. The government should also support basic studies in science and technology. Finally, the global competition in technological development cannot be considered the responsibility of the private sector alone.

In view of the history of technological development in Korea, however, the government should avoid putting too much emphasis on the domestic development of technology. A balance should be reached between the acquisition of foreign technology and the employment of domestic research and development as the source of technological development.[12] Priority should be given to the cultivation of technologies that will eventually help industrial development. Active government participation is necessary for those technological development projects that generate large external economies. The best examples are the capital goods, high-technology, and information industries. On the other hand, projects, even in these industries, that offer immediate profit opportunities for related firms are better left to the private sector.

In view of recent changes in the research capabilities of firms and universities, the past concentration of government research funds in certain government research institutions is no longer desirable. Research units of private firms and universities should be allowed to compete for research funds for national R&D projects. The government should also provide financial aid for acquisitions of equipment needed for research.

The Development of Manpower to Facilitate Restructuring To promote faster technological progress, high-quality manpower is crucial. In this respect, the government's education policy should put more emphasis on the training of a highly qualified labor force. Education policies in the past have emphasized expanding equal education opportunities instead of promoting open competition. Reform of the education system, including changes to the curriculum, entrance examinations, and size of various university departments, is necessary to adjust to changing economic conditions.

Since future employment demands will be generated by technology-intensive and knowledge-related industries, the manpower supply system for engineers, scientists, and technicians should be consolidated to address the changing demands. To this end, the quality of graduate education in the fields of science and engineering should be improved. More attention should also be redirected from entry-level training toward promotional training and retraining. By expanding scholarship assistance and tax incentives, vocational schools may be able to attract more highly qualified applicants.

Preparing for the Information Society In formulating industrial policy, implications of the so-called information revolution have to be considered, because information and knowledge will be the core of economic activities. General policy measures to help prepare for the coming information society must be developed. The government should publicize its vision of the information society and educate the general public to prepare it to contribute to such a society. It is also important to increase the supply of qualified scientists and engineers in the field of information technology. The development of the information industry is essential in fostering the application of information technology in various industries. Without proper development of the domestic information industry, the hardware and software suitable for the domestic environment cannot be developed. Among the various subsectors of the information industry, the promotion of the software industry should be the government's top priority, since domestically required software cannot be adequately supplied by foreign firms. The measures to promote this industry should, however, exclude those that hamper market competition. Trade and entry barriers are not desirable. Instead, the government should try to support manpower training and R&D in the field.

Since an efficient information network is a prerequisite for the development of an information society, the government should accelerate the construction of information networks to improve the quality of public services. The information network business should eventually be open to all private firms.

Establishing a New Private-Public Interface

In the continuing debate over the competitiveness of nations, Michael Porter (1990) argues, no topic engenders more debate or creates less understanding than the role of government. Many see the government as an essential helper or supporter of industry, employing a host of policies to contribute directly to the competitive performance of strategic or target industries. Others accept the "free market" view that the operation of the economy should be left to the workings of the "invisible hand."

Both views are incorrect, Porter continues, since either followed to its logical outcome would lead to the permanent erosion of a country's competitive capabilities. Advocates of government help for industry frequently propose policies that would actually hurt companies in the long run and only create the demand for further assistance. Advocates of a diminished government presence ignore the legitimate role government plays in shaping the context and institutional structure surrounding companies and in creating an environment that stimulates companies to gain competitive advantage. Porter's suggested role for government is somewhere in between the extremes, and it is fair to say that the government's appropriate role shifts as the economy progresses and passes through the various stages of competitive development. In view of the history of Korea's economic growth, this is a critical point that requires a fundamental change in the private-public relationship. The direction of this change should be the promotion of more competition. To accomplish this policy objective, the government will have to do at least the following: strengthen its antitrust law enforcement, promote competition and enhance efficiency by deregulating industries, and design policies to promote efficiency of public enterprises. Since the first issue deals with the main body of competition policy and requires a separate in-depth study, I confine myself to the other two issues in this chapter.

Deregulatory Reform toward a Freer Market System Many would argue that the Korean government's involvement in the economy has been quite substantial and extensive in comparison to government involvement in other market economies.[13] Most economic regulations in Korea were introduced by the government in order to implement certain industrial policy goals rather than to prevent potential market failures and inefficiencies. This kind of regulation typically took the form of protective regulations, resulting in many undesirable side effects, in particular the suppression of market competition. Many regulations were also introduced to prevent "excessive competition" and to maintain "market order."[14] This type of regulation has been demanded frequently by industries, in many cases resulting in the arbitrary distribution of economic privileges (economic rents).

Many industrial regulations in Korea require firms to apply for government permits or licenses. In certain cases, however, the procedures and requirements to obtain them are highly subjective and judgmental. Thus, the bureaucrats have large discretionary power, and the decisions have tended to be arbitrary and abusive. Some regulations require only notification of or registration with the government. However, the government has at times refused to accept registration, in effect creating a licensing procedure. Furthermore, regulatory practices exist which are not even included in the laws. Many business activities are regulated through the government's unofficial interventions and recommendations, often called "administrative directives." Although there is no legal penalty for disobeying, no business person in Korea would dare violate such directives.

Since the early 1980s, however, the regulatory environment in Korea has undergone substantial change. First, there has been a change in the general perception of the government's role in the economy. Many people, especially those in business, began to realize the limits of the government's ability to control the economy. As the economy became larger in size, it became difficult for the government to manage it as effectively as before. A few policy mistakes also contributed to this change in perception. Second, there was a change in the attitude of the private sector toward government regulations. Until the early 1980s, most of the big firms in Korea grew very rapidly thanks to the government's export-oriented protective policies and regulations. As a result, they welcomed and demanded such protection and support from the government. However, as firms became more independent of government protection and grew internationally competitive, they realized that the government's intervention was not always a blessing, and that regulations and bureaucracies could be a burden. Some of them wanted certain government regulations reduced. Furthermore, Korea has undergone significant social and political change since 1986. Because an existing state of regulations can be viewed as a result of interest group politics and as a reflection of the status quo in the society at any particular time, a deregulatory reform can have a better chance of being successful when sociopolitical changes are taking place. In this regard, one can be optimistic about the government's current efforts to deregulate and reform the old regulations.

In response to these changes in the regulatory environment, an interministry working group was formed to discuss and determine ways to promote competition and reform regulations. Changing an economic regulation would normally involve more than one government agency, and one agency's refusal to cooperate in the past would damn the whole effort to failure. This working group was formed to avoid such problems and break down bureaucratic sectionalism. In March 1989, the group announced a comprehensive plan to reform government regulations, including 87 provisions to reduce government intervention and promote competition in the market. In May 1989, the group also announced measures to deregulate ten industries that had been selected earlier in 1988 as the top priority industries for deregulation (see J. S. Kim 1989). The government lifted the entry restrictions on some of the industries earlier designated as "industries to be rationalized" under the Industry Development Act. New entries and increased competition are expected in these industries. Last, and perhaps most important, many offices and agencies in the government are now actively and voluntarily proposing changes to reform economic regulations and to liberalize the market, at times even in the absence of policy directives from government leadership.

Although there seems to be consensus on the need to reform economic regulations and promote competition in Korea, some problems and issues still remain to be resolved. Generally, two types of effects are to be expected from deregulation: promotion of competition through the removal of protective regulations, and reduction of regulatory burdens on businesses to make business activities more efficient. Current reform efforts are aimed more at promoting competition than at reducing regulatory burdens. Social regulations are actually increasing, and Korea will eventually have to extend its reform efforts to include social regulations in order to really see the full effects of deregulation. As democratization continues in Korean society, more interest groups will try to influence government decisions through political processes. This political change may increase the possibility of yet another kind of regulatory failure, one common in Western democracies. We may be facing the regulatory problems caused by political interventions.

Promoting Efficiency in Public Enterprises The public enterprise sector in Korea has continuously expanded and its share of the national economy has grown considerably, giving rise to several problems. The sector's inefficiency is sometimes evident in many aspects of investment behavior, managerial control, and managerial performance. Government price controls on goods and services sold by public enterprises guarantee monopolistic profits, which at times leads to overinvestment. There are also problems of over- and underregulation.

Efficiency of public enterprises should be enhanced in several ways. Government-owned public enterprises must be privatized wherever possible, since the inefficiency largely results from government's over-intervention. Selective privatization should be carried out after considering economies of scale and availability of goods. In selecting public enterprises to be privatized, standards for competitiveness and managerial ability must be established objectively and adhered to strictly. Furthermore, autonomous management must be guaranteed for public enterprises for which privatization is unfeasible. This will infuse principles of independence and responsibility into public enterprise management and will prevent over-intervention by the government. A competition promotion plan within public enterprises which divides up operating systems according to regions or businesses must also be pursued.

Trade Policy Options and the Search for a New International Role

The Korean economy is now one of the most trade-dependent in the world. In 1988, exports of goods alone amounted to $59.7 billion, 35 percent of GNP. Trade in nonfactor services has also grown, with exports amounting to 6 percent of GNP in 1988, although imports were considerably less. Thus, Korea trades heavily not only in goods but also in nonfactor services. Internationally, however, Korea has just begun to carry its weight as a trade partner. This applies especially to trade relations with Japan, the United States, Australia, and Canada. Korea's share in the trade of other countries is considerably smaller, especially in the external trade of EC countries.

Prospects for Korea's Trade Structure Table 18.7 shows the prospects for Korea's overall trade in the coming decade. A rapid structural shift toward capital- and technology-intensive products has accompanied the rapid growth of Korea's manufactured exports (see Table 18.8). As of 1988, the export share of electronic products such as television sets and semiconductors exceeded that of textile products.

Table 18.7
Overall growth of trade (US$ billion)

	1989–92	1993–96	1997–2000
Total exports	97.2	147.6	208.3
Total imports	95.4	144.8	204.4
Trade balance	1.8	2.8	3.9
Annual export growth (%)	12.5	11.0	9.0
Annual import growth (%)	16.5	11.0	9.0

Source: KIET (1989).
Note: The values of exports and imports represent those for the last year in each period.

Table 18.8
Estimated Korean export structure (US$ billion dollars and percentage)

	1988	2000
Electronics	15.7 (25.9)	73.2 (35.1)
Textiles	14.1 (23.2)	21.6 (10.4)
Iron and steel	3.8 (6.3)	9.6 (4.6)
Footwear	3.8 (6.3)	n.a.
Motor vehicles and parts	3.6 (6.0)	18.5 (8.9)
Marine	1.9 (3.1)	n.a.
Ships	1.8 (2.9)	n.a.
Chemicals	1.6 (2.7)	7.1 (3.4)
Plastics	1.3 (2.1)	n.a.
General machinery	1.2 (2.0)	23.6 (11.3)
Subtotal	48.9 (80.5)	n.a.
Total exports	60.7	208.3

Source: KIET (1989).
n.a. = not available.

The other leading exports are mostly capital- and technology-intensive products, such as steel, passenger cars, ships, and general machinery. By the year 2000, the share of these products in total exports will increase considerably.

Imports have been crucial to Korea's economic development, primarily as a source of raw materials and capital goods (see Table 18.9). In 1988, raw materials accounted for 54 percent of total imports, while capital goods accounted for 37 percent. Consumer goods, half of which were grains, accounted for only 10 percent. The structure of imports is not expected to exhibit any significant change in the near future.

Korea's three most important trade partners continue to be the United States, Japan, and the EC (Table 18.10). The developed countries as a group account for about 70 percent of Korea's trade. The United States, in particular, has always provided Korea with by far its largest export market, while Japan has been Korea's largest source of imports. Thus, Korea has had a large structural trade deficit with Japan and a large surplus with the United States, the two more or less offsetting each other. The structural deficit and surplus with these two countries peaked in the mid-1980s and have been declining ever since. These structural imbalances are expected to be reduced in the 1990s.

The International Trading Environment Until the early 1980s, Korea had remained a relatively insignificant participant in the international trading system. With respect to its trade and exchange rate policies, Korea enjoyed virtually complete autonomy under the benign neglect of the developed countries. It could claim exemption under the GATT Article XVIII, Section B, waiver of the Article XI prohibition against quantitative import restrictions. Korea was also able to maintain a protectionist trade policy regime, while enjoying most-favored nation access to the markets of developed countries. Since the early 1980s, however, Korea's status in the in-

TABLE 18.9

Estimated Korean import structure (US$ billion dollars and percentage)

	1988	2000
Raw materials	24.2 (46.6)	95.6 (46.8)
For export processing	11.6 (22.4)	40.3 (19.7)
For domestic uses	12.6 (24.3)	55.3 (27.1)
Crude oil	3.7 (7.1)	14.8 (7.2)
Capital goods	19.0 (36.7)	70.3 (34.4)
Consumer goods	4.9 (9.5)	23.7 (11.6)
Total imports	51.8	208.3

Source: KIET (1989).

ternational trading system has been changing. Korea has been losing its trade policy autonomy and has come under foreign pressures, especially from the United States, to remove restrictions on imports and foreign direct investment and to remedy other allegedly unfair practices. With the emergence of a current account surplus in 1986, Korea also came under U.S. pressure to revalue the Korean won.

In a sense, these developments reflect Korea's growing weight in the international economy and thus were inevitable. There are three main aspects of the country's growing international economic weight: Korea's share in world trade is rising; it has been rapidly catching up with the developed countries in exporting an increasing number of high value-added products; and it has tended to accumulate current account surpluses over the long term. These three aspects of Korea's growing international economic position have been interacting with two important features of the developed economies (excluding Japan) to generate protectionist as well as policy adjustment pressures. One such feature is the developed economies' failure to adjust adequately to foreign competition, which in turn reflects microeconomic rigidities found in these countries. The other relevant feature of the old industrialized countries is the chronic global economic imbalance associated with the huge trade deficits of the United States, due partly to the failure of the U.S. government to manage fiscal, monetary, and exchange rate policies with prudence and flexibility.

It is unlikely that the old industrialized countries will significantly improve their structural adjustment capacity and increase the flexibility of their resource allocation in the near future. The potential for such improvements is found in EC 1992, but it remains uncertain as to whether this potential will materialize. Also, most predictions are that the U.S. trade deficit will continue to persist in the foreseeable future. It is, then, safe to assume that in the 1990s Korea will continue to experience various trade frictions, in the form of the protectionist pressures of the 1980s, on the one hand, and in the form of pressures for currency appreciation and

Table 18.10
Estimated exports and imports by region (US$ billion and percentage)

	Exports		Imports		Balance	
	1988	2000	1988	2000	1988	2000
U.S.	21 (35)	57 (27)	13 (25)	55 (27)	8	2
Japan	12 (20)	45 (22)	16 (31)	46 (22)	−4	−1
EC	8 (13)	29 (14)	6 (11)	28 (14)	2	1
Others	20 (32)	77 (37)	17 (33)	75 (37)	3	2
Total	61	208	52	204	9	4

Source: KIET (1989).

market opening, on the other. The United States will continue to strengthen its so-called process protectionism and will furthermore continue to press for the appreciation of the won and accelerated opening of the markets for agricultural products and services.[15]

The United States will not be the only developed country with which Korea has trade disputes. The EC is very likely to invoke its protectionist antidumping provisions more frequently while further strengthening its local content regulation of foreign direct investment to ease the problem of adjustment attendant on the 1992 program. In fact, the EC is already following the United States in demanding the reciprocal opening of Korea's markets. Korea fears that the trade tension with the EC may further escalate as it continues to increase its share in the European markets. Moreover, the EC countries' movement to unify their internal markets under the Single European Act seems to be of profound significance to the future of the international trading system as well as of the Korean economy. The 1992 program certainly encouraged the EC to assume a policy of bilateral reciprocity similar to that of the United States. These developments could seriously affect all countries outside the EC, and the Asian NIEs and Japan would be among the most seriously affected by a "Fortress Europe."

Korea is not currently experiencing any serious trade tensions with Japan and other Pacific Basin developed countries. One reason for this is that Korea's market opening for U.S. goods and services is automatically extended to these countries on a most-favored nation basis. Another reason is that these countries have thus far adhered to multilateralism rather than bilateralism. Moreover, Korea runs trade deficits with these countries, which should make them more tolerant of the trade barriers they may face in the Korean market. But this is not to say that these Pacific Basin countries will continue to stand out as clear exceptions to the present global trend toward protectionism. A brief review of Korea's international trading environment reveals a system that is becoming increasingly discriminatory and fragmented. Process protectionism is spreading, and bilateralism and possibly regionalism seem to be on the verge of blossoming. In either case, the victim will be the multilateral trading system for which the GATT stands. In the context of these developments, Korea has all but lost its special and differential treatment in the international trading system. It instead faces increasingly discriminatory treatment in the markets of the developed countries. In addition, it no longer holds true that Korea need not reciprocate access to its markets. Still, there are difficulties at home inhibiting full reciprocation, increasing uncertainty concerning access to markets abroad.

Trade Policy Options For the past three decades, the international trading system has served many trading countries well, helping them pursue export-led economic growth with varying degrees of success. Korea, along with other Asian NIEs, provides a shining example in this respect. The recent developments toward a fragmentation and weakening of the system are, however, threatening the very basis of Korea's continued economic success.

Such developments have already affected Korea, indicating that the country will continue to encounter this global trend toward discriminatory protectionism. Over the past several years in Korea there has been an unending series of measures, including trade liberalization, to move toward a more open trading regime. Nonetheless, Korea's trade policy regime still carries many vestiges of the earlier developmental mercantilism, and this together with Korea's well-publicized economic success has prevented the country from receiving praise for these reforms. Rather, they have earned Korea the reputation of having achieved economic success on the basis of unfair trade practices and, despite all evidence to the contrary, of trying to continue to do so.

What, then, should be Korea's strategy in coping with the international economic environment of the 1990s? One can think of this strategy as having five components. First, Korea should continue to make the current account adjustment to avoid a large surplus. This will not only avoid unnecessary trade policy conflicts but also be conducive to the domestic policy objective of greater social equity, since both require an increase in domestic absorption as well as a consequent increase in imports. In this sense, Korea should be pursuing "trade-led" economic growth instead of export-led growth in the 1990s.

Second, and more immediately, Korea should push for the successful conclusion of the Uruguay Round and utilize those negotiations to rationalize and clarify as many rules as possible in order to minimize room for process protectionism. Domestically, it is urgently necessary to reform industrial policy measures, in particular for agriculture and service industries, since the subsequent market opening after the Uruguay Round will have a significant impact on the economy.

Third, along with Japan and other NIEs, Korea should make efforts to remove all its nontariff barriers of questionable legitimacy, thus eliminating the grounds for accusations of unfair trade practices. For this purpose, various commercial as well as administrative practices should be critically reviewed.

Fourth, one way of overcoming protectionist barriers is to invest abroad. For this reason, overseas direct investment in the industrialized countries may be encouraged, especially in the United States and the EC. Investment in these countries may be used as a means of acquiring advanced technology, thus bypassing technology protectionism.

Fifth, economic relations should be diversified. In particular, markets in Japan, the EC, China, and other socialist countries should be explored. There is much room for the mutual opening of markets in the Asia-Pacific region, and the process may be further accelerated by expanded direct investment flows among the regional economies. Thus, overseas investment in other Asia-Pacific countries should be given special emphasis.

In coping with the international economic environment of the 1990s, Korea should, in fact, do more than just pursue these five objectives. As one of the dynamic Asia-Pacific economies, Korea should further pursue the broader objective of making active and creative contributions to the management and prosperity of the global economy. The future of the international trading system will depend critically on the roles played by Japan, Korea, and other Asian NIEs, in particular. These economies are the most dynamic exporters in the world; as such, they have also been the main source of adjustment pressure on the economies of the old industrialized countries. In this sense, they have also been a prime cause in the weakening of the international trading system, since the rise of the new protectionism has largely been a response to the emergence of these economies as dynamic exporters.

Such failure by new exporters to reciprocate has in turn evoked many of the allegations of unfair trade practices against them. Whether such failure should be regarded as unfair behavior is neither clear nor relevant in the present context. What matters is the fact that, had the new dynamic exporters more fully opened their domestic markets and subsequently shared greater responsibility for the maintenance of a liberal international trading system, the system itself would have been better preserved than it actually has been. This point being stated, fuller market opening by Korea and other dynamic exporters, not to mention Japan, is called for.

NOTES

1. For a slightly different scenario, see KDI (1987), which presents the sources of economic growth, 1973–2010.
2. The electronics, automobile, and shipbuilding industries provide typical examples of this pattern of industrial development.
3. For export manufacturing, tariffs applied to raw materials and parts were waived through a tariff drawback system. Machines used for export production were also subject to very low tariffs.
4. Technological capability can be categorized by the following: production capability, investment capability, and innovative capability. Of these three, Korea has become most competitive in production capability. See Lee (1989) and KDI (1990) for further details.
5. For example, the market size of new materials industries in the year 2000 is estimated to be around US$600 billion, whereas the market for industries that utilize new materials is expected to reach $6 trillion.
6. The computer industry, for example, started by producing CRT terminals on an OEM basis. The foreign partner provided the necessary designs and software. The technical know-how needed by domestic firms was very similar to that used in the production of television sets. The combination of advanced foreign technology and domestic mass production capabilities created a very competitive industry. Some domestic firms were able to develop their own design capabilities and sell under their own brand names.

7. In the early stages of industrial development, there were only a few cases of declining industries in the manufacturing sector. Most manufacturing industries enjoyed constant growth, with a few exceptions such as the plywood and wig industries.

8. The prominent examples are promotion of heavy and chemical industries in the early 1980s; rationalization of structurally depressed enterprises, including shipping, overseas construction, and shipbuilding in 1984; industry-specific rationalization efforts based on the Industrial Development Law of 1986; and the provisions for insolvent firms in the Tax Reduction Exemption Law.

9. The Industrial Development Law, which is the policy guide for incentives for the manufacturing sector, is an integration of seven previous industry-specific promotion laws and thus can be considered an improvement in that it is a movement away from selective incentives for certain industries. Still, it is important to guarantee equitable and publicized application of the law.

10. See Presidential Commission on Economic Restructuring (1988:55–70) for further details.

11. The ratio of total R&D investment to GNP increased to 2 percent in 1986 from 0.9 percent in 1980. The proportion of the government investment in total R&D investment, however, declined to 26 percent in 1986 from 68 percent in 1980. See Presidential Commission on Economic Restructuring (1988:82).

12. The Korean firms' marketing strategy of following the leading firms of advanced countries must be continued for the time being until Korean firms accumulate more advanced technological capabilities.

13. According to one survey conducted by the Federation of Korean Industries, there are 1,013 regulations on business activities in the manufacturing sector, found in 64 laws: 220 regulations on entry and exit, 420 on production, 163 on purchase and sales, and 210 on personnel and labor.

14. One may argue that the concepts of excessive competition and market order are too ambiguous.

15. According to Schott (1989), most U.S. trade legislation since 1979 has been devoted to elaborating the criteria and requirements for import relief. The protective intent of such provisions is hidden in "generic" amendments to U.S. trade law which apply to all industries, even though the change was formulated to meet the interests of a particular industry. In most instances, these changes have increased the likelihood that an industry can gain relief from imports, thus masking the increased protectionism that has become embedded in the administrative "process" of determining import relief.

REFERENCES

Denison, Edward F., and William K. Chung. 1976. *How Japan's Economy Grew So Fast.* Washington D.C.: Brookings Institution.

Kim, Jong Seok. 1989. "Regulatory Reform in Korea: Toward a Freer Market System." Unpublished mimeo. KDI, Seoul.

Kim, Kwang Suk. 1990. "Industrial and Trade Policy Regimes in Korea: Past, Present and Future." Presented at the Workshop on Comparative Analysis of Development Policies in China, Japan, and Korea, Seoul.

Kim, Kwang Suk, and Joon-kyung Park. 1985. *Sources of Economic Growth in Korea: 1963–1982*. Seoul: Korea Development Institute.

Korea Development Institute (KDI). 1987. *The Future Course of Industrial Development and Policy Response*. The final report of the Future Industry Task Force. Seoul.

Korea Development Institute. 1990. "The Korean Economy in the 1990s: Policy Issues and Reforms" (in Korean). Unpublished mimeo, Seoul.

Korea Institute for Economics and Technology (KIET). 1989. *Prospect for Korea's External Trade in the Year 2000 and Long-Term Trade Policy Directions* (in Korean). Seoul.

Lee, Won-Young. 1989. "The Future Course of Industrial Development in Korea." Unpublished mimeo. KDI, Seoul.

Porter, Michael E. 1990. "The Competitive Advantage of Nations." *Harvard Business Review*, March–April, 73–93.

Presidential Commission on Economic Restructuring. 1988. "Realigning Korea's National Priorities for Economic Advance." Seoul.

Schott, Jeffrey J. 1989. "U.S. Trade Policy: Implications for U.S.-Korean Relations." In Thomas O. Bayard and Soogil Young (eds.), *Economic Relations between the United States and Korea: Conflict or Cooperation?* Institute for International Economics and Korea Development Institute.

Young, Soogil. 1989. "Trade Policy Problems of the Republic of Korea and the Uruguay Round." Working Paper no. 8913. Korea Development Institute, Seoul.

CHAPTER 19

Korean Industrial Policy: Legacies of the Past and Directions for the Future

D. M. Leipziger
World Bank
Peter A. Petri
Brandeis University

Introduction

Industrial policy remains at the center of the debate about Korea's economic future. To some, Korea's industrial policy has lost its creative edge by abandoning selective, strategic support of industry. To others, despite pronouncements to the contrary, the government is still pursuing an interventionist strategy that is poorly suited to Korea's modern, complex economy. And to still others, there is a need for a new model, rooted neither in Korea's past nor in the elusive "laissez-faire" of economics textbooks. But perhaps the most striking contrast with the past is that controversy and even confusion have taken the place of the self-confident, definitive policies of earlier periods.

The central theme of this chapter is that Korean industrial policy, despite its rapid transformation over the past decade, has not kept pace with the enormous change—political and economic, domestic and international—in the country's policy environment. The "right" industrial policy depends on constantly changing factors: the nature of market failures facing the economy, and the scope and effectiveness of policy instruments available to government. Some market failures vanish with economic growth, while others take their place at more advanced stages of development. Instruments appropriate in one economic environment become ineffective, illegal, or too risky in others. And the evolution of political institutions may change how a particular instrument is used, so that, over time, the same instrument may produce different and less satisfactory results.

Korea is at a crucial turning point. Of course, its recent economic performance has been reasonably strong notwithstanding that growth rates have now dropped below the double-digit rates of the mid-1980s. But the increased incidence of conflicts between government and business suggests troubling contradictions in economic policymaking. Korea's policy goals are increasingly those of an advanced industrial economy: to become more competitive in advanced industries and to maintain market shares in key world markets. Yet the most visible instruments of Korean industrial policy, including especially credit policy, have been inherited from a simpler economy. These tools are not well adapted to addressing the country's new economic objectives and are rapidly becoming politicized. As we argue here, this conflict between goals and means is undermining the credibility of industrial policy and is delaying the development of institutions that will have to be important in the economy's next phase of growth.

In this chapter we argue for a "new compact" between business and government as the core of the policy approach of the 1990s. This compact would disengage the government from direct intervention, especially in the financial sector, and shift authority over resource allocation to the private sector. To balance these new freedoms, private firms would be exposed to greater competitive pressure and firmer regulatory oversight. Government would focus its attention on maintaining a firm but predictable regulatory environment, building greater consensus around a vision of a fair and sophisticated economy, and developing the human and technological resources required to make this vision a reality.

A shift to such a compact is consistent with the policy experiences of the several major industrial economies reviewed in this chapter. As in France, such a compact may be difficult to develop because the bureaucracy, comfortable in its traditionally important (and highly successful) leadership role, will be reluctant to relinquish authority. Yet the need for a shift could become especially urgent—and even more difficult to engineer—if the ongoing democratization process puts an end to the insulation of Korea's technocratic bureaucracy.

The Industrial Policy Menu

Rationales for Intervention

Just why an economy should utilize industrial policy is subject to much confusion. Some authors treat the question of industrial policy almost as a choice between religions—between the "old" Anglo-Saxon economics of competitive markets and the "new" political economy of government-directed capitalism. This is a false dichotomy. Modern analysis provides both rigorous rationales for industrial policy and arguments against interventions based on several popular justifications.

Some of the frequently cited goals of industrial policy are not supported by rigorous analysis. For example, although there are good reasons to shift resources from slow to fast-growing sectors in the course of economic development, this does not itself require an active industrial policy, because market forces (barring critical distortions) also generate such shifts. Still other popular goals provide a recipe for losses rather than benefits. One popularly cited goal is to raise the value added of domestic industry by supporting high-value-added branches. Yet this typically requires the transfer of capital from productive uses in labor-intensive (and therefore low-value-added) industries to relatively unproductive uses in capital-intensive (and high-value-added) industries. For example, Yoo (1990) has estimated that in the early 1970s capital was used approximately four times as productively in Korea's clothing and footwear sector as in other manufacturing sectors.

Over the 1980s, however, rigorous arguments for industrial policy have been developed. One category of arguments focuses on externalities associated with specific industries. Some activities create technology or improve resources in such a way that the investing firm cannot fully capture the benefits as private profit. In these cases, protection or subsidization can expand the scale of the externality-generating activity and create social gain. At early stages of industrialization, a new firm may create externalities simply by importing a foreign technology and proving to other firms that foreign techniques can be successfully adapted to local conditions. In more advanced economies, externalities are likely to be limited to newer, technology-intensive industries. In mature economies, industrial adjustment may also involve externalities; for example, under the social arrangements of advanced economies, much of the cost of maintaining and relocating unemployed workers is borne by the state. In this context, industrial intervention may be designed to smooth the private adjustment process in order to minimize the socially borne costs of unemployment.

A second category of arguments focuses on strategic support for domestic firms in global, oligopolistic markets. In this setting, appropriate government intervention can help domestic firms capture (from foreign firms) a larger share of the international "pool" of excess profits. These strategic arguments apply most directly in internationally concentrated markets such as aircraft. Even in this "ideal" industry, empirical studies do not suggest that countries have been able to capture large benefits from strategic trade policy. The case is weaker for relatively competitive sectors such as automobiles and semiconductors, where all but a few companies fail to make significant profits.

Thus, although it is now recognized that industrial policy can be justified, it is also clear that many conventional arguments for it do not pass analytical scrutiny. The case for intervention is strongest for new, export-oriented industries (which facilitate the diffusion of foreign technology) in developing economies and new technology-intensive industries (which result in inappropriable gains to other firms and sectors) in advanced economies. Intervention may be also justified in declining sectors if some rigidity distorts the economy's internal ability to adjust. Yet the arguments for industrial intervention are typically subtle. There is little justification for using such simple indicators as sectoral growth rates or value-added ratios to direct industrial policy; the rationale has to be based on estimates of elusive externalities.

Costs of Intervention

The key argument against intervention is that faulty intervention is worse than neutrality; poor targeting diverts resources from economically beneficial activities to inefficient ones. Governments often follow a hunch to support a particularly prestigious or difficult technology, even though there is no clear evidence of market failure. Examples of such mistakes abound in the industrial policies of Europe (Concorde) and Japan (artificial intelligence), and they have also resulted in costly mistakes in Korea. Instances of faulty targeting have continued even after the costly "white elephants" of the heavy and chemical industry promotion drive; the Korean government was slow to support the development of microcomputers and memory chips, which now appear to be major winners, but it did support the development of a minicomputer that is unlikely to find a market beyond government-related procurement (Clifford 1991).

In some policy environments, industrial policy may not even get a fair chance to be successful, because targets are chosen on political rather than economic criteria. To a greater or lesser extent, political institutions tilt intervention in favor of powerful, rather than economically meritorious, industries. Established, "sunset" sectors often have an especially strong advantage against emerging "sunrise" sectors. Moreover, given the possibility that politically strong groups can manipulate industrial policy, the support for an active approach is likely to be greatest in countries that have powerful special interests. For these reasons, in some political circumstances industrial policy is more likely to be misdirected than accurately targeted.

Even correctly targeted intervention has costs. The taxes required to finance industrial subsidies, for example, withdraw resources from other activities and distort economic decisions in the taxed sectors of the economy. Alternatively, policies that raise a targeted sector's revenues through protection tend to distort the consumption decision and reduce welfare. And intervention can draw substantial resources into nonproductive activities such as lobbying.

Thus the decision to adopt an active industrial policy ultimately involves the weighing of costs and benefits. The question is not whether a particular industrial objective is desirable, but whether industrial policies make the achievement of the objective more likely, and whether the incremental contribution outweighs the risks and costs involved. Korea's future policies must be evaluated with these demanding criteria in mind. There is no single, durable conclusion in the industrial policy debate; past successes provide little guidance for the future. The answers vary across industries, countries, and time.

Instruments of Intervention

The effective implementation of industrial policies requires sophisticated institutions for setting policy goals and efficient instruments. Targeting requires a great deal of information and difficult technical judgments. Thus active industrial policies require a powerful, capable, technocratic institution that is, on one hand, sheltered from the political process, and on the other, well connected to industry expertise. This requirement has been met in only a small number of countries, including Korea. As we discuss below, it appears that economic decision making is becoming politicized in Korea, and that the business-government relationship is now more strained than is desirable from the viewpoint of information flows. Much will depend on how Korea's democratization process evolves—specifically, whether it moves toward the stable, single-party model that has helped to keep the bureaucracy insulated in Japan.

In a market setting, industrial policy also requires instruments that substantially change the incentives facing industry. This can mean lowering input costs or increasing revenues. The instruments that operate on costs include direct subsidies on (or preferential access to) capital, energy, imports, and other key inputs. The main instruments that operate on revenues are protection from domestic or foreign competition and government procurement. Because an economy with relatively small markets (Korea fits this category for many of the advanced products it now makes) is limited in using its own markets to support the development of new industries, Korea has relied largely on cost-reducing instruments to implement its industrial policies, including especially directed credit.

The range of available, legal instruments has sharply narrowed over time. Many of the instruments of industrial policy have been controlled or declared illegal by international agreements. Protection through tariffs has been gradually eroded by successive GATT rounds. The direct use of subsidies in export-oriented industries has been curtailed under the GATT Subsidies Code and in the face of aggressive countervailing actions by the United States and other countries. The Procurement Code has also begun to limit the extent to which governments can give preference to their own producers. Finally, for reasons of domestic economic efficiency, most countries have liberalized trade and permitted greater competition in domestic markets, further limiting the scope for setting industrial incentives. As a result of these changes, the industrial policies of most advanced countries have shifted either toward greater neutrality (as in the case of Germany and Japan) or toward greater reliance on credit policy, competition policy, and functional support for technology as the main instruments of industrial policy.

Industrial Policies in Advanced Countries

A comparison of industrial policies across industrial economies reveals a surprisingly wide range of institutions and policies. The main trends in industrial policy are outlined in Tables 19.1 and 19.2 for the four largest industrial countries. Table 19.1 shows that the objectives of policy have varied widely, both across countries and within countries over time.

France has had highly variable policies, including periods of aggressive intervention in the 1960s and early 1970s, and again in the mid-1980s. Industrial interventions were scaled back substantially outside these periods. German policies have

TABLE 19.1 Objectives and institutions of industrial policy

	United States	West Germany	France	Japan
Historical evolution	Emphasis on maintaining neutral, competitive environment and on defense capability. Since early 1980s relaxation of antitrust policy and ad hoc interventions to support declining and import-threatened industries. Debate on more focused industrial policy remains unresolved.	Neutral until mid-1960s; from 1966 on, concerted focus on high-technology industries. Substantial support for declining industries in late 1970s; shift to greater neutrality and privatization in 1980s.	Increasingly ambitious plans until mid-1960s; starting in 1966 emphasis on concentrating investments in national champions. From mid-1970s retrenchment to narrower portfolio of high-technology projects. In 1980s broad nationalization effort tried and abandoned; focus now on technology and privatization.	Emphasis on heavy industry until late 1960s and on knowledge-intensive industry since. Gradually relinquished most selective instruments: abandoned exchange controls in 1962 and formally liberalized trade between 1960 and late 1970s. Policies now concentrate on new technologies.
Dominant policy objectives	Maintain competition; develop defense technology; prevent system-threatening bankruptcies; moderate import threat.	Promote new technology; support declining industries and promote adjustment.	Develop "industries of the future"; achieve international competitiveness; facilitate adjustment; foster national champions.	Develop technology for knowledge-intensive industry; facilitate adjustment.
Implementing institutions	Department of Defense; trade representative and other trade-oriented agencies; ad hoc legislative pressure and presidential commissions.	Economics Ministry; "concertation" councils with government-business-union representation.	Ministry of Industry, Planning Commission; economywide and sectoral plans; state-owned banks and firms; dialogue with industry.	MITI; "Visions"; business-government-public sector councils; dialogue with firms and industry.

Source: Entries for each country are based on the following: *United States:* Wachter and Wachter (1981), Wescott (1983), Behrman (1984), OECD (1989c); *West Germany:* Weiss (1984), Wagenhals (1983), USITC (1984), Smith (1983), Legler (1990), OECD (1986), OECD (1989b); *France:* Franko and Behrman (1984), USITC (1984), Adams and Stoffaes (1986), OECD (1989a), DeWitt (1983); *Japan:* Lee and Yamazawa (1990), Taylor and Yamamura (1990), USITC (1983), Fukushima (1984), Behrman (1984), Adams and Ichimura (1983), Komiya, Okuno, and Suzumura (1989).

TABLE 19.2 Instruments of industrial policy

	United States	West Germany	France	Japan
Credit policy	Private banks and private equity, bond and venture capital markets finance industry. Government guarantees are provided in exceptional system-threatening circumstances.	Most industry financing is handled by large private banks, which also oversee management through equity positions. The government directly provides export credit and some venture capital.	Directed credit pervasive during early 1980s. Government owned or controlled financial in stitutions (esp. Caisse de Depots and Credit National) accounted for significant share of credit provided to business. Additional funds available for specific policy purposes. Aggressive denationalization and decontrol under way.	Group-related banks provide most capital. Direct lending through the Japan Development Bank modest since early 1960s. Until liberalization in 1980s the cost of capital was below world levels. Various policies promote savings. Entry in financial sector is restricted and banks are subject to "window guidance" from Bank of Japan.
Taxes and subsidies	Accelerated depreciation promoted investment in 1980s; new investment incentives now modest due to equalized earned income and capital-gains tax rates.	Special tax benefits are used to implement regional objectives and energy policy, and to support declining industries such as coal and steel.	Various tax exemptions are used to promote new investment and mergers. There is a substantial tax credit for R&D. Subsidies provided for state-owned industry.	Although tax credits and deferrals played an important role in early industrial policy, tax rates have become relatively uniform across industries since mid-1970s.
Protection	Antidumping and subsidy laws and 301 clause give leverage for negotiating VERs and import expansion by other countries.	Protection has declined, except in politically important sectors such as agriculture, forestry, mining, and textiles.	Tariffs and quotas set by EEC, but special procedures used to protect favored industries. Foreign operating investment invited in high-tech areas but controlled strategically.	Formal barriers modest. Low rate of manufactured imports suggests invisible barriers, likely through the distribution system. Foreign investment surprisingly limited.
Competition policy	Until early 1980s antitrust policy was aggressively aimed at preventing market dominance. Policy has been more permissive since and antitrust exemptions are available for joint research.	Anticartel policy has been in force since the early 1950s, but exemptions have been granted in distressed industries and some mergers were encouraged in the 1970s.	Mergers were encouraged between the mid-1960s and early 1980s to create "national champion" firms.	Mergers encouraged until mid-1970s. Anticartel policies weak; relatively high prices suggest producers exercise market power in domestic markets. Officially sanctioned cartels operate in depressed industries.
Science and technology	Considerable R&D financed by Defense Department, but government resists redirecting these funds to non-military applications.	Extensive support is offered to research from the government directly and from commercial R&D spurred by fiscal incentives.	Specific industries designated "industries of future." Ministry of Industry coordinates research and industrial policies and greater R&D spending.	MITI-sponsored joint industry research projects have been linked to major improvements in the competitiveness of key industries.
Government participation	Defense procurement plays an important role in high-technology demand.	Government ownership in several major firms divested in the 1980s. Government procurement favors domestic products.	Half of economy, including all major banks, nationalized in early 1980s. Government procurement supports domestic producers. Aggressive privatization now under way.	Little direct ownership. Government procurement favors domestic industry.

Source: See Table 19.1.

experienced more moderate shifts, with a period of relatively intense involvement in the 1970s preceded and followed by more neutral policies. Japan's industrial policies moved gradually from intensive intervention in the 1950s and 1960s to general, functional approaches in the 1980s. Throughout, however, Japan has maintained powerful institutions for facilitating dialogue and information exchange between government and industry. The United States has no central institutions charged with setting industrial policy. Considerable research support is provided through defense-related procurement and research, and from time to time the government has also become involved in industrial adjustment and rescue efforts through ad hoc interventions. Overall, the U.S. policy stance has been pro-competitive and relatively neutral.

Some general conclusions appear to hold for all four economies. First, the use of directed credit has declined over time, spurred by the increased sophistication and international integration of capital markets. France, which departed from this trend briefly in the early 1980s by nationalizing its major banks and establishing policy priorities for the allocation of credit, paid a high price in accelerated inflation, payments deficits, and lost growth.

Second, policies that have encouraged mergers and combinations and discouraged combinations involving foreign firms have also been largely abandoned. In the United States, policy trends have also favored market decisions: antitrust policies are used with declining frequency to prevent mergers even of horizontal competitors. In recent years, both national and international merger activity have accelerated in anticipation of the single European market and under the pressure of international competition.

Third, subsidies and preferential government procurement remain important, notwithstanding international agreements that limit the use of these instruments for internationally traded commodities. Table 19.3 shows that subsidies are equal to approximately 2 percent of GDP in Europe, 1 percent in Japan, and 0.6 percent in the United States. The composition of subsidies (as shown for Germany in Table 19.4) generally favors declining sectors such as agriculture, mining, and ship-

Table 19.3
Subsidies in OECD countries

	General government, % of GDP	
	1982	1988
France	2.2	1.9
Germany	1.8	2.2
Japan	1.4	1.0
United States	0.8	0.6

Source: OECD (1989b).

building; basic social sector industries such as transportation, education, housing, and health; and one infant industry, aerospace.

Fourth, policies aimed to promote technology have become more prominent. As Table 19.5 shows, R&D spending increased in the 1980s in each of the four developed economies analyzed in comparison with Korea. The private sector performs two-thirds of this R&D in the private sector in Europe and the United States, and nearly all in Japan, but in all countries private R&D spending is vigorously encouraged by tax advantages. Whereas subsidies favor declining industries, not surprisingly, R&D spending favors new and emerging sectors. As Table 19.6 shows, R&D expenditures were highest in such industries as aerospace and computers; intermediate in heavy industries subject to rapid change, such as automobiles and chemicals; and lowest in stable industries such as foods and beverages, shipbuilding, and oil refining.

Despite considerable variations in the thrust and intensity of industrial policies, it is difficult to find a relationship between industrial policy and economic

Table 19.4
Structure of subsidy rates, Germany

	Subsidy as % of value added	
Sector	1973–74	1979–82
Agriculture, forestry	88	180
Electricity, gas	4	3
Coal mining	30	93
Other mining	16	19
Iron and steel	1	4
Oil refining	4	4
Shipbuilding	12	30
Aerospace	65	32
Food and beverages	0	0
Construction	1	2
Trade	1	1
Railways	168	100
Shipping	28	21
Other transport	16	17
Postal services	4	10
Credit institutes	3	1
Insurance	5	10
Housing	51	57
Education service	22	18
Health and veterinary service	13	17
Other services	2	2

Source: OECD (1986).

Table 19.5

R&D spending in OECD countries and Korea (percentage)

	1963	1975	1981	1987
Share of R&D in GDP				
France	1.50	1.80	1.97	2.28
Germany	1.40	2.22	2.42	2.71
Japan	1.20	1.96	2.32	2.78
United States	2.90	2.27	2.45	2.72
Korea		0.42	0.64	1.78
Share of R&D financed by industry				
France		—	68	68
Germany		—	82	84
Japan		—	98	98
United States		—	68	66
Korea		33	56	80

Source: Wescott (1983), Nelson (1990); data on Korea is from the Korean Ministry of Science and Technology.

Table 19.6

Structure of R&D expenditures, 1980

	R&D spending as % of output			
	France	Germany	Japan	U.S.
Aerospace	14.1	21.6	1.0	36.1
Office machines	10.1	6.5	5.9	19.3
Electronics	11.4	8.1	6.2	14.4
Pharmaceuticals	5.1	8.3	8.8	9.5
Scientific instruments	2.5	2.1	2.8	10.5
Electrical machinery	1.6	8.1	3.5	7.3
Automobiles	2.1	2.7	2.8	3.0
Chemicals	1.9	3.4	3.0	1.7
Other manufacturing	—	5.4	—	—
Nonelectrical machinery	0.6	2.3	1.7	1.8
Rubber, plastics	1.6	1.6	1.2	1.2
Nonferrous metals	0.6	0.6	2.3	0.7
Stone, clay, glass	0.5	0.7	0.9	1.0
Food, beverages	0.1	0.2	0.4	0.2
Shipbuilding	0.2	0.6	3.6	—
Oil refineries	0.5	0.5	0.3	0.7
Ferrous metals	0.3	0.6	1.1	0.6
Fabricated metals	0.5	0.7	0.5	0.6
Paper, printing	—	0.2	0.1	0.4
Wood, furniture	—	0.2	—	0.3
Textile, footwear	0.1	0.2	0.2	0.3
Average	2.0	2.1	1.6	2.6

Table 19.7
Export shares of technology-intensive products (percentage)

	1965	1975	1984
France	7.3	8.4	7.7
Germany	16.9	16.8	14.5
Japan	7.3	11.6	20.2
United States	27.5	24.5	25.2
Korea[a]	0.0	0.5	2.9

Source: McCulloch (1990), World Bank estimates.
[a]Estimates based on exports of electrical goods, electronic equipment, and transport equipment.

Table 19.8
Total factor productivity growth (percentage per annum)

	1960–73	1973–79	1979–86
All manufacturing			
France	5.3	2.9	1.4
Germany	3.4	2.4	1.4
Japan	5.6	3.5	4.2
United States	2.5	0.3	2.7
Korea[a]	—	—	2.7
Machinery/equipment			
France	3.8	3.3	-0.2
Germany	2.4	2.2	1.3
Japan	6.2	6.0	9.2
United States	5.2	0.5	
Korea[a]	—	—	4.0

Source: OECD (1989a), Zeile (1991).
[a]1972–85.

performance, either across countries or over time. Since industrial policies were typically aimed to increase the production of advanced manufactured goods, it is surprising to see that France, Germany, and the United States had essentially constant market shares in the world exports of technology-intensive goods over the 1965–84 period (Table 19.7). Japan substantially increased its market shares over this time, and especially so during the most recent decade, under moderating and increasingly functional interventions. There is also no obvious relationship between policy approaches and productivity growth (Table 19.8). In France, productivity growth was slowest during the period of the most intense industrial policy activity, and especially so in the machinery and equipment industries targeted by French policies. The United States, which had no coordinated industrial policies at any time during this period, lagged behind Europe in the 1970s but outperformed Europe in the 1980s.

Overall, there is a tendency for interventions to moderate with economic maturity. This trend is evident in the pattern of intervention across the four industrial countries, and also within Germany and Japan over time. Other similarities between Japan and Germany, the two most successful industrializers of the past fifty years, may be much more important than their approaches to policy. In these countries national policy goals were shared by business and labor and easily implemented through effective relationships between industry and the financial sector. Special linkages between banks and firms in these economies helped to finance risky, long-term investments without government intervention. Both countries also pursued policies that were largely market-conforming, and both eventually converged on R&D support as the centerpiece of their industrial policy.

Korea's Industrial Policy Environment

Evolution of Korean Policies

The broad outline of Korean industrial policy is captured by the three-period approach popularized by the World Bank (1987). In the first phase, which began in the mid-1960s, policies favored exports in general, without specific sectoral biases. The exchange rate was set competitively and a wide range of interventions helped to offset the anti-export bias of the trade regime (Westphal 1978). Credit allocations favored exporters, reflecting higher social returns on export-oriented investments than on import-substituting investments. This regime rewarded size and growth with access to scarce capital and set the stage for the formation of large family-owned firms and the future trend toward the concentration of Korean industry.

The second policy phase, spanning the mid-1970s, was characterized by intense, selective interventions favoring heavy and chemical industries (HCI). No other period in Korea's recent economic history has produced as much controversy as this episode. Initially treated as a fiasco by most Korean scholars, it has been reevaluated in recent years in a more neutral (World Bank 1987) and even favorable light (Amsden 1989; Auty 1991; Wade 1990). The HCI policy was implemented through directed, subsidized credit, selective protection, regulations affecting industrial entry, and direct government involvement in industrial decision making. The regime had some of the expected negative consequences: inappropriate industry choices, excessively capital-intensive investments in the targeted sectors in an otherwise capital-starved economy, and the retardation of trade and financial liberalization. But it also had positive results: a discrete jump in Korea's "level of industrialization," the development of some potentially world-class firms, and inroads into lucrative, Japanese-dominated markets (Petri 1988; Leipziger and Song 1991).

The third policy phase began as Korea abandoned HCI preferences during the traumatic economic adjustments of 1979–81 (see Cho 1988; Leipziger and Petri 1989; Zeile 1990). The policy shift was hastened by severe problems in the nontargeted, labor-intensive sectors of the economy and by the balance-of-payments crisis created by the second oil shock. The shift away from intensive interventions in heavy industry was well timed. It permitted Korea to take advantage of the boom in manufactured exports in the mid-1980s and allowed it to embark on a trade liberalization path that was essential for maintaining a cooperative relationship with the United States. Korea also began to liberalize its financial sector, but, as shown below, much less progress was made in this field.

The functional thrust of Korea's new industrial policy was formalized by the Industrial Development Law of 1985 and the simultaneous repeal of selective industrial promotion laws. Support for research and technology replaced directed credits as the mainstay of policy. Yet government did not abandon ad hoc industrial interventions. It restricted entry into industries where size was thought to be necessary for export success; for example, Samsung was prohibited from entering the automobile market several times in the 1980s. The government sharply disciplined Kukje (the sixth largest *jaebul* at the time) but came to the rescue of other conglomerates heavily involved in shipbuilding, machinery, and other overextended industries. It also helped to rationalize sunset industries such as shipping and overseas construction with government-mandated mergers, divestitures, and closings.[1] Most important, it kept the badly damaged financial sector solvent.

Under the Industrial Development Law, eight industries have been rationalized.[2] Textiles were given three years to adjust, and dyeing two; and both were granted access to subsidized loans to modernize their equipment.[3] Two other industries designated for rationalization, ferro-alloys and fertilizers, were both uneconomic in Korea as far as one can judge. The former was treated in a fashion analogous to Japanese restructuring under the Depressed Industries laws.[4] Specifically, two existing copper-smelting firms were merged into a domestic monopoly, future entry was barred, and the industry was thus "saved." In manganese steel, three firms were designated to supply the Pohang Steel Company on a long-term, exclusive basis, under a contract arranged by MTI.

One basic question that arises is whether an independent banking sector would have been willing to finance these restructurings. If not, was some fundamental market failure involved? The fact is that it is difficult to find here the externalities that would usually justify industrial policy. With the possible exception of dyeing, none of these industries was pursuing new activities where learning or dynamic economies of scale might have been important. As in other countries, these interventions probably reflected political considerations and fears of the effects of large corporate failures on the banking system. It is fair to say that the Korean government has been more successful in disengaging itself from sunrise industries than from sunset industries.

The government has also remained closely involved in credit policy. Moreover, its basic role in rationing credit has in turn forced it to become involved in many additional ad hoc regulations. In 1989, for example, the government became concerned that the *jaebul* were using bank credit to speculate in real estate rather than to invest in manufacturing. It is understandable why they should have wanted to do so: since the profitability of real estate investments was in effect determined by the high cost of funds in the nonpreferred sectors, the *jaebul* could earn very attractive margins on money borrowed at commercial bank rates. Thus the government had to invent a new decree that required conglomerates to divest themselves of "excess land holdings," and it eventually bought land from the companies at handsome prices.

Efforts to limit the *jaebul* share to 65 percent of new low-cost bank loans have created a similar chain of unintended interventions. Faced with the deteriorating export performance of several major companies, the government sought a way to make additional funds available for productive investment. To justify the additional credit, the *jaebul* were told to select three core operations for specialization, which would be exempted from credit limits. Many chose their most capital-intensive activities, including especially petrochemicals—certainly not the industries Korea needs to foster for the future. It is not clear whether the government simply aimed to make more credit available to the *jaebul* and used the specialization directive merely to make the policy more palatable.

What is clear is that access to credit remains rationed and politically determined, and it repeatedly involves the government in questionable new pronouncements and regulations. Controlled systems are always subject to abuse, as several recent incidents illustrate; the interest differentials that arise from domestic and international capital controls produce a great temptation for selling access to bank credit and for bringing foreign capital into domestic capital markets.

These pressures suggest a need for new approaches to financial policy, as well as clearer policies of regulatory control. In Korea's increasingly politicized environment, reformed institutions much more than bureaucratic oversight are needed for economic supervision. Also at stake is the government's relationship with the *jaebul*. Each new effort to control *jaebul* behavior generates new mistrust between business and government—a trend that is reinforced by popular resentment against *jaebul* economic power. Yet these developments reduce the likelihood of a cooperative business-government relationship such as exists in Germany or Japan.

Domestic Environment in the 1990s

There was more political change in Korea during the last of the 1980s than in the previous two decades, and the transformation of the country's political institutions is likely to proceed rapidly in the future. A similar acceleration of change is evident in the international economic environment, where the emergence of new regional blocs and the challenges of socialist transition are likely to trigger major global economic realignments. These forces require new approaches with regard both to policy goals and to the instruments used to pursue them.

Sophistication Savings rates are setting new records, and investment remains high in both physical and human capital. The relative size of the technology-intensive sector has expanded, and the economy's manufacturing sector is becoming far more sophisticated and diversified. Many Korean firms now rank among the world's largest and are becoming more thoroughly integrated into the world economy through corporate alliances and foreign investments. The growing complexity of the economy implies a larger gap between the technical information available to firms and that available to the government. Moreover, more sophisticated markets and larger firms are better able to evade or circumvent government directives.

The changing capabilities of the economy also affect the rationale for intervention. The objectives of the 1960s and 1970s—gaining experience in risk taking and in the acquisition of foreign technology—are less applicable today. Korea has acquired enormous experience with importing technology; its private sector is alert to new opportunities and understands its own capabilities. Korean companies are experienced in international markets and no longer need the stimulus of government intervention to look abroad.

The new directions of the economy suggest, however, that technology-related market failures may be increasingly important. New technology inevitably leaks out, to the benefit of firms other than those investing in it. New industries may involve learning externalities: one firm's experience facilitates the growth of the whole industry through human capital investments or the development of subcontractors. Evidence of such externalities can be found in the extensive geographic and national clustering of high-technology industries. An especially important source of market failure is human capital. Because Korean workers move a great deal from company to company (like U.S. workers, but unlike Japanese workers), individual firms have insufficient incentive to invest in human capital. This leaves this important form of investment to private capital markets, which are notoriously flawed in financing human capital investment.

Changing Goals Economic progress is likely to remain a preeminent goal in Korea, but the relative importance of other, competing factors is rising. Rising incomes allow people to pay more attention to issues such as the environment, housing, health, and equity. In addition, the relative political weight of the middle and working classes is increasing as the political process becomes more open. Thus government is under great pressure to show improvements in the standard of living and in the distribution of the fruits of economic progress. There is also pressure to avoid policies that might raise the suspicion that specific companies or individuals are being helped to become rich at the expense of society.

It is tempting to argue that these changing attitudes will shift priorities from investment to consumption. Yet the experience of high-growth countries, including Japan, demonstrates that savings and investment can remain high even as income levels rise. During rapid growth, incomes outpace households' ability to increase consumption and savings rise. However, countries experiencing rapid growth often find their stock of social investments to be insufficient, and they are thus likely to shift the structure of investment toward public goods such as infrastructure, housing, safety, and the environment. Social investments are capital-intensive and, like the HCI investments of the 1970s, could lead to a general scarcity of capital in other branches of economic activity.

Pluralism Korea's economic ministries, like those of Japan, have a tradition of considerable decision-making capacity and authority. Economic policy has been implemented by relatively independent ministries, with little day-to-day intervention from the political process. But Korea's ability to maintain this Japanese-like separation between politics and economic decision making is under challenge; the government's political position is more fragile. Through the inclusion of the opposition in the Democratic Liberal Party, the architects of Korea's political process are clearly aiming to achieve the stability that underpins Japan's political model. Whether this initiative will succeed is unclear; Korea's societal structure and political process are more adversarial than those of Japan and, at least for now, seem to involve more direct conflict over economic objectives. This foreshadows much greater political involvement in future economic decisions. In such a political context, it has been argued in the United States, it is preferable to have no strong instruments of industrial policy that are vulnerable to political manipulation.

External Environment in the 1990s

Korean industrial policy must face various worldwide changes that affect the incidence of market failures and restrict the utility of various policy instruments.

Technology Recent technological trends have dramatically shortened the life cycles of products, especially in electronics, machinery, and automobiles. These trends are changing the importance of various factors of production: know-how is becoming more valuable, and raw labor less so. To remain internationally competitive, a company must pioneer, or at least rapidly copy, new features in its product line. Japan has emerged as a leader in these skills and is developing new competitive approaches—for example, made-to-order automobile manufacturing—which are designed to increase the importance of technology and design. Computer-aided design and manufacturing contribute to these trends, since they reduce the time and cost involved in implementing rapid product changes.

In some industries product turnover is associated with increasingly large and risky technological investments. In semiconductor manufacturing, for example, there are multiple technical solutions for achieving a particular product, and unless a company pursues all approaches it may risk not participating in a given generation of technology and perhaps falling far behind for many years. To a lesser extent, similar considerations apply even in conventional industries such as automobiles, where each model now has to generate substantial sales over a shrinking life cycle in order to break even. Under these circumstances, large companies in all major countries have begun to establish alliances and partnerships for sharing the risks involved in developing new technology.

To participate in this high-level competition, Korean firms must be comparable in size and capability to their foreign competitors. In fact, Korea's *jaebul* are quite successful in attracting major foreign partners; consider, for example, the collaborations between Hyundai and Mitsubishi, Ssangyong and Daimler-Benz, and Goldstar and Hitachi. Samsung is perhaps the most successful example of a firm that has reached a global stage of development; it manufactures a broad range of products and has now succeeded as one of the first companies in the world to develop the 64-megabit DRAM memory chip. Thus Korea's electronics output in 1991 was the fourth-largest in the world (behind the United States, Japan, and Germany) and nearly double that of Taiwan (Clifford 1991).

It is sometimes argued that Taiwanese development patterns, which were less favorable to large firms, have also resulted in internationally competitive industries. (Unlike Korea, Taiwan used market interest rates to provide relatively equal access to credit by all sectors.) Indeed, Yoo (1990) has found that, despite the credit preference given to heavy and chemical industries in Korea, the two countries were roughly equally successful in increasing their export shares to the OECD in heavy and chemical industries. It appears that Taiwan's smaller, equity-financed companies have been faster at responding to new market opportunities. But a closer examination of the evidence also shows that Taiwan has been less able to maintain its market positions over a longer period of time and has had to shift production abroad to keep down labor costs (Mody 1989). Many experts judge the long-term prospects of Korean companies to be superior.

Yet the lessons go both ways. As a result of directing credit to larger companies, Korea has a much weaker infrastructure of small-component and parts suppliers than Taiwan. Its larger companies are too diversified and need to become nimbler. At the same time, Taiwan has begun to foster larger-scale investments, for example, through a publicly funded venture capital fund.

More International Players Competition in international manufacturing is expanding, reflecting the declining cost of communications and a worldwide trend toward more open, investment-friendly policies. The new manufacturing powerhouses include not only China and ASEAN but also Latin American economies such as Mexico and Chile, and eventually, one expects, the formerly socialist economies of Eastern Europe. These countries cannot yet challenge the technological lead of Korea, Taiwan, and Singapore in key manufacturing industries; but with the support of sizable direct investments from Japan, other advanced countries, and the NIEs themselves, they are rapidly moving into advanced manufacturing.

The internationalization of manufacturing is facilitated by the "disaggregation" of manufacturing processes into several stages, with each stage implemented in the most advantageous locale. Computers and advanced communications now make it possible to coordinate increasingly complex production chains. Such chains might include, for example, the manufacturing of sophisticated components in Japan, the manufacturing of more standardized components in Thailand or Indonesia, and final assembly or marketing activities in a low-wage country or in a final market such as the United States. In some cases, technological hubs such as Singapore coordinate the manufacturing operations by sourcing components throughout East Asia.

These technological trends are strongly reinforced by the internationalization of the Japanese economy, which is driven by the high yen, high savings, and shortage of labor in Japan. Capital outflows have also been facilitated by the liberalization of Japanese finance; Japanese investors are aggressively exploiting the large differentials between domestic and foreign rates of return which emerged under earlier financial constraints. The pace of investment in East Asia has slowed in the early 1990s, but the underlying trends are robust, and they are likely to spread to other parts of the world which achieve a suitably stable and open economic environment.

New Regional Alignments European integration, now planned to encompass a single market of 250 million people and a still wider free trade area, will create a large but perhaps also less easily accessible market. The North American Free Trade Area will generate a market of similar size, and with time it might also include several Latin American countries. The truly novel feature of these regional alignments is that each includes its own potential low-wage manufacturing base. Thus the agreements may divert investment away from traditional manufacturing bases such as East Asia and into Latin America and Eastern Europe, which enjoy more secure access to European and North American markets.

Pacific Asia, at the same time, is steadily becoming more important as both a market and a source of supply. Despite such proposals as the East Asian Economic Grouping, no major, formal economic agreement is likely to emerge in the near term (Petri 1992), but ongoing market forces will continue to increase actual economic integration. Especially rapid progress is likely in some "growth triangles"—including perhaps a triangle that links Korea with Pacific Russia and western Japan—which involve small free trade areas designed to exploit intense, local trading opportunities. Eventually, these small trade zones may provide further impetus for general liberalization. The ultimate impact of these trends cannot be assessed precisely, but Korea's trade, too, is likely to shift toward Pacific Asia.

With or without blocs, the trading environment in Europe and North America is likely to become more demanding, in part because Korean industry is increasingly competing directly against European and American firms. After the Uruguay Round, there will also be new disputes over the implementation of developing country agreements on market access, especially in services. The enforcement of subsidies and other disciplines is likely to become stricter. The financial sector is bound to play an increasingly contentious role in trade diplomacy, both because it represents a key service and because preferential access to credit is a form of subsidization. These trends will further constrain Korea's traditional tools of industrial policy.

In sum, the foregoing yields five key conclusions on the objectives and implementation of industrial policy:

1. The rationale for intervention is shifting from conventional infant industry arguments to technological and strategic issues. The latter are best addressed by functional rather than selective interventions.

2. The key instruments of selective industrial policy—especially directed credit—are becoming ineffective because they can be evaded by large, sophisticated, internationally connected companies. Continued efforts to rely on these instruments undermine the government's credibility and lead to a deterioration of business-government relationships.

3. Although they create problems for the execution of industrial policy, large companies are essential for building Korea's international competitiveness in technology-intensive industry.

4. Selective interventions are also constrained by domestic perceptions of unfairness and an increasingly contentious international trade policy environment.

5. The risks involved in maintaining a system of selective interventions are growing because (a) the government is less able to guide Korea's increasingly complex economy, and (b) Korea's economic decisions are increasingly shaped by political rather than economic considerations.

In the remaining sections of this chapter we analyze the implications of these conclusions for future policy directions.

Korean Industrial Policy in the 1990s

Despite substantial adjustments during the past decade, Korean industrial policy continues to be dominated by the goals and instruments of the 1970s. These are less effective in the 1990s, and they undermine the government's efforts to establish a long-term economic strategy. In the interest of greater clarity and predictability, a new approach needs to be developed, including a new compact between business and government.

A key problem that underlies many of the contradictions of recent industrial policy is the government's ambivalence toward the *jaebul*. We have argued that Korea needs strong, independent companies to pursue global technologies and markets. The government appears to recognize this point and has given the *jaebul* considerable support. Yet it is also concerned about the power of the *jaebul* and has been reluctant to abandon financial and other instruments that allow it to control their behavior. The result has been inconsistent, ad hoc interventions, as well as conflicts and policy mistakes. This dynamic is damaging the government's credibility in economic policy, and it undermines efforts to establish a cooperative business-government relationship.

The key question is, Who should guide the industrial sector—the financial sector, industry itself, or government? In most successful advanced economies, decision-making authority rests in the hands of those best able to judge market opportunities—industrial firms and the financial sector. Inevitably, Korea must also move in this direction. But as lender of last resort, the government also has the responsibility to ensure that financial markets exercise appropriate discipline. Strong, independent monitoring agencies are required for this task.

Putting this another way, we favor giving conglomerates full responsibility for their futures, but only subject to transparent and rigorously enforced rules. We favor independence for banks, but also subject to regulations that ensure safety through adequate capital and supervision. Adopting this approach would represent a radical departure from Korea's past policies. It would require the strengthening of independent regulatory institutions, such as the Bank of Korea, Korean Fair Trade Commission, and the Office of Bank Supervision and Examination, as well as the creation of new ones, such as bank examination offices for nonbank financial institutions and government banks.

Financial sector reform is complicated by the fact that the financial system has not adequately dealt with the losses it suffered during earlier periods of government-directed lending. Yet this is not a reason for maintaining a high level of government involvement in financial sector governance. The legacy of past financial crises should be tackled, once and for all, by bold, transparent solutions to the problem of nonperforming loans, such as the issue of new government debt to replace irretrievably lost assets. As part of the deal that makes the commercial banks viable, they should be given full authority and responsibility for maintaining sound portfolios in the future.

At the same time, the government's profile should rise in other areas. Above all, the government must ensure that the policy environment is stable and predictable—that is, conducive to rational private planning and high rates of saving and investment. This requires, in addition to the well-known macroeconomic policies, new institutions of dialogue between business, labor, and government. It also requires efforts to improve public perceptions of economic progress in such areas as tax policy, infrastructure development, and social programs.

Education and applied research, including cooperative ventures that improve the dissemination of technology within Korea, represent likely areas of market failure and should be supported vigorously. The government should also encourage private investments in technology-intensive industries. Many of these policies can be implemented through a modern, functional incentive system—for example, through investment- and education-oriented tax policies. The government also needs to be aggressive in assuring access to key markets through negotiations and aid.

These changes would shift the focus of government activity but by no means diminish its overall role in economic affairs. The government would pursue economic progress by clarifying its vision of a technology-based society, enhancing the country's technological resource base, and encouraging private investment and technological progress. It would also foster a consensus-oriented decision-making system by disengaging itself from the increasingly acrimonious relationship with private business and by focusing more attention on public goods such as safety, environmental protection, and infrastructure. To do so requires the strengthening of financial institutions to provide the oversight of the use of the nation's considerable savings and a clear regulatory structure to ensure its fair application.

Jaebul Policy

Korea's large, closely held conglomerates cast a long shadow over many aspects of industrial policy. Financial sector policies, for example, are closely linked to the *jaebul* issue because the government has relied on the credit allocation process to influence *jaebul* behavior. Regulatory policy is also tied to *jaebul* policy because the conglomerates exercise market power in many sectors of the economy. Because the *jaebul* are largely owned by individuals (see Table 19.9), policies toward them are inevitably colored by issues of equity and social justice.

Yet the *jaebul* have played a central role in Korea's industrial development and are vitally important to the future of Korea's technology-intensive industries. Policy toward the *jaebul* is also complicated by the fact that these companies are highly leveraged and have enormous appetites for investment capital. In the face of these conflicting demands on policy, the government's attitude has been ambivalent. Efforts to liberalize the financial system have been slowed by the goverment's desire to make low-cost capital available to the *jaebul* and to control their behavior. Share ownership has been restricted and the selection of bank managers has been heavily influenced by the government in order to keep the *jaebul* from assuming

Table 19.9
Ownership of large business groups

	Share of ownership (%)		
Group	Individuals	Group companies	Total clan control
Hyundai	27.5	40.3	67.8
Daewoo	9.8	40.6	50.4
Samsung	8.5	44.7	53.2
Lucky-Goldstar	7.6	30.6	38.3
Hanjin	27.7	24.3	52.0
Ssangyong	7.6	34.4	42.0
Sunkyung	21.5	29.1	50.6
Korea Explosives	10.5	30.8	41.4
Daelim	7.6	31.6	39.2
Lotte	3.6	20.0	23.6
Average of top 5 groups	—	—	52.4
Average of top 10 groups	—	—	48.2
Average of 61 large business groups	—	—	47.1

Source: EPB data submitted to National Assembly. Data as of April 1991.

control over the banks. And as we have shown, efforts to ration credit to the *jaebul* in the face of their inevitably high demand for below-market-rate credit have led to a chain of contradictory interventions.

The *jaebul* dilemma has driven Korean industrial policy into gridlock. The government is reluctant to transfer decision-making authority to market institutions because it fears that the *jaebul* will capture the banks and abuse their power. At the same time, the government's continuing role in the economy prevents the emergence of independent private institutions, such as powerful banks, which could impose financial discipline on *jaebul* behavior. In the meantime, the government's instruments of control are becoming less effective, and the relationship between the government and business, instead of moving toward harmony, is turning confrontational.

The best way to address this dilemma is to relax direct financial controls on the *jaebul* and to shift the job of controlling them to independent regulatory bodies, and to greater private sector competition in both the financial and industrial sectors of the economy. This new compact would give the *jaebul* more freedom in raising and spending money, both at home and abroad. At the same time, it would subject them to stricter regulation and greater competition. The result would be checks on *jaebul* behavior administered by private institutions and markets instead of government. This would free the government to pursue broader micro- and macroeconomic objectives.

With greater private sector autonomy, some of the distortions that now lead to conflict and uneconomic actions could, with appropriate oversight, be eliminated. Interest differentials between bank and nonbank instruments would narrow, removing the temptation for arbitrage. With greater private participation (even if by the *jaebul* themselves) the banks would assume greater responsibility in lending and in corporate oversight. Of course, these changes require "cleaning up" the inherited capital structures of both firms and banks, which would otherwise not be viable in a commercial context. None of these changes would have to be implemented overnight—unlike Eastern Europe, the Korean economy is functioning very well—but a predictable, preannounced strategy is needed to signal a viable transition trajectory.

Financial Sector Policy

The financial sector has not yet achieved the level of maturity common in other East Asian countries, let alone the OECD countries.[5] Until recently, for example, Korea had a virtually nonexistent equity market. With government's desire in the 1980s to reduce the leveraging of Korean firms, the stock market expanded, with *jaebul* issuing equities but retaining large shares for individual owners. Almost three-quarters of Korean equity shares in 1988 were held by individuals, compared to a quarter in Japan (see Hahn 1989). Japan has made the transition from first-generation ownership, and now approximately 73 percent of shares are held by corporate owners (e.g., banks, trusts, and corporations), compared to a mere 31 percent in 1949 and 57 percent in 1970.

There are, of course, many different models for organizing the relationship between "banks" and "industry"; but in each of the advanced countries there is substantial, independent decision-making authority vested in financial institutions. A weak financial sector may have suited Korean policymakers in the past, because it permitted government to pursue an active industrial policy. It is now a liability that undermines the country's resource allocation process.

The issue of financial liberalization is intricately linked to industrial policy. Before 1988, half the funding for the corporate sector was derived from bank and nonbank debt issues, 20–25 percent from borrowing from abroad, and approximately a quarter from stock issue. Much of this credit was subject to an elaborate credit control system established in 1974, which has allowed government to exercise considerable control over the flow of credit to specific industrial activities and different types of industrial borrowers.

Despite several rounds of liberalization since 1974, credit-based interventions have remained important in the 1980s and early 1990s. In 1984, for example, government froze the credit share of the largest 30 firms and cut off credit altogether to firms with debt–equity ratios above 500 percent. These policies were eventually reversed, though restrictions continued on the real estate or cross-corporate investments of the 49 largest conglomerates. In 1987 the government "urged" 82 firms with 50 billion won or more in bank loans to repay a total of 1 trillion won by issuing public stock. And in 1991 it ordered them to select three core business lines, promising to provide these with better access to credit.

The key to eliminating the need for these interventions is to make the financial sector independent. In a private financial system, effectively regulated and supervised, firms would have clear financial incentives to issue equity, to pursue promising business ventures, and to abstain from high-risk investments. One argument frequently used against the full privatization of the banks is that they would be controlled by the *jaebul* themselves. According to the Office of Bank Supervision and Examination, the top 10 conglomerates officially own about 20 percent of the top six commercial banks. As Table 19.10 shows, the role of large shareholders is even greater in nonbank financial institutions (NBFIs). Conglomerates also increased the number of NBFIs they owned—the top 10 owned 31 NBFIs in 1989—because the credit obtained from them is not subject to the same credit controls as normal bank credit.[6]

To prevent *jaebul* ownership, the government limits bank credits to a single customer and bank ownership by a single customer to 8 percent of capital. Because corporate ownership is hard to trace, this restriction probably does not limit ownership as much as it appears. But if the 8 percent rule did work, it would distribute ownership responsibility so widely across different owners that banks would face little effective shareholder oversight.

As S. W. Nam (1990) has argued, it would be better to regulate the behavior of banks and the *jaebul* than to limit bank ownership. Indeed, since NBFI ownership is currently unregulated, it makes good sense to develop a comprehensive system of prudential regulation instead of ownership rules that have questionable merit, are difficult to enforce, and lack credibility. We now examine the implications of such a regulatory regime for the central bank, bank supervisory agencies, and the financial intermediaries themselves.

Central Bank The advantages of central bank autonomy are well known; studies have shown that independent central banks tend to be associated with low-inflation environments because they are more insulated from the political process (Cargill 1988). In Korea, maintaining a low rate of inflation has been a traditional national policy objective, and the Bank of Korea (BOK), much like the Bank of Japan, has pursued this objective despite its close ties to the Ministry of Finance. With recent political changes, however, the case for insulating the BOK from political pressures, more along the model of Germany or the United States, is becoming stronger.

Commercial banks would have been unable to provide policy-based loans without the backing of the BOK. The BOK has provided substantial overdraft privileges, reaching at times 7–10 percent of the commercial banks' asset base, and a special window to rediscount policy loans. Rather than calling in nonperforming loans, commercial banks have been able to pass on their balance sheet problems to

TABLE 19.10

Ownership structure of financial intermediaries, end of 1989 (percentage)

	Five NCBs	Provincial banks	Investment/ finance	Securities	Merchant banking	All listed companies
Securities companies	3.4	2.8	1.4	2.7	9.6	5.1
Insurance companies	14.2	3.5	0.8	2.8	0.4	2.6
Other financial intermediaries	3.2	1.9	6.2	7.5	35.4	3.2
Nonfinancial corporations[a]	17.2	20.7	18.3	24.8	14.2	20.6
Foreigners	0.0	2.7	0.7	1.8	23.8	2.1
Domestic individuals	61.8	68.5	72.4	60.3	16.4	54.6
Total	100.0	100.0	100.0	100.0	100.0	100.0[b]
Small shareholders	77.7	76.0	66.6	65.5	55.1	–
Corporations	14.5	11.2	10.5	14.2	40.3	–
Individuals	63.1	64.8	58.1	51.4	14.7	–
Largest stockholders	5.8	9.4	16.1	26.2	17.6	–
Other stockholders	16.5	14.6	17.3	8.3	27.2	–
Corporations	16.0	11.5	7.7	6.8	25.2	–
Individuals	0.5	3.0	9.5	1.6	2.0	–

Source: Nam (1990).

Note: Includes listed companies only: 10 provincial banks, 29 investment and finance companies, 22 securities companies, and three merchant banking corporations. Figures are simple averages.

[a]Includes securities investment companies.

[b]Includes 11.8 percent held by government-invested companies.

the BOK, shifting the cost of policy errors to the least transparent portion of the financial system—the central bank's income statement. In the new regulatory regime, the BOK should abstain from lending to financial institutions, except according to guidelines that reflect the bank's responsibilities for monetary policy and the safety of Korea's financial system.

Industrial policy has also affected financial sector policy in the sphere of interest rate determination. Interest ceilings have enabled preferred creditors to borrow at rates well below those available to others. Minister Sakong's liberalization program of 1988 was only partially carried out, and a recent study found that "lending rates and most rates in the primary securities market are still very rigid and unresponsive to market conditions, indicating that the Korean financial market is still far from being fully integrated and operating purely on a competitive basis. This phenomenon seems to be partly due to limited interest rate deregulation and partly to an inertia and mentality inherited from the time when most financial institutions were run like public enterprises" (Nam 1991:15). Further interest rate deregulation is thus required, particularly since the capital market will eventually have to be opened to foreigners.

Bank Supervision The legacy of government intervention is still evident in the balance sheets of commercial banks. Korean banks are marginally profitable, but serious portfolio problems have been rolled over for many years.[7] Past attempts to clean up balance sheets have not been fully successful, nor has provisioning against potential losses been as vigorous as needed. Between 1985 and 1988 alone some 9.8 trillion won in financial assistance was provided to restructured firms at government behest.[8] Thus, at the end of March 1988, 16 percent of commercial bank loans were to firms designated under official rationalization programs. Of 650 billion won in uncollected interest payments by commercial banks, more than two-thirds was owed by rationalized firms. These losses depressed bank net profits relative to total assets, which reached an all-time low of 0.19 percent. Reforms in loan loss provisioning, capital requirements, and lending rules are essential for strengthening banks and introducing greater discipline in the financial sector.

The supervision of commercial banks in Korea is the responsibility of the Office of Bank Supervision and Examination, an agency affiliated closely with the BOK. The NBFI sector, which now intermediates 60 percent of financial savings, is regulated by the Ministry of Finance. In most developed countries, bank supervisory agencies are independent and subject to transparent reporting requirements. To be sure, regulatory independence is not always sufficient for proper oversight, as is so evident in the case of the U.S. savings and loan crisis. But it is also true, as demonstrated by the recent financial scandals in Japan, that ministries of finance have too many other conflicting goals to operate effectively as an overseeing body. A separation of the regulatory/supervisory functions from government business and political influence is a necessary, although not sufficient, requirement for effective supervision.

Supervision is made difficult in Korea by the widespread practice of cross-corporate guarantees. Affiliates of the *jaebul* endorse each other's liabilities, so that the distinction between active and contingent liabilities is blurred. BOK data submitted to the National Assembly suggest that conglomerates in Korea have offered payment guarantees on liabilities equal to at least three times their net worth. For the top five *jaebul*, their potential liabilities exceed their net worth by a factor of 3.7 (see Table 19.11). Banks are not able to say with clarity what capital is being pledged as collateral for a given liability. Overall lending by conglomerates is not tallied in a way that makes it possible to assess the risks facing a bank's portfolio. This problem is exacerbated by the blurred line between personal borrowing by *jaebul* owners and corporate borrowing, weak corporate disclosure requirements, and generally weak coordination among regulatory agencies (see S. W. Nam, Chapter 10 in this volume).

Many of these issues have been addressed by supervisory agencies and by the CAMEL system of the Bank for International Settlements (BIS).[9] The BIS recommends a risk-adjusted approach to capital adequacy. The approach requires banks to categorize their assets by type of risk. In the Korean context, for example, loans for speculative real estate purchases would be rated differently from plant and equipment investment, as would loans backed by tangible assets from loans guaranteed by other *jaebul* affiliates. Appropriate risk-based capital requirements would encourage the risk-adjusted pricing of capital and would make it unnecessary to apply special ad hoc constraints on bank portfolios or lending activities.[10]

Bank and Nonbank Intermediaries Bank management is still not independent in Korea, with most CEOs appointed or recommended by government. According to Nam (1991), policy loans still account for almost half of domestic credit, including the lending of government banks to industry, agriculture, and housing. Banks and NBFIs cannot charge risk-based prices for capital. Entry into the banking sector is restricted and price competition is limited. These factors have retarded the development of independent financial intermediaries. Banks and other financial institutions

Table 19.11
Net worth and debt payment guarantee of core business of conglomerates, August 1991

Group	Net worth (bil. won) (A)	Debt payment guarantee (bil. won) (B)	Guarantees per won of net worth (B/A)
Hyundai	1,332	2,168	1.6
Daewoo	1,218	5,364	4.4
Samsung	1,195	5,782	4.8
Lucky-Goldstar	1,295	4,507	3.5
Hanjin	390	2,108	5.4
Ssangyong	1,052	1,980	1.9
Sunkyung	759	689	0.9
Korea Explosives	734	1,974	2.7
Daelim	3	631	233.7
Lotte	235	29	0.1
Average of top 5 groups	5,430	19,929	3.7
Average of top 10 groups	8,213	25,232	3.1
Average of top 30 groups	12,413	38,433	3.1

Source: BOK data submitted to National Assembly.

have not been able to exercise purely commercial judgments or develop commerical lending expertise.

The effect of a repressed financial sector on industrial development is hard to quantify, but given Korea's present stage of development it is almost certainly negative. Compared to either Japanese or Taiwanese statistics, Korea's financial deepening is low, as measured for example by the ratio of domestic financial assets to GNP. Although equity financing is increasing, the debt–equity ratios of Korean firms still make them vulnerable to interest rate cycles. These problems not only affect the allocation of resources but also severely constrain the use of monetary policy as a tool of macroeconomic management. In addition, the slow development of the financial sector makes it difficult to liberalize the service and capital accounts, despite growing international pressure in these areas.

In sum, Korea needs to develop a stronger, more competitive, independent banking sector. This will require settling on a one-time basis the questionable portfolios of commercial banks. It will also require a transfer of decision-making authority to shareholders and the managers who represent them. To check the potential abuse of these new opportunities, supervisory practices will have to be strengthened and barriers to entry reduced. These changes cannot occur overnight, but far more rapid progress is possible than experienced during the 1980s. With such changes, the Korean financial sector can begin to accumulate the authority and experience needed to manage resource allocation privately, following the successful models of Germany and Japan.

Competition Policy

The structure of industrial ownership in Korea is the result of deliberate policies that concentrated capital in the hands of fast-growing firms. Size became an especially important objective during the HCI drive of the 1970s. Intercompany shareholding was also permitted, leading to further concentration of ownership. In the wake of these policies, the *jaebul* have assumed a commanding position in Korean industry. The top 10 *jaebul*, for example, own half of the 100 largest firms and account for 62 percent of the value of manufacturing shipments (Lee and Lee 1990).

When measured by traditional concentration ratios, however, business concentration in Korea is similar to that in other countries and has even declined in the past decade.[11] Nor do the *jaebul* seem to focus their activities exclusively in highly concentrated industries (Table 19.12). But they do play an important role in a majority of those commodies identified as "market dominating" by the Korean Fair Trade Commission (KFTC), that is, in the 131 markets where one producer accounts for more than 50 percent of output or the top three exceed 75 percent of output. More than two-thirds of these products were dominated by the largest 30 *jaebul* in 1989 (see Lee and Lee 1990). In more than 80 percent of these markets, a conglomerate had to compete with at most one other conglomerate taken from the top 20 firms. In effect, a small number of *jaebul* share markets with each other in a wide variety of industries. In this setting the temptation to contain competition must be very high.

The first regulatory action of consequence in Korea, the Price Stabilization and Fair Trade Act of 1975, was initiated not to improve competition but rather to halt inflation. The focus was to "stabilize" markets by designating monopoly products for surveillance and subsequent price action if the price was found to be excessive. Unfair trading practices were defined as unwarranted price movements rather than market domination. Worried by the increased size of the conglomerates, the government introduced the Monopoly Regulation and Fair Trade Act in 1980 to curb big business power. The KFTC was strengthened in 1986 with rules designed to limit economic concentration by restricting intercompany ownership[12] and regulating, for the first time, anticompetitive mergers by business groups. The KFTC took a step toward independence in 1989, but it is still affiliated with the Economic Planning Board.

Although the concentration in the manufacturing sector declined and intercompany investments fell in the 1980s, the policy changes did not dramatically change the competitive environment. In the KFTC's first decade (1980–89), over 2,000 business mergers were approved and only two rejected. The number of business group subsidiaries has dramatically increased; according to KTFC data, there have been 532 horizontal mergers, 369 vertical mergers, and 1,102 diversifications into new business areas. Nor was much progress made on reducing entry barriers. The government's own assessments indicate that 89 key industries were subject to

Table 19.12

Business concentration, 1982 and 1987

	Number of markets (and %)					
	Top 5 groups		Top 10 groups		Top 30 groups	
Market share	1982	1987	1982	1987	1982	1987
Over 80%	33	42	48	64	74	103
	(7.2)	(6.5)	(6.9)	(7.4)	(6.6)	(6.9)
60–80%	31	38	39	47	58	81
	(6.7)	(5.9)	(5.6)	(5.4)	(5.2)	(5.4)
40–60%	74	82	92	98	121	151
	(16.1)	(12.7)	(13.2)	(11.3)	(10.8)	(10.1)
20–40%	87	141	120	186	190	291
	(18.9)	(21.8)	(17.2)	(21.4)	(16.9)	(19.4)
Less than 20%	236	345	398	494	678	873
	(51.2)	(53.2)	(57.1)	(56.8)	(60.3)	(58.2)
Total	461	648	697	869	1,125	1,499

Source: Lee (1986) and Lee and Lee (1990).

regulatory entry barriers in 1988. Some 218 regulatory statutes in 54 laws affected these industries, with many regulations on entry, standards, pricing, lines of business, production capacity, and geographic markets (EPB 1991:6).

In international perspective, Korean competition policy appears to lie closer to that of the EEC than that of the United States. U.S. antitrust laws actively discouraged monopolistic and collusive behavior by preventing mergers among competitors and by dissolving monopolies such as Standard Oil, American Tobacco, and more recently AT&T. U.S. deregulation policies promoted vigorous competition, which in the case of airline deregulation has produced particularly large-scale entry and exit from the industry. Competition policy has been less vigorously enforced in the post-Reagan era.

Audretsch (1989) notes that, in the EEC, industrial policy encourages size for international competitiveness, while competition policy discourages market-dominating positions. Individual European countries, however, have taken a permissive approach. France actively encourages mergers to create national champion firms. In Germany, cartels can be legal if registered; 241 cartels existed in Germany in 1983 (Audretsch 1989), of which 52 were focused on foreign markets.

In Japan the total number of legal cartels was 505 in 1982, including 59 export cartels. In both Germany and Japan structurally depressed industries are eligible for rationalization programs, including government-organized cartels. Though the fair trade concept in Japan is patterned on U.S. antitrust laws, in reality antitrust exemptions and legal cartels are much closer to the norm (see Caves and Uekusa 1976 and Audretsch 1989 for further discussion). Small and medium-industry cartels, often regional rather than industry-specific, exist for long periods, as do rationalization cartels created under depressed industry laws.

Like other countries with ambitious industrial policies, Korea has consistently encouraged its conglomerates to be competitive internationally and has not intervened aggressively to create competition at home. In 1987 only 44 percent of Korean domestic markets (by sales volume) were classified as competitive, with "competitive" defined as the top three firms controlling less than 60 percent of the market (Lee and Lee 1990). Evidence on the degree to which firms exploit their oligopoly positions is not available, but Korea may fall into that group of countries where many consumer goods (including consumer goods made in Korea) seem to be more expensive in Korea than in other countries.

Should Korea pursue a more aggressive approach toward competition? The answer is "somewhat." Although present policies appear to benefit producers at the expense of consumers, consumers' losses can be limited without vigorous competition policy simply by setting the barriers to imports at a low level. Since most large companies actively compete in foreign markets, they have a strong incentive to improve productivity and reduce costs. The key is to provide adequate regulatory incentives for true gains to be passed on to domestic consumers as well. In theory, as long as import barriers are relatively low, competition policy is redundant; foreign competition can provide market discipline at low administrative cost. Experience in other countries has shown, however, that import discipline can be circumvented, and it is important for Korea to avoid this trap. Moreover, it may be even more important to focus competition policy on nontraded industries.

Trade Policy

Trade policy must be closely integrated with industrial policy. Korea's exceptional success in international markets argues for careful adjustments that maintain the momentum of past achievements. Particularly important are policies that maintain market access to Korea's key export markets, such as the United States; initiatives that diversify Korea's trade toward countries emerging as important new markets; and policies that maintain the competitiveness of Korean companies. Below, we consider the implications of the industrial policy issues examined above for export policy and import policy.

Export Policy Although the fundamental features of Korea's pioneering export promotion system (an unusually effective drawback system implemented through the domestic letter of credit and automatic access to low-cost export finance) remain in place, the direct subsidies implemented during the early stages of export promotion (such as tax advantages to exporters, excessive wastage allowances on duty-free imports, and highly subsidized access to long-term capital) have long since been dismantled. This is a good thing, since such policies would have made its exports to the United States and other countries vulnerable to countervailing penalties. It should be anticipated that export incentives will weaken somewhat if interest ceilings are lifted on bank credit.

The major new role of government in the 1980s on the export side has been as gatekeeper for domestic industries and negotiator vis-à-vis major markets for access. The proportion of Korean exports subject to voluntary export restraints has grown significantly and now accounts for a major percentage of exports. The issue of "voluntarily" limiting exports cannot be separated from access to Korea's market and leads to the difficult policy area of managed trade. What is clear is that there remains a legitimate economic and political role for government in promoting market access and seeking to maximize national welfare gains.

Import Policy After a substantial liberalization of the import system in the late 1960s, the share of commodities subject to restrictions increased up to the late 1970s. In the 1980s Korea sharply expanded the list of liberalized commodities; today more than 95 percent of all commodities, including virtually all manufactured commodities, are "automatically approved." Some progress has also been made in abolishing special laws that restrict even automatic approval commodities.

Still, questions remain about the openness of the Korean market. The volume of consumer goods imports remains low, and the prices of imported goods, especially higher-quality goods, are high in comparison to other markets. Reportedly the government has taken direct action—including income tax investigations—against purchasers of foreign luxury goods such as passenger cars. There are also programs that provide low-interest loans to reduce imports ("localization") and to shift imports from Japan to the United States ("diversification") for selected commodities. In general, the government initially tended to handle the trade imbalances of the past few years with new policy interventions rather than rapid adjustments in the exchange rate, both on the upside in 1987–88 and on the downside in 1990–91.

These questions notwithstanding, Korea is very open by international standards, and one cannot argue that import restrictions are compromising the economy's linkages with world markets. The export ambitions of Korean companies have kept them intensely engaged in international competition, with visible benefits in technological progress and productivity. Thus the question whether interventions should continue hinges on other policy goals.

Korea's future import policy should be guided by four broad objectives. On the side of continued protection, the main argument is that some infant industry protection may be justified in selected new industries. We would prefer other, functional policies for this purpose. It is also worth noting that Korea has done exceptionally well in the past in introducing new products into international markets without significant prior domestic sales (perhaps because other instruments bore the brunt of the support of new industries).

Three other objectives suggest a further relaxation of restrictions. First, exposure to international competition is a better approach for controlling the economic power of the *jaebul* than an aggressive and acrimonious competition policy. Second, improved access to imported consumer goods would provide consumers with an important symbol of Korea's increased standard of living. (As in Japan, high-quality consumer goods may also act as a substitute for increasingly expensive goods in relatively fixed supply, such as real estate and housing.) Third, a liberal import policy is essential for maintaining market access in the United States and Europe, and it could help Korea develop new markets in Eastern Europe and Asia. On balance, these arguments call for continued progress on trade liberalization, which in turn implies a greater role for exchange rate adjustments in handling cyclical adjustments in the balance of payments.

Toward a New Business-Government Compact

Korean industrial policy, which has guided the Korean economy through nearly three decades of spectacular growth, is showing its age. The policy has not been adjusted fully to the new challenges facing the economy, and it has not recognized the obsolescence of its key instruments. In this chapter we have argued that the time has come, as in other advanced industrial countries, to disengage the government from managing the economy's structural development and to adopt a new compact to delineate the responsibilities of business and government.

Under this compact, responsibility for allocating investable funds would be shifted fully to the industrial and financial sectors, but at the price of greater competitive discipline and regulatory oversight. Establishing this new framework presents an enormous challenge to policy. In addition to compexities of the transition, the government will have to maintain macroeconomic stability and the momentum of savings and investment, tackle the "new" market failures associated with Korea's rising technological level, and develop new institutions to increase the flow of information, reduce conflict, and ensure the equitable sharing of the fruits of economic progress.

What "model" industrial policy is to be sought for Korea today? It is not U.S.-style policy, since the role advocated here envisions a more direct and coordinated involvement in the development of technological resources and the supervision of the financial system. It is not French-style policy, since it advises against strong interventions through government-arranged mergers and large-scale policy lending. Of the models reviewed in this paper, it is closest to the German and Japanese models. These countries are unique in having exceptionally close working relationships between the financial and industrial sectors. These relationships assure the availability of long-term capital for the development of new products and industries and also impose close supervision and considerable financial discipline on industrial companies. It is hard to see how a government could improve on the results of these mechanisms, and in both countries the government has essentially withdrawn from influencing the allocation of credit.

As the Korean financial sector develops into a stronger, independent entity, it may well generate German- or Japanese-style relationships between financial institutions and their industrial clients. If the independence of the financial sector is achieved under present restrictions (effectively enforced) on maximum share ownership, the result will approximate the German model, with powerful, independent banks playing the lead role in the relationship between industry and the financial sector. There may well be transitional difficulties with this model, because under dispersed ownership it will take time to establish strong, private control over bank operations, and the government, as lender of last resort, will have a strong incentive to maintain control. It may therefore be necessary to use Korea's traditional corporate strength to create (nonfamily) banking *jaebul* to develop Korea's banks into respectible world-class financial institutions. Though unconventional, this may be the most effective way to strengthen domestic financial institutions.

If the independence of the financial sector is achieved in the absence of limits on share ownership, the result is likely to approximate the Japanese financial setup, with industrial companies closely linked to their group bank through cross-ownership ties. In this scenario, each major *jaebul* might acquire and develop a group bank; and being responsible for its safety and profitability, it would have a strong incentive to use the bank to impose strict financial discipline on its various subsidiaries.

Korea has used the lessons of Japanese experience very effectively in developing its own policies in the past. The Japanese model remains attractive at this juncture, but some important differences are becoming significant. In its early stages, Japanese industrial policy relied on some of the same instruments Korea later adopted to encourage investments in infant industry and to develop home markets as a base for international competitiveness. But in its later stages, Japanese policy has moved away from intervention, focusing instead on information sharing and coordination and on indirect, functional support for new activities. In this context, and deprived of its earlier powerful tools, Japanese industrial policy has relied heavily on the cooperative relationships that bind Japanese business and government and Japanese business and labor.

Can Korea base its industrial policy on similar relationships? We would argue, not yet. John Zysman (1983) suggested that an effective industrial policy requires (1) a national consensus on broad economic goals, (2) effective policy instruments, and (3) a forceful bureaucracy. It is worth reviewing briefly how Korea stands on these criteria.

Korea had a consensus on economic policy through the Fifth Republic, primarily because the government was strong enough to impose its vision on all critical actors. No similar cohesiveness seems to exist today. A particularly divisive issue is the distribution of gains from Korea's phenomenal growth. Long considered a model of equitable growth, Korea is now facing a widening distribution of wealth (Leipziger et al. 1992) and a less equal distribution of income. Koreans are no more able to afford housing today than they were twenty-five years ago. Due to minimal taxes on capital gains and on earnings on financial assets, many see the tax system as inequitable. There is considerable public resentment of the skewed distribution of wealth, and especially of the family-owned *jaebul*. These concerns can easily explode in protest, as they did in the massive strikes of 1988 and 1989.

We have shown that Korea's traditional policy instruments, including especially directed credit, are becoming less approximate and effective. Moreover, given an increasingly pluralistic political process, it is now likely that industrial policy will be drawn into the political arena, where it will lead to conflict and debate rather than to concerted action. Given this risk, it is best for government to focus its energies on a broad vision of technological development—consensus surely exists on this—leaving the more contentious allocational issues to private market forces.

Finally, although Korea's bureaucracy remains highly competent, it too needs to adjust to new political and economic realities. Despite its elite status, the bureaucracy's power is declining relative to the legislature and business. Government officials are now frequently called to testify before the National Assembly, and business and social leaders are increasingly willing to criticize government policies in public. Rightly or not, the bureaucracy is sometimes viewed as authoritarian and arbitrary. Policies that exacerbate the conflict between the government bureaucracy and different elements of the public—policies that involve promulgating rules and decisions and disciplining individuals or companies, even if these enjoy general popular support—will ultimately reduce the government's effectiveness as a coordinating agent.

Thus, the role of the bureaucracy itself needs to be strengthened by shifting its functions toward predictable, regulatory, coordinative activities rather than ad hoc policy measures. The government will need to bridge the interests of producers and consumers, of business and politicians. These objectives will be best achieved through ongoing consultations and predictable actions based on statutory powers rather than political imperatives.

NOTES

1. For details of the shipping rationalization program, for example, see World Bank 1987:vol. 2).
2. See J. H. Kim (1990) for a complete review.
3. See World Bank (1987:vol. 2) for a case study of the textile industry.
4. The Law of Special Measures for the Stabilization of Specific Depressed Industries was adopted in 1978, with a five-year horizon, and was then replaced in 1983 by the Law of Special Measures for the Structural Improvement of Specific Industries. See Peck, Levin, and Goto (1985), and World Bank (1987:vol. 2) for details.
5. For a review of financial issues, see S. W. Nam (1990, 1991, and Chapter 10 of this volume).
6. The conglomerates have also used their NBFIs to circumvent regulations, such as the 27 September 1980 decree halting further real estate puchases by the *jaebul*.
7. Profitability is directly related to the share of nonperforming loans in nationwide commercial banks, according to P. J. Kim as reported in Nam (1991).
8. This included, according to Office of Bank Supervision and Examination data reported by Nam (1991), funds to subsidize interest rates for restructured industries, extended grace periods on repayments, fresh concessional funds to firms taking over unprofitable firms as part of official workout and placement of firms, and straight writeoffs.
9. CAMEL refers to examinations of a bank's capital, assets, management, equity, and liquidity.
10. Direct controls on real estate lending activity have also proved ineffective in Japan, where banks founded special (for the most part wholly owned) subsidiaries to circumvent restrictions on their real estate portfolios. Many of these subsidiaries are now in severe financial trouble.

11. Lee and Lee (1990) report that the percentage of shipments accounted for by the largest 100 firms fell from 45 to 39 percent between 1977 and 1987 and that the employment shares by the top 100 fell from 24 to 20 percent over the period.

12. Investments by large business groups in other companies of the group cannot in total exceed 40 percent of the net assets of the company.

REFERENCES

Adams, F. Gerard, and Shinichi Ichimura. 1983. "Industrial Policy in Japan." In F. Gerard Adams and Lawrence R. Klein (eds.), *Industrial Policies for Growth and Competitiveness.* Lexington, Mass.: Lexington Press.

Adams, William J., and Christian Stoffaes, eds. 1986. *French Industrial Policy.* Washington, D.C.: Brookings Institution.

Amsden, Alice H. 1989. *Asia's Next Giant: South Korea and Late Industrialization.* New York: Oxford University Press.

Audretsch, D. 1989. *The Market and the State.* New York: New York University Press.

Auty, Richard M. 1991. "Creating Competitive Advantage: South Korean Steel and Petrochemicals." *Tijdschrift voor Economische en Sociale Geografie* 82:15–29.

Behrman, Jack N. 1984. "Industrial Strategies in the United States." In Robert E. Driscoll and Jack N. Behrman (eds.), *National Industrial Policies.* Cambridge, Mass.: Oelschlager, Gunn and Hain.

Brander, J., and B. Spencer. 1981. "Tariffs and the Extraction of Foreign Monopoly Rents under Potential Entry." *Canadian Journal of Economies* 14:371–389.

Cargill, T. 1988. *Central Bank Independence and Regulatory Responsibilities.* Seoul: Monetary Economics Institute.

Caves, Richard, and Masu Uekusa. 1976. *Industrial Organization in Japan.* Washington, D.C.: Brookings Institution.

Cho, Y. J. 1988. "Effect of Financial Liberalization on the Efficiency of Credit Allocation: Some Evidence from Korea." *Journal of Development Economics* 29.

Clifford, Mark. 1991. "Taking on the Titans." *Far Eastern Economic Review,* 31 October, 66–69.

De Melo, Jaime, and David Roland-Holst. 1990. "Industrial Organization and Trade Liberalization: Evidence from Korea." PRE Working Paper Series, no. 518.

DeWitt, Francois. 1983. "French Industrial Policy from 1945–1981: An Assessment." In F. Gerard Adams and Lawrence Klein (eds.), *Industrial Policies for Growth and Competitiveness.* Lexington, Mass.: Lexington Books.

Eads, G., and K. Yamamura. 1987. "The Future of Industrial Policy." In K. Yamamura and Y. Yasuba (eds.), *The Political Economy of Japan,* Vol.1. Stanford: Stanford University Press.

Economic Planning Board (EPB), Republic of Korea. 1991. *Economic Bulletin,* no. 91–07 (July): 6.

Franko, Lawrence G., and Jack N. Behrman. 1984. "Industrial Policy in France." In Robert E. Driscoll and Jack N. Behrman (eds.), *National Industrial Policies.* Cambridge, Mass.: Oelschlager, Gunn and Hain.

Fukushima, Kiyohiko. 1984. "Public Use of Private Interests: Japan's Industrial Policy." In Robert E. Driscoll and Jack N. Behrman (eds.), *National Industrial Policies.* Cambridge, Mass.: Oelgeschlager, Gunn and Hain.

Hahn, Daewoo. 1989. "Analysis of Ownership and Control in the Large Corporations." *Monthly Economic Review* 404. Korea Development Bank.

Holloway, Nigel, and Mark Clifford. 1991. "Creaking Conduits." *Far Eastern Economic Review*, 13 June, 64–68.

Kim, J. H. 1990. "Korea's Recent Experiences with Industrial Restructuring in Response to Trade Friction." Mimeo. Korea Development Institute, Seoul.

Kim, K. H. 1991. "Housing Prices, Affordability and Government Policy in Korea." Asia Regional Discussion Paper, World Bank, Washington D.C.

Komiya, Ryutaro, M. Okuno, and K. Suzumura, eds. 1989. *Industrial Policy of Japan*. New York: Academic Press.

Krugman, Paul. 1979. "Increasing Returns, Monopolistic Competition, and International Trade." *Journal of International Economics* 9:395–410.

Lee, Chung H., and Ippei Yamazawa. 1990. *The Economic Development of Japan and Korea*. New York: Praeger.

Lee, Kyung Tae. 1991. "Policy Measures to Reduce Industrial Concentration and Concentration of Economic Power." In Lee-Jay Cho and Yoon Hyung Kim (eds.), *Economic Development in the Republic of Korea: A Policy Perspective*. Honolulu: East–West Center.

Lee, Kyu-uck. 1986. "The Concentration of Economic Power in Korea: Causes, Consequences, and Policy." In Lee Kyu-uck (ed.), *Industrial Development Policies and Issues*. Seoul: Korea Development Institute.

Lee, Kyu-uck, and J. S. Lee. 1990. *Kiupjipdan Kwa Kyungjeryuk Jipjoong* (Business groups and economic power concentration). Seoul: Korea Development Institute.

Legler, Harald. 1990. "The German Competitive Position in Trade of Technology-Intensive Products." In Gunter Heiduk and Kozo Yamamura (eds.), *Technological Competition and Interdependence*. Seattle: University of Washington Press.

Leipziger, D. M., and Peter A. Petri. 1989. "Korean Incentive Policies toward Industry and Agriculture." In J. G. Williamson and V. R. Panchamukhi (eds.), *The Balance between Industry and Agriculture in Economic Development*. New York: St. Martin's.

Leipziger D. M., and S. Y. Song. 1991. "A Review of Korea's Trade Pattern." Asia Regional Discussion Series, World Bank, Washington, D.C.

Leipziger, D. M., et al. 1992. *The Distribution of Income and Wealth in Korea*. Washington, D.C.: World Bank.

McCulloch, Rachel. 1990. "The Challenge to U.S. Leadership in High Technology Industries." In Gunter Heiduk and Kozo Yamamura (eds.), *Technological Competition and Interdependence*. Seattle: University of Washington Press.

Mody, Ashoka. 1989. "Institutions and Dynamic Comparative Advantage: Electronics Industry in South Korea and Taiwan." Industry and Energy Department Working Paper no. 9. Washington, D.C.: World Bank.

Nam, S. W. 1990. "Institutional Reform of the Korean Financial System." Mimeo. Seoul: Korea Development Institute.

Nam, S. W. 1991. "Korea's Financial Policy and Its Consequences." Mimeo. Seoul: Korea Development Institute.

Nelson, Richard R. 1990. "What Has Happened to U.S. Technological Leadership?" In Gunter Heiduk and Kozo Yamamura (eds.), *Technological Competition and Interdependence*. Seattle: University of Washington Press.

Organization for Economic Cooperation and Development (OECD). 1986. *Economic Surveys: Germany*. Paris.

Organization for Economic Cooperation and Development (OECD). 1989a. *Economic Surveys: France*. Paris.

Organization for Economic Cooperation and Development (OECD). 1989b. *Economic Surveys: Germany*. Paris.

Organization for Economic Cooperation and Development (OECD). 1989c. *Economic Surveys: United States*. Paris.

Peck, M., R. Levin, and A. Goto. 1985. "Picking Losers: Public Policy towards Declining Industries in Japan." Mimeo. New Haven: Yale University.

Petri, Peter A. 1988. "Korea's Export Niche: Origins and Prospects." *World Development* 16(1).

Petri, Peter A. 1992. "One Bloc, Two Blocs or None? Political Economic Factors in Pacific Trade Policy." In Kaoru Okuizumi, Kent E. Calder, and Gerrit W. Gong (ed.), *U.S.–Japan Economic Relationship in East and South East Asia*. Washington, D.C.:CSIS.

Sakong, Il, and Leroy Jones. 1980. *Government, Business, and Entrepreneurship in Economic Development: The Korean Case*. Cambridge: Harvard University Press.

Smith, Eric Owen. 1983. *The West German Economy*. New York: St. Martin's.

Swann, Dennis. 1983. *Competition and Industrial Policy in the European Community*. London: Methuen.

Taylor, Sully, and Kozo Yamamura. 1990. "Japan's Technological Capabilities and Its Future." In Gunter Heiduk and Kozo Yamamura (eds.), *Technological Competition and Interdependence*. Seattle: University of Washington Press.

Uekusa, Masu. 1987. "Industrial Organization: The 1970s to the Present." In Kozo Yamamura and Yasukicki Yasuba (eds.), *The Political Economy of Japan: The Domestic Transformation*, Vol. 1. Stanford: Stanford University Press.

U.S. International Trade Commission (USITC). 1983. *Foreign Industrial Targeting and Its Effects on U.S. Industries. Phase I: Japan*. Publication 1437. Washington, D.C.

U.S. International Trade Commission (USITC). 1984. *Foreign Industrial Targeting and Its Effects on U.S. Industries. Phase II: The European Community and Member States*. Publication 1517. Washington, D.C.

Wachter, Michael L., and Susan M. Wachter, eds. 1981. *Toward a New U.S. Industrial Policy?* Philadelphia: University of Pennsylvania Press.

Wade, R. 1990. *Governing the Market*. Princeton: Princeton University Press.

Wagenhals, Gerhard. 1983. "Industrial Policy in the Federal Republic of Germany: A Survey." In F. Gerard Adams and Lawrence Klein (eds.), *Industrial Policies for Growth and Competitiveness*. Lexington, Mass.: Lexington Books.

Weiss, Frank D. 1984. "Industrial Policy and International Competitiveness in West Germany." In Robert E. Driscoll and Jack N. Behrman (eds.), *National Industrial Policies*. Cambridge, Mass.: Oelschlager, Gunn and Hain.

Wescott, Robert F. 1983. "U.S. Approaches to Industrial Policy." In F. Gerard Adams and Lawrence Klein (eds.), *Industrial Policies for Growth and Competitiveness*. Lexington, Mass.: Lexington Books.

Westphal, Larry. 1978. "The Republic of Korea's Experience with Export-Led Industrial Development." *World Development* 6(3).

World Bank. 1987. *Korea: Managing the Industrial Transition*. Washington, D.C.

Yoo, Jung Ho. 1990. "The Industrial Policy of the 1970s and the Evolution of the

Manufacturing Sector in Korea." Working Paper no. 9017. Seoul: Korea Development Institute.

Young, Soogil, and Jungho Yoo. 1982. "The Basic Role of Industrial Policy and the Reform Proposal for the Protection Regime in Korea." Mimeo. Korea Development Institute.

Zeile, William. 1990. "Industrial Policy and Organizational Efficiency: The Korean Chaebol Examined." Program in East Asian Culture and Development Research Working Paper Series, no. 30. Davis: Institute of Government Affairs, University of California.

Zeile, William. 1991. "Industrial Targetting through Government Rationing: The Korean Experience in the 1970s." Program in East Asian Culture and Development Research Working Paper Series, no. 41. Davis: Institute of Government Affairs, University of California.

Zysman, John. 1983. *Governments, Markets and Growth*. Oxford: Martin Robertson.

Zysman, John. 1991. "Productivity Growth in Korean Manufacturing Industries, 1972–85." Program in East Asian Business and Development Working Paper Series, no. 38. Davis: Institute of Government Affairs, University of California.

PART VIII

The Relationship between Labor and Management

CHAPTER 20

Korean Labor-Management Relations

Sookon Kim
Kyung Hee University

Introduction

There is a general consensus that the unprecedented rapid economic development of the past three decades in Korea has rested on the ability to develop and utilize the nation's abundant human resources. Ironically, however, little study has been made of this essential source of economic development. Korea's labor-management relations, being a means and end of human resource management, have become a focal point of international attention as well as domestic politics since the June 29 declaration of democratization in 1987. From that time until the fall of 1989, neither the government nor the opposition parties would have been likely to support any policy suppressing labor unions, even including the pervasive and illegal wildcat strikes. But a backlash in public sentiment opposing the violent labor movement coupled with the merger of three parties to become the majority at the beginning of 1990 has led to more positive intervention by the government in labor disputes. Actions taken were, however, more expedient than rational and lacked an assessment of long-term consequences. It is unclear whether government policy toward labor is swinging back to the old style of authoritarianism or to a new synthesis that will accommodate the needs of both labor and management. These circumstances make this study on the future of labor management policy timely.

A widely shared concern since 29 June 1989 is that, if harmonious labor-management relationships are not maintained, Korea's recovery from the economic slump of 1991 will be endangered. Is this concern based on a belief that past successful performance in economic development was caused by amicable, harmonious, and modernized labor-management relationships in Korea? Few people would answer affirmatively. Then why do people believe that labor-management relations will be a bottleneck for future economic development in Korea? This question is addressed later in the chapter.

It is difficult to determine whether a country's labor-management relations are a cause or a consequence of its economic development, because they mutually reinforce each other. It cannot be denied, however, that past success in Korea's economic development has taken advantage, wittingly or unwittingly, of premodern, underdeveloped practices of the industrial relations system.[1] However, for the reasons discussed in the following section, namely, a transition from an excess supply of labor to a scarce supply, contemporary organizations cannot be managed in the traditional style. As the clock cannot be turned back, so the dynamic labor market conditions of Korea cannot be returned to the old norm, which can be viewed as a paradise for traditional, authoritarian management. Therefore, it is Korea's task to find ways to accommodate the rising economic and social-psychological needs of Korean workers without sacrificing continuous economic development. My purpose in this chapter is to develop a model for achieving such a goal through institutional development. In the process, Korea will have to reexamine its historical experiences of labor-management relations.

The Dynamics of the Korean Labor Market

Export-oriented industrialization resulted in a rapid increase in nonfarm employment at an annual rate of 10 percent during the 1960s and 1970s, reducing the nonfarm unemployment rate from 16.4 percent in 1963 to below 5 percent in the mid-1980s. By 1977 or 1978, all the readily available supply of labor was absorbed, and the official national unemployment rate was merely at the level of frictional unemployment of 3.2 percent. At that time, the Korean labor market went through the Lewisian turning point, moving from an unlimited labor supply to a scarce labor supply. There were several indicators of this phenomenon. The vacancy ratio went up rapidly, as did monthly real wages (Bai 1982).

Thanks to the rising demand for labor in industries, monthly separation and accession rates of the manufacturing sector in the late 1970s went up to 5.9 percent and 6.3 percent, respectively. Such fluid labor market conditions were the causes and consequences of employers' common practice of "pirating" workers and of workers' low level of commitment to their employers, which may be called a rational labor market. These trends tend to increase labor mobility among firms, industries, and regions, resulting in an efficient allocation of human resources. Without freedom of labor mobility over geographic areas, firms, and industries, human resources could not have been allocated so efficiently.[2]

During the past three decades the educational composition of the labor force has also changed significantly. The proportion of those with a high school education or above rose from 35 to 42 percent. The implications of such a labor market transformation are several: the traditional style of authoritarian management is no longer effective in motivating the new workforce; wages have to be adjusted constantly to keep pace with the prevailing wages in the labor market; and workers' demands for participation in managerial decision making through collective bargaining institutions have to be accommodated.

The mode of recruitment also has changed. In one of the rapidly expanding plywood companies in Pusan, the personnel manager indicated that his whistle had been his best instrument of recruitment before. But the whistle was no longer effective (it had "rusted") because no more readily available female workers were around to be called in for employment at the factory gate. To meet the company's labor requirements, recruiters had to be dispatched to rural areas where teenage boys and girls were marginally employed in the agricultural sector. Soon afterward this company went out of business, and the plywood industry is no longer profitable in Korea.

Due to a rapid increase in college enrollment in 1981, there was an excess of college graduates in 1985. For the first time in Korea, college graduates' unemployment rate exceeded that of high school graduates. Some college graduates, unable to find jobs corresponding to their educational level, now enter blue collar jobs in the hope that they can become labor union leaders someday. Some of them are political activists and therefore alienated from the mainstream of business unionism of the FKTU (Federation of Korean Trade Unions). As the democratization movement progresses, it remains to be seen how policies will be formulated to deal with the touchy issue of a student-labor alliance in the future.

Before management had begun to adjust itself to the new tide, the political democratization movement had already brought about a sweeping liberalization of the trade union movement in Korea. How well was Korean management prepared for this? Very poorly during the years immediately after the declaration, but steadily improving thereafter, particularly since 1991. Still, disaster lies ahead if traditional, authoritarian management techniques are reapplied to the new workforce, who discovered their potential power to influence employers during the summer of 1987. A new industrial relations approach is required—one of accommodation of the new workforce and its demands for a more democratic, participatory institutional framework for joint decision making through collective bargaining.

Historical Background of the Korean Labor Movement

The first labor violence ever recorded in the history of the Korean labor movement was in 1886 at Cho San Station, where laborers protested against government officials rather than employers for their harsh treatment of the people. There was no employer as such in that premodern agrarian society. Subsequent labor strikes, such as the ones at Unsan gold mine or Wonsan Harbor, were not aimed against the Korean business establishment, which did not yet exist, but against foreign capitalists and Japanese colonial authorities (Y. W. Kim 1982). In fact there was no indigenous Korean capitalism at the time, since capital formation did not take place in Korea until the end of World War II. In the absence of indigenous capital formation, the labor union movement started at the turn of the century, and in the 1920s the national federation of trade unions was organized. The primary objective of the trade union movement at that time was to fight Japanese colonialism. Hence, the more violent and bloody the fight against Japanese establishments and their colonial government, the more it expressed patriotism and commitment to the cause of liberation of the mother country. The uncompromising and violent nature of the Korean labor union movement is rooted in this tradition of a bloody resistance movement for political independence.

Trade unions resurfaced during the U.S. military occupation. Although the U.S. occupation forces in Korea did not have clear policy directives from headquarters in Tokyo, which was preoccupied with the democratization of Japanese politics, politically oriented labor union leaders in Korea actively pursued hegemony in the political vacuum created by the Japanese surrender. Even though the U.S. government intended to encourage a kind of business unionism in Korea patterned after the American tradition of tripartitism by introducing conciliation, mediation, and arbitration in labor dispute settlement, it was difficult to do so because there was little resemblance between Korea and the United States (Macmillan 1987).

Labor union leaders who resurfaced from underground were generally more interested in political activities than in bread-and-butter labor issues. Among them were several left-wing communist agitators working in conformity with directives from Pyongyang. As the prelude to the Cold War era opened on the Korean peninsula, the U.S. military government hurriedly switched its interest from democratization of the labor movement to defense against communist infiltration into the Korean trade union movement.

Dae Han No Chong, predecessor of the current Federation of Korean Trade Unions (FKTU), was formed to compete with the communist-led trade union Joun Pyung. By 1949, Joun Pyung was completely dismantled. In the process of competing against Joun Pyung, Dae Han No Chong gained strength and influence through its cooperation with the government. This was the beginning of the government's exercise of influence on union affairs, and trade unions' disentanglement from politics has become ever more difficult since then. The term *euh yong nojo*, "sweetheart union," was used to describe such an entanglement with the government, and this term of abuse is still used to describe any union with whom one does not agree or whom one does not support.

At the close of the Korean conflict, President Syngman Rhee's government enacted three major pieces of legislation that have had lasting effects on Korea's labor relations policies: the Labor Union Law, the Labor Standards Law, and the Labor Dispute Adjustment Law. However, actual operation of collective bargaining and its administration did not materialize for a long time, and the labor policies promulgated in 1953 had little effect on labor practices of the day.

These laws were essentially copied from the West via emulation of Japanese labor statutes. The laws were also designed to demonstrate that the South was a "better paradise" than the communist North in protecting laborers (S. Kim

1983c:95–139). Labor standards were set so high that, if every condition stipulated in the statute was observed by an employer, he would be unable to run a business. As a result, delinquency became commonplace in labor law enforcement: the businessman became a lawbreaker, the union leader became a "sweetheart" who would not exercise the labor rights as guaranteed by the law, and the government official became guilty of deliberate negligence of law enforcement. Corrupt union leaders, business-dominated enterprise unions, and government control of the FKTU led to havoc within the labor movement.

In 1960 workers participated in a demonstration that led to the fall of the Rhee government. After the coup of 16 May 1961, General Park Chung Hee banned trade unions. The ban was lifted shortly thereafter, and a new FKTU, under close government supervision, was formed. The unions were structured into industry-wide national unions affiliated with the new FKTU. The free collective bargaining practices that were permitted during the 1960s were again suspended in December 1972 with the promulgation of the Emergency Decree on National Security.

During the 1970s, under the emergency decree, unions were required to secure government approval before engaging in wage negotiations. This meant that a union's right to collective bargaining was suspended, simply as a result of policymakers' ignorance about the industrial relations profession. The Labor Dispute Adjustment Law was also suspended, to be replaced by direct government intervention in all labor disputes. All collective work actions were prohibited. These practices became so deeply entrenched in contemporary labor-management practices that even after the suspension of the emergency decree in 1981 the government's interference with labor disputes was quite extensive. Only since the summer of 1987 has the government taken the position of not interfering with labor-management disputes.

In spite of statutory protection of legal rights vis-à-vis economic strike or work stoppage, not a single lawful dispute was recorded until 1986; in that incident, as soon as the Ministry of Labor made it clear that it would not intervene in the dispute, management conceded to the union's demand in its entirety. After the announcement of democratization on 29 June 1987, the labor movement was quickly reactivated. Freed from government interference, 3,300 cases of "collective actions" (meaning unlawful collective labor actions, such as wildcat strikes, picketing, and street demonstrations) were recorded during the months of July and August. In September 1987 the government had to step in because of the pervasive unlawful violence. Labor unrest was so severe that normal business activities were virtually stopped; the opposition parties as well as the majority party encouraged the government to take firm action. The general public's sentiment against the radical labor unions' violence enabled the government to take steps to separate the labor union movement from political activities. At present, the spirit of political unionism is declining steadily and the seed of business unionism is beginning to germinate in conservative political soil.

The Role of Government in Korean Labor-Management Relations

Direct Intervention

Unlike Western industrialized countries, the Korean government's involvement in labor-management relations has always been thorough and extensive, so much so that there was little room left for union leaders to exercise their power, whether in the area of union organization or in the dispute adjustment process. Given this historical background, what has existed in Korea has been labor-government relations rather than labor-management relations.

The role of the Korean government in labor-management relations has been one of direct intervention and control even though every member of the government officially in charge of labor has emphasized the importance of neutrality and noninterference. The inconsistency between what was practiced and what was said by government officials created a credibility gap. The government has only recently, since the summer of 1987, seemed to be trying a hands-off policy with labor disputes. However, as can be seen by the government action in September 1987, the prevalence of wildcat strikes and the lack of collective bargaining experience make it highly unlikely that the government will be able to disentangle itself from intervention in labor-management relations soon.

The government's position has consistently been "develop first, share later." Such a policy inherently favors employers at the expense of labor. Here again the party's announced platform has been different from the actual policy pursued by each regime. The Liberal Party under the leadership of Syngman Rhee pronounced its power to be based on laborers, in contrast to the conservative Nationalist Party. Yet, in fact, the Liberal Party's labor policy has always favored business over labor, and labor's demands for rights have frequently been denied for the sake of anticommunism. President Park Chung Hee, who came to power extolling liberal causes that favored farmers and labor rather than business, in practice manifested the belief in the "develop first, share later" policy. It was during Park's regime that Korean capital formation took place. The Democratic Justice Party under the leadership of President Chun Doo Hwan also called for construction of a welfare society. But the economic growth-oriented policy has never changed. Throughout the past forty years of the republic's history an openly declared conservative party has never come to power, but all those liberal or apparently progressive parties, when they came to power, turned out to be closely tied to business interests. To a considerable extent these ties may have been inevitable from the standpoint of the government-initiated export-led industrialization policies the parties pursued, which appeared in the eyes of laborers to favor business interests more than labor's. Declared policy has always been liberal in favor of labor, but actual implementation has always favored business. This contradiction has reinforced workers' dissatisfaction and distrust of parties in power. The reason labor union leaders advocate a constitutional amendment that includes more detailed labor-protection provisions than those adopted by any other country is precisely politicians' lack of credibility.

No doubt there is a degree of sincere commitment among political leaders and high-ranking government officials to liberal and progressive ideals. These ideals have not, however, been evident in the process of policy implementation. The beliefs of President Park and the technocrats can be summarized as follows: Until Korea becomes an advanced country, labor unions should be deprived of the right to bargain and strike. Instead, the government should deliver welfare benefits to the workers in amounts the economy can afford. Thus, rather than conflict in labor-management relations, cooperation, as can be observed in the Japanese industrial relations system, should be emphasized. Although both government and business advocated enterprise corporatism, state corporatism was increasingly practiced.

Development technocrats did not understand that conflict and cooperation are inherent parts of the industrial relations system—like two faces of the same coin, like husband and wife. They are mutually indispensable and therefore quarrel sometimes; quarrels may on occasion lead to divorce, but in most cases they cooperate and love each other. By denying their freedom to quarrel and the presence of conflict, one may deprive them of an opportunity for true cooperation. Furthermore, the look-at-Japan policy has often been based on a shallow and superficial observation of the Japanese industrial relations system (Koike 1987:289–330).

Under such circumstances, therefore, laborers could not be satisfied with the welfare package delivered at the hands of government officials no matter how good it was, because they did not have a sense of having won it through their own efforts. Laborers as well as union leaders tended to think that, had they exercised their right to strike, they would have gotten a better package.

The apparent chaos in labor-management relations during the summer of 1987 and thereafter was thus to a substantial degree due to lack of experience in direct negotiation between the parties without government intervention. The government's position during July and August was to take an absolute hands-off policy. This laissez-faire policy was the antithesis of the previous interventionist policy. Then the government intervened in the Hyundai shipyard strike; this developed into a citywide riot in September 1987. During 1988, unions undertook an active organizing drive, emphasizing lawful actions within the legal framework. But the unions' basic intent was to demonstrate their ability to strike rather than to achieve a slice of the economic pie, so union leaders carefully followed the procedural requirements of the Dispute Adjustment Law. But with the reoccurrence in 1988 of long, violent strikes at Hyundai shipyard (122 days), Poong San, and Dae Woo shipyard, the government once again intervened. With the slowdown in the economy as a whole in 1989, the government declared an "economic crisis" and served notice that further violence in labor-management relations would not be tolerated. This policy might have been better accepted by professionals in industrial relations as well as by labor if much-needed institutional reform measures had been implemented beforehand.

Incomes Policy

The validity of using incomes policy to interfere with labor-management relations at a macro level needs objective consideration because the government is likely to take that course in the future. The question here is not so much whether the incomes policy is effective, but what the rationale behind such a policy is. In the late 1970s the level of union demands for wage increases was very high, ranging from 40 to 50 percent, reflecting the high inflation rates of the time. Employers' initial offers were on the average less than half of what the union demanded (Table 20.1). During the stabilization period after 1981, labor demands fell rapidly from 27.5 percent in 1982 to 17 percent in 1985. Employers' offers also fell rapidly to one-digit

TABLE 20.1

Union demands, employer offers, negotiated wage increases, and wage drifts, 1977–1993 (percentage)

	Union demand (1)	Employers' offer (2)	Negotiated wage increase (3)	Employers' concession rate (4) = (3) − (2)	Year end nominal wage increase (5)	Wage drift (6) = (5) − (3)
1977	48.7	n.a.	36.0	n.a.	32.1	−3.9
1978	55.9	21.5	29.7	8.2	35.0	5.3
1979	52.4	19.5	26.8	7.3	28.3	1.5
1980	48.6	15.9	21.5	5.6	23.4	1.9
1981	58.0	14.5	16.1	1.6	20.7	4.6
1982	27.5	8.2	9.5[a]	1.3	15.8	6.3
1983	17.5	6.4	6.9[a]	0.5	11.0	4.1
1984	13.4	3.0	5.3[a]	2.3	8.7	3.4
1985	17.0[b]	5.2[b]	6.9	1.7	9.2	2.3
1986	18.4	5.0	6.4	1.4	8.2[b]	1.8
1987[b]	26–27	6–7	17.2	10.7	10.1	−7.1
1988	29.3	7.5–8.5	13.5	5.5	15.5	2.0
1989	26.8	8.9–12.9	17.5	6.6	19.4	1.9
1990	17.3–20.5	7.0	8.5	1.5	18.8	10.3
1991	17.5	7.0	10.5	3.5	17.5	7.0
1992	15.0	4.7–6.9	6.5	0.8	15.2	8.7
1993	12.5	4.5	6.8	2.3	12.0	5.2

Source: Federation of Korean Employers' Association (annual); *Dong-A Ilbo*, 21 December 1984; FKTU (various years).

[a]Ministry of Labor, Korea (1982).

[b]*Cho Sun Ill Bo*, 13 March 1987.

rates of increase, reflecting price stability. Thus the gap between labor demands and employers' offers narrowed somewhat. The employer concession rate, defined as the collectively agreed wage rate increase less employer's initial offer, was above 6 percent until 1980 but declined thereafter.

For the first time since 1977, the negotiated wage increase superseded the year-end nominal wage increase in 1987, thanks to the union organizing thrust of that year. However, this initial gain was quickly followed by a wage drift phenomenon (the year-end nominal wage increase was greater than the negotiated wage increase). Is this because of diminishing union power after 1987? To the contrary, it was the threat of the unions to organize unorganized firms that led employers in the unorganized firms to yield higher wage increases—a threat effect.

Careful examination of Table 20.1 reveals that before 1987 there was hardly any union effect on wage increases that might have had a cost-push inflationary effect. In 1977, when the negotiated wage increase was higher than the year-end nominal wage increase, it is difficult to detect a union effect. Nevertheless it is interesting to note that the union penetration rate was at its highest point in 1977 (see Figure 20.1). Only since 1989 has any real effect of the trade union movement on wage increases been felt—either directly through collective bargaining or indirectly through the threat effect. However, whereas the employer concession rate decreased from 5.5 percent in 1988 to 2.5 percent in 1993, wage drift increased from 2.0 to 5.2 percent over the same period, showing the diminishing effect of unionization on wage increases after the initial organizational drive.

The government has on several occasions adopted wage guidelines. The first time was in 1977, when Deputy Prime Minister Nam Duck Woo announced: "Among the monopolistic firms whose product prices are under government control, if any price increase is requested as a result of higher labor cost, only 15 to 18 percent of the cost increase in the wage factor will be approved" (*Han Kook Ilbo*, 16 February 1977). This statement made clear the degree to which the government was willing to interfere with the private sector's wage settlements. It was one of the most articulate wage policy statements announced by the government.

Still, there was criticism of the statement because it constituted a de facto wage guideline. Fortunately or not, there was not a single instance of denial of a request for price revision by the government on these grounds. Compared to later wage guidelines, this first de facto wage guideline did have some teeth with which to enforce its policy, but it had no meat to bite. Subsequent wage guidelines took a very subtle and indirect form, and even the existence of wage guidelines has been denied, not to mention teeth or meat to bite.

The Economic Planning Board announced that it would withhold any wage increase for civil servants in 1980. Subsequently the Korea Bankers' Association adopted a resolution on 21 November 1980 to refuse any new loans to firms that (1) increased wages in spite of financial deficiency; (2) increased wages in spite of expecting no long-term profit, though not in deficiency on current account; or

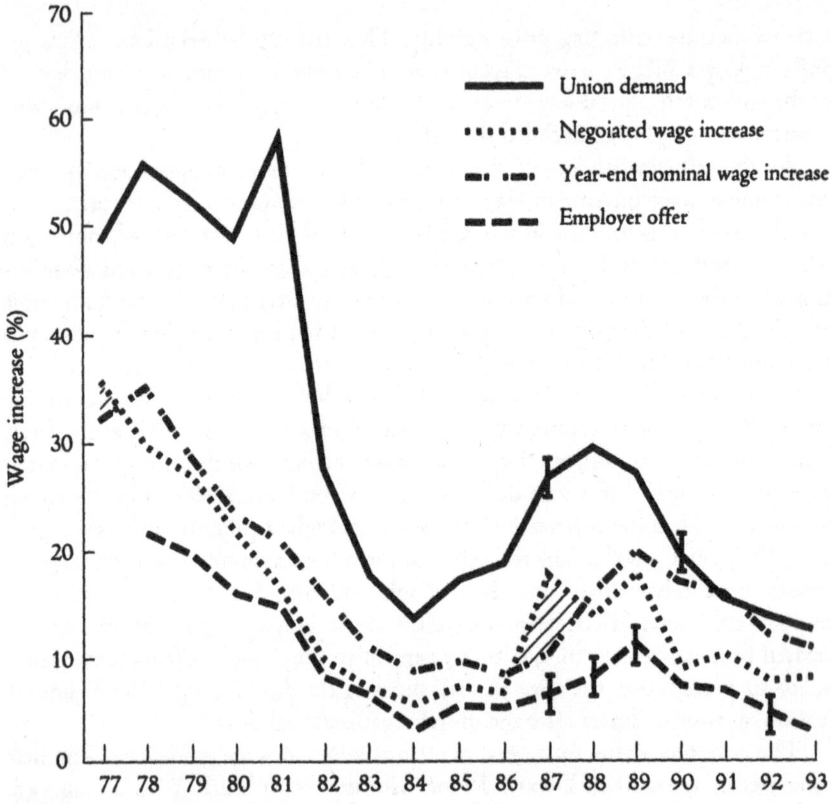

FIGURE 20.1 Union demand, employer offer, negotiated wage increase, and year-end nominal wage increase, 1977–1993.

(3) increased wages beyond the level of increase in labor productivity, even if the firm made a profit in its current account. On 5 February 1981, the FKTU formally protested the action of the Bankers' Association and requested that the resolution be withdrawn, since it was beyond the association's authority to interfere with the process of wage determination (FKTU 1982:51, 174).

The association's resolution seemed to have no effect on wage settlements, however. The Bank of Korea instructed all banks to enforce the association's resolution. In response, the president and vice presidents of the FKTU visited the deputy prime minister's office to lodge a formal protest against the Bank of Korea. The deputy prime minister replied that, since the Bankers' Association resolution was that body's private matter, it did not constitute a public wage guideline and thus was not legally binding. The deputy prime minister took the position that the government would honor wage decisions reached through negotiation between the parties involved. Similar types of wage guidelines were issued repeatedly every year, followed by FKTU's protests.

One wonders who won the game and who lost what. FKTU gained nothing but the government's verbal promise that it would not intervene in private wage negotiations. But the employers now knew that government was behind their position to increase wages as little as possible to cooperate with the antiinflation campaign. The government has come to have two faces: a noninterference position, taken by the Ministry of Labor, and a position of moderate encouragement for employers to resist wage demands from the Finance Ministry. The unfortunate consequence is that, with no single voice from the government as far as incomes policy is concerned, the future direction of government involvement on incomes policy is totally ambiguous. And this ambiguity has left no room for logical debate either for or against this kind of indirect incomes policy. In appearance FKTU succeeded in the game, and union leaders regard any type of wage guideline as an evil in itself (J. W. Kim 1987).

Labor Union Organization

It has been an undeniable fact of life in the Korean trade union movement that, whenever a new political regime comes into power, trade union activities are either stopped for some time or leaders are purged for their "sweetheart" connections or corruption. Thus, trade union activities are closely linked to the political atmosphere of the country. Trade unions are organized on an enterprise basis. Local unions in the same industry have established industrial federations, 21 of which constitute the FKTU. Where organization of a local union is inappropriate at an establishment due to the special characteristics of the business, such as in the garment industry, where each firm has only a handful of employees, workers may form an area-wide union in the same city or province by geographic criteria.

There were some 2,658 local unions in the country representing a total of 1,036,000 members recorded by the Ministry of Labor in 1986 (Tables 20.2 and 20.3) (total union membership reported to the Ministry of Labor was not based on payment of union dues to FKTU). The union penetration rate has declined abruptly since 1980 for several reasons, including decline in business activities in the early 1980s and the amendment of the Labor Union Law in December 1980. This amendment was purported to convert industry-based unions into enterprise unions patterned after Japanese practice. Hence union locals were reorganized on an enterprise basis, and statistics on the number of union locals and chapters are therefore not directly comparable before and after the 1980 amendment. After 29 June 1987, unions were rapidly organized along with the democratization momentum.

By the amendment of the Labor Union Law in 1980, collective bargaining was in principle carried out at an enterprise level, and an industrial federation, categorized initially as the "third party," was not allowed to step into enterprise-level collective bargaining.[3] The amendment also outlawed any closed shop and union shop agreements except in the stevedore union. As a result, the size of FKTU membership declined rapidly, to 1,004,000 in 1985. The union penetration rate

TABLE 20.2
Labor union membership, 1963–1990

	Total nonfarm permanent employees (10^3)	Union members reported to the Ministry of Labor		
		Number (10^3)	Growth rate[a] (%)	Organization rate[b] (%)
1963	1,106	224	—	20.3
1965	1,349	302	35.0	22.4
1970	2,363	473	57.0	20.0
1971	2,520	497	5.0	19.7
1972	2,529	515	3.6	20.4
1973	2,683	548	6.4	20.4
1974	2,974	565	3.1	22.1
1975	3,258	750	32.7	23.0
1976	3,630	846	12.8	23.3
1977	3,922	955	12.9	24.3
1978	4,389	1,055	10.5	24.0
1979	4,609	1,088	3.1	23.6
1980	4,728	948	–12.9	20.1
1981	4,946	967	2.0	19.6
1982	5,160	984	1.8	19.1
1983	5,594	1,010	2.6	18.1
1984	6,031	1,011	0.1	16.8
1985	6,397	1,004	–0.7	15.7
1986	6,666	1,036	3.2	15.5
1987	7,316	1,267	22.3	17.3
1988	7,772	1,707	34.7	22.0
1989	8,270	1,932	13.2	23.4
1990	8,682	1,887	–2.3	21.7

Source: FKTU (1987); Economic Planning Board and Ministry of Labor, Korea (annual).

[a]Percentage increase over previous year.

[b]Number of union members as a percentage of total nonfarm employment.

declined from 23.0 percent in 1975 to 15.5 percent in 1986, but it began to gain again thereafter, reaching 22.3 percent in 1989, and began to level off from 1990. The rate increased more sharply in 1987, thanks to the democratization trend (see Figure 20.2).

Article 13 of the Labor Union Law (as amended in 1980) stipulated that workers had the right to organize a trade union with the approval of a minimum of 30 workers or one-fifth of the total workforce. Prior to the amendment there

TABLE 20.3
Unionization, 1980–1990

	Total establishments with 10 or more employees	Local unions		
		Number	Growth rate[a] (%)	Organization rate[b] (%)
1980	38,176	—	—	—
1981	38,355	2,141	—	5.58
1982	42,593	2,191	2.3	5.14
1983	47,552	2,238	2.1	4.71
1984	52,120	2,365	5.7	4.54
1985	56,642	2,534	7.1	4.47
1986	62,204	2,658	4.2	4.26
1987	67,830	4,086	53.7	6.00
1988	73,562	6,142	50.3	8.33
1989	78,016	7,883	28.3	10.12
1990	—	7,698	−2.3	—

Source: FKTU (1987); Economic Planning Board and Ministry of Labor, Korea (annual).

[a]Percentage increase over previous year.

[b]Number of union members as a percentage of total establishments with ten or more employees.

was no such clause defining the minimum number of workers required to organize a union. A subsequent amendment of 1989 abolished this minimum requirement. Theoretically speaking, therefore, even two people can organize a labor union, provided that its registration is accepted by the government.

It is important to note, however, that once any union comes into existence with the completion of its registration with the government, it automatically has the right to demand collective bargaining with the employer. If the employer refuses to bargain, he can be charged with unfair labor practices. The confusion and conflict of multiunion rivalry were prevented by Article 3, Section 5, of the Labor Union Law, which was designed to prevent problems of multiple unions in a single plant. A union's entitlement to collective bargaining depends on its being registered with the government, but the government may refuse to register a union if that union is considered to have an intention to interfere with the normal activities of a preexisting bona fide labor union.

It is entirely possible under the law that Union B, with the support of half an enterprise's workforce, might not be able to register because that union is considered by a government official as intending to interfere with preexisting Union A's

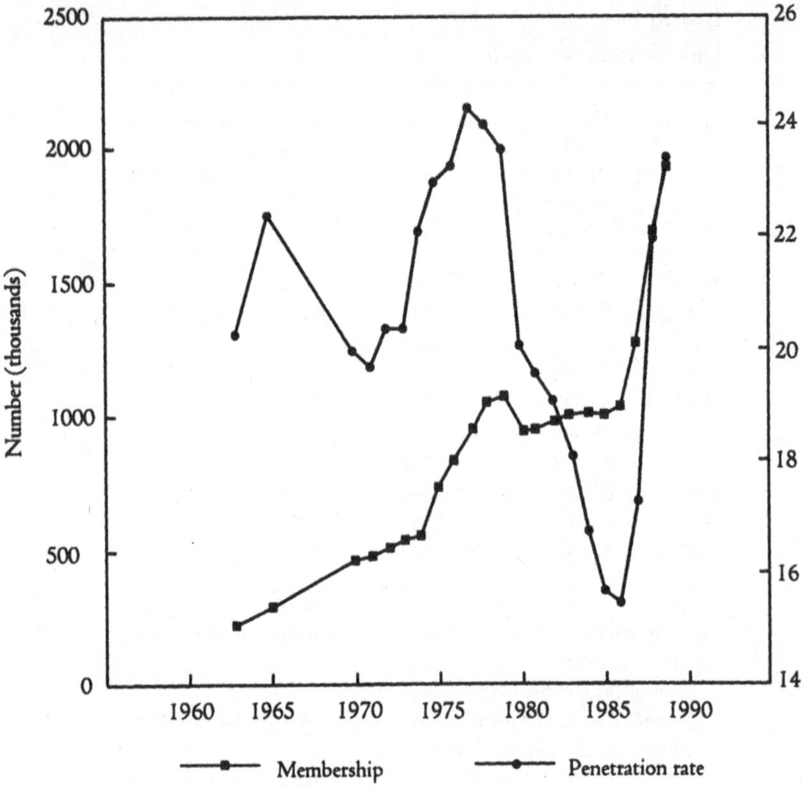

FIGURE 20.2 Union membership and penetration rate.

normal activity, even if Union A has the support of only one-fifth of the workers. In such a case, Union A may rightfully be termed a "sweetheart" union. Intraunion disputes in which one faction characterizes the other as a "sweetheart" have been the source of labor unrest in the past—for instance, the mineworkers' disputes in Sabook and the Dae Woo auto industry's strike activity.

By 1987 the Hyundai shipyard had been in existence for fourteen years without labor unions. In 1974 a huge labor dispute at this shipyard lasted for several days with work sabotage and violence. After that incident, management felt the need for an organized voice of the workers to be channeled to top management, but it was firmly opposed to organizing a labor union. Instead, a labor-management council was established from the shop level up to the departmental level. A case report showed that under the circumstances this council operated quite well in lieu of a labor union (Park 1982:384–456).

In addition to the labor-management council, a new labor union was organized, and its registration was completed on 21 July 1987 by the president of the union,

Osung Kwon. A week later another group of laborers led by Shim Soo Kim demonstrated against Kwon's union. After four days of demonstration, the employer agreed with the new union to expel Kwon's organization. Kim, who called his labor group the Democratic Labor Union Steering Committee, blamed Kwon for his previous record of "sweetheart union" activity with the employer. Kwon, however, claimed that his group was the legitimate labor union and had completed its union registration in accordance with the Labor Union Law. As of 6 August 1987 the Democratic Labor Union Steering Committee had obtained 15,000 membership applications from workers. The number of Kwon supporters was not known. Officials of the Ministry of Labor tried unsuccessfully to mediate between the two factions.

A member of the Kwon faction is reported to have said that "to call us a sweetheart union and try to push us out of the union would constitute an obvious interference with normal activities of a bona fide labor union," and so his union was willing to fight in the courts. Confronted with this stubborn resistance, the Democratic Labor Union Steering Committee decided to demand that the employer implement the agreement to expel the preexisting union. But the employer was no longer able to do that (*Cho Sun Ill Bo*, 7 August 1987).

Because the employer could not take any action to expel the preexisting union, on 8 August representatives of eleven Hyundai conglomerates located in the Ulsan area met under the leadership of Yong Mock Kwon and organized the Association of Hyundai Group Labor Unions. In the meantime, the Hyundai shipyard announced plant closure without recognizing the newly elected president of the so-called Democratic Labor Union, whose membership far outnumbered the previously registered, legitimate union. Dissatisfied over this action, tens of thousands of workers from all eleven Hyundai conglomerates came to demonstrate in the rain on 17 and 18 August. There was imminent danger of a man-made disaster if chemicals and heavy machines mobilized by the workers got out of control. The vice minister of labor stepped in to mediate the situation. The demonstration ceased with the promise that the employer would negotiate with the newly elected president of the Democratic group, Hyung Keun Lee, on the terms of wages and working conditions before 1 September. However, this promise was not kept to the union's satisfaction, and Hyundai conglomerate unions in the Ulsan area rose up again, burning the city hall and breaking windows. This violence could not be tolerated by the government, and police were called in.

This is precisely the kind of labor dispute that had been predicted for a long time under the current legal system (S. Kim 1983a:1–61). But little attention has been given to addressing the source of these disputes. The discussions center on who is versus who is not a sweetheart rather than trying to create any institutional reform. The easiest analysis of these labor-management problems has been to emphasize the cultural commonality among the Far Eastern, Confucian countries and to copy the Japanese practices. Such an easy way out has deterred the development of institutional reform.

Labor Disputes and Conflict Resolution

The number of labor disputes increased sharply in 1987 in the atmosphere of democratization. Previously there had been about a hundred labor disputes each year, except during times of political instability, when the number was higher. There were 407 cases in 1980 in the political vacuum after the death of President Park. This unrest is attributable to the country's lack of experience with institutional means to deal with bread-and-butter issues between labor and management. Arthur Ross (1957) once described American trade unions as "political institutions working in an economic environment." In the case of Korea, past experience leads one to describe the Korean union as "a semi-economic political institution working in a political environment," because of the union members' as well as the leaders' sensitivity to the political atmosphere. This phrase also describes the characteristics of mainstream FKTU, in contrast to the minority radical unionists, whose goal may be political action rather than basic issues.

Almost one-third of all labor-management disputes arise from disagreements on wage increases and working conditions (interest disputes), whereas another third are caused by wage delinquency (Table 20.4). The rest are caused by other factors such as plant closures, layoffs, and unfair labor practices by employers

Table 20.4

Number of labor disputes by cause, 1975–1992

	Wage delinquency	Wage increase	Plant closure	Layoff	Unfair labor practice	Working conditions	Piece adj. in tax; ind.	Other
1975	32	42	7	10	19	4	0	19
1976	37	31	8	3	8	4	0	19
1977	30	36	4	4	6	2	0	14
1978	29	45	3	1	2	0	0	22
1979	36	31	5	6	3	0	0	24
1980	287	38	11	5	0	14	0	52
1981	69	38	11	9	4	32	0	23
1982	26	7	4	2	0	21	0	28
1983	35	8	9	6	0	19	0	21
1984	39	17	2	5	7	14	12	17
1985	61	62	12	22	12	41	22	27
1986	48	75	11	34	16	48	13	44
1987	45	2,629	11	51	65	566	n.a.	382
1988	59	946	20	110	59	136	n.a.	543
1989	59	742	30	81	10	21	n.a.	673
1990	10	167	6	18	—	2	n.a.	119
1991	5	132	—	7	—	2	n.a.	88
1992	27	134	—	4	—	—	n.a.	70

Source: Ministry of Labor, Korea (1990). n.a. = not available.

Table 20.5
Labor disputes by type, 1975–1991

	Work refusal	Occupation of workplace	Demonstration	Other	Total
1975	49	44	10	30	133
1976	45	45	15	5	110
1977	58	30	5	3	96
1978	55	26	3	18	102
1979	60	43	2	0	105
1980	98	204	47	58	407
1981	88	40	32	26	186
1982	67	16	3	2	88
1983	62	27	6	3	98
1984	62	46	3	2	113
1985	108	154[a]	3	0	265
1986	138	112	21	5	276
1987	1,226	2,426	88	7	3,749
1988	675	1,178	5	15	1,873
1989	632	898	1	85	1,616
1990	261	43	1	17	322
1991	205	24	3	2	234

Source: Ministry of Labor, Korea (1990).
[a]Twelve of these involved occupation of government buildings.

(rights disputes). Over the years the number of interest disputes has tended to increase, particularly during upturns in the business cycle. But it should be recognized that many labor disputes occur, not because of a single factor such as wages or a rights dispute, but for several reasons.

Labor disputes have taken the form of sit-ins, hunger strikes, refusals to work, and various types of demonstrations (Table 20.5). Sometimes a group of laborers occupied government buildings; at other times they went into the streets and even blockaded strategic locations such as railroad crossings to attract public attention and force the government to step in quickly. In the past, ironically, such illegal labor disputes more often occurred in workplaces where no union was organized. It is also true that the government's prompt response to such illegal occupation of strategic spots has further reinforced labor unions' tendency not to follow legal procedures for dispute settlement.

Labor disputes since 1987 have some shared characteristics (Federation of Korean Employers' Association 1987:63):

- Disputes were caused by wage negotiations.
- They were initiated by "disguised workers" such as former college students who had entered the blue collar workforce to lead a new labor union movement and who frequently became radical in their approach.

- Laid-off workers and radical students collaborated against employers in disputes.
- Besides demands for wage increases there were also political demands, to amend labor laws and for the resignation of the minister of labor, for instance.
- Disputes were spread to neighboring firms through calls for sympathy strikes.
- Disputes did not follow legal procedures stipulated in the Labor Dispute Adjustment Law and therefore were resolved through means other than labor-management institutions.

It is possible to strike a company without violating the law if the following steps are taken: parties must notify the administrative authorities; conciliation and mediation must be found ineffective; parties must not agree to bring the matter to arbitration; and the government must decide not to intervene because the dispute is not considered to be a national emergency. But practice shows that parties rarely go through such procedures to exhaust all legal requirements. As one of the union leaders stated, "If you wait until legal procedures are exhausted, by the time you need mass action, the workers will be already out of steam and cooled off, so you cannot mobilize them against the employer." Hence the dispute becomes illegal and violent, and then the government steps in.

Many potential disputes do not develop into lawful collective actions because employers fear that strikes would force them to make larger concessions. A second factor is the general public's inability to distinguish between a legal strike motivated by economic concerns and an illegal strike motivated by political reasons. Third, the government's strong intention is often to prevent work stoppage by any means. If labor unions could not strike, employers would not make genuine concessions; instead they would try to reduce labor costs by inviting government intervention in the name of stability. However, when it is practically impossible for an employer to lock workers out because of the government's intervention to maintain employment, the union will not compromise but will stick to its original demand. Too frequently political expediency has dictated quick solutions in labor disputes, thus depriving the parties of opportunities to make agreements.

At no time in Korea's industrial history have so many labor disputes taken place during so short a time span and with so little government interference as in the summer of 1987. Employers were making concessions to an unprecedented degree because they could no longer look to the government for help. At the same time, the unions were demanding too much too soon in the mood of the political democratization movement. Employers as well as the government seem to regret that the institutional rules of the game on industrial relations had not been developed sooner. Since 1990, however, the number of labor disputes has declined significantly to what may be an ordinary level of 322 cases. The Ministry of Labor called the year the beginning of the era of industrial peace. An even lower number of disputes (234) was recorded in 1991.

The current Labor Dispute Adjustment Law is unrealistic in many respects, given the peculiar characteristics of the Korean industrial relations system such as the face-to-face relationship between employer and employee, the seniority-related wage and promotion system, and the lack of union activity in the past. These circumstances necessitate reconsideration of the dispute resolution system with reference to other countries' experiences.

A Model for Emerging Labor-Management Relations

Korean politics is said to be underdeveloped relative to the country's stage of economic development. But there is an area that is even less developed than politics in Korea: labor-management relations. The primary reason for underdevelopment in labor-management relations is the north-south division of the peninsula into communist and democratic regimes.

In contrast to Japan, where there was no division of the country into two ideologically opposing regimes, the Korean peninsula not only was divided by the will of the big powers but also became a bloody battleground of the Cold War. The Cold War between the world powers became a hot war in Korea. Because of the danger of war, with its connotation of class struggle, tensions could not be relaxed—military, political, or in the labor movement. Any repressive policy by the government toward either the opposition party or the labor union movement could easily be justified in the name of defense against communist subversion. Law-abiding moderate citizens even refrained from teaching and studying about the labor movement or labor-management relations in colleges, although these activities were not officially prohibited. Consequently, the current generation of managers, those between 40 and 60 years of age, is paying a high toll for not having learned about industrial relations. The pervasive turmoil since the 1987 declaration of democratization is, to a great extent, attributable to popular ignorance about industrial relations.

In such an atmosphere, a handy strategy for an employer has been to suppress the free labor union movement simply by blackmailing workers involved by threatening to label them "pink." To the extent that such a strategy was effective, the tensions of the Cold War may have helped managers deprive workers of their basic rights.

Figure 20.3 is useful in illustrating a model of transitions in industrial relations (see Seashore 1954). Workers at stages B and C feel that they are threatened by management, whereas those at stages A and D feel that managers are their friends and work for common goals of mutual interest. If workers who distrust management are not cohesive, they tend to show a high level of productivity (stage B). But workers who distrust management and yet have a high degree of group cohesiveness, perhaps because of union organization, tend to show low productivity (stage C). At stages A and D, where workers consider managers their friends working for common goals, an opposite relationship found: low cohesiveness and low productivity (stage A), and high cohesiveness and high productivity (stage D).

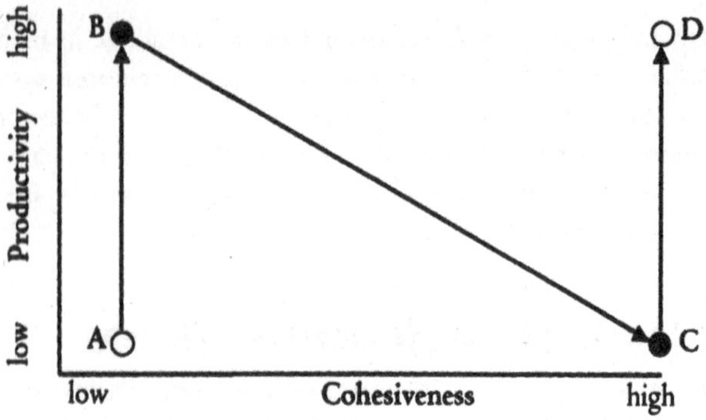

FIGURE 20.3 Dynamics of industrialization.

If we look at Korea's industrial relations system in light of this model, its labor-management relations before democratization were situated at stage B, where unionization is cursory and worker cohesiveness is weak. If they acted vigorously in union organization, workers were threatened by possible unemployment and by characterization as communists. Fear of the authoritarian management thus led Korean workers to demonstrate the high level of performance that took the world by surprise. The Korean labor market passed through a Lewisian turning point (recall the term "rusting whistle") in the mid-1970s, so the threat of unemployment was no longer an effective tool for managers. The discretionary power of managers to give or not give overtime work had been the sole source of their authority and the means by which they controlled their subordinates. After the turning point of 1987, however, workers no longer wanted to work overtime, thus diminishing management effectiveness in supervising laborers. Futhermore, after June 1987 workers started to enjoy full freedom to organize labor unions, and thus a high cohesiveness among the working groups developed. These two factors, absence of the likelihood of unemployment in the labor market and strong cohesiveness among workers through newly organized trade unions, brought Korean labor-management relations to stage C.

Real wages went up over 12 percent in 1989, compared to 7 and 8 percent in the preceding two years, but the rate of increase in worker productivity declined from 11.6 percent in 1987 and 12.2 percent in 1988 to 6 percent in 1989. Whereas the export increase in physical terms stopped during the year, full-time regular employment in the manufacturing industry declined by 3.3 percent during the first half of 1989. These developments led foreigners to scoff that "Korea has opened the champagne too soon."

From stage C in the figure, should Korea move back to B, where high productivity was manifested? Or should it move to D, where advanced industrial and post-industrial countries, such as Japan and some Western European countries, are located. To managers who suffered from their employees' violence and lawlessness in the workplace after democratization, there is strong nostalgia for stage B. And some shortsighted managers surely would like to take advantage of recent government intervention in labor-management relations and swing back to B.

But Korea should not and cannot go back to stage B. Even if political expediency in response to a middle-class backlash against labor violence operated to move it in that direction, today's labor market conditions preclude the possibility of the old paradise for management, the time of the "unrusted whistle." The Korean industrial relations system, which has become so vital to the life and death of the Korean economy, will either have to move to stage D or risk peril at stage C, like so many troubled Latin American countries. I make several concrete recommendations for institutional reform measures to depart C and reach D in the final section. But first it is worthwhile to examine the major characteristics of stages B, C, and D in reference to the main actors of Korea's industrial relations system—managers and their representatives, labor and the unions, and the government.[4] I omit any discussion of A, the preindustrialization stage in which there is no separation of roles among management, labor, and government. I hope, however, to discover some universal characteristics of development from stage B through C to D which are applicable to other developing countries.

Stage B: Before the Turning Point

During the 1960s and 1970s, the overall economic and political environment was highly favorable to Korean management. Not only was the world market conducive to Korean manufactured commodity exports, but the domestic labor market also constantly supplied an abundant well-educated labor force of about 600,000 every year. The stability of the labor market and the political favoritism given to management were definite advantages for Korean employers during the initial takeoff in industrial development.

In this period at stage B, the embryonic entrepreneurship of an early capitalistic economy was in harmony, ideologically, with the political regimes of Park and Chun, thus accelerating the speed of economic development. As long as the economic pie was growing quickly, there was no room for ideological conflict. An added factor was the impact of the Cold War, which, in its extreme form in Korea, helped to suppress Marxist ideology. This situation tended to breed an intellectual bankruptcy in labor-management relations vis-à-vis future development into stage C.

Management Managers at this stage were generally believers in Douglas McGregor's (1960) "Theory X": the average worker is by nature indolent, lacks ambition, dislikes responsibility, prefers to be led, and is self-centered, indifferent to organizational needs, resistant to change, gullible, and not too bright. Working from this characterization, managers regarded authoritarian paternalism as more effective than democratic leadership. In the prevailing Machiavellian atmosphere, they thought of workers as a perishable resource in the industrialization process—as seen by the high industrial accident rates—rather than as growing human capital to be developed constantly. They were little interested in worker training beyond the basic skills.

Accordingly, top managers were reluctant to decentralize authority and allowed little room for workers to participate in corporate decision making. The chief motivations used by managers were threat of discharge and all sorts of extrinsic factors. A web of workplace rules and regulations was imposed by management without consent of the workers. The individual employment contract was the sole basis on which managerial authority was derived.

Laborers and Unions Workers in general at this stage were unskilled and not highly educated. Their wage was barely at the subsistence level, but they could not negotiate any better terms of employment because of the high unemployment rate in the external labor market. As the economy continued its growth, employment opportunities became increasingly abundant and unsatisfied workers began to quit; thus the turnover rate rose in the manufacturing sector (S. Kim 1983b). Where the labor union movement was suppressed by force, only "sweetheart" unions could survive. In this atmosphere of forced harmony between labor and management, labor's true sentiments could not be detected on the surface, and an explosive feeling of betrayal by union leaders, combined with distrust of management, arose among rank-and-file workers.

Government Government leaders subscribed to the principle of "develop first, share later." The government, as the locomotive of economic growth, pursued an export-oriented low-wage policy combined with suppression of the trade union movement. Leaders were justified as benevolent dictators able to mobilize every bit of resources for rapid development under the banner of a "can do" spirit. It was believed that the government could deliver a better welfare package than a labor union could get through collective bargaining. By encouraging individual employment contracts, the government kept mobility of labor highly fluid. Free movement of the workforce among industries and firms contributed greatly to the development of Korean industry through efficient allocation of human resources. An antipirating bill was suggested by employer organizations several times in vain, thwarted by government officials' strong belief in a free market economy in human resources. The Cold War in many ways helped the government suppress the labor movement, thus assisting the business community in the end.

Stage C: After the Turning Point

At stage C, subsequent to democratization, the general environment became unfavorable to business. After this political turning point, politicians became conscious of a pervasive antibusiness sentiment among the public and dared not stand up for management interests. In Korea especially, international trade barriers have become a serious bottleneck for business growth into the 1990s.

As for ideology at stage C, because of the long suppression of liberalism at stage B, no sooner had business unionism started than radical activists began to blackmail middle-of-the-road, moderate business unionists, calling them "sweethearts." As a defense against such an extremist, aggressive, class-oriented campaign, the average labor leader has had to equip himself with a seemingly more aggressive attitude and a more radical tone in his speech to appease the rank and file. In this general mood, the labor movement has become more politically oriented than in the past. There is a valid concern that, if things are left as they are, politically motivated labor unions may come to dominate the labor movement as a whole, which is then likely to shy away from business altogether. At stage C there is a mood of great uncertainty regarding ideology, and this mood can be dominated by political power games. Rank-and-file blue collar workers in general are not inherently interested in political ideology or class struggle; they are more conservative and concerned about bread-and-butter issues. But if the chance for their voice to be heard becomes slim or even nonexistent, they are willing for practical purposes to support political activists in their union.

Management Management at stage C is still feared by workers, and its basic assumptions about human work behavior are the same as at stage B (i.e., Theory X). The only difference from stage B is the fact that workers have gained enough power to counteract management. Laborers feel that no man is an angel, and therefore checks and balances are inevitable between labor and management. Workers believe that managers are so selfish that only through a labor union's countervailing force is it possible to share the economic pie. The emergence of militant unionism sometimes forces management to abdicate managerial prerogatives by lowering work standards; the result is lower productivity. The hierarchical chain of command in the organization also begins to break down, to be replaced by the union's political leadership. In spite of increasingly open conflict, there are few game rules established for reconciliation.

Rising labor costs make it a managerial imperative to go through an extensive industrial restructuring process and invest anew in labor-saving machines and high technology. But, even so, there are no guarantees that radical union leaders will not emerge and block employment rationalization. Afraid of redundancy problems in the future, businessmen are reluctant to reinvest, despite the critical necessity to do so at stage C. And there is a need to move quickly. The longer society stays at stage C, the less likely it is to make the leap to stage D, since business people may lose all hope and simply give up.

Laborers and Unions At stage C, distrust and confrontation become a way of life in the workplace. Machiavellian tactics are used not only by management but also by labor leaders. Due to a strong union organizing drive, not only the number of local unions but also the union concentration rate and the number of labor disputes increase rapidly. In this process, intraunion rivalry become an everyday matter. Because collective bargaining experience has not yet been accumulated, collective bargaining is considered a game that one party must win rather than a venue for establishing compromise. As a gesture of dedication to labor's cause, union leaders frequently resort to extreme, unachievable demands, and the struggle continues until management surrenders. Employees slowly learn the consequences of such one-sided, extreme demands—plant closures and unemployment. Until numbers of workers actually experience unemployment among their close friends, they refuse to believe the true financial position of the company. However, if the government does come in and bail out the company's debt—thus saving employees' jobs—it just takes that much longer for rank-and-file workers to learn the lesson.

Government In Korea, without adequate preparation for economic unionism at stage B, society abruptly shifted into stage C. Here, the government takes a completely laissez-faire attitude, under the principle of noninterference in labor-management relations. In the midst of lawlessness and turmoil, there is no room for any rationale but "collective selfishness"; the people tend to believe that "whenever a collective voice wins, that is justice and democracy." Whereas democracy as a way of life has generally evolved through institutions of family, workplace, and government in Western countries, none of these three evolved along with Korea's material modernization of the past three decades.

Stage D: Joining the Advanced Industrial Countries

Korean society has not yet experienced stage D, which is to some extent only an ideal yet to be fully realized anywhere. But its characteristics can be derived from the experiences of advanced countries such as Japan, West Germany, and some segments of the United States and the United Kingdom. At stage D, labor-management conflicts are resolved by institutions of law and order and long-established customs, and through compromise rather than confrontation. Not only do labor and management recognize each other, but each appreciates the other's presence and the roles by which their common interests for survival are optimally served.

The majority of the people share a middle-class consciousness and believe that they are being equitably compensated, because the rewards they obtain are equal to their contribution to their job and their work organization. As for the ideological component, at stage D there is no more bipolarized extremism. The chief concerns are how to save the global environment from the deterioration due to industrialization and how to improve workplace conditions.

Management At this stage, managers try to motivate workers according to the assumptions of Theory Y, rather than Theory X: work is not necessarily always a painful thing; the average man and woman are not gullible and are willing to sacrifice present pleasure for the sake of a greater good in the future if they are so motivated. A participative management style develops in business, with joint decision making between union leaders and the management team, who resolve conflict through compromise.

Management regards workers not as perishable goods but as human capital; the more investment made in them through retraining and development, the more contributions they make to the organization. Therefore, higher skill is respected and rewarded, facilitating not only technological innovation but also a shift toward career employment of workers.

Laborers and Unions Having learned through the democratic process of internal union operations that the trade union is instrumental in achieving equality with management at the bargaining table and in executing collective agreements, worker distrust of both management and union leaders tapers off at stage D. The number of trade union locals and rank-and-file members does not increase as much as at stage C, and the number of strikes and average duration of strike substantially decrease.[5]

Labor unions in general find it in their interest to avoid radical fights with management; they seek to promote the pragmatic interests of employees rather than any dogmatic ideology. Labor leaders have learned how to make tradeoffs in negotiations between wage increases and member unemployment. Since industrial restructuring is an ongoing process at stage D, the key concerns of labor leaders are structural unemployment and the necessity for higher productivity, which is a prerequisite to higher real wages. Leaders negotiate with management to enable technological innovation and consider management blueprints for retraining programs to safeguard rehiring of redundant workers and prevent manpower obsolescence among the membership. Unions in particular become more conscious of quality-of-life issues, such as preventing industrial accidents and diseases and environmental degradation. For all these purposes, ever-closer cooperation is needed between labor and management leaders.

Government Government policy at this stage is "develop and share simultaneously," in the belief that the labor-management relationship is not a deterrent to well-balanced economic growth but a facilitator. The government tries to maintain domestic industry's international competitive strength by promoting a balance between real wage increases and productivity increases. Investments in human capital are made by both government and business to meet the requirements of a high-technology society. In principle the government policy toward labor management is noninterference. If a dispute becomes serious enough to threaten the welfare of the citizens and economy, the government has to step in. That decision must be made from a long-range perspective, looking at industry as well as the evolution of labor-management behavior vis-à-vis government involvement in free collective bargaining. If wage guidelines become absolutely necessary, they are enacted only on a temporary basis.

Proposals for Institutional Reform

To achieve distributional justice without sacrificing the functional efficiency of society, several reforms can be recommended. This goal is achievable through fair competition, egalitarianism, and humanitarianism. These three elements are both causes and consequences of the mature industrial relations systems depicted in stage D. The institutional reforms I recommend in this section would help achieve such goals and expedite the transition from stage C to D.

Intraunion Rivalry and Elections

We saw earlier that Article 3, Section 5, of the Labor Union Law has been the source of frequent intraunion rivalry disputes.[6] To avert this problem, I recommend the following measures:

1. Article 3, Section 5 of the Labor Union Law should be amended such that, when competing factions purport to represent the workers within the same establishment, the government must conduct an election for representation. The group that obtains the majority vote (through a run-off election between the two top-ranking factions if necessary) duly represents all the establishment's workers at the bargaining table.
2. For any disagreement between employer and worker representatives as to the appropriate boundaries of the exclusive bargaining unit for the purpose of collective bargaining, a local labor relations committee should be given authority to adjudicate. In determining the appropriate boundaries of the bargaining unit, consideration should be given to the following criteria: (a) bargaining customs in the industry, (b) occupational and educational similarity for wage determination, (c) technical relations among jobs, (d) common characteristics of internal and external labor markets, and (e) practical usefulness of delineating the bargaining unit.
3. I propose that local union presidents who have the right to bargain with their respective employers (at the time of this amendment) under the old law should be automatically granted the right to continue under the new law to represent the same union as if there were no other contestants.
4. Finally, once an exclusive bargaining representative is selected by the government procedure, his or her right to bargain on behalf of the employees of the bargaining unit should not be challenged for at least one year.

The proposed election procedure would not only eliminate the legislative grounds for blackmailing a rival union faction as a "sweetheart" union but also significantly reduce the abundance of wildcat strikes in Korea.

The Management Representative

Just as a labor union delegate needs full authority to represent the entire group of workers in the bargaining unit, so does the management representative need such authority at the bargaining table. But in many instances the management delegate has had no authority to make concessions at the bargaining table, because he or she has been given too narrow a discretionary power by top management (frequently the owner of the company). Agreements reached at the bargaining table and signed by the delegates can then be disapproved by the top management, thus leading to a wildcat strike. Such a situation may be partly attributable to the traditional management culture in Korea. But, unless authority is delegated to professional management in the area of industrial relations, true industrial democracy in contemporary complex organizations can never come about.

Therefore, I recommend that labor union's collective action (in an orderly work stoppage) should not be seen as constituting an unfair labor practice on the part of the union if that action is taken in protest against top management's refusal to accept a collective agreement signed by both the labor representative and the management representative whom the top management authorized in written form. Such a provision would enable future management representatives to work more professionally, independent of arbitrary, authoritarian decision making by top management.

Unfair Labor Practices by Labor Unions

Up to now only employers have been liable for unfair labor practices. Article 39 of the Labor Union Law stipulates five types of unfair labor practices on the part of employers: (1) dismissal of an employee for union activity, (2) yellow dog contracts, (3) refusal to bargain with a legitimate labor union leader, (4) interfering with union operations or subsidizing the expenses of a labor union, and (5) disadvantaging employees in any way for joining legitimate collective action.

There are, however, no provisions to deal with unfair labor practices on the part of laborers or labor unions. The lack thereof has been justified on grounds that laborers and their representatives are weak relative to employers in Korean society. That has been true by and large in the past. But after democratization, the new trade union movement gained legitimate power and also frequently committed acts of violence and lawlessness in the name of freedom to act, protected by the Labor Union Law as well as the constitution.[7] The pendulum of power has swung from employer to labor. In the absence of fair rules of the game between labor and management, it is unjustified to limit unfair labor practice provisions to employers. It is abundantly clear that labor unions should also be subject to such provisions, so as to keep the balance of power between employer and employee. I therefore recommend that the following be considered unfair labor practices:

1. Extracting payment from an employer for work not performed. This is consistent with the principle of "no work, no pay" discussed below or for work not to be performed in the future, either in the form of payment of a union officer or in any other form thereof. (This change is consistent with Article 3 of the Trade Union Law and would represent an anti-featherbedding provision.)

2. Engaging in a secondary boycott for the purpose of (a) forcing an employer to coerce any politician to resign or to pursue or not pursue a particular policy; (b) forcing an employer or a self-employed person to join a labor union or to cease doing business with any third party; (c) forcing an employer to recognize an uncertified union as the bargaining representative of his or her employees; or (d) forcing an employer to recognize a union when his or her employees are already represented by another union.
3. Slowing down regular operations or occupying the working premises while on strike.[8]
4. Coercing members not to provide regular service to an employer simply to support a neighboring union (i.e., sympathy strike).
5. Forcing an employer to abdicate any management prerogative not subject to collective bargaining. This does not preclude a laborer as an individual or a union as a group from participating in management decisions if both parties so agree.

The Principle of "No Work, No Pay"

Irrational though it might be, there has long been a practice in Korean industrial relations for employers to pay workers 40–65 percent of regular wages during stikes. This practice not only violates the principle of "no work, no pay," which is fundamental to the freedom of contract, but it also induces workers to prolong strikes and to resort to a wildcat strike for any grievance. There are several historical reasons for such payments: (1) Economic strikes were rare in the past. (2) In the past the government, thinking that the accumulation of a strike fund on the part of a union tends to facilitate strike action, which it considered an evil in itself, ordered unions to dissolve all existing strike funds. (3) Paternalistic managers believed that to withhold wages during a strike was contrary to Confucian benevolence; they justified the payment of wages during a strike on grounds of "good human relations."

Like many other companies, the Daewoo Shipbuilding Company pledged not to pay wages for lost time due to strike in 1988. But at the time of final settlement, 50 percent of regular wages was granted under the guise of a "stipend for productivity increase." The 1989 convention of the Korean Employers' Federation adopted the principle of "no work, no pay," and a campaign for this principle was vigorously carried out by both employers and the government.[9] It is difficult to assess the degree to which employers actually adhere to the principle, because there can be any level of disguised, under-the-table deals between union and employer. Therefore, even if a piece of legislation is passed to outlaw making payments during a strike period, its enforceability is in question. Nevertheless, it seems appropriate to recommend that Article 24 of the Trade Union Law be amended to eliminate the maximum ceiling of union dues at 2 percent, so as to facilitate the accumulation of strike funds.

A test case was with the Hyundai Auto Company at the end of 1989. The enterprise union was led by a newly elected president, Sang Bum Lee, an ambitious young man leaning toward what was called (self-named) a "democratic union." Intending to affiliate with a newly emerging national federation (Chun-No-Hyup) not legally approved by the Ministry of Labor, the union launched a wildcat strike from December 19 through 23 to demand an extra bonus of 150 percent. The company announced that it would stick with the no-work, no-pay principle for those five days of walkout. The 17,000 workers who joined the strike by walkout, slowdown, or sit-ins (of a total of 29,000 employees) had an average of 60,000 won per person deducted from their December wages. The company announced that it must withhold payment for nonwork because of strike-related financial losses and that it would do so again if there was further unlawful labor action.

Union President Lee conceded failure, apologizing that because of his lack of experience, combined with the belief that "if you push hard, you can gain," he had launched an unsuccessful strike. However, he added, "This is not to concede to the principle of no work, no pay, which we will pursue in the coming collective bargaining session in the spring" (*Cho Sun Ill Bo*, 6 January 1990, 11; *Dong-A Il-Bo*, 8 January 1990, 11). Ambiguity remains on both sides as to how to apply the principle to a lawful strike resulting from failure to reach an agreement at regular bargaining sessions. At the least, this case demonstrates that the principle of no work, no pay is workable in the case of an unlawful wildcat strike in Korea—a clear milestone.

Grievance Arbitration Procedures

In Korea the typical collective bargaining agreement is one year in duration. But during the 1987 and 1988 calendar years it was not uncommon for Korean firms to have two or three periods of negotiation: for example, one for an annual pay increase in March, another regarding summer vacation sometime in June, and still another on the annual bonus increase at the end of a year. Consequently, employers were under constant pressure to negotiate at any time the labor union might choose. The same was true for firms with no union organization. Under Article 11 of the Labor Management Council Law, employers are required to meet with representatives of the labor union at least once every three months. This law was not intended for the representatives of employees and employer to negotiate wages or terms of employment, but for employers to seek cooperation and productivity increases from workers. In actual experience, however, when worker representatives meet with management, requests tend to have labor-cost implications. Therefore, employers have been reluctant to come to such council meetings, and they often try to fulfill their legal obligation superficially by taking four phony pictures around a table on one occasion and then reporting to the government as if four meetings had been convened that year. But when such meetings are actually held, they have yielded some benefits to the employees. There has been no tradition of collective bargaining, but the experience of such labor-management councils has not lessened the desire of laborers to demand more and more whenever they can.

As discussed earlier, rival union leaders may surface to bring up rank-and-file workers' dissatisfactions over negotiated wages and other terms of contracts previously negotiated by the incumbent head of the union. Internal union politicking is often so severe that not a month elapses before a rival comes up with a promise to win a better package or new terms of contract of a different kind. The solution proposed earlier in this chapter is to guarantee the stability of the union representative in collective bargaining for at least one year by not allowing any no-confidence votes during the 12-month duration of the contract.

I therefore recommend that Article 35 of the Labor Union Law be amended as follows: A collective agreement shall be valid only if its duration is more than 12 months; if the duration is shorter than that, the agreement must be approved by the government. Only under a mutual agreement between management and labor union can a valid renegotiation take place during the duration of the contract.

Current law—illustrative of previous labor administrators' lack of experience and failure to understand the nature of industrial relations—assumes that wage negotiation differs from other types of collective bargaining. A wage package must be inseparable from negotiations on other collective bargaining items such as housing allowances, retirement, hours of work, and many other matters. I therefore recommend that Article 35 of the law make no distinction between wage negotiations and "other collective bargaining."

In addition to collective bargaining once a year, or once every two years if the parties so wish, a grievance arbitration mechanism should be institutionalized in Korean industrial relations. The current grievance mechanism is nothing more than a goodwill gesture on the part of benevolent managers toward their employees. According to one survey (see Kim and Ha 1983), in the typical grievance mechanism employees petition for some monetary or nonpecuniary favor from an employer on a personal basis, rather than contesting an issue by interpreting terms of the contract and so on. This behavior is quite characteristic of the traditional style of Korean community behavior, and I do not mean to alter it here. But when a conflict over the interpretation of an employment contract or a collective bargaining agreement arises, such informal relationships cannot truly resolve the problem. I therefore urge that the following changes be made to Article 35: for a collective agreement to be valid, the parties should set up a grievance arbitration procedure to safeguard the selection of a neutral party who will deliver an award with professional authority in any controversy between employer and employee arising out of interpretation of the collective agreement and related laws. Such an institution would be likely to lessen the number of wildcat strikes on rights issues, which are extremely common today.

Limitations on Strike Activity

Section 3 of Article 12 stipulates that dispute activity (a strike) should not take place other than on work premises. This means that strikers must stay at the workplace and may not demonstrate in the streets or at other places, such as government offices. This section was passed in 1980 with the intention of containing strike activities, which are likely to develop into political demonstrations, to the workplace. This is contrary to the standard practice in Western countries, where strikers are not allowed into the workplace and therefore usually picket the company they are striking at the factory gate or its equivalent. Strikers contained on the work premises easily become violent and often engage in various work disturbances, such as disconnecting electric power.

In principle, an interest dispute arises from disagreement over the terms of a contract. A strike of this kind is a collective refusal to provide labor, which should automatically preclude workers' physical presence at the workplace. Therefore, Section 3 should be eliminated.

Union Political Activity

The purpose of Article 12 of the Labor Union Law (Prohibition of Political Activities) has been to encourage the development of business unionism free of government interference. However, this article not only violates the constitutional rights of labor but is also unfair, because there is no such restriction on employers and their representatives. Labor unions as representatives of laborers should have the right to exert some pressure on Congress and in other political arenas.

The current law stipulates in Article 12, Section 1: "A trade union shall not be allowed to conduct any act in the election of any public office, in order to support a specific political party or have a specific person elected." Section 2 stipulates: "A trade union shall not be able to collect political funds from its members. And Section 3 stipulates: "Funds for a trade union shall not be diverted to political funds." I recommend that Section 3 be retained while Sections 1 and 2 be deleted and replaced by "Political activities by union members are not permitted at the workplace, in order to maintain orderliness and peace." This kind of reform would allow Korean trade unions to have positive effects on social policy at the macro level, which their Japanese counterparts were unable to do.

Arbitration Procedures on Economic Issues

The democratization declaration recognized labor unions' right to strike, a right that was exercised almost unconditionally in 1987, when there were 3,749 strikes. The pro-strike climate was so feverish that rank-and-file members, feeling that they had long been deprived of their basic rights, thought that any union leader who did not exercise this right was a "sweetheart." It is no surprise, therefore, that the unions' tactic in 1987 and 1988 was "strike first, negotiate later."

However, as Mario Bognanno has said, "misuse [of rights to strike] is anarchy and their overuse is economic ruin" (1988:110). Exercise of the right to strike should be civilized, within the web of rules and regulations. If the reforms I have proposed above—the prohibition of strikes for union recognition and the institution of a grievance arbitration procedure—are widely utilized, the number of rights disputes is sure to decrease. But when we consider the question of interest disputes over wages and terms of contract, current impasse resolution procedures are inadequate and confusing.

Under the current law as amended in 1987, arbitration can commence (1) if both parties agree to resort to arbitration by the labor commission of their jurisdiction; (2) if one of the parties so requests under the provision of the collective bargaining agreement; or (3), for firms in the public sector, by compulsory arbitration initiated by the minister of labor or the chairman of the labor commission. This does not prevent parties in the private sector from resorting to an independent arbitration panel selected by themselves. Therefore, a private company can be struck on economic issues only if (1) the parties do not have a voluntary arbitration procedure as part of their collective agreement, and (2) the parties do not agree to refer the impasse to a labor commission for arbitration. Resorting to a voluntary impasse resolution is desirable in the private sector because it tends to encourage free collective bargaining.[10]

Once arbitration has commenced, a 15-day cooling-off period is imposed on the parties in addition to the previous cooling-off period of 10 days for the private sector and 15 days for the public sector.

An arbitration panel is composed of three people appointed by the labor commission chairman on the recommendations of the parties involved in the interest dispute. When the parties cannot reach an agreement about whom to recommend for the panel from among the public representatives of the labor commission, the chairman of the commission is free to choose any public representative of the commission for the arbitration panel. Because it is difficult for the parties to select the panel jointly, the chairman exercises great power in finally selecting the arbitration panel. This naturally creates a lot of distrust toward the panel from the parties, which tends to weaken the effectiveness of the implementation of the arbitration awards. I therefore recommend that selection of the panels for any level of arbitration should follow these steps:

1. The central as well as the local labor commissions appointed by the minister of labor should maintain a large list of professional arbitrators, consisting of professionals in labor and industrial relations who can serve as neutral parties.
2. Selection of an arbitration panel should be made not by either the government or the chairman of the Central Labor Commission but by the parties themselves, on the basis of a rule such as the following: from the list of neutral arbitrators, labor and management representatives in the case involved should alternately strike out the names of undesired persons, with the last remaining person or persons becoming the arbitration panel.

This method would guarantee that arbitrators who betray their professional integrity or the neutrality vital to their profession would in the long run be selected out. This arbitration procedure should be followed in workplaces where strikes are legally prohibited, such as the government or defense-related industries, or in places where work stoppages cannot be practically tolerated because of the nature of the work.

Emergency Procedure

Chapter 6 of the Labor Dispute Adjustment Law stipulates an emergency procedure for any labor dispute in the public sector or for one that is likely to hurt the national economy or endanger the daily life of citizens. With the amendment of 1989, the cooling-off period for the emergency procedure was shortened from 30 to 20 days. This can be compared with the Japanese norm of 50 days and the U.S. emergency procedure cooling-off period of 80 days. Not only is 20 days inadequate, but the requirement for mediation under the emergency procedure is also unnecessary (Article 42). Much of the current emergency procedure is redundant to the procedures under Chapters 4, 5, and 6, namely conciliation, mediation, and arbitration as already discussed. This is probably why not a single case has been handled under the emergency procedures. The purpose of the emergency procedure is quite different from the previous impasse resolution. Therefore, I recommend that the current emergency procedure be supplemented by a final-offer arbitration (called "pendulum arbitration" in the United Kingdom) procedure by more effectively utilizing a fact-finding board as follows:[11]

1. Article 41 should be retained, except that the 20-day fact-finding period should be extended to 30 days, and Articles 42 and 43 should be deleted.

2. From the list of professional arbitrators kept by the Central Labor Commission (as discussed above), a fact-finding board panel should be appointed by the chairman of the Central Labor Commission within three days after the decision is made, on the basis of Article 40. This panel should consist of at least one employer representative, one employee representative, and one public representative from the Commission.

3. The fact-finding board should hold hearings, make on-site visits, request any necessary data from the parties, and then deliver its recommendations to the minister of labor within 20 days of the board's appointment. The minister of labor should make the board's recommendations available to the public.

4. If the parties do not come to an agreement voluntarily after the fact-finding board's recommendations, the parties should select the panel of arbitration within four days, according to the same rule as described above (by the method of striking out undesired arbitrators) without including anyone who was already on the fact-finding board for the same case.

5. Also within four days, parties should make final revision of their demands in reference to the fact-finding board's recommendations.
6. On the fifth day after the fact-finding board's recommendations are issued, the arbitration board should assemble and choose any one of the three—the fact-finding board's recommendations, the employer's final offer, or the employees' final demand. This choice should be final and binding and have the effect of a collective agreement.

Summary and Conclusions

In this chapter I have examined labor-management relations in the light of Korean history and also in comparative perspective. Recognizing that idiosyncratic cultural factors play a significant role in conditioning a country's managerial environment, I have offered a model for Korea's industrial relations system in developmental context, particularly after the democratization of 1987. I indicated earlier that Korean industrial relations would "have to move to stage D or risk peril at stage C." There has been some movement in that direction in recent years, especially after 1992: the number of labor disputes has decreased, and workplace violence has virtually disappeared. Thanks to a scarce labor supply, employers have become quite aware that, unless they treat workers humanely as their equals, they will not get genuine cooperation at the workplace. As the labor shortage has accelerated, Korean job search behavior has become choosier, with "dirty, difficult, or dangerous" jobs more often avoided. This situation will have to be overcome by restructuring the Korean wage system in such a way that these "three-D" jobs as well as productivity are reasonably compensated; currently, educational certificates and seniority are the sole criteria for wage determination. Also noteworthy is the 1 April 1993 agreement between national union (FKTU) and employer (KEF) federations on a wage increase guideline of 4.7–8.9 percent to be followed by individual bargaining units for 1993 wage negotiations. Though noncompulsory, this is the first time in Korean industrial relations history that employer and union federations have voluntarily reached such a "social consensus." Whether it can be repeated in the coming years remains to be seen, but such consensus is a good omen.

With equity and efficiency as my guiding principles in this world of unlimited competition, I have proposed several institutional reform measures, mostly aimed at the extensive amendment of existing labor laws. If these recommendations are followed, harmonious rather than adversarial industrial relations may be realized in the near future—stage D in my model. Without such legal and institutional innovation empowering workers to participate responsibly in decision making, it will not be possible to extract high commitment from the workers. Without repeating the details, let me summarize the highlights here:

1. An exclusive union representation election system should be adopted so that intraunion rivalry disputes can be minimized.
2. Management should delegate full authority to its representative at the bargaining table.
3. Regulations concerning unfair labor practices on the part of unions should be introduced so as to keep the balance of power between labor and management. Unfair labor practices by unions include (a) featherbedding, (b) secondary boycotts, including recognition strikes, (c) slowdowns or sit-in strikes, (d) sympathy strikes, and (e) forcing an employer to abdicate management rights.
4. The principle of "no work, no pay" should be strictly adhered to, and the maximum ceiling on union dues must be done away with so that unions can accumulate their own strike funds.
5. A grievance arbitration procedure should be made part of every collective bargaining agreement.
6. Union political activity in supporting or raising funds for friendly candidates should be allowed, but the use of union funds for political campaigns should continue to be prohibited as stipulated in current law.
7. Striking workers should not be allowed to occupy the workplace.
8. All arbitration panel members should be selected not by the chairman of the labor commission but by the contending parties themselves by the method of alternatively selecting out undesired person's names from the list of professional arbitrators.
9. The interest arbitration (final offer or pendulum arbitration) method should be adopted for the emergency procedure.

The following more general policy approaches would also expedite modernization of the Korean industrial relations system:

Labor and Trade Unions

- should fall into the hands of neither political activists nor "sweetheart" union leaders subservient to the management. A free labor union movement should stick to bread-and-butter issues for workers.
- should conduct extensive educational programs for workers.
- should participate jointly with managers in making decisions on (a) technological change and relocation, (b) rationalization of employment, (c) deployment procedure (reallocation of employment), (d) training and retraining programs, (e) prevention of industrial accidents and diseases plus alleviation programs for the victims, and (f) environmental protection measures.
- should assume as much social responsibility as the management is asked to assume.

Management

- should not only recognize the existence of a union once it comes into existence but also accommodate it as a joint decision-making partner without abdicating management rights.
- should change its traditional method of motivation. It should try to motivate contemporary workers more through intrinsic factors such as decentralization of authority and responsibility, thus making the work itself more interesting and rewarding psychologically. Management in every workplace is also encouraged to use a system of reinforcements (whether they be wages or other benefits) in such a way that employees perceive an equity between their input and outcome ratio comparable to that of their co-workers.
- should carry out management development programs, especially in human resource management and labor relations.
- should work toward the adoption of courses on wage and salary administration.

Government

- should search for policy alternatives. With the passage of the turning point in the Korean labor market, Korean industries must inevitably undergo an extensive restructuring process. Government should be able to cope with such structural unemployment problems with unemployment insurance and retraining programs.
- should protect the rights of both management and workers vis-à-vis layoffs. As the rationalization of employment becomes inevitable, the government should protect an employer's right to lay off redundant workers, just as it should protect laid-off workers by providing them with retraining opportunities for reemployment elsewhere.
- should avoid unnecessary intervention in industrial disputes. Conflict and cooperation, like labor and management relations, are two faces of the same coin. Employers frequently induce the government to intervene so as to avoid direct confrontation with labor. Employers often try to avoid increasing wages beyond their initial offer, ostensibly because of the government's wage guidelines. This is why I describe Korean labor relations as *labor-government* relations rather than labor-management relations. Reinstalling management prerogatives in the minds of Korean managers is a most urgent task if genuine cooperation between labor and management is to be achieved. In the midst of the rapid transition in labor market conditions, nothing seems more urgent than to strengthen both the management team and labor leaders so as to enable them to work together to enlarge the size of their pie and to agree on their fair share of it without government intervention. Government policy should be directed to this end: to have as little intervention as possible and to keep the power balance between the parties.

Finally, even with all these rational suggestions for institutional reform in effect, it may still not be possible to guarantee genuine harmony between labor and management. Rationality must also be supplemented by good human relations between employer and employee in the workplace. The egalitarian philosophy and brotherly sentiment that are widely shared among Korean workers also demand a high level of commitment on the part of managers toward their workers' welfare; this cannot be achieved easily unless managers are truly motivated by humanitarianism, which is one of the implications of the present report. Only when the two vital elements of logos and pathos are combined can the modernization of Korean industry succeed.

NOTES

I acknowledge my indebtedness to Professor K. Koshiro of Yokohama University, Professor Mario F. Bognanno of the University of Minnesota, and Dr. Jung Hyun Whang, Vice President of the Korea Federation of Employers, for their valuable comments and criticisms on an earlier draft of this chapter.

1. I use the term "industrial relations" interchangeably with "labor-management relations," although to be more precise the latter is a subset of the former.

2. Sometimes this high worker mobility is blamed by employers for a worker's tendency to lack commitment to the firm. But employers who pirate workers are also to be blamed. High turnover is a cost to the employer, but the high workforce mobility that is bad for employer A may be good for employer B and for society as a whole.

3. Subsequently, under pressure from the FKTU, the government announced that the industrial federation would thereafter not be considered a third party. The concept of a third party is very arbitrary. Employers disliked the presence of an industrial federation representative at the bargaining table even if he had been asked to attend by the president of the local chapter organized within his company. The local chapter president usually has been an employee of the company for many years, and therefore it is easier for him than for an outsider coming from the industrial federation to deal with management. The federation representative is more likely to be concerned with the general industry-wide wage level than with a specific enterprise's ability to pay. It is therefore very natural for any employer to dislike the federation representative. However, because of the daily face-to-face relationship between the employer and the local union president, it is extremely difficult and embarrassing for the latter to make any bold demands to his employer at the bargaining table without hurting their personal relationship. Therefore a local union president uses the federation representative as a scapegoat for the demands he actually wants to make. This being the case, the labor union vigorously protested the amendment, which had been interpreted by employers as categorizing the industrial federation as a third party. In response to this protest, the ministry announced that the industrial federation would not be considered a third party, but that other groups from the labor movement, such as the urban industrial league and religious groups not under the FKTU umbrella, were categorized as third parties.

4. According to John T. Dunlop (1958), the three key elements of any country's industrial relations system are *actors, environment*, and *ideology*. I analyze stages B, C, and D according to Dunlop's framework for its heuristic value.

5. See the experiences of the U.S. industry analyzed in Bognanno (1988).

6. A description of the Hyundai experience is provided above. At this same workplace, Hyundai shipyard, in early 1988, the same sort of intraunion rivalry dispute erupted again, resulting in a work stoppage of 112 days. The so-called labor-labor dispute (*ro-ro boon jaeng*) was a fight between a legitimate union with minority support and an unauthorized union with majority support (*hap-bup* vs. *shil-sae* union dispute). The long-lasting dispute was ended only by the government's forceful intervention and replacement of the minority leader with a new, middle-of-the-road leader through a new election. Had there been an amendment to Section 5 of Article 3 in such a way as to institute a representation election system in November 1987, we would have avoided this long labor-labor strike, not to mention numerous work stoppages over the years caused by similar problems elsewhere.

7. Note that the U.S. Taft-Hartley Act not only outlawed closed shop agreements but also stipulated unfair labor practices of unions to equalize the obligations of employers. The following six actions were outlawed as unfair labor union practices: (1) to deny an employee's right not to participate in the union (anti-closed shop agreement); (2) to cause an employer to discriminate against employees because of their union activity; (3) to refuse to bargain collectively with an employer; (4) to engage in a secondary boycott for the purpose of (a) forcing an employer or self-employed person to join a labor union, (b) forcing an employer to recognize a union not certified as a bargaining representative, (c) forcing an employer to recognize a union where the employees are already represented by another union, (d) forcing an employer to assign work to members of one union rather than another; (5) charging excessive dues; and (6) extracting payment from an employer for work not performed (featherbedding). Further, in 1959 the Landrum-Griffin Act outlawed a union's picketing for the purpose of forcing an employer to recognize a union without an election (Sandver 1987:193–200).

8. This proposal deserves special attention on the ground that a slowdown is actually nothing but a kind of sabotage, which results in greater damage to the employer. In Korea picketing on streets is prohibited for political reasons, and therefore striking workers must stay within the factory premises.

9. Many experienced union leaders admitted the validity of the principle of "no work, no pay." But they insisted that during the transitory period a subsistence amount should be given while a strike fund accumulates. Publicly, however, they all speak with one voice against the principle, in solidarity with young and more vocal members of the union. Some argue by the following analogy: "Do you stop feeding a hen on the days she does not lay eggs?"

10. According to this article, arbitration can commence (1) if it is requested by both parties, (2) if one party requests it on the basis of their existing agreement, or (3) if, in a public enterprise, either public authority or the Labor Relations Commission requests it.

11. I am indebted to my friend and colleague, Professor M. F. Bognanno, for his suggestions on this issue; see also Bognanno (1988).

REFERENCES

Bai, Mooki. 1982. "Structural Changes in Korean Labor Economy." Paper presented at the Seminar on the Korean Economy's Structural Changes, sponsored by the Economic Research Institute, Seoul National University.

Bognanno, Mario F. 1988. "Korea's Industrial Relations at the Turning Point." Paper prepared for the Korea Development Institute, December.

Dunlop, John T. 1958. *Industrial Relations Systems.* New York: Henry Holt.

Economic Planning Board, and Ministry of Labor, Republic of Korea. Various years. *Employment Statistics.* Seoul.

Federation of Korean Employers' Association. 1987. *Yearbook of Labor Economics.* Seoul.

Federation of Korean Employers' Association. Various years. *Labor Economics Almanac.* Seoul.

Federation of Korean Trade Unions (FKTU). Various years. *Annual Report of the Federation of Korean Trade Unions.* Seoul.

Kim, Jae Won. 1987. "Manpower Implications of the Sixth Five-Year Economic Plan." Presented at the Korea-Germany Seminar on Employment Effects of Technological Development, 7–8 March, sponsored by the Frederick Ebert Foundation and the Korean Labor Economic Association. Seoul.

Kim, Sookon. 1983a. "Current Status of Labor-Management Relations and the Direction of Institutional Reform." In Sookon Kim (ed.), *Labor-Management Relations and Task before Us: With Special Reference to Necessary Institutional Development.* Seoul: Korea Development Institute.

Kim, Sookon. 1983b. "Is the Japanese System of Lifetime Employment Applicable to a Developing Country Such As Korea?" Paper presented at the Sixth World Congress of the International Industrial Relations Association, Kyoto, Japan.

Kim, Sookon. 1983c. "Foreign Influence upon Development of Labor Management in Korea." In *Korean Social Development Studies,* no. 10. Seoul: Asiatic Research Center, Korea.

Kim, Sookon, and Tae Hyun Ha, eds. 1983. *Ro-Sa-Kwan-Kye Sa-Rye Youn-Koo* (A case study on labor-management relations). Seoul: Korea Development Institute.

Kim, Yoon Whan. 1982. *Han-kook no-dong woon-dong-sa* (History of the Korean labor movement). Seoul: Chung Sa Publishing.

Koike, Kazuo. 1987. "Human Resource Development and Labor-Management Relations." In Kozoo Yamamura and Ysukichi Yasuba (eds.), *The Political Economy of Japan,* vol. 1. Stanford: Stanford University Press.

Macmillan, Michael E. 1987. "Labor Policy under the American Military Government in Korea, 1945–1948." Ph.D. diss., Department of History, University of Hawaii.

McGregor, Douglas. 1960. *The Human Side of Enterprise.* New York: McGraw Hill.

Ministry of Labor, Republic of Korea. 1982. *Yearbook of Labor-Statistics.* Seoul.

Ministry of Labor, Republic of Korea. 1990. *Current Labor Status.* Seoul.

Park, Funkoo. 1982. "Shipbuilding Industry." In Sookon Kim and Tae Hyn Ha (eds.), *Case Studies on Labor-Management Relations.* Seoul: Korea Development Institute.

Ross, Arthur M. 1957. *Trade Union Wage Policy.* Berkeley: University of California Press.

Sandver, Marcus H. 1987. *Labor Relations: Process and Outcomes.* Boston: Little, Brown.

Seashore, Stanley E. 1954. *Group Cohesiveness in the Industrial Work Group.* Ann Arbor: Institute for Social Research.

Chapter 21

Industrial Relations and Human Resource Policy in Korea: Options for Continued Reform

Thomas A. Kochan
Massachusetts Institute of Technology

Introduction

Two different stories emerge from most descriptions of the evolution of industrial relations and human resource management in the Republic of Korea. The first describes an economic development miracle—a success story of a highly educated, hard-working, low-cost, and disciplined workforce (Steers, Shin, and Ungson 1989; Amsden 1989). This story stresses the fact that, as shown in Table 21.1, Korea has produced consistent improvements in real wages since 1960 and, until recently, enjoyed double-digit rates of economic growth. The second is a story of suppression of labor and worker rights, authoritarian managerial rule, long hours of work in an environment where labor standards and health and safety conditions are not enforced, and violent repression of independent or democratic unionism (Deyo 1989; Ogle 1990). Both descriptions provide accurate but partial caricatures of the pre-1987 situation and to a lesser extent the current state of industrial relations and human resource management practices in Korea.

Yet there is widespread agreement among experts from all perspectives that the Korean industrial relations system is undergoing an important transition that makes neither of these caricatures viable for the future. With the announcement of democratic reforms in 1987, Korea took a major first step toward modernizing and democratizing its industrial relations system. The task, however, is far from complete. Thus, the next few years will be a period in which policymakers in Korea must decide the type of system that best suits the economic and socials needs of its workforce, economy, and society.

Making informed choices is especially important at this juncture in Korea's development. Indeed, some observers see labor relations as the pivotal issue affecting Korea's future economic performance—or as the *Economist* put it, the "Achilles

TABLE 21.1
Gross domestic product and real wage changes (1985 prices)

	Gross domestic product (billion won)	Real wages, all manufacturing (monthly won)
1960	10,922	
1961	11,561	
1962	11,808	
1963	12,887	
1964	14,133	
1965	14,945	
1966	16,765	55,306
1967	17,754	60,917
1968	19,766	70,000
1969	22,503	82,868
1970	24,475	91,089
1971	26,726	93,320
1972	28,314	95,090
1973	32,398	108,398
1974	34,961	118,004
1975	37,230	119,931
1976	42,151	140,068
1977	46,749	169,946
1978	51,289	199,371
1979	55,102	216,906
1980	53,989	206,889
1981	57,615	204,618
1982	61,821	219,216
1983	69,101	237,725
1984	75,606	251,292
1985	80,847	269,652
1986	90,868	286,464
1987	101,804	310,383
1988	113,492	346,305
1989	120,429	410,035

Source: IMF (1990).

heel" in economic policy. The dimensions of the issue can be stated as follows. Since approximately 30 percent of the country's GNP is derived from exports, Korea must remain competitive in world markets. Yet it is rapidly losing the comparative advantage used to establish its strong position in world markets; it is now in a position of high labor costs relative to other newly industrializing countries of Asia and Latin America (Table 21.2). Thus, Korean industry must place greater

Table 21.2
Relative hourly compensation costs for manufacturing production workers

	1975	1980	1981	1982	1983	1984	1985	1986	1987	1988	1989	1990
United States	100	100	100	100	100	100	100	100	100	100	100	100
Korea	6	10	10	10	10	10	10	11	13	18	25	28
Brazil	14	14	15	15	10	9	9	11	10	11	12	19
West Germany	100	125	97	88	85	75	74	101	126	130	123	144
Hong Kong	12	15	14	14	12	13	13	14	16	17	20	22
Japan	48	57	57	49	51	51	50	70	81	92	88	87
Mexico	—	—	—	—	—	—	12	8	8	10	11	12
Pakistan	3	4	3	3	3	2	2	3	—	—	—	—
Portugal	25	21	19	16	13	12	12	16	19	19	20	24
Singapore	13	15	17	17	18	20	19	17	17	19	22	25
Taiwan	6	10	11	11	11	11	12	13	17	20	25	27

Source: U.S. Bureau of Labor Statistics (1991).

emphasis on technology, innovation, product quality, and human resources as sources of competitive advantage in the future.

At the same time, Korean society is deeply committed to continuing along the path of democratic reforms and aspires to become a more respected member of the international community; accordingly, it expects to have its labor policies judged against democratic International Labour Organisation (ILO) standards. Korean workers do more than share this interest in democratization; they, along with students, have led the fight for broader democratic rights and for improvements in their standards of living and remain militant in their demands for improved wages and working conditions.

Thus, stated succinctly, the challenge for Korea is to move from its dependence on a low-wage development strategy to a high-productivity, high-value-added strategy while simultaneously sharing more of the benefits of economic growth with its workforce and continuing along the path of democratic reforms.

How, then, can Korea adapt its industrial relations and human resource practices to achieve these objectives? This debate is well under way within the academic, policymaking, and practitioner communities in Korea. Foremost in these debates is the question of what insights, if any, can be gained from models of industrial relations and human resource practices in other countries. Of particular interest are the practices found in Japan, the United States, and Germany. This focus seems appropriate, because, as I note later in this chapter, current industrial relations in Korea feature a mixture of practices borrowed from these three systems but embedded in a unique Korean culture and historical setting.

My purpose in this chapter is to analyze the relationship of current labor policy and practices and proposed reforms to these alternative models and to draw implications for future strategies for reform in Korea. Readers are referred to Sookon

Kim's contribution to this volume (Chapter 20) for a more detailed description and analysis of the historical development and current features of the Korean industrial relations system. The present chapter, a companion to Professor Kim's, seeks to bring an outsider's perspective to the range of alternatives open to the parties for proactively shaping their future. In doing so it applies a strategic choice model of industrial relations (Kochan, Katz, and McKersie 1986). This perspective is particularly appropriate now because Korea's traditional policies and institutions were opened up to scrutiny and change by the announcement of democratic reforms on 29 June 1987 by President Roh Tae Woo and by the subsequent growth of labor unrest and unionization. Thus, the system is not in a stable equilibrium. Instead, it is moving through a historic juncture similar to that experienced in the United States in the 1930s, in Japan in the early 1950s, and in Germany in the early postwar years. Periods like this offer greater room for strategic choice on the part of labor, management, and government than do periods of political and economic stability when institutions are more resistant to fundamental change.

One other perspective needs to be made explicit. I believe it is important to see industrial relations and human resource practices at the firm and as regulated through government policy as a closely related system of practices and institutions. Indeed, one of the problems with most of the literature on Korea, and much of policymaking and enterprise-level practice, is that labor-management relations and human resource policy are treated as separate domains. The analytical approach developed in this chapter argues that industrial relations and human resource policies and practices make their greatest contribution when treated as a single system and integrated with the competitive strategies and governance arrangements of the firm and the economic and social policies of the country.

Figure 21.1 presents the generic framework used to organize my analysis of industrial relations and human resource practices at the level of the firm. The framework differentiates among policies and practices at (1) the highest or strategic level of the firm where long-term values, basic competitive strategies, and governance arrangements are determined; (2) the functional or personnel policy level where standard personnel policies such as training, compensation, and staffing practices are determined; and (3) the workplace level where job designs, employee participation, and the nature of day-to-day labor-management relations are carried out. Within these levels, Figure 21.1 outlines a set of generic principles that contemporary theory suggests are needed to achieve the twin goals of an economy that is competitive in world markets with a high and advancing standard of living.

Although this framework emphasizes firm-level policies and practices, not all these choices are within the sole discretion of the individual firm, either unilaterally or collectively with labor organizations. The role of government policy, in conjunction with market forces, technological opportunities and requirements, and the larger values of society or cultural influences all affect the viability of different firm choices. Indeed, the interconnections between firm-level and government

Strategic Level
Supportive management values and organizational culture
Competitive strategies that emphasize value added
Effective integration of human resources in strategy making and organizational governance
Broad sharing of information

Functional (Personnel Policy) Level
Supportive management reward and development system
Contingent compensation system
Commitment to employment stabilization and adjustment policies
Comprehensive training and development policies

Workplace Level
Highly educated, skilled, and committed workforce
Broad, flexible job designs and teamwork
Employee participation and empowerment to solve problems
Cooperative labor-management relations

FIGURE 21.1 Generic principles for gaining competitive advantage from enterprise-level human resource and industrial relations policies.

policies complete the analysis of the institutional structure of an industrial relations system.

No two countries follow the same set of practices in structuring these activities. Indeed, we can use this framework to characterize the broad differences among alternative industrial relations systems and thereby highlight and evaluate various alternatives available for designing industrial relations policies and practices. I now turn to this task by comparing three distinctive approaches to structuring industrial relations, found in the United States, Germany, and Japan.

Alternative Models of Industrial Relations

The United States: From a Traditional to a Transformed Model

The industrial relations system in the United States is often described as an example of a "pluralist" system since it relies heavily on a decentralized approach that emphasizes the rights of labor and management to negotiate and resolve conflicting interests and to pursue areas of common interest with minimal government involvement (Clegg 1976). Under the pluralist model, the government serves as a mediator of these private interests by establishing the procedural rules for collective bargaining and labor-management interaction. Out of the free interplay of these competing interests should emerge substantive outcomes that promote and balance the twin goals of democracy and economic efficiency.

Although the basic legal doctrines on which the system rests date back to the New Deal labor legislation of the 1930s, since the early 1980s the parties have been seeking to introduce reforms in an effort to transform the system in fundamental ways (Kochan, Katz, and McKersie 1986). Thus, in presenting the U.S. model and assessing its relevance for current and future policies in Korea, we need to distinguish between traditional and transformed U.S. industrial relations practices.

The traditional New Deal model rests on three basic principles corresponding to the three levels of activity outlined in Figure 21.1. The centerpiece of the traditional model is collective bargaining: in 1935, workers and their representatives gained the right to form unions of their own choosing to negotiate wages, hours, and conditions of employment. In return, for accepting the procedures established for union elections and recognition, management maintained the right to make the strategic decisions affecting the firm's long-run values, competitive strategies, and other organizational policies without the need to consult with or involve workers or their representatives. At the workplace this collective bargaining system was supported by written labor contracts that are legally enforceable through a private grievance and arbitration system. When it first emerged in the 1930s, the system inherited a strong legacy of scientific management and industrial engineering and translated these job design principles into what eventually turned out to be a rather rigid set of rules which my colleagues and I have described as "job control unionism."

This model gradually expanded across manufacturing, transportation, communications, and utility industries in the aftermath of the Great Depression so that by the early 1950s approximately 35 percent of the American workforce was unionized and a significant number of nonunion firms followed personnel practices that were similar to many of those found in the unionized sector. The system worked well because it could bring labor-management stability through negotiations and grievance arbitration and because wage rules evolved that helped to "take wages out of competition" among workers in competing labor and product markets. Since the economy was expanding, labor showed little interest in influencing strategic management policies. Rather, it was content to let management manage and to use the formal negotiations process and the controls built into job control unionism at the workplace to achieve job security and economic advancement for its members. One of its most important early achievements was its success in reducing the deep worker unrest and protests associated with sitdown strikes and violent labor-management battles over union recognition by establishing formal election procedures and principles under which workers could choose their representatives and an impartial government agency administered the voting and recognition process.

This traditional system experienced significant difficulties in recent years as the U.S. economy was affected by increased international competition, the need for greater flexibility in job structures, and the growing range of strategic choices open to American firms regarding where to invest, where to locate production or service facilities, and whether or not to continue to accept union representation in new establishments or firms. The separation of management's strategic actions from labor's rights embedded in the New Deal model posed significant hardships on workers and unions as employers acted to restructure their way out of high-cost locations or market positions. The fact that American labor policy continues to follow an "employment at will" doctrine which leaves management free to dismiss workers without prior consultation (except in the case of mass layoffs or plant closings, for which 60 days advance notice is now required) reenforces rigidities in internal labor markets because it heightens workers' concerns for control over their specific job rights at the workplace (Osterman 1988).

As a result, the 1980s was characterized by both a great deal of conflict over the principles associated with the traditional system and a great deal of innovation as companies and unions experimented with ways to transform their practices. The United States now has a system in which unionization continues to decline (currently approximately 16 percent of the American workforce is unionized) but with pockets of innovative relationships in which labor and management engage in greater consultation over long-run policies at the strategic level of the firm, introduce greater direct employee involvement and participation at the workplace with more flexible, team-based work redesign principles, and give greater emphasis to training, employment security, and flexibility in wage setting and structures.

Thus, the traditional American industrial relations system has been under siege in a world dominated by global markets and strong international competitors, changing technologies, and the requirements of a system of human resource management that can help firms gain competitive advantage from their human resources. Yet this transformation process is far from complete, in part because American policymakers are caught in a political stalemate over whether to support reforms of the traditional system or to maintain their traditional pluralist position of leaving business and labor to work out their competing interests on their own. Indeed, recognition of the institutional weaknesses in the traditional American system and the slowness of diffusion of the transformed model or practices is now leading many American scholars, practitioners, and policymakers to look abroad—first to Japan and more recently to Germany and other European nations—for alternative models from which the United States might learn.

The Japanese Model

So much has been written about Japanese industrial relations that they need to be only briefly reviewed here in the context of the institutional framework outlined in Figure 21.1. The Japanese model defies any single-term description. Though it is decentralized and enterprise-based, it is more centralized than the U.S. model since broad corporate values and principles are more influential in the conduct of industrial relations and human resources in specific business units and workplaces than in the United States.

The strategic level of Japanese industrial relations starts from a model of the firm that elevates employees as stakeholders to a higher level of influence and consideration than is the case in the United States (Dore 1992). Top executives are under strong social and moral expectations, as well as some legal and financial pressures and incentives, to manage the firm in ways that promote long-term growth, employment stability, and employee commitment and cooperation at the workplace (Shirai 1983). Japanese financial markets encourage this long-run view with large equity and debt positions held by banks that have long-term relationships with the large firms.

Human resource executives and human resource policies therefore enjoy considerably higher status in Japan than in the United States, and this supports a closer integration of human resource and industrial relations policies and strategies with the competitive strategies and long-term or top-level decisions within the firm (Aoki 1988). These features are viewed as important sources to firms and economies that seek competitive advantage from the development and utilization of their human resources in support of competitive strategies that emphasize flexibility and adaptability, technological innovation, and product differentiation and quality.

At the level of personnel policy, Japanese firms have long maintained a commitment to employment continuity and thus an equally strong commitment to continuous training and career development of its workforce. In turn, rather than long-term, fixed-wage contracts, wages are adjusted annually through the "Spring Wage Offensive" and base wages are supplemented with annual bonuses, which theoretically at least if not always in practice can vary according to the performance of the firm and the economy. Thus, employment adjustment in Japan is less responsive in the short run to cyclical variations in labor demand than is the typical case in the United States. Positive adjustment policies have, however, helped the Japanese economy move out of declining industries effectively over time without major economic or social disruptions (Dore 1986).

Unions in Japan are organized on an enterprise basis and include blue and white collar workers in the same organization. In fact, many top-level executives are former union leaders (Shirai 1983). Although recently a new national federation of unions has been formed, labor-management relations remain largely enterprise-based. The most significant exception to this is the annual round of government, business, and labor consultations and subsequent labor-management negotiations during the Spring Wage Offensive. The results of the key wage settlement, usually in the railroad or steel industry, then sets the basic pattern or norms for enterprise-specific wage negotiations (Dore 1992).

At the workplace the long-term employment security commitment of the firm and the need for continuous training and development produce a more flexible job structure in which both blue and white collar employees are rotated across a wider array of jobs and departments as part of the training and career development process (Cole 1989). Widespread use of quality circles and other forms of employee involvement in problem solving are other features of the workplace in Japan that serve to promote continuous improvement in productivity and product quality.

Although labor-management relations remain largely enterprise-based and there are no formal or legal structures for tripartite consultations over government, labor, human resource, or economic policymaking, a variety of national institutions such as the Ministry of Industry and Trade, the Japanese Productivity Center, and the Japanese Institute of Labor produce large amounts of information and analyses in support of labor and human resource policymaking and negotiations.

It should be noted that these features of Japanese employment relations do not apply equally to all firms or workers. Japanese law prohibits employment discrimination against women and minorities, but by custom Japanese women and most foreign workers have been excluded from the lifetime employment system and have not attained the higher-level jobs in most large and small corporations. The lifetime employment system also does not extend to many smaller firms or subcontractors of the large enterprises, nor is it as prevalent in the fast-growing technical and service occupations and firms in Japan. Indeed, this partial diffusion of the Japanese model continues to be a source of tension and pressure within the country, especially as Japan experiences labor shortages. Currently, debates over the role of immigrant labor, career opportunities for women, the retirement age, and workers' standards of living are placing pressures on the system to adapt to a more diverse workforce and the need to offer Japanese workers more leisure time and a stronger voice for workers' interests in macroeconomic and social policymaking.

The German Case: Formalized Governance Sharing

The German industrial relations system contrasts with the U.S. and Japanese systems in its emphasis on formal, legally mandated structures for worker representation and participation in decision making at the strategic and personnel policymaking levels of the enterprise and in government policymaking and administration. Thus, although it is more decentralized than some of its northern European neighbors, it is often used as an example of a "corporatist" industrial relations system that has achieved an effective social partnership among government, business, and labor (Streeck 1991).

Workers are formally represented at the strategic level of decision making within German firms through their rights to codetermination, that is, representation on the supervisory boards of German companies. One of the key functions of this board is to appoint top corporate managers including the *Arbietsdirektor*, or personnel director. This individual must be approved by the majority of the worker representatives on the supervisory board. Thus, worker interests and human resource issues are formally integrated into the governance structure and strategic decision-making processes of German firms.

At the personnel policy level, legally mandated works councils provide additional employee consultation rights and input into the design and administration of such issues as training, layoffs and employment adjustment, technological change, safety and health, and other personnel issues. Collective bargaining in Germany takes place largely outside the firm at the industry and regional levels through a structure of industrial unions and corresponding employer associations. In addition, German law provides for the extension of basic wage agreements to all workers in an industry, thereby further institutionalizing the practice of taking wages out of competition within the domestic economy.

Workplace industrial relations in Germany are tightly linked to the country's well-developed system of apprenticeship training and education. Over 60 percent of all German workers have completed apprenticeships and met the standards set for these occupations by oversight committees of employer and union representatives. Thus, internal labor markets are organized around these occupational structures. The high quality of the preparation provided German workers leads to an internal labor market with relatively few status distinctions between blue and white collar workers, fewer supervisors than are typically found in American or other European firms, and few rules governing the allocation of work. Flexibility in internal labor markets is supported by public policies that require firms to develop a social plan with their works councils before laying off workers or closing facilities. These features, along with a strong work ethic embedded deep in the German culture, give Germany its reputation for having a cooperative, flexible, productive, and well-integrated industrial relations and human resource management system.

These enterprise structures are supported by a tradition of a labor-business-government partnership in overseeing the training and human resource development policies within specific industries and at the national level. German unions and employers are therefore consulted on and involved in the administration of a wide range of labor, social, and economic policies of the country. Friedrich Fuerstenberg provides a succinct description of the German case: "Union policy is 'co-operative' insofar as the unions receive information and are consulted about all major areas of social and economic policy. This extends to practically all public policy relating to the quality of life of the working population and their dependents. Though the unions are technically neutral in party politics, their political presence is obvious. Thus, the West German unions are not only powerful partners in collective bargaining, but they also exert great influence on political and social life" (1987:169).

This role is similar to that in more centralized systems such as those in Sweden, Austria, and Denmark, where strong labor and social democratic political parties with strong ties to the labor movement provide the political power and centralized discipline needed to support a corporatist model over an extended period of time (Katzenstein 1985; Swenson 1989).

Shared Features of Advanced Industrial Relations Systems

In addition to their distinctive practices and institutions, these three industrial relations systems share characteristics found in all advanced democratic market-based economies. All systems start by respecting the bedrock principle of workers' rights to organize into unions of their own choosing. The structures and relationships of unions with employers and government differ in each country, but all recognize workers' rights to choose whether or not to be represented, and if so, which union to join. Second, all advanced industrial relations systems are held accountable and evaluated against their effectiveness in meeting the dual objectives of equity and efficiency (Barbash 1984; Meltz 1989). Stated differently, national policies and enterprise practices need to support both the effective negotiation and resolution of disputes where the parties' interests conflict and the pursuit of joint gains on issues where the parties share common goals or interests (Cutcher-Gershenfeld 1991). These, therefore, are the broad standards against which Korean policies are evaluated both in this chapter and, more generally, by the world community.

The Korean Industrial Relations System

Any comparison of the three industrial relations systems reviewed above with Korea's must acknowledge that in many ways the latter is at its very early stages of development. Only since 1987 have the commonly accepted democratic standards and criteria for evaluating the effectiveness of an industrial relations system begun to be recognized there. Prior to the announcement of democratic reforms on 29 June 1987, one criterion dominated—economic growth. Government policy was described as "develop first, share later" (S. Kim, Chapter 20).

My interviews with employer, government, and labor representatives suggested that it is not yet clear whether Korean policymakers fully accept the need to evaluate their industrial relations institutions against these broader standards of democracy, equity, and distributive justice. For example, the government still does not accept the basic principle that it is workers, not government or business, who should determine which union (if any) is to represent them in collective bargaining and political affairs. Instead, government policies continue to suppress unions affiliated with Chonnohyup (the Korean Trade Union Congress) or Chunkyojo (the Korean Teachers' Union). Thus, a starting point for *any* reforms of industrial relations policy must be an acceptance of these basic criteria or standards. Without this, none of the institutional alternatives discussed in this chapter, in Professor Kim's, or elsewhere (e.g., Bognanno 1988; Ogle 1990; Im 1990; M. B. Lee 1991) are likely to be feasible or acceptable.

One of the most important features of Korea's remarkable economic development process has been the strong role played by state policy, particularly in its ability to discipline and influence large businesses that dominate the Korean economy (Amsden 1989). The state has played an equally dominant role in Korea's industrial relations system, both before 1987 and currently. The key question for the future is whether the state will be able to continue to play this dominant role in the future or whether, given the dissatisfaction with government that seems to be building up among both business and the Korean public, business and to some extent labor will more forcefully challenge government initiatives. Thus, we start our analysis of contemporary practices and options for the future by considering the role of the Korean government.

Macroeconomic, Human Resource, and Labor Policy

For an advanced industrial relations system to contribute to macroeconomic and social welfare, its policies must be effectively integrated into national economic policymaking. This is the national level counterpart to the firm-level principle that human resource plans and policies must be well integrated into an enterprise's competitive strategies and planning processes.

Recently, efforts have begun in Korea to achieve this objective by attempting to create a "social partnership" among labor, business, and government similar to the corporatist arrangements found in Germany and other European counties. Indeed, the draft of the government's Seventh Five-Year Economic and Social Development Plan would establish the development of a social partnership as an explicit policy objective. The hope is that a German style of corporatism might evolve that will produce consensus, wage moderation, and stable labor-management relations and thereby contribute to continued economic prosperity.

In 1989 the government attempted to take a first step in this direction by proposing a tripartite national commission to recommend or possibly even decide on wage increases for different industries. This effort failed when the Federation of Korean Trade Unions (FKTU) rejected the proposal, arguing that the commission was simply a government effort to impose wage restraints (Im 1990). In place of this tripartite commission emerged the bilateral (labor and management without formal government participation but including several academic experts) National Social and Economic Council. This council has met several times and discussed a wide range of economic, social, and labor issues. At a 1991 meeting the council issued a statement of broad principles for achieving "stable labor-management relations." The main points in this declaration are these:

- Labor and management should solve problems through voluntary dialogue.
- Both parties should recognize their social responsibility to lead sound management and labor activities.
- Employers should work hard to distribute the fruits of growth in a fair way and to expand workers' welfare.
- Employers should strive to develop technology and invest in facilities.
- Employees should boost their work ethic and become more responsible workers.
- Both labor and management should demand that the government stabilize prices, solve the housing problem, eradicate land speculation, pursue consistent economic policies, and accelerate democratic reforms.

These principles reflect the values and standards expected of an advanced industrial relations system, but the real question is whether Korean policymakers are ready to accept these challenges and whether the institutional structures are able to implement them. There is a vast literature on the emergence and sustainability, and more recently on the decline, of corporatism in Western Europe (Pizzorno 1978; Offe 1981; Maier 1985; Katzenstein 1985; Goldthorpe 1985; Im 1990). The features most often cited as necessary for corporatism to evolve include (1) a government and management environment that accepts labor as a legitimate and valued partner in policymaking; (2) a government in which labor enjoys considerable political influence and access; (3) a high degree of unionization; (4) a centralized and unified union structure and movement; and (5) an equally centralized peak association that can represent and enforce commitments among employers. Some also believe that corporatism can survive only in an economy that has favorable long-term rates of economic growth that can be reasonably projected to continue into the future. In addition to these basic features, the social partnerships in both Germany and Japan are supported by well-developed and respected information and policy analysis infrastructures that supply the data, analysis, and expertise needed for informed policy debates and decision making.

As noted earlier, there is considerable interest in achieving a corporatist style social partnership in Korea among government, business, and labor interests. However, just listing the features necessary to make such a partnership feasible makes it obvious how few of the preconditions are present in Korea and thus highlights some of the issues that will need to be addressed if the parties wish to move in this direction.

One of the primary weaknesses in Korea's efforts to promote a social partnership is the lack of integration between macroeconomic policymaking and analysis and the administration and policymaking processes that govern labor and human resource issues. Macroeconomic policymaking lies within the domain of a small set of economists who advise the president and the Economic Planning Board (EPB). The EPB is responsible for long-range planning. This agency also serves as the coordinating body that oversees the budgets of the various government ministries, including the Ministry of Labor. Most of the macroeconomists who staff these agencies lack significant background in labor economics or industrial relations. Indeed, labor economics was not taught in most graduate or undergraduate economics departments in Korean universities until very recently. Thus, these macroeconomists have a relatively narrow and perhaps superficial view of the substance and scope of labor and human resource issues.

My interviews with officials of the EPB and other government policymakers reinforced this concern. When asked for their views on labor policy, EPB economists focused almost exclusively on the need to contain and lower the growth of wages in order to keep firms competitive in world markets. Even here, the government was seen as having limited tools at its disposal. Little, if any, consideration appears to be given to the need to develop labor and human resource policies that support a transition to an economy that competes on the basis of high value-added products and services.

Discussions with other economists and labor policy experts indicated a deep dissatisfaction with the level of economic analysis of labor issues occurring in national policymaking circles. In the absence of strong analysis, labor policy was described as being determined solely on the basis of short-run political needs and expediency. The labor minister is basically expected to hold the lid on labor conflict rather than to develop a coherent long-term approach to labor policy and its development. Policy seems to be determined more by purely political needs and influenced by the mass media than informed by economic analysis. Thus, there is a critical need to upgrade the quantity and quality of labor and human resource policy analysis in the government or to develop institutions that coordinate economic, labor, and human resource policymaking.

This approach to policymaking often leads to piecemeal enactment of social and labor policies which serves to drive up labor costs without due consideration for the benefits to workers or the economy. One example is the proposed program to have employers set aside 3 percent of profits to be allocated to various worker welfare programs. This policy was proposed by the government in the same year it was asking employers to adhere to a "one-digit wage policy." The result of such an approach is to misallocate resources by forcing employers to put more of their labor costs into government-mandated areas rather than putting these scarce won into areas that respond to labor market signals or are jointly negotiated in collective bargaining.

Though one might expect the Ministry of Labor to serve as lead agency for labor policy analysis, the ministry suffers from the problem of having to enforce a set of labor relations laws that are viewed as illegitimate by a substantial portion of the unions in the country. Thus, the labor minister is called on to join with police and the Department of Justice in deciding whether to arrest and prosecute union leaders who engage in strikes or other activities outside the current law.

Indeed, the number of arrests of union leaders and activists has increased substantially since 1988 after the government decided to abandon its noninterventionist policy of 1987. Between 1988 and May 1991 more than 1,200 union leaders and activists were arrested (*Labor Weekly*, April 1991). Given his role in the enforcement of an unpopular law, it is difficult for the minister of labor to oversee policy research that is deemed to be credible. I return to this issue in the final section on policy options by suggesting that the Ministry of Labor or some other institution with greater credibility will need to conduct and disseminate data and research that has broad utility for policy debates and decision making.

Fundamentals of Labor Law

Regardless of who conducts the policymaking process, all advanced democratic governments are expected to support policies that conform to the basic right of workers to choose who, if anyone, is to represent them at the workplace. From papal encyclicals to ILO conventions to generally accepted norms for a democratic government and society, this right is viewed as a basic and fundamental worker and human right. The mechanisms used in different countries to implement and protect this right varies considerably, but all policies are expected to meet the tests of the principles spelled out in ILO Convention 87 (Figure 21.2).

Whether Korean labor law conforms to these international standards is a source of great controversy within the country. Indeed, the law is sufficiently complex that it is best to rely on the words of Korean experts to summarize its provisions. Professor Young-Ki Park (1991), a senior Korean labor scholar, describes Korean labor law as follows:

> The Labour Union law (L.U.L.) regulates the crucial areas of labour relations such as labour unions, collective bargaining and unfair labour practices. Under the L.U.L. a union is defined as "a voluntary organisation or a federation of organisations formed at the initiative of the workers with the aims of maintaining and improving working conditions and seeking the enhancement of their economic and social status" (L.U.L. Article 3).
>
> Various impediments are placed in the way of unions which are not officially approved, thereby making it very difficult for approved unions to assist in their activities. First, the L.U.L. stipulates that unless a workers' organisation receives an official registration certificate it cannot "be authorized to request an adjustment of labour disputes by the Labour Relations Commission" (L.U.L. Article 7-1) and further, that "only an organisation formed in pursuance of this law may call itself a labour union" (Article 7-2). No legal protection is applied to unions whose jurisdiction overlaps with an existing officially recognized union, or where the purpose of a union is to hamper the ordinary operation of an existing labour union (L.U.L. Article 3, proviso 5). . . .
>
> . . . When a new local union is formed, the law requires the new local first to obtain written recognition from the appropriate national industrial federation.
>
> . . . Regarding the representation of the union at the bargaining table, the L.U.L. makes it possible for only the chief executive of the union, or the worker representative duly empowered by the union, to have the right to bargain.

The provisions critics find the most objectionable and inconsistent with democratic standards are those that (1) require new unions to be part of the existing Federation of Korean Trade Unions; (2) the prohibitions on the use of "third party" advisors by unions in negotiations; (3) the exclusion of teachers and other civil servants from the right to organize; and (4) the limits on political activities of union leaders. These features serve to divide the labor movement, since the FKTU is seen as benefiting from the recognition provisions and the newer unions that have attempted to organize after 1987 are excluded from recognition unless they join and do not compete with an existing FKTU organization. Given this interunion

Part I. Freedom of Association

Article 1

Each member of the International Labour Organisation for which this Convention is in force undertakes to give effect to the following provisions.

Article 2

Workers and employers, without distinction whatsoever, shall have the right to establish and, subject only to the rules of the organisation concerned, join organisations of their own choosing without previous authorization.

Article 3

1. Workers' and employers' organisations shall have the right to draw up their constitutions and rules, elect their representatives in full freedom, to organise their administration and activities and to formulate programmes.
2. The public authorities shall refrain from any interference which would restrict this right or impede the lawful exercise thereof.

Article 4

Workers' and employers' organisations shall not be liable to be dissolved or suspended by administrative authority.

Article 5

Workers' and employers' organisations shall have the right to establish and join federations and confederations and any such organisation, federation and confederation shall have the right to affiliate with international organisations of workers and employers.

Article 6

The provisions of Articles 2, 3 and 4 hereof apply to federations and confederations of workers' and employers' organisations.

Article 7

The acquisition of legal personality by workers' and employers' organisations, federations and confederations shall not be made subject to conditions of such a character as to restrict the application of the provisions of Articles 2, 3 and 4 hereof.

Article 8

1. In exercising the rights provided for in this Convention workers and employers and their respective organisations, like other persons or organised collectivities, shall respect the law of the land.
2. The law of the land shall not be such as to impair, nor shall it be so applied as to impair, the guarantees provided for in this Convention.

Article 9

1. The extent to which the guarantees provided for in this Convention shall apply to the armed forces and the police shall be determined by national laws and regulations.
2. In accordance with the principles set forth in paragraph 8 of article 19 of the Constitution of the International Labour Organisation the ratification of this Convention by any member shall not be deemed to affect any existing law, award, custom or agreement in virtue of which members of the armed forces or the police enjoy any right guaranteed by this convention.

Article 10

In this Convention the term "organisations" means any organisation of workers or of employers for furthering and defending the interests of workers or of employers.

Part II. Protection of the Right To Organise

Article 11

Each member of the International Labour Organisation for which this Convention is in force undertakes to take all necessary and appropriate measures to ensure that workers and employers may exercise freely the right to organise.

FIGURE 21.2 International Labour Organisation: Convention (No. 87): Concerning Freedom of Association and Protection of the Right to Organise (1948).

conflict, efforts to create a social partnership with a credible and unified labor movement are unlikely to be successful. This does not necessarily imply, however, that at some stage in the institutional development of Korea national dialogue cannot be fruitfully pursued.

Industrial Relations and Human Resources in Korean Enterprises

Managerial Values and Corporate Governance

Managerial values and the structure and governance of Korean corporations reflect the strong influence of the country's Confucian heritage. This heritage has been viewed as a source of competitive strength for Korean industry in the past but one that requires significant adaptation to be compatible with the democratization of society and industrial relations (Steers, Shin, and Ungson 1989; Ogle 1990; Cho 1991; M. B. Lee 1991). The challenge therefore lies in adapting managerial styles and decision-making structures to promote human resource development and labor-management relations in ways that are compatible with the positive and enduring aspects of Korean culture and traditions.

The Confucian heritage implies that top executives are expected to treat their employees in a paternalistic fashion and in return to receive cooperation, respect, loyalty, and acceptance of managerial authority. This set of values translates into a tradition of highly centralized decision making and strong hierarchical control. This tradition of centralized control is reinforced by the strong role of family owners or founders in many of the large *jaebul* and other Korean firms.

Management style has traditionally been highly authoritarian. Individual managers traditionally had little discretion in their job assignments or in decisions about whether to accept a job transfer. Indeed, it is quite common for managerial assignments and transfers to be determined by the company president rather than by group or department managers. Hours of work have tended to be longer in Korea than other industrialized countries and other comparable industrializing countries in Asia. The average workweek in Korea declined from 54 hours in 1980 to 48 hours in 1989, but managers are expected to work as much as 70 or 80 hours per week (Steers, Shin, and Ungson 1989:107). All these traditional customs, values, and practices are now open to more direct challenge as Korea "democratizes" its society, government, and industrial relations system. Which of these can or should be modified is impossible to conclude at this point without considerably more detailed knowledge, experimentation, and analysis of company-specific efforts to reexamine their own traditions and practices.

An example of a firm that has undertaken this type of self-examination and change was provided in interviews with managerial representatives of one of the large *jaebul*, Lucky-Gold Star. Top management of this company recognizes that to compete in the world economy requires greater decentralization and delegation of decision making to lower levels of management. As a result, management commissioned McKinsey and Company, an American consulting firm, to propose changes in the management structure and process needed to achieve these objectives. As a result of this study, the corporation has now embarked on what it refers to as a long-term effort to change the culture of the company and its traditional top-down, centralized decision-making processes. It has divided the company into twenty-six different "cultural units." Each of these units in turn has been given the task of developing strategies and the managerial capabilities for meeting the broad objectives and values of the overall corporation. In the area of human resource policy, for example, this means that policies such as the type of welfare programs to implement (vacations, education and training, sick pay, etc.), which in the past were made by the president of the overall corporation, are now decentralized to the cultural unit level.

Although in general this new autonomy was welcomed, a good deal of confusion appeared among middle managers over how to function in this new environment. For example, a board composed of middle managers was established within one major division of the corporation to identify and propose solutions to problems experienced by middle managers in making the transition to a more decentralized system. However, this board experienced considerable difficulty because its members were afraid to make decisions without first knowing the preferred outcomes of their higher-level managers. As a result, the board lost the confidence of lower-level employees and had to be reconstituted.

This example is symptomatic of any large organization attempting to delegate decision making to lower levels after years of more centralized hierarchical control. Yet greater managerial autonomy is essential to support the democratization of the economy and society and to respond to the demands of more differentiated product markets. But this must be done within a culture that has historically not challenged managerial authority.

Achieving these changes will require considerable investment in managerial training and organizational development. Yet one must be cautious about adopting too many U.S. managerial policies and practices, since most American management consultants are unlikely to fully understand the Korean culture and context and are likely to carry over to Korea the strong union avoidance ethic or value system that dominates their client base in the United States. This type of managerial advice will only increase adversarialism and labor-management conflict in Korea. For these reasons, Korean managers must be careful to choose managerial models and advisors committed to labor and human resource management principles and practices that involve workers and labor representatives as joint stakeholders and partners.

Training and Human Resource Development

Korea has recognized the need for continuous training and skill development of its workforce. A strong commitment to education and individual development is another of the strengths of Korea's Confucianist heritage that has contributed to its economic development. Its high literacy rate and the generally high quality of its primary and secondary schools combine to produce an exceptionally well prepared entry-level labor force. This should continue to serve as a source of competitive advantage, provided that the supply of labor adjusts somewhat to fill areas of emerging skills shortage.

A 1990 report on vocational education in Korea (Ministry of Labor, ROK, 1990) sees the greatest shortages occurring in the technical and skilled blue collar occupations, which are traditionally filled by high school graduates who do not go on to college. For these reasons, the vocational training, apprenticeship, and continued training programs and institutions serving skilled blue collar and technical workers are most central to the next phase of institutional reform and development of industrial relations and human resource policy in Korea.

Korea already has a rather well developed vocational education system. The 1976 Basic Law for Vocational Training requires firms with 300 or more employees to provide basic skill training to a fixed percentage of employees per year or, if they choose to not train at this level, to pay a training tax to the government. Thus the infrastructure to promote the type of investment in human resources necessary to support the movement to a high-value-added, high-productivity, and high-wage economy already exists.

Unfortunately, there appears to be weak government enforcement of the provisions of this law and little business and labor commitment or direct involvement in oversight of the training and skill development process and occupational standards. This is one of the key institutional features of the German system, one that experts (Streeck 1987) believe contributes significantly to the long-term success of the system.

The evidence suggests that the amount of training and the quality of private sector training has declined over the period 1979–85, the most recent years for which data are available. Kim, Kim, and Ihm (1990) report that between 1977 and 1985, while the number of firms subject to the law increased more than 34 percent, the training ratio declined from 5.7 to 1.73 percent, and the total number trained declined by more than 60 percent. Moreover, the quality of the in-company training seems to be significantly lower than the quality of the vocational training when judged by the standards of the percentage of employees who took the government's craft certification tests and the percentage who passed these tests. In 1979 only 10 percent of those who were supposed to have completed their craftsman training from in-company training programs actually took the certification test, and of those that took it only 67 percent passed compared to 90 percent of those who received their training from public vocational programs. The numbers and percentage passed declined further in 1983. In that year only 59 percent passed compared with 68 percent of those who completed their training in vocational programs.

Thus, although the basic legal infrastructure to promote training exists, steps need to be taken to increase employer use and the quality of its outputs. One way to do this would be to include labor and management representatives in the overall governance of the training system, as is done in Germany and in some innovative firms and union relationships in the United States. Shifting from a business-government interaction to a tripartite training board governed by preestablished, jointly developed criteria should raise both the incentive to upgrade the quality and the number of workers who participate in training.

An equally important form of training necessary to support the democratization of industrial relations is management development. Korean firms report spending a great deal on training new managerial recruits, but to date most of this training involves socialization to the traditional values, culture, and managerial practices of the company (B-C. Lee 1991). At the end of the socialization process these new recruits are assigned to jobs chosen by managerial superiors, often with little or no say on the part of the recruits. Moreover, the heavy emphasis on socialization leaves little room for developing the managerial skills needed to foster the greater decentralization, participation in decision making, and creativity that will be increasingly important to the competitive strategies of Korean organizations as they move from low-cost to value-added competitive strategies. Thus, a major rethinking of the initial socialization, job assignment, and career development process of Korean managers may be called for as part of the broader democratization and economic adjustment process.

Educational Infrastructure

Individual firms cannot be expected to produce managers with knowledge of human resource and labor management relations on their own. Universities need to take a more active role in this process both within their business and economics programs and in those institutes that specialize in industrial relations (Bognanno 1988). Korea currently has no certified graduate programs that produce this type of training and research. In the 1930s and 1940s, U.S. colleges such as Wisconsin, Cornell, Minnesota, MIT, Illinois, California, and UCLA all responded to the wave of labor unrest by establishing interdisciplinary centers for teaching and research on industrial relations. Indeed, many of the leading Korean Ph.D. researchers in labor economics and industrial relations now active in Korea graduated from these programs. Though continued use of these foreign universities should be encouraged for the training of *researchers* at the Ph.D. level, they cannot produce an adequate supply of managers professionally trained in labor and human resource management. Nor can foreign universities provide the ongoing training, development, and research links to companies, unions, and national policymakers needed to support continuous learning and analysis required for the further development of the industrial relations system in Korea. Thus, development of interdisciplinary programs such as these are essential to the development of an effective industrial relations and human resource management system.

Women in the Labor Market

One of the more controversial issues related to labor force utilization involves the role of women in the labor market. Here there is a clear struggle between Korean tradition and the aspirations of the large number of highly educated Korean women for broader economic opportunity. Female workers are mainly found in low-skilled manufacturing or service sector jobs or in clerical and secretarial jobs, but few women have advanced to managerial, professional, or executive positions. Large gaps in male and female wages also exist. Indeed, until recently the gap between male and female wages was larger in Korea than in most other developing or highly developed countries (Amsden 1989). Currently at 56 percent, the female-to-male wage ratio is clearly larger than it has been in the past but still lags most other developed nations (the current average wage of women in the United States is approximately 68 percent of the average male wage).

The limitations on women's careers are deeply ingrained in the culture and practices of management, particularly with respect to women in office and white collar professions. The typical practice in the large companies has been for young women to be employed as secretaries until they marry. At that point they are expected to quit to attend to their responsibilities at home and to make room for other young, single women. This not only leads to severe limitations on career and income opportunities for young women but also represents a significant misallocation of human resources.

As labor markets for professional, technical, and skilled blue collar workers tighten and as the key sources of productivity and activity move from unskilled production and assembly work in the factory to maintenance and servicing equipment and customers and from the factory to the field and office functions in marketing, product development, design, human resource management, and information technology, these white collar professions will take on increased strategic importance. Thus, continuing to limit access of women to these occupations and career opportunities will serve as an increasingly costly drag on Korea's productivity and competitiveness. Moreover, opening these jobs and careers to women could help ease the upward pressures on wages that are now beginning to be felt from the tight labor markets for blue collar, professional, and technical employees.

For all these reasons, the practices, not the specific letter of the law, governing women's careers need to be addressed. This may require a deeper examination of Korean cultural values than is possible from the vantage point of this outsider. It is important for the parties at the workplace to address this issue directly among themselves.

Though the evidence is not yet clear, one might expect that the increased power or threat of unions in Korea should advance the cause of women just as labor unions have served to shock management into giving more attention to other aspects of their human resource policies. Regardless of the effects of unions on gender equality to date, this topic deserves a prominent place on the agenda of labor-management relations in the years ahead. Clearly a binding commitment to women's rights embedded in law and privately negotiated contracts is a positive first step. Still, addressing the issue and producing continuous improvement requires significant cultural change and examination of both the formal personnel policies and practices that heretofore have limited women's opportunities and the more subtle, informal organizational norms that often remain in place even when formal policies are reformed. In short, a significant cultural change in management and organizational behavior is needed to produce continuous improvement in the opportunities and achievements of women in corporate life (Kanter 1977; Bailyn 1992). This, therefore, appears to be a topic well suited to ongoing discussion by a broadly representative forum in the organization—a forum similar to the labor-management councils now mandated by law.

Closing the gender gap will also require changes in university education patterns. Whereas nearly 40 percent of current M.B.A. students in the United States are female, almost no women major in business or management at the undergraduate or graduate level in Korea. This too requires dialogue within universities and among universities, employers, and women students.

Wage Structures and Policies

Wage determination practices are at the center of intense debate among Korean labor leaders, employers, and government policymakers. All parties seem to be quite dissatisfied with the current process and outcomes of wage determination in Korean firms. Despite the rapid rise in wages experienced since 1987, workers and labor leaders continue to argue that wages are still too low. This is not surprising given the country's low-wage strategy legacy and the rapid rise in housing costs experienced in recent years. Thus, pressures for real wage improvement will continue to be strong in the years to come.

In addition to their concern over the effects of rising wage levels on the competitiveness of Korean firms in international markets, Korean employers and government representatives are highly dissatisfied with the current wage structure and wage-setting practices. The major concern raised with respect to the process of wage setting is that wages are negotiated several times a year. As in Japan, annual wage increases are normally determined during the Wage Offensive. Then, however, over the course of the year compensation is again adjusted for bonuses due on Korean Thanksgiving Day, the end of the year, and the Lunar New Year. Sometimes the labor management council also becomes a forum for negotiations of additional wage increases. Thus, wage bargaining is not a periodic or fixed event that produces wage outcomes that remain constant for a definite period of time but appear to employers to be a rather unpredictable but continually evolving process. As a result, nominal wage increases or wage drift in recent years far exceeded the levels of wage increase announced by the parties after the Wage Offensive.

These concerns over the process are related to concern over the structure of wages. The "bonuses" appear to be rather inflexible and are apparently not tied to any measure of firm or national economic performance. A survey of collective bargaining agreements by the Korea Employers' Federation (KEF 1991a:3) found that agreements in 80 percent of the companies surveyed provided for bonus payments over the course of the year. The survey also found that bonuses increased steadily since 1975 as a proportion of monthly wages and showed no evidence of varying in response to variations in profits, although there is some evidence that bonuses were somewhat more sensitive to changes in business cycles than were base wages (M. B. Lee 1992). In 1989 the average bonus equated to approximately two months' wages. Thus, bonuses were not only downward rigid but also growing in importance as overall wage levels increased in the latter half of the 1980s.

Employers and government representatives have expressed strong interest in introducing flexible wages for both their firm-specific and their macroeconomic benefits (Weitzman 1984). They look to the successful introduction of a flexible system in Singapore and to a lesser extent to the Japanese enterprise-level practice of bonuses, which are more closely tied to economic performance than is the case in Korea.

The literature on wage flexibility (e.g., Weitzman 1984; Blinder 1990; Lawler 1990; Lesieur 1957) suggests that a flexible wage system must meet the following criteria to be successful: it must supplement, not substitute for, an adequate base wage level; it must be understood and accepted as equitable by those covered; it must be close enough to the workplace and timely enough to motivate workers to achieve its micro-level effects of improving motivation, work effort, and labor-management cooperation; and it must be accompanied by some form of negotiation, participation, and ongoing information sharing.

Significant changes in Korean management and wage policies are needed to meet these criteria. Worker dissatisfaction with the low level of base wages will continue to be a problem. To attempt to implement a flexible wage system when levels are low will add further conflict to an already highly conflictual industrial relations system. Further, the current bonus system was introduced unilaterally by management without significant union or worker participation or negotiation. Thus, when unions gained real bargaining strength they felt no commitment to the principles of the bonus system and simply used the preexisting bonuses as means of raising what they and their membership viewed as unacceptably low wage levels. Thus, any system of flexible wages must be introduced with more participation and negotiation. Finally, the labor-management council system still does not function well in sharing economic information—a necessity for a successful flexible or contingent wage system.

Introducing a flexible wage system would also require consensus on the type of system (profit sharing, employee stock ownership, establishment-level gains sharing, etc.) and on whether to focus on flexibility through macroeconomic policy as in Singapore, at the firm level as envisioned in most profit-sharing or gains-sharing programs, or through individual or group bonuses based on some agreed-on performance evaluation system as promoted by many behavioral scientists and personnel consultants.

Significant education of union representatives, effective communication with workers, and changes in managerial styles are required for any system of flexible wages to be sustained over time. Experience shows that these systems require considerable managerial attention and effort. Management needs to both share information with union leaders and develop a workplace climate where workers not only understand and trust the information provided but see it in their interest to contribute to the success of the enterprise in their daily work activities. Thus, the authoritarian management style and culture must change to a more participatory style if flexible wages are to have any chance of working.

A study by the Korean Employers' Federation (KEF 1991a) noted that, whatever system is introduced, it must have the features noted above. The KEF goes on to suggest that, consistent with the Asian emphasis on teamwork rather than individual differences, company- or group-based incentive programs are likely to be more consistent with the culture than are individual incentives.

In summary, few of the conditions needed for successful implementation of a sustainable, productive, flexible wage system are present in the current Korean industrial relations system. Thus, the institutional reforms noted above must either precede or be introduced as part of any process for designing and implementing flexible wage strategies.

Workplace Industrial Relations

The eruption of a large number of strikes after the 29 June 1987 announcement of democratic reforms indicated that the relatively low strike record of the previous years was not a valid indicator of Korean workers' attitudes toward their working conditions. After the massive strike waves and the period of government nonintervention in 1987 and 1988, the government began to once again take a more interventionist approach to labor policy. As a result, 1,211 union leaders were arrested between January 1988 and March 1991 (Park 1991). Strikes subsequently declined considerably from the peak number of 3,617 in 1987 to 322 in 1990, and it appears the downward trend continued in 1991. Only 70 disputes were recorded as of May 1991. Part of this decline is undoubtedly due to the slowdown in economic growth, part may be due to the belief on the part of some Korean workers that the labor-management conflicts of 1987 and 1988 had gone too far, and some of it is likely due to the increased government crackdown on union leaders.

This pattern of strikes fits the longer historical trend in Korea (Table 21.3). Unlike its Asian neighbors of Taiwan, Hong Kong, and Singapore, which all experienced reductions in strike activity as their economies expanded from the 1960s through the 1980s, Korea experienced periods of relatively low strikes that were interrupted three times by short periods of explosive conflict: 1960–61, 1978–81, and 1984–88 (Deyo 1989). Each of these high conflict periods coincided with periods of political change and upheaval: 1960 was the collapse of the Syngman Rhee government, 1979 the end of the Park Chung Hee regime, and 1984–87 the buildup and transition to the cur-

Table 21.3
Industrial conflict in South Korea, 1960–1989

	Work stoppages	Workers involved (thousands)	Working days lost to stoppages (thousands)
1960	256	64	—
1961	122	16	—
1962	0	0	—
1963	70	20	—
1964	7	1	2
1965	12	4	19
1966	12	31	41
1967	18	3	10
1968	16	18	63
1969	7	30	163
1970	4	1	9
1971	10	1	11
1972	0	0	—
1973	0	0	—
1974	58	23	17
1975	52	10	14
1976	49	7	17
1977	58	8	8
1978	102	11	13
1979	105	14	16
1980	206	49	61
1981	186	35	31
1982	88	9	12
1983	98	11	9
1984	114	16	20
1985	265	29	64
1986	276	47	72
1987	3,617	935	6,946
1988	1,873	294	5,401
1989	1,616	397	6,351

Source: ILO (various years).

rent period of democratic reforms. Thus, the decline of visible strike activity from mid-1989 to the present most likely means that labor-management conflict has once again gone underground temporarily rather than subsided permanently.

Several different surveys have documented the lack of confidence of rank-and-file workers in current unions and their leaders. For example, a survey of the "Causes and Consequences of 1987 and 1988 Labor Disputes" showed that 63 percent of workers believed that the FKTU had not represented workers' interests properly. Similarly, a survey by the KEF (1991b) found that only 40 percent of union members were satisfied with their unions. Interviews with management representatives of Lucky-Gold Star indicated that surveys conducted by their unions revealed a similar level of dissatisfaction. Thus, although there is little hard empirical data to draw on, one gets the picture of workplace labor-management relations as characterized by a relatively low level of trust and a degree of suppressed conflict. One can only wonder whether some future political or economic event will not once again serve as the spark to ignite the tensions smoldering under the surface.

Korean Labor Unions

A more detailed description of the trends in trade unions in Korea after 1987 is contained in Chapter 20, and thus only the critical points in this recent history need to be noted here to lay the foundation for a discussion of policy options. Between 1986 and 1990, union membership increased dramatically from 15.5 to 23.4 percent of the labor force. While the vast majority of union members (1.9 million) belong to unions affiliated with the FKTU, somewhere between 400,000 and 600,000 are members of various independent unions. Approximately 150,000–200,000 of these workers are organized under the newly formed Korea Trade Union Congress (KTUC) (Chonnohyup), and another 200,000–400,000 are organized into independent unions or under a loose affiliation called the Solidarity Council of Large Enterprise Unions.

The unions outside the FKTU lack official status since one of the provisions of prevailing labor law requires that a union be affiliated with a national federation to be registered by the Ministry of Labor. The FKTU is the only national federation recognized by the ministry for this purpose.[1] As Sookon Kim and others point out, the need to belong to a nationally recognized federation is one of the most controversial provisions of current Korean labor law.

The unions outside the FKTU are often referred to as "democratic [*minju*] unions." They are viewed by most Koreans as more militant and radical than the FKTU unions and are more closely allied with student movement groups and various religious leaders who have worked with worker groups over the years to promote worker and union rights (Ogle 1990). Interviews with several representatives of the democratic unions and of the FKTU illustrate the unstable nature of current trade union law and interunion relations. Representatives of the democratic unions generally view the FKTU leaders as failing to admit that before 1987 they were government controlled, even though most of the current FKTU leaders were elected after 1987. In contrast, FKTU leaders see the leaders of the democratic union movement as radicals more interested in political change than in advancing workers' economic interests.

Leaders of the democratic unions argue that the process of democratic reform in Korea will not be complete until workers are given full rights to choose to be represented by whatever union they prefer. Moreover, they acknowledge that many of their leaders are former or current student activists, some of whom advocate radical political change. This radical element competes with others within the democratic unions who prefer to focus on more moderate trade union economic and social objectives. But the more the government suppresses the efforts of these moderate union leaders by arresting them for illegal union activities or leading illegal strikes, the more it strengthens the leadership positions of the more radical leaders. Thus, leaders of the democratic unions argue that reforming labor law to allow for union organizing outside the FKTU structure would enable the more moderate union-oriented leaders to prevail.

Regardless of these internal and interunion debates, the democratic union leaders and most Korean labor scholars argue that the entire body of current labor law lacks legitimacy, since workers have had no voice or opportunity to participate in the political process leading to its passage or implementation. Although several reforms were introduced and passed by Parliament in 1990, the bill was vetoed by President Roh Tae Woo. Thus basic reform of labor law is seen as a necessary condition for moving forward with the process of democratizing Korean society and creating a stable and effective industrial relations system.

Conclusions and Options for Further Reform

With the announcement of its 29 June 1987 reforms, the Korean government took a major step toward establishing an industrial relations policy suited to the needs of a democratic society. Yet much remains to be done. Current policy is still governed largely by the pre-1987 politics of labor control and by an economic policy focused primarily on efforts to control labor costs. To continue moving along the path of democratic reform of society, significant changes in the mindset of top government leaders and economic advisors is needed.

Control over worker rights to organize needs to be replaced by a strategy of allowing workers to choose their own leaders and structuring the environment in ways that encourage union leaders and employers to develop cooperative relationships based on mutual trust. The emphasis on avoiding strikes or other forms of labor-management conflict in the short run must give way to a long-term strategy of building a basis for cooperative labor-management relations. Economic policy must focus on developing human resources and encouraging high-productivity, value-added competitive strategies and must give as much emphasis to the structure and degree of flexibility in wage adjustments as it does to simply controlling the level of wages.

Although I suggest here that the experiences and institutions of Europe, Japan, and the United States offer insights for further reforms, the specific reforms that work best are often ones the parties themselves design and agree on. Thus, the alternatives for further reform outlined below are presented with these substantive and procedural considerations in mind and should only be viewed as a framework for ongoing debate among the parties of interest rather than as a detailed prescription for action.

A Model for Adaptive Learning

Recent reform efforts in Australia suggest a promising strategy for learning from, debating, and then adapting practices that appear to have worked well in other countries. Lansbury and Zappala (1990) provide a useful summary of the Australian system along with an analysis of its relevance to Korea; I focus here on the relevance of the process by which Australian labor, government, and business leaders have gone about analyzing foreign experiences and using them to introduce reforms in their traditional system.

In 1987 a joint team of government and labor leaders and researchers conducted a study tour of several European countries to examine these countries' industrial relations and human resource policies and institutions. The joint report produced on the basis of that tour, *Australia Reconstructed* (ACTU 1987), has since served as a reference point for adapting and implementing a broad series of reforms in Australia's industrial relations system which range from the macroeconomic policy (modifications of their labor-management "Accord") to a form of productivity-based principles to guide the national arbitration tribunal ("structural efficiency principle") to workplace reforms in the organization of work and training and human resource development policies.

The specific adaptations made by the Australians to European policies and practices may not be appropriate for Korea, but the adaptive learning process may serve as a model for how a country can best learn from abroad and then adapt institutions or practices that work well in other systems to fit their own customs, traditions, and needs. Since Korea has historically borrowed concepts from Japan, the United States, and European systems, such a study tour and adaptive learning process would need to cover these systems. In concluding this chapter, I therefore point out what aspects of these different systems appear to hold the most relevance or promise for the task of moving forward along the path of further reforms in Korea.

Role of the Government

Just as the dominant model of economic development in Korea in the past has been one of state-led capitalism, the change to a high-trust industrial relations and human resource management system requires a government commitment to completing the process of democratizing its labor markets and labormanagement policies and institutions. Only then will Korea have a viable chance of developing the type of social partnership called for in the government's Seventh Five-Year Plan.

The starting point for the next phase of democratization lies in addressing the fundamental flaws in the basic labor law so as to bring them into conformance with the ILO conventions and accepted international standards. Foremost in this area is the need to reform the union recognition and certification provisions of current law to allow workers to choose their own representatives regardless of affiliation with a national union confederation. If the goal is to represent democratic worker rights at the workplace, there is no further justification of carrying over a provision from the pre-democratic period which requires the new union to be part of the FKTU or any other national federation.

Neither can there be justification for limiting who can advise or represent workers in negotiations. Limitations on involvement of "third parties" not only serve as a symbol of pre-democratic efforts to control worker access to information and expertise but also constrain the development of the type of third-party infrastructure and professional community that has been crucial to the development of other industrial relations systems in their formative years. A positive case can be made for expanding the base of third-party expertise and involvement in educating, advising, and developing the leadership of worker and employer representatives.

Thus, government policy could go beyond the simple lifting of limitations on third-party involvement to examine how other countries have built up a cadre of knowledgeable experts and a professional community of third parties who work with both labor and management to develop orderly principles of negotiations and conflict resolution suited to their particular needs. This is the legacy of the generation of U.S. scholars who were active in the War Labor Board during World War II and other public and private labor-management forums during the formative years of the post–New Deal industrial relations system (Taylor 1948; Dunlop 1984). It is also the legacy of professional associations such as the Industrial Relations Research Association and the formation of the various industrial relations research and teaching programs in major universities (Derber 1949). Active government support for the development of this type of third-party institutional structure in Korea seems timely; it carries a history that bears further exploration by a Korean study team.

Finally, the role of public employees must be addressed at an early point in the reform process. Democratic governments vary considerably in their policies regarding the right of public employees to strike and the scope of bargaining, but they are expected to extend the principle of the freedom of association to public employees (Treu et al. 1978). This still leaves ample room for the parties to work out alternative dispute resolution procedures for occupations or situations where strikes would threaten the public safety or health. Excluding public employees from the right to some form of collective association and bargaining will only encourage further defiance and militancy and risk producing exactly the type of adversarial labor-management relations that government and the public would prefer to avoid.

Others have offered specific proposals to reform these aspects of labor law which draw heavily on the features of U.S. labor laws (Bognanno 1988). Although I have no basic quarrel with these proposals, I would leave it to the joint analysis of the parties involved to decide on the specific approaches that best fit the Korean environment. This, therefore, is an area of U.S. experience that bears careful examination from a multiparty Korean study team.

Labor law changes are necessary, but they would be far from a sufficient condition for the needed reform. The Korean government must go on to integrate its labor and human resource policies with its long-term economic strategy. Although the conditions for a full-fledged corporatist approach or development of a well-functioning social partnership are not present in Korean society or industrial relations, various steps can be taken to develop a better integration of these areas of policymaking. One clear step would be to strengthen the links among institutions such as the Korean Institute of Labor, the Korea Development Institute, the Ministry of Labor, and the Economic Planning Board. The staffs of these agencies should work together to provide the data and information base required for informed policymaking. A useful model worthy of closer examination is the data gathered and coordinated by the Japan Productivity Center before the Spring Wage Offensive (Dore, Ingami, and Sako 1991). These data serve to both inform and educate a broad range of labor, management, and government leaders on the needs of the economy and the workforce and thereby provide a useful analytic foundation for negotiations, consultation, and policymaking.

Steps might also be taken to gradually create the incentives, opportunities, and pressures on unions and employers to contribute more effectively to the development of labor and human resource policy at the national level. Here the approaches used in Japan and Germany to gather and share information and analyze labor and human resource policy issues appear to be most relevant.

Prime candidates to experiment with this approach to policy development include development of an effective and trusted mediation and arbitration system and set of professionals, a wage and labor market equity board designed to promote the integration and development of women, a safety and health commission linked to worker and employer improvement efforts at the workplace, a training and development policy and set of institutions that involve business and labor representatives, and a tripartite commission to explore options for compensation structure reforms. These are among the substantive labor and human resource issues that must be attended to in a more comprehensive and integrated fashion and that require the commitment of the parties involved if they are to be successful. If issue-specific experiments at involvement of the social partners are successful, they will produce the insights needed to design a more lasting and broad-based social partnership in Korea.

The Role of Employers

Given the strong role played by large firms in Korea, industrial relations and collective bargaining are likely to remain enterprise-based rather than centralized at the industry level. Thus, although employer federations such as the KEF must continue to coordinate employer involvement in policymaking forums and provide research and training services, the human resource and industrial relations policies and professionals within the individual firms will be dominant in shaping management's approach to industrial relations and human resource policy. The development of strong human resource and industrial relations skills and expertise within Korean management is therefore critical. The first tendency for Korean managers is to turn to the writings of U.S. scholars and management consulting firms for advice on how to adapt their traditional structures and practices to meet these new challenges. One must be cautious here, however, and learn from the weaknesses in the traditional American management practices which recent experiences have exposed. By studying the efforts of leading companies and unions that are well along in their efforts to transform this traditional system, one might bypass this 50-year American history of arms'-length collective bargaining.

The common feature of these transformative efforts lies in effectively integrating labor and human resource policies and practices into management responsibilities at all levels of the enterprise. Most experts agree that before 1987 Korean managers did not have to develop many labor relations or human resource management skills, since unions were either nonexistent or ineffective in most Korean firms, decision making was highly centralized, and authoritarian managerial styles prevailed. Since 1987, however, Korean management has been going through what has been described by American scholars as the "shock effect" period: the increased presence and vigor of unions has forced management to professionalize its approach and to develop formalized policies for coping with labor relations (Slichter, Healy, and Livernash 1960). The challenge is to use this shock effect to educate line managers and all human resource professionals in the principles of effective human resource management, negotiations, and conflict resolution. The mistake made in the United States was to overspecialize the industrial relations function and thereby to insulate both the industrial relations specialists and labor leaders from understanding and coping with the competitive pressures of the business and to limit the opportunities for broader forms of employee participation to develop. Here is where the Japanese and the German models have greater relevance for organizational practice than the U.S. model, since both Japanese and German management structures and career development paths are less specialized and promote more interaction between line managers, employees, and labor representatives.

The Korean labor-management council system might potentially serve as a vehicle for promoting this type of interaction. Although in its present form it largely duplicates the union-management negotiation structures and processes, if expanded to resemble European-style works councils with representatives of all classes of workers—blue and white collar, managerial and technical employees, men and women—it might serve as a more effective consultative body and support the integration of human resource considerations with other policies and strategies of the firm. A careful study of the structure and functioning of works councils in Germany should provide useful insights on how this type of institution might be better adapted to fit into Korean enterprises.

The career development strategies of Japanese firms and some U.S. firms that have been attempting to transform their traditional practices may also be helpful for avoiding marginalizing and overspecializing the management of industrial relations. This approach ensures that the development path of managers includes some time in the industrial relations and human resources functions. Another practical way of providing a perspective and exposure to labor and human resource issues is to ensure that most managers serve as either employee or management representative on the labor-management council.

Regardless of specific functional responsibilities, the fundamental managerial requirement is to hold all managers accountable for the human resource and labor-management performance of their unit and to collect systematically and share widely data on these performance outcomes. Embedding these principles in the management systems will help to elevate the influence and distribute the responsibility for human resource management across management. From this setting the appropriate formal structures or consultative forums needed to institutionalize employee participation and human resource planning will more easily and naturally emerge.

Labor's Role

The basic challenge facing the labor movement in this period of democratic reforms is to allow rank-and-file workers to choose the leaders they view as most compatible with their needs and values. Continuation of the process of democratization and reform will undoubtedly be accompanied by increased competition among union leaders advocating different political views and strategies for representing workers. If workers are allowed to choose freely among these competing views, local union leaders who are most effective in solving workers' daily problems and advancing their economic interests will emerge and survive. In short, the successful leaders will be ones who can function effectively in the industrial relations system that is created. If this system encourages and supports leaders who can negotiate, consult, and cooperate with employers, this style of leadership will dominate. If, however, the system requires periodic demonstrations of militancy followed by government suppression and jailing of leaders, then union leaders capable of functioning in this fashion will dominate. Thus, in Korea as in other countries, employer and government policies are likely to influence the types of union leaders workers elect.

In the short run it may not be possible to combine unions with diverse views into a single national federation. Indeed, multiple union federations continue to exist in many industrialized countries. What is more critical than structural unification is the avoidance of a prolonged period of interunion conflict that limits the potential for effective labor-management-government negotiations and consultation.

Thus, developing a dialogue and eventually a forum for interunion cooperation on both enterprise-specific and national issues is essential to the orderly development of Korea's industrial relations system. This is another area where third-party advisors and participants from the broader community of industrial relations professionals can play a constructive role.

What is being proposed here does not neatly conform to either the pluralist or corporatist models of industrial relations. Indeed, as Streeck (1987) and others have argued, these models no longer capture the essence of what it takes for a modern industrial relations and human resource management system to contribute to the economic and social advancement of a society. Instead, what appears to be emerging are new combinations of neocorporatist, liberal, and decentralized models that sample from the lessons alternative systems have to teach and then go on to adapt these lessons to fit their particular setting. If history is any guide, out of this adaptation process will emerge the next generation of innovations from which others can learn and adapt. Korea now has a landmark opportunity to embark on this learning, adapting, and innovating role.

NOTES

I thank the many employer, labor, and government representatives who provided the data and interview material used in preparing this chapter. I also thank Michael Byungnam Lee, George Ogle, and Ronald Rodgers for their helpful comments on an earlier draft and Marc Weinstein and Gil Preuss for their very helpful research assistance. The views expressed are, however, solely my own.

1. Actually, one other small federation is now also recognized, the Council of Union Federation in Trade, composed of a union of insurance workers and a union of finance and clerical workers.

REFERENCES

Amsden, Alice. 1989. *Asia's Next Giant: South Korea and Late Industrialization.* New York: Oxford University Press.

Aoki, Masahiko. 1988. *Information, Incentives and Bargaining in the Japanese Economy.* New York: Cambridge University Press.

Australian Confederation of Trade Unions (ACTU). 1987. *Australia Reconstructed.* Canberra: Australian Government Publishing Service.

Bailyn, Lotte. 1992. "Changing the Conditions of Work: Responding to Increasing Work Force Diversity and New Family Patterns." In Thomas Kochan and Michael Useem (eds.), *Transforming Organizations.* New York: Oxford University Press.

Barbash, Jack. 1984. *The Elements of Industrial Relations.* Madison: University of Wisconsin Press.

Blinder, Alan. 1990. *Paying for Productivity.* Washington, D.C.: Brookings Institution.

Bognanno, Mario. 1988. "Korea's Industrial Relations at the Turning Point." KDI Working Paper no. 8816. Seoul: Korea Development Institute.

Cho, Lee-Jay. 1991. "Ethical and Social Influences of Confucianism." In Lee-Jay Cho and Yoon Kyung Kim (eds.), *Economic Development in the Republic of Korea: A Policy Perspective.* Honolulu: East-West Center.

Clegg, H. 1976. "Pluralism in Industrial Relations." *British Journal of Industrial Relations* 13.

Cole, Robert. 1989. *Strategies for Learning: Small Group Activities in American, Japanese, and Swedish Industry.* Berkeley: University of California Press.

Cutcher-Gershenfeld, Joel. 1991. "The Impact on Economic Performance of a Transformation in Workplace Relations." *Industrial and Labor Relations Review* 44(2).

Derber, Milton. 1949. "Preface." In Milton Derber (ed.), *Proceedings of the First Annual Meeting, Industrial Relations Research Association, 1948.* Champaign, Ill.: Industrial Relations Research Association.

Deyo, Frederic. 1989. *Beneath the Miracle: Labor Subordination in the New Asian Industrialism.* Berkeley: University of California Press.

Dore, Ronald. 1986. *Flexible Rigidities.* Stanford: Stanford University Press.

Dore, Ronald. 1992. "Japan's Version of Managerial Capitalism." In Thomas Kochan and Michael Useem (eds.), *Transforming Organizations.* New York: Oxford University Press.

Dore, Ronald, Akeshi Ingami, and Mari Sako. 1991. *Japan's Annual Economic Assessment.* London: Campaign for Work.

Dunlop, John. 1984. *Dispute Resolution: Negotiation and Consensus Building.* Dover, Mass.: Auburn House.

Fuerstenberg, Friedrich. 1987. "The Federal Republic of Germany." In Greg Bamber and Russel Lansbury, *International and Comparative Industrial Relations: A Study of Developed Market Economies.* London: Allen & Unwin.

Goldthorpe, John. 1985. *Order and Conflict in Contemporary Capitalism.* New York: Oxford University Press.

Im, Hyug Baeg. 1990. "State, Labor, and Capital in the Consolidation of Democracy: A Search for Post-Authoritarian Industrial Relations in South Korea." Mimeograph. Seoul: Seoul National University.

International Labour Organisation (ILO). Various years. *Yearbook of Labour Statistics.*

International Monetary Fund (IMF). 1990. *International Financial Statistics Yearbook.* Washington, DC: International Monetary Fund.

Kanter, Rosabeth. 1977. *Men and Women of the Corporation.* New York: Basic Books.

Katzenstein, Peter. 1985. *Small States in World Markets: Industrial Policy in Europe.* Ithaca: Cornell University Press.

Kim, Sookon, Jae-Won Kim, and Chonsun Ihm. 1990. *Human Resource Policy and Economic Development: Republic of Korea.* Manila: Asian Development Bank.

Kochan, Thomas, Harry Katz, and Robert McKersie. 1986. *The Transformation of American Industrial Relations.* New York: Basic Books.

Korea Employers' Federation (KEF). 1991a. "Wage Flexibility in Korea." *KEF Quarterly Review.*

Korea Employers' Federation (KEF). 1991b. "Survey of Manufacturing Workers' Attitudes." *KEF Quarterly Review.*

Lansbury, Russell, and John Zappala. 1990. *Recent Developments in Industrial Relations: General Perspectives for Korea with Special Reference to Australia.* Seoul: Korea Labor Institute.

Lawler, Edward. 1990. *Strategic Pay: Aligning Organizational Strategies and Pay Systems.* San Francisco: Jossey-Bass.

Lee, Byeong-Cheol. 1991. "Understanding Outcomes of the Organizational Entry Process: A Comparison of the Situationist, Individualist, and Interactionist Perspectives." Ph.D. diss., Massachusetts Institute of Technology.

Lee, Michael Byungnam. 1991. *Industrial Relations around the World: Labor Relations for Multinational Companies.* New York: Walter de Gruyter.

Lee, Michael Byungnam. 1992. "Profit Sharing and Productivity: Employee Bonus Programs in South Korea." Unpublished paper, Georgia State University.

Lesieur, Fred. 1957. *The Scanlon Plan: A Frontier in Labor-Management Cooperation.* Cambridge: MIT Press.

Maier, Charles. 1985. "Preconditions for Corporatism." In John Goldthorpe (ed.), *Order and Conflict in Contemporary Capitalism.* London: Clarendon Press.

Meltz, Noah. 1989. "Industrial Relations: Balancing Efficiency and Equity." In Jack Barbash and Kate Barbash (eds), *Theories and Concepts in Comparative Industrial Relations.* Columbia: University of South Carolina Press.

Ministry of Labor, Republic of Korea. 1990. *Vocational Training in Korea.* Seoul: Ministry of Labor.

Offe, Claus. 1981. "The Attribution of Public Status to Interest Groups: Observations on the West German Case." In Suzanne Berger (ed.), *Organizing Interests in Western Europe.* New York: Cambridge University Press.

Ogle, George. 1990. *South Korea: Dissent within the Economic Miracle.* London: Zed Books.

Osterman, Paul. 1988. *Employment Futures.* New York: Oxford University Press.

Park, Young Ki. 1991. "South Korea." Mimeograph. Seoul: Sogang University.

Pizzorno, Alessandro. 1978. "Political Exchange and Collective Identity in Industrial Conflict." In Colin Crouch and Allesandro Pizzorno (eds.), *The Resurgence of Class Conflict in Western Europe since 1968.* New York: Macmillan.

Shirai, Taishiro, ed. 1983. *Contemporary Industrial Relations in Japan.* Madison: University of Wisconsin Press.

Slichter, Sumner, James Healy, and Robert Livernash. 1960. *The Impact of Collective Bargaining on Management.* Washington, D.C.: Brookings Institution.

Steers, Richard, Yoo Keun Shin, and Gerardo Ungson. 1989. *The Chaebol: Korea's New Industrial Might.* New York: Harper and Row.

Streeck, Wolfgang. 1987. "The Uncertainties of Management in the Management of Uncertainty: Employers, Labor Relations and Industrial Relations in the 1980's." *Work, Employment, and Society* 1(3).

Streeck, Wolfgang. 1991. "The Federal Republic of Germany." In John Niland and Oliver Clarke (eds.), *Agenda for Change: An International Analysis of Industrial Relations in Transition.* North Sydney: Allen & Unwin.

Swenson, Peter. 1989. *Fair Shares: Unions, Pay, and Politics in Sweden and West Germany.* Ithaca: Cornell University Press.

Taylor, George. 1948. *Government Regulation of Industrial Relations.* New York: Prentice Hall.

Treu, Tiziano, et. al. 1978. *Public Service Labour Relations: Recent Trends and Future Prospects.* Geneva: International Labour Office.

U.S. Bureau of Labor Statistics. 1981. *International Survey of Labor Costs in Manufacturing.* April.

Weitzman, Martin. 1984. *The Share Economy: Conquering Stagflation.* Cambridge: Harvard University Press.

PART IX

Conclusions

Chapter 22

A New Vision for Institutional Reforms

Lee-Jay Cho
East-West Center
Yoon Hyung Kim
Hankuk University of Foreign Studies

Introduction

On 18 December 1992, in the last year of the Sixth Republic, the general election of the 14th president was held under the auspices of a nonpartisan cabinet. When Kim Young Sam, the Democratic Liberal Party's candidate, won the election, Korea was in the midst of serious economic challenges, both internal and external.

The new government was given a historical mission, with responsibility for redressing the economic imbalace that now hampers further economic growth in Korea. In the early 1960s, when the nation embarked on industrialization, the general population was poor and almost everyone sought ways to improve their low social and economic status. Today, thanks to rapid industrialization, all segments of society have acquired higher standards of living. Income and wealth disparities have, however, widened substantially between social strata, geographic regions, and the urban and rural sectors. The sense of relative deprivation among alienated low-income workers resulted in social conflict and ultimately explains the acrimonious labor-management disputes that erupted in the spring of 1989. Disruptive strikes led by Korea's labor unions, along with what the government considered to be democratic wage increases, weakened management's enthusiasm for business enterprise and labor's will to produce and work. Consequently, the international competitiveness of the Korean economy has been declining.

While the Korean society has been preoccupied with internal conflicts, the country entered a fight for its economic life in a new international environment where military contest has been replaced by economic competition in globalized world markets. Just as the fall of the Berlin Wall in 1989 marked the end of the old confrontation between capitalism and communism, so the integration of the European Common Market in 1993 marked the beginning of a new economic competition on a global scale. Indeed, we now face world competition between different cultures and forms of capitalism. The severe competitiveness of this international environment allows little tolerance for system inferiorities.

The central task facing Korea's new government is to construct a harmonious national economy and at the same time to regain Korean competitiveness. This task can be defined by two goals: a new adaptation of Korean capitalism befitting Korea's unique culture, values, and institutions, and the selection of the most appropiate system of national economic management for the next stage of Korea's economic development.

Building Cooperative Capitalism

To cope with internal conflicts and the current international challenges, Korea must carry out timely and thorough institutional reforms in order to pursue equitable distribution while simultaneously sustaining economic growth. This goal stimulates debate over which model of capitalism will best achieve efficiency and equity at the same time. Korea can learn from the experiences and theories of advanced industrialized countries, but it is most likely to succeed if it concentrates inductively and empirically on its own history, culture, and exprience.

In Anglo-American economic theory, efficiency and equity are regarded as mutually conflicting goals; income generation becomes inefficient if the government intervenes in the free market mechanism to promote equity. As Alice Amsden (Chapter 4), John Zysman (Chapter 5), and Thomas Kochan (Chapter 21) have indicated, however, both Japanese and West German versions of capitalism actually augmented economic efficiency by activating the logic of equity.

After World War II, the Japanese and German societies undertook the painful process of reconstruction. These two defeated nations recognized the failings of their prewar political and economic systems and accordingly gave up much of them. In this postwar period, the two countries developed new adaptations of capitalism, referred to by Lester Thurow (1992) as "communitarian capitalism." To Germans and especially Japanese, economic prosperity was reinterpreted as economic betterment for all members of society. All sectors of society cooperated toward the goal of an industrialized society characterized by fair distribution of income and wealth and by social harmony, through the synergy of efficiency and equity. Accordingly, we call this economic system "cooperative capitalism."

Reducing inequality was not only an ethical good for its own sake but also a new source of productivity. Thurow (1985:125) called this new productivity, derived from motivation, cooperation, and teamwork, "soft" productivity, distinguishing it from "hard" productivity, which can be increased through equipment investment and R&D. U.S. manufacturing productivity is lower than that in Japan or Germany, he argued, because of poorer soft productivity—in other words, because of defects in the management of American workers.

Thurow's emphasis on human relationships in the workplace recalls Friedrich List's earlier theories. In contrast to Adam Smith, who viewed the division of labor as the cause of the increase of wealth, List argued that improved productivity is effected not by the division of labor but by the essential unification of labor. By unified labor, he meant the unification of the productive forces and power of individuals, and so he attached great significance to the unified efforts of a collection of individuals. In List's own words, "Whenever individuals are engaged in wars, the prosperity of mankind is at its lowest stage, and it increases in the same proportion in which the concord of mankind increases" (1841:124).

List made a significant contribution to economic theory with his insight that mere accumulation of material capital is of minor importance compared with the organization of the productive forces of society. According to his theory, mental capital—"the accumulation of all discoveries, inventions, improvements, perfections, and mental exertions of all generations which have lived before us," that is, the accumulation of all intellectual and ethical powers—generates mental productive power, which improves material productive power. Intellectual power is capability in science and technology; ethical power is the morality that promotes social cohesion. Whereas the productive power of individuals grows in proportion to the maximization of intellectual power, the union of productive powers among individuals is achieved through the maximization of ethical power. Clearly, the strengthening of intellectual power and ethical power is an essential condition for national survival. It is mental power that promotes social well-being, which in turn produces national wealth. Ultimately, then, morality is the cohesive quality that holds a society together.

In his reactionary theory of ethics based on economics, Max Weber argued that the country that maintains the mental power capable of suppressing and controlling social conflict and greedy fetishism, which inevitably accompanies capitalism, will undoubtedly become an advanced country. Whereas Karl Max asserted that ideology is entirely determined by underlying economic causes, Weber accepted not only the materialists' assertion that material conditions inevitably influence the success or failure of religious and political movement but also the spiritualists' assertion that ideas can and sometimes do have an independent and decisive influence on the economic order. Weber became convinced of the indispensability of ethics in explanations of the rise of industrial capitalism (Weber 1930, 1979).

What do these theories of List and Weber and subsequent propositions by Thurow imply for Korean capitalism in transition? The Korean society urgently needs to abandon the paradigm of Anglo-American economics, which argues for a trade-off between efficiency and equity, and adopt the cooperative Japanese-German variant of captitalism, which assumes that efficiency and equity are complementary goals.

The principal elements of a free market economy as manifested in Anglo-American economics may have been appropriate for the initial developmental stage of productive capacity expansion in Korea, when the economy was struggling to overcome national poverty. But the pluralistic American model forces a trade-off between equity and efficiency, and so it may be unsuited to present-day Korea. The uneven distribution of wealth has emerged as an important social issue in Korea. The economy is moving toward a new stage in which growth needs to be accompanied by distributive justice. Efficiency may have been the most important factor in the early stage of growth, but now it seems clear to many economists that the country must focus more on its Confucian ethical values of fairness within the family and the community. Unlike Western society, where social justice means creating equal opportunity for the individual, Korea's long history has been guided by social harmony. Thus, with the success of modernization, Koreans must now seek to define and restore traditional values within a modern environment. Cooperative capitalism, with its combination of free market capitalism and humanitarianism, has overshadowed America's focus on short-term economic efficiency and profit. It may well be that this strategic synergy of competition and cooperation is best suited for the new Korea.

A new national vision for the twenty-first century that Korea desperately needs will then be the construction of a kind of modified cooperative capitalism based on a unified theory of economics and ethics. But equity as a logic of social harmony cannot be borrowed from others; Korea must define a clear standard of equity based on the Confucian values of fairness within the family and the community. Guided by that standard of equity and economic efficiency, all the existing economic institutions and policies should be reformed. And such restructuring of the Korean economy cannot be achieved simply by the rational choices of free competitive market forces. It also requires political will and leadership.

The institutional reforms for building cooperative capitalism will inevitably require the concession of vested interests. But the "haves" may violently resist any reform of existing economic institutions and policies for economic fairness. History offers few examples of empowered elites willing to sacrifice for the betterment of those below them in social status—unless they are threatened by a systemic crisis such as the Great Depression or a social collapse because of internal revolution or external military defeat. In the history of Western civilization, few nations have modernized without passing through the painful process of collapsing vested interests through either civil revolution or defeat in war. For example, England's Civil War of the 1640s, the French Revolution of 1783, the American War of Independence of 1776, and the American Civil War of the 1860s preceded industrial revolutions and modernization in these countries.

Somewhat different from the modernization pattern of "civil revolution first and industrial revolution later," Germany and Japan embarked on industrialization as their first step in the modernization process. It was only after defeat in World War II that their vested interests weakened. Subsequently, West Germany and Japan achieved economic and political democratization. In the coming years, Korean modernization may continue to follow the the Japanese and West German course. But if Korean capitalism can accomplish economic democratization autogenously and gradually, without the national throes of revolution or defeat in war, the Korean success story will be an interesting example in the world history of modernization.

How will it be possible for Korean capitalism, at this historical crossroads, to correct inequitable institutions and policies? Who is to initiate the sweeping reform of all the existing legal systems and institutions based on Korean standards of economic fairness for social harmony. In this regard, Michio Morishima (1983) asserts that once a powerful and legitimate political leadership system presents a national goal, then a national consensus can be easily established in a Confucian society characterized by strong family and community values. The national goal can then receive popular support by activating the pragmatic elements of Confucian ethics and thereby mobilizing all of the national energy.

The new govrnnment headed by President Kim Young Sam has been given the challenge of restructuring Korea's political economy. Strong political leadership is essential to enlighten the public about the urgency of meeting the emerging threats to the nation's well-being. If internal conflicts continue, Korea will lose international competitiveness and fail in the international marketplace. Nationwide public education through regular public forums, open seminars, and hearings is needed to convince most Koreans that appropriate reforms are indispensible to making the Korean economy competitive in the world economy.

A new sense of national morality should also be aroused in Korean society. Entrepreneurs must awaken from the illusion of constructing private kingdoms of wealth; working people must restrain requests for welfare and become diligent and thrifty, remembering the old days of absolute poverty. Koreans in all walks of life should be ready to share the pains of a temporary drop in living standards necessary to restore the international productive strength. In this regard, Korea can learn from the success story of the Singapore economy. Confronted with the loss of international competitiveness during the deep recession of 1985 and 1986, which was caused by the controversial wage correction policy and overinvestments in construction projects, the Singapore government designed and implemented a comprehensive set of policy changes which included no net increase in average wage costs for two years. Singaporeans accepted a temporary lower standard of living because they thought they were treated fairly when economic sacrifices were assigned to different groups (see Economic Committee 1986). And a most important factor was the strong political leadership of Prime Minister Lee Kuan Yew, who directed a government that was reputedly efficient as well as honest.

A strong, efficient political leadership is urgently needed to present Koreans the construction of cooperative capitalism as a new vision for Korea in the twenty-first century. The vision could create hope, greater moral cohesion of society, and a new bond of national unity. History shows us that the construction of cooperative capitalism can be accomplished by a social accord between capital and labor. In Sweden in the early 1930s, a social accord was successfully established in which the propertied class accepted the concept of equalization through welfare capitalism, and the working class acknowledged the legitimacy of the existing accumulated wealth. These two success stories from Singapore and Sweden illustrate Thurow's "soft" productivity and his proposition that the perception of equity is the essence of efficiency. If members of Korea's vested interests can be convinced of this argument, they will be more receptive to decisive policy changes and institutional reforms so as to achieve a social accord in Korea.

Several major institutional reforms are proposed in this book. As a first example, the present tax system should be restructured from the economic growth-supportive system (which has aggravated unequitable distribution) to a system oriented toward public welfare. The basic direction of the a reform must be toward correcting the distributional inequity in taxation and raising the welfare revenue sources for low-income brackets (see Chapters 6–7). Income from financial assets such as interest and dividends as well as wages should be brought into the global income tax system to correct the unfair distribution of tax burdens between the propertied class and the working class. Along with implementing the global income tax system, a central task in achieving economic fairness is to complete the recently introduced real-name system of financial transactions (see Chapters 6 and 9). As real estate and other physical assets become substitutes for financial assets as means of multiplying wealth, the global property tax system should be established to ensure that all physical assets owned by a single person are aggregated. Moreover, the effective tax rates should be levied based on a realistic property-value assessment system. To prevent the hereditary transfer of full personal wealth from generation to generation and therefore enhance equity in wealth distribution, it is urgent that the present system of inheritance and gift tax be made more efficient by drastically curtailing special provisions for deductions and exemptions.

We also propose that the welfare program be extended to satisfy a comfortable level of basic needs for Koreans in all walks of life, through expansion of educational opportunities, low-cost housing, medical insurance benefits, and public transportation. In particular, the housing issue is of keen interest to Koreans caught in the move from a middle-income industrializing country to an advanced industrialized country. The welfare policy should be formulated in such a way that in the long-run minimum housing space is guaranteed to all Koreans.

The new adaptation of Korean capitalism can benefit from some elements of Germany's "coformation of capital" by labor and management. This policy is the system of labor's participation in the capital formation of newly created means of production without altering the ownership relationships of the existing means of production. When labor and management conclude an agreement on wage increases, the wage increase is permitted to exceed labor productivity. But this excess of wage increase over labor productivity is then converted to production capital in the form of "investment" wage as distinct from "cash" wage. This property-formation policy for workers not only permits them to own the means of production jointly with management but also becomes the basis of cost-neutral wage policy as one of the economic stabilization measures.

In reality, however, the German economy recently suffered from high wage increases that include welfare benefits. Although growth encourages wage increases, it is extremely difficult to lower wages when the economy is in a business downturn. Consequently, Germany and other European countries are presently faced with high wages as constraints on economic growth, and many German firms have lost their competiveness. In contrast, the Japanese system of bonus payments helps Japanese firms maintain their competitiveness. Japanese companies pay two annual bonuses beyond regular salaries; when the recession sets in, these bonuses are suspended. Another suggestion made in this book is that a mixture of the German and Japanese systems would be a more appropriate blueprint for Korea.

Finally, the new government's policy toward the conglomerates should be formulated in the direction of inducing the separation of ownership and management gradually, by institutionalizing independent management systems for *jaebul*-affiliated companies, dispersing the ownership of the *jaebul* through public offering of stocks, and so forth.

Overall, Korea's new vision should consist of a comprehensive set of decisive policy changes and institutional reforms designed to minimize the internal conflicts between social strata and at the same time to sharpen Korea's edge in the international competitition for productivity. If the national consensus is established that the relative apportionment of economic sacrifices which the integrated reform proposal imposes on different groups of society is fair and that the new wealth created thanks to the economic sacrifices of all will be equitably distributed later, this vision as a national goal will ignite a new motivation among the people, thereby releasing national energy.

National Economic Management

If the cooperative form of capitalism is the most suitable blueprint for Korea to cope with internal conflicts and external threats, then the important issue becomes the choice of the best market system of national economic management. A useful approach to this issue can be found in the history of cooperative capitalism—in the distinction between state-led capitalism and state-oriented capitalism.

State-Led Capitalism In the early stages of industrialization among the latecomers—Germany, Russia, Italy, Hungary, and Meiji Japan are the primary historical examples—the government was dominant in selecting industries for promotion, in building infrastructure, in arranging the institutional framework for industrial growth, and in supplying both capital and entrepreneurial guidance to industrial enterprises. The state was also instrumental in activating spiritual culture, be it nationalism or religious ethos or idealogy, to catalyze rapid economic growth.

State-Oriented Capitalism As nations succeeded in industrializing under the guidance of the state, as the size and scale of economies increased, the state's role became less dominant. In the case of Germany, such institutional innovations as investment banks took over the state's functions of capital disposition and management of enterprise. This diminishing explicit state role was a consequence of the very success of state intervention in industrial development. Implicitly, the state continued some functions, and in a variety of forms. The Japanese "admiminstrative guidance" instituted during the 1930s under the military-industrial alliance for colonial expansion continues even today, an illustration of the move from the visible to the invisible guiding hand. Since the state is the largest investor in social infrastructure and the primary policymaker for regional planning and resource allocation, large industrial enterprises still direct considerable attention toward the government and its leaders. This government-business relationship and the cooperation that follows from it can be said to be the main feature of state-oriented capitalism.

The institutional structure of Korea's national economic management was state-led capitalism, also known as "state corporatism," during the 1960s and 1970s (see Chapter 2). A powerful bureaucratic organization under the political leadership of President Park Chung Hee energetically and persistently pushed forward a future-oriented, outward-looking strategy for industrialization under state guidance. Within a short period, Korea achieved rapid industrialization and high-speed economic growth, thereby eliminating absolute poverty and transforming itself from Asia's poorest country into a semi-industrialized nation. But although the Park regime's political authoritarianism and state-led capitalism produced economic progress, they were not able to foster political development because of suppression of the opposition party, restriction of human rights, and control of the press.

After the death of President Park, the subsequent administrations should have adopted a new institutional structure of national economic management by reinforcing the merits of the state-led market economy and correcting its limitations. But both the Fifth and Sixth Republics attempted to abandon this variant of market economy and to adopt the American pluralist market economy as their ideal model. The American model is based on laissez-faire economic liberalism, which advocates unlimited competition and free market principles. In the 1980s, the doctrine of economic liberalism gained ground in dominant mainstream economics in the concrete shape of Reaganomics and Thatcherism. But the laissez-faire policy that the Chun Doo Hwan and Roh Tae Woo administrations adopted as the new principle of national economic management was institutionally inappropriate to Korean conditions then prevailing and consequently it resulted in frictions and contraditions.

The poor fit between the American model and Korean circumstances appears in several ways. Korean attitudes and behavior in the early 1980s, broadly speaking, differed greatly from the type of rational perspective Anglo-American economists argue is a precondition for constructing a successful market economy. Moreover, Korean society was—and still is—quite traditional and conventional in its social outlook.

As Alice H. Amsden indicates in Chapter 4, the American model is fundamentally inconsistent with Korea's path to industrial development. Whereas the United States pioneered new techonology to become a successful international competitor, Korea has been following the early development processes of Japan and Germany, which promoted industrialization by borrowing and learning technology commercialized by firms from advanced industrialized countries. According to Amsden, Korean industries still have not advanced to the degree that their international competitiveness is based on the capability of initiating major technological innovation. To achieve this goal, the Korean economy should continue to develop along the line of the Japanese and German economies, that is, as a refined variant of the late-industrialization model of the capitalist developmental state. Amsden strongly recommends that Korea "follow in the footsteps of Germany and Japan and catch up with the world technological frontier."

After World War II, the Japanese and West German governments shifted toward state-oriented cooperative capitalism, or "societal corporatism," as a basic principle of national economic management. Today's Japanese and German models are institutionally reformed versions that combine the merits of state corporatism and Western liberalism and harmonize these merits with their traditional ways of thinking and acting. The societal corporatist market economy can be viewed as a system of "organized private enterprise" (Shonfield 1969), which the Japanese and Germans perfected by grafting their unique organizational principles onto the American "free enterprise system."

Chalmers Johnson asserts in Chapter 3 that the Japanese societal corporatist market economy has been more effective in solving economic imbalances and more efficient for economic development than the American pluralist market economy. In international economic battles, the Japanese-German model defeated the American model by combining the free market and individual initiatives with social organizations. But Korean capitalism still functions as a small developing economy trying to catch up with other countries and has a long way to go before it is fully industrialized. Accordingly, state-oriented cooperative capitalism, with its focus on the long-term benefit of all citizens, would be best for Korea's national economic management.

In retrospect, the Fifth and Sixth Republics should have continued to refine corporatist national economic management, with an intermediate institutional structure between the Park regime's state-led capitalism and American liberalism, rather than trying to directly switch over to a free enterprise system in the Anglo-Saxon mode. Unfortunately, the Chun and Roh administrations discarded some of the Park administration's important and creative high-growth institutions and policy measures appropriate to actual circumstances in Korea. In general, it seems, they did not quite provide the required leadership and were not effective in the national economic management of the 1980s.

Even though the doctrine of economic liberalism became the basic principle of economic policies during the Fifth and Sixth Republics, many of the state corporatist institutions and legal systems survived the political democratization of 1987 and still dominate the actual operation of the Korean economy today. Confusion in national economic management due to the coexistence of liberalism and state corporatism has certainly contributed to the loss of international competitiveness and to the trade deficit. The government was not concerned about strategic industrial policies, and the big business groups were preoccupied with vying against each other to secure special privileges from the government. Unfortunately, there were no social groups in the Korean society to stand guard over long-term national interests. Consequently, Korean capitalism failed to evolve an appropriate industrial structure which would generate dynamic comparative advantage in world markets. As the DPL put it, Korea was entering the 1990s confronted with "overall national difficulties."

The gist of these arguments and reviews of past policy is that the national economic management system most appropriate to the present developmental stage of Korean capitalism is neither liberalism nor state-led capitalism but some adaptation of the Japanese-German model of state-oriented capitalism. It is by virtue of the existence of industrial policy that the state-oriented market economy can be clearly distingushed from the liberal market economy. The German and especially Japanese industrial policies, basically founded on the typical "catch-up" philosophy, first established their own visions of the future of their industries, with the developmental patterns in the industrial structure of the Anglo-American countries as a model. Next, they intentionally intervened to restructure the existing industrial structure to achieve their goals. Thus, the Japanese and German industrial policies are theoretically based on the principle of dynamic, rather than static, comparative advantage; they keep an eye to future comparative advantage.

The main differences between the German and Japanese models can be found in the industrial decision-making processes. German industrial policy is implemented by highly organized private associations, and the central government keeps close and intimate relations with these institutionalized social "partners." On the other hand, in Japan industrial policy is managed by a government-business cooperative system under the government initiative. In the decision-making process of Japanese industrial policy, the central role is played by the Minstry of International Trade and Industry (MITI) on the government side and by business associations for the private sector. To mediate between these two are forums of institutionalized "deliberative councils" and "investigative councils." These council consists of business leaders, financiers, retired bureaucrats, press leaders, and a few university professors, who are appointed by the minister of MITI. MITI assigns the special policy task to the "deliberative council" and then makes a policy decision based on a written report submitted by the council.

Japan's powerful bureacracy directs and guides the industry by a system called *amakutari*, which literally means "power of Heaven." Retired senior government officials from various economic ministries are given executive positions in the business world, which creates a network of elite government officials and retired bureaucrats who maintain effective communication and cooperation between government and business. This system functions especially well in Japan's cultural milieu, where jobs in the public or private sectors are often available after retirement from administrative service.

Like Japan, Korea during the Park Chung Hee administration established a powerful bureaucratic organization and created business groups that would cooperate with the nation's industrialization strategy. As part of a "purification" drive, however, the Chun Doo Hwan regime purged nearly 8,000 civil servants in July 1980, thereby leading to some loss of adminstrative capability accumulated during the development period of the 1960s and 1970s. Moreover, in the early 1980s when the doctrine of economic liberalism became the basic ideal of economic policy, the big business groups no longer heeded what the government said.

The situation was quite different in postwar Japan, where ownership and management were completely separated with the dissolvement of the *zaibatsu* (the Japanese conglomerates) and the purge of the top management of these enterprises carried out by the headquarters of the occupation forces as part of economic democratization. New Japanese managers, who were young, non-owners, and employed, pursued the expansion of business rather than maximization of profit and adopted the philosophy that management and labor are bound by a common fate and common interests. This management style was based on family values deep-rooted in the samurai society, which emphasized the prosperity and continuity of an individual warrior family. The Japanese call this *kyodotai*, meaning upholding a collective entity in times of peril as well as in times of prosperity. The idea functions beyond blood relationships in a strict hierarchy, independently and autonomously. Stressing "we" over "they," *kyodotai* enforces the responsibility of each member of the group for the whole organization and minimizes assignments of specific duties.

In contrast to Japan, in Korea company management still tends toward the owner-governed system in which the company manager is keen to serve the owners by striving for great profits, with less concern for long-term stability. Management-labor relations are often adversarial. Especially since the political democratization in 1987, Korea's big business groups have exerted an enormous amount of influence on society through their contributions to political campaigns. In general, we might say that Korean corporations have grown but not matured as much as those in Japan.

Under such circumstances, it is not easy for the government bureaucracy to lead the design and implementation of the nation's industrial strategy for the long term. Besides, officials throughout the industrialized world, especially in the United States, would charge unfair trade practices if Korea's government became "directly" involved in making industrial policy. Moreover, the Japanese practice of the "deliberative council" as a government-business forum may not fit local conditions in Korea. As it is, Korea has numerous councils or committees in every economic ministry, but their operations tend to be superficial formality.

In the meantime, Korea's business groups have been nurtured as one of the most organized, powerful social groups in the process of rapid industrialization during the past thirty years. Much of the national energy of Korean society is now concentrated in the big business groups' capital, management, technology, and information. Accordingly, the new framework of the national economic management should be restructured in the direction of activating the latent energy within the business groups. But activating this energy also means appropriately regulating it. To make government-business cooperation workable under Korean conditions, it would be highly desirable to institutionalize this framework not merely by custom (as in Japan) but also by law (as in Germany). At the present time, Korea lacks effective mechanisms for coordinating industrial policies. Korean society has not progessed to a level where legal sanctions can effectively regulate business corporations. For this reason, the Japanese and German models must be examined carefully for clues to establishing laws, legal institutions, and precedents that will be effective and realistic by being founded in Korean cooperative values.

The German constitution gives national industrial associations consultative or semiofficial status as subsidiary organs of policymaking and allows them to participate in the decision-making process (Shonfield 1969; Hardach 1980; Zysman 1983). By providing such a status only to the associations which have nationwide authority, the government intentionally promotes the centralization of interest representation. In Germany the industrial associations link German businesses to the government in an elaborate and centralized fashion. These associations collect comprehensive data on each industry, carry out the forecasting function for the industry concerned, and perform an important public role by considering the protection of the long-term interests of German industry as their political responsibility. One of the merits of the German model of the organized private enterprise is that the participation of the industrial associations in policymaking is legally institutionalized. When the government formulates the economic policy, it is required by the federal constitution to receive the opinions of the authorized industrial associations. The German parliament is likewise obliged to receive the opinions of related private associations at the time of legislation. Thus the industrial associations are crucial in shaping sectoral economic policy; their advisory hearings do not proceed as mere formalities but are legally institutionalized.

If Korea adapts the German model to its local conditions, the government may then be able to carry out industrial policy indirectly by maintaining close relations with the highly organized industrial associations. Since individual companies have no windows to the government, each company needs representation by the industrial association. Moreover, because each company will be organized in a hierarchical system of industrial associations, adjusting investment by industry and promoting international competitiveness can be achieved autonomously. The central task facing Korean capitalism in transition is to induce an independent management system for *jaebul*-affiliated companies and to promote specialization by the big business groups. These tasks could be accomplished within the framework of the state-oriented market economy in the German spirit. At the same time, the government's economic policy would to a certain degree be insulated from political influence by big business.

There are, of course, limitations to this framework. The government's vision may be "tunnel vision" and its policies shortsighted if it relies only on industrial information collected and reported by industrial associations and if public opinion is shaped through them. To overcome this shortcoming, it would be desirable to set up a non-government, non-business economic advisory organ that keeps aloof from interest groups, draws professional judgments, and considers the basic problems of the national economy from an independent, long-term perspective. In Germany the councils of economic experts, councils of academic advisors, and economic research institutes are legally institutionalized to perform such functions as evaluating government policies that have already been implemented and offering alternatives (Shonfield 1969). These organizations are needed by the government to convince the concerned industrial associations and the public, so they provide not only judgments about past policies but also guidelines for the future.

Under the Park administration, a body of economic advisors at arm's length from the government such as the Economic Science Council and a group of professors was assigned to evaluate government policies. The government could heed or ignore their advise. Such advisory groups functioned effectively until the mid-1970s. Once again, Korea urgently needs an economic advisory mechanism, charged with the duty of evaluating government policies and offering alternative choices to the government.

The central element of the Japanese and German systems of "organized capitalism" is the bank (Zysman 1983). German banks play a major tutelary role in the industrial structure as guardians of the German industry, through their governing market power over all sources of corporate finance, their direct ownership of substantial stock in corporations, and their exercise of proxy votes for other shareholders. Like the German case, the Japanese financial system as a whole is oriented toward bank financing of the corporate sector. In this bank-oriented, credit-based system of corporate finance, Japanese banks are pivotal in the *zaibatsu* with which they are affiliated yet independent. Both Japanese and German banks perform the role of prefects of business firms by blocking takeovers of business firms and promoting specialization.

Whereas in the Japanese system of corporate finance the bank and companies affiliated to the same business group are independent and cooperate through mutual stock owerships, in the German system the bank is deeply involved in the company's management strategy as a majority stockholder. The leading bank of the company has representives on the company's supervisory board, and representatives of the bank exercise strong control on the day-to-day management of the company. Each of the big German banks has representatives in several other banks and in a large number of industrial enterprises, and representatives affect the management strategy of German industry (Shonfield 1969).

Korea has not yet created an institutional source and supply of qualified financial experts. Accordingly, a modified framework of national economic management must be adapted to Korea for a transitional period before Korean banks can play such leading roles in corporate financing. In Chapter 19, D. M. Leipziger and Peter Petri point out that, if the Korean government accelerates financial sector liberalization while maintaining the present upper limit on *jaebul* ownership of outstanding bank shares (set at 8 percent), the bank-business relationship would converge to the German model. On the other hand, if the Korean government removes the restriction, the bank-business relationship will approximate the Japanese model. In this regard, Il SaKong (1993) proposes the promotion of the financial groups that specialize in financial services, by eliminating the upper limit on owning outstanding bank shares, except for the business groups. These new financial groups should be legally institutionalized to keep them separate from the conglomerates. As noted above, management and ownership of the big business groups in Korea are not yet separated as in Japan. Since public sentiment opposes an even greater concentration of economic power around the *jaebul,* including ownership and control of national commercial banks, some combination of the Japanese and German models seems appropiate. In particular, the role of German banks as prefects and guardians of business firms seems suitable for Korean capitalism.

Since the government's direct involvement in the management of industrial strategy will not be desirable in future national economic management, restructuring Korea's political economy is urgently needed so that industrial associations and banks can fill in the vacuum and perform a pivotal role in pursuing the interests of Korean industry over the long term. This role as guardians and prefects of industrial enterprises is indispensable for creating dynamic comparative advantage for Korean industry.

The institutionalization of the economic policy decision-making process, through cooperative efforts of the government, industrial associations, banks, economic advisory organs, and the mass media, would be the most effective system of mobilizing the national energy. To overcome the "overall national difficulties," the central task for today's Korean political leaders is to design practical adaptations of these Japanese and German examples—with modifications suitable to Korean circumstances.

Finally, there is a social factor that must be recognized by Korean leaders as they prepare the nation to participate in a globalized world economy. In East Asia the Confucian qualities of harmony and social stability that bind the various segments of society are held in high esteem. Once national goals are established, these states achieve them through a national consensus. As mentioned in Chapter 1, a "rich nation and strong army" were achieved relatively quickly in Meiji Japan because government leaders used precepts from the Confucian classics such as the Analects in combination with Western technology to sponsor national development. Education was the major force behind Japan's modernization, and the emperor's formal edict "Kyoyuku Choku Go" inspired the entire country to preserve Japanese culture while developing its own kind of capitalism. Korea's political leadership has demonstrated a similar social and national commitment to achieving rapid economic development beginning with the period of President Park's administration in the 1960s and 1970s. These decades demonstrated that an educated population is essential for Korea to effectively compete and cooperate with other countries, be they developed or developing.

Faced with increasing globalization and regionalization, Koreans need to internationalize their thinking, their language, and their behavior. The new political leadership must also provide an atmosphere that encourages private sector leaders, government officials, and the people to work vigorously toward the goal of guaranteeing Korea a major position in a new world order. Korea's society has the potential to transform its respect for the past into a modern civic religion that aims for national development. If its leaders can sense the global trends and rhythms of history, they can guide the entire nation to seize the economic opportunities of the upcoming twenty-first century.

REFERENCES

Cho, Lee-Jay, and Yoon Hyung Kim, eds. 1991. *Economic Development in the Republic of Korea: A Policy Perspective.* Honolulu: East-West Center and University of Hawaii Press.

Economic Committee, Ministry of Trade and Industry, Singapore. 1986. *The Singapore Economy: New Directions.* Singapore: Ministry of Trade and Industry.

Hardach, Karl. 1980. *The Political Economy of Germany in the Twentieth Century.* Berkeley: University of California Press.

List, Friedrich. 1841. *The National System of Political Economy.* Translated from the original German. London: Longmans, Green.

Morishima, Michio. 1982. *Why Has Japan "Succeeded"? Western Technology and the Japanese Ethos.* Cambridge: Cambridge University Press.

SaKong, Il. 1993. *Korea in the World Economy.* Washington, D.C.: Institute for International Economics.

Shonfield, Andrew. 1969. *Modern Capitalism.* New York: Oxford University Press.

Thurow, Lester C. 1985. *The Zero-Sum Solution: Building a World-Class Economy.* New York: Simon and Schuster.

Thurow, Lester C. 1992. *Head to Head: The Coming Economic Battle among Japan, Europe, and America.* New York: Morrow.

Weber, Max. 1930. *The Protestant Ethic and the Spirit of Capitalism.* Translated from the original German. Chicago: University of Chicago Bookstore.

Weber, Max. 1979. *Economy and Society.* 2 vols. Translated from the original German. Berkeley: University of California Press.

Zysman, John. 1983. *Governments, Markets, and Growth.* Ithaca: Cornell University Press.

Index

About the Book

Over the past three decades, South Korea has moved along a path of strong economic growth and political democratization, attracting worldwide attention and providing valuable lessons for other developing economies. Yet Korea still must grapple with many intractable problems fueled by its rapid industrialization and uneven growth, including unbalanced distribution of wealth, concentrated economic power, and adversarial relationships between management and labor.

Within the context of these sweeping changes, this volume explores options for economic and social institutional reform in Korea. Drawing on models of economic development from Japan, the United States, and Europe, a distinguished group of Asian and Western scholars relates the experiences of previously industrialized economies to each facet of Korea's economic system, including national management; taxation and banking; land ownership and use; trade and industrial strategy; and relations among business ownership, management, and labor. In so doing, the contributors provide valuable insights and fresh proposals for a viable model of social and economic modernization.

Throughout the volume, the contributors emphasize the importance of Korea's cultural heritage—not only in explaining the nation's recent growth but also as a key element of its continued success. By providing an overview of the evolution and interaction of Korean economic, political, and sociocultural institutions, the contributors make clear how these structures mediate the movement between cultural values and economic progress.

About the Book